Critical Issues
in Special Education

Critical Issues in Special Education

THIRD EDITION

James E. Ysseldyke
University of Minnesota

Bob Algozzine
University of North Carolina at Charlotte

Martha L. Thurlow
University of Minnesota

HOUGHTON MIFFLIN COMPANY   **BOSTON   NEW YORK**

Senior Sponsoring Editor: Loretta Wolozin
Associate Editor: Lisa Mafrici
Editorial Assistant: Carrie Wagner
Project Editor: Gabrielle Stone
Senior Production/Design Coordinator: Jennifer Waddell
Senior Manufacturing Coordinator: Priscilla Bailey
Senior Marketing Manager: Pamela Laskey
Associate Marketing Manager: Jean Zielinski DeMayo

Cover Design: Catherine Hawkes, Cat & Mouse

Printed in the U.S.A.
Library of Congress Catalog Card Number: 99–71908
ISBN: 0-395-96127-0
123456789–CS–03 02 01 00 99

To our children: Amy, Heather, Kathryn, Mike, Lisa, and Rob

Contents

Chapter 8
Early Intervention   208

Preface

The state of the art in any field should be evaluated periodically. American public education received little systematic analysis in the two hundred years of its history, but more recently, the system has been under continuous scrutiny. Increased diversity in the schools, heightened concern for educational outcomes for all students, and growing challenges from alternative practices like school choice, charter schools, and inclusion created growing interest in taking stock of how America's schools were doing. The field of special education has been part of recent inspection efforts. This text is a comprehensive revision of our earlier works addressing critical issues in the provision of services to individuals with disabilities. It is a straightforward analysis of important conceptual and practical issues that face professionals involved in special education. The content represents our thinking and reflects perspectives derived from the results of much of our research (and that of others) on problems associated with providing special education to children and youth with disabilities.

In regularly examining the status of special education, our goal is to present a thought-provoking analysis that will stimulate debate and discussion to serve as a catalyst for change when it is needed. The kinds of questions professionals ask tell much about the developments in their field. In many areas, our analysis results in more questions than answers. Although we do not offer solutions to all problems, we believe we have done a good job identifying the critical areas of concern and the kinds of questions that need to be asked when evaluating special education.

Audience

The text has served well in graduate courses in special education, school psychology, and counseling. The heightened interest in collaboration and educating students with disabilities with their neighbors and peers without disabilities makes it a very good addition to graduate coursework in general education as well. Undergraduate students preparing to teach also represent an appropriate audience for what we have written.

About This Edition: New Features and Coverage

There are many dramatic new critical issues in special education today, and in this book we have captured them in what we believe is a captivating and thought-provoking manner. This edition is not just an update, it is a major revision that recognizes that special education has a variety of new forces impinging on it. Highlights of major revisions in this third edition include the following:

- **The virtually new Chapter 10, "School Reform and Special Education,"** examines the key issues surrounding school reform and special education including new topics like the reform movement in general education, discussion of the

Goals 2000: Educate America Act, the National Council of Disability's report, and Choice in Education.

- **An entirely new Chapter 11, "Home-School-Community Agency Partnerships,"** offers in-depth coverage of recent issues surrounding home-schoolcommunity agency partnerships with new research on the effects of disabilities on families, the debate about ways to increase parent involvement, overcoming challenges to home-school collaboration, and barriers to home-school collaboration.

- **Significant new content, updated coverage, and relevant analyses** permeate the entire book.

- **New part and chapter organization** (described below) makes the flow of topics more logical than ever before.

- **Improved discussion question pedagogy** at the end of each chapter encourages student reflective thinking.

This edition is organized in three parts. **Part I, "Foundations of Contemporary Practice,"** offers an up-to-date analysis of fundamental guiding practices illustrating the background and status of contemporary special education. First, we review the foundations of current practice. Then, we describe competing perspectives that shape special education today. We also provide an analysis of the current context in which services for individuals with disabilities must fit, the status of efforts to provide special education, and the important debates that drive questions about who shall receive services and where they shall be provided.

Chapter 1, "Competing Perspectives," contains completely updated perspectives on inclusion, as well as new material on component or separate systems, educational service or teacher relief, and full or selective exclusion.

Chapter 2, "Special Education in Context," contains in-depth new analyses of such essential topics as characteristics of families, coverage of issues surrounding the national educational goals, the key changes in IDEA, and current legal developments related to special education.

Chapter 3, "Special Education Today," provides current information on special education categories, including autism and traumatic brain injury, who receives special education, and who provides special education. It also offers new analysis of the questions faced by every generation of educators, such as who succeeds in special education and what continuing services are needed?

Chapter 4, "Definitional Debate," offers new and expanded coverage of key issues pertaining to the ongoing definitional debate. These issues examine essential questions such as where does ADD or ADHD belong? and what are the definitional criteria for ADHD?

Chapter 5, "Placement Controversy," provides a new, in-depth analysis of issues such as where special education should take place, the push and pull of the general education classroom, and the fact that places still mean problems for people with special needs.

Part Two, "Contemporary Issues and Practices," focuses on key practices central to the effective provision of special education services. The latest thinking in assessment, instruction, early intervention, transition, and school reform is presented. In this section of the book, we analyze important issues and practices in areas of central concern in providing special education in contemporary settings.

Chapter 6, "Issues in Assessment," provides completely new coverage of assessment issues. This chapter offers insights on topics such as current decision-making practices, the many kinds of assessment information used in schools, contemporary influences on assessment practices, issues in making classroom and entitlement decisions, and issues in making large-scale assessment and accountability decisions.

Chapter 7, "Issues in Instruction," offers new and expanded material on the many issues in instruction. Included in this chapter is comprehensive coverage of prereferral intervention, effective instruction, and why intervention research doesn't get translated into practice.

Chapter 8, "Early Intervention," is a comprehensive study of current issues in early intervention. New to this edition is coverage of topics such as assumptions of early intervention, preprimary enrollment, services for infants and toddlers, and minimal practices for developmentally appropriate classrooms to meet the needs of young children with disabilities.

Chapter 9, "Transition," contains new information on all aspects of movement in and out of schools, with a comprehensive look at the issues surrounding transition into school, dropping out of school, and transitions beyond high school.

Chapter 10, "School Reform and Special Education," a virtually new chapter, examines the many complex issues surrounding school reform and special education. Among the many new topics of analysis are the reform movement in general education, with coverage that introduces readers to the fourth wave of educational reform; discussion of "Goals 2000: Educate America Act" and reform rhetoric of the late 1990s; the National Council of Disability's report, which was designed to assess the progress of disability policy in setting an agenda for the future; and choice in education, which looks at the schooling choices available for special education students. In addition, this chapter offers insights into the Kentucky Educational Reform Act and change in education.

Part Three, "Issues Reflected in Practice," provides an analysis of social, political, legal, and economic activity reflected in special education practice. New and expanded coverage on valued partnerships, legal issues, economic interrelations, outcomes of schooling, and continued concerns are addressed in this section.

Chapter 11, "Home-School-Community Agency Partnerships," is entirely new. This chapter offers comprehensive coverage of recent issues surrounding home-school-community agency partnerships. A range of essential topics are explored, with new research on the effects of disabilities on families, the debate about ways to increase parent involvement, overcoming challenges to home-school collaboration, and barriers to home-school collaboration.

Chapter 12, "Legal Issues," explores historical and current legal issues, with new insights on the definition of provision of services and disciplining students with disabilities.

Chapter 13, "Economic Issues in Special Education," focuses on the leading economic issues in special education, offering expanded coverage of payment for special education services and funding incentives and disincentives. Additionally, it raises the question, are we spending too much on special education?

Chapter 14, "Results of Schooling," provides current information and research on the results of schooling. Among the many key issues in this section is new coverage on identifying desired educational results, with examples of state standards in science, grading the standards, graduation requirements, material for retention in grade/social promotion, and grading practices.

Chapter 15, "Continuing Challenges," addresses new issues and perspectives surrounding the future of special education. New to this chapter are insights on current personnel needs and preparing people versus preparing professionals.

All chapters contain completely updated references.

Acknowledgments

As we indicated in the last edition, the initial impetus for a book evaluating special education came while we were sitting in a diner in Dinkytown, Minnesota. Behind the counter was a new broom in a cellophane wrapper on which was written, "This broom sweeps four times better." We wondered, "Better than what?" and "When was the contest?" The broom is still there, still wrapped in its glory, but is now somewhat tattered from years of service. The claim of enhanced performance continues to provoke discussions among the three of us about promises made in special education. We thank the manufacturers of that broom for reminding us to examine issues that should not be "swept under the rug."

We also thank the many people who have helped to keep this project on the front burner. Loretta Wolozin accepted and supported the original idea, believed in the importance of doing it again and again, and consistently challenged us to make it better. Carrie Wagner's editorial support made doing the third edition a real treat. Susan B. Hasazi, University of Vermont; David R. Johnson, University of Minnesota at Twin Cities; Ellen L. Nuffer, Keene State College; and Deanna J. Sands, University of Colorado at Denver, provided valuable criticism and advice that greatly improved the meaning and the message.

This book continues to be a collaborative effort in the fullest sense, and it speaks for all of us. We enjoyed revising it. We hope you will enjoy reading it.

James E. Ysseldyke

Bob Algozzine

Martha L. Thurlow

Critical Issues
in Special Education

Part

1

Foundations of Contemporary Practice

Chapter 1
Competing Perspectives

Toto, I've a feeling we're not in Kansas anymore.
—*The Wizard of Oz*

Special education has passed a crossroads in its development. In the early years, simply standing up and being recognized were the primary goals of professionals concerned with students with special learning needs. As special education approached adolescence, problems in the system related to gaining independence and growing too big to ignore were being addressed. Early concern for access to free appropriate education has been replaced by radical and mature perspectives that put people with special learning needs in regular classes to be educated with everyone else. At the same time, professionals are beginning to question whether special education is effective in efforts to improve the lives of individuals with disabilities.

Other questions are surfacing as well. Is special education a right or a privilege? What is the proper focus of special education intervention? Who should receive special education? Is special education a method, or is it just a vehicle for receiving services? How should special education services be delivered? Is special education an art or a science? Is it a profession or a practice? These and other conceptual as well as practical questions form the basis for the various, often competing perspectives that characterize and drive its practices. In discussing competing points of view with regard to these concerns, we hope to stimulate change and continued improvement in special education. We also intend this discussion as a prologue to the broader, more detailed coverage of issues that make up the central focus of this book.

To present these competing perspectives, we use a variety of strategies. In some cases, we give both sides of the question "equal time." When the preponderance of proof or support falls on one answer, we present information that is biased by evidence. In rare cases, we simply frame an issue, as a question, or state a problem. Sometimes, leaving an important and critical question unanswered or problem unresolved is the best way to stimulate an answer or a solution. Put another way, special education is different things to different people. Our goal is to evenhandedly set forth a broad set of perspectives that influence special education and the people who practice it. Some issues have more relevance than others.

To some parents who have children failing in school and needing special services, special education is a promise of renewed progress. The system becomes a problem when children "fall between the cracks" and present unusual cases that do not meet accepted eligibility standards or when placement in special education fails to produce desired benefits. Legal issues and issues related to assessment, intervention, choice, reform, and transition have considerable relevance to these parents.

To children, placement in special education is sometimes a symbol of difference that they want to avoid when they think placement means they have done poorly in school. (The dividends gathered by participating in this special system, however, often override the disappointment experienced by many of the children.) Categorical debate and placement controversies as well as issues in assessment, instruction, and transition create concerns for students with special needs.

To teachers working with students who receive special education, it means working closely with other professionals in ways that are not necessary for students who do not receive special education. This close collaboration creates problems in decision making, intervention, and home/school relations. Working with students with special needs, especially those who are very difficult to teach, is taxing, and as a result teachers of students in special education face professional concerns (e.g., attrition) that are less common than those faced by their colleagues in general education.

For the administrator, with constituencies that are often at odds, special education classes are places for learners perceived to be slow, disruptive, or atypical, havens for the hard-to-teach. Seemingly endless hassles involved in arranging special transportation and class schedules, debating teacher responsibilities, and managing parent conferences cause headaches, too. When responsibility for special education is shared, the partnership may cause conflicts between administrators, who are affected by the same broad issues as parents, teachers, and students.

CONCEPTUAL ISSUES

The concerns about special education that affect parents, students, teachers, and administrators grow, in part, from conceptual issues. For instance, is special education a right or a privilege? Is it a component of regular education or a separate system? What is the appropriate focus of special education intervention: treatment or prevention? Who receives services? What drives interest in disabilities, deficits, dysfunctions, and disadvantages?

Right or Privilege

With the passage of the Education of All Handicapped Children Act (Public Law [PL]94-142) in 1975, a free appropriate education became an expected, established right for people with disabilities. The act established principles and guidelines for the delivery of special education services. Public Law 101-476, passed on October 30, 1990, reauthorized, revised, and renamed the law the Individuals with Disabilities Education Act. In 1997, the Individuals with Disabilities Education Act Amendments reauthorized and further amended the law. These laws reaffirmed a national intent to support alternative education for students with special learning needs. Prior to passage of these laws, there was no guarantee that special education would be provided in public school programs. Exclusionary clauses, refusal to provide services, special charges for services provided free to other students, and segregationist practices all occurred and were documented during hearings prior to enactment of the law (Lipsky and Gartner, 1989; Rothstein, 1990; Ysseldyke & Algozzine, 1990). The social and political action that led to the act grew out of parents' and professionals' dissatisfaction with the type and kind of services students with special learning needs were receiving (Biklen, 1989; Ysseldyke, Algozzine & Thurlow, 1992).

Unfortunately, mandating changes in educational systems and practices does not always make them happen. In addressing the extent to which a "disabled student today [is] getting more than a student with a similar disability educated before 94-142," Adrienne Asch made the following comments:

> Running throughout my conversations with disabled students, parents, and professionals is the message that today's education is still largely separate and rarely equal. Separate means not only the segregated school or class but the *separate standards* used to measure the opportunities provided, or the progress made, by the student with a disability who is physically integrated. Whether speaking of such "basics" as reading, writing, mathematics, science labs, organizing ideas and organizing time, or such "frills" as physical education, field trips, computer literacy, art, music, home economics, industrial arts, driver education, or enrichment programs, the nation's disabled students are deprived. In many instances, standards of

> attendance, discipline, participation, and performance are different and lower for disabled students than for nondisabled members of the same class, grade level, school district or state. (1989, pp. 183–184)

Inequities such as these have a long-established history in education. A study of formal education prior to the development of public schools revealed that early schooling was directed toward a specific segment of the population (males, nobility, or the leisured, monied, privileged, upper class or trainees for high-status positions such as the priesthood), and it often included the teaching of ethics, moral conduct, or religion (Ysseldyke & Algozzine, 1995). When schools became public, these practices continued; emphasis was on educating a selective, limited population—the white, male children of upper-class families (Henley, Ramsey, & Algozzine, 1998; Smith, Price, & March, 1986). The select few are still the major beneficiaries of education, and it is still more a privilege than a right, federal laws to the contrary notwithstanding.

Component or Separate System

Who is responsible for educating students with special learning needs? Who is responsible for students in special education? Where should special education services be delivered? Who should provide special education services? Answers to these questions depend on whether special education is a component of general education or a separate education system.

Traditional organizational practices promoted the separation of general and special education students and programs. An elaborate system of assessment and classification evolved to support the need and conduct of separate systems of education. From the moment children entered school, formal and informal assessments were carried out to order and explain individual differences that not so long ago passed as normal products of childhood. Lipsky and Gartner suggested that "the establishment of a separate system of education for the disabled is an outgrowth of attitudes toward disabled people" (1987, p. 72).

The history of providing care for people with disabilities has only recently evolved to stages of progressive integration because not everyone supports the principle of a separate but equal special education system. In a report to the secretary of the U.S. Department of Education, Assistant Secretary Madeleine Will presented cogent arguments to support her belief that, although much has been accomplished in special education programs, "problems have emerged which create obstacles to effective education of students with learning problems" (1986, p. 4). She did not mean the term *obstacle* to "imply that special programs have failed dismally in their mission to educate children with learning problems" or to suggest that the "existing general system of education for these children warrants radical reform and redesign" (Will, 1986, p. 4). She did use the term to "convey the idea that the creation of special programs has produced unintended effects, some of which make it unnecessarily cumbersome for educators to teach—as effectively as they desire—and children to learn—as much and as well as they can" (Will, 1986, p. 4) Will's perspective profoundly influenced the direction of special education.

First, she identified several types of problems. The first is the result of a fragmented approach that has failed to provide services to many students who are "often not served adequately in the regular classroom and are not 'eligible' for special education or other special programs because they do not meet State or Federal eligibility requirements" (Will, 1986, p. 5). A second type of problem grows out of duel (perhaps dueling) administrative systems for special programs that "contribute to a lack of coordination, raise questions about leadership, cloud areas of responsibility, and obscure lines of accountability within schools" (Will, 1986, p. 6). A third type is created by segregating students from their peers and attaching labels to the segregated students, which sometimes result in lowered expectations for success that "have been fully described in the literature" (Will, 1986, p. 7). And a fourth type results from a decision-making process that sometimes turns a valuable partnership between parents and teachers into a series of "adversarial, hit-and-run encounters" (Will, 1986, p. 7) that leave everybody tallying points instead of considering students' unique learning needs and the most appropriate ways to meet them.

In describing "a solution to the problem," Will qualified her argument: "Although for some students the 'pullout approach' may be appropriate, it is driven by a conceptual fallacy; that poor performance in learning can be understood solely in terms of deficiencies in the student rather than deficiencies in the learning environment" (1986, p. 9). She believed that creating new educational environments as the primary way to improve student performance is a flawed approach; the alternative she advocated would "adapt the regular classroom to make it possible for the student to learn in that environment" (Will, 1986, p. 9). In closing, she challenged states "to renew their commitment to serve [children with learning problems] effectively," and she defined that commitment as a "search for ways to serve as many of these children as possible in the regular classroom by encouraging special education and other special programs to form a partnership with regular education" (Will, 1986, p. 19).

The principles embodied in Will's call for a partnership between general education and special education in meeting the special learning needs of students became known as the "regular education initiative." Called the "hottest debate in special education" (Viadero, 1988, p. 1), deciding whether and how to improve services provided to students with disabilities has sparked controversy throughout the field (Lipsky & Gartner 1989; Stainback & Stainback, 1989). Conferences, professional presentations, and numerous articles and special journal issues were devoted to praising or maligning professionals who believe that general education should assume more responsibility for students with special learning needs (cf. Kauffman, Gerber, & Semmel, 1988; Kauffman, Lloyd, & McKinney, 1988; Keogh, 1988; Lloyd, Crowley, Kohler, & Strain, 1988; Wang, Reynolds, & Walberg, 1987; Wang & Walberg, 1988). Kauffman characterized the regular education initiative as a flawed policy lacking the support of critical constituencies. He called the movement a "trickle-down theory of education for the hard-to-teach" and suggested that "it rests on illogical premises, ignores the issue of specificity in proposed reforms, and reflects a cavalier attitude toward experimentation and research" (1989, p. 256). His position was reaffirmed and critically reviewed by other professionals (cf. Goetz & Sailor, 1990; Kauffman & Hallahan, 1990; McLeskey, Skiba & Wilcox, 1990; Pugach, 1990). But after all the dialogue, the question of where best to educate special education students still remained and was renamed "the inclusion debate" when the rhetoric heated up.

The emotions stirred by inclusion are evident in the discourse surrounding it. Those supporting the position that students with disabilities can be educated to a greater extent in general education settings have been characterized as demagogues intent on bringing special education down (cf. Kauffman & Hallahan, 1995). Their opponents view themselves as saviors bearing the weight of traditional special education practices on their shoulders. Brantlinger (1997) delimited beliefs undergirding each point of view (see Table 1.1). Traditionalists write in support of a continuum of special education services and are very wary about inclusion and the direction it has taken in contemporary practice. Inclusionists believe that experiences for the people with disabilities and those who live and work with them can be improved by changing the current system of special education to support more experiences with natural neighbors and peers. And the enemy of progress is not ideas but the steel grip of intractible opinions and beliefs.

Remediation, Compensation, or Prevention

The practice of special education is a three-stage process. Students are first declared eligible for special education services, then they are treated or taught differently, and finally their progress is evaluated (Ysseldyke & Algozzine, 1995). The terms *treatment* and *teaching* are used as synonyms by many professionals because in the early development of services for people with disabilities, medical perspectives dominated more than educational ones did. Treatment of students with special learning needs serves many purposes. Remediation and compensation are two of them.

Many students receive special education as a correction for their special learning needs and problems. The term *remediation* is derived from the word *remedy,* something that "corrects, counteracts, or removes" something that has gone wrong. Physicians treat people by using certain medications in an effort to correct, repair, or cure certain conditions. Regardless of whether the medicines work, they are often called remedies. In special education settings, this medical model obtains, and the focus of "treatment" is often on remediation. Specific skills, such as reading or math, are taught in an effort to overcome deficiencies in academic skill development. Or emphasis may be placed on remedying specific deficits in abilities, such as memory or perception of sounds. If students who are being asked to solve multiplication problems are shown to have deficits in the skill of adding numbers, they may be given training (or treatment) in adding numbers. Students with trouble reading may be provided perceptual-motor training because some professionals believe learning to track a target visually or discriminate visual images will overcome reading problems.

A second purpose of treatment is *compensation.* The term derives from the word *compensate,* which means "to make up for." If you do not own an automobile, you can make up for it by taking buses, riding bicycles, or getting rides from people who have cars. People who do not have the use of their legs compensate by getting around in wheelchairs, and those who lose the use of their voice may compensate by writing down what they want to say. Usually, compensatory treatments are employed when overcoming a problem seems impossible or when compensating for a condition seems easier than trying to correct it.

Many special education treatments are compensatory. Compensatory activities are usually most apparent in the treatment of sensory or physical disabilities, but they are often used with students with other disabilities. The most obvious

TABLE 1.1 **Perspectives on Inclusion**

Traditionalist	Inclusionist
Disabilities are innate conditions that require treatment to correct them.	Diversity is an inherent human condition, but people are more alike than different.
Students who achieve above or below normal expectations should be sorted into groups.	Diversity is natural and expected; sorting students into groups is unnecessary and can be damaging.
Disabilities create problems for schools and society.	Diversity contributes positively to classroom climate, learning outcomes, and community quality.
Academic and behavioral supports are provided most effectively in special education settings.	Diversity is managed best in inclusive learning environments where all children are active and valued and where families are welcome.
Students who achieve below expectations will improve only if they receive special education.	Diversity enhances the performance of individuals of varying achievement levels, competence, and behavioral patterns when they learn together.
Special education teachers are more successful than general education teachers in meeting the needs of students with disabilities.	Diversity is a challenge for all teachers, who should be prepared to include and engage successfully all learners in their classrooms.

SOURCE: Adapted from E. Brantlinger (1997). Using Ideology: Cases of Nonrecognition of the Politics of Research and the Practice of Special Education. *Review of Educational Research, 67,* 425–459. Reprinted by permission of the American Educational Research Association.

compensatory treatments are those in which students who do not see well are taught to communicate using braille, students who do not have the use of their arms are taught to write holding a pencil in their toes, or students who do not hear well are taught to communicate using sign language or finger spelling. Yet compensatory treatment is also used when students who have difficulty reading and/or writing are allowed to take oral, rather than written, examinations; when "talking books" (on audiotapes or CDs) are given to students who have visual disabilities; or when students who have difficulty taking notes are allowed to tape-record lectures.

Special education is also seen as prevention when intervention is designed to reduce the probability of a problem becoming a disability or to control problem behaviors that sometimes result in classification of students with disabilities. For example, early interventions can result for students who are at risk for school failure, and specialized interventions can be used early in life with students who are blind or deaf to prevent serious problems later in school.

Deciding whether to use remediation, compensation, or prevention can present challenges when the goals of treatment conflict with the goals of general classroom instruction. For example, controversy periodically surfaces about whether people who are deaf should be taught to compensate for their limited verbal abilities with alternative communication systems or taught to correct faulty communication so they can be accepted in the hearing world. Similarly, questions about fairness and appropriateness of testing and instructional modifications for students with learning disabilities are raised regularly in school districts and other settings.

Mild or Severe Disabilities

More than 90 percent of students receiving special education in recent years were those placed in special education categories of specific learning disabilities, speech and language impairments, mental retardation, or serious emotional disturbance (U.S.D.E., 1988b, 1989b, 1990b, 1996, 1997). The term "mild disabilities" is sometimes used to refer to these students. However, it is not used to imply that these students do not have serious learning problems or that they are less important than those of any other students. We think the term has come to be used for this group of students because many of their characteristics overlap, they require less intensive treatment than some others, and many of them can be served in regular classroom environments or resource rooms with assistance from special education teachers (U.S.D.E., 1989, 1990, 1997; Ysseldyke & Algozzine, 1995).

Students classified with learning disabilities, mental retardation, or emotional disturbance account for more than two-thirds of all students with disabilities (U.S.D.E., 1997) and they share many characteristics (Hallahan & Kauffman, 1977). For example, students with learning disabilities often have problems with reading comprehension, language development, interpersonal relations, and classroom behavioral control (Lerner, 1996). These same characteristics are presented in descriptions of students with mental retardation (Coleman, 1986; Fessler, Rosenberg & Rosenberg, 1991; Kauffman, 1997; Robinson & Robinson, 1982) and many students with no recognized disabilities (Ysseldyke & Algozzine, 1995). Because many of their characteristics are not severe and because they overlap in conditions with different names, students with learning disabilities, mental retardation, and emotional disturbance are sometimes grouped together and called "mildly handicapped." Some common and unique characteristics of these students are presented in Table 1.2.

In a widely accepted definition, people with severe disabilities are described as constituting the lowest 1 percent of the population on any measure of intellectual functioning (Brown & York, 1974; Sailor, 1989). Clearly, this is a small group of people, but these students do not inspire optimism in administrators who feel forced to deal with them. For example, Sailor recounted an anecdote related to discussions of how to implement key special education provisions in a number of midwestern states.

> Not all of these directors were certain, by any stretch of the imagination, that this law and its extensive regulatory language was such a good idea. The LRE [least restrictive environment] portion particularly rankled some participants. One vociferous administrator, in an oratorical denunciation of the process shouted, "the logical extension of this LRE stuff is that we are going to be forced to put vegetables in the regular classroom!" (1989, p. 53).

TABLE 1.2   **Unique and Common Characteristics of Students with Disabilities Referred to as Mild**

Characteristics	Condition		
	LD	MR	ED
Cognitive	Average IQ, memory problems, information deficits	Below average IQ, memory problems, information deficits	Varied IQ, memory problems, information deficits
Achievement	Below average, reading problems, math deficits, writing problems	Below average, reading problems, math deficits, writing problems	Below average, reading problems, math deficits, writing problems
Language	Often delayed	Often delayed	Often delayed
Social	Hyperactivity, non-attention, interpersonal problems	Hyperactivity, non-attention, interpersonal problems	Hyperactivity, non-attention, interpersonal problems

SOURCE: Derived from Henley, M., Ramsey, R., & Algozzine, B. (1998). *Characteristics of and Teaching Strategies for Student with Mild Disabilities,* Boston: Allyn and Bacon.

Less than 10 percent of all special education students have severe disabilities (Ysseldyke & Algozzine, 1995). But controversy and questions surrounding their education complete with those that drive education for other people with and without disabilities. Where should people with severe disabilities be educated? Who should be responsible for providing services to them? To what extent should schools be expected to bear all the costs of their education? What benefits can be expected? Are the benefits worth the costs when compared to those associated with meeting the needs of gifted and talented students or students with mild handicaps? How early and how long should services be available? Today, more than ever before in history, the answers to these questions reflect the opinion that people with severe disabilities should be treated just like everybody else.

Dysfunction or Disadvantage

Oliver Sacks, the author of *The Man Who Mistook His Wife for a Hat and Other Clinical Tales* and *Awakenings,* noted in the former work that "neurology's favourite word is 'deficit,' denoting an impairment or incapacity of neurological function: loss of speech, loss of language, loss of memory, loss of vision, loss of dexterity, loss of identity, and myriad other lacks and losses of specific functions (or faculties)" (1985, p. 3). Special educators find plenty of room for deficits, disabilities, dysfunctions, and other disadvantages in their vocabulary as well.

Deficits such as an inability to process visually presented information or disabilities such as the loss of an arm can greatly influence performance in school activities. So can dysfunctions (the effects of these deficits and disabilities) and disadvantages (unfavorable situations or circumstances). When problems of people with special learning needs are being considered, differing opinions about deficits, disabilities, dysfunctions, and disadvantages affect perceptions and influence the behaviors of people who receive special education and those who interact with them (Ysseldyke & Algozzine, 1995).

Those competing opinions often break down along nature versus nurture lines, and the perceived cause of special learning needs influences the actions and reactions that result from them. Nature theorists believe that special learning needs are the result of deficits, disabilities, and dysfunctions within people and that students are born with them. Nurture theorists believe that conditions outside people (i.e., disadvantages) cause special learning needs. According to this view, being unsuccessful in school is evidence of an unfavorable and/or unproductive environment for learning. McGill-Franzen (1987) noted that current explanations for school failure have changed over time, and she presented evidence that a shift from "disadvantagement" to "disability" characterized changes in explanations of reading failure.

A passage from an early report on the conditions of exceptional people in Massachusetts illustrates the perspective created when nature is blamed for disabilities:

> Idiocy is found in all civilized countries, but it is not an evil necessarily inherent in society; it is to an accident; and much less it is a special dispensation of Providence; to suppose it can be so, is an insult to the Majesty of Heaven. No! *It is merely the result of a violation of natural laws,* which are simple, clear and beautiful; which require only to be seen to be known, in order to be loved; and which, if strictly observed for two or three generations, would totally remove from any family, however strongly predisposed to *insanity or idiocy,* all possibility of its recurrence. (Howe, 1848, p. 2, emphasis added)

The tone of Howe's message and the presumed cause of insanity and idiocy probably reflected the actions and reactions of people during his time. Nevertheless, beliefs about natural causes of exceptionality are still prevalent today (cf. Hallahan & Kauffman, 1989; Kauffman, 1997; Rhodes & Tracy, 1972; Ysseldyke & Algozzine, 1995). The aim of those who treat people with disabilities that are viewed as violations of nature is to rearrange biological and physical dysfunctions to produce improved behavior and learning.

"Insanity is inherited; you get it from your kids." This seemly contradictory prophecy makes great copy for T-shirts and bumper stickers. We like it because it is a paradox, a statement with seemingly inconsistent content. We inherit characteristics from our parents, or we learn behaviors from our children. Professionals who support nurture theories believe that special leaning needs are learned, not inherited. They argue that environmental events result in increases and decreases in behaviors and that the appropriateness or inappropriateness of these behaviors is the basis for special education needs. Nurture theories differ from nature theories in regard to four fundamental assumptions about behavior: what behavior is, what causes behavior, how to change behavior, and how to measure behavior (Alberto & Troutman, 1986; Criswell, 1981; Johnson & Pennypacker, 1980; Kauffman, 1989a, 1997).

The views people hold about the causes of behavior influence the opinions they hold about the people exhibiting the behaviors. Most of us can recall at least one time when our reactions to another person were influenced by knowledge of that person's condition. Most people are more tolerant of crabbiness or other minor, annoying behaviors in friends when the friends are "a little under the weather." That people's views about the cause of a problem influence outlooks about the problem is suggested in the results of at least one research project. Farina, Thaw, Felner, and Hust (1976) arranged an experiment in which undergraduate students gave mild electric shocks to labeled confederates. The shocks given to a confederate thought to be organically (i.e., naturally) retarded were shorter and less intense than those given to a subject thought to be normal or mentally (i.e., not organically) ill. When reactions to these categories were compared in other research, organic impairments (those believed to be caused by physical ailments) were considered more acceptable than functional impairments (those with unknown cause but obvious effects) (Ysseldyke & Algozzine, 1982).

PRACTICAL ISSUES

Practical issues in special education are no less fraught with controversy, and conceptual differences of opinion often spill over into the practical arena. For example, is special education a place to receive services, or is it the actual service being received? Is the focus custodial care or altered educational services? To what extent are services provided simply to offer relief for general classroom teachers? What effects does special education have on core curriculum concerns? What is the best place to provide special education? Continuing dialogue and attempts to resolve practical issues such as these form the foundation for many of the practices that characterize contemporary special education.

Administrative Arrangement or Instructional Method

When many teachers refer students for special education, their primary goal is placement in programs outside the general classroom. These teachers believe that an alteration in instructional placement will be a sufficient basis for improving the educational opportunities of the student with special learning needs. General education teachers come to believe that there are others in the system who are better able to teach students with academic or learning problems. They assume that students should be sent to places where they can benefit from the services of these other people. As a result, many teachers see placement and altered instructional programs as synonymous. This view has been fostered by continuing inservice education presentations designed to inform and enlighten general education teachers to the needs and benefits of special education. Professionals in special education perpetuate this perspective when they argue that process training, learning strategies, behavior modification, or any other instructional methods can and should be delivered only by special education teachers in special classes.

Some students do require specialized instruction to meet their special learning needs. Mobility training for students with visual limits, manual communication training for students with problems hearing, and communication boards for students with an inability to speak are a few examples of instructional needs and methods that make special education special (Ysseldyke & Algozzine, 1995). But there is no reason to believe that such altered instructional methods must be provided in special classes or segregated administrative classroom arrangements. Conversely, assignment to a special class does not guarantee receipt of an altered instructional program. For example, Allington and McGill-Franzen (1989) reviewed research on the quality of reading instruction provided in special programs and concluded that participation in special education programs, even when students with mild disabilities were mainstreamed, did not ensure access to larger amounts of reading instruction. Algozzine, Morsink, and Algozzine (1989) found few differences in instructional behaviors of general classroom teachers and teachers working with students classified with learning disabilities, mental retardation, or emotional disturbance.

Service or Custodial Care

A history of the way society has cared for people with disabilities can be captured in four words: ignorance, isolation, insulation, and integration. Earliest records reveal ignorant, inhumane treatment of people with disabilities. Boring holes in the head to let out evil spirits, burning at the stake as a test of witchcraft, and imprisoning without consideration for civil rights gave rise to a countermovement for moral treatment. Brookover noted that "moral treatment was never clearly defined, possibly because its meaning was self-evident during the era in which it was used; it meant compassionate and understanding treatment of innocent sufferers" (1963, p. 12). Ullman and Krasner pointed out that moral treatment represented "the first effort to provide systematic and responsible care for large numbers of deviant people" (1969, p. 126). And certainly Dorothea Dix's (1843) plea to the Massachusetts legislature for "insane" people, whom she described as being "in cages, closets, cellars, stalls, pens, chained, naked, beaten with rods, and lashed into obedience" can be viewed as evidence of movement into a new era of treatment for people with disabilities. Unfortunately, as Brookover also noted, interest in providing facilities for treatment may have been responsible for the false notion that "institutional treatment is better treatment" (1963, p. 17).

The limited perspective on care created by isolation in large public institutions is evident in this quote:

> These early institutions were in a sense a branch of the public school system, boarding schools having for their purpose the education of the mentally defective. . . . When these early education methods proved less fruitful than had been anticipated in the intellectual rehabilitation of the mentally defective, the institutions . . . were forced to face reality in the demands made upon them for the custodial care of many relatively unimprovable cases, and they entered upon that second and familiar stage in which custodial care and segregation were most prominent. (Davies, 1925, p. 210).

Davies added that isolation as custodial care arose because of a fear in society about what people with disabilities might do if left to their own devices.

As attitudes toward people with disabilities improved and concern for providing adequate care became more of a social issue, perspectives changed from protecting members of society to protecting people with disabilities from society. Practices akin to sheltering, nurturing, and shielding were part of the movement to provide insulation from the ills of society. Special classes with related special curricula and specially trained teachers were hallmarks of this historical phase (Hendrick & Macmillan, 1989; Ysseldyke & Algozzine, 1982).

Recently, special education entered a period when custodial care and service were viewed either as separate and independent activities or as related aspects of treatment in special education. The perspective that care should provide service caused parents, teachers, and other professionals to assess critically the developments created by providing services that were not much like those received by normal students. This led to the birth of PL 94-142 and the requirement of an appropriate placement in the least restrictive environment (Lipsky & Gartner, 1989). A 1983 Sixth Circuit Court of Appeals decision helps illuminate the LRE concept: "Where a segregated facility is considered superior, the court should determine whether services which make the placement superior could feasibly be provided in a nonsegregated setting. If they can, the placement in the segregated school should be inappropriate under the Act [PL 94-142]" (*Ronicker* v. *Walker*, 700 F. 2d, 1058, cert. denied, 104 S. Ct. 196). Concepts of normalization (making life as much like other people's as possible), mainstreaming (ensuring that education is as much like other people's as possible), least restrictive environments (providing service in places as much like those provided for other people), and inclusion (enjoying life experiences with people without disabilities) remain the goals and objectives of improved special education systems during the integration phase that continues today (Asch, 1984; Lipsky & Gartner, 1989; Ysseldyke & Algozzine, 1995).

Educational Service or Teacher Relief

What purpose is served by special education? Some argue that it is a service provided to students with special learning needs to help them acquire more fully the benefits of education and schooling (Hallahan & Kauffman, 1997; Heward & Orlansky, 1989; Kirk & Gallagher, 1986, 1989; Ysseldyke & Algozzine, 1995). From this perspective, special education is delivered in a variety of settings by specially trained professionals, and the provision of special education services is a benefit of an improved educational system trying to accommodate people with special learning needs. But special education was not always seen this way, and not everyone sees it this way today.

To some people, special education is a means of providing relief for general classroom teachers and students; it is a reprieve from the rigors of working and learning with students who are difficult to teach. This perspective has its origins in the early history of special education (Hendrick & Macmillan, 1989). For example, in evaluating the outcomes of alternative education programs, Lincoln (1903) pointed out that by removing many trying pupils from the regular classes, the special education movement accomplished precisely what it set out to accomplish. The implications of comments made by Elizabeth Daniels Nash at the turn of the century remain as challenges today: "Of all the schools that have recently sprung up in this country for the instruction of various classes of unfortunate children, perhaps none have met with so hearty a welcome from the public school teacher as the special class for the mentally deficient" (1901, p. 42).

Indeed, many general education teachers have been opposed to including students with disabilities in their classrooms (Hudson, Graham, & Warner, 1979; Jones, Gottlieb, Guskin, & Yoshida, 1978; Knoff, 1985; Miles & Simpson, 1989;

Williams & Algozzine, 1979). In some cases, however, their opinions became more positive when they had some say in decision making (Miles & Simpson, 1989). Placing students with disabilities in general education classrooms for all or part of the school day (i.e., inclusion) faces obstacles because segregationist thinking is still prevalent today (Brantlinger, 1997; Fuchs & Fuchs, 1994; Kauffman & Hallahan, 1995). Efforts to encourage general and special education teachers to work together (i.e., consultation) to meet the special learning needs of students with disabilities (Morsink, Thomas, & Correa, 1990) and other efforts to "merge" special and regular education systems (cf. Stainback & Stainback, 1984) share the burden of this type of thinking as well. If efforts to educate students with disabilities are to be successful in general classrooms, shared responsibilities and mutual respect for individual differences among parents, teachers, and students are essential (Brantlinger, 1997).

Core Curriculum or Special Curriculum

Special education exists to provide educational opportunities to people with special learning needs. In the early days, the curriculum in special education was based on educational principles established in Europe. It centered on physical (motor and sensory), intellectual (speech and academic), and moral (socialization) training (Talbot, 1964; Ysseldyke & Algozzine, 1982). Although this looks similar to the curriculum being provided in general classrooms, closer inspection reveals important differences. For example, Fort described the "course of instruction" in special classes this way:

> The elementary training must of necessity be specially adapted to the child and, as far as my own experience goes, I would limit the primary work to reading and writing with special work in arithmetic that could simply be supplementary to what I am a firm believer in as the proper sphere of such children, viz. manual training. . . .
>
> The choice of instruction when we come to manual training is large and continually growing. For the younger children, all the occupations of the kindergarten; for the older boys, woodwork, basket-weaving, machine sewing, cane-seating, brush and broom making; the girls, needle-work, cooking, and laundry work with some of the lighter handicrafts usually taught the boys. (1900, pp. 33–34)

This perspective on curriculum was prevalent because a common view held that the future for students with special learning needs was very limited: "Learn to expect little from your deficient child" (Nash, 1901, p. 47).

Today the view of most professionals in special education are radically different and clearly more optimistic. They are shaped by "inclusive" perspectives presented over the years. For example, in his opening address to the First International Conference on Special Education, in Beijing, China, the president of China Welfare Fund for the Disabled presented the purpose of special education as preparing people with disabilities to fulfill social obligations (Lipsky &

Gartner, 1989). Earlier, Lipsky and Gartner argued for seeing people with disabilities in new ways—as "capable of achievement and worthy of respect" (1987, p. 69). Partly as a result of concern for the efficacy of special education and partly as a result of the changing population of students eligible for special education, concepts such as normalization, mainstreaming, and inclusion are uppermost in the views held by many contemporary special educators (Biklen, 1989; Brantlinger, 1997; Stainback & Stainback, 1989; Ysseldyke & Algozzine, 1995).

This shift in outlook brings with it a concern for curriculum. The idea that people with disabilities ought to be allowed to live as normal a life as possible (i.e., normalization) and the implementation of this principle in schools through education of students with disabilities in general classrooms whenever possible have greatly influenced what is and should be taught in special education programs.

Students with disabilities are entitled to special eduction; it is a right provided to them by federal laws. As Abeson and Zettel indicated, "On the opening day of school . . . [it became] a violation of federal law for any public education agency to deny to a child [with a disability] in need of a special program an appropriate program" (1977, p. 115). The mechanism used to ensure that students with disabilities receive a free appropriate public education is the individualized education program (IEP). Students who receive special education have IEPs that delimit what teachers and other professionals will do to meet their special learning needs (Kirk & Gallagher, 1989; Lipsky & Gartner, 1989). The IEP is one factor that differentiates special education from general education (Ysseldyke & Algozzine, 1990). It is "in some ways the most important step in the [special education] process, for it has the potential to make or break the child's educational future" (Rothstein, 1990, p. 201). An IEP, however, is not a guarantee that acceptable levels of performance will be achieved after a specified period of time (Rothstein, 1990; Ysseldyke & Algozzine, 1990). It is a statement of goals and related services that will be used to meet them and a reflection of the curriculum that a student in special education will receive—a "blueprint for appropriate instruction, and delivery of service" (Smith, 1990, p. 85).

Unfortunately, research has demonstrated that the IEP process and the documents that accompany it are inadequate, ineffective, and incomplete (Comptroller General, 1981; McBride & Forgnone, 1985; Pyecha et al., 1980; Schenck, 1980; Smith & Simpson, 1989). Often key objectives in IEPs show little correspondence between the core curriculum in general education and the alternative curriculum in special education (Biklen, 1989). The following quote illustrates the curricular dilemmas created by IEPs.

> In educating a student with a hearing impairment, for example, a major focus is on communication. Curricula are likely to include instruction in sign language or oral communication [such as] techniques, auditory training instruction from a specialist; amplification systems; . . . special seating; . . . captioned films, good acoustics, and someone to take notes in class; and modified curricula. . . . The IEP will specify each of these items. But the IEP will leave many unanswered questions, all related to the student's place in school. How does the student's curriculum fit with

the curriculum of the other students, the curricular goals of the school, and the education atmosphere of the school? What are the attitudes of teachers and peers about disability and other perceived differences? How obtrusively or unobtrusively are special services presented? (Biklen, 1989, p. 15).

Stay Put Placement or Pull Out Program

In attempts to "assure that all children with disabilities have available to them . . . a free appropriate public education which emphasizes special education and related services designed to meet their unique needs" (U.S. Dept. of Education, *Annual Report to Congress,* 1996, p. 2), federal government programs provide supplementary funds for states to use in educating children and youth with disabilities. The federal government provides support for children and youth aged three to twenty-one under provisions of Part B of the Education of the Handicapped Act (EHA-B). Support is also provided to children and youth from birth through age twenty in programs operated by state agencies through Chapter 1 of the Education Consolidation and Improvement Act—State-Operated Programs (ECIA-SOP) authorization. These two initiatives "share the common feature of primarily serving children who have not been successful in general classrooms through specialist teachers who remove children from the general classroom for some part of the school day" (Allington & McGill-Franzen, 1989, p. 75). In recent years, more students in every category except speech impairments, visual impairments, other health impairments, and orthopedic impairments were educated in resource rooms or separate special education classes than in general classrooms (U.S. Dept. of Education, 1996).

Not everyone is satisfied with the existence and perpetuation of separate, and sometimes unequal, special education programs and facilities (Heller, Holtzman, & Messick, 1982). Educators are being challenged to work together in identifying and implementing alternatives for meeting the special learning needs of children and youths in general classrooms (Wang, 1989; Wang, Reynolds, & Walberg, 1986; Will, 1986; Ysseldyke & Algozzine, 1995). Efforts to meet the challenge are evident in federal funding initiatives and recent literature, both of which illustrate a growing movement to adapt instruction so that the services traditionally provided in separate programs can be incorporated into general education (cf. Fuchs & Fuchs, 1994; Gartner & Lipsky, 1987; Stainback, Stainback, & Forest, 1989; U.S. Dept. of Education, 1989, 1990; Wang, 1989).

Adaptive instruction means increasing the capabilities of schools so they can better accommodate diverse students' characteristics and provide instructional interventions that improve every student's ability to choose from the menu of experiences provided in America's schools (Wang, 1989). Effective adaptive instruction includes the following features:

1. Assessed capabilities of students are the basis for instruction. Teachers provide varied amount and types of instruction in meeting needs identified by individualized assessments.

2. Instructional methods and materials provide opportunities for students to master content being presented at their own pace.

3. Continual systematic assessment is the basis for feedback on mastery of content and student progress.

4. Students take increasing responsibility for their educational experiences.

5. Alternative activities and materials are available.

6. Students have opportunities to make choices about goals, learning activities, and learning outcomes.

7. Students cooperate in achieving group educational goals. (Wang & Lindvall, 1984)

Clearly, the intent that students "stay put" in general education programs, rather than be placed in "pullout" special education environments, is evident in efforts to adapt instruction to meet individual learner needs and in efforts to enhance the education of difficult-to-teach students in the mainstream (Fuchs & Fuchs, 1994; Kauffman & Hallahan, 1995; Kaufman, Kameenui, Birman, & Danielson, 1990; Wang, 1980, 1981; Wang & Birch, 1984; Wang & Walberg, 1988). This is true despite equivocal support for these practices:

> Assuming we have not missed reports of successful implementations of the [adaptive learning environment model], we believe currently there is insufficient cause to view it as a successful, large-scale, full-time mainstreaming program. (Fuchs & Fuchs, 1988, p. 126)

> Perhaps the "hardest" evidence of the [model's] feasibility and effectiveness is its successful implementation by hundreds of teachers in a variety of school settings for more than a decade. (Wang & Walberg, 1988, p. 132)

ISSUES REFLECTED IN PRACTICE

The adage that the more things change, the more they stay the same has continuing relevance in special education. When mainstreaming, individualized education programs, resource rooms, and other "innovations" were introduced, they were promoted as significant educational reform for the ills that characterized special education. And, indeed, much has been accomplished. Special education is no longer seen as an evil or as a distant relative of general education. People with special learning needs are participating more actively in experiences that are as much as possible like those of their peers without disabilities. They are being viewed as "full-fledged human beings, capable of achievement and worthy of respect" (Lipsky & Gartner, 1987, p. 73). And professionals are calling for more and more changes. But despite movement in a favorable direction, competing perspectives on important issues continue to be reflected in the practice of special education. People still argue about who should receive special education. There is continuing concern for the character of special education (e.g., is it a practice applied to people or the people themselves?). And who is responsible for it?

Full or Selective Exclusion

The competing ideals of inclusion and exclusion have been evident throughout the history of education in America. The earliest schools were exclusionary, developed to serve a selective group in society (i.e., white male children of upper-class families). With progressive inclusion of "broader ranges of students (e.g., girls, children of color, children of noncitizens, children of slaves and nonproperty owners), states began to prohibit exclusion of ordinary students by passing compulsory attendance laws (Ysseldyke & Algozzine, 1982). The stage for the development of special education was set by the requirement that all children attend school and by the recognition that schools (as currently or historically conceived) were not for everybody.

Around the turn of the last century, James Van Sickle, superintendent of schools in Baltimore, noted that "before the attendance laws were effectively enforced, there were as many of these special cases in the community as there are now; few of them, however, remained long enough in school to attract attention or to hinder the instruction of the more tractable and capable" (1908–1909, p. 102). Students with special learning needs were always (and always will be) part of the national education system. Social policies forced them to go to school, and once there, efforts to provide benefits segregated them from their natural class peers (Lipsky & Gartner, 1989; Stainback, Stainback, & Forest, 1989; Ysseldyke & Algozzine, 1982). Inclusion, the process whereby students with special learning needs receive all or part of their education in general classes, does not mean that all children with disabilities will be retained in or returned to regular classes without special education supports. But it does reflect the view that the experiences of these students should be as much as possible like those of their peers without disabilities.

With the enactment of the Education for All Handicapped Children Act of 1975, each state was directed to establish

> procedures to insure that, to the maximum extent appropriate, handicapped children, including children in public and private institutions or other care facilities, are educated with children who are not handicapped and that special classes, separate schooling, or the removal of handicapped children from the regular education environment occurs only when the nature or severity of the handicaps is such that education in regular classes with the use of supplementary aids and services cannot be achieved satisfactorily (PL 94-142, 1975, sec. 612, 5, B, p. 125).

These principles remained unchanged in the Individuals with Disabilities Act of 1990 (PL 101-476) and the Individuals with Disabilities Education Act Amendments of 1997 (PL 105-17), which reauthorized discretionary programs established by PL 94-142 (NASDSE, 1990). Not only is free education of students with disabilities compulsory, the law mandated that it must be as similar as possible to the education provided to students without disabilities. As is true with any law, the principles embodied in legislation to provide assistance to people with disabilities are subject to interpretation.

As Stainback and Stainback (1989, p. 41) point out:

> We appear to be at a point in history wherein we are no longer satisfied with just discussing the mainstreaming or integration of some students into regular education. Rather, we have begun to analyze how we might go about integrating or merging special and regular education personnel, programs, and resources to design a unified, comprehensive regular education system capable of meeting the unique needs of all students in the mainstream of regular education (Forest, 1987; Gartner & Lipsky, 1987; Lipsky & Gartner, 1987; Stainback & Stainback, 1984, 1985, 1988).

This radical perspective is different from the more traditional view, which states that moving students with mild disabilities into the general education classes for part of their educational experiences was acceptable.

Despite continued attack from traditionalists, the belief that adaptive instruction in general education is possible for all students with disabilities continues to capture the interest of many special educators. Of course, the opinions of some professionals reflect the alternative perspective as well. For example, Braaten, Kauffman, Braaten, Polsgrove, and Nelson (1988) argued that (1) some students *require* special education, (2) these students can be identified in many cases on the basis of their problem behavior(s), (3) these students require different educational technology, (4) teachers of these students need different skills than most teachers, and (5) the efforts to develop partnerships with general education to provide services to students with special learning needs jeopardizes the meager services already available and probably would cause many of them to be shunted out of education altogether. According to Brantlinger (1997, p. 429), efforts to engage in more extensive, full inclusion (i.e., "integration of students with moderate and severe disabilities in general education") are viewed as an even less favorable practice:

> Kauffman and Hallahan (1995) introduce their critique of integrating students with disabilities as "a tool to warn of the dangers of embracing the illusory rhetoric of full inclusion" and "for informing educators, advocates for students with disabilities, and policymakers of the disaster that we can still avoid—if we quickly, forcefully, and effectively unite to steer the full inclusion bandwagon away from its collision" (p. x). Semmel, Gerber, and MacMillan (1995) add that "[l]ooking simultaneously at the past and at the future, we fear that contemporary reform rhetoric about 'full inclusion,' as well as about consultative and collaborative models of service delivery, will not only fail to benefit from the tragic past experience, but also will command such little real commitment of resources as to be a farce" (p. 43).

Practices or People

Special education is an alternative means of meeting the educational demands of students with special learning needs. For most children, school begins as fun and games—something like the life they led before entering the hallowed halls of learning. And for these children, "satisfactory" progress is the outcome of these early school experiences. But for some children, report cards carry unsatisfactory ratings, and school becomes a difficult place to demonstrate competence and gain self-esteem. Special education was developed to meet the needs of these students. And if it were possible to deliver special educational services without assigning names to students and without seeing the special education system as distinctly different from general education, the world would probably be a better place (Biklen, 1989; Biklen, Ferguson, & Ford, 1989a, 1989b; Ferguson, 1989; Ferguson & Asch, 1989; Stainback & Stainback, 1989). Unfortunately, special education is not simply a set of practices applied to students to make them do better in school. Special education is also a complex system of names and labels assigned to students before they can receive special services. The practice of assigning names has caused significant problems for adolescents with special learning needs and for the professionals who serve them.

Students who are labeled with learning disabilities, mental retardation, or emotional disturbance do share some characteristics. For example, they often experience academic difficulties and similar behavior problems. Of the differences used to describe and classify these students, performance on intelligence tests seems to be the main differentiating characteristic. But even this is of little value because any two children with different scores on an intelligence test may be similar in their abilities. The commonly reported overlap in other characteristics of ED, LD, and MR students also influences the extent to which actions and reactions to those conditions vary (cf, Hallahan & Kauffman, 1977; Neisworth & Greer, 1975; Ysseldyke & Algozzine, 1982).

Katz investigated people's attitudes toward and reactions to specific kinds of disabilities. He concluded that

> attitudes toward persons with physical disorders tend to be ambivalent. On the friendly, compassionate side, there appears to be concern for those who suffer, respect for persons who cope with adversity, and acceptance of a norm of kindness toward the sick and injured; on the critical, rejectant side are apparent tendencies to dislike anyone who arouses fear or guilt and to perceive [people with handicaps] as inferior, as perhaps responsible for their fate, as marginal people who should know their place and refrain from testing the limits of acceptance. (1981, p. 21)

Balancing the benefits of special education practices with the difficulties people assigned to special education encounter is not easy. Consider the following:

- As much as 80 percent of the students in some schools can be classified as having learning disabilities by one or more sets of criteria presently in use across the country.

- Many of the characteristics associated with some conditions of special education are evident in large numbers of students who never require special services to be successful in school.
- People with varying degrees of disabilities are successful in all walks of life.
- Being declared eligible for special education does not guarantee that the services provided will be qualitatively different from those received by regular education students in some classrooms.
- People with disabilities consistently report that their biggest problem is overcoming negative attitudes held by other members of society.

Differentiating people from practices in special education is difficult for several reasons. Special services are not available to all students. To receive special education a student must be assigned a label and declared eligible for services. This act often separates the person from the practice. People are referred to by their disability names (e.g., the mentally retarded, the learning disabled), and the focus of concern shifts to what people cannot do, rather than what they can do.

Special or General Responsibilities

During the 1990s, more than 5 million students each year received special education services. In some states, groups of these students (e.g., with learning disabilities) more than doubled during this same period (U.S. Dept. of Education, 1990b, 1996). At the same time, professionals argued that significant portions of some categories of students (e.g., seriously emotionally disturbed) were radically underserved (Braaten et al., 1988), and data indicated that some groups (i.e., Hispanic students with special needs) were radically underserved (Fradd & Correa, 1989). Each year, more and more people seem to need special education. The "medically fragile," those with attention deficit–hyperactive disorder (ADHD), the gifted and those with learning disabilities, "crack babies," children born with acquired immune deficiency syndrome (AIDS), children who transfer between schools, Hispanic students with special needs, and adults with learning disabilities are among the latest people at risk for special education to have their collective pasts and futures exposed and debated in the professional literature (Barnes, 1986; Byers, 1989; Cantwell & Baker, 1991; Centers for Disease Control, 1987a, 1987b; Fradd & Correa, 1989; Interagency Committee on Learning Disabilities, 1987; Jason et al., 1990; Shaywitz & Shaywitz, 1991; Stevens & Price, 1991).

Justified concern for burgeoning masses of people at risk for significant school failure is complicated by the broad issues currently affecting special education (Figueroa, Fradd, & Correa, 1989; Fradd & Correa, 1989; Rueda, 1989). For example, Rueda pointed out that issues affecting Hispanic students with special learning needs "cannot be considered outside the larger institutional context of special education as a whole" (1989, p. 121). Concerns identified by Figueroa, Fradd, and Correa as evidence that "miseducation of many bilingual children with disabilities may well be the norm" (1989, p. 175) are broadly representative of issues in special education in general (see Table 1.3).

All these concerns are also complicated by issues that beg questions of responsibilities for meeting the needs of students who fail to profit in regular classes. Who should pay for special education? How do fiscal and budget concerns influence special education services? Why don't all students receive some form of special education? To what extent do biased assessment practices, untrained psychologists, limited access to related services, the absence of model programs, the inability to hire competent aides, and administratively fragmented programs force some students into special education that they do not need? Will there ever come a time when all students receive special education? Who will control the growth? Who should teach students in need of special education? Who is responsible for students receiving special education? Who should be accountable when they fail to meet IEP objectives or when they are not employable after school? Whose students are they anyway?

Profession or Practice

In professional conversations, it is not uncommon to hear debate about whether the profession of teaching is an art or a science, a profession or a practice (Dunkin, 1987). It has been said that the character of a profession can be measured by the nature of training required to do it. For example, learning about impressionism, cubism, and realism probably has very little to do with whether an artist becomes an impressionist, a cubist, or a realist. Art, or becoming an artist, has probably less to do with what a student studies in school and more to do with what that student can do without it; people become artists in spite of schooling. Scientific professions, in contrast, are characterized by recognizable bodies of knowledge that are essential for acceptance and competence. Principles of mechanics, motion, and stress are taught to young people as a basis for assimilation into a society of professional engineers. Of course, practicing the principles in real-life situations helps an engineer to mature and profit, but as in most sciences, fundamental knowledge is required before practice is expected or permitted.

Arguments in support of the art or science of teaching usually lead to discussions of the purposes and functions of teacher training programs and the relevance of improving teaching without considering its origins and base. For example, Gallagher (1970) argued that teaching is an art but that it should become more of a science. He also believed that improvement of teaching would be more likely if some of the mystery typically associated with art was removed by identification of the scientific aspects of teaching. Gage (1978) believed the real issue in understanding and improving teaching is to identify its scientific basis. He was concerned with the extent to which scientific methods could be employed in studying teaching. The nature of the scientific basis, according to Gage, will be "established relationships between variables in teaching and learning" (1978, p. 22), and the stronger these relationships are, the more likely teaching will be improved.

TABLE 1.3   **Findings from Minority Research Institutes**

Assessment Concerns	Instruction Concerns
1. Language proficiency is not seriously taken into account in special education assessment. 2. Testing is done primarily in English, thereby increasing the likelihood that achievement or intelligence discrepancy will be found. 3. English-language problems that are typical of second-language learners (poor comprehension, limited vocabulary, grammar and syntax errors, and problems with English articulation) are misinterpreted as handicaps. 4. Learning disability and communication handicapped placements have replaced the misplacement of students as educable mentally retarded during the 1960s and 1970s. 5. Psychometric test scores from Spanish or English tests are capricious in their outcomes, though, paradoxically, internally sound. 6. Special education placement leads to decreased test scores (IQ and achievement). 7. Home data are not used in assessment. 8. The same few tests are used with most children. 9. Having parents who were born outside the United States increases the likelihood that a student will be found eligible for special education. 10. Reevaluations usually lead to more special education.	1. The behaviors that trigger teacher referral suggest that English-language-acquisition stages and their interaction with English-only programs are being confused for handicapping conditions. 2. Few children receive primary language support before special education; even fewer, during special education. 3. The second and third grades are critical for bilingual children in terms of potential referral. 4. Prereferral modifications of the regular programs are rare and show little indication of primary language support. 5. Special education produces little academic development. 6. Individual education plans had few, if any, accommodations for bilingual children. 7. The few special education classes that work for bilinguals are more like good regular bilingual education classes (whole-language emphasis, comprehensible input, cooperative learning, and student empowerment) than traditional behavioristic, task-analysis driven, worksheet-oriented special education classes.

SOURCE: From Findings from Handicapped Minority Research Institutes by Figueroa, R. A., Fradd, S. H., & Correa, V. I. *Exceptional Children,* 56, 1989; p. 176. Copyright © by The Council for Exceptional Children. Reprinted with permission.

If the nature of a profession is evident in the character of the training provided novice practitioners, teaching is more an art than a science. Significant certification requirements reflect the belief that coursework and experience are important but that coursework is essential. But teachers consistently complain about the irrelevance of undergraduate and graduate education training (if there is a scientific basis for teaching, it is not being presented or perceived as such by people learning to teach). Large portions of coursework have little to do with a science of teaching; there are few principles taught that apply directly and uniformly to solution of problems in classrooms, and much professional literature contains "almost nothing in the way of specific, practical help for teachers" (Swart, 1990, p. 317). People who enter teaching from other professions, without formal pedagogical training, often turn out to be exemplary teachers. People who stay in teaching for many years often report that few changes occur during their tenure in classrooms (Swart, 1990).

A brother of one of the authors is a clinical pharmacist in a large hospital. He is an active agent in providing medical assistance to patients. He is responsible for monitoring the effects of remedies prescribed by physicians. His knowledge needs and his levels of knowledge attainments have grown significantly during his tenure in his profession. As is true for most hospital pharmacists, he "had to keep pace with the development of new products, assimilate new findings about old ones, and learn to use new tools within new systems" (Swart, 1990, p. 315). Similar levels of professional growth are not necessary or common in the teaching profession.

Teaching is the systematic presentation of content assumed necessary for mastery of the subject matter being taught. A practice is a set of principles that can be applied in the solution of problems. If we use these definitions, we can conclude that teaching in special education is a practice that requires general professional training. Preservice training in special education is a mixture of courses similar to those taken by general education students and some "professional" courses within a specialized program of training. For example, prospective elementary school teachers take foundations and general methods courses (e.g., introduction to education, social and/or psychological foundations of education, elementary school curriculum) and specific methods courses (e.g., teaching reading, mathematics, social studies); they also spend some time student teaching. Prospective special education teachers take background courses in the foundations of education (e.g., introduction to education, social and/or psychological foundations of education, elementary school curriculum) and then specialize in foundations and methods of exceptional student education; they also spend some time student teaching (Ysseldyke & Algozzine, 1982). Marston (1987) found that the focus of a special education teacher's certification (e.g., mental retardation versus learning disabilities) had little to do with the nature of the instruction provided to students. Interestingly, training programs for school psychologist offer courses in the same general areas (Brown, 1979; Curtis & Batsche, 1991;

Ysseldyke, Dawson, Lehr, Reschly, Reynolds, & Telzrow, 1997) and some evidence suggests that their practices are not categorically different either (Ysseldyke & Algozzine, 1995). In recent years, inservice training in special education has focused on procedures for compliance with federal laws (e.g., writing acceptable IEPs), rather than on innovative ways to organize and present content. New products do not enter special education at a pace that makes inservice training essential or practicing teachers' knowledge deficient to an extent that matters.

Paralleling development in other professions, several hundred organizations have formed to support the development and maintenance of services to people with disabilities. Groups consist of teachers who serve special students, related services personnel, administrators, parents of children with disabilities, and people who have disabilities themselves (Ysseldyke & Algozzine, 1995). Often several organizations serve the same category of special education students, but their members may work in slight opposition to one another. For example, members of the Association for Children and Adults with Learning Disabilities, the Council for Learning Disabilities, the Division for Learning Disabilities of the Council for Exceptional Children, the Society for Learning Disabilities and Remedial Education, and the Orton Society all serve people with learning disabilities. State departments and any or all of these professional organizations may hold different perspectives on eligibility criteria for learning disability services and the kinds of treatment students should receive in special education.

Similarly, disagreements among members of organizations occur because different types of people join for different reasons. Parents may be charter members of one group and advocate quite different things than university professors who are the founders of another similarly named group. This does not mean that one organization is better than another. It simply is a final illustration of the variety of perspectives that drive a profession and practice as diverse as special education.

Whether viewed as a profession or a practice, information about competing perspectives and issues is valuable for people interested in special education. From a professional point of view, information about issues that affect special education practices serves as foundation knowledge for organizing the development of professionals. From a practical point of view, information about issues that affect special education professionals serves as foundation knowledge for improving practices.

EDUCATION AT THE MARGINS

Special education and general education share common goals. As more and more students are served by people in special education, the boundaries between the two systems become less distinct, and the unique characteristics of special education become harder to specify. When more and more students are considered at risk, the concept of specialized instruction to meet individual learning needs becomes moot. As more students are identified with special learning needs, multiple, even competing perspectives all begin to make sense.

Special education is a subsystem of education that exists to enhance experiences of people with special learning needs. Because it is not available to everyone, special education is a controversial practice. The controversy takes up issues of access, availability, and accountability. Concerns about access ask who should receive special education. Concerns about availability center on where special education should be provided and what should be provided. Concerns about accountability address the extent to which special education makes a difference. The rest of this book looks at the evolution of special education services, the condition of special education today, and the issues and concerns that professionals who practice special education face each day.

Discussion Questions

1. Special education is a subsystem of education organized to provide alternative experiences for students with special learning needs. What views held by general education teachers support this practice? Why do some professionals argue for less use of pullout programs in special education?

2. In the beginning, the curriculum in special education classes was different from that provided in general classrooms. Today, people who have spent considerable time in special education programs complain that their education is inferior to that of their regular class peers. Should the curriculum in special education be the same as that provided in general education?

3. How do people at your school view special education? Do students in other programs think teaching is an art or a science? Do they see teaching as a profession or a practice? What do faculty members in other departments think about faculty in special education and other education programs?

Chapter 2
Special Education in Context

The foundation of every state is the education of its youth.

—Diogenes

In this chapter, we examine the mission of schooling in America and the extent to which the mission differs according to the type of student. We review the social, political, and legal bases for both general and special education. Inasmuch as the current mission of schooling has evolved over the decades, a brief history of important educational events offers a beginning perspective on the basis for special education.

Because large numbers of students are failing to accomplish the goals and objectives of America's schools, this chapter also examines the objectives of American education and the failure to achieve them. We provide some current evidence on the progress of education and some information on those students who are failing to accomplish the objectives set for them by parents, teachers, and other members of society. We also describe briefly the legal precedents that have evolved in support of society's willingness to help failing students.

EDUCATION'S MISSION

Many of the issues that emerged when schools (or society through its schools) were perceived as failing in their obligations to the nation's children and youths have their origins in the evolution of the school's mission and purposes in American education. Because the provision of special services emerged as one way to improve educational opportunities for students who were difficult to teach, special education's history can perform the same function of clarifying how special education has come to its current crossroads.

According to Hendrick and Macmillan, the first special education classes were justified politically on two grounds:

> First, the larger social and political force of progressivism in American life called for humane treatment of poor and disadvantaged children. Second, even if politicians were unmoved by the humanitarian motive, probably they would be persuaded that it was in society's best interest to provide educational opportunities to children who otherwise might grow up with antisocial tendencies. (1989, p. 395)

Humanitarian reform and social control were not the only reasons for expanding the mission of the public schools at the turn of the last century to include students with special needs. Practical problems played a part as well: "Although the age-graded plan of pupil organization and promotion was well in place in 1900, large, urban school systems were groping for ways to cope with an increasingly large and diverse student population" (Hendrick & Macmillan, 1989, p. 399).

As the need for special classes was increasingly met, the need for definitions, criteria, and curriculum for students who would be served there intensified as well. The development and use of intelligence testing helped early educators to address questions about definitions and criteria (Sarason & Doris, 1979; Ysseldyke & Algozzine, 1995). Curriculum took the form of more physical engagement than was the case within general classrooms: "Instead of books, copy books, and written questions to answer," students with special learning needs "[made] toys, play[ed] games, and work[ed] with things" (Hendrick & Macmillan, 1989, p. 401). Even though the content of special education was different, early pioneers believed the methods that worked with normally achieving students would work for students needing special education (Farrell, 1908).

Early educators did consider students with special learning needs different from their peers:

> In all its work the ungraded class emphasizes, for the purpose of preserving and enhancing his self-respect and his personal esteem, those things which the [special student] has in common with his more fortunate brothers and sisters, it believes his differences are already too apparent; it preaches as well as practices its belief and

> knowledge that his mental power is like theirs only of less degree. By having one such class in an elementary school it is possible to get the moral support of the whole body of pupils in developing and molding the child who is "different." (Quoted in Hendrick & Macmillan, 1989, p. 397)

Today, however, it is less appropriate to speak of differences as primary characteristics of people with disabilities because it is widely recognized that all people are more alike than different. A central concern within special education is to make the curriculum provided to students with special needs as much like that received by their peers as possible (Brantlinger, 1997; Lipsky and Gartner, 1989; Ysseldyke & Algozzine, 1995). Yet despite significant and continuing efforts to reform education, the signs of failing schools are still evident everywhere (Sarason, 1990). Dropout rates continue to increase despite massive federal, state, and local expenditures supporting programs to keep students in school (Seligmann, 1990). In many urban areas and for some groups of students with disabilities, the rate exceeds 50 percent of the student body that should graduate (Macchiarola, 1989; U.S. Dept. of Education, 1996). Because the failures cut across all education, let us start by scrutinizing the original purpose of schooling and the extent to which schools do what they purport to do.

Foundations of Education

The first schools in this country were secondary schools established in Massachusetts in the early seventeenth century. Called Latin grammar schools, largely because of their curricula, the first one was established in Boston, Massachusetts, in 1635. The sole purpose of the Latin grammar schools was to prepare students to enter Harvard College, America's first institution of higher education, which was established in 1636. The pattern of schooling followed that established in Europe, where higher education in general was reserved for the top two classes in society—the landed nobility and the landed gentry. When John Adams attended Harvard, students were ranked according to social standing, not academic achievement. He was near the bottom. The curricula of the Latin grammar schools consisted almost entirely of the study of Latin and Greek, an emphasis that had its historical roots in the early religious basis of education to train youths to read the Old and New Testaments.

Between 1634 and 1638, the first laws were enacted for the public support of education; they enabled the Commonwealth of Massachusetts to tax its populace and assume responsibility for schooling. The Commonwealth took on the responsibility of public education because parents were allegedly doing an inadequate job of educating their children at home. The first laws establishing public support of education had a religious basis, as evidenced in the Massachusetts law of 1647, often called "the old deluder, Satan, Act." This law read, in part, as follows:

> It being one chiefe project of that old deluder, Satan, to keepe men from the knowledge of the Scriptures, as in former times by keeping them in an unknown tongue, so in these latter times by persuading from the use of tongues, that so at least the

true sence and meaning of the originall might be clouded by false glosses of saint seeming deceivers, that learning may not be buried in the grave of our fathers in church and commonwealth, the Lord assisting our endeavors.—

It is therefore ordered that every township in this jurisdiction, after the Lord hath increased their number to 50 householders, shall then forthwith appoint one within their towne to teach all such children as shall resort to him to write and reade, whose wages shall be paid either by the parents or masters of such children, or by the inhabitants in general, . . . and it is further ordered that where any towne shall increase to the number of 100 families or householders they shall set up a grammar schoole, the Master thereof being able to instruct youth so farr as they shall be fitted for the University, provided that if any town neglect the performance hereof above one year, that every such town shall pay five pounds to the next school till they shall perform this order (Cubberley, 1934, pp. 18–19)

Virtually the only kind of public secondary school in America until the middle of the eighteenth century was the Latin grammar school. But a significant change occurred in 1750 when Benjamin Franklin opened his academy (later the University of Pennsylvania). Franklin believed that students should be educated in modern languages, especially English, and in practical subject matter such as navigating, surveying, and kite flying. Franklin's school also included instruction in history, geography, rhetoric, logic, astronomy, geometry, and algebra.

SCHOOL AND SOCIETY

To study education and the ideals that motivate it and contribute to its sense of mission and purpose is to study society and culture (Silberman, 1970). Inasmuch as schools reflect culture, it is not surprising to find educational ideals reflecting societal ideals. Three ideals have guided the development of education in America and are evident in all aspects of schooling (although, of course, as with any generalization, exceptions can readily be found).

Ideals of Education

One of the primary characteristics of American society is that it is democratic. Countless books have been written on the meaning of democracy, but it can be described quite simply as a system in which the individual is perceived as central and in which all political, social, and economic institutions serve the individual's well-being. Many people readily repeat Abraham Lincoln's words in the Gettysburg Address—"government of the people, by the people, and for the people"—to define democracy. Corollaries of the democratic ideal include beliefs in the individual's worth, equality of opportunity, freedom of thought, and faith in reason. Based on this societal ideal, "we are committed to the democratic proposition that each child—genius or moron, black or white, rich or poor—should be educated to bring out the best that is in him [or her]" (Callahan, 1961, p. 145). As you will see in this chapter as well as in others, the democratic ideal that *all* should be appropriately educated has directed much educational thinking, especially that related to the schooling of minority students and students with disabilities.

A second ideal, one that characterizes American society and through it American education, is nationalism. Americans regard this nation as the center of the universe, and for many this implies a strong loyalty symbolized by the American flag as well as the national anthem, heroes, myths, and legends. Nationalism is developed and nurtured through the process of education, both in and out of schools. When children learn to read English, they encounter national symbols in their earliest readers, and teachers tell them the stories of George Washington and the cherry tree, Paul Bunyan and his blue ox, and Thanksgiving. Children learn the pledge of allegiance and the national anthem, and they study the lives of American presidents. Yet American education is often caught between fostering nationalism and promoting respect for and concern with other nations, understanding their rights, and recognizing their contributions, especially when numbers of immigrants from particular countries become concentrated political forces in cities and towns across the country.

The third characteristic of American society is individualism. The schools' emphasis on individualism has led to an emphasis on achievement or success. Because individual success is a dominant value in American society, it is nurtured in the schools and forms the basis for evaluation of schools and their students.

Characteristics of Society

Just as the American ideals of democracy, nationalism, and individualism shape the nature of American education, the specific social and economic characteristics of American society direct and constrain the purposes of schooling (Callahan, 1964). American society is scientific and technical, and the curricula of its schools reflect the role of science and technology in the development of modern America. Although in principle this is a classless society and America is called a "land of equal opportunity," vocation, income and source of income, family background, and type of house or residential area do indeed establish class membership and the boundaries between classes. Class membership often determines the amount of schooling a person receives, and membership in a particular class is in turn influenced by the amount of a person's schooling.

America is also segregated by race, despite the belief in equality and equal opportunity. In most sections of the country, cities are divided into neighborhoods on the basis of ethnicity and race. Although segregation in schools has been declared unconstitutional, it still exists to a considerable extent.

American society is also industrial. Industrialization has encouraged increases in population because there are more resources to feed and clothe people, has created high-density population centers around industries with large work forces, and has led to the organization of labor unions. Schools are patterned after industry and often adopt such industrial goals as operational efficiency, increased productivity, and inservice training.

American society is further characterized by mass education. Conformity and uniform standards for education are emphasized, and only recently have individual learning needs and efforts to devise individualized education programs been recognized.

Finally, American society is characterized by capitalism. Competition is basic to this society, and commercialism flourishes. Schools no longer exist solely to prepare students for the next level of education; they are also expected to prepare students for different roles in the world of work. In most secondary schools the offerings include business, commercial, and vocational curricula.

School as a Social Institution

The establishment of schools presumes that human beings lack the general knowledge, morals, and intellect necessary to culture; that people are capable of learning and attending to the presentation of knowledge; that they wish to learn; and that "there is a body of knowledge and skill to be taught" (Broudy, 1978, p. 25). Wallace defined school as follows:

> School is an institution which deliberately and systematically, by the presentation of symbols in reading matter, lectures, or ritual, attempts to transform from a condition of ignorance to one of enlightenment of the intellect, the morality, and the technical knowledge and skills of an attentive group of persons in a definite place at a definite time. (1973, p. 231)

A number of implications follow from the preceding definition of school. As a social institution, the school is charged with instilling in children society's beliefs and knowledge base. This charge presupposes that school instruction is both systematic and deliberate.

As a social reflection, school has a class system, segregation, and competition, and the administrative model parallels that of industry. School conforms to standards set by local, state, and federal governments to ensure uniformity, productivity, and efficiency, and school models the social values it is designed to instill and cultivate.

As a social organization, a public school is an instrument for the public good. It is a place where societal ideals can be inculcated and to which society has entrusted a valued resource—its youths. School is a first-line defense against poverty, ignorance, and other ills. Because of this, a school is a tough place for people to live. To achieve the "greater good," a school must operate within parameters that sometimes compete with individual educational needs and ideals. For example, classroom rules are necessary and prominent components of any school program. But the order achieved by having rules often competes with and sometimes cancels out individual goals of independence and freedom of expression.

The American school is a graded organization. Rights of passage between grades are controlled by scores obtained on performance indicators presumed to be important (e.g., tests). Achievement of rights of passage (promotion) is valued by members of society. Success and promotion serve as important sources of competition within American schools, much as they do within American business (Glasser, 1990; Sarason, 1990). Often, important interpersonal skills (e.g., cooperation) are devalued as a result (Deming, 1982).

Effective Schools

Much has been written about the characteristics of effective schools (cf. Edmonds, 1982; Lezotte, 1989; Purkey & Smith, 1985; Robinson, 1983). Most professionals agree that effective schools share five common characteristics:

1. They have an effective leader (generally the principal) or leaders.
2. They have a well-articulated instructional focus.
3. They offer safe, orderly climates for teaching and learning.
4. People in them have high expectations for student success.
5. Student achievement is monitored regularly.

In recent years, this taxonomy has offered the promise of educational reform to many professionals.

But despite the progress that has been made in articulating the characteristics of effective schools and in improving what goes on in them, concern for the future of education remains. For example, Sarason argued that schools are intractable to change and that efforts at educational reform will fail as they have in the past.

> There are two basic issues. The first is the assumption that schools exist primarily for the growth and development of children. That assumption is invalid because teachers cannot create and sustain the conditions for the productive development of children if those conditions do not exist for teachers. The second issue is that there is now an almost unbridgeable gulf that students perceive between the world of the school and the world outside of it. Schools are uninteresting places in which the interests and questions of children have no relevance to what they are required to learn in the classroom. Teachers continue to teach subject matter, not children. Any reform effort that does not confront these two issues and the changes they suggest is doomed. (1990, p. xiv)

There are no simple answers in education. Recognizing that special education is a subsystem of education helps to illustrate why there are no simple answers in special education either. Issues created by the social, political, and economic characteristics of schools influence special education in complex ways. For example, English is the primary language of American society, and transmission of the proper grammatic rules of English is an important curricular goal in America's schools. When large numbers of students enter school from home in which English is a second language, special education becomes a dominant alternative in the search for ways to meet the special learning needs created by diversity among students. Similarly, achievement and school performance are sometimes considered reflections of the educational health of a nation. Note the interest generated when the College Entrance Examination Board periodically makes public the distribution of Scholastic Aptitude Test (SAT) scores for high school students.

Every fall, state education officials wait impatiently for the College Board to release the latest figures on high school students' performance on the SAT. Much like the arrival of the first report card of the year (SAT reports typically appear in September), these proclamations from the College Board sometimes bring misery and fear to even the most optimistic educators. For example, when his state moved from fiftieth to forty-ninth in the national rankings provided by the College Board, a spokesperson for the South Carolina Department of Education said, "We've lived in this misery for all these years. Now it's somebody else's turn" (Morell, 1989, p. 1A). At the same time, officials in North Carolina (bumped to the bottom in 1989 by South Carolina's two-point gain) said the state superintendent would outline a plan for improvement immediately. Next year, when scores of students climbed from last place to forty-ninth, the North Carolina superintendent of public instruction, Bob Etheridge, was quick to take credit: "I'm pleased that North Carolina is no longer at the bottom of the heap. . . . We promised progress and we delivered some measure of progress and, in the next few weeks, I plan to issue a report to keep the heat on so we can continue to make progress" (*Charlotte Observer,* August 28, 1990, p. 1A). South Carolina schools superintendent Charlie Williams partly blamed private schools and said, "Hurricane Hugo could have played a role" in scores in his state falling from 838 to 834 (*Charlotte Observer,* August 29, 1990, p. 5A). Because SAT scores are treated as indicators of the quality of education in America as well as reflections of intelligence and objects of devotion for individual students, they have accrued a power completely out of proportion to what they actually reflect.

Concern for achievement and the relationship between achievement and perceptions of effectiveness are powerful forces in education. Their effects on the development and progress of special education are illustrated in opinions about "how the raising of reading standards, coupled with social expectations that schools help America's cold war effort and also sort students for future work roles in a stratified economy" led to the creation of the category of learning disabilities (Sleeter, 1986, p. 48).

A significant escalation of standards for academic achievement followed the launching of *Sputnik I* in 1957 and the related "race for space" that captured the intellectual interests of technicians, practitioners, and the public. According to Sleeter, recommendations during this time for

> reforming American education included (a) toughening elementary reading instruction . . . ; (b) introducing uniform standards for promotion and graduation and testing students' mastery of those standards through a regular, nationwide examination system . . . ; (c) grouping students by ability so the bright students can move more quickly through school and then go on to college and professional careers, while slower students move into unskilled or semiskilled labor . . . ; and (d) assigning the most intellectually capable teachers to the top group of students. (1986, p. 48)

When students failed to keep up, few blamed the raising of standards. Instead, the students were blamed for their failure (Brantlinger, 1997; Sarason & Doris, 1979; Ysseldyke & Algozzine, 1982). Once traditional and existing categories of special education (e.g., mental retardation, emotional disturbance) became suspect as inappropriate classification for many of these students, the way was paved for the emergence of learning disabilities as a category, which became increasingly popular. Using underlying process disorders as the reason for discrepancies between ability and achievement as well as other deficits, dysfunctions, and academic disadvantages made infinitely good sense to many people (especially parents frustrated by the search for reasons for their children's lack of achievement in school), and education was changed forever.

Characteristics of Families

Because the family is the fundamental social unit in this society, the larger social changes that have affected education have also affected the family. And the opposite is also true: the evolving nature of the family is modifying, sometimes profoundly, educational practice and philosophy. A report of the House of Representatives Select Committee on Children, Youth, and Families provided clear evidence of the extent and ways families are changing.

In the past 30 years, America has witnessed significant changes in family constitutions believed to influence negatively the lives of children. The greatest effects have to do with increases in the number of divorced or never-married parents and the increasing numbers of mothers entering the workforce. Rises in the number of children being raised by single parents have been accompanied by other trends as well (Brooks-Gunn, Denner & Klebanov, 1994; Hodgkinson, 1992; Sautter, 1994).

- Between 1940 and 1960, 6 to 8 percent of child and youth below the age of 18 were living in mother-only families; during the 1990s, this figure was 3 times larger. Increases in the divorce rate accounted for a portion of this increase.

- In 1960, about 2 percent of single-parent families were the result of divorce; that figure was 4 times higher during the 1990s.

- By the age of 16, 40 percent of European-American children and 75 percent of African-American children will have lived in single-parent households.

- During the 1990s, more than one-quarter of all births were to unmarried mothers.

- Households headed by single or never-married mothers are much more likely to be poor than households with two parents; additionally, family income decreases substantially following a divorce.

- The number of women in the workforce who had children under the age of 6 more than doubled from the 1960s to the 1990s.

Family changes are thought to result in redistribution of family resources. Working parents have less time to spend with children, and divorce reduces the contact children have with noncustodial parents. All of this often washes over into school experiences. School adaptation, including appropriate engagement in schooling, ability to regulate behavior, competence in peer interactions, and general achievement, is influenced by what happens at home (Brooks-Gunn, Denner, & Klebanov, 1994; Hodgkinson, 1992). The problem is long-standing.

Hodgkinson (1985, 1992) has written extensively on the changing nature of families and their impact on the schools. More students from minority cultures with a greater diversity of languages are present in today's classrooms, as are more children from families in stress. Many students come to school with limited educational support. Others are sophisticated, "streetwise," and skeptical; most are less willing to be directed without acceptable reasons. A demographic profile of children attending school at the height of the school reform movement is presented in Table 2.1. Because students have diverse backgrounds and attitudes, making a difference in their lives is hard work. Teachers need high levels of creativity, energy, and effort to make classrooms full of these students work. Given the current nature of schools, many children and youths go there and fail. And at a time when students are requiring more varied and comprehensive programs to be successful, political support for schools is undergoing detrimental changes. Today only about 20 percent of the nation's taxpayers have children in school, and many of these parents are taking advantage of opportunities to place their children in schools of choice (Goens & Clover, 1990; Hodgkinson, 1992). Coupled

TABLE 2.1	Demographic Profile of Students in America's Schools	
Characteristic		**Percent**
Children from families in poverty		25
Children of teenaged mothers		14
Children from immigrant families that speak a language other than English		15
Children of unmarried parents		14
Children from broken homes		40
Latchkey children		25–33

SOURCE: Hodgkinson, H. L. (1985). *All One System*. Washington D.C.; Institute for Educational Leadership. Used with permission.

with the diverse characteristics students are bringing to school, this potential lack of funding support makes finding productive ways to meet special learning needs an increasingly critical concern in America's schools.

GOALS AND OBJECTIVES OF EDUCATION

The ideals of American society and the nation's social and economic characteristics have interacted to shape and influence the nature of American education. What, then, are the goals or objectives of American education?

Stated broadly and in nonoperational terms (as most statements about school philosophy or objectives are), schools in America exist to educate all children; inculcate in them an appreciation of democratic principles, a sense of nationalism, and a belief in the worth of the individual; and educate them to their utmost capacity. There is little disagreement over these general goals. But because objectives are statements of preferences, choices, or values, they change over time, and they vary from one social group to another. Thus, the public, according to Broudy, is not a singular entity: "It is no longer possible to speak meaningfully of a public school serving a public good. For there are as many publics as there are constituencies vocal enough to make their expectations— often conflicting—known to local, state, and federal educational agencies" (1978, p. 24).

Because there may be considerable debate over the specific objectives of schooling and considerable variance in objectives among states and among local education agencies, let us look at the educational goals of representative national groups. In the past, the first formally stated educational goals or objectives were the seven cardinal principles of education identified in 1918 by the Commission on Reorganization of Secondary Education of the National Education Association: (1) health, (2) command of the fundamental processes, (3) worthy home membership, (4) vocation, (5) citizenship, (6) worthy leisure, and (7) ethical character.

In 1938, the Educational Policies Commission of the National Education Association proposed a new classification of educational objectives. These were based on four domains: (1) development of the individual; (2) development of home, family, and community life; (3) response to economic demands; and (4) development of civic and social duties. Four groups of objectives with related subdivisions were formulated (see Table 2.2). For example, the objectives of "self-realization" indicate that the "educated person has an appetite for learning" and "can speak the mother tongue clearly." The objectives of "human relationships" indicated that the "educated person can work and play with others" and "is skilled in homemaking." More recent purposes, goals, objectives, and educational priorities for all students have included the "ability to think," the "development of rational powers," and the ability to learn how to learn, attack problems, and acquire new knowledge."

TABLE 2.2   **National Education Association Classification of Educational Objectives**

The Objectives of Self-Realization

The inquiring mind. The educated person has an appetite for learning.
Speech. The educated person can speak the mother tongue clearly.
Reading. The educated person reads the mother tongue efficiently.
Writing. The educated person writes the mother tongue effectively.
Number. The educated person solves his problems of counting and calculating.
Sight and hearing. The educated person is skilled in listening and observing.
Health knowledge. The educated person understands the basic facts concerning health and disease.
Health habits. The educated person protects his own health and that of his dependents.
Public health. The educated person works to improve the health of the community.
Recreation. The educated person is a participant and spectator in many sports and other pastimes.
Intellectual interest. The educated person has mental resources for the use of leisure.
Esthetic interests. The educated person appreciates beauty.
Character. The educated person gives responsible direction to his own life.

The Objectives of Human Relationships

Respect for humanity. The educated person puts human relationships first.
Friendships. The educated person enjoys a rich, sincere, and varied social life.
Cooperation. The educated person can work and play with others.
Courtesy. The educated person observes the amenities of social behavior.
Appreciation of the home. The educated person appreciates the family as a social institution.
Conservation of the home. The educated person conserves family ideals.
Homemaking. The educated person is skilled in homemaking.
Democracy in the home. The educated person maintains democratic family relationships.

The Objectives of Economic Efficiency

Work. The educated producer knows the satisfaction of good workmanship.
Occupational information. The educated producer understands the requirements and opportunities for various jobs.
Occupational choice. The educated producer has selected his occupation.
Occupational efficiency. The educated producer succeeds in his chosen vocation.
Occupational adjustment. The educated producer maintains and improves his efficiency.
Occupational appreciation. The educated producer appreciates the social value of his work.
Personal economics. The educated consumer plans the economics of his own life.
Consumer judgment. The educated consumer develops standards for guiding his expenditures.
Efficiency in buying. The educated consumer is an informed and skillful buyer.
Consumer protection. The educated consumer takes appropriate measures to safeguard his interests.

The Objectives of Civic Responsibility

Social justice. The educated citizen is sensitive to the disparities of human circumstance.
Social activity. The educated citizen acts to correct unsatisfactory conditions.
Social understanding. The educated citizen seeks to understand social structures and social processes.
Critical judgment. The educated citizen has defenses against propaganda.
Tolerance. The educated citizen respects honest differences of opinion.
Conservation. The educated citizen has a regard for the nation's resources.
Social applications of science. The educated citizen measures scientific advance by its contribution to the general welfare.
World citizenship. The educated citizen is a cooperating member of the world community.
Law observance. The educated citizen respects the law.
Economic literacy. The educated citizen is economically literate.
Political citizenship. The educated citizen accepts his civic duties.
Devotion to democracy. The educated citizen acts upon an unswerving loyalty to democratic ideas.

SOURCE: Educational Policies Commission (1918). *The Purposes of Education in American Democracy,* Washington, D.C.: National Education Association and the American Association of School Administrators, pp. 50, 72, 90, 108. Used with permission.

The Latest Goals of American Education

B y the year 2000, all children will start school ready to learn.

- The high school graduation rate will increase to at least 90 percent.

- All students will leave grades four, eight, and twelve having demonstrated competency in challenging subject matter, including English, mathematics, science, history, and geography; and every school in America will ensure that all students learn to use their minds well, so they may be prepared for responsible citizenship, further learning, and productive employment in our modern economy.

- The nation's teaching force will have access to programs for the continued improvement of their professional skills and the opportunity to acquire the knowledge and skills needed to instruct and prepare all students for the next century.

- Students in the United States will be first in the world in mathematics and science achievement.

- Every adult American will be literate and will possess the knowledge and skills necessary to compete in a global economy and exercise the rights and responsibilities of citizenship.

- Every school in the United States will be free of drugs, violence, and the unauthorized presence of firearms and alcohol and will offer a disciplined environment conducive to learning.

- Every school will promote partnerships that will increase parental involvement and participation in promoting the social, emotional, and academic growth of children.

SOURCE: From National Education Goals Panel, 1997. *The National Education Goals Report.* Washington, D.C.: Author.

News reports throughout the country during the 1990s featured stories about the national goals agreed to by "the education presidents" and chief state officials. For the first time in two hundred years of education history, the public was provided with an educational mission of national prominence. The broad goals deal with inculcating school readiness, increasing school completion rates, bettering student achievement, improving the teaching force, making the United States first in the world in mathematics and science achievement, increasing adult literacy, making schools safe places for learning, and improving partnerships with families to support the education of all children (see the box on this page).

In 1990, the National Education Goals Panel was created to monitor the amount of progress made by the nation and the states toward the National Education Goals. More than two dozen core indicators (e.g., percentage of infants born with one or more health risks, percentage of teachers reporting participation in professional development programs) were established to convey progress in each goal area. According to the 1997 National Education Goals Report, progress was slightly better than in previous reports (National Education Goals Panel, 1997). There were improvements in some indicators, no change in several indicators, and less than encouraging news in other indicators (see Table 2.3).

TABLE 2.3   Summary of Progress Toward National Education Goals

Areas of Improvement

- More infants were born with a healthier start in life.
- More 2-year-olds were fully immunized.
- More families were reading and telling stories to their children on a regular basis.
- Mathematics achievement has improved among students in grades four, eight, and twelve.
- More students are receiving degrees in mathematics and science.
- School incidents of threats and injuries to students have decreased.

Areas in Which Conditions Have Stayed the Same

- The gap in preschool participation rates for high- and low-income families has not changed.
- The percentage of students reporting use of alcohol has not changed.
- The high school completion rate has remained the same.
- The gap in college enrollment rates for white and minority students has not changed.
- The gap in college completion rates for white and minority students has not changed.

Areas of Concern

- Reading achievement at grade twelve has dropped.
- Fewer secondary school teachers hold a degree in their main area of teaching.
- Fewer adults with a high school diploma or less are participating in adult education.
- Student drug use and attempted sales of drugs at school have increased.
- Threats and injuries to teachers have increased.
- More teachers are reporting that disruptions in their classrooms interfere with their teaching.

Regardless of the progress or lack of it in efforts to evaluate the national goals crusade, the effort is a source of concern for professionals in varied fields of education.

Kagan (1990), for instance, identified questions related to assessment and effectiveness in ongoing programs for young children as central to practical issues in meeting the "readiness" goal. Racial and cultural differences in the economic and social effects of dropping out of school continued to justify interest in improving graduation rates (Gage, 1990). Concerns that reduced the likelihood of American students leaving grades four, eight, and twelve having demonstrated competency in challenging subject matter were evident in issues identified by Darling-Hammond (1990). Rotberg (1990) criticized the representatives of samples used to compare math and science achievement across national groups, and Mikulecky (1990) presented a pessimistic view of the likelihood of success for the literacy goal based on the dismal success of past programs. Finally, Hawley (1990) presented competing perspectives on the extent of the "drug" problem as evidence of concern for achievement of the drug-free schools goal. Issues in special education practice reflected in the national goals are illustrated in Table 2.4.

In addition to general educational objectives, such as those outlined by presidents Bush and Clinton and the nation's governors, schools take on other objectives, many of which are more than simple compliance with ideals of intellectual growth, development, and responsibilities. Goodlad observed that

> our school system, a huge enterprise, operates as though its social purpose is exclusively educational; it sets goals that are educational, and it is evaluated as though what it does is educational. Meanwhile, it serves purposes appearing to be other than educational, performs functions other than educational, but it is generally not evaluated by criteria that are other than educational. (1979b, *What Schools Are For,* p. 8)

Although objectives and resources for doing so are seldom provided, members of society call on schools to solve such problems as racism, unemployment, divorce, poverty, drug abuse, and war. And assessments of what schools have done are not always complimentary:

> Some who would rewrite American educational history say that they also have served to select winners and losers on the basis of circumstances of birth: to increase the gap between the haves and have-nots in our economic system: to turn off certain kinds of talent while fostering others; and to lower the self-concept of those who do not adjust easily to the expectations and regimens of schooling. What schools have done is not necessarily what they should have done. (Goodlad, 1979b, p. 2)

A fundamental goal of American schools is the education of students regardless of race, religion, gender, national origin, creed, lifestyle, or disability. But on almost any standard at almost any time in history, schools have failed to educate significant numbers of students, or significant numbers of students have failed to profit satisfactorily from schooling. The double-edged nature of the preceding sentence indicates the multidimensional nature of the problem.

TABLE 2.4   **National Education Goals Issues Reflected in Special Education Practices**

Goal	General Education Concerns	Special Education Issues
Readiness	Assessment practices to determine readiness have been challenged. School entry is individualized and school services are homogenized.	Assessment Instruction Early intervention Families
School completion	Effects of dropping out are not singular. Definitions for dropouts are varied. Causes for dropping out are varied.	Assessment Instruction Transition Results of schooling
Student achievement	Curricula in American schools are not challenging. Testing is overused and misused in decision making.	Results of schooling Instruction Assessment Transition
Teacher education	Content of education coursework is seen as inadequate. Teaching out-of-field is a continuing problem.	Continuing challenges
Math and science achievement	Representativeness of samples used in comparisons is questionable. Test scores are not accurate reflection of productivity. Narrow definitions lead to trivial solutions.	Assessment Results of schooling Instruction School reform
Adult literacy	Success of past programs is dismal.	Transition Results of schooling
Safe schools	Competing perspectives on extent of problem and effective solutions.	Instruction Assessment Families School Reform
Parent participation	Parents sometimes viewed as unwilling collaborators. Adversarial roles are difficult to challenge.	Families Law and legislation The economy

THE CHANGING AND UNCHANGING FACE OF EDUCATION

During the 1980s, member of society became more fully aware of the range of critical issues facing education. As noted in *A Nation at Risk,* "The educational foundations of our Society are presently being eroded by a rising tide of mediocrity that threatens our very future as a Nation and a people" (U.S. Dept. of Education, 1983, p. 5). Not unlike other times throughout history, criticism stimulated rhetoric, research, and reform regarding effective schools. Descriptions of effective schools cropped up everywhere, and "school reform" became the catch phrase of the decade. But despite all this activity, the answers to questions about how well schools are really doing are mixed (Forgione, 1998).

Student Progress and Outcomes

A student's ability to read is essential to educational success. If students fall behind in reading proficiency, they may find it difficult to profit from other areas of instruction. Poor readers may also have difficulty participating successfully in a society and economy requiring increasing levels of literacy competence. Trends in reading performance provided by the National Center for Education Statistics (1998) reveal persistent concerns and issues:

- Overall, reading proficiency for 9-year-olds improved between 1971 and 1980, declined between 1980 and 1990, and was stable between 1990 and 1996. Little change occurred from 1971 to 1996 at ages 13 and 17, although scores for 17-year-olds increased slightly between 1971 and 1984.

- Females continued to outscore males in reading proficiency across all age groups.

- For all three age levels (i.e., 9-, 13-, and 17-year-olds), average scores for African-American students rose by about 20 or more scale points between 1971 and 1988, and in 1996, the average scores were higher than those in 1971. The gap between scores of white and black students consequently decreased at ages 9 and 17 between 1971 and 1996.

- In general, average reading proficiency levels do not reflect high levels of competence developing over time (see Figure 2.1).

Mastering mathematics is also an important outcome of education. Knowledge of mathematics is critical to success in science, computing, and numerous other related areas of study. In a technology-heightened world, proficiency in basic arithmetic facts, numerical operations, and multistep problem solving is a critical component of occupational competitiveness. Analyses of mathematics proficiency provided by the National Center for Education Statistics (1998) reveal consistent trends:

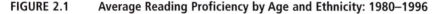

FIGURE 2.1   **Average Reading Proficiency by Age and Ethnicity: 1980–1996**

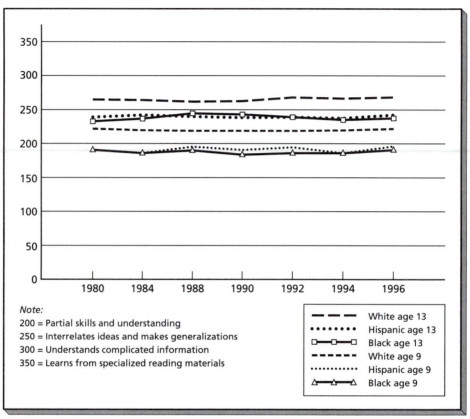

Note:
200 = Partial skills and understanding
250 = Interrelates ideas and makes generalizations
300 = Understands complicated information
350 = Learns from specialized reading materials

- Average mathematics performance improved between 1973 and 1996 (see Figure 2.2). The average overall level of proficiency for 9-year-olds was relatively low (i.e., below mastery of numerical operations and beginning problem solving).
- Average mathematics performance for white students was consistently higher than that for African-American or Hispanic students.
- Several states reported significant increases in average mathematics scores.

Effective writing skills are important in all stages of schooling. Students at almost all grade levels are expected to convey simple and complex ideas and information in clear, succinct prose. Inadequate writing skills inhibit achievement across all curriculum areas and in occupational careers. Proficient writing skills help students convey ideas, deliver instruction, analyze information, solve problems, and

FIGURE 2.2   **Average Mathematics Proficiency by Age and Ethnicity: 1973–1996**

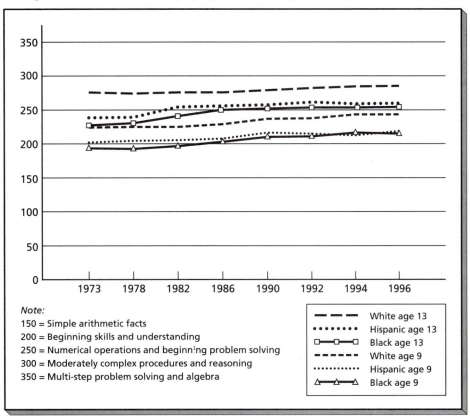

Note:
150 = Simple arithmetic facts
200 = Beginning skills and understanding
250 = Numerical operations and beginning problem solving
300 = Moderately complex procedures and reasoning
350 = Multi-step problem solving and algebra

White age 13
Hispanic age 13
Black age 13
White age 9
Hispanic age 9
Black age 9

motivate others. Trends in writing performance provided by the National Center for Education Statistics (1998) reveal persistent concerns and issues:

- From 1984 to 1996, average writing proficiency remained relatively stable for fourth-grade students, while eighth-grade scores fluctuated and eleventh-grade scores declined (see Figure 2.3).

- Girls have outscored boys in writing proficiency at all grade levels since 1984.

- On average, whites have demonstrated more proficiency in writing (although consistently below complete, sufficient writing and effective, coherent writing levels) than African-American and hispanic students at all grade levels assessed.

- In 1996, 31 percent of eleventh graders were generally able to write complete, sufficient responses (level 300) and 2 percent provided effective, coherent responses (level 350).

FIGURE 2.3   **Average Writing Proficiency by Age and Ethnicity: 1984–1996**

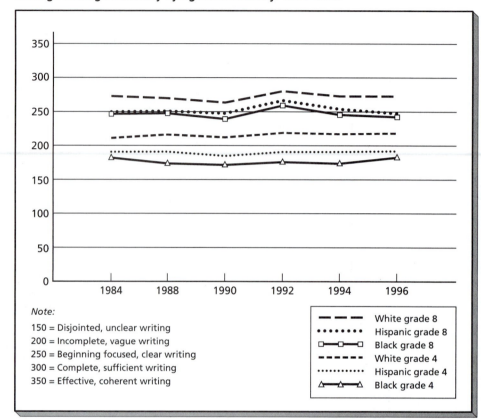

Note:
150 = Disjointed, unclear writing
200 = Incomplete, vague writing
250 = Beginning focused, clear writing
300 = Complete, sufficient writing
350 = Effective, coherent writing

– – – White grade 8
• • • • • Hispanic grade 8
□—□—□ Black grade 8
– – – White grade 4
• • • • • Hispanic grade 4
△—△—△ Black grade 4

Consistent progress through school is a characteristic of academic success. On average, performance of students in America's schools reflects low levels of progress and competence. For example, levels of reading and writing proficiency have remained relatively constant for almost two decades (NCES, 1998). Similarly, reading competency levels of many young students (especially African-American and Hispanic 9-year-olds) are consistently below the "partial skills and understanding" criterion used in measuring national progress (NCES, 1998). Persistent failure to demonstrate adequate academic progress is a common cause for referral for special education services. Trends in reading, mathematics, writing, and content area proficiency among general education students create continuing needs for specially designed instruction to correct or compensate for learning problems or prevent further failure. Additionally, factors in the backgrounds of students and other characteristics of learners and their families provide a continuing basis for special education within the broader context of schooling.

Social Context of Schooling

Children in American schools come from varied family environments, income levels, and cultural backgrounds (Grissmer, Kirby, Berends, & Williamson, 1994; Young & Smith, 1996). Of the 4 million babies born each year, nearly one out of eight is born to a teenage mother, one out of four to a mother with less than a high school education, almost one out of three to a mother who lives in poverty, and one out of four to an unmarried mother (Young & Smith, 1996). Family income, especially conditions of poverty, are related to enrollment rates in preschool programs and achievement throughout the school years. Students from racial and/or ethnic minority backgrounds are more at risk for poor school outcomes, and conditions created by cultural differences have been an educational concern for some time (Ralph, 1989). The diversity evident in today's classrooms creates challenges that are more unique than ever before for teachers concerned with providing equal educational opportunities for all students.

The social context of schooling (i.e., factors such as family structure, parental education, family income, race, ethnicity, and English proficiency) is associated with educational access and outcomes. Consider a few facts (cf. Young & Smith, 1996):

- Children in single-parent homes are more likely to experience school problems than are children in two-parent families.
- Children in single-parent homes are less likely to participate in early literacy activities than are children in two-parent families.
- Parental education level is strongly associated with child achievement.
- Poverty is negatively associated with enrollment rates in early childhood education programs.
- High school graduates from high-income families are more likely to go directly to college than are graduates from low-income families.
- Median family income in black and Hispanic households remains at about 60 percent of that in white households.
- Minority students are more likely than white students to attend resource-poor schools.
- Students with difficulty speaking English are more likely to drop out of school.

Minority students and those from diverse backgrounds are projected to make up an increasing share of the school-age population during the coming decades, having increased substantially during the last twenty years. Between 2000 and 2020, the numbers of students from diverse minority backgrounds is projected to grow much faster than the number of children from white majority backgrounds (see Table 2.5). While learning environments are enhanced by students and families with varied backgrounds and interests, diversity also creates challenges that often present problems for students and educators alike (Young & Smith, 1996).

In 1995, 13 percent of students aged 5 to 17 spoke a language other than English at home, and 5 percent had difficultly speaking English (NCES, 1997).

Students who have difficultly speaking English already start school at a disadvantage, and although retaining these students may be a way to allow them to catch up to their neighbors and peers, it may also further stigmatize and alienate them. Because studies have shown that students who repeat at least one grade are more likely to drop out of school, referral for special education services provides an alternative with more promise than less acceptable options (i.e., retention) for many of these students.

The importance of the social context of schooling is also evident in facts about early school problems (NCES, 1997). For example, parents of black first and second graders (32%) were more likely than their white (16%) and Hispanic (18%) peers to report that their children had behavior or academic problems in school. Parental education level was also related to school problems: parents with a high school diploma or less were generally more likely than parents with an undergraduate degree or higher to report that their children had academic or behavior problems. Children who experience problems early are more likely to experience similar problems later in school. Children with poor academic proficiency and higher levels of misbehavior often require more time from teachers. They are also the primary candidates for referral for special education services (Ysseldyke & Algozzine, 1995).

TABLE 2.5	Change in School-Age Population by Race and Ethnicity	
	Percentage Change	
Race/Ethnicity	1993 to 2000	2000 to 2020
White		
Age 5–13	2.9	−11.2
Age 4–17	10.1	−10.3
Black		
Age 5–13	12.9	15.4
Age 4–17	11.5	20.0
Hispanic		
Age 5–13	29.8	47.0
Age 4–17	23.6	60.6
Other		
Age 5–13	32.5	67.2
Age 4–17	45.1	73.3

SOURCE: National Center for Education Statistics, 1996. *Youth Indicators, 1996.* Washington, D.C.: U.S. Department of Education, Office of Educational Research and Improvement.

Financial Resources

Support for public education is provided by a combination of federal, state, and local revenues. The share provided by different sources is determined by factors such as public perception of the role of governmental bodies, taxes, tax bases, and competing demands for revenues. Funding of education is accomplished through formulas and equations that vary from state to state and even within school districts. In recent years, state funds have accounted for larger percentages of the costs of education, and federal funds have consistently remained below 10 percent of total costs. This pattern of funding is largely due to expanding federal efforts to improve education without supporting the costs these efforts entail. As federal requirements for mandated programs alter the costs of education, funding patterns change. For example, when free lunch programs are supported as part of a national initiative to control the effects of poverty, states and local agencies bear the burden unless federal financial support follows a mandated function. If a national initiative to meet the needs of more students with special learning needs is not coupled with increased levels of federal financial support, state and local education agencies bear the burden of compliance with national directives.

Concerns about equity surface when financial and human resources are studied (NCES, 1996, 1997; Parrish, Chambers, & Matsumoto, 1994; Rothstein & Miles, 1995). Interest in varying levels of educational resources received by different types of students in various schools and communities heightened with the publication of Jonathan Kozol's *Savage Inequalities*. He painted a bleak picture that reflected the effects of different levels of resources on the lives of individual children. The Improving America's Schools Act of 1994 (IASA) reauthorized the Elementary and Secondary Education Act (ESEA) and put in place procedures and changes considered the most significant since the ESEA was first passed in 1965 (see Figure 2.4). The IASA set a number of national goals in terms of the results of schooling, and the renewed emphasis on outcomes revived interest in issues related to equality of educational opportunity for all students. Of course, all concerns about equity and the distribution of local, state and federal monies are grounded in data reflecting differences within the infrastructure of education. For example:

- Students in high-poverty schools are less likely to have gifted and talented programs or extended day programs than students in low-poverty schools.

- Students in mathematics classes in high-poverty schools are less likely to be taught by teachers who majored or minored in mathematics than students in low-poverty schools.

- Public schools with high levels of students in poverty are less likely to be connected to the Internet than schools with lower levels of students in poverty.

- Teacher salaries are higher in low-poverty schools than they are in high-poverty schools.

- Relatively low-wealth public school districts spend less per pupil in general and more on capital investment than do school districts with more wealth. (NCES, 1997)

FIGURE 2.4   **Summary of Improving America's School Act of 1994**

Signed on October 20, 1994 by President Clinton, the law authorizes about $11 billion for most federal K-12 education programs in 14 areas
• **Title I:** Helping Disadvantaged Children Meet High Standards $7.4 billion for the Title I compensatory education program and related special programs
• **Title II:** Dwight D. Eisenhower Professional Development Program $800 million for several programs to promote personnel development
• **Title III:** Technology in Education $250 million for improvement of education technology programs
• **Title IV:** Safe and Drug Free Schools and Communities $655 million to implement crime and drug abuse prevention programs
• **Title V:** Promoting Equity $173 million for desegregation, women's educational equity, and school dropout programs
• **Title VI:** Innovative Education Program Strategies $370 million for additional technology, literacy, and reform projects
• **Title VII:** Bilingual Education, Language Enhancement, and Language Acquisition Programs $350 million for improving programs for individuals needing second language instruction
• **Title VIII:** Impact Aid $775 million to districts with lost revenue due to presence of federal property or workers
• **Title IX:** Indian, Native Hawaiian, and Alaska Native Education $91 million for districts with high concentrations of specific minority children
• **Title X:** Programs of National Significance $400 million for a variety of school improvement programs
• **Title XI:** Coordinated Services Permits use of up to 5% of ESEA money to coordinate education, health, and social services
• **Title XII:** School Facilities Infrastructure Improvement Act $200 million for school construction, renovation, and repair
• Other Support and Assistance Programs to Improve Education

The face of education has changed over the past few decades (NCES, 1997). The student population in America's schools is more diverse than ever before. The structure of families is shifting away from two biological parents bringing up children. The percentage of children from minority backgrounds is increasing, as is the percentage of children who have difficulty speaking English. Black and Hispanic children remain much more likely than white children to be living in poverty, a factor associated with poor results in school. Minority students are more likely to attend schools with a high level of poverty, which is significant because the climate in these schools is less conducive to learning than that in low-poverty schools. Similarly, high-poverty schools are, on average, worse off than low-poverty schools with regard to financial and human resources. Efforts to improve and restructure educational conditions are among those being addressed by federal, state, and local policy makers and practitioners.

How will students with disabilities fare in a restructured system of education? There is reason to believe that they may fall further behind if standards for achievement are raised, unless sufficient resources are redistributed in attempts to reform education. Largely as a result of previous inequities, per pupil expenditures in special education are growing faster than those in general education (Chambers, Parrish, Lieberman, & Wolman, 1998; Rothstein & Miles, 1995). However, most special educators believe that students with disabilities will not fare well in a restructured education system, and they want assurances that a free, appropriate education will remain a central part of special education's services. This concern and desire for assurances is grounded in the history and legal basis for special education.

LEGAL BASIS FOR SPECIAL EDUCATION

The first piece of legislation containing specific provisions related to people with disabilities was an 1827 act setting aside land in Kentucky for the location of an asylum for people who did not hear or speak. The first substantive law establishing a government hospital for the insane was not passed until 1857. The facility, located in Washington, D.C., and later named St. Elizabeth's Hospital, was designed primarily for delivery of services to members of the army and navy who became "insane." Also, in 1857, Congress passed an act to establish an institution for people who were deaf, dumb, and blind in Washington, D.C. Almost one hundred years later, in 1954, this institution became Gallaudet College, a school that continues to provide higher education to students who are deaf or hearing impaired (La Vor, 1979).

In 1858, Congress provided the first funds for education of students with disabilities when $3,000 per year for five years was appropriated for maintenance and student tuition at the Columbia Institution for the Instruction of the Deaf and Dumb and Blind. In 1879, Congress appropriated $250,000 for purchase of supplies and materials for education of blind students throughout the United States. Such supplies and materials were to be provided by the American Printing House for the Blind, another organization that still exists.

For the next forty years, there was very little legislation specifically relevant to people with disabilities. Following World War I, however, Congress passed the Soldier's Rehabilitation Act (1918), which enabled vocational rehabilitation of veterans disabled as a result of the war. But that act was restricted to services for veterans because Congress maintained that rehabilitation of people with disabilities other than veterans was not a federal responsibility. Two years later, however, Congress passed the Citizens Vocational Rehabilitation Act providing counseling, job training, and job placement, and supplying artificial limbs and other prosthetic devices (La Vor, 1979). World War II furnished a different impetus for provision of services. As large numbers of men and women entered the armed services, a labor shortage developed in industry. In response, Congress passed legislation providing job training and rehabilitation for people with disabilities to enable them to fill positions in industry.

During the late 1950s and early 1960s, a significant increase occurred in federal legislation for exceptional persons. Some of the laws were enacted after advocacy groups put pressure on Congress to meet their needs. Yet much of the legislation was initiated by President John F. Kennedy and Vice President Hubert H. Humphrey. As La Vor noted:

> Possibly the biggest assist that the handicapped received in terms of public acceptability, the stimulus for further legislation, was the fact that President Kennedy had a retarded sister and Vice President Humphrey had a retarded grandchild. As a result of personal commitments on the part of both men, in 1961 the President appointed the "President's Panel on Mental Retardation" with a mandate to develop a national plan to combat mental retardation. Two years later legislation was passed that implemented several of the panel's recommendations.
>
> In the years that followed, legislation was passed providing funds for states to develop state and community programs and to construct facilities to serve the mentally retarded. Funding was also made available to establish community mental health centers and research, to provide demonstration centers for the education of the handicapped, and to train personnel to work with the handicapped. (1979, p. 99)

In 1958, following the Soviet launching of *Sputnik I,* Congress passed the National Defense Education Act, a defense-oriented piece of legislation designed to promote education of mathematicians and scientists. The law implied that gifted and talented students should receive extra educational services. In 1961, Congress passed legislation to support the preparation of teachers of the people who were deaf and in 1963 amended the legislation to provide for preparation of teachers of students with hearing impairments, speech impairments, visual impairments, emotional disturbance, physical impairments, and other health impairments.

Beginning in 1963, there was a significant increase in legislation relevant to the education of students with disabilities. At that time, funds were provided to states to enable provision of vocational education, and in 1965, Congress passed the Elementary and Secondary Education Act (ESEA). Title I of ESEA was amended to establish grants to state agencies to enable them to provide a free, appropriate public education to students with disabilities. In 1967, ESEA was amended again to provide even more services for these students. Regional resource centers for testing students with disabilities and deaf-blind service centers were established. Funds were authorized to facilitate both personnel recruitment and information dissemination of special education services. In 1968, the Handicapped Children's Early Education Act was passed, funding model demonstration programs for preschool children with disabilities. On April 13, 1970, provisions related to gifted and talented children were included as amendments to ESEA.

In 1972, the Vocational Rehabilitation Act was extended, and state rehabilitation agencies were required to give first service priorities to those with the most severe disabilities. During the late 1960s and early 1970s, there was a dramatic increase in court cases directly related to the education of students with disabilities. This litigation led eventually to passage in November 1975 of the Education for All Handicapped Children Act, Public Law 94-142 (subsequently reauthorized and amended as the Individuals with Disabilities Education Act in 1990 and 1997). More legislative action addressing other special education concerns followed. Major practices today (ranging from the inclusion of individuals with severe disabilities in educational programs to barrier-free architecture and nondiscriminatory employment practices) might not have occurred without this and other ground-breaking work (Rothstein, 1990; Yell, 1998).

Fundamental Court Action

Continuing changes in laws and specific court cases have brought about modification of special education services. The landmark case of *Brown* v. *Board of Education* (1954) forcefully established a philosophy of integration in America's schools based on constitutional principles established by the Fourteenth Amendment, which provided that people could not be denied "equal protection of the laws" or deprived of "life, liberty, or property, without due process of law." The *Brown* decision "recognized that educating black children separately, even if done so in 'equal' facilities, was inherently unequal because of the stigma attached to being educated separately and because of the deprivation of interaction with children from other backgrounds" (Rothstein, 1990, p. 2). The view that separate education was wrong for people with disabilities followed the movement away from racial segregation in the schools.

In 1975, it was estimated that more than half of the children and youths with disabilities were receiving either inappropriate or no educational services (Lynn, 1984). Common practices that characterized special education and led to the passage of PL 94-142 were summarized by Rothstein (1990): identification and placement of children with disabilities were haphazard, inconsistent, and generally inappropriate; blacks, Hispanics, and some other groups were often stereotyped and disproportionately placed in special education programs; parental involvement was generally discouraged; special education placements were often made with the goal of avoiding disruption in the general classroom; both special educators and regular educators were competitors for resources, and consequently the two groups did not work in a spirit of cooperation.

Court action addressed these problems and focused on a person's right to a free appropriate education by establishing guidelines for states' rights to educate students (Gilhool, 1989). In *Hanson* v. *Hobson* (1967), the court ruled that educational placements based on pupil performance on standardized tests was unconstitutional. In *Mills* v. *Board of Education* (1972), the court asserted the right of students with disabilities to due process before they could be excluded from a school; their right to an appropriate education was upheld in *Mills* as well as in *PARC* v. *Commonwealth of Pennsylvania* (1972). Misclassification of students from minority and non-English-language backgrounds was the issue in *Diana* v. *State Board of Education* (1970). As a result of this case, schools in California agreed to test all children in their primary language and to reevaluate those minority students and children from non-English-language backgrounds who had been enrolled in special classes based on their performance on standardized intelligence tests.

Fundamental Legislation

There is no federal constitutional provision establishing a national education system or rights to education. When state rules and regulations provide education, the Fourteenth Amendment comes into play. This means that education must be provided to all citizens on an equal basis, and it cannot be denied without due process of the law. The Education for All Handicapped Children Act of 1975 (Public Law 94-142) established principles for how these rights and responsibilities were to be exercised for people with disabilities. Reauthorization and amendments have maintained and extended its guiding principles.

PL 94-142 required that a free appropriate education be made available to all students with disabilities between the ages of three and twenty-one by September 1980. It prohibited exclusion of these students from school and mandated that federal funds be made available only to those school districts that complied with these provisions. This law provided assurances protecting students with disabilities and their parents or guardians through due process, protection in evaluation procedures (PEP), least restrictive environment (LRE), and individualized education program (IEP). The right to due process and the PEP provisions were attempts to deal with problems in eligibility for and classification in special education. The LRE and IEP provisions focused on decisions concerning placement of classified students and on how learning would differ from that of the general curriculum. All provisions of PL 94-142 affected aspects of decisions made about progress in special education programs.

Public Law 101-476

On October 30, 1990, President Bush signed into law the Education of the Handicapped Act Amendments of 1990 (PL 101-476). This action reauthorized the discretionary programs under Parts C through G of the Education for All Handicapped Children Act; made certain changes in Parts A, B, and H of the act; and renamed the EHA as the Individuals with Disabilities Education Act (IDEA) (Lewis, 1990). In addition to changing the title of the law, the reauthorization modified the general provisions of the act to reflect contemporary perspectives. For example, all references to "handicapped children" were replaced with "children with disabilities." Two new categories (autism and traumatic brain injury) were added to the definition of "children with disabilities," and the following comprehensive definition of "transition services" was added to Section 602(a)(19):

> A coordinated set of activities for a student, designed within an outcome-oriented process, which promotes movement from school to post-school activities, including post-secondary education, vocational training, integrated employment (including supported employment), continuing and adult education, adult services, independent living, or community participation. The coordinated set of activities shall be based upon the individual student's needs, taking into account the student's preferences and interest, and shall include instruction, community experiences, the development of employment and other post-school adult living objectives, and when appropriate, acquisition of daily living skills and functional vocational evaluation.

On June 4, 1997, President Clinton signed the Individuals with Disabilities Education Act Amendments (PL 105-17). This law reauthorized and revised the IDEA. To improve the law, Congress passed the most significant amendments to the IDEA since original passage in 1975 (Yell & Shriner, 1998).

The IDEA Amendments restructured the law, changing the original nine subchapters, parts A through H, into four subchapters, parts A through D.

- Part A contains the general provision of the law, including definitions, findings, and purposes.
- Part B details the requirements of states to ensure a free appropriate public education consisting of special education and related services to all qualified students with disabilities.
- Part C extends Part B protections to infants and toddlers with disabilities and strengthens incentives for states to provide services to infants and toddlers. Part C, which was originally Part H, was added to the IDEA in 1986 with the passage of PL 99-457.
- Part D contains the discretionary or support programs that formerly were Parts C through G.

A summary of other changes in PL 105-17 is presented in Table 2.6.

TABLE 2.6 **Key Changes in IDEA**

Targeted Improvement	IDEA Enabling Action/Requirement
General Provisions	• Word *serious* omitted from emotional disturbance category out of concern that it may have derogatory connotations.
	• Assignment of disability deemed inappropriate if child lacks only instruction in reading, math, or other content area or speaks English as a second language.
	• Attempt made in state funding formula to eliminate any incentive for educators to over-identify children with disabilities.
	• Requires states to identify and count students with disabilities attending private and parochial schools.
	• Local education agencies required to serve students with disabilities in charter schools in the same manner as students with disabilities in other schools.
	• In an effort to reduce paperwork, IEP team and other qualified professionals may determine that a child is still eligible for special education services by reviewing existing assessment evaluation rather than conducting complete reevaluation once every three years.
Strengthening Roles of Parents	• Informed consent required before initial evaluation.
	• Participation in placement decisions must be ensured by local education agencies.
	• Participation required in individualized education program (IEP) planning.
	• Must be informed of progress toward annual goals as often as parents of students without disabilities are informed of the progress of their children.
	• Guarantees access to all records.
Ensuring Access to General Education	• Provides nonadversarial means for working out differences.
	—Mediation must be available.

TABLE 2.6	**Key Changes in IDEA (Continued)**
Targeted Improvement	**IDEA Enabling Action/Requirement**
	—Participation is voluntary. —State must provide list of qualified, trained, impartial mediators. —State must pay costs of mediation. —All discussions are confidential and all agreements are in writing. • General education teacher is a required participant in IEP planning (if student is or may be in general education), but may not need to be involved in all aspects of team's work (e.g., related services). • Individual knowledgeable about general education curriculum and its relation to special education is required IEP team participant. • IEP team must document portions of general curriculum, including goals, standards, and accountability demands, relevant to each special education student. • Extent of participation in state- and district-wide assessments, including necessary modifications, must be documented.
Focusing on Teaching and Learning	• Requires states to establish performance goals for students with disabilities that are consistent with those of students without disabilities and indicators to assess progress toward the goals. • State Education Agency (SEA) required to report to public on state- and district-wide assessment performance of students with disabilities as often and in the same detail as it reports on performance of students without disabilities. • Beginning when student is age 14 and updated annually, IEP must include a statement of transition needs to be provided after age 16. • SEA must include, at the minimum, the number of children participating in general assessments, the number of children participating in alternate assessments, and the performance of children with disabilities on general and alternate assessments.

TABLE 2.6	Key Changes in IDEA (Continued)
Targeted Improvement	IDEA Enabling Action/Requirement
	• School officials may discipline a student with a disability in the same way(s) they discipline students without disabilities, except: —Unilateral change of placements are permitted for disciplinary purposes to the extent they are used with other students. —Suspensions may not exceed 10 days, unless student brings a weapon to school or a school function or possesses, uses, or sells illegal drugs or controlled substances, in which case 45 days becomes the limit. —Hearing officers may order change of placement and/or time limits extended if students with disabilities present danger in current placement(s). • IEP teams are required to consider proactive interventions for students with disabilities exhibiting behavior problems, regardless of category. • Requires states to continue providing services to students who have been suspended or expelled for disciplinary purposes. • Paraprofessionals must be appropriately prepared and supervised in accordance with state law, regulation, or written policy.

Continuing Legal Concerns

Special education is driven in part by laws that have established provision of services to students with special needs. Because of the abusive conditions that have existed in special education, the intent of the most recent legislation was massive educational reform for students with disabilities and their families. The major provisions of PL 94-142 (retained in the IDEA) targeted different steps in a three-step process: declaring students eligible for special education services, providing special treatment for them, and periodically evaluating the extent to which they are making progress. Due process provisions protected individual rights and together with the PEP provisions addressed concerns at the eligibility/classification decision-making step. These provisions attempted to reduce the problems inherent in trying to decide who should receive special education. The LRE and IEP provisions targeted treatment practices, and all the provisions addressed aspects of the progress evaluation phase of the special education process.

Of course, passing a law does not guarantee that changes will occur in the ways the law directs. Interpretation of the law influences what effect the law has on practice. Indeed, Bersoff observed that "legislation itself may serve as a springboard to future litigation, as parties seek to define, implement, and enforce its provisions. Federal and state statutes may evoke what may be called 'second generation' issues" (1979, p. 103). Legal cases that followed the enactment of PL 94-142 challenged the procedures by which schools assessed and made placement decisions and the practices that were used to educate students with disabilities (Gilhool, 1989; Rothstein, 1990; Ysseldyke & Algozzine, 1990).

The best known of these court decisions, *Larry P. v. Riles*, was rendered in 1979 in response to a California case that began in 1971. Plaintiffs in that case represented the class of black children in California who had been or in the future might be wrongfully placed and maintained in special classes for students with mental retardation. The plaintiffs challenged the placement process, particularly the use of standardized intelligence tests in the decision-making process. The plaintiffs contended that the IQ tests used were biased and discriminated against African-American children. Plaintiffs cited as evidence the disproportionate placement of African-American students in these classes. The defendant in the case was Wilson Riles, California superintendent of public instruction.

In January 1975, the California State Department of Education voluntarily imposed a moratorium on IQ testing for *all* children regardless of race. In January 1977, the plaintiffs filed an amended complaint reflecting recent legislative concerns, and in August 1977 the U.S. Department of Justice entered the case as *amicus curia* (friend of the court), contending that provisions of PL 94-142 and Section 504 of the Rehabilitation Act of 1973 had been violated. The Justice Department maintained that intelligence tests had not been validated for the purpose of diagnosing mental retardation and that the use of such tests had a disproportionate impact on African-American children. Judge Peckham concluded his opinion by stating:

> Whatever the future, it is essential that California's educators confront the problem of the widespread failure to provide an adequate education to underprivileged minorities such as the African-American children who brought this lawsuit. Educators have too often been able to rationalize inaction by blaming educational failure on an assumed intellectual inferiority of disproportionate numbers of black children. That assumption without validation is unacceptable, and it is made all the more invidious when "legitimized" by ostensibly neutral, scientific I.Q. scores. (*Larry P.*, pp. 109–110)

In *Crawford v. Honig* (1994) the U.S. Court of Appeals for the Ninth Circuit vacated the *Larry P.* on IQ testing for the purpose of placing African-American students in special education. The case was brought on behalf of African-American students who sought to have standardized IQ tests administered so that they could qualify for the category of learning disabled. The appellate court, however, let stand the original *Larry P.* ruling against using IQ tests to place black students in classes for those with mental retardation. This decision seemed to indicate that neither the individuals with Disabilities Education Act nor Section 504 prohibits the use of IQ tests per se in special education evaluations (Yell, 1998).

The issue of bias in assessment clearly was not settled by the *Larry P.* case because the issue continues to be debated in the nation's courtrooms. A case of significant note, *PASE* v. *Hannon* (1980), was a class-action suit brought by Parents in Action on Special Education on behalf of "all black children who have been or will be placed in special classes for the educable mentally handicapped in the Chicago school system." Plaintiffs observed that while 62 percent of the enrollment of the Chicago public schools was black, black students made up 82 percent of the enrollment in classes for students with mental retardation. The plaintiffs claimed that the misassessment of children was caused by racial bias in the standardized intelligence tests they were given.

At issue in *PASE,* as in the *Larry P.* case, was the detrimental effect on students of placement in classes for students believed to be retarded: "an erroneous assessment of mental retardation, leading to an inappropriate placement of a child in an EMH class, is nearly an educational tragedy. However beneficial such classes may be for those who truly need them, they are likely to be almost totally harmful to those who do not" (*PASE,* p. 4).

Judge Grady, who presided in this case, took a unique approach to the issues. He systematically examined every item on the Stanford-Binet and the Wechsler Intelligence Scale for Children—Revised (WISC-R). He read every item into the court record and rendered his own opinion on the extent to which each item was biased against blacks. Judge Grady said:

> It is obvious to me that I must examine the tests themselves in order to know what the witnesses are talking about. I do not see how an informed decision on the question of bias could be reached in any other way. For me to say that the tests are either biased or unbiased without analyzing the test items in detail would reveal nothing about the tests but only something about my opinion of the tests. (*PASE,* p. 8)

The judge ruled in favor of the defendants, stating that he could find little evidence that the tests were biased. He further stated that poor performance on these items alone was not sufficient to result in the misclassification of black students as having mental retardation.

The other post—PL 94-142 court cases addressed legal issues of critical importance to special education. *Frederick L.* v. *Thomas* (1976, 1977) was a class-action suit in which the Philadelphia school district was charged with the failure to provide students with learning disabilities with appropriate education. Using a 3 percent incidence of learning disabilities as a criterion, the plaintiffs charged that the schools were serving too few such children. They said that 7,900 students (3 percent) should be identified with learning disabilities, yet only 1,300 students were being served in special programs. The schools argued that other students who had not been referred were being served appropriately in general classrooms. The court ordered the school district to engage in "massive screening and follow-up individual psychological evaluations" designed to identify students with learning disabilities.

Lora v. *New York City Board of Education* (1978) was a class-action suit brought by black and Hispanic students. The plaintiffs asserted that their statutory rights were violated by the procedures and facilities used by New York for the education of children whose emotional problems led to severe acting out and aggression in school. In his opinion, Judge Weinstein held that (1) the process of evaluating students to determine if they should enter "special day schools" violated students' right to treatment and due process; (2) to the extent that students were referred to largely racially segregated schools, there was a denial of equal educational opportunity in violation of Title VI; and (3) New York City's monetary problems did not excuse violation of the students' rights. In both *Lora* and *Frederick L.*, the schools were mandated to engage in more extensive assessment and evaluation. Thus, the two cases forced school systems to spend more money and change current practices. A summary of other legal developments subsequent to the passage of PL 94-142 is presented in Table 2.7.

SPECIAL EDUCATION: WHY NOW AND WHAT FOR?

As the review of the history of education in America reveals, there was a time when people with disabilities were treated poorly by other members of society, and children were excluded from school solely on the basis of a disability. Today, education is a guaranteed right for students with disabilities. According to Gilhool (1989, p. 244), the linchpin of recent disability enactments was the "integration imperative expressly articulated in PL 94-142," which required that all states establish procedures to ensure

> that to the maximum extent appropriate, handicapped children, including those children in public or private institutions or other care facilities, are educated with children who are not handicapped, and that special classes, separate schooling, or other removal of handicapped children from the regular educational environment occurs only when the nature or severity of the handicap is such that education in regular classes with the use of supplementary aids and services cannot be achieved satisfactorily.

Recent federal legislation has also taken the civil rights of people with disabilities to unprecedented levels. The Americans with Disabilities Act (ADA), which was signed into law in July 1990, gave protections to people with disabilities that were the same as those provided to people on the basis of race, sex, national origin, and religion. The ADA guaranteed equal opportunity in employment, public accommodations, transportation, government services, and telecommunications (U.S. Department of Justice, 1990). Requirements established by the ADA are presented in Table 2.8.

TABLE 2.7   **Legal Developments Related to Special Education**

Case	Precedent
Battle v. *Commonwealth* (629 F 2d 269, 3rd Cir. 1980)	Established that educational policies would violate the Education of All Handicapped Children Act if they denied students with disabilities a free appropriate public education.
Board of Education v. *Rowley* (458 U.S. 176, 1982)	Established that an "appropriate" education exists when a program of special education and related services is provided such that the individual benefits and due process procedures have been followed in developing it.
Honig v. *Doe* (108 S. Ct. 592, 1988)	Established that expulsion from a school program for more than 10 days constitutes a change in placement, for which all due process provisions must be met; temporary removals are permitted in emergencies where student(s) and staff are in danger.
Zobrest v. *Catalina Foothills School District* (113 S. Ct. 2462 1993)	There is no general prohibition against providing special education services at parochial schools.
Light v. *Parkway School District* (21 IDELR 93; 8th Cir. 1994)	Disruptive students with disabilities do not actually have to cause harm before removal from school; rather, they have to be judged substantially likely to cause harm.
Cefalu v. *East Baton Rouge Parish School Board* (25 IDELR 142; 5th Cir. 1996)	A school district is not required to provide a sign language interpreter at a parochial school; a school district offering free, appropriate public education is under no further obligation to parent-placed, private school students with disabilities.

SOURCES: Rothstein, 1990; Yell, 1998.

But despite legal guarantees of rights that have belonged for some time to people without disabilities, life is still not rosy for many people with disabilities (Asch, 1984; Brightman, 1984; Fine & Asch, 1988). The negative beliefs held by some members of society about special education and labels assigned to people with disabilities contribute to this state of affairs. As Lipsky and Gartner (1989) pointed out:

TABLE 2.8   **Requirements Established by Americans with Disabilities Act**

Employment

- Employers may not discriminate against a person with a disability in hiring or promotion if the person is otherwise qualified for the job.
- Employers can ask about a person's ability to perform a job but cannot inquire if someone has a disability or subject a person to tests that tend to screen out people with disabilities.
- Employers have to provide "reasonable accommodation" to people with disabilities. This includes steps such as job restructuring and modification of equipment.
- Employers do not need to provide accommodations that impose an "undue hardship" on business operations.
- All employers with 25 or more employees must comply, effective July 26, 1992.
- All employers with 15–24 employees must comply, effective July 26, 1994.

Transportation

- New public transit buses ordered after August 26, 1990, must be accessible to people with disabilities.
- Transits authorities must provide comparable paratransit or other special transportation services to people with disabilities who cannot use fixed route bus services unless an undue burden would result.
- Existing rail systems must have one accessible car per train by July 26, 1995.
- New rail cars ordered after August 26, 1990, must be accessible.
- New bus and train stations must be accessible.
- Key stations in rapid, light, and commuter rail systems must be made accessible by July 26, 1993, with extensions up to 20 years for commuter rail (30 years for rapid and light rail).
- All existing Amtrak stations must be accessible by July 26, 2010.

Public Accommodations

- Private entities such as restaurants, hotels, and retail stores may not discriminate against people with disabilities, effective January 26, 1992.
- Auxiliary aids and services must be provided to people with vision and hearing impairments or other people with disabilities unless an undue burden would result.
- Physical barriers in existing facilities must be removed if removal is readily achievable. If not, alternative methods of providing services must be offered if they are readily achievable.
- All new construction and alterations of facilities must be accessible.

State and Local Government

- State and local governments may not discriminate against qualified people with disabilities.
- All government facilities, services, and communications must be accessible consistent with the requirements of Section 504 of the Rehabilitation Act of 1973.

TABLE 2.8   **Requirements Established by Americans with Disabilities Act (Continued)**

Telecommunications
- Companies offering telephone service to the general public must offer telephone relay services to people who use telecommunications devices for the deaf or similar devices.

SOURCE: U.S. Department of Justice, Civil Rights Division, Coordination and Review Section, (1990). *Americans with Disabilities Act Requirement: Fact Sheet.* Washington, D.C.: Author.

The assumptions underlying such beliefs can be tersely summarized: "(1) disability is a condition that individuals have, (2) disabled/typical is a useful and objective distinction, and (3) special education is a rationally conceived and coordinated system of services that help children labeled disabled. . . . This view of students labeled as handicapped adversely affects expectations regarding their academic achievement. It causes them to be separated from other students, to be exposed to a watered-down curriculum, to be excused from standards and tests routinely applied to other students, to be allowed grades that they have not earned, and, in some states, to be awarded special diplomas. (1989, p. 259)

Costs of Inclusion

The canary in the special education coal mine heralded the need for reform and reconstruction many moons ago. Legal precedents created conditions for repair, restructuring, and renewal. Educating students in least restrictive environments grew deep roots in efforts to provide free appropriate public education. As a result, inclusion became a widespread practice of choice in special education programs across the country. It is deeply rooted in the least restrictive environment (LRE) provision of the IDEA. It is typified by a student's participation in a regular class with education of that student shared by general and special educators (Sailor, Gee, & Karasoff, 1993). Implementations vary, from students having a general education homeroom assignment with some pull-out instruction for special problems, to full-time participation in general education with special education support on an as-needed basis (McLaughlin & Warren, 1994). The practice is not without its critics, despite little data demonstrating that doing it is wrong (cf. Brantlinger, 1997; Kauffman & Hallahan, 1995).

Does inclusion make sense in the broad scheme of education? Does it cost more than traditional programming? Does it create risks for extant personnel and resources? Who benefits from inclusion? "Although inclusion has been extensively discussed in the literature, information is notably absent regarding how allocations of resources change as a result of moving to inclusion" (McLaughlin & Warren, 1994, p. 1). Special educators are pushing forward with inclusion, however, because they believe it is the right thing to do, and preliminary research provides some interesting answers regarding inclusion in the context of special education.

- Initial implementation of inclusion is likely to require additional resources.

- Start up costs, such as increased professional development, increased use of paraprofessionals, and capital modifications, can put demands on district special education and general operational budgets.

- When the costs of providing services in home schools are considered *relative* to the costs of transportation and educational services in cluster programs or specialized schools, inclusion may very well be less expensive.

- Transportation is one area where districts may recognize significant cost savings over time.

- Over the long term, the number of personnel will likely increase with a move toward inclusion.

- Proponents believe that students with disabilities have a basic right to share their everyday lives with students without disabilities.

- Schools and communities strongly supporting diversity share the notion that inclusion has positive effects on communication and social adjustment.

- The primary motives in support of inclusion appear to be rooted in concepts of social justice and equity of opportunity. (McLaughlin & Warren, 1994)

Capable of Achievement and Worthy of Respect

As Justice Brennan noted in *School Board of Nassau County* v. *Arline* (1987), "Society's accumulated myths and fears about disability and disease are as handicapping as are the physical limitations that flow from actual impairment" ("On cases of contagion," 1987, p. A21). If the situation is going to change, positive alternative views of people with disabilities must gain the upper hand. Beliefs that disabilities cause impairments and limitations must be replaced by views that disabilities cause challenges that many people overcome. Negative social attitudes toward people with disabilities must be replaced by opinions, perspectives, and points of view that reflect acceptance, agreement, and approval of differences as characteristics of all people. The human service practices that cause providers to believe that clients (students) have inadequacies, shortcomings, failures, or faults that must be corrected or controlled by specially trained professionals must be replaced by conceptions that people with disabilities are capable of setting their own goals and achieving or not. Watered-down curricula, alternative grading practices, special competency standards, and other "treat them differently" practices used with "special" students must be replaced with school experiences exactly like those used with "regular" students. Conceptions of teaching as control and coercion must be modified to reflect cooperative, collaborative, and common perspectives. The direction for significant reform in educational practices is relatively clear. The only nagging question that remains is why the process labors so tediously and takes so long.

Discussion Questions

1. Special education has recently become a prominent topic in general education. Why has it taken so long for special education to gain this attention? What factors account for this increase in interest among professionals in general education?

2. What problems will special educators face in meeting the eight goals for education suggested by President Clinton?

3. What are some characteristics of present-day families? How might these characteristics affect the way students learn?

4. What are some of the challenges faced by teachers whose classrooms have more students from diverse backgrounds?

5. What differences characterized legal actions that preceded PL 94-142? What legal actions are likely as PL 105-17 is implemented?

Chapter 3
Special Education Today

I can complain because rose bushes have thorns or rejoice because thorn bushes have roses. It's all how you look at it.

—J. Kenfield Morley

During the last two decades, the country became increasingly aware of a broad range of issues facing educational professionals. Low achievement, teacher qualifications, school violence, drugs and alcohol, teenage pregnancy, dropping out, and teacher effectiveness were among the problems identified as critical for solution if education was to improve in this century. Special education was not exempt from critical review, nor should it be. The state of the art in special education has to be reviewed periodically if progress is going to be made. Toward this goal, we review two important aspects of contemporary special education in this chapter. We describe the current categories of special education and the current condition of special education as summarized in the most recent reports to Congress on the implementation of the Individuals with

Disabilities Education Act (IDEA). The categories represent the building blocks that give special education form and structure. The periodic reviews provide the essential and continuing monitoring necessary for special education to gain respect and to progress as a practice.

CURRENT SPECIAL EDUCATION CATEGORIES

Special education means specially designed instruction to meet the unique needs of a child with a disability, including instruction conducted in the classroom, in the home, in hospitals and institutions, and in other settings and instruction in physical education (IDEA, 1997). In general, the term *child with a disability* means a child with visual impairments (including blindness), hearing impairments (including deafness), orthopedic impairments, other health impairments, autism, traumatic brain injury, mental retardation, emotional disturbance, speech or language impairments, or specific learning disabilities. These names represent the categories of special education and each has a definition and characteristics associated with it. The definition and characteristics are used to formulate identification practices and provide a context of needs addressed when planning, managing, delivering, and evaluating specially designed instruction provided in special education. The IDEA also permits providing special education for children ages 3 through 9 who are experiencing developmental delays, as defined by state education agencies and measured by appropriate diagnostic instruments and procedures, in one or more of the following areas: physical, cognitive communication, social or emotional, or adaptive development. Students who are gifted and talented are provided special education, but not under provisions directed in the IDEA.

Visual Impairments

By law, students with visual impairments, including blindness, and partial sight, are eligible for special education services. Definitions of visual impairment rely on *visual acuity,* or the ability to see things at specified distances. Visual acuity is usually measured by having the person read letters or discriminate objects at a distance of twenty feet. A person who is able to read the letters correctly is said to have normal vision. Visual acuity is usually expressed as a ratio, such as 20/90, which tells us how well the person sees. The ratio 20/90 means that the person can read letters or discriminate objects at twenty feet that a person with normal vision can read to discriminate at ninety feet. The expression "20/20 vision," which is familiar to most people, is used to describe normal, or perfect, vision; it means that the person can see at twenty feet what people with normal vision see at twenty feet.

People with visual impairments are those with visual acuity greater than 20/200 but not greater than 20/70 in the better eye with correction. For all practical purposes, any student who has visual acuity with correction of less than 20/70 is eligible for special services for visual impairments. All cases employ the standard "with correction." This simply means that if the condition can be corrected with glasses or contact lenses, the student is not eligible for special services.

The term *partial sight* is used to refer to people who are able to use vision as a primary learning modality.

A legal definition of blindness was established in 1935 by the Social Security Act, and the definition continues to be used today in decisions about who is blind. The act specifies that *blindness* "is visual acuity for distant vision of 20/200 or less in the better eye, with best correction; or visual acuity of more than 20/200 if the widest diameter of field of vision subtends an angle no greater than 20 degrees" (National Society for the Prevention of Blindness, 1966, p. 10). A person who can see, with correction, at twenty feet what a person with normal vision can see at two hundred feet or more is considered blind. The second part of the definition includes people with restricted visual fields; such people are said to have *tunnel vision.*

Hearing Impairments

Students who are deaf, which means they are unable to understand speech even with the assistance of a hearing aid, or who have significant hearing impairments are eligible for special education services. Hearing impairment falls on the continuum between normal hearing and deafness, and it is the degree of hearing loss that defines the extent to which people are eligible for special services.

As with visual acuity, *hearing acuity* is measured in reference to an objective standard. People hear sounds at certain levels of loudness, or intensity, which is measured by an audiometer. Loudness is expressed in *decibels (dB)*; larger dB numbers refer to increasingly louder sounds. In addition to differing degrees of loudness, sounds also occur at different frequencies, or pitch. Frequency is measured in *hertz (Hz)*, or cycles per second. In educational settings, the extent to which a person can hear sounds within the frequency range for conversational speech, a range from five hundred to two thousand hertz, is the generally accepted standard.

Moores offered the following definitions of hearing problems:

A "deaf person" is one whose hearing is disabled to an extent (usually 70 dB or greater) that precludes the understanding of speech through the ear alone, without or with the use of a hearing aid.

A "hard of hearing person" is one whose hearing is disabled to an extent (usually 35 to 69 dB) that makes difficult, but does not preclude, the understanding of speech through the ear alone, without or with a hearing aid. (1982, p. 5)

For practical purposes, *deafness* means the absence of hearing in both ears, *hard of hearing* means significant difficulties in hearing, and *hearing impairment* means a problem hearing that adversely affects educational progress but is not included under deafness or hard of hearing definitions.

Orthopedic and Other Health Impairments

A number of terms have been used to refer to students with orthopedic and other health-impairing conditions. The terms generally indicate little about the needs of the students, but they do reflect conditions grounded in differences among people that can be objectively identified (Reynolds & Birch, 1982). For example, *arthritis* is a measurable inflammation of a joint that makes movement difficult, painful, and limited in scope. *Cerebral palsy* is paralysis resulting from brain damage. *Epilepsy* is also a brain disorder, and it results in measurable convulsive episodes and periods of unconsciousness.

In recent years, approximately 60,000 students were identified with orthopedic impairments, and the category of "other health impairments" grew substantially (U.S.D.E., 1996). The increase in the number of students with other health impairments was due to an expansion of the service population. In many states, the increase was primarily due to increased provision of services to students with attention deficit disorder (U.S.D.E., 1996). It is also due to improved health care technology—babies with significant impairment are living well beyond infancy. Increasingly, students with orthopedic and other health impairments are receiving special education in general education classrooms.

Autism

Autism is a relatively small category, accounting for less than 1% of all students with disabilities. The U.S. Department of Education (1997) reported that about 30,000 students with autism between the ages of 6 and 21 received special education in the public schools, an increase of more than 6,000 students from the previous year.

Autism is a developmental disability significantly affecting verbal and non-verbal communication and social interaction, generally evident before age 3, that adversely affects a child's educational performance. Other characteristics often associated with autism are engagement in repetitive activities and stereotyped movements, resistance to environmental change or change in daily routines, and unusual responses to sensory experiences. The term does not apply if a child's educational performance is adversely affected primarily because that child has a serious emotional disturbance.

The fourth edition of the *Diagnostic and Statistical Manual of Mental Disorders* of the American Psychiatric Association (1994, pp. 70–71) lists the following diagnostic criteria for autism:

A. A total of six (or more) items from (1), (2), and (3), with at least two from (1), and one each from (2) and (3):
   1. Qualitative impairment in social interaction, as manifested by at least two of the following:
      a. Marked impairment in the use of multiple nonverbal behaviors such as eye-to-eye gaze, facial expression, body postures, and gestures to regulate social interaction.
      b. Failure to develop peer relationships appropriate to developmental level.

    c. A lack of spontaneous seeking to share enjoyment, interests, or achievements with other people (e.g., lack of showing, bringing, or pointing out objects of interest).

    d. Lack of social or emotional reciprocity.

2. Qualitative impairments in communication as manifested by at least one of the following:

    a. Delay in, or total lack of, the development of spoken language (not accompanied by an attempt to compensate through alternative modes of communication such as gestures or mime).

    b. In individuals with adequate speech, marked impairment in the ability to initiate or sustain a conversation with others.

    c. Stereotyped and repetitive use of language or idiosyncratic language.

    d. Lack of varied, spontaneous make-believe play or social imitative play appropriate to developmental level.

3. Restricted, repetitive, and stereotyped patterns of behavior, interests, and activities, as manifested by at least one of the following:

    a. Encompassing preoccupation with one or more stereotypic and restricted patterns of interest that is abnormal either in intensity or focus.

    b. Apparently inflexible adherence to specific, nonfunctional routines or rituals.

    c. Stereotypic and repetitive motor mannerisms (e.g., hand or finger flapping or twisting, or complex whole-body movements).

    d. Persistent preoccupation with parts of objects.

B. Delays or abnormal functioning in at least one of the following areas, with onset prior to age 3 years: (1) social interaction, (2) language as used in social communication, or (3) symbolic or imaginative play.

C. The disturbance is not accounted for by Rett's Disorder or Childhood Disintegrative Disorder.

Most children with autism (about 75%) receive special education in separate classes or separate schools; younger children (ages 12 to 21) with autism were slightly more likely than older children (ages 12 to 31) with autism to be educated in general education settings (U.S.D.E., 1997).

Traumatic Brain Injury

Traumatic brain injury is another relatively small category, accounting for less than 1% of all students with disabilities. The U.S. Department of Education (1997) reported that less than 10,000 students with traumatic brain injury between the ages of 6 and 21 received special education in the public schools, an increase of more than 2,000 students from the previous year.

    Traumatic brain injury refers to an acquired injury to the brain by an external force, resulting in total or partial functional disability or psychosocial impairment, or both, that adversely affects educational performance. The term applies to open or closed head injuries resulting in impairments in one or more areas, such as cognition; language; memory; attention; reasoning; abstract thinking; judgment; problem solving; sensory, perceptual, and motor abilities; psychosocial behavior; physical functions; information processing; and speech. The term does not apply to brain injuries that are congenital or degenerative, or brain injuries induced by birth trauma.

Children with traumatic brain injury are more likely than children with autism to be educated in general classrooms or resource rooms in neighborhood schools (U.S.D.E., 1996). Their educational needs typically involve four areas: cognition, speech and language, social and behavioral skills, and neuromotor and physical functioning (Ponsford, Sloan, & Snow, 1995). Individuals with a brain injury may be unable to remember or retrieve newly acquired information; they may also not be able to attend to simple or complex tasks for sustained periods of time. Speech may be difficult (e.g., unintelligible, slurred, labored) for these individuals; they may know what to say but have difficulty expressing it. Many individuals experience changes in their personalities and behaviors as a result of traumatic brain injury. Increased irritability, decreased motivation, and an inability to restrict inappropriate behavior are common. Neuromotor problems, such as poor eye-hand coordination, as well as physical problems, such as impaired balance, reduced energy, and paralysis, create frustration and additional need for support for some individuals with traumatic brain injury (Ponsford, Sloan, & Snow, 1995).

Mental Retardation

The Manual on Terminology and Classification in Mental Retardation provides a succinct definition of *mental retardation:* "Mental retardation refers to significantly subaverage general intellectual functioning existing concurrently with deficits in adaptive behavior, and manifested during the developmental period" (Grossman, 1973, p. 11). The manual also defines the key elements of mental retardation. They are *intellectual functioning,* which "may be assessed by one or more of the standardized tests," and *significantly subaverage* scores, which reflect "performance which is more than two standard deviations from the mean or average of the tests" (Grossman, 1973, p. 11).

To be included in the mental retardation category, a person must perform very poorly on an intelligence test. The person must also demonstrate deficits in adaptive behavior. Because the term *adaptive behavior* refers to the way in which a person functions in his or her social environment, many different measures of adaptive behavior have been developed. The judgment that a person is deficient in adaptive behavior is subjective. You may view the behavior of a given person as adaptive, whereas several classmates may view the same behavior as maladaptive. Trying to define adaptive behavior is like trying to define normal behavior. The requirement that people demonstrate a deficit in adaptive behavior is included in the definition of mental retardation so that people who perform poorly on intelligence tests but manage to adapt or adjust to their environment, thus functioning adequately outside school, will not be included in classes for students with mental retardation.

Emotional Disturbance

In the current federal definition, *emotionally disturbed* is defined as follows:

> (i) The term means a condition exhibiting one or more of the following characteristics over a long period of time and to a marked degree, which adversely affects educational performance: (a) an inability to learn that cannot be explained by intellectual, sensory, or health factors; (b) an inability to build or maintain satisfactory interpersonal relationships with peers and teachers; (c) inappropriate types of behavior or feelings under normal circumstances; (d) a general pervasive mood of unhappiness or depression; or (e) tendency to develop physical symptoms or fears associated with personal or school problems. (ii) The term includes schizophrenia. The term does not apply to children who are socially maladjusted, unless it is determined that they have a serious emotional disturbance.

Interestingly, this definition is similar to that used in the early 1960s and to a more recent description of less serious emotional or behavorial problems (cf. Bower, 1982; Kauffman, 1997). Professionals make up the definitions based on research and implications drawn from it; professionals also decide if the definitions represent serious or ordinary versions of the disorders.

The Individuals with Disabilities Education Act (PL 101-476) placed increased emphasis on meeting the needs of students with serious emotional disturbance. Specifically, the first amendments to PL 94-142 established a new program of support for projects to improve special education and related services to children and youths with serious emotional disturbance. The projects studied services provided; developed methods, curricula, and strategies to reduce the use of out-of-community residential programs; and increased the use of school district–based programs. At the time of the latest reauthorization, there was continuing use of effective collaboration among educators, related services personnel, and others charged with meeting the special learning needs of students with emotional problems. Federal initiatives were also proposed to develop innovative approaches to prevent children with mild emotional and behavioral problems from developing serious emotional disturbance. Whereas learning disabilities was the category of growth in the 1970s and 1980s, emotional disturbance has held that position in the 1990s.

Speech and Language Impairment

Current federal regulations indicate that students with *speech and language impairments* are those with a communication disorder such as stuttering, impaired articulation, a language impairment, or a voice impairment *that adversely affects* educational performance. Language articulation, fluency, and voice are primary areas in which these students are eligible for special education services, and norm-referenced tests are used to determine whether a student has a speech or language impairment. Speech and language pathologists' caseloads consist primarily of students who receive services for language articulation problems (less than 5 percent is comprised of students with voice and fluency disorders). Students with language disorders may have difficulty with semantics (vocabulary, comprehension, following directions), syntax (grammar), or pragmatics (following social conversational rules). Most speech and language pathologists work closely with classroom teachers by providing services in general education settings rather than pull-out programs. Approximately 20 percent of students with disabilities served in recent school years were included in the speech and language impairments category (U.S.D.E., 1997). There were more students in this category than in all others except learning disabilities.

Learning Disabilities

Learning disabilities (LD) is the most recent addition to the categories of special education. Since the category's inclusion, it has grown to include the largest groups of students receiving special services. In some states, more than half the students enrolled in special education are classified with learning disabilities. The most commonly accepted definition of *specific learning disabilities* is that they comprise

> a disorder in one or more the basic psychological processes involved in understanding or in using language, spoken or written, which may manifest itself in an imperfect ability to listen, think, read, write, spell, or do mathematical calculations. The term includes such conditions as perceptual handicaps, brain injury, minimal brain dysfunction, dyslexia, and developmental aphasia. The term does not include children who have learning problems which are primarily the result of visual, hearing, or motor handicaps, of mental retardation, or emotional disturbance, or of environmental, cultural, or economic disadvantage. (IDEA, 1997)

For the most part, students with learning disabilities have average or above-average scores on intelligence tests and below-average scores on at least one achievement test. When the differences between ability and achievement are large, classification is likely.

Recent years have witnessed significant efforts to identify subgroups of students with learning disabilities. For example, Kirk and Gallagher (1986) distinguished developmental from academic learning disabilities: attention, memory, perceptual, perceptual-motor, thinking, and language disorders are primary characteristics of developmental learning disabilities, and disorders in reading, spelling, written expression, handwriting, and arithmetic characterize academic learning disabilities. Others differentiated among types of academic and developmental behavior problems of students with learning disabilities (Lyon, 1983, 1985; McKinney, 1984, 1988; McKinney & Speece, 1986; Rourke, 1985; Short, Feagans, McKinney, & Appelbaum, 1986; Speece, McKinney, & Appelbaum, 1985). McKinney, for instance, "discovered that children with LD could be classified into more specific subgroups according to their patterns of behavioral strength and weakness, and that those patterns were prognostic of developmental trends in academic progress" (1989, p. 148). We believe fractionating categories of special education is largely an academic exercise of little practical consequence. We mention it here as evidence of the pursuits that engage professionals who believe the names assigned to students are indications of real characteristics, rather than words accepted as indications of presumed differences between people.

Gifted and Talented Students

Children who do more than expected have always been part of the educational system. Whenever a standard for achievement is set, some performers will miss the mark and others will excel. Horn, in the first textbook about exceptional children, pointed out why highly endowed students were often overlooked: "The special education of [these children] is in a far less advanced state than that of the dull and feeble, partly because [they] do not force themselves as a problem on the consciousness of the teacher and the school administrator" (1924, p. 24). Cubberly, however, suggested they should not be overlooked.

> We know that the number of children of superior ability is approximately as large as the number of the feeble in mind, and also that the future of democratic governments hinges largely upon the proper education and utilization of these superior children. One child of superior intellectual capacity, educated so as to utilize his talents, may confer greater benefits upon mankind, and be educationally far more important, than a thousand of the feeble-minded children upon whom we have recently come to put so much educational effort and expense. (1922, p. 451)

In the Gifted and Talented Children's Act of 1978, *gifted and talented* students were defined as those

> who are identified at the preschool, elementary, or secondary level as possessing demonstrated or potential abilities that give evidence of high performance capabilities in areas such as intellectual, creative, specific academic, or leadership ability, or in the performing and visual arts, and who by reason thereof, require services or activities not ordinarily provided by school.

The definition of gifted (and talented) students has gone through numerous variations. Early definitions were based on scores on intelligence tests alone (Newland, 1980). Later criteria included evidence of superior performance in areas other than solely intellectual ones (Renzulli, 1987).

Official federal policy toward gifted and talented students recommends but does not mandate (that is, legally require) the provision of special educational services for these students. The government encourages a cooperative venture between private and public sectors in the establishment and funding of programs for gifted and talented students. Nevertheless, the primary responsibility for developing and implementing services lies with the states and school districts; the national role is one of technical assistance and support (cf. Reynolds & Birch, 1982; Gallagher, 1988). Recently, interest has been shown in gifted students who show evidence of other exceptionalities and in gifted members of minority groups (Patton, Prillaman, & Van Tassel-Baska, 1990; Richert, 1987; Van Tassel-Baska, Patton, & Prillaman, 1989).

Categories of the Future

Although a disorder currently known as attention-deficit—hyperactivity disorder (ADHD) has been part of clinical practice since the 1930s, interest in ADHD within educational practice has only recently peaked (Silver, 1990). Indeed, the most controversial issue addressed during debate leading to the passage of the Individuals with Disabilities Education Act of 1990 was the proposal to add attention deficit disorder (ADD) as a separate category or subcategory under the law (Johns, 1991). At the final passage of the first amendments, ADD was not added as a new category, however; input from professional organizations, parents, and others concerned with this group of students was solicited, and the secretary of education was directed to fund one or more centers designed to organize, synthesize, and disseminate current knowledge relating to children and youths with ADD. Information to be disseminated includes: assessment techniques, instruments, and strategies for identification; location, evaluation, and measurement of progress; competencies needed by professionals providing special education and related services; conditions needed for effective professional practice; developmental and learning characteristics; and instructional techniques, strategies, and activities.

Recently other factors have been associated with serious learning problems in infants, children, and youths. According to Greer, children exposed to cocaine and other drugs

> will be prominent among the next generation of special ed students and each of them may be a neurochemical time-bomb, likely to experience the same dysphoria and thought and mood disorders as a recovering addict, which is what the child is. We do not have anywhere near the knowledge base or the educational technology to even begin to create the appropriate support structure for dealing with these children. (1990, p. 383)

Children with AIDS and fetal alcohol syndrome as well as those suffering because of homelessness, child abuse, continuing need of medical treatment, and other traumatic and difficult life events are among the constituencies likely to need special education (Stevens & Price, 1991; U.S.D.E., 1997).

Growing numbers and types of children with medical, social, and educational problems will tax special education's resources as never before in history. Greer (1990) identified the following six ways to "get ourselves ready" for the future and the increasingly complex group of students who will likely need special education; they remain current today:

- First, no single human service agency, including the schools, has the human and fiscal resources to meet the needs of these children and their families. A full-scale coordination effort must begin now to integrate the institutions and agencies providing policy/rulemaking/legislative leadership at community, state/province, and national levels.

- Second, because we don't even know the full extent of the problem, we have to begin immediately to collect data on these children to serve as the foundation for programming and personnel training. Every educator must be involved in information gathering and sharing. Fortunately, mechanisms such as the ERIC Clearinghouse and ECER (Exceptional Children Education Resources) already exist to support this task. They must be fully utilized.

- Third, every special education degree-granting institution has to get a grip on this problem now. Our profession's academic leadership will need all of its imagination and skill to train a new generation of teachers to deal with a whole new category of disability.

- Fourth, school district administrators, teachers, principals, parents, and others must begin to rethink the meaning of a "free, appropriate public education" in this new context. We need to ensure that assessment teams are prepared for the mounting wave of referrals and prepared to set up IEPs and programs.

- Fifth, the drug babies are going to reintensify the need for vigorous and successful "child find" activity to make sure that the spectrum of agencies with which they are likely to come in contact closes up the holes in the safety nets.

- Sixth, at a time when "excellence is king" as a result of the preoccupations of the 1980s school reform movement, there will be resistance to curriculum additions. That resistance must be met and overcome. There will also be added impetus for using these children collectively as an excuse for backing away from many special education initiatives such as mainstreaming and plug-in programs. But we cannot afford to lose ground now. (1990, pp. 383–384)

CURRENT CONDITIONS OF SPECIAL EDUCATION

Since 1975, when mandatory special education legislation was first enacted, educational services for students with disabilities have changed dramatically. Substantial progress has been made toward meeting the original goal of providing a free, appropriate public education for all children with disabilities.

Before IDEA and its predecessors were enacted, 1 million children with disabilities were excluded from school, and many others were housed in institutions that did not address their educational needs. Today, one of the basic goals of the law—ensuring that children with disabilities are not excluded from school—has been largely achieved. Almost 5.5 million children and youth with disabilities are receiving special education services. All states and jurisdictions now provide services to preschoolers with disabilities, and all states and jurisdictions now ensure full implementation of programs for infants and toddlers with disabilities. During the previous two decades, results for children with disabilities have improved (U.S.D.E., 1997). Graduation rates are higher. More students are going to college. Today, half of all adults with a disability have completed some college or received a degree, compared with only 30 percent in 1986. More than half of all youth with disabilities (56 percent) are competitively employed within 5 years of leaving school. The number of children served in costly state institutions has declined significantly; today, just over 1 percent of all children with disabilities live in institutions.

A central purpose of IDEA is to ensure an effective and individual education designed to address each child's unique needs in the least restrictive environment. IDEA requires that students with disabilities be educated in general education classrooms with appropriate aids and services. The goal is to provide students with disabilities an education with their natural neighbors and peers in their neighborhood school, unless the nature or severity of the disability is such that education cannot be achieved satisfactorily there with use of supplemental aids and services. States and school districts have made and continue to make progress in meeting this goal. States report that an increasing proportion of students are served in general classes. Where students with disabilities are appropriately educated in inclusive environments, research shows that students—both those with disabilities and those without disabilities—benefit academically and socially (U.S.D.E., 1997).

The *Eighteenth Annual Report to Congress* (U.S.D.E., 1997) marked the twentieth anniversary of the passage of PL 94-142. We use it as a basis for analyzing the condition of special education after two decades of progress in providing a free, appropriate public education to students with disabilities.

Who Receives Special Education?

A total of 5,439,626 children and youth with disabilities, ages 3 to 21, were served under the IDEA during the 1994–1995 school year (U.S.D.E., 1997). This represented an increase of 167, 779 (3.2 percent) from the previous year. The rate of growth in the numbers of students receiving special education continued to exceed the rate of growth in the ages 3 to 21 resident population (which increased by 793,570, or 1.1 percent, in the same year) and the rate of growth in the number of children enrolled in school (which increased by 671,161, or 1.5 percent, in the same year).

The two largest age groups served under the IDEA were 6- to 11-year-olds (2,520,863) and 12- to 17-year-olds (2,154,963), representing 46 percent and 40 percent, respectively, of all students with disabilities ages 3 to 21 (U.S.D.E., 1997). Students ages 6 to 21 comprised about 90 percent (4,915,168) of the identified special education population (see Table 3.1).

When reporting to Congress, Department of Education personnel include the following twelve disability categories (U.S.D.E., 1997): specific learning disabilities, speech or language impairments, mental retardation, emotional disturbance, multiple disabilities, other health impairments, hearing impairments, orthopedic impairments, visual impairments, autism, deaf-blindness, and traumatic brain injury. Multiple disabilities means concomitant impairments (such as

TABLE 3.1   **Number and Percentage Change of Students Ages 6 to 21 Served 1993–1995**

	Number		Change		Percentage of Total Ages 3–21
Age	1993–1994	1994–1995	Number	Percentage	
3–5	491,685	524,458	32,773	6.7	9.6
6–11	2,458,924	2,520,863	61,939	2.5	46.3
12–17	2,079,094	2,154,963	75,869	3.6	39.6
18–21	242,144	239,342	−2,802	−1.2	4.4
3–21	5,271,847	5,439,626	167,779	3.2	100.00

SOURCE: U.S.D.E. (1996). *Eighteenth Annual Report to Congress.* Washington, D.C.: Office of Special Education Programs.

mental retardation–blindness or mental retardation–orthopedic impairment), the combination of which causes such severe educational problems that people with these disabilities cannot be accommodated in a single category of special education programs (IDEA, 1991). Deaf-blindness means concomitant hearing and visual impairments, the combination of which causes such severe communication and other developmental and educational problems that they cannot be accommodated in special education programs solely for children with deafness or children with blindness (IDEA, 1991).

The numbers of students in each disability category are presented in Table 3.2. Students with specific learning disabilities account for more than half of all students receiving special education. Students with speech or language impairments (20.8 percent), mental retardation (11.6 percent), and emotional disturbance (8.7 percent) make up an additional 41.1 percent of students ages 6 to 21 with disabilities. Together, these students, sometimes referred to as those with "mild disabilities" or "high prevalence disabilities," account for 92.2 percent of all students receiving special education (U.S.D.E., 1997).

From 1990–1991 through 1994–1995, there was a 12.7 percent increase across all categories of disabilities (U.S.D.E., 1997). Trends in numbers of students with mild/high prevalence disabilities served in special education are presented in Figure 3.1. Greater increases (17.3 percent) are evident for specific learning disabilities and emotional disturbance (9.6 percent) than for speech or language impairments (3.6 percent) or mental retardation (3.6 percent). Trends in numbers of other students with low prevalence disabilities served in special education are presented in Figure 3.2. The increases within several categories were greater than the 2.8 percent increase across all categories (see Table 3.2). The largest increase occurred in the category of traumatic brain injury, which grew 33.2 percent. Large increases also occurred in the categories of other health impairments and autism. Growth in the number of students with traumatic brain injury and autism is due mostly to the newness of the categories in federal

TABLE 3.2   **Number and Percentage Change in Categories of Students Ages 6 to 21 Served 1993–1995.**

Category	Number		Change		Percentage of Total Ages 3–21
	1993–1994	1994–1995	Number	Percentage	
Specific learning disabilities	2,428,062	2,513,977	85,915	3.5	51.1
Speech or language impairments	1,018,208	1,023,665	5,457	0.5	20.8
Mental retardation	553,869	570,855	16,986	3.1	11.6
Emotional disturbance	415,071	428,168	13,097	3.2	8.7
Other health impairments	83,080	106,509	23,429	28.2	2.2
Multiple disabilities	109,730	89,646	−20,084	−18.3	1.8
Hearing impairments	64,667	65,568	901	1.4	1.3
Orthopedic impairments	56,842	60,604	3,762	6.6	1.2
Visual impairments	24,813	24,877	64	0.3	0.5
Autism	19,058	22,780	3,722	19.5	0.5
Traumatic brain injury	5,395	7,188	1,793	33.2	0.1
Deaf-blindness	1,367	1,331	−36	−2.6	0.0
All disabilities	4,780,162	4,915,168	135,006	2.8	100.0

SOURCE: U.S.D.E. (1996). *Eighteenth Annual Report to Congress.* Washington D.C.: Office of Special Education Programs.

reporting and the resultant technical assistance provided to districts in identifying students to fill the categories (U.S.D.E., 1996). The increase in the number of students with other health impairments is likely due to increases in the provision of special education services to students with attention deficit disorder, which is not currently recognized as a separate disability grouping.

What Services Are Provided?

In accordance with earlier provisions of IDEA, states were required to report the number of students receiving related services druing the school year. The total number of students receiving various types of related services is reported in Table 3.3. Testing services (i.e., diagnostic services, counseling services, psychological services) represented a large portion (42 percent) of the related services provided

FIGURE 3.1   **Growth Trends for Students with Mild High Prevalence Disabilities (Number Served in Thousands)**

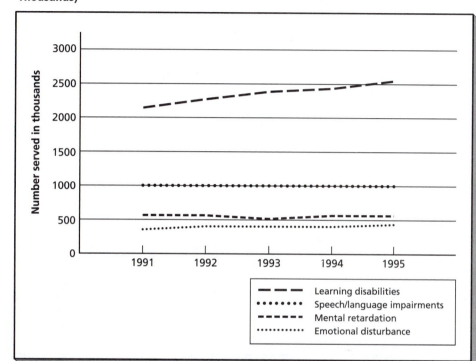

to students with disabilities. Transportation and related special assistance (e.g., school social work and speech/language pathology) were also among the most frequently received related services. Occupational therapy and physical therapy were not received by many special education students.

Where Are Services Provided?

People in special education believe that exceptional students are more like normal students than different. This leads to the belief that students should be provided ample opportunities to receive all or part of their education in the same settings as their neighbors and peers. The principle used in deciding where a student should receive special education is called the *least restrictive environment* (LRE). Special education students are expected to be educated in environments that are as much like normal, or as least restrictive, as possible. The assumption is that settings (places) and programs (what goes on in settings) are synonymous; of course, this is not always true (cf. Tucker, 1989).

LRE does not mean that all special needs students must be placed in general classrooms, even through many are enrolled full time in general classes. Other students are enrolled primarily in general classes but leave these rooms

FIGURE 3.2   **Growth Trends for Students with Severe Low Prevalence Disabilities (Number Served in Thousands)**

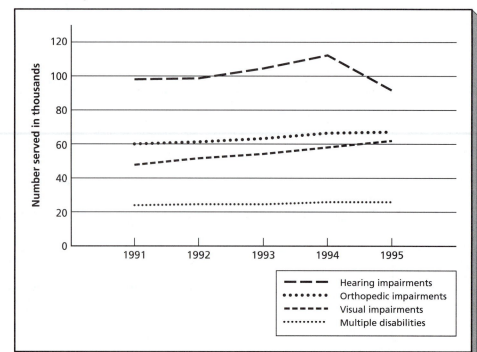

part of the time to go to other locations where they receive direct services from special education teachers or related-services personnel such as social workers, occupational therapists, or psychologists. Still others are enrolled primarily in special education classes, but to the maximum extent possible they attend general classes for part of the school day for certain instructional activities. Some students are enrolled full time in special education settings and receive all their instruction in those settings. Some exceptional students are educated in hospitals or at home when they cannot attend their general classes because of illness or other medical problems. Still others receive their instruction in a residential (institutional) setting in classes run and staffed by personnel from local school districts. The most restrictive setting for students with disabilities is one in which they live in a residential school or institution and receive education services from a staff employed by that school or institution.

The federal government uses the following six distinctions in reporting numbers of students with disabilities served in different educational environments: regular class, resource room, separate class, public or private separate school, public or private residential facility, and homebound/hospital placements (U.S.D.E., 1996) *Regular class* includes students who receive the majority of their

TABLE 3.3   **Numbers of Students Receiving Related Services**

Related Service	Number of Students	Percent of Services
Diagnostic services	777,436	17
Counseling services	620,262	13
Transportation services	569,673	12
Psychological services	557,119	12
School social work services	472,785	10
Speech/language pathology	432,157	9
School health services	419,237	9
Recreational services	215,435	5
Other related services	186,849	4
Audiological services	184,817	4
Occupational therapy	106,710	3
Physical therapy	87,888	2

SOURCE: U.S. Department of Education. (1988b.) *Tenth Annual Report to Congress on the Implementation of the Education of the Handicapped Act.* Washington, D.C.: Author, Table 6, p.23.

education program in a general education classroom and receive special education and related services outside the general education classroom for less than 21 percent of the school day. *Resource room* includes students who receive special education and related services outside the general education classroom for at least 21 percent but no more than 60 percent of the school day. *Separate class* includes students who receives special education and related services outside the general education class for more than 60 percent of the school day. *Separate school* includes students who receive special education and related services in a public or private separate day school for students with disabilities, at public expense, for more than 50 percent of the school day. *Residential facility* includes students who receive special education in a public or private residential facility, at public expense, for more than 50 percent of the school day. *Homebound/hospital* environment includes students placed in and receiving special education in a hospital or homebound program.

Placement patterns in these different environments vary considerably by disability (see Table 3.4). The majority of students with speech and language impairments are served in general education settings. Students with speech and language impairments are more likely than students with any other disability to spend the majority of their day with peers who do not have disabilities. Students with learning disabilities, orthopedic impairments, other health impairments, emotional disturbance, and traumatic brain injury are generally placed within the

TABLE 3.4   **Percentage of Students with Disabilities Ages 6 to 21 Served in Different Educational Environments, by Disability: School Year 1993–1994**

	Regular Class	Resource Room	Separate Class	Separate School	Residential Facility	Homebound/ Hospital
Speech or language impairments	87.5	7.6	4.5	0.3	0.04	0.05
Visual impairments	45.2	21.3	18.3	4.1	10.6	0.5
Other health impairments	40.0	27.0	21.3	1.8	0.4	9.4
Specific learning disabilities	39.3	41.0	8.8	0.6	0.1	0.1
Orthopedic impairments	37.4	20.7	33.3	5.3	0.5	2.9
Hearing impairments	30.6	20.0	30.6	7.0	11.6	0.2
Traumatic brain injury	22.3	23.5	30.2	18.3	2.6	3.0
Emotional disturbance	20.5	25.8	35.3	13.4	3.2	1.8
Mental retardation	8.6	26.1	57.0	7.0	0.7	0.5
Autism	9.6	8.1	54.5	23.4	3.9	0.5
Multiple disabilities	9.1	19.8	44.1	21.8	3.2	2.0
Deaf-blindness	7.7	8.0	34.6	24.3	23.2	2.2
All disabilities	43.4	29.5	22.7	3.1	0.7	0.6

SOURCE: U.S.D.E. (1996). *Eighteenth Annual Report to Congress.* Washington, D.C.: Author.

regular school building, but then students are spread across regular classes, resource rooms, and separate classes. It is likely that many of these students spend a portion of their day in classes with peers who do not have disabilities, but are pulled out for extended resource room support or alternative academic courses. Separate classroom placements are most prevalent for students with mental retardation (57.0 percent), autism (54.5 percent), and multiple disabilities (44.1 percent), although resource room placements are also commonly used to serve students with mental retardation and multiple disabilities. By definition, those in separate classroom placements may spend up to 40 percent of the school day in a general education classroom.

The percentage of students with disabilities served in general education classrooms has increased considerably in recent years (U.S.D.E., 1996, 1997). Regular classroom placements are still used primarily with elementary students as well as those with speech or language impairments, visual impairments, other health impairments, learning disabilities, and orthopedic impairments.

Who Provides Services?

The average rate of increase in the number of students receiving special education services during the last decade was about 3 percent a year (U.S.D.E., 1997). The increase in the number of students enrolled in special education classes occurred at the same time that enrollment in general education decreased. This growth, coupled with a high turnover rate, meant that plenty of new instructional and noninstructional professional positions were available in special education. For example, using a conservative average of fifteen students per class, approximately 3,500 to 4,500 new teachers were needed each year of the 1990s.

In recent years, about 93 percent of special education positions were held by fully certified teachers, 6 percent of special education teachers were employed on a provisional or emergency basis, and only 1 percent of funded positions were vacant (see Table 3.5). The largest group of teachers (28 percent) provided

TABLE 3.5   **Special Education Teacher Positions Funded to Serve Students Ages 6 to 21 Under IDEA, Part B, by Employment Classification: School Year 1993–1994**

Disability/Other Classification	FTE Employed		Vacant Positions	Total Positions
	Fully Certified	Not Fully Certified		
Specific learning disabilities	85,853	6,897	771	93,522
Mental retardation	39,342	2,530	353	42,225
Speech or language impairments	36,807	1,655	1,097	39,559
Serious emotional disturbance	26,171	3,608	373	30,151
Multiple disabilities	7,118	520	67	7,705
Hearing impairments	5,738	285	84	6,107
Orthopedic impairments	2,684	239	126	3,049
Visual impairments	2,433	1,439	68	2,640
Other health impairments	2,065	239	43	2,347
Autism	1,418	285	24	1,727
Traumatic brain injury	110	23	2	136
Deaf-blindness	102	13	3	118
Cross-categorical[a]	84,534	4,501	559	89,594
Other classification[b]	15,962	119	74	16,155
Total	310,338	21,054	3,643	335,035

[a] Three states (Idaho, Massachusetts, and Texas) report all special education teachers as cross-categorical.
[b] Includes counts of special education teachers for the five jurisdictions—Oregon, Pennsylvania, South Dakota, Palau, and the Commonwealth of the Northern Mariana Islands—not using federal disability categories.

NOTE: The total FTE shown in both the row and column totals may not equal the sum of the individual states and outlying areas because of rounding.

SOURCE: U.S.D.E. (1996). *Eighteenth Annual Report to Congress.* Washington, D.C.: Author.

services to students with learning disabilities; this category also accounted for the largest group (33 percent) of not fully certified teachers. The next largest group taught in cross-categorical classes in which students with different disabilities were grouped for instruction. The largest number of vacant positions was in the area of speech and language impairments (30 percent), followed by specific learning disabilities (21 percent) and cross-categorical (15 percent) programs. About 87 percent of the employed, fully certified teachers and 63 percent of the not fully certified teachers were retained for employment.

Teacher aides accounted for 60 percent of all personnel positions other than teachers (see Table 3.6). Psychologists, nonprofessional staff, and other professional staff were the next largest groups of professionals providing services to students with disabilities in recent years. Nearly one-third of all reported related services personnel vacancies were in positions requiring occupational therapists, physical therapists, and psychologists. Growth in the numbers of students in the categories of autism, other health impairments, orthopedic impairments, and traumatic brain injury account for some of the growth in these employment positions.

Who Succeeds in Special Education?

Few national data exist reflecting levels of performance of students with disabilities in special or general education programs. Since 1993, data on the following indicators have been gathered for individuals exiting special education (U.S.D.E., 1996): graduation with diploma, graduation with certificate, reached maximum age, returned to general classrooms, dropped out, moved (known to be continuing), moving (not known to be continuing), and died. Of the total exiters in recent years, about 35 percent graduated with diplomas or certificates. Students with low prevalence disabilities were somewhat more likely to graduate with a diploma than were students in high prevalence categories.

Numbers and percentages of students with disabilities who graduated, reached the legal age limit, dropped out, and died are presented in Table 3.7. Of these outcomes, more than 60 percent of students in all categories except emotional disturbance graduated with a diploma or certificate. Students with multiple disabilities, autism, deaf-blindness, and traumatic brain injury are more likely to reach the legal age limit of special education than students with other disabilities. Students with mild disabilities (i.e., learning disabilities, emotional disturbance, speech or language impairments, or mental retardation) are more likely to drop out than students in all other categories except other health impairments. Mortality rates are somewhat higher for multiple disabilities, orthopedic impairments, other health impairments, and deaf-blindness categories.

In recent years, approximately 60,000 students with disabilities returned to general education (U.S.D.E., 1996). Students with learning disabilities represented the largest group (57 percent) to return to general education classes. Students with speech or language impairments (14 percent), emotional disturbance (13 percent), other health impairments (8 percent), and mental retardation (4 percent) were among the next largest groups to leave special education and

TABLE 3.6   Special Education Personnel Positions Other Than Teachers Funded to Serve Students with Disabilities Ages 3 to 21 Under IDEA

Disability/Other Classification	FTE Employed			
	Fully Certified	Not Fully Certified	Vacant Positions	Total Positions
Teacher aides	189,011	12,968	1,286	203,265
Psychologists	20,104	424	336	20,864
Nonprofessional staff	18,844	1,452	165	20,461
Other professional staff	18,053	3,002	139	21,194
Supervisors/administrators (LEA)	14,502	344	161	15,007
School social workers	11,026	463	106	11,595
Diagnostic and evaluation staff	8,464	76	167	8,707
Counselors	7,269	127	108	7,504
Occupational therapists	5,331	207	459	5,997
Physical education teachers	4,971	251	60	5,282
Vocational education teachers	4,123	115	97	4,335
Physical therapists	3,536	131	390	4,057
Interpreters	2,209	470	60	2,739
Work study coordinators	1,407	85	42	1,534
Supervisors/administrators (SEA)	1,021	10	39	1,070
Audiologists	836	22	22	880
Recreational and therapeutic recreational therapists	256	61	8	325
Rehabilitation counselors	179	6	8	193
Total	311,142	20,214	3,653	335,009

SOURCE: U.S.D.E. (1996). *Eighteenth Annual Report to Congress.* Washington, D.C.: Author.

return to their former classes. Relatively small numbers of students with orthopedic impairments (2 percent), multiple disabilities (1 percent), and hearing impairments (1 percent) left special education to return to general education; less than 1 percent of students in each of the visual impairment, autism, deaf-blindness, and traumatic brain injury categories returned to their former classrooms.

Approximately 125,000 students with disabilities exited special education programs as a result of personal or family mobility (U.S.D.E., 1996). Students with learning disabilities (55 percent), emotional disturbance (25 percent), and mental retardation (12 percent) were more likely to leave special education by moving than any other categories (less than 5 percent each).

TABLE 3.7   **Distribution of Special Education Student Outcomes**

Special Education Category	Graduated	Received Certificate	Reached Legal Age Limit	Dropped Out	Died	Total
Specific learning disabilities	76,735	10,871	891	44,244	438	133,179
	58%	8%	1%	33%	0%	60%
Mental retardation	13,900	9,117	2,307	10,270	361	35,955
	39%	25%	6%	29%	1%	16%
Speech or language impairments	3,423	473	121	1,875	31	5,923
	58%	8%	2%	32%	1%	3%
Emotional disturbance	11,251	1,649	331	17,370	184	30,785
	37%	5%	1%	56%	1%	14%
Multiple disabilities	1,254	675	553	531	133	3,146
	40%	21%	18%	17%	4%	1%
Hearing impairments	2,209	391	48	570	11	3,229
	68%	12%	1%	18%	0%	1%
Orthopedic impairments	1,557	285	133	412	82	2,469
	63%	12%	5%	17%	3%	1%
Other health impairments	2,250	191	44	1,005	97	3,587
	63%	5%	1%	28%	3%	2%
Visual impairments	931	105	53	195	19	1,303
	71%	8%	4%	15%	1%	1%
Autism	169	120	80	55	3	427
	40%	28%	19%	13%	1%	0%
Deaf-blindness	34	26	8	8	6	82
	41%	32%	10%	10%	7%	0%
Traumatic brain injury	232	45	25	73	3	378
	61%	12%	7%	19%	1%	0%
All disabilities	113,945	23,948	4,594	76,608	1,368	220,463
	52%	11%	2%	35%	1%	100%

SOURCE: U.S.D.E. (1996). *Eighteenth Annual Report to Congress.* Washington, D.C.: Author.

What Continuing Services Are Needed?

The Individuals with Disabilities Education Act requires that the Secretary of Education collect data every three years on anticipated services needed for students aged 12 to 21 who are exiting the educational system (U.S.D.E., 1996). The intent is to provide state education agencies with information to improve transition planning and the postschool lives of individuals with disabilities. Data are gathered using the Performance Assessment for Self-Sufficiency (PASS) system, in which need for more than a dozen anticipated services are reported for individuals in states selected to participate. In the most recent data collection, the most prevalent primary need was case management (80 percent of sample). Alternative education, including programs in continuing education, adult education, adult basic education (ABE), general educational development (GED), adult high school diploma programs, and adult compensatory or special education, was the next most common primary need. Communication services (e.g., speech/language therapy, interpreter services, reader services, braille assistance) and recreation services were considered primary needs for over one-third of the sampled students. Vocational preparation and job placement were reported as a primary need for relatively low percentages of students, and only 6 percent reported no anticipated services (U.S.D.E., 1996).

A POSITIVE IDEA?

For many people, disability is a natural part of life. Disabilities do not diminish the rights of individuals nor do they have to reduce opportunities to participate in or contribute to society. Mastery of basic skills, achievement of academic competence, and independence in daily living are among the educational goals of schooling for all students. Improving these educational outcomes for children with disabilities is an essential element of our national policy of ensuring equality of opportunity, full participation, independent living, and economic self-sufficiency for individuals with disabilities. Before enactment of Public Law 94-142, the Education for All Handicapped Children Act of 1975, the canary in the special education coal mine heralded a condition requiring drastic change. The needs of children with disabilities were not being fully met; more than one-half of children with disabilities in the United States did not receive appropriate educational services; more than 1 million children with disabilities were excluded entirely from the public school system and did not go through the educational process with their peers; many children with disabilities participated in school programs but did not have a successful educational experience because their disabilities were undetected; and because of the lack of adequate services within the public school system, families were often forced to find services outside the public school system, often at great distance from their residence and at their own expense.

A key objective of enactment and implementation of the Education for All Handicapped Children Act of 1975 (and its subsequent amendments) was ensuring that all children with disabilities have access to a free, appropriate public education designed to meet their unique needs and prepare them to achieve the goals of education. Each year since 1975, the total number of children and youth with disabilities receiving special education services has increased (U.S.D.E., 1997). During recent school years, approximately 12 percent of elementary and secondary school students received special education services (a 44 percent increase since the beginning of the program). Access is a necessary, but not sufficient condition for improving educational results for children with disabilities.

Is all this extra education producing positive results for individuals receiving it? Is the condition of special education improving? Like the optimists who see the glass as half full, many believe the system is working. Results for students with disabilities have improved dramatically during the past 20 years (U.S.D.E., 1996). Too often, such beliefs are offered in the absence of data reflecting changes in areas other than numbers of students receiving special education as opposed to evidence illustrating attainment of other educational outcomes (e.g., improved literacy skills, improved academic achievement, improved functioning in daily living skills). There are many others who believe special education is not working. Their arguments are grounded in the conspicuous absence of data illustrating that special education makes a difference in terms of achievement of important personal, social, and academic outcomes (e.g., improved independence, relationships, or literacy scores compared to students not receiving special education). We believe there is a broad and immediate need for more information on outcomes (not just access) before making a reasoned decision on the condition of special education. But, clearly, it's all how you look at it.

Discussion Questions

1. Students in some categories represent large numbers of the people who receive special education, while students in other categories require more intensive services than others. What effects do these facts have on social, political, economic, and educational attitudes, perspectives, and practices?

2. Special education is a subsystem of general education. How does the condition of special education influence the condition of general education?

3. What information should be used to judge the condition of special education? Who should be responsible for collecting, compiling, and reporting it?

4. What effect does growth in numbers of students classified with learning disabilities have on the condition of special education?

5. Why are there so many categories in special education? Are there students with special needs who do not fit in the current categorical system? What problems are created if a student is eligible for special services in more than one current category?

Chapter 4
Definitional Debate

HARDWARE VERSUS SOFTWARE
Blindness
Deafness
Physical and Health Impairments
Changing Definition of Mental Retardation
LD or Not LD?
Variance in Gifted and Talented Identification
EBD, ED, EH, BD, SM, SED, SLBP, EI, or EIEIO

PERSPECTIVES ON CLASSIFICATION
Categorical Labeling
Categorical Drift
Numbers Tell a Story
Make Mine Mild
In Search of Students with Real Disabilities

WHERE DOES ADD OR ADHD BELONG?

DISCUSSION QUESTIONS

"When I use a word," Humpty Dumpty said, in a rather scornful tone, "it means just what I choose it to mean—neither more nor less."
—Lewis Carroll, *Through the Looking Glass and What Alice Found There*

ategories of special education do not exist in and of themselves. They are constructs given meaning and life through comparison of performance to criteria. *Blindness* is a name assigned to visual performance judged different from that called *average* or *normal*. *Giftedness* and *mental retardation* are names assigned to intellectual performance judged different from that called *average* or *normal*. Criteria accepted as evidence for a condition form the cornerstones of a definition. Definition is the cornerstone for the existence of the condition. For all practical purposes, without definitions there are no categories. Myers and Hammill put it well with regard to learning disabilities:

> Before 1965, local, state, and federal education agencies did not officially recognize learning disabled as a category of handicapped individuals, that is, as a *defined* group of individuals whose special education or other treatment needs could be paid for with public money. As a result, there were few classes for learning disabled children, fewer remedial or habilitation facilities for youths and adults, and almost no college preparation programs in the learning disabilities area. (1990, p. 3; emphasis added)

They also remarked that with formal definition, learning disabilities has become "a legally constituted category of handicapped students, the use of the term has become pervasive in American education, and the number of students said to have learning disabilities is larger than any other group of handicapped students" (p. 3). (How things change with official definition and sanction!)

Clearly, definitions drive conditions; without definitions there are no conditions in ways that are important to a profession (e.g., funding, teacher preparation programs, facilities). Yet there are significant difficulties associated with these conditions. These difficulties affect all aspects of special education. This issue was highlighted in a study about students with disabilities in standards-based reform conducted by the National Research Council (McDonnell, McLaughlin, & Morison, 1997):

> Currently the criteria for identifying many of the categories of disability are not well defined or reliable, even though these criteria affect important decisions about which students are eligible for legal rights and special education services under the IDEA. (p. 110)

Classifying students and assigning labels to them are not benign activities. They affect the people who do the labeling and the people who receive the labels; they also affect the people who live and work with people who receive the labels. Blackman referred to children who receive special education because they *have* or *have been assigned* a disability as "children with negative school labels" (1989, p. 459)

This situation raises several questions: What criteria form the basis for assigning these labels? What concerns and debates consistently surface when definitions are developed and evaluated? Have all categories of children with negative school labels been similarly affected by labeling? Clearly, debate about defining and classifying students according to the definitions has not produced negative effects in terms of growth or interest. But such debate has consistently been a source of task force formulations and professional flagellation in some areas of special education more than in others.

HARDWARE VERSUS SOFTWARE

The function of definitions in special and remedial education is to provide a conceptual model for understanding the condition(s) created by the act of defining. In addition, definitions provide the bases from which identification practices evolve. When we know what we are looking for, we have some indication of how to find it. Note, however, that the categories or names assigned to the observed differences in other people do not represent real "things." The meanings of the terms used to refer to these categories (for example, idiocy, mental retardation, learning disability, blindness) depend on purposes the people who use the terms have for assigning them to students. Bodgan and Taylor offered the following examples:

> Some have argued [that] mental retardation is a social construction or a concept which exists in the minds of the "judges" rather than in the minds of the "judged." . . . A mentally retarded person is one who has been labeled as such according to rather arbitrarily created and applied criteria.
>
> *Retardation,* and other such clinical labels, suggests generalizations about the nature of men and women to whom the term has been applied. . . . We assume that the mentally retarded possess common characteristics that allow them to be unambiguously distinguished from all others. We explain their behavior by special theories. It is as though humanity can be divided into two groups, the "normal" and the "retarded." (1976, p. 47)

Sarason and Doris put it this way: "Mental retardation is not a thing you can see or touch or define in terms of shape and substance. It is a *concept* serving two major purposes: to separate a group of people; and to justify social action in regard to those who are set apart" (1979, p. 11; emphasis added).

The position we take is that learning disability, emotional disturbance, underachievement, blindness, deafness, and other special education categories are simply terms people use to refer to concepts that they have constructed to confirm a belief that people in this society differ from one another. These categories are also used to explain people's behavior.

The definitions created to describe people with special learning needs fall into two groups: those definitions that have a sensory basis and functional disability (that is, blindness, deafness) associated with them and those that have a psychometric basis and assigned disability (that is, learning disabilities, mental retardation) associated with them. Conditions in special education have different origins or bases. Some conditions are grounded in performances measured primarily by hardware (i.e., machines or instruments) that provides objective scores. For example, visual functioning is evaluated by machines such as the Keystone Telebinocular and the Lomb Orthorater. When screening instruments such as a Snellen Wall Chart are used, decision making becomes more subjective.

In decision making for categories such as blindness and deafness, multiple measures of the same type of performance do not generally provide different results. For example, a person typically does not have 20/60 vision on a vision screening based on the Snellen Wall Chart and 20/80 based on another instrument. Similarly, it is not the case that a person is blind with one instrument and normally sighted with another or that normally sighted people are consistently misidentified using certain vision tests. In sensory based conditions, there is a widely accepted standard for measuring performance, and criteria for identification are more likely to be universally accepted. The procedures for identifying some of these conditions are so transparent and universally accepted that professionals have endorsed home versions (see the box on p. 96) for distribution in popular magazines (Yeager, 1990).

In contrast, almost any published test, observation, or interview can be used in making decisions about conditions (e.g., mental retardation, emotional disturbance) that have a psychometric basis, and considerable controversy surrounds special education categories that are based primarily on scores on commercially

The Reader's Digest Home Eye Test

By Robert C. Yeager

Technical associates:
Weylin G. Eng, O.D., and George W. Weinstein, M.D.

TEST NO. 1: ADULT "E" TEST

GOAL: To measure your visual acuity.

1. Fasten the "E" chart to the wall at eye level.
2. Stand ten feet from the chart. Wear any lenses you normally use.
3. Cover your left eye.
4. Begin with the largest E's. Can you tell which direction their "legs" are pointing? Continue to the lowest line on which you can clearly see at least half the E's.
5. Repeat with the other eye.

If you can read line 4 or lower, you've passed. If you can't read line 4, or can't make out the same line with each eye, schedule an appointment with your eye doctor.

TEST NO. 3: CHILD'S "E" TEST

GOAL: To help determine if your child needs glasses or has amblyopia—lazy eye.

1. Have the child stand ten feet from the "E" chart, wearing any lenses he normally uses.
2. Gently cover his left eye. (Watch out for peeking.)
3. Tell the child to pretend the E's are tables and to point in the same direction as the table legs. Begin with the largest E. (You may need to point to each letter.)
4. Stop when the child reaches the lowest line on which he can clearly identify at least half the E's.
5. Repeat with the left eye. To guard against memorizing, have the child read the rows backward.

Scoring for visual acuity is the same as in the adult "E" test. If the pinhole test improves the child's vision, he may simply need glasses. If, however, one eye scores more than two lines poorer than the other, your child may have amblyopia or another eye problem, and should see a vision specialist at once.

available pencil and paper tests or on classroom observations and interpersonal interviews. To illustrate, consider that a student can be classified as having emotional disturbance in a school district that uses one behavioral checklist, but not classified in a neighboring district that uses a different checklist of screening procedure. And even though this could happen to students with visual impairments, it seldom does. Similarly, student are identified as having a learning disability if differences between scores on tests of intelligence and academic achievement are significant. Virtually any test of intelligence and any test of academic achievement can be used in making this decision, and the magnitude of the difference can be determined by any number of commonly used practices.

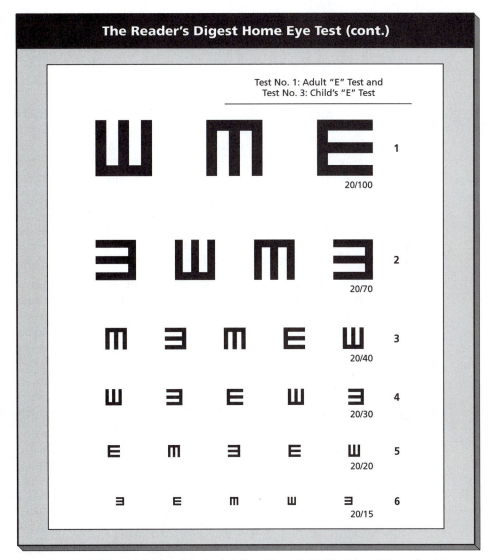

The Reader's Digest Home Eye Test (cont.)

Test No. 1: Adult "E" Test and
Test No. 3: Child's "E" Test

Source: Excerpted with permission from "The Reader's Digest Home Eye Test" by Robert C. Yeager, *Reader's Digest,* September 1990, pp. 93–100.

The flux created when such educational software is the basis for special education identification is evident in decision-making practices with unacceptable validity and reliability. Instruments that produce scores that are open to large degrees of interpretation produce soft signs of disability and create problems for professionals concerned with the integrity of the identification system. Such use permits criteria that vary with the whims of society. "Both the label and definition can lead to different conceptualizations of what constitutes a disorder depending upon how one understands and uses them" (Center, 1990, p. 141). An analysis of current special education conditions illustrates the basis for identification and provides information about the historical dilemmas associated with definitions for these categories.

Blindness

Blindness was first legally defined in 1935 by the Social Security Act (Hatlin, Hall, & Tuttle, 1980). Students with visual impairments represent less than 1 percent of those receiving special education (U.S. Dept. of Education, 1997; Ysseldyke & Algozzine, 1995). The National Society for the Prevention of Blindness offered the following definitions of blindness and partial sight:

> Blindness is generally defined in the United States as visual acuity for distance vision of 20/200 or less in the better eye, with acuity of more than 20/200 if the widest diameter of field of vision subtends an angle no greater than 20 degrees.
>
> The partially seeing are defined as persons with a visual acuity greater than 20/200 but not greater than 20/70 in the better eye with correction. (1966, p. 10)

The exact criterion (20/200 rather than 20/100) for blindness or partial sight is subjective but is founded on objective standards that reflect similar functional difficulties among people who are similarly defined. Application of these criteria has not resulted in excessive numbers of students being classified, and little controversy has surfaced with regard to the appropriateness of using them.

Deafness

Moores gave two definitions of people with sensory problems related to hearing. Each differs from the other on the extent of hearing loss;

> A "deaf person" is one whose hearing is disabled to an extent (usually 70 dB ISO or greater) that precludes the understanding of speech through the ear alone, without or with the use of a hearing aid.
>
> A "hard of hearing" person is one whose hearing is disabled to an extent (usually 35 to 69 dB ISO) that makes difficult, but does not preclude, the understanding of speech through the ear alone, without or with a hearing aid. (1978, p. 5)

The definitions of blindness and deafness and associated functioning have changed little over time. Students in each of these categories represent less than 1 percent of those receiving special education (U.S. Dept. of Education, 1997; Ysseldyke & Algozzine, 1995). Defining conditions of special education through the use of hardware has produced conditions characterized by little definitional controversy and relatively low prevalence rates.

Physical and Health Impairments

In recent years, about 2 percent of students receiving special education have been classified as orthopedically or other health impaired (Ysseldyke & Algozzine,

1990). Definitions for these conditions illustrate the functional impairments associated with some special education categories. For example, federal rules and regulations define orthopedic handicap as an "impairment which adversely affects a child's educational performance. The term includes impairments caused by congenital anomaly (e.g., clubfoot, absence of some member, etc.), impairments caused by disease (e.g., poliomyelitis, bone tuberculosis, etc.), and impairments from other causes (e.g., cerebral palsy, amputations, and fractures or burns which cause contracture)."

Because of the obvious nature of some of their problems, people with physical disabilities have been mistrusted and mistreated in the past. As a result of the medical, measurable nature of some of their problems, however, people with orthopedic and health impairments (other than attention deficit hyperactivity disorder) are less often misidentified than people with disabilities whose assignation is based on psychometric performances. Because range of motion and other bodily functions are measured using clinical hardware, definitions for specific conditions fluctuate little, and specific types of orthopedic and health impairments are seldom confused. And even though controversy surrounding these conditions has arisen (e.g., autism, currently a category in its own right, formerly was considered a health impairment, and before that was considered part of emotional disturbance and more generally, part of developmental disabilities), it has been minimal.

Changing Definition of Mental Retardation

The *Manual on Terminology and Classification in Mental Retardation* defined mental retardation as "significantly subaverage general intellectual functioning existing concurrently with deficits in adaptive behavior, and manifested during the developmental period" (Grossman, 1973, p. 11). This definition is similar to others that have been devised since the development of intelligence tests: mental retardation is a condition characterized by abnormal intellectual functioning. The basis for this conception was the work of Binet and Simon, who recognized the need for a *"precise basis for differential diagnosis. . . .* We do not think that we are going too far in saying that at the present time very few physicians would be able to cite with absolute precision the objective and invariable sign, or signs, by which they distinguish the degrees of inferior mentality" (1916, p. 335). What would probably come as a surprise to Binet and Simon is that there is no absolute, objective, and invariable sign of mental retardation; indeed, intelligence, the sign that comes the closest and is the most frequently used, is also a construct that has defied definition and remains the center of controversy (cf. Gardner, 1983; Sarason & Doris, 1979; Sternberg, 1985; Thorndike & Lohman, 1990).

When Binet discovered a way to measure a construct that was thought to reflect an important social concern, his work became the basis for subsequent conceptualizations of mental retardation. Over time, professionals have struggled with defining levels of intelligence and identifying cutoff scores for establishing a category. As Robinson and Robinson noted:

> The most significant change in 1973 as compared with the 1959 definition [of mental retardation] is a return to a *more traditional cut-off score,* two standard deviations below the mean. The 1959 definition had defined "borderline retardation" as intelligence only one standard deviation below the mean and thereby had tended to shift the emphasis from the severely retarded to the much larger group with mild and borderline retardation. (1976, p. 31)

From 1959 to 1973, a student with subaverage general intellectual functioning that was one standard deviation below the mean was likely to be classified as retarded; after 1973, that same student was not considered retarded. The label then applied only to students whose intellectual functioning was at least two standard deviations below the mean. Thus, many students ceased to be retarded simply by a pen stroke of the American Association on Mental Retardation. As one might guess, changes continued to be made to the definition. In 1983, the eighth manual on classification and terminology (Grossman, 1983) emphasized the importance of clinical judgment and adjusted the developmental period as being from conception to age 18. In 1992, the definition looked considerably different:

> Mental retardation refers to substantial limitations in present functioning. It is characterized by significantly subaverage intellectual functioning, existing concurrently with related limitations in two or more of the following applicable adaptive skill areas: communication, self-care, home living, social skills, community use, self-direction, health and safety, functional academics, leisure and work. Mental retardation manifests before age 18. (American Association on Mental Retardation, 1992, p. 1)

Despite its new look, the definition continued to include the same three major components as previous definitions (intellectual limitations, problems in adaptive behavior, and age of onset) (Beirne-Smith, Ittenbach, & Patton, 1998). The new ways of thinking about limitations in functioning in the 1992 definition (based on need for support rather than IQ) were not readily acceptable, and alternative definitions soon emerged (e.g., Jacobson & Mulick, 1996). Even though reasons for changing criteria make sense (e.g., too many minority students placed in programs; federal, state, and local litigation; excessive demand relative to teacher supply), the ease and acceptability with which change occurs illustrate problems inherent in using purely psychometric criteria in decision making.

LD or Not LD?

According to the most recent definition by the U.S. Department of Education, the term *specific learning disability*

> means a disorder in one or more of the basic psychological processes involved in understanding or in using language, spoken or written, which may manifest itself in an imperfect ability to listen, think, read, write, spell, or to do mathematical calculations. The term includes such conditions as perceptual handicaps, brain injury, minimal brain dysfunction, dyslexia, and developmental aphasia. The term does

not include children who have learning problems which are primarily the result of visual, hearing, or motor handicaps, or mental retardation, or emotional disturbance, or environmental, cultural, or economic disadvantage.

Although the primary manifestation of specific learning disability is imperfect ability in important school-related areas, the definition itself offers no basis for differentiating a child with learning disabilities from a school underachiever. The criteria for determining the condition of learning disability, which are outlined in the same *Federal Register,* add very little to the specifics necessary to identify imperfect abilities and/or to quantify achievements that is not commensurate with assumed ability. Although these guidelines for applying the federal definition of learning disability suggest that the discrepancy between ability and achievement should be severe, no standards for determining when a discrepancy is "severe" are given; thus local or state education agencies must flesh out the skeletal structure offered by the federal agency. So, like early educators faced with carrying out decisions relating to the nation's "simpletons," contemporary educators dealing with other, more subjective, highly prevalent, and popular notions of disability or deviance must also rely on a standard that can be "adapted to different localities and conditions of society" (see Howe, 1848, p. 13).

In work at the Institute for Research on Learning Disabilities, Ysseldyke and his colleagues examined overlap among categorical groups in performance on psychometric measures and the extent to which diagnostic personnel could differentiate clinically among special education groups. In one such investigation, more than forty tests were administered to forty-nine students identified as having learning disabilities by their schools and to fifty low-achieving students who scored below the twenty-fifth percentile on a group-administered achievement test. Performances on intellectual, achievement, and perceptual-motor tests; on measures of classroom behavior; and on self-concept tests showed an average of 96 percent overlap between groups, thereby making it difficult psychometrically to differentiate between low-achieving students and those with the learning disability label (Ysseldyke, Algozzine, Shinn, & McGue, 1982). In a follow-up study (Ysseldyke & Algozzine, 1983), professionals were asked to review the scores of students with the learning disability label and low-achieving students and to use clinical judgment to identify those students with learning disabilities. Using both school placement and the federal definition as criteria, professionals consistently were right about half the time. Both investigations provided evidence that professionals had difficulty trying to differentiate, either psychometrically or clinically, between low-achieving students and those school personnel had labeled as having learning disabilities.

In an article in the *Journal of Learning Disabilities* addressing screening and diagnosis in the "future of the LD field," Algozzine and Ysseldyke summarized their research related to classification:

While many school-identified learning disabled students do meet commonly applied criteria (e.g., 15 point difference between ability and achievement, subtest scatter), some do not. . . . Many low-achieving students, never classified as LD, also meet these same criteria . . . and many normal students are classifiable using these criteria. . . . In fact, the overlap in scores for many of these students is so great . . . that it is difficult for them not to be classified when commonly used criteria are applied to performance estimates on commonly used assessment devices. (1986, p. 396)

Many LD professionals were not happy with these conclusions, and these findings were attacked (see Kavale, Fuchs, & Scruggs, 1994), and the attack was rebutted (see Algozzine, Ysseldyke, & McGue, 1995). Much of the controversy seemed to grow out of a fear that the learning disability category needed to be viable for students to get help (Fuchs & Fuchs, 1995). Continued attempts to redefine LD have done little to create a condition with diagnostic purity greater than that created by operationalizing the commonly used federal definition.

Variance in Gifted and Talented Identification

There is much disagreement about concepts underlying the definition of gifted and talented and in procedures applied to identify students who are gifted and talented (Algozzine & Algozzine, 1990; Gallagher, 1988; Hagen, 1980). According to Algozzine and Ysseldyke:

The history of classification is replete with examples of definitional changes and dilemmas provoked by dissatisfaction with the current practice; those who champion the cause of gifted students argue over the appropriateness of intellectual cut-off scores and how much creativity, task, commitment, and other variables should be considered in diagnostic efforts. (1987, p. 55)

Cohn, Cohn, and Kanevsky (1988) in their discussion of giftedness pointed out that the variety of definitions, strategies, and instruments that can be used to identify or select students is infinite; "this diversity contributes to the confusion one meets in attempting to estimate the number of truly gifted individuals" (p. 460).

The extent to which the category of gifted and talented varies from state to state and in relation to the major special education classifications was investigated by Shriner, Ysseldyke, Gorney, & Franklin, 1993). They studied the variability among states in their definitions of gifted and talented students and the subjective use of these definitions as evidenced by state criteria and guidelines for classification. They found that a majority of states followed the current federal definition, which included "children who give evidence of high performance capability in areas such as intellectual, creative, artistic, leadership capacity, or specific academic fields and who require services or activities not ordinarily provided by the school in order to fully develop such capabilities." Some states still followed the 1978 federal definition, which included psychomotor ability as a qualifying area, and other states developed their own definitions using the federal definition as a point of reference. States actively sought subjective data and subjective evaluations in identification procedures for the gifted; at least eight states

(Hawaii, Minnesota, Tennessee, New Jersey, Idaho, Iowa, Maryland, and Virginia) identified "subjective data" or "expert opinion" as necessary in determining eligibility, and one state included the phrase "inclusion of 5–10% 'gut instinct' in the rating, selection, and placement sections of their guidelines" (p. 37). Shriner et al. also found that definitional variability and subjectivity had been highlighted as key issues in gifted identification practices, and they demonstrated that, depending on the statistic of choice, the category of gifted was as variable as, if not more than, the categories of learning disability, educable mental retardation, and emotional disturbance. This is hardly a surprise given the "soft" base that characterizes definitions of gifted and talented and identification practices that necessarily derive from them.

EBD, ED, EH, BD, SM, SED, SLBP, EL, or EIEIO

Verbal subjectivity and word play that may be fine for fairy tales and children's stories present significant problems when evident in definitional practices in special education. For instance, as we indicated in chapter 3, serious emotional disturbance is defined as follows:

> (i) The term means a condition exhibiting one or more of the following characteristics over a long period of time and to a marked degree, which adversely affects educational performance: (a) an inability to learn which cannot be explained by intellectual, sensory, or health factors; (b) an inability to build or maintain satisfactory interpersonal relationships with peers and teachers; (c) inappropriate types of behavior or feelings under normal circumstances; (d) a general pervasive mood of unhappiness or depression; or (e) a tendency to develop physical symptoms or fears associated with personal or school problems. (ii) The term includes children who are schizophrenic. The term does not include children who are socially maladjusted, unless it is determined that they are seriously emotionally disturbed.

Prior to this definition, autism was included within the definition of serious emotional disturbance. Autism became a category in its own right, however, another instance of political pressures determining conditions of disability. With the 1997 reauthorization of IDEA, the definition of serious emotional disturbance remained the same, but the word *serious* was deleted from all but the first reference to the condition, a word play intended to "eliminate the pejorative connotation of the term 'serious'" (Cahir, 1998, p. 2).

Interestingly, the current government definition is similar to that used in the early 1960s and to a more recent description of children who have less severe emotional handicaps or behavior problems (cf. Bower, 1969, 1982; Kauffman, 1980, 1989a; Nelson & Rutherford, 1990; Reinert, 1967; Shea, 1978). Bower (1982) noted that the first section of the federal definition was an exact restatement of his earlier work. He also indicated that section (ii) did not appear in the original definition and appeared to him to be a "codicil to reassure traditional psychopathologists and budget personnel that schizophrenia and autism are indeed serious emotional disturbance on the one hand, and that just plain bad boys and girls, predelinquents, and sociopaths will not skyrocket costs on the other hand" (p. 56). Unquestionably, especially with moderate and high-prevalence conditions, social, political, and economic motives may drive practice more than do sound pedagogical policies or profound principles (Ysseldyke & Algozzine, 1995). Because people make up the definitions, they can decide who is included and excluded by the words they write and the categories they imply.

The exclusion of social maladjustment from the category of serious emotional disturbance created significant concern among professionals engaged in special education of students with behavioral disorders (cf. Bower, 1982; CCBD, 1990a; Center, 1990; Cline, 1990; Nelson & Rutherford, 1990; Weinberg & Weinberg, 1990; Wood, 1990). As Nelson and Rutherford pointed out, "One of the factors affecting the abilities of policy makers and researchers to clarify this issue is the lack of a generally accepted definition of social maladjustment" (1990, p. 38). The problem is clear-cut: the definition of serious emotional disturbance excludes a group of students without defining them. It is as if professionals had defined mental retardation as significantly subaverage intelligence without having an accepted standard for intelligence. And the problem is further complicated by the absence of any valid evidence or thought justifying the separation of social maladjustment and emotional disturbance (Grosenick & Huntze, 1980).

The consequences of definitional confusion are professional debate and practical absurdity. For example, "vast differences exist among the states regarding the percentage of special education students served as seriously emotionally disturbed" (Weinberg & Weinberg, 1990, p. 149). Estimates have varied from less than 1 percent to more than 25 percent of the student population in some states (U.S. Dept. of Education, 1988b), and "varying interpretations" of the federal definition have been blamed for these disparities (Weinberg & Weinberg, 1990, p. 149). It is not difficult to see that different numbers of students will be identified based on how the social maladjustment exclusionary clause is interpreted; there is evidence that it is completely ignored in many state definitions (Center, 1990; Mack, 1985).

Likewise, educators regularly debate alternative explanations for observed differences. Hallahan, Keller, and Ball (1986) compared prevalence rates for categories of exceptional students. They reported that the category of learning disabilities was less variable than other categories and concluded that "definition and identification criteria for learning disabilities are at least as well articulated, and perhaps more so, than those for other categories in special education" (1986, p. 13). Algozzine and Ysseldyke took issue with the Hallahan et al. analysis and argued that high-prevalence categories (learning disability, speech/language impairment, mental retardation, emotional/behavioral disturbance) had more variable prevalence rates because they were more subjectively defined than were low-prevalence categories (physical and other health impairment, hearing impairment). Algozzine and Ysseldyke stated that "the conclusions one makes about variance in prevalence are a function of the methods one uses to examine differences among prevalence rates" (1987, p. 32).

The consequences of using software-based decisions is clearly evident in efforts to identify and classify students as having a behavioral disorder, emotional disturbance, serious emotional disturbance, emotional handicap, emotional/behavioral disorder, or other psychometrically based condition. Professionals argue about the terms to be applied to the condition, and typically there is no universal acceptance of a term across service delivery systems (i.e., states and agencies within them). This softness spills over to produce wide variation in number of students served in different locations (see Table 4.1) and to create considerable disagreement among professionals as to what exactly is a (insert a category name of your choice in appropriate form) student. For example, in addition to continued debate over similarities and differences between students with learning disabilities and other low-achieving students, professionals identify subtypes of students as more or as less evidence of "real" students with learning disabilities. And arguments about the importance of creativity, motivation, task commitment, and intellectual ability continue to motivate and frustrate people concerned with educating students who are gifted. And the answer to the question "Who are the *real* (insert label) students?" is, "Nobody knows."

TABLE 4.1   **Variation in Numbers of Students Served**

	Condition				
State	Learning Disability	Speech/Language Impairment	Mental Retardation	Emotional Disturbance	Total Overall
Hawaii (7.60%)	3.90	1.29	1.04	0.73	92%
Idaho (8.22%)	4.87	1.39	1.07	0.22	92%
Arizona (8.51%)	5.06	1.58	0.72	0.57	93%
Kansas (9.78%)	4.22	2.29	1.17	0.97	88%
Ohio (10.73%)	4.04	2.69	2.44	0.60	91%
Nebraska (11.89%)	5.10	3.12	1.70	0.94	91%
West Virginia (12.82%)	5.76	3.59	2.30	0.61	96%
New Jersey (14.33%)	7.93	3.86	0.30	1.02	91%
Rhode Island (14.41%)	8.83	2.84	0.61	1.14	93%
Massachusetts (14.85%)	9.19	2.38	1.34	1.23	95%
All states, D.C., and Puerto Rico (10.63%)	5.44	2.26	1.15	0.91	91%

NOTE: Numbers are percentages based on estimates of enrollment. Numbers in parentheses are totals for all conditions. The Total Overall column if the percentage of the total represented by the four conditions.

SOURCE: U.S. Department of Education (1997). *Nineteenth Annual Report to Congress on the Implementation of the Individuals with Disabilities Education Act.* Washington D.C.: Author, Table AA13.

PERSPECTIVES ON CLASSIFICATION

Each year, personnel in the U.S. Department of Education assess progress in the provision of services to children and youths with disabilities and prepare a report of findings for dissemination. Initially, these annual reports provided a "detailed description of the activities undertaken to implement the [law] and an assessment of the impact and effectiveness of its requirements" (U.S. Dept. of Education, 1989b, p. xiii).

National statistics reported by states to the Office of Special Education Programs (OSEP) are provided in the annual report. These statistics include numbers of students with disabilities, disaggregated in various ways (by category, by age and category, by placement, etc.), as well as information on how students exit from special education (e.g., drop out, graduate) and the number and characteristics of personnel who provide services to the youngsters. Special concerns (e.g., postschool success of students with disabilities, participation of students with disabilities in state assessments) and other evidence of federal initiatives and support (e.g., services provided to infants, toddlers, and preschool children with disabilities; federal monitoring activities) are described in other chapters. In the twentieth year after the enactment of the law to provide a free and appropriate public education to students with disabilities, the annual report was redesigned using "a conceptual model that provides a framework for understanding the various factors that affect educational results for students with disabilities" (U.S. Dept. of Education, 1997, p. xv). In this framework, educational results were viewed as products of three sets of factors: "the context and environment in which education is provided, the characteristics of students, and school programs and services" (p. xv). These factors define the organization of the annual report.

The federal government provides support for children and youths aged 3 to 21 under provisions of Part B of the IDEA. The OSEP uses many sources to evaluate the extent to which funding achieves its purpose. The number of students served in special education categories is one source used in making these judgments. Even states that do not have categorical programs (e.g., Massachusetts) provide data in categorical form.

In recent years, more than 5.5 million students have received special education in programs developed and maintained in part by principles initially embodied in PL 94-142. When the *Nineteenth annual report to Congress on the implementation of the Individuals with Disabilities Education Act* was published, it documented the continued increase in children and youths served. During the 1995–1996 school year, twenty years after passage of PL 94-142, 5,619,099 children and youths with disabilities from ages 3 to 21 were served under IDEA, Part B. Another 177,673 infants and toddlers received early intervention services through Part H funds (which, starting in 1998, were provided through Part C funds). These numbers continue to reflect a steady increase in the percentage of youngsters receiving special education services. The U.S. Department of Education described these changes as follows:

During the first 10 years of the program, the growth in the IDEA, Part B, count occurred while population and enrollment counts were decreasing. Early growth in special education counts occurred as IDEA was more fully implemented, and services were expanded to more fully serve the eligible population.

During the second 10 years of the program, growth in the special education counts coincided with increases in enrollment and population. However, the percentage of students enrolled in special education has increased at a slightly higher rate than has the total school age population. (U.S. Dept. of Education, 1997, p. II-28)

Analyses of the primary disabilities of youngsters receiving special education services continue to show that the largest categories are specific learning disabilities (51.2 percent), speech, and language impairments (20.2 percent), mental retardation (11.5 percent), and serious emotional disturbance (8.6 percent). These four categories account for 94 percent of all children and youth served under Part B.

Identifying students by category permits official agencies to allocate assistance and provide progress reports. It also provides financial incentives for school personnel to identify and label certain students with certain disabilities. For example, if funds are linked to numbers of students served, regardless of category of disability, the temptation of receiving more money because more students are labeled is very real. Similarly, if special funding is provided for special groups of students (e.g., preschool students with disabilities), the pressure to identify specific disabilities can be very compelling.

Categorical Labeling

Scholars predict that Lenny Ng will become America's best mathematician. There is nothing very remarkable about such a prediction, except that it was made when Lenny was in elementary school. He took the Scholastic Achievement Test at age ten; his score on the quantitative items was 800. Lenny's talents are not limited to numbers. He plays tennis, writes stories, and composes music. He seldom watches television or goes to the movies. "I'm just not that kind of person," he says. His perspective on being gifted and labeled is revealing. "It's fun to do this stuff. . . . There are no ill effects as long as people don't call me a nerd" (*Parade* Magazine, December 2, 1990, p. 5).

Classifying and labeling students are fundamental activities in contemporary special education. Each year more than 250 million standardized tests are administered to the 44 million public school students in America's schools. The purpose of much of this testing is identification of students performing below expectations. Every category of special education, except gifted and talented, has poor performance in school as a central or peripheral part. Concern would be minimal if being labeled had only positive effects, but as Ysseldyke and Algozzine (1982) indicated, perspectives on categorical treatment center on the extent to which the negative effects of being labeled outweigh the positive ones.

Effects   The effects of labeling must be studied from two perspectives: the impact of the label on the perceptions and behavior of the person being labeled and the

FIGURE 4.1   Model for Examining the Effects of Labeling

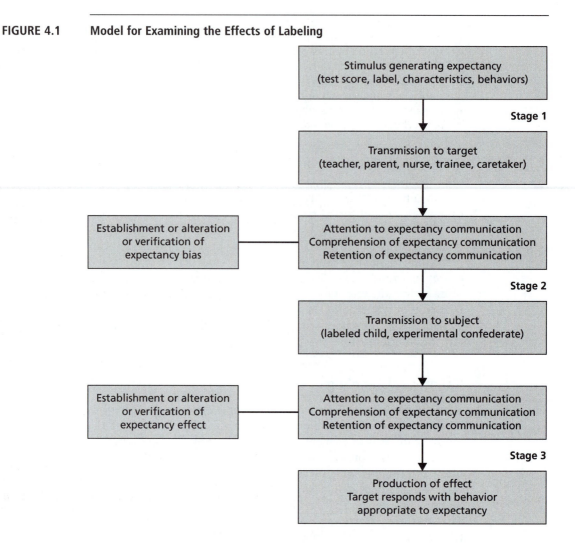

impact of the label on the perceptions and behavior of those who interact with the person being labeled. This perspective on labels and their effects is illustrated in Figure 4.1. Labels serve as sources of perceptions and behaviors, which in turn serve as the basis for the labeled individual's personal expectancies and performance. People connected with labeled individuals—friends, family, educators—form perceptions, modify behavior, and shape performance expectations for the individual according to the ascribed labels. Perceptions, behavior, expectations, and performance represent personal and interpersonal aspects of the effects labels have on the people who are labeled. Labeling is justified by its presumed advantages and challenged by its presumed disadvantages.

Advantages Foremost among the *presumed advantages* of labels is that they serve as admission tickets to alternative educational services. According to Gorham, Des Jardins, Page, Pettis, and Scherber, "Practically speaking, 'good' labels are those marshaling resources on [the student's] behalf" (1978, p. 155). Supporters of labeling believe the labels that serve as "passports" to improved educational services are ideal. Gallagher pointed out that labels serve other purposes as well. In his discussion, he suggested the "sacred" uses of labeling as follows:

1. A means for beginning a classification, diagnosis, and treatment sequence peculiarly designed to counteract certain identifiable negative conditions.

2. The basis for further research which will give more insight into etiology, prevention, and possible treatment applications of such conditions in the future.

3. A means of calling attention to a specific problem in order to obtain additional resources through special legislation and funding. (1976, p. 3)

Gallagher's first use parallels the use of labels in medicine. When a physician labels a patient as diabetic, the classification and diagnostic process sets a prescribed treatment sequence in motion. The analogy is that once a student is labeled learning disabled, the classification and diagnostic process sets prescribed treatment sequences in motion as well.

The second item in Gallagher's list also has a base in medical practice. Once the profession accepted a specific set of symptoms as acquired immune deficiency syndrome, a significant basis was available for continued research into the causes, cures, and courses of AIDS. Giving symptoms a name facilitates systematic research to understand better what the name means.

Reports that more than 5 million students receive special education, and that more than 1.5 million of them are classified as having learning disabilities, serve as evidence of the continuing need for special allocations of funds, Gallagher's third list item. The problem is seen as very large, and this means only that more must be done. Unquestionably, there is strength in numbers.

Disadvantages   The *presumed disadvantages* associated with labeling are generally viewed along two dimensions: the extent to which labels lead to expected and desired outcomes (e.g., improved educational services) and the extent to which labels are actually harmful (i.e., result in undesired effects). Many professionals have argued that labeling does not necessarily lead to improved education treatment. Hallahan and Kauffman noted widespread disenchantment with labeling, commenting that "there is no rational basis, in terms of instructional efficacy, for grouping children in accordance with some of the categorical labels now in use" (1977, p. 139). From this perspective, labels appear at best to serve merely as passports that do not guarantee differential or improved educational treatment. Labels provide excuses for not meeting the special learning needs of individual students. At times, the decreased willingness of teachers to work with students borders on total abdication of responsibility to modify instruction to meet individual needs.

There is evidence that labels may be harmful. According to Gorham et al., "Labels have damaged many children, particularly minority group children whose cultures and lifestyles differ sufficiently from the 'norm' to make any measurement of their abilities and aptitudes by norm-biased scales a certain disaster for them" (1976, p. 155). In addition to the harm done to students, Gallagher (1976) noted other "profane" uses of labeling, such as using labels to restrict opportunities for minority group children and to avoid addressing complex social and ecological conditions. Labeling students is not a benign activity nor is it a necessary evil, as school officials and others sometimes claim. Despite a presumed need for them, labels are an unfortunate by-product of a system that attaches money to acts, thus resulting in classifications and categories. Labels are often irrelevant to the instructional needs of students. Furthermore, labels become real attributes that prevent meaningful understanding of actual individual learning needs. By causing some to believe that students labeled as having mental retardation cannot perform certain tasks, the act of classifying condemns these students to a life of lesser expectations and performance. Labels require official sanction. Resources diverted to the process of identifying and classifying students are extensive. Time and money spent on labeling are time and money not spent on teaching; time spent being labeled is time not spent on being taught or learning.

Research on the effects of labeling is no longer prevalent. Today, professionals are more concerned about the appropriateness of placement (see Chapter 5) or understanding the disproportionate representation of minority students in special education (Reschly, 1997; U.S. Dept. of Education, 1997).

Categorical Drift

Definitions used to create categories in special education are based on prevailing professional opinions about the nature and characteristics of students who fail to profit from the educational experiences provided in regular education programs. Because these opinions are constantly changing, special education's categories should be considered ephemeral representations for people with special learning needs that leave the field susceptible to categorical drift. This situation is evident when professionals name and rename groups of students to meet socially accepted value systems and thereby please important constituencies. Recently, we have seen autism pulled out of the serious emotional disturbance category to become a new category. The same happened with traumatic brain injury, which previously was included in the other health impairments category. In the 1997 reauthorization of IDEA, the term *developmental delay*, previously created for children ages 3 to 5, was extended to children through age 9, in part to "avoid locking children into an incorrect category" (Cahir, 1997, p. 1).

Categorical drift is evident when students move easily among supposedly distinct groups and thereby begin to look like a psychometric Dow Jones average rather than clinical cases (e.g., special education increased substantially for the fourth year in a row; fueled in large part by continuing and large increases in learning disabilities, coupled with corresponding but smaller decreases in mental retardation, special education remains the growth profession of the 1990s). Categorical drift surfaces when similarities between groups blend to the extent that larger, less specific names (e.g., developmental delay, mild disabilities, educational handicaps) serve as generic titles for classrooms and students. Categorical drift can also be found for some conditions of special education more than others.

Definitions based on hardware are founded, at least, on measurable phenomena; that is, the distance a person can see or the level at which a person can hear can surely be measured more objectively than the information a person knows or the intelligence level a person demonstrates. The former conditions are much less susceptible to categorical drift. Even so, it is still difficult to define them. For example, what is the appropriate definition for a person whose measured hearing is 68 dB ISO (within the hard-of-hearing range of 35–69 dB ISO) but whose ability to hear is disabled to the extent that it precludes understanding speech through the ear alone? More pervasive problems relative to mashing of categories are evident in the use of definitions based on software such as those for learning disabilities, emotional disturbance, and mental retardation.

Numbers Tell a Story

One important reason for defining categories of disabilities is that people are then able to evaluate the extent or pervasiveness of the problem. For example, having defined blindness, researchers can count the number of people who fall within that definition and are therefore "blind" and then can determine the course and direction of the social policies for these individuals with disabilities. Similarly, having defined a condition, professionals can estimate the extent of the problem and construct programs to remedy it. Numbers change over time as categories are created (often by removing specific conditions from existing categories, such as autism from serious emotional disturbance), or new conditions added to existing categories (such as attention deficit hyperactivity disorder being "recognized" as a health impairment). Reasons proposed for changes in numbers of students illustrate that categorical drift is a product of contemporary policy and practice (U.S. Department of Education, 1997):

> The largest relative increases from 1994–95 to 1995–96 occurred in the traumatic brain injury (30.1 percent), autism (27.2 percent), and other health impairments (24.5 percent) categories. Most states attributed the increases in the two newest categories, traumatic brain injury and autism, to reclassification of students during the time of triennial re-evaluations. The increase in the other health impairments category was generally attributed to increased service to students with attention deficit/hyperactivity disorder. (p. vi)

Broader strokes have been used to explain interstate variation in percentages of students served in special education (U.S. Department of Education, 1990).

> It may be that State-to-State variation in the percentage of students served is related to State classification procedures, resulting in greater or lesser numbers of students identified as requiring special education services. Use of pre-referral interventions in some States may reduce the number of students assessed or identified for special education service needs. Other causes of State-to-State variation may include: data reporting practices; State funding formulas; and differences in student populations. (p. 2)

When people admit that definitions are at best arbitrary attempts to objectify social, political, and moral constructs, they will have a better basis for understanding the problems created by such a system. Until that time, considerable effort will likely be expended in a search for the "right" students to place in special education classes; we predict that such effort will be largely unproductive.

Make Mine Mild

All the ambiguity created by efforts to come up with a precise basis for differential diagnosis generates controversies in special education that cause professionals to redefine and question practice. Note the consistent use of the term *mild disability* without a widely accepted definition for it and without a justifiable basis for using it (i.e., there is nothing mild about a student three or five years behind in school, or functioning socially at levels significantly below those of peers, or suffering serious childhood depression). As boundaries between categories meld, questions of instructional effectiveness and appropriateness become relevant, and at the highest levels distinctions between special and regular education become questionable (Lipsky & Gartner, 1989; Stainback, Stainback, & Forest, 1989; Will, 1986; Ysseldyke & Algozzine, 1995).

In Search of Students with Real Disabilities

The history of special education is replete with controversy over *the* definition of mental retardation, *the* definition of learning disabilities, and *the* definition of all other types and kinds of special children and youths. As soon as someone comes out with *a* definition, it stimulates other persons to criticize, convene, propose a new definition, and take their turn on the defensive. The main implication of this continuing discussion among professionals is that these definitions do not exist in a vacuum: each change in definition directly or indirectly affects the identification and treatment of children and youths with learning problems. At a roundtable conference on the assessment of students with learning disabilities, Lovitt captured the dilemma of professionals when he said:

> I believe that if we continue trying to define learning disabilities by using ill-defined concepts, we will forever be frustrated, for it is an illusive [elusive] concept. We are being bamboozled. It is as though someone started a great hoax by inventing the term and then tempting others to define it. And lo and behold scores of task forces and others have taken the bait. (1978, p. 3)

Similar problems surface with regard to emotional disturbance: "Definition provides the basis for prevalence" (Kauffman, 1980, p. 524). We add that definition is the basis for the existence of the conditions and for the interest in them; without definition, for all practical purposes, there is no category or problem! Lambert recounted an example of the way in which labeling a condition creates interest in it. She stated that during the early 1960s, she and Bower were writing a summary of research in California on students with emotional handicaps in preparation for legislation to be introduced in the state legislature in the winter of 1961. They described different levels of intervention for students based on the degree of handicap:

> Inasmuch as the children we had studied who needed the small group instruction most, and benefited most from it, were those who were significantly behind in their academic subjects, we called them "learning disability groups." When this name appeared in California special education parlance, the search was on to find the deficit responsible for the failure rather than the method to teach the child. It was only a matter of time before the discovery would be made that explanations for significant discrepancies between ability and achievement were many, chief among them failure of the instructional program to provide an appropriate level of tasks for the child as well as appropriately modified regular class learning situations. (1981, p. 200)

Once defined, the importance of the category becomes a function of the number of children assigned to it. For years, the U.S. government estimated that 2 percent of the school population was "disturbed" but recent "child counts" indicated that the figure was actually 0.8 percent (Dept. of Education, 1988b.) Kauffman argued that the reported difference in prevalence stemmed from the differences in identification practices brought about by federal rule making:

> If federal law has had and will continue to have a suppressing effect on identification of most disturbed children, then it is obvious that legal precedent is supplanting, or at least is being used to define, clinical judgment in our society's view of deviance. Bureaucratic-legal domination of our thinking about disordered behavior and the tacit assumption that extralegal considerations are the least pressing issues in special education today may represent advancement or regression, depending on one's view of what forces should move the field forward. To the extent that extralegal judgment is trusted, one could argue that the bureaucratic-legal approach will result in the unfortunate denial of services to many mildly and moderately disturbed children who would benefit from identification and intervention. To the extent that legislation, bureaucratic control, and litigation are trusted as the best means for defining children's deviance, one could rejoice in the fact that social institutions such as schools will be required to tolerate behavioral difference unless it violates standards of conduct that are unassailable in court. (1980, p. 526)

Thus, for instance, if the federal government or any other group of professionals for whatever reason decides that it is time to serve individuals with severe disabilities and either through outright changes in definitions or through financial grants and contract bargaining establishes an interest in children and youths with severe handicaps, interest in identifying and serving youngsters with more moderate or mild disabilities will diminish.

In an editorial entitled "What Happened to Mild and Moderate Mental Retardation?" in the *American Journal of Mental Deficiency*, Haywood noted that despite the plans and good intentions that must have been the basis for the shift in the emphasis of research and service from mild to severe retardation, the outcome has been unfavorable:

> It is practically certain that the individuals who pleaded for increased attention to severely and profoundly retarded persons hoped that the increased attention would represent a total increase in scholarly interest, public funds, and service for the entire field of mental retardation, i.e., that additional funds, research, and services directed toward severely and profoundly retarded persons would be "added on" to the existing levels of support for the entire field. What has happened instead has been a shift of resources away from mildly and moderately retarded persons, to such a marked degree that it is frequently quite impossible to obtain public funds to support both research and services in this important area unless one promises to give primary emphasis to those individuals who are severely or profoundly handicapped. (1979, p. 429)

Students receiving special education sometimes exhibit behaviors that interfere with progress in school, and this fact seldom creates controversy within the field. Problems do arise when professionals try to assign names to clusters of behaviors or characteristics and thereby create categories that can be subjected to initial analysis and review. The problems are compounded when names assigned to students serve as signals for lowered expectations for parents or teachers. These problems are not easily resolved.

WHERE DOES ADD OR ADHD BELONG?

The most recent evidence of professionals' willingness to be seduced by categories and individual differences is provided by concern for the placement of students with attention deficit disorders (ADD), or the more recently named condition of attention deficit–hyperactive disorder (ADHD). Prior to the 1940s, students having difficulty in school were considered emotionally disturbed, mentally retarded, or physically disabled (e.g., blind, deaf). Research during that time illustrated the relationship between a person's performance on a variety of measures and "soft signs" of abnormal brain functioning (Strauss & Lehtinen, 1947; Werner & Strauss, 1941). The term *minimal brain dysfunction* was coined to refer to the syndrome evidence by children exhibiting soft signs of neurological dysfunctioning. As Silver indicated, "Using current concepts, the term minimal brain dysfunction referred to children with (a) learning disabilities; (b) difficulties with hyperactivity, distractibility, and impulsivity; and (c) emotional and social problems" (1990, p. 395). The term *attention deficit disorder* was used in *DSM III* to refer to this same group of people, and two subtypes were used to differentiate disorders with and without hyperactivity (American Psychiatric Association, 1982).

The term *attention deficit–hyperactive disorder* (ADHD) replaced ADD in *DSM IV* (American Psychiatric Association, 1994), and a complex set of criteria was put forth for a person to be considered as having ADHD (see Table 4.2). Clearly, large numbers of students will be eligible for services when a definition built on these software-based characteristics undergirds the condition. In fact, all three authors of this book agree that one of the three authors fits these criteria for ADHD perfectly! Although these characteristics could be indicative of a person having ADHD, one could argue to some extent that professionals should be concerned when a child does not demonstrate these characteristics before the age of seven. Observations of characteristics such as "loses things" or "easily distracted" can be made, but standards for inappropriate levels of such behaviors are nonexistent. Further evidence of the futility of using broad psychometric characteristics such as those used to define ADHD is illustrated by the "interventions" commonly recommended for teaching students with conditions like ADHD: for example, provide supervision and discipline, provide encouragement, place the student near the teacher's desk, make sure the student comprehends the task before beginning, etc. (CHADD, 1988). Almost any student can profit from these recommendations, and there is only a marginal link between the condition and the teaching strategies. Nevertheless, considerable interest continues to be shown in students with the label ADD or ADHD (Abikoff, 1991; Barabasz & Barabasz, 1996; Cantwell, 1996; D'Alonzo, 1996; Fiore, Becker, & Nero, 1993; Forness, Youpa, Hanna, Cantwell, & Swanson, 1992; Gardill, DuPaul, & Kyle, 1996; Maag & Reid, 1994; McKinney, Montague, & Hocutt, 1993; Pelham, 1993).

The passage of the IDEA Amendments of 1990 was delayed by serious debate about whether ADD should be made a separate category of eligibility for special education services (Reynolds, C.J., 1991). Proponents argued that creation of a new (within IDEA) category would serve a growing number of students who needed specialized instruction and who were currently inappropriately labeled as emotionally disturbed or learning disabled. Opponents argued that the category ADD faced serious questions with regard to definition and identification practices. The Council for Exceptional Children's response to inquiry (cf. *Federal Register,* November 29, 1990, p. 49598) regarding issued related to ADD clearly delimited concerns of professionals in opposition to creating a new category. This organization maintained that adding ADD to the list of handicapping conditions under part B of IDEA was unnecessary because students diagnosed with ADD who manifested symptoms severe enough to impair educational performance were currently being served with existing categories. The organization also contended that strategies recommended for teaching students with ADD could easily be implemented in regular classrooms and probably would benefit any students receiving education there.

TABLE 4.2   **Definitional Criteria for ADHD**

To be considered as having ADHD, a person must meet at least one of two sets of criteria.

(1) Six (or more) of the following symptoms of *inattention* have persisted for at least 6 months to a degree that is maladaptive and inconsistent with developmental level:

Inattention
(a) Often fails to give close attention to details or makes careless mistakes in schoolwork, work, or other activities
(b) Often has difficulty sustaining attention in tasks or play activities
(c) Often does not seem to listen when spoken to directly
(d) Often does not follow through on instructions and fails to finish schoolwork, chores, or duties in the workplace (not due to oppositional behavior or failure to understand instructions)
(e) Often has difficulty organizing tasks and activities
(f) Often avoids, dislikes, or is reluctant to engage in tasks that require sustained mental effort (such as schoolwork or homework)
(g) Often loses things necessary for tasks or activities (e.g., toys, school assignments, pencils, books, or tools)
(h) Is often easily distracted by extraneous stimuli
(i) Is often forgetful in daily activities

(2) Six (or more) or the following symptoms of *hyperactivity-impulsivity* have persisted for at least 6 months to a degree that is maladaptive and inconsistent with developmental level:

Hyperactivity
(a) Often fidgets with hands or feet or squirms in seat
(b) Often leaves seat in classroom or in other situations in which remaining seated is expected
(c) Often runs about or climbs excessively in situations in which it is inappropriate (in adolescents or adults, may be limited to subjective feelings of restlessness)
(d) Often has difficulty playing or engaging in leisure activities quietly
(e) Is often "on the go" or often acts as if "driven by a motor"
(f) Often talks excessively

Impulsivity
(g) Often blurts out answers before questions have been completed
(h) Often has difficulty awaiting turn
(i) Often interrupts or intrudes on others (e.g., butts into conversations or games)

In addition, four other criteria are used: (1) some of the symptoms noted above must be present before age 7 years; (2) impairment resulting from the symptoms must be present in two or more settings; (3) clear evidence of clinically significant impairment must exist in social, academic, or occupational functioning; and (4) the symptoms do not occur exclusively during the course of a pervasive developmental disorder, schizophrenia, or other psychotic disorder and are not better accounted for by another mental disorder (e.g., mood disorder, anxiety disorder, disassociative disorder, or personality disorder).

The controversy surrounding ADD and ADHD has continued, to the point where the 1997 Annual Report to Congress (U.S. Department of Education, 1997) included a module on students with attention deficit–hyperactivity disorder, even though it was still not recognized as a separate category under IDEA. By this time, there was some agreement that students with ADHD were eligible for services under the other health impairments category, with the justification being that this was appropriate when "the child's disorder is a chronic or acute health problem that results in limited alertness and adversely affects his or her educational performance" (U.S. Department of Education, 1997, p. II-37). When this was not the case, it was proposed that these youngsters could be served as having learning disabilities or emotional disabilities. If those conditions were not appropriate, Section 504 of the Rehabilitation Act of 1973 was proposed as a way to meet these youngsters' needs.

Despite not being a category in its own right, considerable funds have been devoted to studying the condition. The Office of Special Education Programs has funded research syntheses on characteristics, assessment, school-based interventions, and medications (see Burcham & Carlson, 1994; Dykman, Ackerman, & Raney, 1994; Fiore, 1994; McKinney, Montague, & Hocutt, 1994; Swanson, 1994), and the National Institute of Mental Health conducted a study of the long-term effectiveness of various treatments.

The controversy continues. Is ADHD a disability? If it is, why subsume it under another category name? Will it follow the path of autism and traumatic brain injury, eventually becoming a recognized category of disability? If it is not a disability, why not? If it is not a disability, what is it? These and other questions continue to be asked as ADHD reflects the legacy of confusion, controversy, and debate surrounding definitions in special education.

Discussion Questions

1. The category of learning disabilities grew more than any other category of special education during the ten years following the implementation of PL 94-142. How do you explain this growth? Why did other categories decrease or stay about the same during the same time period?

2. Why are some professionals opposed to including social maladjustment in definitions of emotional disturbance? What effect does including or excluding subgroups have on a category? What evidence illustrates that exclusionary practices permeate other definitions with psychometric bases?

3. Passage of the IDEA Amendments in 1990 was delayed by debate that focused on including a new category. Why would members of a professional group oppose development of a new category? Why was similar opposition not evident when the learning disabilities category was created and added to federal special education practices?

4. What dangers are there in using subjective criteria to define a category of special education students?

5. If you had to argue that ADHD should be a recognized disability category, what would you say? If you had to argue that ADHD should *not* be a recognized disability category, what would you say?

Chapter 5
Placement Controversy

Comparisons do ofttime great grievance.
—John Lydgate

It is not a benign activity to label a person as emotionally disturbed, learning disabled, mentally retarded, blind, deaf, silly, or dumb. Quite simply, assigning names to people creates conditions that foster comparisons not always beneficial. Doing so in school is most often justified by promises of needed and improved educational services. Despite good intentions, "with rare exceptions, today's adults with disabilities who recall segregated facilities, separate classes, or home instruction cannot say enough about how inadequate was their academic training" (Asch, 1989, p. 183). Clearly there is a dilemma here: people who see, hear, walk, talk, and manage tasks in school differently from their neighbors and peers may need special assistance, but sometimes it comes at a great personal cost, if it comes at all. Creating categories for people also makes problems when professionals argue about the best place to provide special education.

NAMES STILL MEAN PLACES FOR STUDENTS WITH SPECIAL NEEDS

When I first started teaching I was called the "retarded teacher." When I taught boys who couldn't read I was called the "disabled reading teacher," students with emotional problems, the "emotionally disturbed teacher," incarcerated young adults, the "prison teacher." Never had the good fortune of being known as the "gifted teacher."

There was a time when very few people with unique abilities received special education. In the old days, segregated treatment was reserved for "special cases" that attracted attention because it was believed they hindered the instruction of their "more tractable and capable" peers (Van Sickle, 1908–1909, p. 102). As education became more formalized and people were required to attend school, the need for special education became greater. As Sarason and Doris noted, "These two educational developments that called for a lock-step progression of pupils through class-graded schools, and forced attendance of all children within a given age range, immediately confronted the educator with the problem that not all children were capable of maintaining the necessary rate of progress required by the lock-step instructional system (1979, p. 137). And what began as a noble effort to bring order to public education has become a massive alternative educational system with elaborate diagnostic classification systems, powerful professional advocacy groups and significant numbers of students being served each year. Today, more students receive special education than receive undergraduate education in America's two-year colleges and universities (National Center for Education Statistics, 1998).

Special education exists to serve people with special learning needs. Access to this alternative education system is controlled by identification and classification practices. A procedure similar to that in medicine has emerged: catalogues of symptoms of various conditions are accepted, and diagnostic information is collected to determine the extent to which a person has characteristics similar to those of the known conditions. The picture that emerges during a diagnostic evaluation serves as a basis for classification and subsequent treatment. Simply put, students classified as having mental retardation are treated in MR programs; students classified as having serious emotional disturbances receive all or part of their education in SED programs; and so it goes for students with other disabilities.

But there is a difference from medicine. When a person receives a medical diagnosis, treatment for the condition is provided in an appropriate setting. But the setting is not the treatment, which is much more specific than a setting or a program. The effects of the program are often more short-lived, and the outcomes are often much more obvious. For example, a diagnosis of diabetes does not render life all that different from life before the diagnosis. In medicine, classification links directly to treatment.

Children and youths receive special education because parents and other professionals believe it is important for them to do so. Students are entitled to special education because federal laws guarantee them a free, appropriate individualized education program based on their needs. These beliefs and mandates have created difficulties within the educational system. Concerns have emerged relative to the appropriateness of large numbers of students (especially those with learning disabilities) receiving special education, the best place to provide special education services, and the link between placement and treatment.

ENVIRONMENTS AND PREVALENCE

It might be expected that the prevalence of students with various disabilities would be linked to the environments in which students receive special education services. A district having mostly students with learning disabilities, for example, might be expected to serve more of them in general education settings than a district having mostly students with significant cognitive disabilities. Danielson and Bellamy (1989) presented data showing the considerable variance among states in the number of students placed in separate facilities. There are two alternative explanations for this type of observed variance in prevalence: either the variance is due to differing understandings of the LRE concept (see Tucker, 1989), or it is due to diversity in applying clearly understood concepts (see Blackman, 1989).

Where Should Special Education Take Place?

In early American educational history, few students received special education services and the push for inclusion in general education settings was minimal or nonexistent. In these circumstances, there was little need for much differentiation in the locations where special education services were provided. A dual-track system compensated for differences in students' rates of learning: a student either received and profited from instruction in lock-step graded classes or was educated in a special school or class. To tailor instruction to the learner's needs, educators placed students in homogeneous groups, assuming that those with similar characteristics should be taught using the same instructional methods or techniques. Special education classrooms were self-contained.

In the late 1950s and early 1960s, the efficacy of self-contained special classrooms for students with disabilities was seriously and continually challenged. Investigators demonstrated again and again that students who received special education services did not improve academically and socially over those peers with disabilities who were kept in general education classrooms and were not offered special educational interventions. Although early efficacy studies were plagued with methodological problems (for example, failure to demonstrate that the groups were comparable), they did cause educators to question the efficacy of self-contained programs for students with disabilities (see meta-analyses conducted by Carlberg & Kavale, 1980; Madden & Slavin, 1983).

At the same time that educators were questioning the benefits of special education, especially of self-contained classrooms, they recognized that there were as many variations within categories of students as between them. This recognition returned the focus of education to individual differences rather than keeping it on categories.

Special education soon evolved to the point where educators were speaking of "continua of placements" and of a "variety of alternative placements and services." Over time, names for places changed as well, with the most conspicuous being the change from "regular" to "general" to refer to the mainstream classroom. The common perception of placement was a continuum from general education class placement with tutorial or resource teacher assistance, to isolation from the general education program. Deno (1970) pictured the continuum of placements as shown in Figure 5.1. Students with special needs are sifted out of the regular classroom to settle downward in various increasingly restrictive environments. Reynolds (1978) elaborated and refined Deno's cascade model by developing a triangular conception with regular education placement as the base (Figure 5.2). This conception goes beyond the "places" where special education occurs to consider the delivery methods of instructional services. Students move individually and deliberately up from regular classroom placement, with the goal of returning as soon as possible to regular classroom placement.

PL 94-142, the Education for All Handicapped Children Act of 1975, specified that all students with disabilities have the right to a free, appropriate public education to meet their particular needs. Simply placing students in classes or programs for students with disabilities is not enough; schools must ensure that the instruction delivered is appropriate to the needs of each learner. It must be provided in the least restrictive environment (LRE) possible. In the words found in PL 94-142, this meant that:

> to the maximum extent appropriate, handicapped children, including children in public and private institutions or other care facilities, are educated with children who are not handicapped. (PL 94-142, 1975, sec. 612, 5, B, p. 123)

As might be imagined, what this really implied was not interpreted in the same way by everyone, and over time, much discussion occurred about what LRE really entailed (Cruickshank, 1977; Daniel, 1997; Dwyer, 1990; Lockwood, 1978; Miller & Miller, 1979; Nietupski, 1995; Nix, 1977; Raines, 1996; Stein, 1994). Yet in the 1997 reauthorization of the Individuals with Disabilities Education Act (the new name, as of 1990, for the Education for All Handicapped Children Act), as in past reauthorizations, the basic concept of LRE remained unchanged and an integral part of the law. The federal government has consistently documented places in which youngsters receive special education services in an attempt to monitor LRE compliance. Time spent in general and special settings is used to define alternative placements (see Table 5.1).

Where Does Special Education Take Place?

During the past two decades, there has been a trend toward the increased placement of students with disabilities in general classroom programs (see Table 5.2), even though federal placement data apparently underestimate general class placements (Roach, Halvorsen, Zeph, Giugno, & Caruso, 1997). The trend is evident

FIGURE 5.1 **Cascade Model of Special Education Service**

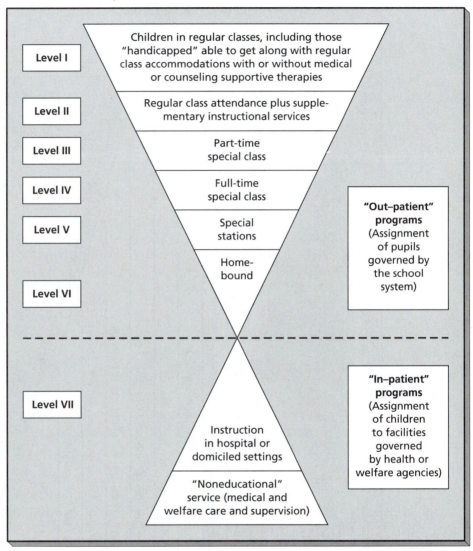

SOURCE: From Special Education as Developmental Capital by E. Deno. *Exceptional Children, 37,* 1970, 229–237. Copyright 1970 by The Council for Exceptional Children. Reprinted with permission.

for every category of disability except deaf-blindness (National Center for Education Statistics, 1997). To some extent, these trends are tied to changes that have occurred in some disability categories. For example, the other health impairments category now includes those students with ADD or ADHD, thereby accounting for much of the large jump in students in general class and resource room placements.

FIGURE 5.2   Reynolds's Triangular Conceptualization of Instructional Alternatives

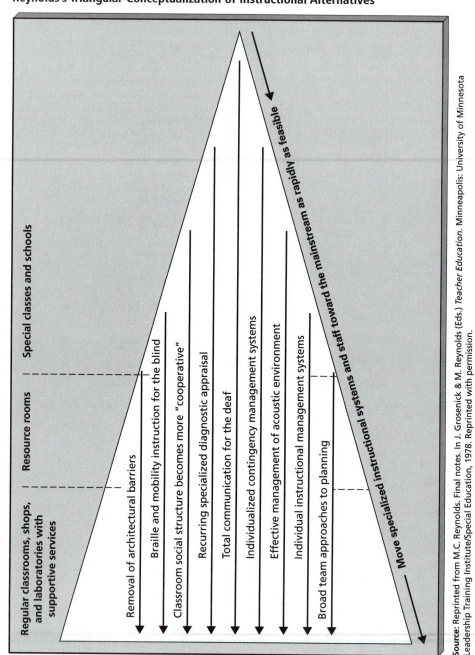

SOURCE: Reprinted from M.C. Reynolds. Final notes. In J. Grosenick & M. Reynolds (Eds.) *Teacher edu-cation*. Minneapolis: University of Minnesota Leadership Training Institute/Special Education, 1978. Reprinted with permission.

TABLE 5.1   **Definitions of Placement Categories Used by the Federal Government**

Placement	Definition
Regular class	Includes students who receive a majority of their education in a regular class and receive special education and related services for less than 21 percent of the school day (approximately 72 minutes of a 6-hour day). It includes students placed in a regular class and receiving special education within the regular class as well as students placed in a regular class and receiving special education outside the regular class.
Resource room	Includes students who receive special education and related services for 60 percent or less of the school day and at least 21 percent of the school day (from 76 minutes to about 3½ hours of a 6-hour day). This may include resource rooms with part-time instruction in the regular class.
Separate class	Includes students who receive special education and related services for more than 60 percent of the school day (more than 220 minutes of a 6-hour day) and are placed in selfcontained special classrooms with part-time instruction in regular class or placed in self-contained classes full-time on a regular school campus.
Separate school	Includes students who receive special education and related services in separate day schools for the handicapped for more than 50 percent of the school day (more than 3 hours of a typical school day).
Residential facility	Includes students who receive education in a public or private residential facility at public expense for more than 50 percent of the school day (more than 3 hours of an average day).
Homebound/ hospital	Includes students placed in and receiving education in hospital or homebound programs.

SOURCE: Adapted from U.S. Department of Education. (1990b). *Twelfth Annual Report to Congress on the Implementation of Education of the Handicapped Act.* Washington, D.C.: Author.

Small changes over time in the percentages served in general classes, such as for students with speech or language impairments, reflect the fact that these students have almost always been served primarily in these types of placements. To some extent, placement continues to be tied to the category of disability.

    Information like that presented in Table 5.2, however, hides other characteristics of placement. For example, the 1997 Annual report to Congress on the implementation of IDEA (U.S. Department of Education, 1997) indicates that placements vary according to state. For example, rural states tend to place more of their students in general and resource room classes, where there are more than

90 percent in these placements, than states with larger urban populations, where there are fewer than 60 percent in these placements. In addition, students with disabilities who are between the ages of 6 and 11 are more likely to be found in general class placements than are older students. The U.S. Department of Education also reported that over a five-year period from 1990–91 to 1994–95, general class placements increased (from 32.8 percent to 44.5 percent) and resource room placements decreased (from 36.4 percent to 28.7 percent). These kinds of numbers reflect to some extent a move toward more "inclusive" environments, but whether they reflect changes made to ensure that students receive the best education possible or changes made to reduce costs remains a question.

TABLE 5.2   **General Education Class/Resource Room Placements of Students with Various Types of Disabilities**

| | Selected Years | | | |
Types of Disability	1986	1990	1994	Overall Change
Deaf-blindness	26.0	24.6	15.7	−10.3
Hearing impairments	43.8	45.3	50.5	6.7
Mental retardation	28.8	26.5	34.7	5.9
Multiple disabilities	20.6	20.5	28.8	8.2
Other health impairments	47.6	53.4	67.1	19.5
Orthopedic impairments	48.0	48.6	58.1	10.1
Serious emotional disturbance	44.1	43.5	46.2	2.1
Specific learning disabilities	77.8	76.8	80.4	2.6
Speech or language impairments	94.7	94.6	95.1	0.4
Visual impairments	62.6	62.8	66.4	3.8

NOTE: Numbers are percentages based on the number of public school children with each type of disability. The Overall Change column is the difference between the 1986 and 1994 percentages.

SOURCE: Adaptation of Table 46–3 from the National Center for Education Statistics (1997). *The Condition of Education 1997*. Washington, D.C.: U.S. Department of Education, p. 296.

THE PUSH AND PULL OF THE GENERAL EDUCATION CLASSROOM

Since the passage of PL 94-142, the field of special education has seen students with disabilities pushed out of the general education classroom and pulled out for resource room services, and students *without* disabilities pulled *into* special settings. It has also seen the use of global terms like regular education initiative, mainstreaming, integration, and inclusion. Special education started as a way to ensure that students with disabilities received some type of education rather than none. As access to education was attained, however, and as the concept of disability was broadened to include students with, for example, learning disabilities, educators and advocates began to think about where education occurred.

Placement Reflecting Philosophy

Discussion about where students with disabilities should receive their special education services have come to reflect philosophies about students and about special education. In 1984, then Assistant Secretary of Education Madeline Will urges that there be shared responsibility for educating students with disabilities. Will's position on developing partnerships to meet the special learning needs of students was not particularly radical, but it generated considerable professional debate.

The principles embodied in the regular education initiative, the term used to describe Will's (1986) position, involved four fundamental changes in how special education was provided (Davis & Maheady, 1990).

1. Students with learning problems would receive more instruction in regular, as opposed to special education, settings.
2. General, compensatory, and special education teachers would work collaboratively to provide "special" education in integrated settings.
3. All instructional resources (i.e., financial, educational, and personnel) would be pooled under a single administrator.
4. Administrative policies and procedures would be developed to encourage placement of students with special learning needs in regular classes.

Unfortunately, empirical study of problems associated with these principles was sparse, and what had been done was criticized for ignoring important constituencies (e.g., teachers, students, administrators). For example, McKinney and Hocutt pointed out that "regular educators, who constitute the largest single group to be affected by these proposals, have not had significant input" (1988, p. 15), and Kauffman, Gerber, and Semmel added that "data reflecting attitudes of regular classroom teachers toward proposed changes in the structure of general and regular education" have been "conspicuously absent" from literature supporting the regular education initiative (1988, p. 9).

To the optimist, a proposal for adopting shared responsibility in teaching students with unique abilities offers a virtual, empirical "gold mine" of opportunities for improving practice. But in the context of previous efforts at school reform, the same proposal may be perceived as simply another opportunity for widespread disappointment and failure. To professionals engaged with students with disabilities, interesting practical questions emerge as driving concerns at the student, classroom, and system levels of practice (Maheady & Algozzine, 1991).

Perhaps the first question that can be asked is, can a heterogeneous group of students, some with serious problems, be taught effectively in general education classrooms given existing instructional resources? Related issues concern the conditions in which such populations can be taught and the limits of accommodation, both with and without additional instructional resources or more powerful interventions. On a social level, issues remain about the effect that students with and without disabilities have on each other in the same classroom. Indeed, whether students with disabilities prefer integrated or segregated placements remains a fundamental, yet unanswered, question.

For years, teachers have been told that homogeneous grouping (by age, ability, or behavior) was a preferred practice, and most of them have desired classes with as few problem students as possible. In light of this, which teachers really welcome students with learning and behavior problems into their classrooms, and does anybody really want to teach them? Even though resources for teaching students with problems are readily available (Algozzine, 1992), many questions still remain about how often "effective" strategies are actually used by classroom teachers, how acceptable these procedures are, and whether they can be generalized to other students with problems and to general classrooms.

Inclusion as More Than Placement

Many of the philosophies and arguments attached to the regular education initiative followed similar efforts to bring students with disabilities into the mainstream of education. The inclusion movement perhaps is the strongest yet of the efforts to normalize the educational experiences of students with disabilities.

Heated debates have addressed the topic of inclusion, yet not much light has been shed on efforts aimed at changing the opinions of those on either side of the argument. The debates are clouded by definitional discrepancies. They are also clouded by a failure to differentiate between what inclusion means for students with mild disabilities, for students with severe disabilities, and for the range of students between the two. Regardless, the move toward inclusion has resulted in more students with disabilities being served in general education classrooms (Council for Exceptional Children, 1995).

From various definitions provided by people using either the term *inclusion* or a similar term (e.g., Lipsky & Gartner, 1989; NASBE, 1992, 1995; Vandercook, Walz, Doyle, York, & Wolff, 1995), we get a sense of many of the foundational ideas for the concepts driving efforts to decide where special education should be delivered. According to York and Tundidor (1995), these include having students with disabilities (1) attend the same schools as their neighbors and siblings, (2) assigned to chronological age–appropriate grades and classes, (3) receiving an individual education program with appropriate instructional adaptations, and (4) providing all services in general school and community environments. Uses of the term *inclusive* or *inclusion* are broader than the meaning of the term *inclusion* as it was first used. Initially, inclusion referred to learners with severe and multiple disabilities in general education classrooms and other integrated learning environments in their home schools, and to those students receiving instruction in general education settings with special education support. Unfortunately, researchers have not used a common definition while they have looked at the effects of inclusion.

Inclusion is deemed by nearly all who discuss it to be based on a certain attitude about what is right for individuals with disabilities. A common belief is that for individuals with disabilities to learn to live in society, they need to be educated with their peers who do not have disabilities. Commonly identified attitudes required for successful inclusion are an accepting and caring attitude by staff, an accepting attitude and active involvement by students with disabilities, and a community with cultural diversity (York & Tundidor, 1995). Others have referred to the need for a "no rejection" policy (Hunt, Farron-Davis, Beckstead, Curtis, & Goetz, 1994) and to supportive, nurturing communities that really meet the needs of all children within them (Sapon-Shevin quoted in O'Neil, 1994/1995).

Nearly all who think that inclusion has been successful refer to the need for commitment to a long-term change and restructuring process (e.g., Salisbury & Chambers, 1994; Schnepf, 1994). There is need for a strong educational leader, usually the principal, who is committed to the vision of inclusion (NASBE, 1995), but there is also a need for greater numbers of paraprofessionals (Salisbury & Chambers, 1994) and for paraprofessionals who are adequately trained (York & Tundidor, 1995). Furthermore, there must be a system of communication with the parents of students without disabilities in the inclusive setting, as well as with the parents of students with disabilities (NASBE, 1995).

Beyond viewing inclusion as a placement, Salisbury and Chambers (1994) referred to inclusion as a logical extension of effective schooling practices. Time for common, collaborative planning among teachers and others is seen as a critical element of inclusion (Salisbury & Chambers, 1994; York & Tundidor, 1995), as is providing appropriate social interaction opportunities for students, both planned and incidental (Hunt et al., 1994).

Research that has shown positive effects of inclusive educational systems provides clues about some of the critical components of inclusion. This research has shown, for example, that the IEPs of students with severe disabilities are of better quality and have more relevance to the curricular content when students are full-time members of general education classrooms, and that the actual levels of engagement and social interactions of students with disabilities with their peers and with adults are better (Hunt et al., 1994). Research also has demonstrated that there are no significant negative academic or behavioral effects on classmates who are educated in classes with students with severe disabilities (Bricker, Bruder, & Bailey, 1982; Hollowood, Salisbury, Rainforth, & Palombaro, 1994/1995; Odom, Deklyen, & Jenkins, 1984; Sharpe, York, & Knight, 1994). Qualitative research (see Giangreco, Dennis, Cloninger, Edelman, & Schattman, 1993) indicates that teachers who initially had negative reactions to including a student with severe disabilities in their classrooms identified benefits received by the students with disabilities, the classmates of those students, and themselves by the end of the year.

Some positive outcomes have also been reported for students whose disabilities are not considered severe. For example, a pilot study by Rogan, LaJeunesse, McCann, McFarland, and Miller (1995) indicated that teaching learning strategies to students with learning disabilities successfully supported them in immediate school English classes. Both the students with learning disabilities and their peers without disabilities performed successfully. Furthermore, those without disabilities in the inclusion classrooms performed at levels comparable to their peers without disabilities in classes in which no students with disabilities were enrolled.

Vaughn and Schumm (1995) have argued that how a student is educated is more important than where, and that by following certain guidelines for "responsible inclusion" (e.g., student comes first, teachers choose to participate, etc.), many students with learning disabilities can be well-served in full-inclusion settings (see also Garnett, 1996). Schumaker and Deshler (1994/195) reiterate this idea in their argument that students with disabilities who are included in general settings must continue to achieve at levels at least equal to or higher than when they were not in the general classroom (p. 51). This requires use of critical instructional procedures and monitoring of effects.

Strong public attacks on the concept of inclusion (e.g., Shanker, 1994/1995; Fuchs & Fuchs, 1994/1995, 1995) have suggested that there is plenty of research on the negative effects of inclusion. For the most part, the cited research has revealed smaller gains in the performance of students with disabilities when they are in general education classrooms versus when the same students are in special education classrooms (e.g., Fuchs, Fuchs, & Fernstrom, 1993; Marston, 1987–1988). Other than recent qualitative research by Zigmond and Baker (1995), the cited research did not attempt to document the ways in which the general education environment was modified to accommodate the learning needs of the students with disabilities. Unfortunately, while Zigmond and Baker documented the nature of the general education environment for students with disabilities, they did not look at student outcomes and how they might relate to the environment. Thus, despite data-driven arguments, professional perspectives on the value and appropriateness of inclusion continue to reflect conflicting viewpoints (cf. Zigmond, Jenkins, Fuchs, Deno, & Fuchs, 1995).

One of the arguments against inclusion is that it is being used as a tool to reduce the costs of educating students with disabilities. This accusation has been made despite the limited research on the costs of inclusion or on the more needed cost-benefit or cost-effectiveness implications of inclusion. McLaughlin and Warren (1994) noted that while inclusion may have a philosophical basis, it "also can offer a more efficient way to use resources to support the learning needs of a broader group of students" (p. 8). On the other hand, it has also been argued that, if appropriately implemented, inclusion actually should cost more than separate special education but that because resources are scarce and because special education mandates have never been funded adequately, schools have to "cut back their regular programs" (Shanker, 1994/1995, p. 21) to provide for the inclusion of students with disabilities. A comprehensive summary of the literature (McGregor & Vogelsberg, 1998) addresses costs as well as other outcomes of inclusive schooling. The major findings on outcomes derived from that synthesis are summarized in Table 5.3

TABLE 5.3   **Empirically Documented Themes Summarized in McGregor and Vogelsberg's Synthesis of Literature on Inclusive Schooling Practices**

Skill Acquisition for Students with Disabilities

- Students with disabilities demonstrate high levels of social interaction in settings with their typical peers, but placement alone does not guarantee positive social outcomes.
- Social competence and communication skills improve when students with disabilities are educated in inclusive settings.
- Students with disabilities have demonstrated gains in other areas of development when they are educated in inclusive settings.
- Interactive, small-group contexts facilitate skill acquisition and social acceptance for students with disabilities in general education classrooms.

Social Outcomes for Students with Disabilities

- Friendships develop between students with disabilities and their typical peers in inclusive settings.
- Teachers play a critical role in facilitating friendships between students with disabilities and their typical peers.
- Friendship and membership is facilitated by longitudinal involvement in the classroom and routine activities of the school.

Impact on Students Without Disabilities

- The performance of typically developing students is not compromised by the presence of students with disabilities in their classrooms.
- Typically developing students derive benefits from their involvement and relationships with students with disabilities.

(Continued)

TABLE 5.3   Empirically Documented Themes Summarized in McGregor and Vogelsberg's Synthesis of Literature on Inclusive Schooling Practices (Continued)

- The presence of students with disabilities in the general education classroom provides a catalyst for learning opportunities and experiences that might not otherwise be part of the curriculum.

Impact on Parents

- Parent support for inclusion is affected positively by actual experience with this approach to education, although experience alone does not shape attitudes.
- Parents of students with disabilities are looking for positive attitudes, good educational opportunities, and acceptance of their child among educators.

Impact on Teachers

- Although many teachers are initially reluctant about inclusion, they become confident in their abilities with support and experience.
- Support from other teachers is a powerful and necessary resource to empower teachers to problem-solve new instructional challenges.
- Facilitating the inclusion of students with disabilities requires the sensitivity to make on-the-spot judgments about the type and amount of support to encourage participation while not interfering with student interactions.

Program-Related Outcomes

- Some evidence suggests that while startup costs may initially increase the cost of inclusive services, the costs over time decrease and are likely to be less than segregated forms of service delivery.

SOURCE: McGregor, G., & Vogelsberg, R. T. (1998). *Inclusive Schooling Practices: Pedagogical and Research Foundations*. Pittsburgh: Alleheny University of the Health Sciences, pp. 57–69.

"YOU'RE OUT OF HERE": PLACEMENTS OUTSIDE THE MAINSTREAM

The LRE provision of PL 94-142 is a key concept driving efforts to provide special education to children and youths with disabilities (Ysseldyke & Algozzine, 1995). The enabling legislation and implementing regulations require that

> first, educational services appropriate for each child be defined annually in an Individualized Education Program (IEP); and, then, an educational placement be selected from a continuum of alternatives so that the individually appropriate education can be delivered in the setting that is least removed from the regular education environment and that offers the greatest interaction with children who are not handicapped. (Danielson & Bellamy, 1989, p. 448)

The concept reflects the belief that segregating students with disabilities is unsound social, political, economic, and educational practice (Ysseldyke & Algozzine, 1982, 1984, 1990, 1995). The concept brings ideals of normalization and mainstreaming convincingly to life by establishing assistance to states in the form of monitoring, discretionary grants, and technical assistance from the federal government.

Even though significant professional debate abounds about the merits of least restrictive placements, there has been little published research revealing the extent to which alternative placements (e.g., resource rooms, separate classes, separate school facilities) are used to operationalize the ideals inherent in LRE provisions (Blackman, 1989; Danielson & Bellamy, 1989; Tucker, 1989; Ysseldyke & Algozzine, 1995). There are data, of course, on the extent to which segregated placements are used (see Figure 5.3). Earlier analyses of data on the use of alternative placements revealed great variability in estimates provided by individual states (cf. Danielson & Bellamy, 1989). According to Tucker (1989, p. 456), the variability was due more to definitions of LRE than to actual

FIGURE 5.3   **Percentage of Students with Disabilities Ages 6 to 21 Served in Each Educational Environment: 1990–1991 to 1994–1995**

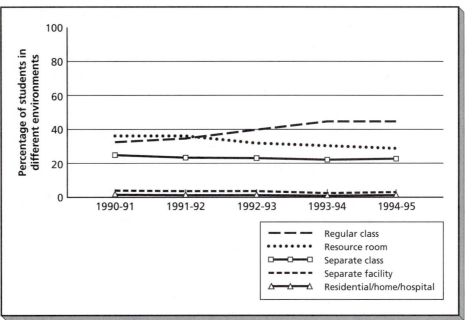

SOURCE: U.S. Department of Education. (1997). *Nineteenth Annual Report to Congress on the Implementation of the Individuals with Disabilities Education Act.* Washington, D.C.: Author.

conditions existing within the states. The variability noted in the earlier analyses continues to be seen today in states' use of segregated placements (U.S. Department of Education, 1997).

Interest in analyzing variation in placement was justified by its policy implications: If state-to-state variability did exist, this would demonstrate potential for improvement in the national effort to educate children with disabilities in less restrictive environments (Danielson & Bellamy, 1989, p. 449). Two assumptions drove this interest. First, data reflective of placements were assumed to be accurate representations of the state of practice (i.e., students in one setting really spent less time in special education than students in another setting did, and the numbers reflected realistic pictures of where students were served). Second, placement and program were used synonymously; therefore arguing that one place was less restrictive than another ignored the possibility that what went on in that place may have been more restrictive regardless of what it was called. The issue at the base of concern generated by such analyses was whether restrictive definitions were creating inappropriate pictures of the benefits accrued by students with disabilities.

The accuracy of the data used to compare variation in placement of students with handicaps was questioned by Danielson and Bellamy: "Of course, some of the variability across states may be the result of measurement error" (1989, p. 453), and "states need to strengthen efforts to improve the accuracy and state-to-state comparability of data" (p. 455). Tucker argued that narrow interpretations of the LRE concept had created conditions calling for *less required energy* in implementation. He used the following example to illustrate that placement should not always be equated with program and that to assume otherwise "sets up a false premise which can serve as the foundation for any number of more restrictive alternatives (e.g., emotionally disturbed students need a separate facility)" (1989, p.457):

> A deaf person needs a program which accommodates his or her loss of hearing. If a hearing aid is all that is *needed* (as defined by the nature and severity of the handicap), then the LRE is any location whatsoever that is normal for a child of that age and other presenting characteristics, *so long as a hearing aid is provided and working.*
>
> If a hearing aid is not sufficient, and one or more alternative forms of communication, such as signing, are needed, than again, the physical location of the person does not determine the least restrictive environment, but rather the conditions surrounding the person. To educate a deaf person with other deaf persons because it is easier to assemble the needed services in one place may be a practical solution to a financial problem, but it does not make the separate facility the least restrictive environment for deaf students. Again, it is the path of least resistance. (p. 457)

Clearly, deciding what is the best environment for providing special education is difficult especially in light of the opinion that *any* environment may be appropriate. Complex social, political, economic, and educational factors enter the decision-making process, and few standards exist for making objective decisions about who should receive special education and where it should be provided (Ysseldyke & Algozzine, 1982, 1984, 1990, 1995).

PLACES STILL MEAN PROBLEMS FOR PEOPLE WITH SPECIAL NEEDS

Now that access to education is expected, guaranteed, and assured, professionals are concerned about the appropriateness of placement, not the effects of labels. The labels have become so ingrained that systematic questioning no longer exists as a topic of educational research.

Before his success with the Simpsons, Groenig wrote a book entitled *School Is Hell,* in which he chronicled his perceptions of the trials and tribulations that faced people forced to be there. Make no mistake, school is not fun for the vast majority of people who attend (Sarason, 1990). Students with disabilities and their families find schools particularly trying places:

> The stigmatizing circumstance under which many deaf persons learned and began using sign language has had its impact on the language and on the level of linguistic sophistication of many sign language users. The signs themselves often tell a story about the frustrations of ineffective education. For example, one composite sign stands for "Too many big words." There are signs that indicate negative self-image, such as "dummy" and "pea-brain," and deaf people often apologize to hearing persons or to more educated deaf persons with comments such as "Me dummy—know nothing." . . . Pat, who emigrated to this country from South America at age 9, said that most of her elementary and junior high school years were spent in special education courses that were far too easy. Comparing special education with mainstream classes, she said: "In ninth grade I had four special education classes. They were very, very easy, I told my mother I wanted out. Now that I'm in all mainstreamed classes, even homeroom, I don't think I'm favored because I'm disabled. I have to work for my grades. Some other disabled kids are passed along." (Asch, 1989, p. 188)

The life experiences of a group of people released from a large institution were analyzed and presented in *The Cloak of Competence* (Edgerton, 1967) more than thirty years ago. We think the comments of many of these people still have relevance. For example, the book presented evidence of "passing," in which individuals disguise their disabilities rather than admit they have them. Passing was, and still is, part of the social behaviors of many exceptional people:

- I don't like to read. It hurts my eyes. I'd rather watch TV" (p. 131).

- When I try to get a job they always ask me where I'm from. I don't tell nobody I'm from there [the hospital]—I say I'm just an outsider like anybody, but I've been working in the East" (p. 151).

- "You know old _____ (another ex-patient). He's always putting on. He went and got these books at the junk shop for ten cents a piece, and now he's got 'em all over his place like he was some kind of millionaire. Well, I went and got me some books too, real classy ones, I paid a dollar for some of 'em. Got all kinds, I think they look real nice" (p. 159).

It is generally recognized that placement issues have a broader base than just those individuals with disabilities. The jump from special education segregation to tracking (or grouping students by their implied level) is not a huge leap, and the effects of tracking have been noted repeatedly, as in the following description.

> Tracking promotes "dumbed-down," skill-drill, ditto-drive, application-deficient curricula. It contributes to the destruction of student dreams and the production of low student self-esteem. . . . These placements can start as early as six weeks into kindergarten; and even though placements supposedly are flexible, they generally are permanent. (Pool & Page, 1995 p. 1)

Dispelling low expectations, in fact, is a common theme in the inclusion literature. For example, teachers speak of the changes in their opinions about children with disabilities.

> Last spring when we discussed the idea of having Zach as a member of my class in the fall, I was fine with this. I could certainly see the benefits for the typical kids—appreciation and awareness of differences, promotion of caring and sharing, etc. However, although I never expressed it at the time, I really did not see the benefits for Zach. I was really under the impression that kids like Zach (with such cognitive delays) did not change much. He taught me differently. I really saw gains in his skills over the school year. I especially saw growth in the way he communicated and played. (Montie, 1989, p. 6)

Similar revelations were described by teachers involved in a middle school integration effort (York, Vandercook, Macdonald, Heise-Neff, & Caughey, 1992, p. 249).

> The experience allowed me to see how a severely disabled learner can learn skills in an integrated environment that previously I felt could not be learned given the success in the special education classroom. Skills and behaviors often reinforced in special education classrooms are often inappropriate in regular classrooms (e.g., talking spontaneously, hugging).
>
> Seeing students in such a different environment was really eye opening. If we build a wall around them so they are in special environments, how do special education teachers and students learn about typical situations and expectations?

Parents of students with disabilities describe their efforts to convince the educational system that their children can learn. They are often forced to go above and beyond what is required of parents of any other students to get placements that work.

> When our daughter Jodi was born with Down syndrome in 1966, I was advised to institutionalize her. I could not do that. . . . She was placed in a segregated class for children with disabilities. We had no alternative. This was disastrous for Jodi. At 11 years of age we decided to pull her out of public school and send her to a Christian day school where she would not be separated. . . . Despite the fact that we were once told that Jodi needed to be separated and that she couldn't learn if she were educated alongside other children, Jodi did learn a great deal. (Bechtold, 1989, p. 36)

While the testimonials about the benefits of moving from segregated to integrated placements are easy to find, there are also plenty about the negatives of such experiences. In reacting to an entire set of less-than-positive case studies on inclusion for students with learning disabilities, Edwin Martin of the National Center for Disability Services made the following comments.

> We do not need to change our philosophy and goals of including persons with disabilities more fully into our society; we just need to avoid simplistic solutions, like focusing on placement and general education improvement rather than improved specially designed instruction and services. Most especially, we must accept the moral obligation to measure what we do in terms that are important and significant to the total lives of our students. Do our programs meet the test of assisting students to attain postschool success and positive self-regard? (Martin, 1995, p. 199)

Discussion Questions

1. At the same time that many parents and professionals applaud the benefits of including students with disabilities in general education classrooms, there are loud voices arguing that inclusion is a disservice to many students with disabilities. Identify two pieces of information or data that would support either of these viewpoints.

2. Placement is not synonymous with program. How would you support or refute this statement?

3. Predict what federal placement data might look like in 2025 by extending either Table 5.2 or Figure 5.3. Give reasons for your predictions.

Part

2

Contemporary
Issues and
Practices

Chapter 6
Issues in Assessment

SUMMARY

DISCUSSION QUESTIONS

You can weigh horse manure on a jeweler's scale and you can slice baloney with a laser beam, but in the end you've still got horse manure and baloney.

—University of Minnesota criminologist Hans Mattick

More than 300 million standardized tests are administered each year to the 44 million students who attend American elementary and secondary schools. In addition, teachers and educational support personnel regularly collect data on students through classroom tests, classroom observations, record reviews, and interviews with students' family members or caregivers. Clearly, assessment, especially the testing dimension of it, is a major activity in America's schools.

Many issues regarding assessment of students, specifically those who have disabilities, and these issues are primarily the result of the considerable importance attributed to testing and test results in American schools and society. Consider for just a moment the decisions made about people, using tests. Eleanor is not allowed to enter school because her performance on a test indicates that she is not "ready" to do so. Heidi is told to repeat second grade because her performance on a set of tests indicates that she has not yet mastered second-grade content. Bill is required to attend summer school because he did not earn a passing score on the eighth-grade basic skills test administered in the state of Minnesota. Jose is assigned to a class for gifted students, while Zeke is placed in a class for students who are learning disabled. Both placements depended on how the student performed on a set of tests.

Students in Texas must pass the Texas Assessment of Academic Skills (TAAS) to receive a high school diploma. Mitchell passes the test. Melvin does not, so he does not receive a high school diploma. Ariel is admitted to Florida State University, but Clem is denied admission because his test scores are too low. Mark, an all-city basketball player, cannot attend a Division I college because his test scores are too low, even though his grades are high enough. Kate earns a high score on a selection test; Esther does not. Kate gets a position with General Mills; Esther does not. Because decisions based on test results often affect people's life opportunities, there is much controversy surrounding how tests and test results are used.

CURRENT DECISION-MAKING PRACTICES

Although tests are administered to students for one or more purposes, testing is only one part of the broader conception of assessment. Testing refers to the sampling of behaviors in students to obtain quantitative indexes (that is, scores) of relative standing. Assessment can be described as a process of collecting data to make decisions about individuals and groups (Salvia & Ysseldyke, 1998). Assessment data come primarily from four sources: norm-referenced and standards-based tests, observations, interviews, and searches of school records.

The decisions made using assessment information are varied and complex. They occur in and out of classrooms. Salvia and Ysseldyke (1998) identified thirteen kinds of decisions made using assessment information. They grouped these thirteen kinds of decisions into four major types: prereferral classroom decisions, entitlement decisions, postentitlement classroom decisions, and accountability/outcomes decisions. Table 6.1 lists the four categories of decisions, the thirteen kinds of decisions made using tests, and the kinds of questions answered for each decision. The categories of decisions are described on pages 143–144.

Prereferral Classroom Decisions

When students show academic, behavioral, or physical difficulties, their classroom teacher typically tries several alternative teaching approaches. In fact, most state departments of education and school districts now require that teachers implement and document the effectiveness of alternative teaching approaches before they are allowed to refer students formally for psychoeducational evaluation. Teachers decide whether to provide special help or enrichment, seek the help of an intervention assistance team, or provide prereferral interventions. Efforts are made to reduce the numbers of students referred for testing and to cut down on misclassification or overidentification of students.

Entitlement Decisions

School personnel make five kinds of entitlement decisions. They may decide whether students:

- Need more intensive assessment
- Should be referred to child study teams for more extensive evaluation
- Meet state criteria for assigning a disability label or label of gifted and talented.
- Have such unique learning needs that special assistance is required to meet goals or standards
- Are eligible for special education services

To be considered eligible or entitled to special education services, students must meet state criteria for assigning a disability label or a label of gifted and talented

TABLE 6.1   DECISIONS MADE USING ASSESSMENT INFORMATION

	Decision Area	Questions to be Answered
Prereferral Classroom Decisions	Provision of Special Help or Enrichment	Should the student be provided with remediation, compensation, or enrichment so that difficulty in learning can be overcome?
	Referral to an Intervention Assistance Team	Should the teacher seek the assistance of an intervention assistance team (composed of other teachers) in planning instructional interventions for an individual student?
	Provision of Intervention Assistance	Should the intervention assistance team provide the student with intensified remediation, compensation, or enrichment?
Entitlement Decisions	Screening	Is more intensive assessment necessary?
	Referral to a Child Study Team	Should the student be referred for formal psychoeducational evaluation, to be conducted by members of a child study team?
	Exceptionality	Does the child meet state criteria for assigning a disability label or a label of gifted and talented?
	Special or Unique Learning Needs	Does the student have special learning needs that require special education assistance so that the outcomes of schooling can be achieved?
	Eligibility	Is the student eligible for special education services?
Postentitlement Classroom Decisions	Instructional Planning	What should a teacher teach and how should he or she teach?
	Setting	Where should students be taught?
	Progress Evaluation	To what extent are students making progress toward specific instructional goals?

(Continued)

TABLE 6.1	Decisions Made Using Assessment Information (Continued)		
Accountability decisions	Program Evaluation		Are specific instructional programs working as school personnel want them to work?
	Accountability		To what extent is education working for students? (Accountability decisions usually are made at the national, state, or school district level.)

SOURCE: Salvia, J., and Ysseldyke, J. E. (1998). *Assessment* (7th Ed.). Boston: Houghton Mifflin.

and have such unique learning needs that they require special assistance to meet state goals or standards.

Postreferral Classroom Decisions

Once decisions are made about the eligibility of students for special education services, educators must make another set of decisions. One decision is an instructional planning decision: they must decide what should be taught and how it should be taught. Second, they must also decide the setting in which instruction will be delivered (e.g., a general classroom, resource room, institutional setting). And they must make decisions about the extent to which students are achieving their individual goals and state or district standards.

Accountability Decisions

School personnel use assessment information to make two kinds of accountability decisions. They gather data for the purpose of deciding the extent to which specific kinds of instructional programs are working as intended. For example, they may want to know whether the new reading curriculum is resulting in higher levels of students competence in reading. They also make decisions about the extent to which education is in its broadest sense is in working for students with disabilities. Accountability decisions are made at the local school, school district, and/or state levels.

THE MANY KINDS OF ASSESSMENT INFORMATION USED IN SCHOOLS

There are only four ways to gather assessment information: (1) observation of students, (2) interviews of students or others in their environments, (3) administration of tests, or (4) reviews of records and permanent products. As far as testing is concerned, it is important that educators recognize that many different kinds of tests are used in schools and that some kinds are used for a single purpose, others for multiple purposes. In this section we differentiate briefly among norm-referenced assessment, standards-referenced assessment, curriculum-based assessment, curriculum-based measurement, performance assessment, and portfolio assessment.

Norm-Referenced Assessment

In norm-referenced assessment, the pupil's performance is evaluated in reference to the performance of others who are like him or her. Standardized measures are used, and the pupil's performance is compared to the performance of those in the normative group. Those who support norm-referenced assessment argue that it is necessary to compare students to their peers, and that knowledge of students' relative standing assists teachers in picking the level at which to instruct students and in grouping students for instructional purposes. Those who call attention to the limits of norm-referenced assessment argue that knowledge of relative standing does not help a teacher decide *how* to teach. They contend that instructional decisions are best made by using curriculum-based approaches or by teaching students and monitoring continuously their progress toward objectives.

Standards-Referenced Assessment

The term *standards-referenced assessment* is relatively new. It is used to refer to the practice of specifying standards for individuals or groups of students and then assessing the extent to which they meet, or are making progress toward meeting, the standards. All states except Iowa have specified state standards. Of those who have specified standards, nearly all use state tests to make judgments about whether students meet the standards. In some states, progress toward meeting standards is scored pass-fail, while in other states scoring rubrics are used to assign values to the level of student performance relative to the standard (e.g., novice, apprentice, proficient, and distinguished).

Curriculum-Based Assessment (CBA)

Curriculum-based assessment, which is sometimes called task analytic mastery measurement (Fuchs & Deno, 1991), is "a procedure for determining the instructional needs of a student based on the student's ongoing performance within existing course content" (Gickling & Havertape, 1981, p. 55). This assessment includes direct observation and analysis of the learning environment, analysis of the processes students use to approach tasks, examination of students' products, and control and arrangement of tasks for students. School personnel break complex tasks into their component parts and analyze the extent to which the student can master each of the components. They teach those components that have not been mastered and integrate the components to teach the complex skill.

Assessment consists of setting terminal and enabling objectives, writing items designed to measure mastery of enabling objectives, administering minitests to students, and charting pupil performance on the tests. Those opposed to the use of these measures argue that the approach is labor intensive and fractionated and that performance on the small tests does not generalize to performance in the broader domain of behaviors that can be assessed.

Curriculum-Based Measurement (CBM)

Curriculum-based measurement is a specific form of curriculum-based assessment devised by Deno and his colleagues at the University of Minnesota. Curriculum-based measurement is characterized by standardized direct measures of the pupil's skills in the content of the curriculum. The measures meet the following criteria: "(1) tied to a student's curricula, (2) of short duration to facilitate frequent administration by teachers/educators, (3) capable of having many multiple forms, (4) inexpensive to produce in terms of time in production and in expense, and (5) sensitive to the improvement of students' achievement over time" (Marston, 1989, p. 30).

Those in favor of the use of curriculum-based measures point out that the measures give valid indications of the student's performance in the curriculum of interest, focus on the broad goals of the curriculum, and enable teachers to monitor student skill development across an entire school year without shifts in measurement devices and procedures. Those opposing the use of these measures maintain that their curriculum specificity limits their use to the specific curriculum being measured.

There is debate about the relative value of CBA and CBM approaches. Shapiro (1996) provides an extensive discussion of the merits and limitations of the approaches. Fuchs and Fuchs (1996) contrasted the CBA and CBM approaches to measuring mastery of IEP objectives, and concluded that CBM approaches were more effective in measuring progress toward short-term goals, and CBA approaches were more effective in measuring progress toward attainment of short-term goals.

Performance Assessment

For the past decade assessors have been moving away from assessment that focuses on pupil performance on multiple-choice tests, sometimes called "paper and pencil," tests, and memorization. They look at problem-solving ability and gather data on pupil performance over longer periods of time. The measurements they use may consist of measuring student performance on tasks that may take as long as a semester to complete, or asking students to work individually or in groups to solve major problems. In doing so, students must frame problems, collect data, and analyze and report results. They may be asked, for example, to study the prices at two supermarkets and determine which supermarket has the lower prices. Performance is evaluated on the bases of how well students work as a group, how well they use math to solve the problem, and so on. This kind of assessment most often is called performance-based assessment, although the terms *alternative assessment* and *authentic assessment* are also used. In 1992 the Office of Technology Assessment, a congressional office, defined performance assessment as "testing methods that require students to create an answer or product that demonstrates their knowledge or skills" (U.S. Congress, Office of Technology Assessment, 1992, p. 17). Elliott (1994) indicated that performance assessments could consist of conducting experiments, writing extended essays, or doing mathematical computations.

Portfolio Assessment

Portfolio assessments are often considered a special form of performance assessment. Portfolios are "collections of products used to demonstrate what a person has done and, by inference, what a person is capable of doing" (Salvia & Ysseldyke, 1998, p. 271). Portfolios are used to document student effort, document growth and achievement, and provide a means of assessing the quality of educational programs. Salvia and Ysseldyke (1998) reviewed common conceptions of portfolio assessments and concluded that they generally have six elements: (1) they target valued outcomes, (2) they use tasks that mirror work in the real world (authentic tasks), (3) they encourage cooperation among students and between teacher and students in solving problems, (4) they use multiple criteria to evaluate student work, (5) they encourage student reflection and critical thinking, and (6) they integrate assessment and instruction (i.e., are inseparable from instruction).

CONTEMPORARY INFLUENCES ON ASSESSMENT PRACTICES

In this section we describe six factors influencing assessment practice: the law, the push for accountability, the push for a national test, international comparisons, and student diversity (especially language diversity).

The Law

Laws have influenced the assessment of students with disabilities at least since President Ford signed the Education of All Handicapped Children Act in 1975. That law specified the Protection in Evaluation Procedures Provisions. According to these provisions, assessment practices must be fair, with no racial or cultural bias. The law also specified, among other things, that:

- There must be a full evaluation of a student's needs before the student is declared eligible for special education services

- Tests must be administered in the child's native language or mode of communication
- Test must be valid for the purposes for which they are used
- Evaluations for special education must be made by a multidisciplinary team

In 1980 Congress passed PL 99-457, an extension of the provisions of PL 94-142 to infants and toddlers. In 1990 Congress passed the Education of the Handicapped Act Amendments (PL 101-476) and enacted changes to PL 94-142. The title (Education of the Handicapped Act) was changed to Individuals with Disabilities Education Act (IDEA), two new disability categories were added, definitions of *related services* and *individualized education program* were clarified, and transition services were added. In 1997 Congress reauthorized the IDEA; clarified the meanings of some of the earlier provisions; and added two new assessment provisions. One provision required participation of students with disabilities in statewide assessments (beginning July 1, 1998), the other required the development of alternate assessments (by July 2000).

The Push for Accountability

Educators, parents, bureaucrats, legislators, and the general public want to know the extent to which students with disabilities profit from their educational experiences. For many years accountability in special education consisted of documenting the numbers of students with various conditions and who received special education services, the numbers of teachers and related services personnel who served them, and the settings (resource rooms, self-contained classrooms, etc.) in which services were delivered. Beginning in the early to mid-1980s, many different constituencies began asking for information that would shift attention away from the process of providing services to the results of those services. The push came under different names. In some places there was a call for "outcomes-based education" or "goal directed instruction," education directed toward the achievement of outcomes or goals and documentation of the extent to which outcomes or goals were achieved. In other places people talked about "standards driven reform" and documentation of the standards toward which students were working and the extent to which they achieved them. In Kentucky the courts declared education bankrupt and called for a statewide overhaul of the educational system, with an accompanying requirement that schools demonstrate accountability for their services based on the results of student performance on statewide tests.

As we noted above, federal laws now mandate that states will include all students, including students with disabilities, in their accountability systems. As we were writing the final copy of this textbook, it was common to read daily newspaper accounts of student performance on state tests, and many of those accounts called attention to the exclusion of students with disabilities from accountability reports and/or the performance of students with disabilities on state and district tests.

International Comparisons

It is important to remember that much of the push for accountability had its origin in the publication of the 1983 report entitled *A Nation at Risk: The Imperative for Educational Reform* (National Commission on Excellence in Education). In that report a distinguished panel of experts called attention to mediocrity in education, the low test performance of America's students relative to that of students in other countries, and the need for significant educational reforms and accountability. The fear that America's students are achieving at lower standards than students in other nations has fueled the move to develop higher standards and to assess progress toward those standards. Many have challenged the contention that America's students or schools are inferior to those in other nations (Bracey, 1998). And many have argued that testing students and holding them responsible for achieving high standards will not motivate them to achieve higher grades.

The Push for National Achievement Test

Early in 1996 President Clinton called for a voluntary national test in reading for all fourth-graders and in math for all eighth-graders. The test was to provide information to the nation on the performance of America's children and provide individual performance information to parents. School districts and states were to decide whether or not to participate. The call for the development and administration of a national test was predicated on the assumption that it would tell us how we are doing as a nation in educating children and youths, and it would serve as a stimulus to improve education. At the time this text was being published, the test was under development, and policy makers were still debating whether to use it.

Student Diversity

The increased diversity of students attending schools, especially their language diversity, is influencing assessment practices. For example, IDEA requires that students be assessed in their primary language or mode of communication. In major school districts today, students speak more than fifty different languages. The California Department of Education lists fifty-four languages other than English, and it collects data on those fifty-four languages. No African languages are listed among the fifty-four, and several of the listed languages (e.g., Native American) could actually encompass several languages. More than eighty languages other than English have been identified by Dade County, Florida (Miami area), students as their home language (Dade County Schools website, **www.dade.k12.fl.us,** 1/27/99).

Assessment of students whose primary language is not English is a formidable task. Assessors struggle with whether to provide translated tests, to provide simultaneous testing in English and the primary language, or to exclude students from testing. For many tests, there are no literal translations.

It is estimated that the range of skill development in most classrooms is extremely broad. It is not unusual for a teacher of fourth-graders, for example, to encounter a group of students whose reading skills cover an eight-year range (from grade 1 to 8). This influences assessment practices. The tests used to assess those youngsters must have easy items that can be answered by the students functioning at the lowest level and difficult items that can challenge students at the highest level. And, of course, the tests must be given in a reasonable time frame.

A third diversity factor has to do with acculturation. Students attending today's schools bring with them a wide array of background experiences and differences in opportunity to learn. Differences in acculturation affect opportunity to learn, the extent to which the student can understand what is presented in the classroom, and the extent to which the student can perform optimally on tests.

ISSUES IN MAKING CLASSROOM AND ENTITLEMENT DECISIONS

The Nearly Automatic Testing of Students Who Are Referred

Is testing for eligibility an automatic consequence of referral? Is being declared eligible for special education services an automatic consequence of testing? Algozzine, Christenson, and Ysseldyke (1982) argued that nearly all students who are referred to child study teams are tested. They also argued that testing led to automatic eligibility. To support their contentions, Algozzine et al. presented the results of a survey of school districts and showed that 92 percent of referred students are tested and 73 percent of tested students are placed in special education.

Ysseldyke, Vanderwood, and Shriner (1998) replicated the Algozzine et al. (1982) study and showed that fifteen years later, the rates were consistent with earlier results: 90–92 percent of referred students were tested, and 70–74 percent of tested students were declared eligible for special education services. They raised issues about the extent to which testing made a difference in eligibility decisions made about students.

The Exclusion of Students with Disabilities from Norms

One of the fundamental assumptions in norm-referenced assessment is that students' performances will be evaluated relative to those of others who have had comparable acculturation (Salvia & Ysseldyke, 1998). Yet students with disabilities are often excluded from the norming population for standardized tests. In most instances, the use of norm-referenced tests to evaluate pupil performance consists of comparison of students to those who are not disabled, and there is little demonstrated validity for making decisions about students with disabilities on this basis. This practice, of course, runs contrary to federal laws, which mandate that tests must have demonstrated validity for the purposes for which they are used. It is critical that students with disabilities be included in test development and norming so that the tests can be used with those students.

A related issue is the failure of test developers to provide assessment accommodations when norming standardized tests. Exclusion from norming often means that users must guess to obtain indices of performance. Failure to include accommodations during the standardization process produces inappropriate norm groups and the exclusion of many students from taking the tests.

Bias in Assessment

A major, and legitimate, issue in assessment is bias. This concern arises directly out of the ways in which American society evaluates the worth of the individual on the basis of presumed intelligence. The IQ has become a very potent yardstick: educators become concerned when a student's achievement is not commensurate with his or her intelligence; parents view their children's IQ scores as if they were measures of worth; and society tries to limit immigration, advocate sterilization, and explain criminal tendencies, mental and physical defects, and degeneracy on the basis of IQ. According to Kamin, "Since its introduction to America, the intelligence test has been used more or less consciously as an instrument of oppression against the underprivileged—the poor, the foreign born, and racial minorities" (1974, p. 1). Kamin illustrated his argument by repeating quotations from early psychologists and congressional witnesses in support of limiting immigration.

This issue of bias also grows out of the different average intelligence test scores achieved by different racial groups. This variance has been fashioned into an instrument of oppression, according to Kamin (1974), and it has also kindled considerable professional controversy over the reason for the observed differences.

Bias is also an issue in the disproportionate representation of minority students in special education classes; this concern is apparent in both litigation and legislation (see Chapter 12), even though neither has changed the situation.

Given the legitimate and necessary concern of professionals with bias in assessment, let us look at how educators and psychologists have addressed the problem. Early observations that minority students earned lower scores on the average than did nonminority students led to long and heated debates on the relative contributions to intelligence of genetic and environmental factors (Bayley, 1965; Bereiter, 1969; Bijou, 1971; Bloom, 1964; Cronbach, 1969; Elkind, 1969; Gordon, 1971; Hirsch, 1971; Jensen, 1967, 1968a, 1968b, 1969b). The debate still goes on, the observed differences continue to exist, and children continue to fail in school.

Observed differences between groups also led to investigations of test fairness. These investigations included large-scale comparative studies of the performances of groups on specific tests (Goldman & Hewitt, 1976; Hennessy & Merrifield, 1976; Jensen, 1976, 1979; Matuszek & Oakland, 1972; Mercer, 1973). Studies of group differences in performances on psychometric devices persuaded other investigators to examine the fairness of specific items used with members of minority groups (Angoff & Ford, 1971; Newland, 1973; Scheyneman, 1976). Specific tests and test items were examined for linguistic bias (Berry & Lopez, 1997; Matluck & Mace, 1973; Vasquez, 1972) and for sex bias (Dwyer, 1976; Tittle, 1973; Tolor & Brannigan, 1975). But major measurement experts have been unable to agree on a definition of a fair test, let alone a test that is fair for members of different groups.

This nation and its researchers have invested considerable effort, time, and financial resources in attempts to develop or identify assessment devices that are not biased against members of racial or cultural groups. Given the history of psychologists' efforts to address the concepts of fairness and their generalized lack of success, it troubles us to see educators these days trying to find *the* fair test to use with specific groups, arguing about the fairness of specific test items, and generating state-approved lists of fair tests. What would it mean if *the* fair test were found? Would bias and abuse in assessment and decision making cease to exist? We think not. Even given a fair test or set of tests, there is considerable evidence that the bias in decision making would not be ameliorated. Indeed, review of testimony before the congressional committee on the Protection in Evaluation Procedures Provisions of PL 94-142 revealed a broader concern with the subject of abuse in the entire process of assessment. Such abuse includes inappropriate and indiscriminate use of tests, bias in the assessment of children with disabilities and in the identification of children as disabled who are not, bias throughout the decision-making process, and bias following assessment. An excerpt from a Senate report on the matter illustrates the depth of concern:

> The Committee is deeply concerned about practices and procedures which result in classifying children as having handicapped conditions when, in fact, they do not have such conditions. At least three major issues are of concern with respect to problems of identification and classification: (1) the misuse of appropriate identification and classification data within the educational process itself; (2) discriminatory treatment as the result of the identification of a handicapping condition; and (3) misuse of identification procedures or methods which results in erroneous classification of a child as having a handicapping condition. . . . The Committee is alarmed about the abuses which occur in the testing and evaluation of children; and is concerned that expertise in the proper use of testing and evaluation procedures falls far short of the prolific use and development of testing and evaluation tools. The usefulness and mechanistic ease of testing should not become so paramount in the educational process that the negative effects of such testing are overlooked. (U.S. Senate, 1975, pp. 26–29)

A corollary concern to bias in assessment is disproportionate minority representation in special education. It is argued that minority students are overrepresented in special education placements. Reschly (1997) indicated that students get extra services when they receive special education services. To the extent that stigma is associated with special education placement and the quality of services in special education are inferior to those in general equation, people become concerned. Thus, concern about overrepresentation is also concern about stigma and the quality of services received.

Reschly also pointed out that when talking about representation in special education, it is always critical to differentiate between the percentage of a racial or ethnic group in special education and the percentage of students in special education who are members of the specific racial or ethnic group. For example, it may be the case in district 283 that 70 percent of the students in special education are African American, and at the same time, that 8 percent of African Americans nationwide are in special education. To interpret whether the figures indicate overrepresentation, one must know the percentage of students in the district who are African American (is it 71 percent or 34 percent?) and the percentage of white students who are in special education (is it 8 percent of 4 percent?). It is more appropriate to talk about disproportionate representation.

Technical Adequacy

Professionals who assess students and thus make decisions about them often use technically inadequate data-collection procedures. We stress this fact because the decisions can have profound effects on the students' lives. Educators are purported to have the best interests of the students at heart when they make decisions, although they often base the decisions on data from technically inadequate tests. Three characteristics determine the technical adequacy of tests: norms, reliability, and validity.

Norms   Norms are standards of comparison. A norm-referenced test is developed by standardizing it on a sample of students that actually represents the population on which the test will be used. The performance of an individual on the test can then be compared with, or evaluated according to, the performance of other members of the population. The nature of the norm group, the group with whom a person is being compared, is important because the norm group's performance is the standard against which the quality of the individual's performance is judged.

To be representative the sample has to be made up of correct proportions of people in the total population—that is, the various kinds of people should be included in the same *proportion* in the sample as in the population (Salvia & Ysseldyke, 1998). The test's norms also must be current. A joint American Psychological Association–American Educational Research Association committee recommended that tests be revised at regular intervals, usually at least once every fifteen years.

Inadequately constructed or described norms skew the judgments educators make about the quality of a pupil's test behavior; the pupil is then being evaluated in reference to an unknown and/or unrepresentative norm group. Some of the most widely used measures of intelligence, achievement, personality, and perceptual-motor functioning were standardized on inadequately constructed and/or described norms (Salvia and Ysseldyke, 1998).

The Hypothetical Typing Test

Suppose that you are the personnel manager for a large industrial firm and that part of your job includes hiring typists. You regularly require applicants for positions as typists to take a typing test, which you score for both speed (number of words per minute) and accuracy. You usually try to hire those applicants who are the fastest and most accurate. But how do you know that you are hiring the best possible typists? You do not unless you have a standard according to which the applicants can be evaluated. Hence, you decide to develop a typing test that requires applicants to type from both handwritten copy and dictation. But even if you give every applicant the same test, you will still need some basis for evaluating the performance. So you decide to standardize your test—that is, develop a set of norms according to which applicant performance can be consistently evaluated.

The way in which you standardize the typing test will affect the evaluation of each applicant's performance. There are several groups on which the typing test can be standardized:

1. All high school seniors in your local school district
2. All high school seniors in your local school district who have been enrolled in a business curriculum and who have taken at least one full year of typing classes.
3. A representative national sample of high school seniors who have been enrolled in a business curriculum and who have taken at least one full year of typing classes
4. All those persons who, over a three-year period, have applied for employment with your company
5. All those persons who, over a three-year period, have applied for employment as typists with your company
6. Persons currently employed as typists in your company who have better than "satisfactory" performance evaluations from their immediate supervisors

The nature of the norm group you select will influence your judgment of an applicant's typing skills. An applicant can look very good compared with high school seniors but very poor compared with currently employed, successful typists. In addition to the test score and norms for evaluating that score, you will still need to know the nature of the norm group. Because the decision to hire or not to hire a person will be influenced by his or her performance relative to the norm group, your decision may well be in error if you do not know the nature of the group on which the test was standardized.

Psychological and educational assessment assumes that the acculturation of the person being assessed is comparable to, although not necessarily identical with, that of the people on whom the test was standardized (Newland, 1980;

(Continued)

Salvia & Ysseldyke, 1998). *Acculturation* refers simply to a person's background experiences and opportunities. This assumption is typically addressed by test developers when they select a sample representative of the population of concern. Representativeness in the testing industry is usually achieved by stratifying a norm sample on a number of characteristics specified in the *Standards for Educational and Psychological Tests* (APA, 1985; see also Salvia & Ysseldyke, 1998). These characteristics include age, grade, sex, acculturation of parents (as usually indicated by some combination of socioeconomic status, income, occupation, and education), geographic region, and race. For achievement tests, the cognitive functioning (intellectual level) of the norm group is also a significant consideration.

Reliability Reliability refers to consistency in measurement. Assessment instruments are said to be reliable when students achieve approximately the same score whenever they take the test. Evaluation of pupil performance depends, in part, on the obtaining of a reliable index of performance. As part of the process, test developers do provide evidence that their tests are reliable. But when Salvia and Ysseldyke (1998) evaluated the evidence for reliability in each test they reviewed, they concluded that there was insufficient evidence of reliability for many tests.

There are standards for reliability, but they change according to the decision being made. Salvia and Ysseldyke (1998) indicated that tests should have reliability coefficients in excess of .60 when the scores are to be used for administrative purposes and when test data are to be reported for groups of individuals. However, when tests are to be used to make decisions regarding individuals, they must have reliability coefficients greater than .90.

Validity Validity refers to how much a test measures what it purports to measure. Evidence for validity is not only considered essential by the *Standards for Educational and Psychological Testing* (American Educational Research Association, American Psychological Association, and National Council on Measurement in Education, 1985) but is also required by law. According to the regulations for PL 94-142, "Tests must have demonstrated validity for the purpose(s) for which they are used." In addition, test developers must provide consumers with evidence of test validity; tests are considered invalid when they provide inappropriate information for decision-making purposes.

The technical adequacy of tests currently used to make decisions on students has been evaluated in several investigations. Thurlow and Ysseldyke (1979) evaluated the technical adequacy of tests used in forty-four model programs for learning disabled students, the Child Service Demonstration Centers. They found that, of thirty tests used by three or more centers, only five (16.7 percent) tests had technically adequate norms. Only ten (33.3 percent) of the thirty tests had reliability adequate for decision making, and only nine (30 percent) had technically adequate validity. The model programs—among the very best special education programs in the nation—made decisions about students by using tests that, for the most part, were technically inadequate.

Much abuse can follow from the use of norm-referenced assessment data to make decisions regarding students. Abuse results from the use of tests for purposes other than those for which they were designed, from comparisons of students who differ systematically in several characteristics, and from the use of technically inadequate tests to collect data on students.

Functional Behavioral Assessment (FBA)

Educators are now required by provisions of the reauthorized Individuals with Disabilities Education Act to engage in functional behavioral assessment as part of new discipline procedures. Functional behavioral assessment is often confused with functional analysis of behavior. Tilly, Knoster, Kovaleski, Bambara, Dunlap, and Kincaid (1998) define functional behavioral assessment as "[t]he process of coming to an understanding of why a student engages in challenging behavior and how student behavior relates to the environment." In conducting an FBA, the IEP team gathers contextual information to pinpoint those factors regularly associated with demonstration of the behavior. The assessments are done to gather data and thus understand better the specific reasons for the student's problem behavior. Tilly et al. (1998, p. 1) suggest that teams ask the following six questions:

1. When is the student most likely to engage in the problem behavior?
2. What specific events or factors contribute to the problem behavior?
3. What functions does the problem behavior serve for the student?
4. What might the student be communicating through the behavior?
5. When is the student most successful and therefore less likely to engage in the behavior?
6. What other factors might be contributing to the student's problem?

There is much confusion about the meaning of the term *functional* in the law. Tilly et al. (1998) identify four alternative meanings of *functional* as it applies to assessment:

1. Functional assessments describe how well an individual is "functioning" in a particular area.
2. Functional assessments describe the status of some intact characteristic of the individual.
3. Functional assessments describe the relationship between a skill or performance problem and variables that contribute to its occurrence.
4. Functional assessment may describe the function or purpose served by an individual's behavior.

Another way to misunderstand functional assessment of behavior is by confusing it with *functional analysis of behavior*. The purpose of functional analysis is "to determine empirically the relationships between the variables controlling the target behavior and subsequently to modify these behaviors" (Shapiro, 1996, p. 49). The process involves selection of treatment variables that are hypothesized to influence (or control) the behavior of concern, implement treatment, and see if the behavior changes. Functional behavioral assessment might be seen as the first step in functional analysis of behavior. Tilly et al. (1998) indicate that functional behavioral assessments should be an integral part of ongoing assessment and intervention efforts, so maybe the two terms have similar meanings. In any event, we expect that the profession will continue to debate these terms for some time.

Student Characteristics Versus Instructional Diagnosis Versus Assessment of Instructional Environments

Assessment can follow three fundamentally different approaches: to diagnose the learner, to diagnose instruction, and to assess the learning environment. Those who conduct assessments tend to concentrate their efforts on one of the three approaches and in most instances the focus is on diagnosing the learner. Tests, or test batteries, are given in an effort to identify what is wrong with students who are first referred by teachers. Elaborate classification systems are used, and varied labels result. When professionals focus on diagnosing instruction, they break it down into component parts, identify specific skill development strengths and weaknesses, and highlight specific instructional needs. According to Engelmann, Granzin, and Severson, "The purpose of instructional diagnosis is to determine aspects of instruction that are inadequate, to find out precisely how they are inadequate, and to imply what must be done to correct their inadequacy" (1979, p. 361). Engelmann et al. argued that "accurate conclusions about the learner . . . can only be reached after an adequate diagnosis of instruction" (p. 356). This type of diagnosis results in a description or an inventory of instructional strengths and needs.

Ysseldyke and Christenson (1994) developed a comprehensive methodology for analyzing the instructional environment—"the interaction of student characteristics, the assigned task, and the teacher's instructional or management strategies" (Christenson & Ysseldyke, 1989, p. 415)—for an individual student. They argued that the instructional environment consists of many factors in addition to curriculum and instructional materials. These factors include the nature of instructional planning, classroom management, instructional presentation, methods and techniques for motivating the learner, clarity of directions, the extent to which teachers check for students understanding, provision of opportunities for practice, feedback, and techniques used to monitor student progress. Ysseldyke and Christenson (1993) developed The Instructional Environment System to enable practitioners to account for these factors in assessment.

In practice, it is probably difficult to identify diagnostic personnel who use one of the three approaches exclusively. It is, however, possible and desirable to characterize specific assessment activities as consisting of one of the three approaches.

The Use of Tests to Classify and Place Students

On paper at least, eligibility, classification, and placement decisions are made on the basis of assessment data. All states have special education rules and regulations that specify eligibility criteria for special education services. The criteria differ considerably among states (Mercer, Forgnone, & Wolking, 1976), and within states there is typically considerable variation in the extent to which local education agencies use the state criteria. Ysseldyke, Algozzine, and Mitchell (1982) tried to identify the kind(s) of decisions made at special education team meetings by videotaping thirty-two meetings and carefully analyzing the contents. They reported that it was impossible to specify the decisions made by the teams. In addition, at the conclusion of meetings the teams did not regularly state or formally write down the decisions they had reached.

The Use and Misuse of Intelligence Tests

The use of intelligence tests has been banned in some school districts and in some states. For example, as a result of rulings in the *Larry P.* v. *Riles* court case in San Francisco, school districts in California were not allowed to administer intelligence tests in the process of declaring black students eligible for enrollment in classes for the mentally retarded. The decision was expanded so that the use of intelligence tests to assess any student for the purpose of placing them in special education classes in California was rendered illegal.

Typically, the argument against the use of intelligence tests is twofold. Opponents maintain that the tests are biased against specific types of students and that the information obtained from the tests is of little or no value in planning instructional interventions.

Issues in Ascertaining Student Gain in Achievement

Assessment information is regularly used to measure gain in achievement. In fact, many school districts report in local newspapers either test scores or gains in achievement for their districts as a whole or for specific buildings within the districts. The use of gain scores, however, has been repeatedly criticized in the professional literature (Cronbach & Furby, 1970). Arguments against the use of gain scores have typically focused on issues of reliability and regression toward the mean. Psychometricians have been able to show that on repeated administration of a test, the student will probably score closer to the population average. With students who are disabled, these arguments take on special meaning because these students typically earn low scores on aptitude and achievement tests. Because there is a higher probability of low scores regressing to the mean as a function of chance, there is then a high probability that these students will evidence at least some gain as a function of chance.

The Directness and Nature of Assessment

Assessment activities differ in their directness and in the nature of inferences made. Sometimes assessors engage in direct measurement of pupil performance. They use terms such as *direct and frequent measurement* to reflect the practice of assessing student performance in the day-to-day activities of instruction. They measure reading to describe pupil performance in reading, they measure math to describe performance in math, and they observe and record interactions with others as a measure of interactions with others. In contrasting direct and indirect approaches to measurement, Ysseldyke and Marston reported that

> direct measures are those that measure precisely the same skills as have been taught and often use the same response mode as was employed in teaching the skills initially. Indirect measures are those in which test items are usually sampled from a larger domain and are not necessarily the items that have been taught. Success on the sampled items is viewed as indicative of mastery of the behaviors from which the samples were taken. (1990, p. 664)

Sometimes assessors engage in projective assessment. They do not sample behaviors directly but instead make large inferences. Such approaches are employed under the assumption that direct assessment may be threatening or that it may result in an inaccurate picture of the student's thoughts, feelings, or behaviors. Students are shown pictures and asked to describe what they think is happening in the pictures. The examiner infers from the student's "story" aspects of how the student feels.

Examiners and educators differ in their positions on what should be assessed. Sometimes the focus is on assessment of student characteristics, traits, or attributes. The assessor administers tests as measures of student intelligence, visual perceptual processing, auditory processing, psycholinguistic processing, attitudes, and so on. The list of possible attributes or characteristics to be assessed is very long. Such attributes or characteristics are assessed under the assumption that the assessment provides important information relevant to pupil performance in school. But those who engage in assessment of student characteristics are forever having to defend their actions and demonstrate the relevance to instruction of their assessment activities.

Sometimes assessment is focused on assessment of pupil progress within the curriculum. Assessment is direct and focused on provision of data on skills acquired and progress toward completion of specific objectives. At other times, assessment does not monitor progress on a direct, frequent basis but instead repeatedly measures the extent to which the student has accomplished specified outcomes. As can be seen from these examples, numerous different perspectives exist on the goal or focus of assessment.

Curriculum progress   The predominant approach in assessment focuses on assessment of student progress in the curriculum. Sometimes this is accomplished by informal recording of pupil completion of assignments, sometimes by collection of the products of pupil's work. Often teachers document progress through the curriculum by using unit mastery tests, especially in basic skills areas such as reading and math. Sometimes data are collected using norm-referenced achievement tests.

Student characteristics   Many practitioners firmly believe that students who experience difficulty in academics do so because of fundamental within-student deficits and deficiencies. Thus, these practitioners advocate collection of data on pupil characteristics (performance on aptitude measures, ability measures, personality measures) and the use of those data in planning interventions for students.

Pupil performance   Still other educators advocate collection of data on pupil performance, rather than on pupil characteristics. They argue that it is more important to know what students do—what they produce—than to know their characteristics. The focus on collection of data on pupil performance is clearly reflected in the work of those who advocate performance assessment.

Pupil outcomes/broad systems indicators   Many practitioners now focus heavily on broad systems indicators in the assessment of students with disabilities. We have seen a move away from demonstrations that services have been delivered and a move toward a focus on the outcomes of service delivery (Finn, 1990). The National Council on Disability (1989) argued that it is time to concentrate on the quality of educational experiences for children and youths with disabilities. To make judgments about educational quality, educators need indexes by which to judge quality.

Another impetus for developing a set of indicators for special education is that general education is proceeding with its own agenda to raise expectations for students and to identify outcomes for "all" students. Although it is clear that educational indicators are needed, there is no consensus on their definition, their uses, and their types. Smith suggested that "most commonly, an educational indicator either assesses or is related to a desired outcome of the educational system or describes a core feature of that system" (1988, p. 487). As is no doubt obvious, many views exist on which data should be used as outcomes indicators. Should indicators be cognitive or affective? Should they focus on mastery of subject matter content, on acquisition of learning and adjustment skills, or on development of positive attitudes and positive self-perceptions? Many different outcomes indicators are currently used by states. The National Center on Educational Outcomes, funded by the U.S. Department of Education and housed at the University of Minnesota, has developed a conceptual framework for evaluating the outcomes of schooling for students with disabilities and is collecting data from states on student performance. More on this activity is described in the section of this chapter focused on large-scale assessment, and more is included in Chapter 14.

The Use of Clinical Judgment

A discussion of issues in assessment techniques would be incomplete without a discussion of clinical judgment. Many assessors argue that they do not rely on test scores in making decisions about students; they rely on clinical judgment. They contend that they take into account pupil performance on many tests, rather than on single tests; integrate this with what they learn through interviews and observations; and make diagnostic judgments based on their own clinical experience and expertise. Epps, Ysseldyke, and McGue (1984) reported the results of an investigation in which they provided test scores to teachers and psychologists and asked them to use clinical judgment to decide whether students were learning disabled; judges were correct about 50 percent of the time.

Who Should Assess Students?

Many different disciplines are involved in the assessment of students with disabilities. Classroom teachers, resource room teachers, school social workers, remedial reading specialists, school psychologists, counselors, occupational therapists, and others administer tests in the process of planning instructional interventions and making other decisions about students. As might be expected, there is disagreement about who ought to administer and interpret which tests.

In some states some assessment activities are governed by licensure and credentialing agencies. For example, in some states a licensed psychologist administers intelligence tests to students. In such cases, deciding who should give which tests should be a relatively simple matter: reading specialists administer reading diagnostic measures, speech and language personnel give and interpret language tests, and so on. But such simplistic reasoning assumes one-to-one correspondence between professional title and professional competence. We have learned that no such correspondence exists. In some districts the best person to give language measures is the speech and language pathologist. In other districts that person does not have the expertise, but the counselor or school psychologist does. We firmly believe that tests ought to be given and interpreted by people who have the necessary competence, regardless of professional title.

RELEVANCE TO INTERVENTION

A major issue in assessment is the link between assessment information and instruction. Heller, Holtzman, and Messick maintained that "the purpose of the entire process—from referral for assessment to eventual placement in special education—is to improve instruction for children. Valid assessment, in our view, is marked by its relevance to and usefulness for instruction" (1982, pp. x–xi). According to Christenson and Ysseldyke, assessment activities should shift away from a simple prediction orientation and toward a broader perspective in which information from multiple sources (the student, the family, the instructional environment, the community) is integrated for the primary purpose of designing appropriate interventions. "Assessment practices in schools would be dramatically improved if (a) student performance was assessed within the context of classroom and home influences, and (b) educators viewed the primary purpose of assessment as intervention planning—or finding ways collaboratively with parents and teachers to teach the child" (1989, p. 410). Unfortunately, much that goes on in the assessment of students with disabilities has very limited relevance to intervention. Our hope is that such activities will diminish and that data collection will be restricted to what is absolutely necessary for planning interventions.

Assessment is a process of collecting data for the purpose of making decisions about students. To the extent that the decisions that are made are viewed as harmful, inappropriate, biased, or limiting students' life opportunities, assessment practices get blamed. In this chapter we have reviewed issues that arise when decisions are made about whom to assess (or whom to exclude from testing), what to assess, the specific techniques and procedures to use, and who should perform assessments. The bottom line in assessment is relevance to intervention. Assessment activities are useless if they do not result in improved instructional opportunities for students.

ISSUES IN MAKING LARGE-SCALE ASSESSMENT AND ACCOUNTABILITY DECISIONS

The Participation of Students with Disabilities in Large-Scale Assessment and Accountability Systems

There are three ways in which students with disabilities participate in district, state, and national large-scale assessment and accountability systems: they may take the regular assessments in the same ways that all other students take them, they may take the tests with accommodations (e.g., large print, separate setting, extended time), or they may take an alternate assessment, about 15% of students with disabilities will need to take on an alternate assessment. It is estimated that 85% of students with disabilities can take large-scale tests with or without accommodations; about 15% of students with disabilities will need to take an alternate assessment.

Vanderwood, McGrew, and Ysseldyke (1998) documented the widespread exclusion of students with disabilities from statewide and national assessments. They reported that students with disabilities were regularly excluded from the National Assessment of Education Progress, the National Educational Longitudinal Survey, and state tests. The reauthorized Individuals with Disabilities Education Act (1997) included a provision requiring that states develop guidelines for participation of students with disabilities in district and state tests; beginning July 1998, states include students with disabilities in their statewide assessments; and states report on the performance and progress of all students. The National Center on Educational Outcomes surveyed states in 1997 and reported that, although thirty-two states indicated that they collected or received data on the numbers of students with disabilities in statewide testing, only fifteen states provided data (Connecticut, Delaware, Florida, Hawaii, Kansas, Louisiana, Maryland, Missouri, New York, North Dakota, Oregon, Rhode Island, South Carolina, Texas, Wisconsin) (National Center on Educational Outcomes, 1997). At the time that this textbook was going to press, forty-one states had written guidelines on the participation of students with disabilities in large-scale assessments, and states were at various stages in developing or revising their participation guidelines. When asked about the status of their efforts, states indicated the extent to which they were working on development or revision. In Table 6.2 we list the states who were at various stages in developing or revising participation guidelines. When reviewing the table, remember that states may be giving little emphasis to development or revision for different reasons. For example, they may already have well-developed current guidelines, or they simply may not be focusing attention on this activity.

State directors of special education indicate several factors that inhibit the participation of students with disabilities. Among the major factors inhibiting participation are the following identified by the National Center on Educational Outcomes (National Center on Educational Outcomes, 1997):

- Teachers, parents, and others wish to "protect" students with disabilities from stressful testing situations.

- The high stakes for districts and states encourage exclusion of students who are expected to perform poorly.

- Implementation guidelines vary widely from district to district and from school to school within districts.

- There is inadequate monitoring of the extent to which students with disabilities participate.

TABLE 6.2   States Developing or Revising Participation or Exemption Policies for Statewide Assessments

No emphasis	2	IA, GA
Little emphasis	2	ID, KY
Some emphasis	9	DE, LA, MS, NE, NV, NH, NM, SD, UT
Moderately high emphasis	10	AK, AZ, IL, MA, MN, MT, NY, ND, PA, TN
High emphasis	27	All states not listed above

- Teachers, parents, and others view large-scale assessment as irrelevant to the education of students with disabilities.

Ysseldyke (1997) identified a set of issues in the participation of students with disabilities in large-scale assessment systems. Among those issues were the following:

- There is disagreement about responsibility for the results of education for students with disabilities. General and special educators debate relative responsibility, and there is concern about responsibility for the performance of students who attend schools in separate settings or in districts other than their district of residence.
- The lack of adequate accommodations keeps many students with disabilities from participating.
- There is disagreement about who (IEP team, principal, teacher) should decide how students with disabilities participate in assessment and accountability systems.

Participation of students with disabilities in assessment and accountability systems is critical. If students with disabilities do not participate, then they are out of sight and out of mind when policy decisions are made based on data about student performance on large-scale tests. If students with disabilities do not participate in assessments, teachers may assume they have no responsibility for instructional results for those students. And this, in turn, can lead to lowered expectations for the performance of students with disabilities. The data derived from large-scale assessments are used to make comparisons among states or nations. If there are differences in the numbers of students with disabilities who participate in assessments, comparisons are bogus.

Definitional Confusion

There is considerable confusion about the meaning of many of the terms used in the 1997 Individuals with Disabilities Education Act. People have different interpretations about what the terms mean, and states define the terms differently in their official policy documents as well as in less formal communication. There is a pressing need to define and differentiate terms such as *accountability systems, assessment systems, alternate assessments, disaggregated scores, accommodations,* and *modifications.* Clear understanding of terms will aid assessment practice as well as improve training, monitoring, technical assistance, and research efforts.

Confusion About Requirements of the Law

There is much confusion among policy makers and practitioners about requirements of the assessment provisions of the IDEA. (These provisions were stated on page 147–148 of this text.) There is also confusion about the requirement that students with disabilities participate in state and districtwide assessment programs. Are students required to participate in districtwide assessments only when a state does not have a statewide assessment? Must students with disabilities participate in all of the assessments given by states (some states have as many as six different state-run assessment programs), or does participation in a single assessment meet the letter and intent of the law?

There is concern about eligibility for alternate assessments. In general, it is agreed that alternate assessments are an option to be made available only to students with the most significant support needs. Both the assistant secretary of the Office of Special Education and Rehabilitative Services and the assistant secretary of the Office of Civil Rights have indicated in a public letter (September 19, 1997) that the alternate assessment is for "the small number of students whose IEPs specify that they should be excluded from regular assessments, including some students with significant cognitive disabilities." Yet the issue of who will be allowed to take alternate assessments is the beginning point for all discussions about alternate assessment. The discussion is linked integrally to the discussion of the extent to which students will need accommodations in typical assessments. The greater the number and kinds of accommodations provided in typical assessments (recognizing that most, but not all, accommodations produce valid scores), the smaller the number of individuals who will be involved in an alternative assessment system.

Provisions found in legal documents that pertain to reporting student scores are also of concern. These documents tend to be vague about issues such as whether it is statistically unsound to report on the performance of students with disabilities. "Statistically unsound," as it is used here, implied being contrary to the best interests of the students. At the core of the issue is the importance of protecting the anonymity of students. Some educators, as a rule of thumb, report scores only if there are more than ten students in a group. The issue of whether to report all student scores or to report selectively in the interest of maintaining student anonymity is, of course, continually debated, and a solution has yet to become apparent.

Lack of clarity about such matters will impede implementation of the new law, and it will impede implementation of inclusive accountability systems. Confusion could lead to exaggerations and distortions of legal requirements that could, in turn, lead to diminished support among educators and the general public for education of students with disabilities. The concern is that substantial agreement about the requirements of the law is needed.

Absence of Consensus on What to Assess

An overriding issue in the design of inclusive assessment and accountability systems is the absence of consensus on a conceptual framework to guide the process. This is the case for accountability systems in general, and it is especially true in efforts to design alternate assessment systems. State assessment and accountability system vary greatly, and there is little consensus both on what ought to be measured and how students with disabilities should be included and reported in the systems.

Two special education organizations have been working on the development of a model or framework for accountability of the results of education for students with disabilities. In the early 1990s, personnel at the National Center on Educational Outcomes worked with hundreds of stakeholders to develop a conceptual model of educational results and indicators to guide the educational accountability process. Outcomes and indicators were developed in eight outcome areas and at six developmental levels (ages 3 and 6; grades 4, 8, and 12; and postschool). Different groups of stakeholders were convened over a two-year period to identify desired results and indicators at each of the six levels.

In 1995 the National Association of State Directors of Special Education (NASDSE) published "Vision for a Balanced System of Accountability" and introduced a model of accountability comprised of three components. (1) system accountability, (2) individual student accountability, and (3) input/process accountability. The NASDSE conceptual model is shown in Figure 6.1. The pivotal concept for this model is that balanced accountability is evident where an educational system is accountable for ensuring that all children, including those with disabilities, benefit from their educational experience through equal access, high standards, and high expectations, and that they become caring, productive, socially involved citizens who are committed to lifelong learning. The fundamental principle of this model of accountability is the dynamic balance between and among the three major components of the system. NASDSE envisions a social system as a triangle and proposes that, in an ideal state, each of the three poles of the triangle is robust and performs its unique function to provide balance. In reality, however, a relative imbalance often prevails, with one pole assuming dominance over the others. For example, an overemphasis on procedural matters can result in high rates of exclusion of students with disabilities from system assessments and inadequate accountability for individual student achievement.

In 1998 the National Center on Education Outcomes revised its model of educational outcomes and created an operational framework for the NASDSE model. NASDSE personnel stopped short of identifying the kinds of data that should or would be collected when measuring the results of education for students with disabilities. NCEO personnel specified the kinds of data to collect in each of six results domains, four educational process domains, and six domains of educational inputs and resources. The conceptual framework can guide the process of collecting data on the results of education for students with disabilities. In its document entitled "NCEO Framework for Educational Accountability" (Ysseldyke, Krentz, Elliott, Thurlow, Erickson, & Moore, 1998), NCEO personnel specify outcomes, indicators, and possible sources of data on outcomes and indicators. The NCEO framework is shown in Figure 6.2.

FIGURE 6.1   NASDSE's Model for a Balanced, Inclusive Accountability System

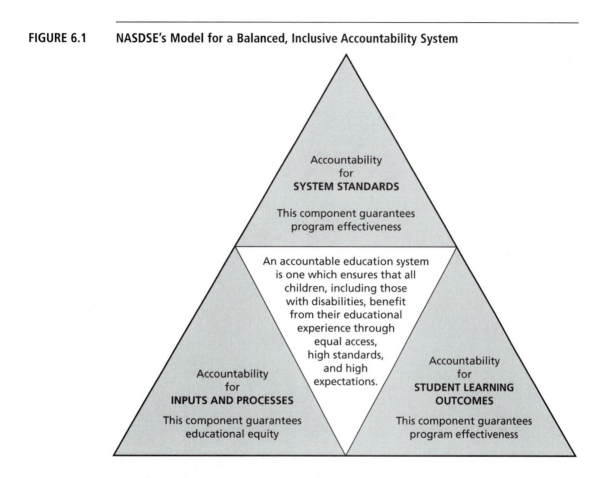

Variability Among and Within States

States are at different points in the development and implementation of their assessment and accountability systems. Some have much farther to go than others to achieve compliance with the law. Since 1990 the National Center on Educational Outcomes has surveyed states and reported on state practices in assessing the results of education for students with disabilities. Six reports of those state surveys are available from NCEO. Since 1988 the Council of Chief State School Officers has conducted an annual survey of state assessment practices. All states except Iowa currently have statewide assessments (Iowa requires district rather than state assessments) (Bond & Roeber, 1998). States differ in the subjects they assess, the kind(s) of tests used, and the grades at which they conduct their state assessments. States also differ considerably in the extent to which they include students with disabilities in their state and district assessments. Effective July 1998, states were to report on the performance of students with disabilities in their state assessments. Only thirty-two states had collected the data by that date.

FIGURE 6.2   A Conceptual Framework for Educational Accountability

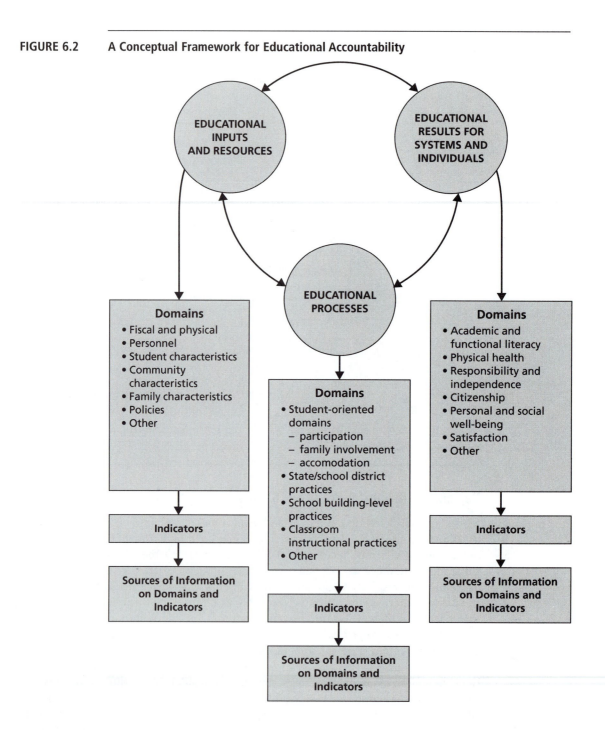

Debate About a National Test

President Clinton and Secretary of Education Riley have suggested that voluntary national tests in reading at grade 4 and math at grade 8 would have a positive consequence on the future of education. The contention is that, if we specify high national standards and measure student performance, achievement will rise. Funding subsequently was allocated to the development of the tests. Then Congress and professionals began to debate the extent to which voluntary national testing would improve education. Some argued that such testing would enable educators to pinpoint problems and take steps to fix them; others contended that we already know the problems and should concentrate our resources and efforts on fixing them rather than identifying them. For example, Linn and Herman (1977, iii) argued that "[c]oupled with appropriate incentives and/or sanctions—external or self-directed—assessments can motivate students to learn better, teachers to teach better, and schools to be more educationally effective." Congressman Goodling, on the other hand, stated that

> If testing is the answer to our educational problems, it would have solved them a long time ago. American students are tested, tested, tested, and the Clinton administration is proposing to test our children again (August 13, 1997).

Goodling suggested that thinking new tests will lead to better students is "akin to claiming that better speedometers make for faster cars" (quoted from Mehrens, 1998). At the time this text went to press, national tests were being developed, many states and cities had volunteered to participate in them, and critics were calling the proposed practice suspect.

The Use of Assessment Accommodations

It is necessary for some students with disabilities to be given specific accommodations so they can participate in large-scale assessments. As this book went to press, thirty-seven states had written guidelines for making decisions about the kinds of accommodations students could be given in assessment. The National Center on Educational Outcomes surveyed states regarding the status of their efforts to develop or revise their accommodation guidelines. Some states were giving this high emphasis; others were giving it low emphasis. Table 6.3 shows the status of state activity in developing or revising accommodations guidelines.

Ysseldyke (1997) identified a set of issues in making assessment accommodations for students with disabilities. Among those issues identified were the following:

- Accommodations that are allowed vary from state to state. Sometimes a state permits an accommodation while its neighboring state prohibits the same accommodation.

- Assessment accommodations should match instructional accommodations, and often this is not the case.
- Many people believe that accommodations simply should not be provided, all students should take tests under the same conditions, and those who cannot do so should be excluded.
- There is disagreement about what "reasonable" means in the term *reasonable accommodations.*
- Each specific kind of accommodation (e.g., use of calculators, large print) raises a specific set of issues.
- There is disagreement (and absence of data) about the extent to which the provision of accommodations changes what is assessed.

TABLE 6.3   States Developing or Revising Their Accommodations Guidelines

No emphasis	5	AL, GA, ID, IA, IL
Little emphasis	1	LA
Some emphasis	13	AZ, DE, KY, MI, MS, NE, NH, NM, NV, NY, SD, TN, UT
Moderately high emphasis	8	KS, MA, MT, ND, OH, PA, WI, WY
High emphasis	23	All states not listed above

Alternate Assessments

By 2000, states will be required to have alternate assessments for students with disabilities who do not participate in statewide assessments. At the time we wrote this text, only two states (Maryland and Kentucky) had alternate assessments, two others were developing them, and fourteen states were discussing the development of alternate assessments. Thirty-six states indicated that they were not emphasizing the development of alternate assessments. The terms *alternate* and *alternative* are often confused, and many states were talking about developing alternative assessments. Alternate assessments are intended for use with a very small proportion of students (probably less than 2 percent) who have significant impairments, and the alternate assessments should be relevant to students' instructional goals. This means that for many students with significant disabilities, the alternate assessments will be measures of the extent to which they are achieving functional standards.

There are many issues regarding the development and use of alternate assessments. Among these issues are the following:

- There is considerable disagreement about who should participate in alternate assessments: (1) students who cannot participate in the typical state test, (2) students who are working toward separate standards, (3) students who are not working toward a "real" diploma, and (4) students who are working toward separate standards *and* a separate diploma.

- There is concern about who (IEP team, principal, teacher) decides whether students take typical or alternate assessments.

- There is concern that large numbers of students with disabilities will be excluded from typical state assessments, these students will be accounted for by means of alternate assessments, and alternate assessments will become "dumping grounds" for large numbers of students.

- There is debate about whether the scores of students on typical and alternate assessments can ever be aggregated.

- There is concern about the cost benefit of developing alternate assessments.

Reporting on the Performance of Students with Disabilities

States and school districts regularly report on the performance and progress of their students, including students with disabilities. Some believe that data on the performance of students with disabilities should be reported separately from the data on the performance of other students. And there is concern about whether data on the performance of students with disabilities who use accommodations can ever be included with data on those who do not use accommodations. Personnel in district and state departments of education say that they are concerned about what increased participation of students with disabilities will do to trends for their districts or states. There is also considerable concern about how to report data in ways that consumers will understand. When high stakes (e.g., rewards or sanctions for districts or schools) are attached to assessments, there are increased incentives to exclude students with disabilities when reporting test performance.

Debate About State Standards and How to Assess Progress Relative to Them

All states except Iowa have specified standards (sometimes these are called outcomes, goals, or essential elements) for student performance. And most states are engaged in developing or using assessments to measure student progress relative to standards. About half of the states indicate that their standards are for all students, including students with disabilities. There are major differences in the breadth of state standards, and these differences affect how the performance and progress of students with disabilities are measured. For example, one state may indicate that upon completion of schooling, students will demonstrate math skills at a level two years beyond ninth-grade algebra, while another may specify that students will demonstrate math skills necessary to be successful in their next environment. Many students with disabilities will take a long time to demonstrate math skills two years beyond ninth-grade algebra. On the other hand, we can measure the extent to which all students with disabilities demonstrate the math skills necessary to be successful in their next environment (postsecondary education, employment in a restaurant, etc.).

States differ in how they measure progress toward meeting standards. In some states, standards for performance at school completion are set, and the progress of schools or districts is measured relative to improvement toward these long-term standards. In other states, the performance of districts or schools is measured at a common point in time, and then performance is measured by assessing a percentage of improvement over this baseline performance.

SUMMARY

Assessment is a process of collecting data for the purpose of making decisions about students. Because many important decisions are made using assessment information, there is considerable controversy about the administration, scoring, interpretation, and use of assessment information. One of the major issues in assessment is a failure to differentiate assessment practices as a function of the kind of decision one is making. Put another way, people try too often to use the same kinds of assessment information to make many different kinds of decisions. In this chapter we described issues that arise when assessment information is used to make classroom and entitlement decisions, and issues that arise when assessment information is used to make accountability decisions.

Discussion Questions

1. Describe briefly the kinds of assessment information that would be needed for purposes of making a decision about whether or not a student is eligible for special education services. Describe the kinds of data that would be needed to decide what to teach a student with disabilities. How would the processes of collecting these data differ?

2. What is the difference between curriculum-based assessment and norm-referenced assessment?

3. How has the push for accountability influenced assessment practices?

4. Obtain a copy of a newspaper article or magazine article on the results of educational testing. What kinds of statements are made about the performance of students? What data are used to support the statements?

Chapter 7
Issues in Instruction

We evaluate the progressivism of a public school system by the number of new things it is doing, rather than concerning ourselves with whether it is doing any of them well.

—Trachtman, 1981

W hat is special about special education? Do students who are exceptional require instruction that is different from that received by students who are not considered exceptional? Who is responsible for teaching and who is best equipped to teach students with special needs? Do students who are exceptional profit from instruction only when it is delivered by teachers who are specifically trained to teach them? What should be the content of instruction for children and youths with disabilities? These and other instructional issues are addressed in this chapter.

Despite considerable disagreement over what should be taught in schools, there is a national consensus that the primary function of schools is to teach students. Thus, educators develop curricula with the general goal of educating all students to their maximum potential, and the curricula are typically designed to meet the assumed capabilities of the majority of students. Because schools are organized according to the students' age or grade, a general core curriculum is made up for each grade. It is the responsibility of the school personnel to adapt these core curricula according to the appropriate emphases for all or for select groups of students. Students who fail to profit from the core curricula developed for their ages and grades are given special or remedial interventions. Those who learn more rapidly than we would expect are given enrichment or provided with service for students who are gifted and talented.

The critical issues in special and remedial instruction are reviewed in this chapter. We begin with a review of alternative perspectives on the reasons for student failure in school and the relationship between causes of disability because the views people hold about the causes of failure and disability affect the instructional interventions they design. We consider the factors that influence the design of interventions and review ways in which treatment decisions are made. We describe the knowledge base on effective instruction, describe competing perspectives on what works in special education, and analyze views on ascertaining the extent to which interventions are effective.

THE RELATIONSHIP OF VIEWS ON CAUSALITY TO TREATMENT APPROACHES

Significant numbers of students fail to profit from the experiences they receive in general education. Educators develop remedial or compensatory interventions or provide alternative schooling for students who fail to profit. The nature of these interventions is very often a direct function of the views that educators hold on the causes of failure.

Differing Attributions for Failure

There are three views of the causes of failure. The first view holds that the schools are doing an inadequate, perhaps deplorable, job of educating students and indeed that the schools are not designed to teach. Baer and Bushell (1981, p. 262) developed this premise after taking a careful look at why students who are poor do not perform well in school. American public schools, they stated, direct considerable time, effort, and energy toward the following societal functions: providing day care for young children, delaying the entrance of adolescents into the labor market, posing difficult problems that children must learn to solve for themselves, and sorting and sifting children into different social positions according to how well they teach themselves to solve academic problems.

The Research and Policy Committee of the Committee for Economic Development took a similar position in its report *The Unfinished Agenda: A New Vision for Child Development and Education*. In that report the committee stated, "Our society has undergone profound economic and demographic transformations, but the social and educational institutions that prepare children to become capable and responsible adults have failed to keep pace" (1991, p. 1).

The second view argues that the schools are designed to teach, that teachers are prepared to do an adequate job of teaching, but that many students simply have too many defects, deficiencies, or disabilities to profit from instruction. These educators contend that students enter school with so many deficiencies that the schools can hardly be expected to overcome them. They maintain that the home situations from which such students come are so problematic that they make it impossible for the students to learn.

The third view attributes student failure to a combination of internal constraints, external pressures, and unattainable objectives in other words, the schools are being asked to do too much. Given the nonoperational nature of many educational goals (for example, to develop self-realization) and society's unwritten goals (for example, to eradicate poverty), the argument says that it is impossible to demonstrate how many, if any, students achieve them. Broudy (1978), for example, noted that education cannot possibly eradicate poverty, unemployment, and war; most people agree with this appraisal of what education can do.

Despite the identification of these three explanations for failure, most educators attribute failure to deficiencies in the students and/or their home environments. In 1979 the research staff of the National Education Association conducted a poll that asked teachers why children did poorly in school. Of the responses, 81 percent blamed the students' home lives, and 14 percent blamed the students themselves; only 1 percent attributed the cause to teachers, and 4 percent blamed the schools. Thus, a total of 95 percent of teachers blamed the students' poor performance on either the students themselves or the students' home lives.

Differing Views on the Causes of Disability

In a survey of assessment and intervention practices for students with disabilities, Quay (1973) said that these practices varied according to the educators' views regarding the causes of disability conditions. He broke these causal explanations down into four general categories: process dysfunctions, experiential defects, experiential deficits, and interaction.

Process dysfunctions   The many educators who believe that the causes of failure reside within the students themselves generally attribute school problems and failure to either process dysfunctions or experiential defects. Quay (1973) described the process dysfunction view as a belief that problems in sensory acuity (for example, deafness), response capability (for example, motoric responses), or internal processes (for example, short attention span, poor visual sequential memory) are the reasons for students' academic difficulties. In this view, process dysfunctions are either expressed (for example, deafness or blindness) or implied (for example, minimal brain dysfunction.) Until recently, many believed that process dysfunctions were unremediable and that they either had to be compensated for or bypassed (for example, teaching deaf students to use manual communication). Since the early 1950s, there have been extensive efforts in special education to remediate certain process dysfunctions (for example, perceptual-motor or psycholinguistic deficits) or symptoms of process dysfunctions (for example, inadequate eye-hand coordination).

Mann traced early views about processes and process dysfunction to the early writings of the Greeks, who attributed specific functions, or appetites (for example, practical, vegetative, speculative, mechanical, and intellectual), to the soul. These functions or appetites were believed to guide behavior. According to Mann:

> Behavioral or psychological processes are, whatever their validity, hypothetical "inner" events or entity constructs. They are usually used to explain behavior, i.e., presumed to cause behavior. While there is nothing that precludes process theorists from identifying their processes with numerical codes, say, 45D, they have usually chosen to name their constructs in a commonsense way—as would the man on the street; the name of a process is usually assigned to it on the basis of the behavior it is presumed to generate. "Intelligent behavior" is the result of intelligence. "Remembering" is brought about by memory; we "perceive' with our perceptual abilities. The famed Roman medical authority Galen (130–200) noted a given faculty "exists only in relation on its own effect.". . . Earlier, Aristotle had attempted a similar operational definition: "Mind must be related to what is thinkable as sense is to what is sensible." Frostig similarly defined perceptual processes, centuries later. (1979, p. 14)

Early thinking about the causes of conditions now associated with special education can be seen in Howe's attribution of idiocy to the violation of natural laws:

> Idiocy is found in all civilized countries, but it is not an evil necessarily inherent in society; it is not an accident; and much less it is a special dispensation of Providence; to suppose it can be so, is an insult to the Majesty of Heaven. No! It is merely the result of a violation of natural laws, which are simple, clear, and beautiful; which require only to be seen to be known, in order to be loved; and which, if strictly observed for two or three generations, would totally remove from any family, however strongly predisposed to insanity or idiocy, all possibility of its recurrence. (1848, p. 2)

Mann described process training activity as follows:

> During the decade leading up to America's bicentennial, there was a process explosion as new areas of psychological investigation proliferated. Witness Neisser's (1967) list of cognitive processes. The visual area includes transient iconic memory, verbal coding, perceptual set, span of apprehension, displacement and rotation in pattern recognition, backward masking, template matching, decision time, visual search, feature analysis, focal attention, preattentive control, figural synthesis, echoic memory, filtering, and perceptual defense. In the auditory area, Neisser lists segmentation, auditory synthesis, recoding, slotting, decay, linguistics, gestalts, and grammatical structure. (Mann, 1979, p. 14)

People who believe that exceptionality is caused by process dysfunctions search for the causes of disorders by studying heredity, nutrition, biochemistry, brain function, and so on (Ullman & Krasner, 1969). To them, remediation is dependent on advances to biochemistry, physiology, pharmacology, and genetic engineering.

Educators have spent a considerable amount of time, effort, and money developing instructional interventions to remediate process dysfunctions. They designed remedial programs to alleviate or ameliorate visual-perceptual, auditory-perceptual, and psycholinguistic deficits, believing that such deficits caused academic difficulties and that children would not (indeed, could not) learn to read, write, and compute until such presumed deficits were overcome. Nevertheless, the history of such efforts consists of a set of pretty dismal findings. Educators have been unable to demonstrate that remediation of process deficits or dysfunctions leads to improved school performance. Those who have reviewed the research on process training or ability training have concluded that there is little empirical evidence to support the efficacy of these practices (Arter & Jenkins, 1977; Ysseldyke; 1973; Ysseldyke & Marston, 1990).

Educators often rely on medical findings to create still other interventions. Evidence suggesting the importance of nutrition to development and learning led to the establishment of school lunch programs, breakfast programs, and vitamin therapy. An entire industry has grown up and prospered in response to the belief and evidence that some conditions of behavioral deviance result from abnormal levels of specific body chemicals.

Mann received the history of efforts to identify and train processes or abilities. He summarized the repeated return to process deficits to explain learning or behavior problems. Mann stated that

> processes come and go; they are evoked or evolved to explain phenomena of interest and then discarded to die or disappear if no one any longer cares about the phenomena they "explain." They are often absorbed into other, newer processes or assume new names according to the changing times or fashions. Frequently they are reinterpreted and given new meanings. Many of the old processes are no longer with us. Where have they gone? Where were the newest of today's processes when we needed them years ago. (Mann, 1979, p. 14)

The idea that academic problems are caused by process dysfunctions leads educators either to give up on efforts to resolve problems (as when educators abandon the education of children who demonstrate cognitive deficits in the belief that intelligence is innate) or to design and implement remedial interventions to alleviate unseen but assumed dysfunctions (for example, visual sequential memory deficits).

Experiential defects   The view that exceptionality is caused by defective experience has led to the investigation of emotional disturbance; these investigations are replete with examples of situations in which researchers hypothesize that "deleterious early experiences (e.g., overinhibition of a child's behavior) produce conditions within the child (e.g., fear and anxiety) that interfere with learning" (Quay, 1973, p. 166). People who ascribe to this view do recognize that certain process dysfunctions or defects (for example, minimal brain dysfunction) exist, but they regard these dysfunctions as the result of experiential defects. Entire special education remedial programs have been developed on the presumption that defective experience (for example, failing to creep and crawl appropriately) causes brain dysfunction and results in academic difficulties. The programs are designed to undo the harm caused by the defective experience.

Experiential deficits   The view that educational difficulties are the result of deficient, rather than defective, experiences arises from the belief that although students have an intact learning apparatus, they have limited behavioral repertoires, which create difficulties. Much has been written on the "disadvantaged" or the "deprived" child and on the effects of deficient early experience on later intellectual, academic, and social development. Educators today believe that deficient experience is a major cause of school difficulties. The Research and Policy Committee of the Committee for Economic Development indicated that "when multiple risk factors, such as poverty, family structure, and race are taken into account, as many as 40 percent of all children may be considered disadvantaged" (1991, p. 3). Whiteman and Deutsch described the view that experiential deficits cause difficulties as follows:

> The child from a disadvantaged environment may have missed some of the experiences necessary for developing verbal, conceptual, attentional, and learning skills requisite to school success. These skills play a vital role for the child in his understanding of the language of the school and the teacher, in his adapting to school routines, and in his mastery of such a fundamental tool subject as reading. (1968, p. 97)

In this view, the locus of the problem is outside the student; even when teachers view the problem as within the student, they consider it caused by outside factors. That is, the student's deviant social behavior, limited vocabulary, and limited reading skills, for instance, are caused by deficient experience and environmental disadvantages. This view is often called the sociological perspective because various social explanations for the development and existence of deviant behavior has been proposed. Each explanation points to rules of social conditions as the source of the problem. For example, social disorganization theory emphasizes differences among communities as the basis for differing levels of abnormal behavior. Levy and Rowitz (1973) reported that the highest rates of mental illness are found in cities' central sections and that the crime rate is likely to be higher in disorganized than in organized communities. Other sociological theorists believe that deviance or dullness is learned through association with deviant or dull people. Proponents of such cultural transmission theories were influential in the early history of American education.

When academic and social problems, school failure, declining achievement, and high dropout rates are viewed as the result of deficient experience, the people holding this view too often limit their explanations to out-of-school environments. As we observed earlier, 95 percent of the teachers who responded in a recent survey attributed problems to home environments and to the children themselves. Nevertheless, more and more blame is now being placed on the schools.

Interaction   The view that disorders or disabilities may result from the interaction of process dysfunctions, experiential defects, and experiential deficits (including inadequate teaching) has yielded a closer look at the selective, rather than the general, effects of both nature and environment. Sarason and Doris, for example, stated, "Not all abusive parents abuse all of their children, and not all parents with characteristics of abusive parents have abused their children" (1979, p. 21). Likewise, referrals for psychological evaluations occur at varying rates for children with similar and different characteristics, children who exhibit the same behaviors often do not receive the same school experiences, and problem behaviors occur in normal as well as deviant children. Sarason and Doris suggested that a "transactional approach" (Sameroff & Zax, 1973) may be useful in explaining such outcomes:

> [From the transactional perspective,] heredity and environment are never dichotomous. It can even be misleading to say they "interact" because that is more often than not interpreted in terms of heredity on environment just as for so long we have paid attention to the effects of parents on children and virtually ignored the influence of children on parents. The transactional approach is always a two-way street. There is nothing in the transactional formulation that denies the existence and influence of genetic processes or the existence of a socially structured context populated by diverse people. (Sarason & Doris, 1979, p. 25)

A similar transactional, or ecological, perspective was suggested by Rhodes (1967, 1970) to explain disturbance. Algozzine, Schmid, and Mercer described this theory as follows:

> Ecological theorists believe that deviance is as much a function of where and with whom a child interacts as it is the nature of the interaction in terms of behaviors which are exhibited by the child . . . ; to these theorists emotional disturbance is in the "eye of the beholder" and is generated or develops when an individual's

behavior is viewed as disturbing or bothersome by others with whom interaction occurs. Deviance, then, is as much a function of reactions to behavior as it is the behavior in and of itself. (1981, p. 168)

An interesting application of ecological theory was suggested by Sarason and Doris in their discussion of iatrogenic retardation:

To the extent that it is appropriate to view the common school as a prescribed cure for the ills of society, we maintain that a considerable proportion of mental retardation encompassed by the term "educably retarded" can be viewed as an iatrogenic disease. By that we mean, just as the administration of certain medications in the treatment of physical disease can cause the appearance of new disease related to the nature of the medication and to the patient's idiopathic response to it, irrespective of its effect upon the original disorder for which it was prescribed, so, in like manner, a considerable part of the problem of educably retarded children derives from the way in which we have devised our educational system. To the extent that we have ignored cultural differences, differences in patterns and tempos of learning, social and affective differences in the temperaments of children, to the extent that we have set goals of achievement for individual children that are either unrealistically high or low, we have ensured the development of that educationally disordered child, with cognitive and social handicaps, that we relegate to the special classroom.

This is not to deny a continuum of competence that may be based on genetic and environmental factors acting together and independent of the educational environment in which society attempts to develop and measure competence. It is to state that the continuum of competence, cognitive and social, existing prior to entry into school becomes distorted by the very system that society has devised for the development and measurement of competence. And that the distortion is of such a nature that individual and social and ethnic class differences interact with the categorical rigidities of curriculum, methods of instruction, and administrative organization to sort out the children not solely in terms of the constitutional and environmentally determined differences existing prior to school entry, but to a large extent independently of such preschool individual differences. (1979, pp. 154–155)

From this point of view, retardation is not simply the consequence of the child's nature or the school's environment; rather, it is the product of transactions between the child's characteristics and school environments, each in response to the other.

Factors That Influence Intervention Decisions

Educators decide to use certain interventions because they believe these interventions will improve students' academic and/or social functioning. No food and drug administration controls this process: any intervention can be used by anyone, and interventions are selected and used as a result of a "bandwagon effect," tradition, cash validity, a "doctor-tested" claim, research findings, or for no known reason.

Bandwagon effect   The bandwagon effect is probably more often the source of special and remedial interventions than any other base.

> The bandwagon effect, wherein an idea or a cause suddenly becomes popular and gains momentum rapidly, may not have been invented in this country, but we have surely perfected it. Our propensity for faddism extends from diets, fashions, and games to major political, educational, or sociological movements. We also tend frequently to be more concerned with the appearance of things than with the substance of things. This is the issue of form versus content. Thus, I wrote elsewhere, "we live in a society which tends to evaluate its devoutness by counting the number of people who go to church rather than the number of people who believe in God. We promote university professors on the basis of the number of publications they have authored, with little consideration for the quality of contents. We evaluate the progressivism of a public school system by the number of new things it is doing, rather than concerning ourselves with whether it is doing any of them well."
> . . . The form versus content issue interacts with the bandwagon effect to produce hastily conceived, poorly implemented innovations or programs, the failure to achieve anticipated goals, and consequent disillusionment with the original idea, or backlash. In turn, backlash may lead to equally precipitous abandonment of meritorious programs and ideas which have not been adequately conducted or sufficiently tried. This situation establishes a state of readiness for the next bandwagon and places us constantly at the mercy of what Hyman (1979, p. 1024) called the panacea mongers. (Trachtman, 1981, pp. 140–141)

Parents have been instrumental in encouraging, and indeed sometimes nearly forcing, educators to get on a variety of bandwagons. To strengthen the bandwagon, parents form clubs or organizations to popularize, promote, and push specific treatments or interventions, and in the process of doing so they push educators to adopt the interventions. Educational fads come and go and are usually adopted with no regard for the empirical evidence of their effectiveness. Then each in turn is replaced by a new, equally untested fad.

Tradition and precedent   In special and remedial education, many practitioners choose to use specific interventions either because of tradition ("We've always done it this way") or because of history ("The treatment worked before"). Some educators employ the same intervention with all students who have academic and social problems simply because they have always used it, and others prescribe a program just because it once worked for another student.

Cash validity   Many educational interventions are adopted because they have "cash validity"—that is, they sell well. Just as school systems use specific group tests because other school districts use them, personnel select interventions because they can be sold. This is one way that bandwagons begin rolling.

Unfortunately, when there is little information on how to treat specific educational difficulties and parents and teachers are looking for simple solutions to complex problems, the environment is ripe for someone to come up with a panacea. Thus, because their developers are looking for profits, many instructional interventions are developed and marketed with no evidence of their effectiveness. Lynn illustrated cash validity by using a statement attributed to Mel Levine:

> I would like to call Doubleday and have them come over here, tell them I'm a Harvard professor and that I've found out, from seeing lots and lots of patients, that air pollution causes learning disabilities and that I'd like to write a book about it. I could have that book done in a few months' time, full of anecdotal evidence about how it hits the kid nearest the city, or tell stories about a kid who lived near a factory and when he moved there his schoolwork got worse, and when he moved away it got better and how that got me thinking. . . .
>
> This book would sell a million copies.
>
> I would then go to Arthur D. Little, which is a consulting firm, to see what they could do about designing me a mask for kids to wear that will filter the air they breathe. Let them design that mask for me, put activated charcoal in the mask so they'll breathe pure air, and then sell these for $15.95 each—you can send away for them—to parents of LD children.
>
> I'll say have them wear the mask at least eight hours a day; kids will go to school with their masks on. I'll have a following around the country—the "Levine Dyslexia Society." It will be extraordinary, with parents who can provide abundant testimony as to how their child's whole life was changed when they started using the Levine method. I'll be famous; I'll get on the "Today" show with my mask; and I'll continue to make money because we'll patent it and sell replacement cartridges that you have to get for $6.95 every six months.
>
> No problem. It will be antitechnological, which is in the spirit of the times; antiauthoritarian (it's those big boards of directors that are poisoning our kids' brains). . . . I'll guarantee you that my air pollution idea will come up within the next three or four years. (1979, pp. 116–117)

Interestingly, Levine may have shown considerable foresight, as we note that residents of the Three Mile Island region in Pennsylvania have claimed that the leakage of the Three Mile Island nuclear power plant may be affecting the learning and behavior of youngsters in that region.

"Doctor tested"   A well-known remedy for hemorrhoids has been advertised as "doctor tested, found effective in many cases." Other medical products use slogans like "Four out of five doctors surveyed recommend. . . ." Of course, such statements do not provide evidence of the effectiveness of a product; they merely try to convince consumers that if a product is doctor tested and used or recommended by a physician, then it is something the consumer should buy. Educators have used many interventions simply because they were "doctor tested"—that is, their use was urged, and no evidence for their effectiveness was provided.

Research   Decisions to use particular interventions should be based on evidence that they are effective. Unfortunately, there are few research findings to support specific interventions. Joyce and Weil stated:

> There have been several hundred studies comparing one general teaching method to another, and the overwhelming portion of these studies, whether curriculums are compared, specific methods for teaching specific subjects are contrasted, or different approaches to counseling are analyzed, show few if any differences between approaches. Although the results are very difficult to interpret, the evidence to date gives no encouragement to those who would hope that we have identified a single, reliable, multipurpose strategy that we can use with confidence that it is the best approach. (1972, p. 4)

Since the days of this 1972 argument, educators have continued to learn that no single approach is always effective with all students (Reschly & Ysseldyke, 1995).

Although we do not have evidence that specific curricula are universally effective, many data support the contention that interventions must be designed for the individual and must be monitored frequently to ensure their effectiveness. Intervention is equivalent to research and is therefore a process of hypothesis testing:

> At the present time we are unable to prescribe specific and effective changes in instruction for individual pupils with certainty. Therefore, changes in instructional programs which are arranged for an individual child can be treated only as hypotheses which must be empirically tested before a decision can be made on whether they are effective for that child. (Deno & Mirkin, 1977, p. 11)

HOW TREATMENT DECISIONS ARE MADE

Those who teach students must decide what to teach. In doing so, they design treatments and decide what the content of instruction will be. These decisions often generate controversies, as do curriculum overload and the use of aversive treatments.

Derivation of Interventions

Any discussion of the critical issues in intervention should start by analyzing the assumptions underlying intervention and the many ways in which educators conceptualize the purposes of intervention. Cromwell, Blashfield, and Strauss (1975) described assessment and intervention as parts of an ongoing process and identified four categories of diagnostic and intervention data, which they labeled A, B, C, and D. Category A consists of historical and/or etiological information, the precursors of currently observed behavior or characteristics (for example, phenylketonuria as a precursor of mental retardation). Category B is made up of data on currently assessable pupil characteristics (for example, "intelligence" or skill in adding single-digit numbers). Category C refers to specific treatments or interventions (or levels of such), and category D comprises the outcomes that result from particular interventions. Use of these four categories enables the interrelations of historical-etiological information, currently assessable pupil characteristics, specific interventions, and the outcomes of those interventions to be examined. The assessment-intervention paradigms proposed by Cromwell, Blashfield, and Strauss are sketched in Table 7.1.

The conceptualization of assessment-intervention programs is useful because it helps to describe the current interventions used in special and remedial instruction and it helps to differentiate valid from invalid assessment-intervention approaches. According to Cromwell and his colleagues, assessment-intervention approaches that include both C and D data (ACD, BCD, CD, and ABCD) are valid because they include treatments on the basis of known outcomes. The three approaches that do not pertain to interventions (AD, BD, and ABD) are not useful in helping to establish a science of instruction. Four approaches (AB, AC, BC, and ABC) have little value for the educator because they describe relationships among historical-etiological data, pupil characteristics, and treatments but pay no attention to the outcomes of differential treatment. Many instructional interventions (AC, BC, and ABC) now used in schools are invalid, assigning students to interventions or treatments with no evidence of their effectiveness or outcomes.

Mercer and Ysseldyke (1977) described five models used by educators in developing interventions: medical, social system (deviance), psychoeducational process, task analysis, and pluralistic. These models are helpful in considering the kinds of instructional interventions employed in schools, and they are outlined in Table 7.2.

Each of the five models has a different definition of abnormality, or perception of deviance from "normal" behavior. In the medical and psychoeducational process models, disorders are traced to pupil disease or dysfunction. Normality is defined as the absence of disease or dysfunction and abnormality as the presence of pathology or process ability deficits. In the other three models, abnormality is traced to environmental (including school) influences on the student. In the social system model, abnormal behavior is perceived as behavior that deviates from society's expectations. In the task analysis model, normal, or abnormal behavior is not defined but is viewed as normal or abnormal only in accordance with the context in which it occurs. In this model, "abnormality is the sort of deviance that calls for and sanctions the professional attention of psychiatrists, clinical psychologists and other 'mental health' professionals" (Ullman & Krasner, 1969, p. 1).

The models for perspectives on intervention programs differ in their assumptions of what causes difficulty and thus lead to the design of different interventions. The medical model views symptoms, difficulties, or problems as originating in the individual's biological condition. The psychoeducational process model sees difficulties as the direct result of underlying process dysfunctions. The social system model assumes that normality and abnormality are role and system specific. The task analysis model views academic performance as the function of an interaction between the particular set of background experiences an individual brings to the learning setting and the demands of the tasks he or she is asked to perform.

TABLE 7.1	**ABCD Assessment-Intervention Paradigms**

Paradigm	Nature of the Paradigm
AB	Describes relationships between historical events or etiologies and current pupil characteristics or behaviors without considering treatment or its outcomes.
AC	Describes relationships between historical events or etiologies and particular treatments or interventions without considering pupil characteristics or treatment outcomes.
AD	Links generalized outcomes to etiology without considering differences among pupils or treatments
ABC	Plans interventions for students according to their history-etiology and current characteristics without evidence of the effectiveness of the outcomes
ABCD	Prescribes treatments with known outcomes or effects according to etiology and current pupil characteristics
BC	Assigns pupils to treatments according to their current characteristics without evidence regarding known treatment outcomes
BCD	Assigns pupils to interventions with known outcomes on the basis of their current characteristics without considering the etiology or historical development of their conditions
CD	Describes relationships between treatments and outcomes without considering etiology or current characteristics
BD	Investigates relationships between student characteristics and instructional outcomes without considering the etiology of the characteristics or the differences in treatment programs

SOURCE: Adapted from Cromwell, R. L., Blashfield, R. K., & Strauss, J. S. (1975). Criteria for Classification Systems. In N. Hobbs (Ed.), *Issues in the Classification of Children: A Sourcebook on Categories, Labels, and Their Consequences.* Vol. 1. San Francisco: Jossey-Bass.

In terms of interventions, proponents of the medical model design interventions to treat the biological organism; when disorders cannot be treated by medical (pharmacological or surgical) intervention, educational programs are designed to compensate for or bypass them. Those who support the social system model and who believe that specific behaviors are abnormal only in that they deviate from role or system expectations design treatments to teach students

TABLE 7.2   Different Assessment Models

Elements of the Models	Medical Model	Social System (Deviance) Model	Psychoeducational Process Model	Task Analysis Model	Pluralistic Model
Definition of abnormal	Presence of biological symptoms of pathology.	Behavior that violates social expectations for specific role.	Psychoeducational process and/or ability deficits.	No formal definition of normal or abnormal. Each child is treated relative to him- or herself and not in reference to a norm.	Poor performance when sociocultural bias controlled.
Assumptions	Symptoms caused by biological condition. Sociocultural background not relevant to diagnosis and treatment.	Multiple definitions of normal are role and system specific. Biological causation not assumed.	Academic difficulties are caused by underlying process and/or ability deficits. Children demonstrate ability strengths and weaknesses. Processes or abilities can be reliably and validly assessed. There are links between children's performance on tests and the relative effectiveness of different instructional programs.	Academic performance is a function of an interaction between enabling behaviors and the characteristics of the task. Children demonstrate more strengths and weaknesses in skill development. There is no need to deal with presumed causes of academic difficulties. There are skill hierarchies; development of complex skills is dependent upon adequate development of lower-level enabling behaviors.	Learning potential similar in all racial-cultural groups. Tests measure learning and are culturally biased.
Nature of treatments or interventions	Treat biological organism. ABCD-type constructs.	Teach child socially expected behaviors. BCD- and BD-type constructs.	Compensatory or remedial ability training. BD-type constructs.	Test-teach-test. Teach enabling behaviors. BC(D)-type constructs.	Nonspecific estimate of performance level. ABD- and BD-type constructs.

SOURCE: Reprinted with permission from J. Mercer & J. E. Ysseldyke (1977). Designing Diagnostic-Intervention Programs. In T. Oakland (Ed.), *Psychological and Educational Assessment of Minority Children.* New York: Brunner/Mazel.

socially expected behaviors. Advocates of the psychoeducational process model design interventions to remediate or compensate for underlying causes (process dysfunctions) of behavior; treatment consists of ability training. The task analysis model emphasizes the teaching of enabling skills, which are subskills necessary to perform more complex behavior.

The perspectives or models of the assessment-intervention process formulated by Cromwell and his colleagues, Mercer and Ysseldyke, and Quay have much in common, and all can be used to analyze the assessment-intervention process and to better understand the interventions used in schools. At issue is the extent to which the alternative approaches have merit and whether schools ought to subscribe to instructional approaches for which there is limited empirical support.

Willingness to Provide Instruction

Perhaps the most fundamental issue in instruction of students with disabilities is the issue of teacher responsibility for instruction. Even though it would be easy to argue that no one wants to teach students with disabilities, this is an overstatement. Both general and special education teachers do want to assume responsibility for teaching certain kinds of students with disabilities, yet at the same time there are some students whom no one wants to teach. Ysseldyke and Algozzine (1995) argued that no one wants to teach difficult-to-teach students. Braaten, Kauffman, Braaten, Polsgrove, and Nelson (1988) argued that only some students with behavior disorders are the responsibility of general education teachers, whereas others are the responsibility of special educators.

Many factors influence teachers' perceptions of responsibility for providing instruction. Among these are the nature of the disability, the presumed cause of the condition, teacher expectations, presumed impact on other students, and the severity of the student's difficulties.

Nature of the Disability

Some disabilities are more acceptable than others to all teachers. Yet there is evidence to suggest that teachers differ in the kinds of students they like to teach and/or will tolerate. At the same time, the stimulus properties of conditions vary; some characteristics are more obvious than others. For example, it is relatively easy to distinguish among racial groups in America. The differentiation is usually made on the basis of one or two obvious characteristics, such as skin color or physical features. But sorting people into groups according to disability conditions is less simple because not all people who have a disability act the same, nor are they differentiated by a simple set of features.

People behave differently toward different kinds of individuals with disabilities largely because of their own reactions to physical or behavioral features. Therefore, specific conditions seldom produce consistent reactions among all people. Some people do not like to interact with individuals who are cerebral palsied, whereas others are not bothered by that condition but prefer to associate with students who are gifted. Still others believe that their compassion for others is displayed when they have a friend who is blind or who has cerebral palsy.

Most teachers express a reluctance to teach students with behavior disorders. In major research projects in which we have tried to integrate into general education students with disabilities, general education teachers have told us that they "should not have to tolerate the crap they take from these students." We have found that teachers are more willing to assume responsibility for instructing students who are mildly mentally retarded, who evidence mild learning problems, or who evidence physical disabilities. They are willing to assume responsibility for educating students with sensory impairments provided they do not have to make major modifications in their lessons. One factor that influences assumption of responsibility for instruction and willingness to have exceptional students in the class is the extent to which the teacher must personally design or redesign instruction. Many teachers indicate a willingness to integrate into their classrooms students with relatively severe physical disabilities. Yet further inspection often reveals that these kinds of students come with their own teacher or with a paraprofessional who assumes instructional responsibility. Teachers are often willing to integrate into their classes students with disabilities provided that someone else is responsible for teaching them.

Presumed Cause

The cause of the condition of exceptionality influences the actions and reactions that result from it. When reactions to categories are compared, organic impairments (those believed caused by physical ailments) are seen as more acceptable than functional impairments (those with unknown causes but obvious effects). Many teachers are more accepting of student learning problems (and more willing to work on remediating problems) if they think that the difficulties are beyond the control of—or not "the fault of"—the student. As we noted in our earlier discussion (see pages 174–183), views of causality affect treatment approaches. Some treatments are remedial (designed to remedy deficient experience); others are designed to overcome experiential defects.

Teacher Expectations

Past experiences help to form teachers' expectations about how students will act or behave. Indeed, expectations are useful for making predictions about what will happen relative to some of those experiences. The relationship between expectations and behavior is cyclical—past actions influence expectations, and expectations influence future behavior—and teachers' expectations can affect students' personal expectations for their own success or failure and, most important, for their own performance.

Teachers are willing to assume responsibility for some students but not for others. Often this assumption of responsibility for instructing students is a direct function of the teachers' expectations for the pupils' performance, expectations that result from prior experiences with similar kinds of students or from hearsay about specific students.

Presumed Impact on Other Students

Observed differences in teachers' willingness to assume responsibility for teaching students with disabilities are often a function of the teachers' beliefs about the extent to which inclusion of a student in classes will interfere with the performance of others. Teachers tell us that they are willing to assume responsibility for teaching individual students who have disabilities as long as they do not have to take time away from other "normal" students or as long as the exceptional students do not interfere with the ability of "normal" students to profit from instruction.

Severity of the Condition

The willingness of teachers to teach students with disabilities is also a function of the severity of the handicap. Some teachers prefer to instruct students with severe handicaps, others to teach students with mild handicaps. We have learned that teachers are most resistant to teaching students who are very difficult to teach, who simply do not profit from very intense instruction.

The Demand for Quick, Simple Solutions

Assumption of responsibility for instructing students is clearly the critical issue in teaching students with disabilities, but a close second place goes to the demand among educators for instant, simple, easy-to-implement solutions to incredibly complex instructional problems. The demand for instant solutions has spawned an interesting marketing enterprise around special and remedial education. Workshops and inservice training programs promise step-by-step directives, and publishers and developers claim to have *the* intervention to assist students who are disabled or failing in school. Educators have demanded, and have been provided with, *the* treatment or intervention that works and have given it widespread use without examining assumptions and/or requiring evidence of the safety or efficacy of the intervention. The professional literature in special and remedial education also publishes examples of instant, easy solutions to problems in the education of students who are disabled. A perusal of several of the most recent issues of the major professional publications in this field was revealing.

Table 7.3 lists the claims made for special and remedial education products. These are verbatim extracts from advertisements for specific instructional programs. The claims illustrate vividly the Madison Avenue approach that has come to characterize the products developed for this profession: claims are repeatedly made for a program as *the* answer, *the* solution to complex problems.

TABLE 7.3 **Claims for Specific Tests and Instructional Programs Found in Professional Journal Advertisements**

"Widely field tested and found to be effective when implemented with normal as well as handicapped and gifted students."

"_____ is the one program that works. It works for *you!* It works for pupils of *every age!*"

"_____ is the one program so thoroughly researched and concisely planned that it gives you every element you need to help pupils achieve a level of reading success never before attained."

"All instruments you'll ever need for evaluation and testing."

"Need an individual test which *quickly* provides a stable and reliable estimate of intelligence in 4 or 5 minutes per form? Has three forms?"

"For the special child you can now diagnose specific Language and Auditory Processing problems—and then prescribe the correct materials for remediation— A great help when making IEPs."

"You can teach the obese mentally retarded person to lose weight—and keep it off— in just 19 weeks."

"Our products and services help you detect the handicapped, identify their particular difficulties, and provide remedial action."

"Can your students become confident spellers in only 15 minutes per day? YES, when you fill the time with lessons from _____."

"With this text, your students will be able to identify appropriate and effective methods for helping children with emotional and behavioral problems."

PREREFERRAL INTERVENTION

Large numbers of students experience difficulty in school, and many who do are referred for psychoeducational evaluation. Educators and related-services personnel in nearly all states institute prereferral interventions to avert placement in set-aside structures for students who can profit from general education placement. According to Carter and Sugai, "The purpose of the prereferral intervention approach is to reduce the number of inappropriate special education placements while identifying interventions which will enable students to remain in the least restrictive setting, usually the regular classroom" (1989, p. 299).

The prereferral intervention model is usually an indirect form of service in which school resource personnel provide resources or assistance to classroom teachers at the point of referral to help the teachers cope with students' difficulties. Fuchs (1991) identified four characteristics of prereferral intervention. First, it is consistent with the LRE doctrine set forth in law; efforts are made to maintain the student in the least restrictive environment. Second, the model is preventive; efforts are made to prevent educational failure at the same time that personnel work to prevent more intensive treatment. Third, prereferral intervention is implemented or coordinated by one or more special service personnel working as consultants. While this typically is the case, new forms of prereferral intervention consist of groups of regular education teachers helping one another to solve problems; such efforts often come under the title of "teacher assistance teams" (Phillips & McCullough, 1989). Fourth, prereferral intervention encourages use of an ecological perspective in which problems are viewed as resulting from an interaction among the individual, instructional approaches, school organization, and home and family factors. The approach downplays a focus on student characteristics and on the assumption that school problems reside within the individual.

Fuchs also identified three factors that have led to the focus on prereferral intervention: the large increase in the number of students who are identified as disabled, the increased frequency of teacher referrals and the "arbitrariness and precipitousness of teacher referral" (1991, p. 242). In short, people attempt prereferral interventions in an effort to stem the tide of the large increase in the provision of special education services in set-aside structures.

There are many models of prereferral intervention. One of the easiest to understand and follow, and one of the few on which there are data, is the model proposed by Graden, Casey, and Bonstrom (1985). This model is shown in Figure 7.1. A carefully articulated set of steps is followed in an effort to alleviate student difficulties and prevent further failure. The important features of prereferral intervention, which have been identified by Fuchs, are illustrated in the figure and are as follows:

1. School systems interested in implementing prereferral intervention must build the activity into the job descriptions of the people they want to implement it. School personnel have other important things to do, and implementation will be facilitated (or even only accomplished) through mandate.

2. Someone must assume leadership and provide overall direction for the prereferral effort.

3. Consultants must receive adequate training in the process of consultation and in implementation of prereferral interventions.

4. The consultation process must be efficient, yet corners must not be cut.

5. The interventions used must be acceptable to classroom teachers.

6. There must be provision for ensuring the "fidelity" of the classroom interventions. Consultants must check that interventions are implemented as they were intended.

7. Data on student or teacher behavior should be collected at multiple points in the prereferral intervention process. (1991, p. 263)

FIGURE 7.1   Prereferral Intervention

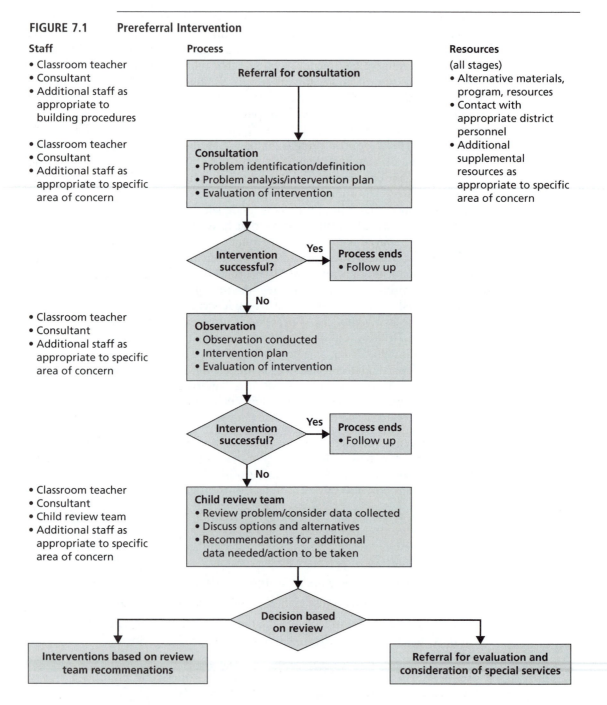

Staff
- Classroom teacher
- Consultant
- Additional staff as appropriate to building procedures

- Classroom teacher
- Consultant
- Additional staff as appropriate to specific area of concern

- Classroom teacher
- Consultant
- Additional staff as appropriate to specific area of concern

- Classroom teacher
- Consultant
- Child review team
- Additional staff as appropriate to specific area of concern

Process

Referral for consultation

Consultation
- Problem identification/definition
- Problem analysis/intervention plan
- Evaluation of intervention

Intervention successful? — **Yes** → Process ends • Follow up

No

Observation
- Observation conducted
- Intervention plan
- Evaluation of intervention

Intervention successful? — **Yes** → Process ends • Follow up

No

Child review team
- Review problem/consider data collected
- Discuss options and alternatives
- Recommendations for additional data needed/action to be taken

Decision based on review

Interventions based on review team recommenations

Referral for evaluation and consideration of special services

Resources
(all stages)
- Alternative materials, program, resources
- Contact with appropriate district personnel
- Additional supplemental resources as appropriate to specific area of concern

Prereferral intervention is catching on in most states and districts. Yet there is limited support for the practice. In those instances in which the practice has been implemented extensively, it has not always been documented and evaluated. The New Jersey Department of Education has had in place since the early 1980s a project designed to assess and improve the quality of the state's special education delivery system. In thirteen school districts, building-based, decision-making teams known as school resource committees were established in each school to strengthen the capacity of general education personnel to serve nonhandicapped students with learning problems. The state has been engaged in pilot studies of modifications to the assessment system, operation of child study teams, and modifications of eligibility criteria for special education. The outcomes of the pilot study were very positive.

Pennsylvania's Instructional Support Team (IST) Model was initiated in 1990–1991, and it is in operation in all school districts in the state. The model emphasizes collaborative consultation among general and special education staff focused on providing services to students in regular classes in their home schools.

In both Pennsylvania and the Minneapolis public schools, prereferral interventions are carried out using a systematic problem-solving approach that emphasizes (1) problem identification, clarification, and analysis; (2) intervention design and implementation; and (3) ongoing monitoring and evaluation of intervention effects. The process is databased, includes specific decision-making points, and emphasizes the use of functional and multidimensional assessment procedures.

Iowa has adopted a statewide reform effort, the Renewed Service Delivery System (RSDS), to change traditional service delivery for special education. School personnel in Iowa use a problem-solving model to define problems precisely, measure behavior directly, design interventions, and monitor student progress frequently as a function of these interventions. Use of the problem-solving model includes proceeding through the following steps (Tilly, Grimes, & Reschly, 1993, p. 12).

1. A problem-centered evaluation and a general education intervention prior to special education referral

2. A review of prereferral intervention data documenting classroom-based attempts to remediate the problem

3. A screening curriculum-based reading assessment (examining grade-level reading performance compared to typical peers)

4. A survey-level curriculum-based reading assessment (examining student skills in multiple levels of the reading curriculum)

5. A specific-level curriculum-based reading assessment (examining reading subskills and enabling skills to determine potential targets for intervention)

6. An observation/examination of the student's current reading instructional program (to determine potential contributions to student performance problems)

7. One or more systematic observations of student performance in the instructional setting during reading instruction

8. Parent, teacher, and student interviews as necessary

9. A review of the student's health, vision, hearing, and educational history

10. Participation in the design, monitoring, and evaluation of an intervention

What are the results of prereferral intervention? Graden, Casey, and Christenson (1985) reported that prereferral intervention resulted in lower referrals for testing, less testing, and fewer students placed in special education. Hartman and Fay (1996) conducted analyses to determine the cost-effectiveness of the IST model in Pennsylvania. They investigated cost-effectiveness by comparing data from the IST and traditional special education programs on effectiveness measures such as number of IST referrals, special education placements, and retentions, and personnel cost measures such as teachers' salaries and benefits. The IST did not show cost savings until the ninth year of implementation. And cost savings were not great. Hartman and Fay argue that the strength of the IST lies in providing increased and better services to more students. In the Pennsylvania IST program, many more students with learning and behavior problems were provided services than those in traditional programs.

In 1985 the Connecticut Department of Education initiated what they called Connecticut's Early Intervention Project: Alternatives to Referral. The project is designed to provide classroom-based services for at-risk students, particularly minority students, experiencing academic or behavior problems. Implementation of the model has resulted in decreased numbers of referrals for special education services and improved services in regular classrooms for students with academic and behavior problems. A minimum of 75 percent of all referrals within each building were either resolved to the teacher and team's satisfaction or continued with assistance within the regular classroom without the need to refer the student for special education evaluation. Tilly and Flugum (1995) surveyed over 2,100 Iowa educators, including special and regular education teachers, administrators, and support staff. The staff were in overwhelming agreement with the view that Iowa's RSDS has had a very positive impact.

After three years of implementing the problem-solving model in the Minneapolis public schools, Minneapolis personnel found a reduction in the numbers of African American students identified as needing special education. Yet many regular education teachers expressed dissatisfaction with the approach, indicating that it relieved burdens for special education teachers and shifted those burdens to regular education teachers. The teachers also indicated that they did not have the time to systematically implement and frequently evaluate a set of interventions.

It looks like the primary benefit of prereferral intervention is improved educational results for larger numbers of students in regular education settings and some reduction in placement of students in set-aside structures. Economic benefits are difficult to demonstrate. Gersten, Vaughn, Deshler, and Schiller (1997) indicate that

[u]nlike medicine, education has no "magic bullets," no chemical cures that destroy micro-organisms and eradicate problems. However, education does have documented instructional practices that enhance students' educational outcomes, just as there are health routines that enhance physical outcomes. (p. 466)

Do We Know What Works?

Appropriate intervention is the "bottom line" in the delivery of services to students with disabilities. Students are assessed for purposes of planning appropriate interventions, they are placed in settings where they will be taught appropriately, and the extent to which they are receiving appropriate instructional interventions is evaluated. Funds are made available for special education so that students may receive appropriate instruction, and laws are enacted to ensure appropriate instruction. Indeed, educators, related-services personnel, and policy makers have spent more time, effort, and energy trying to ensure appropriate assignment to settings and programs than teaching students.

Even though the profession does know which factors enhance the effectiveness of instruction, no one can say with assurance that specific instructional practices will work with all students. Because intervention effectiveness depends on the complex interaction of numerous variables, only a few of which are under the control of the teacher, education is necessarily experimental: educators must form hypotheses for what will work with students, teach in accordance with those hypotheses, and then continually evaluate the effectiveness of the interventions.

Research data on the characteristics of effective reading programs help to identify those factors that interact to determine the effectiveness of any instructional intervention. After an extensive review of the characteristics of successful reading programs, Samuels noted that the difference was greater in administrative arrangements than in curricular methodology and that successful programs differed from unsuccessful ones in their underlying assumptions. Successful programs assumed that "the school *can* have a significant impact on the academic achievement of its students" and that "most children are capable of mastering the basic skills" (1981, p. 2). These assumptions placed the responsibility for student failure on the school. This is not the prevailing mood of the day.

In terms of personnel characteristics, successful programs had strong administrative leaders who provided "time for planning and carrying out decisions, securing financial support, and running interference against counterforces" (p. 4). They also employed teacher aides in direct instruction and reading specialists who worked with teachers and aides to assist them in planning instruction. According to Samuels, the teacher's attitude was critical to success. He found that successful programs were consistently staffed by teachers who, because they were committed, dedicated, and supportive of project goals, devoted considerable time and energy to achieving project goals. They believed that student success and failure depended on what happened in the classroom.

Furthermore, successful reading programs were characterized by practical training and supervision in which regular staff meetings focused on actual problems. Teachers were given the opportunity to observe and model other successful teachers and programs, and they participated in decision making.

Samuels reported that successful reading programs had clearly stated and specific goals and objectives and that the most successful programs used a task analysis (direct instruction) approach as well as creating a warm, friendly classroom atmosphere. These programs emphasized teaching of skills, gave students opportunities to practice those skills, and used instruction and instructional materials relevant to the attainment of the objectives.

Successful programs also provided ample time for instruction, and that time was used efficiently. Instruction was kept at a low level of complexity. Classes were fairly structured. Teachers frequently and directly measured their pupils' progress.

Unsuccessful instructional programs, according to Samuels, were based on the bandwagon effect. The programs were developed more in response to the availability of federal funding or to parental pressure than to demonstrated need. They lacked systemwide commitment, either because they were based on "bottom-up" motivation (teachers were committed to the program, but administrators were not) or "top-down" motivation (the administrators required implementation of programs to which the teachers were not committed). Samuels felt that unsuccessful programs consistently failed to allow enough startup and development time; had narrow, piecemeal approaches; and used time inefficiently.

Samuels's points about effective interventions were made in 1981. Since then, schools have gone in hundreds of directions in efforts to prevent reading difficulties or to teach students to read. The recently published findings of a special National Academy of Sciences Committee on the Prevention of Reading Difficulties in Young Children (National Academy of Sciences, 1998) sound much like those of Samuels 17 years earlier. The committee defined reading as "a process of getting meaning from print, using knowledge about the written alphabet and about the sound structure of oral language for purposes of achieving understanding." There was general agreement among the committee members that early reading instruction should include direct teaching of information about sound-symbol relationships to children who do not know about them, and that it must also maintain a focus on the communicative purposes and personal value of reading. In addressing specifically the issue of preventing reading difficulties, the committee argued that "All children, especially those at risk for reading difficulties, should have access to early childhood environments that promote language and literacy growth and that address reading risk factors in an integrated rather than isolated fashion." The committee recommended that the following be included in home and preschool activities.

- Adult-child shared book reading that stimulates verbal interaction to enhance language (especially vocabulary) development and knowledge about print concepts

- Activities that direct young children's attention to the phonological structure of spoken words (e.g., games, songs, and poems that emphasize rhyming or manipulation of sounds)
- Activities that highlight the relationship between print and speech (p. 321)

One of the arguments we have heard repeatedly at major national conferences is that instruction for students with disabilities is difficult because no one knows what works with those students. This simply is not the case. From an extensive review of the literature in psychology and education (Christenson, Thurlow, & Ysseldyke, 1987; Christenson, Ysseldyke, & Thurlow, 1987; Thurlow, Christenson, & Ysseldyke, 1987; Thurlow, Ysseldyke, & Christenson, 1987; Ysseldyke, Thurlow, & Christenson, 1987), we have drawn several conclusions about instructional effectiveness for students with mild disabilities.

First, there is not one kind of instruction that works best in general education and another kind that works best in special education. And, there are certain instructional factors that must be present and are appropriate for individual students' needs, regardless of setting. A second conclusion is that the literature is replete with academic correlates. It is not very hard to generate a laundry list of factors related to student achievement. . . . A list of factors related to achievement is not very helpful unless it is organized into something that can be implemented by the educator. Third, student achievement is a result of interacting and mutually influencing factors, specifically student, teacher, classroom, instructional, school district, and home characteristics (Ysseldyke & Christenson, 1987, Christenson, Ysseldyke, & Thurlow, 1989).

Christenson, Ysseldyke, and Thurlow (1989) identified nine factors that are critical for student achievement. Instructional outcomes for students are enhanced when:

1. Classrooms are managed effectively.
2. There is a sense of positiveness in the school environment.
3. There is an appropriate instructional match.
4. Goals are clear, expectations are explicitly communicated, and lessons are presented clearly.
5. Students receive good instructional support.
6. Sufficient time is allocated to instruction.
7. Opportunity to respond is high.
8. Teachers actively monitor student progress and understanding.
9. Student performance is evaluated appropriately and frequently.

Algozzine and Ysseldyke published a model of effective instruction in 1992 (Algozzine & Ysseldyke, 1992), and revised it in 1998 (Algozzine, Ysseldyke, & Elliott, 1998) with publication of the second edition of *Strategies and Tactics for Effective Instruction*. The model is shown in Table 7.4. There are four components of effective instruction: planning, managing, delivering, and evaluating. For each component, there are principles of instruction that have been shown empirically to be effective. These principles are shown for each of the components. Teachers have asked us repeatedly to provide specific strategies for implementing the principles of effective instruction. Over time we have identified these strategies, and they are listed in Table 7.4. Teachers have asked us to identify specific tactics for implementing the strategies. Over time we have gathered these from

A Conceptual Framework for Effective Instruction		
Component	**Principle**	**Strategy**
Planning Instruction	Decide What to Teach	Assess to identify gaps in performance Establish logical sequences of instruction Consider contextual variables
	Decide How to Teach	Set instructional goals Establish performance standards Choose instructional methods and materials Establish grouping structures Pace instruction appropriately Monitor performance and replan instruction
	Communicate Realistic Expectations	Teach goals, objectives, and standards Teach students to be active, involved learners Teach students consequences of performance
Managing Instruction	Prepare for Instruction	Set classroom rules Communicate and teach classroom rules Communicate consequences of behavior Handle disruptions efficiently Teach students to manage their own behavior
	Use Time Productively	Establish routines and procedures Organize physical space Allocate sufficient time to academic activities
	Establish Positive Classroom Environment	Make the classroom a pleasant, friendly place Accept individual differences Establish supportive, cooperative learning environments Create a nonthreatening learning environment
Delivering Instruction	Present Information	**For Presenting Content** Gain and maintain attention Review prior skills or lessons Provide organized, relevant lessons
		For Motivating Students Show enthusiasm and interest Use rewards effectively Consider level and student interest

A Conceptual Framework for Effective Instruction (cont.)

Component	Principle	Strategy
		For Teaching Thinking Skills Model thinking skills Teach fact-finding skills Teach divergent thinking Teach learning strategies
		For Providing Relevant Practice Develop automaticity Vary opportunities for practice Vary methods of practice Monitor amount of work assigned
	Monitor Presentations	**For Providing Feedback** Give immediate, frequent, explicit feedback Provide specific praise and encouragement Model correct preformance Provide prompts and cues Check student understanding
		For Keeping Students Actively Involved Monitor performance regularly Monitor performance during practice Use peers to improve instruction Provide opportunities for success Limit opportunities for failure Monitor engagement rates
	Adjust Presentations	Adapt lessons to meet student needs Provide varied instructional options Alter pace
Evaluating Instruction	Monitor Student Understanding	Check understanding of directions Check procedural understanding Monitor student success rate
	Monitor Engaged Time	Check student participation Teach students to monitor their own participation
	Keep Records of Student Progress	Teach students to chart their own progress Regularly inform students performance Maintain records of student performance
	Use Data to Make Decisions	Use data to decide if more services are warranted Use student progress to make teaching decisions Use student progress to decide when to discontinue service

the professional literature and from teachers. *Strategies and Tactics for Effective Instruction* (Algozzine, Ysseldyke, & Elliott, 1998) is a resource containing more than 300 specific tactics that teachers can use with students who are experiencing academic difficulties and who exhibit behavior problems. STEI is accompanied by *Timesavers for Educators* (Elliott, Algozzine, & Ysseldyke, 1998), a set of reproducible worksheets and resources for implementing tactics in classrooms.

Gersten, Baker, and Pugach (1998) reviewed contemporary research on special education teaching and conducted focus group interviews with family members of students with disabilities, general and special education teachers, educators involved in training teachers, prominent educational researchers, and school psychologists. The major concerns expressed by focus group members related to academic instruction, and this included concern about effective instruction of students from culturally diverse backgrounds. Gersten et al. argued that it was very important for teachers to use multiple strategies to achieve a broad array of objectives, and they delineated occasions where intentional use of multiple strategies led to improved results and greater transfer. They also argued that it is important for schools to assist students in learning organizational skills and to teach them organizational strategies, including strategies for accomplishing both academic tasks and daily life tasks (such as remembering which books and assignments to bring home). And they argued that it is important for educators to focus instructional efforts on task persistence. They cite the work of McKinney, Osborne, and Schulte (1993) showing that task persistence is a powerful predictor of achievement for students with learning disabilities, and they suggest that findings from the research on peer-mediated instruction (Fuchs, Fuchs, Mathes, & Simmons, 1997; Greenwood et al., 1992) and socially mediated instruction (Palincsar & Klenk, 1992) are especially helpful in teaching task persistence.

WHAT IS SPECIAL ABOUT INSTRUCTION OF STUDENTS WITH DISABILITIES?

The research on effective instruction has lead us to believe that good teaching is good teaching and that there are no boundaries on where it can occur. But all teaching and teachers are not alike. Individual teachers have their own particular ways of delivering instruction, evaluating instruction, and interacting with their students. This diversity makes the field of education exciting, and it is one of the intangibles that makes teaching so rewarding.

As we have indicated in earlier chapters, there are more similarities than differences between students in special education and those in general education classes. But if students are similar, if good teaching is good teaching, and if individual teachers vary, what is special about special education?

Ysseldyke and Algozzine (1995) identified four factors that make teaching students who are exceptional different from teaching students who are not exceptional:

- Although many of their educational experiences are like those of their age-mates, students receiving special education have individualized education programs; their agemates do not.

- Some students who are exceptional have special learning needs. They receive instruction in skills that their agemates develop without special instruction.

- Although teachers in general and special education perform many of the same tasks, certain instructional methods are used more with students who are exceptional than with students who are not.

- Some students need special instructional adaptations to grow, develop, and prosper from schooling. (p. 123)

Specific individual educational plans, learning needs, methods, and instructional adaptations may be different in special education. Yet most of what we do for students with disabilities can and should occur in the general classroom as well.

Today's educators know a good deal about effective instruction. The principles of effective instruction and improved methods of teaching are being included in teacher training programs. These principles of effective instruction apply to all students—exceptional and nonexceptional. The methods we use for students who are exceptional are much the same as those we use for students who are not exceptional.

Teaching students who are exceptional is a decision-making process in which school personnel decide what to teach and how to teach, and whether adaptive devices are needed. Once these fundamental decisions are made, the principles of effective instruction come into play. Teachers still have to plan, manage, deliver, and evaluate instruction.

More than ever before, general and special education teachers are working together to accommodate students with diverse learning needs in classroom environments that are as much like normal as possible. Through combinations of individualized instruction, small- and large-group instruction, and teacher- and student-directed instruction, teachers are adapting learning experiences for all students.

Teachers are accommodating diversity by:

- Varying the amounts of instruction on the basis of individual student capabilities.

- Using modified instructional approaches, materials, and procedures to enable students to master content at paces suited to their individual capabilities and interests.

- Monitoring pupil progress and providing students with immediate feedback. Instruction is then adapted on the basis of student performance.

- Teaching students to monitor their own performance and identify modifications they need to progress satisfactorily.

- Providing students with opportunities to make choices and decisions about their learning objectives.
- Using peer teaching, in which students assist one another in mastering subject matter content.

We have been in special education for more than 25 years each. Over that time, some of our beliefs about teaching students who are exceptional have stayed the same and others have changed. We have always believed in a simple axiom: good teaching is good teaching. We think the principles of instruction are articulated more clearly today than they have ever been, and there is more and more robust research on good teaching, so we continue to hold this belief. We prefer to see the principles, strategies, and tactics of effective instruction applied in general education classes in efforts to overcome academic and behavior difficulties as a prerequisite to referring students for psychoeducational evaluation or consideration for special education services.

STRATEGY TRAINING VERSUS CONTENT INSTRUCTION

One way in which educators have attempted to intervene with students who experience failure is through training in the use of specific cognitive strategies. Even though the term *cognitive strategy training* has various meanings, Deshler and Schumaker's (1988) Strategies Intervention Model (SIM) is the approach used most often. In the SIM, general and special education teachers work cooperatively to improve the instruction of difficult-to-teach students. The general education teacher works on delivering content, while the special education teacher works on teaching students how to learn and how to succeed in the mainstream class. A number of methodologies are used to teach strategies, including cooperative group instruction, peer tutoring, special feedback systems, and visual and verbal cueing methods. (Schumaker, Deshler, & McKnight, 1991). The SIM also includes routines for teaching content, including the advance organizer routine, the concept teaching routine, the survey routine, factual enhancement routines, and integrative approaches. Some argue that even though strategy training may be effective, it is too difficult for teachers to implement. Indeed, Schumaker, Deshler, and McKnight indicated that following development of the University of Kansas Institute for Research on Learning Disabilities (KU-IRLD) strategy training interventions, classroom implementation rates were "abysmally low." In response, they began working with commercial publishers to include in teachers' manuals examples of strategies to implement and they provided inservice training to teaching staffs. They reported that

> to ensure the adoption of complex educational innovations, training must be offered over a sustained period of time rather than as a one-shot event. Sustained training efforts allow time for modeling, practice, feedback, and ques-

> tions. In addition, teachers need the opportunity to try out the new procedure . . . in their classroom and to debrief with the trainer(s) on problems encountered. Finally, following the formal training session(s), teachers must have the opportunity to receive ongoing support in their efforts to implement the new procedure. (p. 489)

The key, according to Deshler, Schumaker, and their colleagues, is effective use by mainstream teachers of a host of validated teaching routines and devices that can facilitate students' understanding and retention of content information.

ENRICHMENT, ACCELERATION, AND SEPARATION

Historically, gifted and talented students have been served through three educational approaches: enrichment, acceleration, and separation. Enrichment means enhancing the educational experiences of students without changing the setting in which they are educated. Early efforts to educate gifted and talented students consisted entirely of enrichment programs. One of the earliest was established in the Cleveland public schools in 1922; students identified as gifted or talented stayed in the regular classroom in the same grade as their agemates but were given advanced or extra work.

Today enrichment can mean more than within-class tinkering with the curriculum. Students who are gifted can attend special programs at other schools, or they can enroll early in university programs. In Minnesota, for example, the Postsecondary Enrollment Options Program enables students to attend colleges and universities for the purpose of taking advanced coursework. Others participate in after-school coursework in specific subject areas at universities and colleges or in high school settings.

Students also have been treated by acceleration, sometimes called double promotion or the skipping of a grade. Students who are gifted are also sometimes placed in self-contained classes. At issue here is the most effective way to deliver advanced, enriched instruction to students who have already demonstrated competencies that are being taught to their age-level peers in regular classrooms.

AVERSIVE TREATMENTS

The appropriateness of using aversive treatments with students who have disabilities has been a hotly debated topic in special education and one on which major organizations have taken firm positions. Some individuals and associations have argued for a moratorium on the use of behavior reduction procedures. (The Association for Persons with Severe Handicaps, 1981; Donnellan, Negri-Shoultz, Fassbendes, & La Vigna, 1988; Guess, 1988), whereas others (Council for Exceptional Children, 1990; Council for Children with Behavior Disorders,

1990; Favell et al., 1982; Martin, 1975) have argued that the judicious use of behavior reduction may be necessary or even imperative. For example, the Council for Exceptional Children has policies on physical intervention and on corporal punishment, which are as follows:

> *Physical Intervention.* The Council recognizes the planned use of aversive stimulation and negative reinforcement when these options are the treatment of choice, provided that the situations in which they are used are planned between the teacher and the teacher's supervisor, made known to the parents or guardian, applied prudently, and evaluated and modified in terms of the results. The Council also recognizes that at times staff members must physically intervene immediately in the behavior of a child to protect health, safely, or property.
>
> *Corporal Punishment.* The Council for Exceptional Children supports the prohibition of the use of corporal punishment in special education. Corporal punishment is here defined as a situation in which all of the following elements are present: An authority accuses a child of violating a rule and seeks from the child an explanation, whereupon a judgment of guilt is made, followed by physical contact and pain inflicted on the child. The Council finds no conditions under which corporal punishment so defined would be the treatment of choice in special education. (1990, Sections 8.315 and 8.316)

One of the major difficulties in the formulation of clear positions on the use of punishment or aversives, according to Skiba and Deno (1991) is that the terms have multiple meanings; are not clearly defined; and carry with them misconception, misunderstandings, and confusions. They argued for replacing the terms *punishment* and *aversive* with more value-neutral terms because doing so would lead to careful collection of data on methods of behavior reduction and use of the data to make decisions about appropriate behavior reduction procedures.

PL 105-17, passed on June 4, 1997, requires that IEP teams address student problem behaviors in a proactive manner. If a student with disabilities, regardless of the disability category, exhibits behavior that impedes his or her learning, or the learning of others, the IEP must consider positive behavior intervention, strategies, and supports to address these problems. In such situations, a positive and proactive behavior intervention plan, based on a functional assessment of behavior, should be included in the student's IEP. This requirement emphasizes the use of positive interventions to ameliorate problem behaviors.

WHY ISN'T INTERVENTION RESEARCH TRANSLATED INTO PRACTICE?

Gersten et al. (1997) indicate that "[r]esearch findings in education, as in other fields (e.g., health), are embraced by some, ignored by others, and modified to suit the routines and preferences of still others" (p. 466). In this section we describe alternative views on why instructional practices that are shown by researchers to be effective often are not implemented by classroom teachers and related-services personnel.

Some Intervention Research Was Not Done Well

As is the case for many fields, there are often major methodological flaws in research that is carried out on special education interventions. Those who study the effects of interventions often have difficulty finding and using appropriate control groups, carrying out their investigations for long enough periods of time, and demonstrating that the interventions work.

Some Intervention Research Was Not Worth Doing

Research not worth doing is not worth doing well. Many of the studies completed in special education were conceptualized inadequately and addressed unimportant topics or issues. They lead practitioners to the generalized "so what?" conclusion.

Some Intervention Research Is Based on Faulty Assumptions About Acceptability

Sashkin and Egermeier (1993) indicate that much research is based on the faulty premise that people would accept and use the techniques shown to result in improvement. And they point out that researchers often inappropriately assume that teachers can implement effective practices with few adjustments.

Inadequate Communication

Failure to communicate effectively is a factor identified by Gersten et al. (1997) as affecting implementation of research findings. They quote the following statement by Ball (1993):

> Those who would try to change what goes on in schools must figure out how to communicate about change in a way that makes sense and respects where teachers are and yet makes them realize that they are being asked to rethink what they do. (pp. 257–258)

Gersten et al. recommend that researchers deal with teachers as professionals whose knowledge and practice could inform their work rather than as "subjects" or "treatment implementers."

The Intervention Research Does Not Fit "Real" Classroom Instruction

The instructional practices that researchers recommend often do not fit the details of day-to-day practices in classrooms. Gersten and Woodward (1990) called this the "reality principle." Teachers often find themselves saying, "You have got to be kidding; there is no way I could implement this procedure, technique, or strategy in my classroom." And they are often correct.

Scope and Magnitude of the Intended Change Required by the Intervention

Gersten et al. (1997) indicate that recommendations regarding instructional change must be neither too broad nor too narrow. They indicate that sometimes researchers recommend changes in instruction that are narrow and consist of such mere tinkering that they require almost no thinking on the part of teachers. Thus the research findings are not integrated into classroom practice. And they indicate that some of the recommended instructional changes are so major that they stand no chance of being implemented. They quote McLaughlin (1990), who stated that "[p]lanned change efforts . . . need to be sufficient in scope to challenge teachers and kindle interest, but . . . not require too much too soon (p. 12).

Absence of Coaching During Implementation

In some cases, teachers implement research findings but abandon them quickly due to the absence of coaching during implementation. Schools require teachers to attend inservice workshops on research findings and expect that teachers will implement the new practices. When we want students to learn a particular practice, we usually provide them with guided practice, feedback about their performance, and then considerable independent practice. So too, we should provide teachers and related-services personnel with considerable guided practice, coaching, feedback, and independent practice as they attempt to implement interventions that have been shown to work.

Fidelity of Treatment

Some research findings fail to translate into practice because teachers do not implement techniques in the ways shown to be effective by researchers. Interventions are sometimes put into practice and shown to be ineffective. Follow-up reports then show that the interventions were not implemented in the ways researchers had intended.

Teachers Do Not See Positive Results for Their Students

Teachers will implement interventions only for a very short time if they do not see positive results for the students they teach. Gersten et al. (1997) argue that it is critical to teach teachers how to monitor the effectiveness of their efforts directly and frequently, and how to make judgments about the extent to which instructional changes are working.

Discussion Questions

1. The curriculum committee at Jefferson Elementary School has decided to adopt a new program designed specifically to remediate information-processing disabilities for students with learning disabilities and attention deficit disorders. What kinds of information would you want to see before endorsing adoption of the program?

2. Identify at least three arguments for the use of prereferral interventions prior to referring students for psychoeducational evaluation.

3. Members of the Ventura school district administration are interested in putting the latest research findings into practice in their district. Identify three actions the administrators can take to ensure that the research findings are translated correctly into practice.

Chapter 8
Early Intervention

The foundations of a better tomorrow must be laid today.

—Anonymous

Birth statistics are often a fairly good indicator of the challenges facing the special education system. Despite slight improvements during the late 1990s in commonly used risk indicators (e.g., births to teenage or single mothers, infant deaths) (Annie E. Casey Foundation, 1988c), the system remains challenged by children born with fetal alcohol syndrome and other alcohol-related birth defects, as well as by those born addicted to cocaine or those born

FIGURE 8.1   **Percent Low-Birth-Weight Babies, 1975–1995**

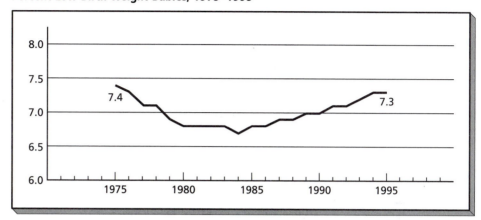

Source: Annie E. Casey Foundation (1998a). *1998 Kids Count. A Pocket Guide on America's Youth.* Baltimore, MD: Author, p.2. Reprinted by permission. Low birth-weight is defined as weighing less than 5.5 pounds at birth.

with AIDS. Medically fragile infants are surviving through extraordinary medical interventions to face life with significant mental and physical impairments. There has been a dramatic rise in multiple births (Ventura, Martin, Curtin, & Matthews, 1998) due primarily to increases in the use of fertility drugs. The number of live multiple births has increased 344 percent since 1980 (Ventura et al., 1998), which in turn is partially responsible for the rise in low-birth-weight babies (see Figure 8.1) and for greater numbers of preterm babies, another risk factor. More than 30 percent of infants in the United States were born with one or more risk factors monitored in the Children's Health Index, which includes (1) late or no prenatal care, (2) low maternal weight gain, (3) maternal smoking during pregnancy, and (4) maternal alcohol consumption during pregnancy (National Education Goals Panel, 1997).

Even children born healthy face the possibility to a greater extent than ever before of poverty, homelessness, or physical abuse. The *Leave It to Beaver* family is gone: more than half of new marriages end in divorce; approximately 15 million children live with one parent, most often the mother (National Center for Education Statistics, 1998); and over 60 percent of women with preschool children now work outside the home, compared to fewer than 40 percent in 1975 (Annie E. Casey, 1998b).

The needs of many youngsters are tremendous even before they reach the age of school attendance. For this reason, educators and policy makers see early intervention as a critical component of meeting the educational goals of this country. Recognition of early intervention's importance is implicit in the first of the national education goals: "By the year 2000, all children will start school ready to learn."

Issues in early intervention have been prevalent for some time, but they have not been as urgent as they are now. In this chapter we describe some fundamental assumptions and trace the history of early intervention, including the downward escalation of services. Issues of assessment and identification are discussed as they relate to young children with disabilities and young children who are at risk for developing disabilities. Several questions are raised about the nature of early interventions, particularly as they apply to younger and younger ages. New constituencies for early intervention are identified, and the tremendous impact of these new groups on intervention are explored.

ASSUMPTIONS OF EARLY INTERVENTION

Two fundamental assumptions—developmental plasticity and cost effectiveness—underlie early intervention for young children. Without these, there would be no reason to intervene before the school-age years.

Developmental Plasticity

From the beginning of his study of intelligence, Binet saw intelligence as something that resulted from an active transaction between the individual and external stimuli (Sarason & Doris, 1979). He viewed intelligence as educable and wrote in 1911 that the educability of intelligence was the basis for pioneering early intervention work. Early interventionists believed that "we can ameliorate, that we can alter, that we can prevent further deterioration of mental function if we start young" (Kirk, 1977, p. 4). At the foundation of all discussions of early intervention programs is the nagging issue of how much, if any, the developmental progress of a child can be changed. To the extent that development is viewed as determined by nature, the individual's behavioral and learning capacities are assumed to be inherited and unchangeable. To the extent that development is viewed as determined by nurture, the individual's behavioral and learning capacities are assumed to be malleable and changeable. When behavior is viewed as changeable, intervention for the young child makes sense. This notion of developmental plasticity is the justification for an array of early intervention programs for children with and without identified disabilities. And the assumption of developmental plasticity directs assessment of young children and the goals of intervention.

Cost Effectiveness

In addition to the belief that lifelong outcomes can be changed through early intervention with high-risk youngsters, there is a belief in "the sooner, the better." According to this view, through early intervention the difficulties a child may face can be avoided, which thereby reduces the number and intensity of interventions that will be needed. This view has implications for the overall costs of providing educational and posteducational services to students. Hirshoren and Umansky stated these views in relation to students with disabilities:

> Early education for children with handicaps offers a number of benefits that warrant serious consideration by school systems. Early intervention with children who have some handicaps may alleviate many of the manifestations of the handicaps that could inhibit development and learning. Furthermore, provision of services in the early years could substantially reduce costs of later education. (1977, p. 191)

Policy reports have regularly noted the cost-effectiveness and cost benefits derived from early intervention. For example, in 1991 the Committee for Economic Development stated:

> Quality preschool programs clearly provide one of the most cost-effective strategies for lowering the dropout rate and helping at-risk children to become more effective learners and productive citizens. It has been shown that for every $1 spent on a comprehensive and intensive preschool program for the disadvantaged, society saves up to $6 in the long-term costs of welfare, remedial education, teen pregnancy, and crime. (p. 28)

Such statements are especially interesting in light of professional articles that question the long-term beneficial outcomes of all but model early childhood programs. For example, Haskins wrote:

> Research has shown that both model programs and Head Start have immediate positive impacts on tests of intellectual performance and social competence but that this impact declines over the first few years of public schooling. The evidence of improvement on long-term measures of school performance such as special education placement is substantial for model programs but thin and inconsistent for Head Start. There is limited but provocative evidence that model programs may have positive effects on life success measures such as teen pregnancy, delinquency, welfare use, and employment, but there is virtually no evidence linking Head Start attendance with any of these variables. Benefit-cost studies show that model programs can produce long-term benefits that exceed the value of the original program investment, but it would be premature to argue that Head Start is cost-beneficial. (1989, p. 274)

Guralnick (1997b) argues that, to some extent, initial evidence of the effectiveness of early intervention programs was a function of the time when the research was conducted—the comparisons made generally were between early intervention and no services or supports. He calls this "first-generation research." Second-generation research, according to Guralnick, should contribute to the design and implementation of early intervention programs, identifying which characteristics of programs make them effective. He cites the work of White and Boyce (1993), who used a prospective, randomized design with controls, and the work of Shonkoff, Hauser-Cram, Krauss, and Upshur (1992), who completed an intensive follow-up of carefully selected samples as examples of good longitudinal research designs. Unfortunately, long-term longitudinal studies that continue for 15 to 20 years are difficult to conduct and are often subject to variable or discontinued funding.

HISTORICAL BACKGROUND

In the early days of American education, compulsory attendance was thought to be the solution to the problems presented by parents who were "indifferent to the public good" and who refused to send their children to school. Nearly one hundred years later, with compulsory education for children and youths aged six to sixteen well established, the need for something special for likely-to-be-failing youngsters was still on the minds of American leaders. The 1960s marked a turning point in the public and governmental response to these issues: with evidence of the scope and effects of poverty (Harrington, 1962; Hurley, 1989), and the pleas of civil rights leaders for quality education for all Americans, educators began designing educational programs for children not yet in school. These educators hoped that compensatory education could begin to counterbalance the negative effects of poverty on the development of young children. These educational efforts were the precursors of early education for students with disabilities (see Table 8.1), and the emergence of early childhood education in the 1960s was called a "rediscovery" by Frost (1968) and a "renaissance" by Shane (1969).

Head Start

In 1964, the Economic Opportunity Act provided massive funding for educational programs for preschool children. During the summer of 1965, 550,000 youngsters (about 10 percent of all children in preschool programs) were enrolled in school programs that were set up as part of Project Head Start. More than 40,000 teachers (many with no experience with preschool children) were hired, and a total of 100,000 adults participated in the programs to "compensate" for the negative effects of poverty likely to hamper some of America's youths. The curriculum in many programs was intense and was based on the assumption that the best way to overcome economic, cultural, and social disadvantage was to start school early. Copperman noted that prior to Head Start, "the primary goal of preschool child care was the normal and healthy psychosocial development of young children, to be achieved through peer-group play and other guided play activities" (1978, p. 57). To counteract the likely effects of social and economic disadvantages, early childhood education specialists recommended that accelerated academic development be adopted as the primary goal of preschool programs. The major effect of this early instruction seemed to be increases in readiness abilities. Nevertheless,

TABLE 8.1   Early Education Programs for Children with Disabilities

Year	Program	Comment
1964	Head Start	Designed to compensate for negative effects of poverty
1968	PL 90-538	Handicapped Children's Early Education Program, including assistance to develop demonstration models for serving all preschool children with handicaps and their families
1968	PL 93-380	Required states to submit plans and timetables for serving all children and youths with handicaps from birth to twenty-one years; also mandated *child find*
1972	Head Start (PL 92-424)	Provided that not less than 10 percent of national enrollment opportunities be designed for children with disabilities
1975	Head Start (PL 92-424)	Changed 10 percent base from national enrollment to state enrollment opportunities
1975	PL 94-142	Provided funding for children with disabilities, aged 3 to 5, who were served; also gave incentive grants for approved plans to serve these children
1986	PL 99-457, Part H— Handicapped Infants and Toddlers Program	Provided incentive money for states to serve infants and toddlers; programs to be phased in over a five-year period, 1987–1991
1991	IDEA (PL 101-476)	Added demonstration and outreach programs for early education; added social work services and requirements for dissemination and training
1997	PL 105-17	Repealed Part H and reauthorized early intervention under revised Part C of PL 101-476; permitted states to extend use of "developmental delay" up to age 9; required transition planning conferences with preschools for children exiting early intervention programs.

> the preponderance of recent research indicates that most of the gains experienced by preschool children in group educational programs disappear by the end of first or second grade. . . . Early intervention produces substantial gains in IQ as long as the program lasts. But the experimental groups do not continue to make gains when intervention continues beyond one year, and, what is more critical, the effects tend to "wash out" after intervention is terminated. The longer the follow-up, the more obvious the latter trend becomes. (pp. 58–59)

When the effects of Head Start seemed to "wash out," a logical follow-up was to provide additional compensatory education programs. In 1969, Congress established the Follow Through program to try compensating for the failings of the compensatory Head Start efforts. Copperman reported that the effects of this program were similar to those of its predecessor; indeed, some evidence indicated that Follow Through produced more negative than positive effects (Stebbins, St. Pierre, Proper, Anderson, & Cerva, 1977). Since the time of these reports, however, gains attributable to the Head Start program have been noted (Lee, Schnur, & Brooks-Gunn, 1988). These latter investigators controlled for initial differences in Head Start and comparison groups and found that Head Start children made larger gains than comparison group children who either were from other programs or had no preschool experience. Yet the greater gains still left the Head Start children behind their peers. Suggestions that the small benefits of Head Start could be due to lower-quality programs (Bryant, Burchinal, Lau, & Sparling, 1994) in part have spurred the infusion of funds to improve the quality of Head Start programs (Bryant & Maxwell, 1997).

HCEEP/EEPCD

With the passage of PL 90-538 (Handicapped Children's Early Assistance Act) in 1968, Congress set the stage for the Handicapped Children's Early Education Program (HCEEP), which was later redesignated as the Early Education Program for Children with Disabilities (EEPCD). The original purpose of the program was to assist in the development of demonstration models for the provision of comprehensive services to all preschool children (birth to eight years) with disabilities and their families (DeWeerd & Cole, 1976; Swan, 1980). This program evolved over time to support (1) comprehensive services for infants and toddlers, birth to age 2, and their families; and (2) expansion of services for children 3 to 8 years old and their families (U.S. Department of Education, 1996).

The HCEEP was originally funded in 1969–1970 with an appropriation of $1 million, which supported 25 grants. Twenty-five years later, the EEPCD supported the 125 projects that addressed demonstration, outreach, inservice training, research, data systems, and technical assistance.

Head Start for Children with Disabilities

In 1972, the Head Start program was expanded by PL 92-424, which provided that not less than 10 percent of the national enrollment opportunities available through Head Start were to be designated for children with disabilities (La Vor, 1972; La Vor & Harvey, 1976). Legislation in 1975 (Head Start, Economic Opportunity, Community Partnership Act of 1974) altered the initial 10 percent enrollment opportunities from a national base to state bases. The change had the "net effect of forcing each state to focus on and meet the needs of children with disabilities within the state" and guaranteed that states would "no longer be able to disregard the minimum 10% requirement by averaging their totals with overall national or regional enrollments" (La Vor & Harvey, 1976, p. 227).

Education for preschool children with disabilities had arrived. And since its arrival, early education for young children with disabilities has continued to grow.

THE DOWNWARD ESCALATION OF EDUCATIONAL SERVICES

The first major legislative support for early education for youngsters with disabilities came from PL 90-538 in 1968 and the establishment of model demonstration programs. PL 93-380 required that the state plans submitted to the Bureau of Education for the Handicapped include timetables and plans for providing services to all children and youths with disabilities from birth through age twenty-one. Similarly, the law mandated states to "establish and maintain efforts to *find* all handicapped children from birth to age 21" (see Cohen, Semmes, & Guralnick, 1979). PL 94-142 provided two sources of funds for preschool programs: states were entitled to funding according to the numbers of children with disabilities in their populations, which could include the number of children in the three- to five-year-old range, and incentive grants were made available to states that provided approved plans to serve children in this age range (Cohen, 1976).

In 1977, Hirshoren and Umansky reported that twelve states offered certification for teachers of preschool children with disabilities. In 1980, Rose found that seven of forty-five states that responded to a survey indicated that their states had specific definitions for preschool children who had disabilities. In the same year, the Office of Special Education reported that sixteen states had mandated services for children aged three to five. By 1987, approximately 261,000 children, in that age range were receiving early childhood special education and related services, a 33 percent increase from 1976–1977. Nearly twenty years later, this number had increased to 548,441, primarily because of increases in the percentage of four-year-olds being served (see Figure 8.2).

The rise of preschool education for children with disabilities did not occur without problems. Karnes and Zehrbach (1977) discussed many of the problems, including difficulties in identifying those who should be served, service models, and staffing patterns. Others expressed concerns about labeling children so young and about specific guidelines for early intervention. Finding effective strategies for individualizing interventions for children and families continues to be a topic of concern, as does the need for information to guide policy decisions about early intervention (Guralnick, 1997a). The field is bound to be challenged

FIGURE 8.2   **Preprimary Enrollment of Three- to Five-year-Olds, by Attendence Status: October 1970 to October 1996**

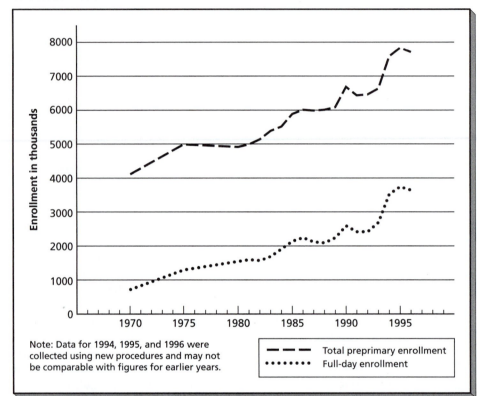

Note: Data for 1994, 1995, and 1996 were collected using new procedures and may not be comparable with figures for earlier years.

- - - - Total preprimary enrollment
· · · · · · · Full-day enrollment

Source: *Digest of Education Statistics 1997.* National Center for Education Statistics (1998), p. 46. Washington, DC: U.S. Department of Education (NCES 98–015).

even more by the emerging risk characteristics of children (e.g., poverty, abuse, low birth weight, and others). Additional issues, such as labeling and the appropriateness of a label like "learning disabled" for children who have not yet reached school age have been addressed by changes over time in the early education laws for children with disabilities.

Services for Infants and Toddlers with Disabilities

In 1986, PL 94-142 was amended by PL 99-457. This law reauthorized assistance for demonstration projects, training, and research and provided greater incentives to states to serve children aged three to five who were not yet being served (the law also extended to these children the rights and protections of PL 94-142 by 1990–1991). In a new Part H, the law provided states with new grant moneys to provide programs for infants and toddlers (i.e., from birth to two years). Along with this money came the requirement that the focus shift toward coordinated interagency planning (made explicit in the IFSP), thereby shifting planning away from a single agency concentrating on the child alone. With the enactment of the Handicapped Infants and Toddlers Program arose questions not only about the services needed by children with disabilities who were this young but about how to begin and then continue effective and meaningful interagency communication about these children (McNulty, 1989; Tingey & Stimell, 1989). Attention was quickly given to as the role of maternal and child health organizations (e.g., Bishop, 1988), the involvement of occupational therapy (e.g., Hanft, 1988), and the relevance of mental health agencies (e.g., Berman & Lourie, 1988).

During the first two years of the Handicapped Infants and Toddlers Program, all states participated (see Figure 8.3). They were required only to (1) provide assurances that funds would be used to assist in planning, developing, and implementing a statewide system of early intervention services; (2) designated a lead agency responsible for the administration of funds; and (3) establish an interagency coordinating council. During the third year of the program, however, states were required to demonstrate that they had adopted a policy that incorporated all the components of a statewide system (see Table 8.2) or had obtained a waiver from the secretary of education. The U.S. Department of Education (1990b) reported that by January 1990, forty-eight applications had been received from states and territories; thirty-two had provided the necessary assurances, and sixteen had requested waivers. Many of the states requesting waivers had done so not because they did not have a plan but because they were awaiting state legislation mandating service to infants and toddlers or final agreements across state agencies or branches of state government. By March 1990, it was becoming clear that many states needed more time to establish programs for infants and toddlers with disabilities (Viadero, 1991). By 1995, however, programs were fairly well established in all states. In fact, in just three years, between 1992–1993 and 1995–1996, the number of these children who received services increased by approximately 23 percent, to 177,873.

Still, there were several continuing issues faced by the programs. One issue was determining ways to count more accurately the number of children served in the programs; duplicated counts had made it difficult to assess accurately how many children the programs actually served (U.S. Department of Education, 1996). How to establish a collaborative structure for administering the programs also continued to be a challenge to programs. Although most states seemed to address this issue by identifying interagency coordinating councils (ICCs) at local levels rather than regionally or at state levels (National Early Childhood Technical Assistance System, 1995), there was no evidence that this was the best approach. Another challenge facing programs was how to increase the number of qualified personnel who could provide needed services. Different states tried different approaches for addressing this problem, yet none seem to have completely solved the problem.

FIGURE 8.3 **Children Served in Preschool Programs for Students with Disabilities**

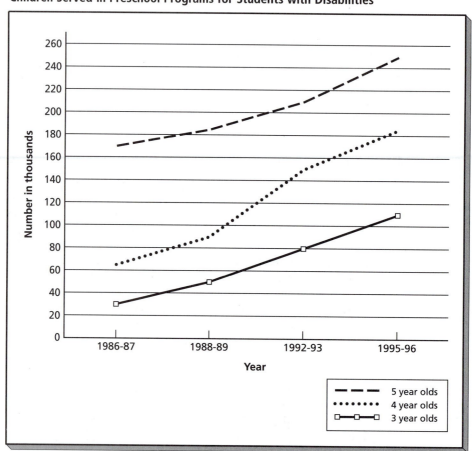

Sources: U.S. Department of Education. (1990b). *To assure the free appropriate education of all handicapped children: Twelfth Annual Report to Congress on the Implementation of the Education of the Handicapped Act.* Washington, DC: Author.
1986-87 and 1989-90: U.S. Department of Education. (1991). *Thirteenth Annual Report to Congress on the Implementation of the Individuals with Disabilities Education Act.* Washington, DC: Author.
1992-93: U.S. Department of Education. (1994). *Sixteenth Annual Report to Congress on the Implementation of the Individuals with Disabilities Education Act.* Washington, DC: Author.
1995-96: U.S. Department of Education. (1997). *Nineteenth Annual Report to Congress on the Implementation of the Individuals with Disabilities Education Act.* Washington, DC: Author.

As the Part H (now the Part C) program reached its tenth year since inception, the need to evaluate the benefits of the program led to the funding of the "Part H Longitudinal Study," generally referred to as PHLS (but perhaps soon to be known as PCLS). This study is designed to answer four questions (U.S. Department of Education, 1997): (1) Who are the children and families being served by Part C? (2) What early intervention services do participating children and families receive? (3) What results do participating children and their families experience? and (4) How do results relate to variations in child and family

TABLE 8.2 **Components of Statewide Early Intervention Services for Infants and Toddlers with Handicaps**

1. Definition of developmental delay
2. Timetable for serving all in need in the state
3. Comprehensive multidisciplinary evaluation of needs of children and families
4. IFSP and case management activities
5. Child find and referral system
6. Public awareness
7. Central directory of services, resources, experts, research, and demonstration projects
8. Comprehensive system of personnel development
9. Single line of authority in a lead agency designated or established by the governor for implementation of:

   a. General administration and supervision

   b. Identification and coordination of all available resources

   c. Assignment of financial responsibility to the appropriate agency

   d. Procedures to ensure the provision of services and to resolve intra- and interagency disputes

   e. Entry into formal interagency agreements
10. Policy pertaining to contracting or making arrangements with local service providers
11. Procedure for timely reimbursement of funds
12. Procedural safeguards
13. Policies and procedures for personnel standards
14. System for compiling data on the early intervention programs

SOURCE: U.S. Department of Education. (1990b). *To Assure the Free Appropriate Education of All Handicapped Children: Twelfth Annual Report to Congress on the Implementation of the Education of the Handicapped Act*. Washington, D.C.: Author.

characteristics and services received? Congress seems determined to continue increasing the funding for early childhood programs in the hope that they will serve a preventative function. It will be nice to have the data to know what is really happening as a result of early childhood interventions.

Prebirth Services?

The mandating of services to children with disabilities from the time of birth leads to the question of whether something should be done before that time. In the realm of medicine, in utero surgery is no longer just a possibility—it is now a reality. Among the more common procedures are the removal of fetal tumors and the correction of diaphragmatic hernias (Adler, 1998). Procedures as complex as surgery in which both the mother and the fetus are opened so that the spinal cord of the fetus can be closed and repositioned are occurring on an experimental basis, and with increasing success in significantly reducing the conditions associated with spina bifida (O'Meara, 1998). Some have argued that virtually certain predictions can be made that a child born to a parent with certain characteristics (e.g., drug abuser) will end up needing special education services. It has been estimated that of the children currently receiving special education services, one-third would have a minor handicap or no handicap at all if adequate medical care had been provided during pregnancy and the first year of life (Hodgkinson, 1989). To what extent are Americans willing to mandate services at birth or before for all children who may need services at some point in their lives? And does this approach provide us with cost savings beyond imagination? Many of these issues arise with greater clarity as professionals talk about the changing population of children in the nation.

EARLY ASSESSMENT

In Chapter 6 we discussed many issues surrounding special education assessment. These included influences on assessment, bias in assessment, who conducts assessment, and the relevance of assessment to intervention. These issues are all relevant to early childhood intervention as well, and many are magnified in the assessment of children who are very young.

Are Neonatal Testing and Preschool Screening Enough?

For most children, the major assessment before school entrance has been the medical assessment conducted at the child's birth. Typically, this assessment includes an Apgar scale rating, measures of weight and length, a phenylketonuria (PKU) exam, and sensory observations. The Apgar scale includes ratings of the infant's color, heart rate, reflex, muscle tone, and breathing. The ratings are made by a hospital staff member (usually a nurse) at one minute and then at five minutes after birth. The PKU exam checks for the PKU metabolic disease, which can be curbed through dietary modification if detected early. Sensory observations confirm that the infant responds to visual and auditory stimuli.

After the initial assessment at the hospital, only those children with regularly scheduled physical examinations and those children participating in preschool screening are assessed for possible developmental disabilities or other conditions putting them at risk for adequate progress in school. Is this enough? Or is a more systematic approach, perhaps a screening program, necessary for infants and toddlers at some point after they leave the hospital?

The aspect of assessment of young children that we know most about (both in terms of having practiced it for the longest time and having conducted research on it) is preschool screening. Screening is a procedure designed to limit the number of children exposed to comprehensive assessments and to help in identifying those who may be in need of special help and should therefore be exposed to comprehensive assessment procedures. The definitions floating around as preschool screening became the subject of study were basically consistent with each other:

- Barnes indicated that the purpose of screening is "to identify those children in the general population who may be at-risk for a specific disability, or who may otherwise need special services or programs in order to develop to their maximum potential" (1982, p. 11).
- Meisels defined early childhood developmental screening as a "brief assessment procedure designed to identify children who, because of the risk of a possible learning problem or handicapping condition, should proceed to a more intensive level of diagnostic assessment" (1985, p. 1).
- Peterson maintained that the purpose of screening is to "identify children who are not within normal ranges of development and need further evaluation and who may be candidates for early intervention programs" (1987, p. 285).

Although the use of preschool screening programs to identify students with disabilities is no longer considered an issue (the demonstrated cost-efficiency of preschool programs implies benefits; see Casto & Mastropieri, 1986; White & Boyce, 1993; White & Greenspan, 1986), how to go about running an efficient, quick, and accurate program remains an important overall issue.

Preschool screening programs can vary significantly from one place to the next, as indicated by a comprehensive study of programs conducted in the mid-1980s (Thurlow, O'Sullivan, & Ysseldyke, 1986). The programs studied were in Minnesota, the first state with a required public preschool screening program (Thurlow & Gilman, 1999). Some programs screened everyone in a district, others systematically eliminated certain children (such as those in day activity centers), and others nonsystematically eliminated some children (such as those who were not on census tract lists, and therefore probably had moved a lot or were homeless). Thurlow et al. also found that the goals of screening programs differed significantly, which in turn affected the number of children likely to be picked up in preschool screening. For example, one program might try to identify only those children with very significant developmental delays. Another program might try to identify all children who could benefit in any way from early childhood educational experiences.

Who Should Be Assessed?

A basic question in preschool screening is, Who should be identified? Should only those young children who are obviously disabled be assessed, or should assessment encompass those young children who are at risk of evidencing a disability later if nothing is done? On one side of this issue are those who argue that the potential hazards of labeling are too great to justify identifying individual children who may be considered at risk (Stixrud, 1982). On the other side are those who promote the benefits of identifying all at-risk children (Meisels, 1985).

The debate continues. Recent changes in IDEA, however, address some of these concerns. One change is that young children with disabilities do not need to be labeled with a category of disability to receive services—the term *developmental delay* can be used to describe children receiving services up to nine years of age. Still, the young children are labeled as different even in this approach.

Previously, children who were attending special education programs for preschoolers and who tended to be in separate early childhood programs, were thus labeled simply by their assignment to these programs. More recently, however, there has been a dramatic push toward the provision of early childhood special education services within general early childhood programs, thus reducing the silent labeling of children.

Several issues must be considered when conducting early assessments. A primary one is the age of the children assessed. The goal of screening programs is to identify children as early as possible. Yet the difficulty of developing and implementing good screening methodologies makes it challenging to assess children at early ages (Thurlow & Gilman, 1999). Similarly, nonparticipants limit the effectiveness of screening programs. One study has suggested that about one-third of young children do not participate in preschool screening in time to benefit from early intervention programs, and that children of color are the most likely not to participate in screening (Wilder Foundation, 1996).

Who Should Conduct Assessments?

As the age of those assessed becomes younger, the "who" of assessment becomes more important. Complications arise when the assessor is an "unfamiliar" individual (see Fuchs, Featherstone, Garwick, & Fuchs, 1984; Fuchs & Fuchs, 1986; Fuchs, Fuchs, Dailey, & Power, 1985; Fuchs, Fuchs, Garwick, & Featherstone, 1983; Fuchs, Zern, & Fuchs, 1983) or an individual with a style and language different from those of the child (Nuttall, Landurand, & Goldman, 1984). In most preschool screening programs, there appears to be differentiation of personnel according to area of assessment (see Table 8.3 on pg. 224). Nevertheless, the professionals involved in the nonphysical areas of assessment are special education personnel and teachers (Ysseldyke, Thurlow, O'Sullivan, & Bursaw, 1986) who may not have adequate training for conducting these assessments.

The role of the parent(s) in assessments of very young children also merits consideration. It has been suggested that parents not be involved in the assessment of preschool children, whereas for younger children (including infants and toddlers) parent facilitation of the assessment is preferable (Salvia & Ysseldyke, 1991).

The participation of volunteers in the assessment process, particularly screening, also produces issues that must be addressed. For example, in a study of preschool screening programs with very high and very low referral rates (Ysseldyke, Thurlow, Weiss, Lehr, & Bursaw, 1985), coordinators indicated that the use of volunteers influenced the frequency with which problems were identified and the eventual referral rates. If this variation is so, how are volunteers trained to identify children needing further evaluation?

What Should Be Assessed and How?

Assessment procedures constitute the largest category of assessment issues. In a survey of model early childhood programs, Lehr, Ysseldyke, and Thurlow (1987) found that the most frequently used procedure for screening was "other" (which included record reviews, observations, and some forms of parent involvement) but that family needs assessments and home visits were considerably less frequent than other procedures.

Assessment instruments are the primary topic of concern, especially in regard to validity, reliability, and representativeness of the standardization population of norm-referenced devices. For example, commonly used readiness tests have been shown to lack the needed levels of reliability for placement decisions (Meisels, 1987). And the instability of performance of young children and the lack of relationship between early measures of intelligence or achievement and later school performance lead to further questions about what to assess.

Preschool screening programs typically have been organized around focus areas similar to those shown in Table 8.3 on pg. 224. However, some early childhood experts suggest that screening areas should be defined by desired outcomes. In this vein, Kagan, Moore, and Bredekamp (1995) proposed five dimensions: (1) physical well-being and motor development, (2) social and emotional development, (3) approaches toward learning, (4) language usage, and (5) cognitive general knowledge. Similar, but slightly different, dimensions have been identified by the National Center on Educational Outcomes (Ysseldyke, Krentz, Elliott, Thurlow, Erickson & Moore, 1998).

Where and When Should Assessment Occur?

The location and timing of preschool screening come with their own set of problems and questions. Although the optimal assessment environment is one with low anxiety and minimal confusion, screening is sometimes done in hallways, with young children moving from one noisy station to the next. Sometimes the same person moves along the stations with the child; sometimes a new assessor greets the child at each station. In some programs, care is taken to assure quiet testing conditions and sufficient preassessment time for getting acquainted with the assessor, but scheduling also has to be taken into account because the schedules of young children include naps and important mealtimes. Of equal importance are the length of the assessment—Peterson (1987) recommended a series of short testing sessions for young children—and the extent to which the timing of assessment is coordinated with further assessment and/or actual initiation of an intervention program (Lichtenstein & Ireton, 1984).

NATURE OF INTERVENTION

The issue of which interventions should be provided is as complex as those regarding who needs early intervention. For young children birth to age three, an established IFSP guides the delivery of services, in part by establishing goals and identifying a case manager. For children between ages three and five, the IEP typically guides intervention efforts.

TABLE 8.3   **Preschool Screening Personnel**

Screening Area	Professional
Physical health	MD Nurse
Hearing	MD Audiologist Nurse
Vision	MD Nurse Optometrist
Speech/language	Speech clinician Special educator/teacher
Motor	Special educator/teacher Occupational therapist
Social-emotional	Special educator/teacher Psychologist
Cognitive	Special educator/teacher

NOTE: Table includes only those roles listed by more than 100 programs.

SOURCE: Ysseldyke, J. E., Thurlow, M. L., O'Sullivan, P., & Bursaw, R. A. (1986). Current Screening and Diagnostic Practices in a State Offering Free Preschool Screening Since 1977; Implications for the Field. *Journal of Psychoeducational Assessment, 4,* pp. 191–203. Used with permission.

Where Should Intervention Occur?

An important aspect of providing early intervention for young children with disabilities is determining where services will be located. Of particular importance are the least restrictive environment for very young children, the flexibility and consistency of services, and the nature of related services incorporated into early childhood services (Administration on Developmental Disabilities, 1988). Should services for the very young be provided at home, in a clinic, or in a school? Should the location vary according to the age of the child or according to some other variable, such as the nature of the disability or its severity? To what extent can the LRE concept be applied to services for very young children with disabilities? This last issue is especially relevant because of the rapid growth in pre-primary enrollment of three- to five-year-olds and the existence of preschool programs into which preschool children with disabilities can be mainstreamed. Several investigators have now provided data on the effectiveness of early intervention inclusion programs (e.g., English, Goldstein, Shafer, & Kaczmarek, 1997; Mills, Cole, Jenkins, & Dale, 1998).

Who Should Receive Services?

That assessors determine intervention is needed does not automatically mean that the child should be the focus of the intervention. Services can be targeted on the child, the family unit, or both. It is important to determine whether the target of intervention efforts changes as a function of the age of the child, the nature of the disability, and/or its severity.

Part C essentially requires that the intervention be family focused in part. But exactly what this means is not clear. A survey of seven states that had written IFSP guidelines by 1988 reported that "all seven required a written plan, a case management system, and identified an IFSP planning process that included family input" (U.S. Dept. of Education, 1990b, p. 57). The extent to which including family input is the same as making the intervention family focused is questionable. As the U.S. Department of Education reported, "Few or none of the policies addressed such issues as the procedure by which the case manager was to be selected or changed; the definition of family; practices that protect the rights of the family; resolution of disputes for payments or services; or resolution of individual or systemic complaints" (p. 57).

Other issues, some of them very emotional, also remain to be resolved. For example, who decides, and how, that developmental delays in an infant are due to inadequate parenting, rather than to a physical condition, and that parent education is required to remedy the infant's delay? Or who determines, and how, that the only intervention for a toddler at a certain age beyond what the parents are already doing is physical therapy?

Who Should Provide Services?

Personnel needs have become an issue as services are provided to younger and younger children. Although an elementary-level teacher can adequately serve a five-year-old, or perhaps even a four-year-old, teachers serving children younger than four are likely to need different skills. The U.S. Department of Education recognized this issue and cited research indicating that "skills required to work with infants and toddlers differ from those required to work with three through five year olds (Bricker & Slentz, 1989; McCollum, 1987)" (1990b, p. 38). An insufficient number of personnel trained to work with preschoolers was already an issue before states began to think about personnel for infants and toddlers with disabilities. To alleviate some of the issues surrounding the lack of personnel, the 1997 amendments to IDEA allowed for states to use appropriately trained paraprofessionals to work in early intervention and preschool programs, as well as to recruit and hire individuals who would complete their training within three years. Furthermore, just as we expect greater involvement of the school nurse as students with more severe disabilities are served in their home schools (National Association of State School Nurse Consultants, 1990), we expect a greater need for nurses able to work interactively with educational personnel in meeting the needs of youngsters involved in early childhood special education.

What Should Be the Focus of Intervention?

Several issues arise about the focus of intervention: the sequence in which motor development, social, and academic objectives should be identified; the length and frequency of services; the maximal amount of services; and the variables affecting this amount. In looking at focus issues, White and Casto (1989), for instance, organized them into seven areas: setting of program, instructional grouping, duration/intensity of services, staffing, type of services, family involvement, and philosophical orientation. They suggested that philosophical orientation underlies all other issues and can vary along such dimensions as teacher-oriented versus child-oriented programming, extrinsic versus intrinsic motivation and reward system, and individualized teaching versus teaching to groups. Bricker (1989) concluded that the three most essential features of early intervention programs in the 1990s are the linking of assessment, intervention, and evaluation; mainstreaming or integration; and program evaluation.

Recent emphases on natural environments for early intervention and inclusion in early childhood education programs for preschoolers has led educators to consider the practices in these settings. In particular, the early childhood classroom has received attention, in part because the National Association for the Education of Young Children (NAEYC) revised its guidelines for what constitutes developmentally appropriate practices in these classrooms (Bredekamp & Copple, 1997). Among the NAEYC guidelines are emphasizing play as the primary means of learning; providing interesting environments for young children; determining activities through child choices; and addressing a wide range of goals through activities and instruction, including social, emotional, and aesthetic skills, in addition to physical and cognitive development. These guidelines stirred up considerable controversy among early childhood educators (e.g., Carta, Atwater, Schwartz, & McConnell, 1993; McLean & Odom, 1993, Wolery & Bredekamp, 1994), generally because of concerns that they would make it difficult to address individualized goals of young children with disabilities. Wolery and McWilliam suggest that, to meet the needs of children with disabilities, there are seven minimal practices that must be used within developmentally appropriate classes (see Table 8.4).

NEW CONSTITUENCIES FOR EARLY SPECIAL EDUCATION INTERVENTION

At the same time that medical advances are enabling America to save increasing numbers of medically fragile infants each year, social problems are increasing the numbers of infants born with significant health problems and hidden disabilities.

Drug- and Alcohol-Exposed Infants

It was the late 1980s before America really began to look at the potential impact of its drug problem. This occurred about the time that *Education Week* (Viadero,

TABLE 8.4   **Minimal Practices for Developmentally Appropriate Classrooms to Meet the Needs of Young Children with Disabilities**

Practice	Research Support
• Ongoing staff development with follow-up into classrooms	Kontos & File, 1993
• Available specialized services	McWilliam, 1996
• Careful program planning, with individualized goals identified across domains, specific instructional strategies, and trained staff	McWilliam, 1992; Wolery & Fleming, 1993
• Embedded instruction on goals that is monitored and adjusted as needed	Bricker & Cripe, 1992
• Challenging behaviors addressed when they are present	Koegel, Koegel, & Dunlap, 1996
• Support for parents' priorities, concerns, and goals, and encouragement of their involvement in curricular decisions	Bailey, 1994
• High-quality curricular activities	Bredekamp & Copple, 1997

SOURCE: From Classroom-based Practices for Preschoolers with Disabilities by Wolery, M. & McWilliam, R. A., 1998. *Intervention in School and Clinic,* 34 (2), 95–102, 117. Copyright © 1998 by PRO-ED, Inc. Reprinted by permission.

1989) reported that an estimated 375,000 children were born each year exposed to cocaine. In a report released in June 1990 (cited in "Crack babies in pre-school," 1990), the U.S. General Accounting Office (GAO) indicated that current estimates of the number of drug-exposed infants being born in the United States were probably much too low. In its study of ten hospitals, the GAO's figures indicated one drug-exposed baby in every eleven births. Researchers generally agreed that the eventual costs of dealing with and helping these children would be significant:

> Whatever the numbers may be, the GAO report agrees that the financial costs of drug-exposed births will be very high, down the line.
>
> For example, the per capita cost in the Los Angeles pilot preschool program for mildly impaired prenatally exposed children is estimated to be $17,000 a year.
>
> For those drug-exposed children who show significant physiologic or neurologic impairment, the Florida Department of Health and Rehabilitative Services estimates that total service costs to age 18 could be as high as $750,000 per child. ("Crack babies in preschool," p. 7)

A study conducted by the National Institute on Drug Abuse followed 300 Chicago-area infants whose mothers used cocaine and possibly other drugs during pregnancy. With the caution that the infants in the Chicago area might be better off than similar children in the general population because their mothers had been motivated enough to seek drug treatment, the researchers found problems as late as age three. They confirmed the findings of several studies that cocaine babies were born smaller and weighed less than their drug-free peers. In addition, they found that cocaine babies spent most of their early weeks crying or sleeping and had a harder time than their peers maintaining a "quiet alert state" during which they could learn about their environment (Viadero, 1990). Although the cocaine youngsters appeared to catch up physically with their peers by age two, they "still tended to score lower than drug-free toddlers on tests measuring their ability to concentrate, interact with others in groups, and cope with an unstructured environment" (p. 15). Early examinations of limited numbers of three-year-old children who were cocaine babies indicated that many were easily distracted and exhibited language and/or behavior problems.

Fetal alcohol syndrome (FAS) was soon identified as a developmental disability characterized by deficient growth, unique facial features, physical anomalies, and occasional evidence of central nervous system dysfunction (Carmichael, Olson, & Burgess, 1997; U.S. Department of Health and Human Services, 1993). The severity of any or all of these manifestations could vary significantly. Furthermore, a variety of cognitive, linguistic, and social impairments seem to emerge as these children age.

Since the late 1980s and early 1990s, the picture of doom for drug- and alcohol-exposed infants has changed considerably. There is now recognition that early forecasts of dire outcomes were often based on false assumptions (Carmichael, Olson, & Burgess, 1997). The current view is that children exposed prenatally to alcohol and other drugs are a heterogeneous group of youngsters, and that their outcomes depend on both risk and protective factors that may exist in their lives (Myers, Carmichael, Olson, & Kaltenbach, 1992; Neuspiel, 1993).

Low-Birth-Weight Survivors

Low-birth-weight infants received attention in a study conducted by Sparling of the Frank Porter Graham Child Development Center at the University of North Carolina. In this largest study ever conducted on low-birth-weight children, 985 infants weighing five and a half pounds or less at birth were followed. As reported in *Education Week*:

> Some of the infants were given only traditional pediatric follow-up care. The rest received such care as well as intensive educational services at home, and later on, in special day-care programs. . . .
>
> By age 3, the researchers report, the children receiving special-educational services had significantly higher I.Q. scores and fewer behavior problems than did the toddlers receiving only health care. (Viadero, 1990, p. 15)

Washington Schools Chief Reveals She Has AIDS Virus

J udith A. Billings, the school chief in Washington state, said last week that she has the AIDS virus. But she vowed to continue working with "energy, zeal, and commitment." . . .

Ms. Billings, 56, said she believes she contracted HIV, the virus that causes AIDS, as long as 15 years ago from artificial insemination using donor sperm. . . .

Ms. Billings said she would like to remain in the public eye because her position would allow her to educate people about AIDS. . . .

Ms. Billings is the vice president of the [Council of Chief State School Officers] and was the group's president last year.

She began working in the state superintendent's office in 1979, when she became the state director of the federal Title I compensatory-education program. From 1987 to 1988, she worked as a policy adviser for a subcommittee of the U.S. House Education and Labor Committee. She was first elected to the superintendent's post in 1988, then was re-elected in 1992.

SOURCE: Ponessa. "Wash. schools chief reveals she has AIDS virus". Reprinted with permission from *Education Week*, Vol. 15, No. 16. Jan. 24, 1996.

Similar positive findings for early intervention with low-birth-weight infants have been demonstrated in several studies since that conducted by the Frank Porter Graham Center (see Blair & Ramey, 1997, for a summary of these studies).

AIDS Babies

Tremendous implications for education accompany the growing number of babies born with the HIV infection that causes AIDS. These children are presumed to be at risk for developing AIDS within seven to ten years, their elementary school years. These children almost certainly will fall within the other health impairment category of special education. The extent to which schools will be able to deal with these youngsters, who may be expected to die regardless of educational treatment and its expenses, is unknown. Today, however, the threat of schools having to deal with thousands of young children with HIV infection has been significantly decreased due to new drugs and identification procedures. According to Cohen, Grosz, Ayoob, and Schoen (1997):

The technology exists to (1) identify mothers with HIV infection with almost 100% reliability, (2) reduce the rates of transmission to newborns by about two-thirds, (3) identify about 80% of newborns who are HIV infected, and (4) identify almost all 6-month-olds who are infected. In addition, this same technology and improvement in treatment since the mid-1980s permit the use of medical interventions that can delay or mitigate some of the adverse effects on the infant of both the HIV infection and the secondary infections that commonly occur. (p. 195)

Research on interventions for these children has been limited. With improved medical interventions, however, the need remains to study long-term outcomes and intervention effectiveness.

Response to the New Constituencies

Despite the increasing recognition of needs among new constituencies of very young children, responses to these needs have been slow to emerge. For example, although an office of fetal alcohol syndrome was established by Congress in 1988, as of December 1990 staff for the office still had not been hired (Karaim, 1990). In response to drug-exposed infants, some states contemplated laws to allow prosecution of mothers of these infants for child abuse (Behrmann, 1990). In a commentary in *Exceptional Children,* Greer wrote, "Already in our schools is the advance guard of what will surely swell into an epidemic in a few short years; the drug babies. The question for today is, what preparation are we making (1990, p. 382)?

The tables have turned for many of the new constituencies facing early childhood programs. While we still hear about the challenges that they create, we no longer seem to be standing with a sense of dread and in awe of the problems that these constituencies create. Rather, there is a sense that we are dealing with basically the same challenges we faced before—the effects of poverty and the effects of medical advances that result in the survival of low-birth-weight babies.

Discussion Questions

1. Do assumptions of developmental plasticity and cost-effectiveness really guide early childhood special education? Are there other assumptions in play as well? If so, which ones?

2. Would there be significant benefits in providing special education services to children at risk of needing services later on?

3. Is there a way to link assessment to intervention for infants, toddlers, and preschoolers?

4. How should services to infants, toddlers, and preschoolers be provided if there is not enough trained and certified personnel? Can educators with alternative certifications be used?

5. Is the issue of new constituencies no longer relevant? Why or why not?

Chapter 9
Transition

TRANSITION INTO SCHOOL
Early Labeling
Alternatives to Traditional School Placements

TRANSITION DURING SCHOOL
Moving Between General and Special Education
Dropping Out of School
Functional Dropouts
Dropout Prevention

TRANSITION BEYOND HIGH SCHOOL
Transition Planning
Anticipated Services
School-to-Work Transition Outcomes
Promise of Self-Determination

DISCUSSION QUESTIONS

Progress begins with getting a clear view of the obstacles.

—Anonymous

Life is a series of transitions. People make the transition from one class to another while in school and survive the transition period between childhood and adulthood known as adolescence. People also move from one place to another, from one type of relationship to another, or from student life to work life. These transitions, though often stressful, are made without much difficulty by most persons. In the 1980s, however, professionals joined parents in realizing that not all individuals make transitions so easily. This realization led to an emphasis on the transition process and the difficulties many individuals with disabilities had in successfully accomplishing transitions. Special efforts were deemed necessary to "transition" the individual with special needs successfully.

Although the transition from school to work has received considerable attention recently in the special education literature, it is not the only critical transition that youngsters with disabilities are required to make. For example, they must accomplish the transition into school in the first place and then negotiate numerous transitions within school. Not only are there the typical transitions from one grade level or type of school to the next, but there are unique special education transitions, such as from one type of placement to another or one school to another and between general education and special education settings. The transition from school to some "adult" endeavor, such as postsecondary training, work, or other form of activity, is another transition that has to be made. In this chapter, we discuss the issues that surround each of the types of transition that youngsters with disabilities face.

TRANSITION INTO SCHOOL

In special education, transition is defined as "the process of moving or changing a child from one service component or delivery system to another" (Lerner, Lowenthal, & Egan, 1998, p. 262). Prior to attending formal school programs, many young children with disabilities participate in early intervention programs that provide support and special education services (cf. Guralnick, 1997b). This increasingly popular action is grounded in the belief of professionals, parents, advocates, and policy makers that it is a societal responsibility to provide early assistance for children with identified disabilities and for those whose development may be compromised as a result of biological or environmental factors. It is also firmly established by the conviction of many that the early years constitute a unique opportunity for preventing developmental problems and providing family support (Guralnick, 1997a). The importance of providing a smooth and effective transition for very young children with disabilities from early intervention programs to other preschool programs is recognized in the Individuals with Disabilities Education Act of 1997 (p. 31).

> By the third birthday of such a child, an individualized education program or, if [appropriate], an individualized family service plan, has been developed and is being implemented for the child. The local educational agency will participate in transition planning conferences arranged by the designated lead agency [for the child].

A critical issue related to transition from early intervention to preschool program is the lack of research investigating effectiveness or components of effective programs (cf. Guralnick, 1997; Lerner, Lowenthal, & Egan, 1998). Research that has been done shows that active participation by family members reduces stress and supports overall transition efforts (Fowler, Chandler, Johnson, & Stella, 1998; Hamblin-Wilson & Thurman, 1990; Lerner, Lowenthal, & Egan, 1998).

Another important change for a young child who has been identified with a disability is the movement from the preschool program into the formal K–12 educational system. At least two issues arise with this transition. First, should the child's disability be made known to the school in which the child will be enrolled? This question, which is most relevant for children with mild disabilities, is highly related to issues of early labeling. Second, to what extent should alternatives to traditional school placements be used for providing services to students with disabilities? Alternative school options, such as transitional kindergartens and junior first grades, are possible choices.

Early Labeling

Although children in preschool special education programs need not be given a specific label of disability, participation in the program itself is a type of label. In a detailed case study analysis of what happened to children as they left their preschool special education programs to move into elementary schools, Thurlow, et al. (1986) found extreme variability in the process. In some districts, program staff visited with staff of the elementary program in which the student was going, discussing in detail the child's strengths and weaknesses and recommending instructional techniques for the child. In one district, all information related to the child's participation in the early childhood special education program was deleted from the child's records, and the child was sent on to the elementary school without any indication of previous special education service. Unfortunately, follow-up of children in early childhood special education programs was a rare event. Informal input from the program in which no information followed the child indicated that nearly 60 percent of the children continued for another year without referral for evaluation for possible special education placement.

We do not have good data on what happens to students for whom extensive preparations are made for entry into the elementary school setting in addition to providing information on the students' special education status. Is it better to label, then drop the label? Is it better to make preparations for a smooth transition when the special education participation will be revealed? Or is it better not to prepare a transition in this way?

Alternatives to Traditional School Placements

Instead of having their children enter public school programs, some parents of young children with disabilities opt to send them to private schools or to schools with special programs, such as Montessori programs. No research has been conducted on either the extent to which this occurs or on the effects of this alternative. Another alternative is to hold the child out of school for a year so that when the child does enter, there is little likelihood of problems arising from immaturity. Some school districts encourage this practice.

Recently, Shepard and Smith (1989) published a book on the effects of retention in grade, more commonly known as flunking. Special grades, such as transitional kindergartens (to which a child goes after unsuccessfully completing a year in kindergarten), or junior first grades (to which a child goes because he or she is not quite ready for first grade), are a form of retention. Special words (transitional, junior) are used to deflate the negative aura that typically accompanies failure.

Some have likened these programs (particularly the practice of holding the child out of school for a year) to the practice of "redshirting" in college sports: a student is kept from playing a varsity sport until sophomore year so that the students' four years of eligibility do not start until then. In the conclusion to their book, Smith and Shepard argued that

> transition programs, which provide an extra year of school between kindergarten and first grade, are no different—in spite of their different philosophies—from simply retaining children for a second year in kindergarten. Although they are predicated on the idea that immature children should be given an extra year to grow or to repeat the pre-first grade experience, controlled studies show that children so treated do no better than their counterparts who are promoted directly into first grade. The findings of no difference or no benefit hold whether the children were selected for retention on the basis of immaturity or low achievement. (1989, pp. 215–216)

From a comprehensive review of the research literature on kindergarten retention, Shepard also noted that

> self-concept or attitude measures, only rarely included in research studies, showed no difference or negative effects from the extra-year placements. In this respect retention, whether it is called by a special name (transition), occurs for special reason (immaturity), or takes place in kindergarten rather than later, is still retention—and still ineffective. (1989a, p. 76)

With this kind of evidence, opposition to such programs has increased. In 1991, the National Association of Elementary School Principals (NAESP) passed a resolution opposing the practice (Cohen, 1991). Those who voted against the resolution noted the need for this transition program for developmentally immature children, despite the arguments of Shepard and Smith and more recent evidence presented by Ferguson of the noneffectiveness of the practice (Early Years, 1991). Ferguson's work is of interest because he looked specifically at children considered to be developmentally slow and included a control group. He found that teachers' ratings of the students revealed no differences in social skills, self-esteem, or rate of placement in special education. The students who went through the transitional program, however, were rated as more aggressive.

When NAESP passed its resolution, it noted the need to seek alternatives to the practice of retaining children through transitional kindergartens or junior first grades. The chairperson of the panel that drafted the resolution, Lillian Brinkley, suggested some possibilities (Cohen, 1991):

- Providing the child with a support system and tutors (peers, adult volunteers, older students)
- Encouraging consultation between teachers
- Pairing slower pupils with higher achievers
- Making classes smaller
- Providing more schooling (summer school or extended-year programs)
- Instituting midyear promotions

TRANSITION DURING SCHOOL

Many of the transitions children and youths make are introduced as they mature, such as movement from smaller classrooms to larger classrooms, from smaller buildings to larger buildings, and from a single teacher all day to seven or eight different teachers during one day. Perhaps because of the ease with which these transitions are made by most students, there has been little research conducted on them. Nevertheless, it is not unreasonable to assume that these transitions are made more easily by children without disabilities than by children with them. Yet no special provisions are made to train students with disabilities in how to make these transitions.

Moving Between General and Special Education

Transitions seem to be required far more often of students with disabilities than of students without them. While the typical elementary school child is in a single room with a single teacher all day, students receiving special education services often leave the special education setting to go to a general classroom or leave the general classroom setting to go to a special classroom to meet with a specialist (most commonly the special education teacher). Sometimes they must go at more than one time to meet with more than one other teacher (e.g., they may see an occupational therapist in the morning and a special education teacher in the afternoon; or they may see two different special educators, one who specializes in academics and one who specializes in behavior). Students leaving the general classroom to meet with these individuals not only have to adjust to dealing with more than one teacher; they also have to adjust to entering and leaving curriculum materials when other students do not. Students have to explain to other students why they leave the classroom and for what purpose.

Students who do not leave the classroom but who find themselves with the special education teacher inside the general classroom may not have to make quite as many transition adjustments as other students with disabilities do, but the adjustments may still be considerable. When this type of integrated service is used by the special education teacher as simply a different location to carry on typical special education activities (e.g., use different materials, drill basic facts, etc.), the students must also learn to concentrate when other students in the same classroom are engaged in completely different tasks, perhaps even listening to a teacher lecturing to the class.

We have already indicated to some extent the difficulties that surround the student for whom special education is separate from general education. We have spoken of the disjointedness of curricula and of the student's having to work with many more adults than the typical student must. We wish to point out here that students who must travel from one classroom to another while classmates continue with the work of the classroom are deprived of a significant amount of time during which they could be learning.

Dropping Out of School

Perhaps the most significant transition that some students make is to move out of school before graduating, an action more commonly known as dropping out. Concern about dropouts is supported by research demonstrating that dropping out of school has a serious impact on students, schools, and society. Unemployment, low income and lifetime earnings, limited cognitive growth, high rates of imprisonment, and low scholastic achievement are among the negative personal consequences for students who leave school (cf. Catterall, 1988; Ekstrom, Goertz, Pollack, & Rock, 1986; Grossnickle, 1986; Kortering & Braziel, 1998; McMillen, 1997; Office of Juvenile Justice and Delinquency Prevention, 1995; Pallas, 1987; Rumberger, 1987). The educational and social consequences of leaving high school without a diploma are also serious. For example, young women who drop out of high school are more likely to become pregnant at young ages and are more likely to be single parents. High school dropouts are more likely to receive public assistance than high school graduates who did not go to college. Billions of dollars lost in tax revenues, increased welfare and unemployment expenditures, and elevated spending of crime prevention funds are additional social effects associated with dropping out of school (cf. Braddock & McPartland, 1993; Catterall, 1998; Hahn, Danzberger, & Lefkowitz, 1987; Kortering & Braziel, 1998; McMillen, 1997).

For some time, the characteristics of those youths dropping out of school were studied and discussed. Factors commonly included within the lists of characteristics were attendance, number of school transfers, participation in free/reduced lunch programs, grade point average, educational level of parents, reading and math scores, ethnic/gender distinctions, language spoken at home, participation in extracurricular activities, pregnancy, and family status (Wells, Bechard, & Hamby, 1989). Characteristics of schools that seemed to produce more dropouts than the norm included overcrowding, low amounts of time that teachers engaged in instruction, weak leadership from the principal, low degree of order and discipline, retention policies, and changes associated with the reform movement in secondary schools (see Fine, 1986; Hess, 1987; Mann, 1986; Massachusetts Advocacy Center, 1986; School Dropouts, 1986).

Of particular note in the literature on dropouts was that policies that frequently affected students in special education programs (such as being held back in grade a second time or being suspended) often encouraged students to leave school permanently (Berlin & Duhl, 1984; Mann, 1986; Massachusetts Advocacy Center, 1986). Another factor associated with students in special education, race or ethnicity, was reported extensively in the literature: minority students (excluding Asian Americans) more frequently left school than did non-minority students (California Dropouts, 1986; Ekstrom et al., 1986; Hess & Lauber, 1985; Stephenson, 1985). Particularly at risk were Hispanic students (Pitsch, 1991b).

Recent government figures reflect that Hispanics continue to drop out at higher rates than do members of other groups. For example, in 1996, 9 percent of Hispanics left before completing high school, compared to 6.7 percent for blacks and 4.1 percent for whites (McMillen, 1997). Consider some other recent findings.

- In 1995, 5 out of every 100 young adults left school without successfully completing their high school program; this rate was consistent with estimates reported over the previous 10 years.
- Only thirteen states report high school completion rates of 90 percent or better.
- Young adults living in families with incomes in the lowest 20 percent of all family incomes were 5 times as likely as their peers in the highest 20 percent of the income distribution to drop out of school.

The dropout literature has been plagued by definitional issues that continue, even though dropping out is acknowledged as a major national problem for American education. Different criteria are often used to define who is a dropout, and different procedures may be used to count dropouts. Variations in criteria can be a function of which students are actually included, the number of days a student must be absent from school to be considered a dropout, the age at which a student can be classified as a dropout, and the grade levels included. For example, some schools do not count students younger than sixteen as dropouts because the law mandates their attendance; this practice seriously underestimates the number of school leavers. Various rationales for exiting school also serve as criteria for defining a school dropout: often students pursuing a GED are counted as dropouts, whereas teenage mothers are not (Cipollone, 1986). In some cases, students in special education are entirely excluded from the calculation of dropout rates. Some researchers make distinctions among school leavers, students who leave school after reaching the legal age limit for attendance, push outs, and dropouts; others do not. Because of these differences, the National Center on Education Statistics obtained agreement from twenty-seven states to use the following definition: a student is a dropout if he or she was enrolled in school during the previous school year but was not enrolled at the beginning of the current year; has not graduated from high school or completed a state- or district-approved program; has not transferred to another public school district, private school, or state- or district-approved education program; has been suspended, expelled, or excused from school because of illness; or has died.

To address some of these concerns, federal agencies have adopted the following definitions when gathering and reporting dropout rates (McMillen, 1997).

- **Event rates** describe the proportion of students who leave school each year without completing a high school program. This annual measure of recent dropout occurrences provides important information about how effective educators are in keeping students enrolled in school.

- **Status rates** provide cumulative data on dropouts among all young adults within a specified age range. Status rates are higher than event rates because they include all dropouts, regardless of when they last attended school. Since status rates reveal the extent of the dropout problem in the population, this rate can also be used to estimate the need for further education and training that will help dropouts participate fully in the economy and life of the nation.

- **Cohort rates** measure what happens to a group of students over time. This rate is based on repeated measures of a selected collection of students with shared experiences and reveals how many students starting in a specific grade drop out over time. Cohort rates can also be obtained by combining rates at different age levels. Typically, cohort rates provide more background and contextual data on the students who drop out than are available through other measures or collection procedures.

Recent event dropout and school persistence (staying in school) rates for different groups of students are presented in Table 9.1. Rates of leaving and staying in school are comparable for males and females, but these rates are different for racial/ethnic, income, and geographic groups. Dropout rates were lower in high-income families and the Northeast. Low-income families and Hispanics have high dropout rates.

Special education dropout rates   The annual dropout rate for students with disabilities (see Table 9.2) ages 14 to 21 was 5.1 percent (U.S.D.E., 1996). Students with serious emotional impairments dropped out at higher rates than any other group of students with disabilities (9.2 percent of all students ages 14 to 21 in this category). Those with the lowest dropout rates included students with autism (1.0 percent), multiple disabilities (1.4 percent), and deaf-blindness (1.4 percent). Students with learning disabilities, serious emotional disturbance, mental retardation, and speech or language impairments represent more than 96 percent of the students with disabilities who drop out of school.

The annual dropout rate for students with disabilities at each individual age can be combined to estimate a cohort dropout rate. The cohort dropout rate estimates the percentage of a group of students (e.g., 14- to 24-year-olds) who will drop out over the course of their entire high school careers. Given current trends, approximately 26 percent of students with disabilities (cohort rate) will drop out of school (U.S.D.E., 1996). The U.S. Bureau of the Census (1995) collects data on annual and cohort dropout rates for students nationwide. The Census Bureau reports an annual dropout rate of 5 percent for students without disabilities in grades 10 to 12, the same as the rate for students with disabilities ages 14 to 21, and a cohort rate of 13.3 percent for persons without disabilities ages 14 to 24. According to the U.S. Department of Education (1996), the discrepancy in cohort rates may be a result of differences in dropout recovery rates among students with (26 percent) and without (13.3 percent) disabilities, which directly influence the cohort dropout rate but not the annual rate.

TABLE 9.1 **General Education Dropout Rates, Persistence Rates, and Distribution of Dropouts Across Different Groups**

Group	Dropout Rate (Percent)	School Persistence (Percent)	Number of Dropouts (Thousands)	Percent of Dropouts (Within Group)
Total	5.0	95.0	485	100.0
Gender				
Male	5.0	95.0	241	49.6
Female	5.1	94.9	245	50.4
Race/Ethnicity[a]				
White, non-Hispanic	4.1	95.9	267	54.9
Black, non-Hispanic	6.7	93.3	103	21.1
Hispanic	9.0	91.0	100	20.6
Family Income[b]				
Low income level	11.1	88.9	145	29.8
Middle income level	5.1	94.9	282	58.1
High income level	2.1	97.9	59	12.1
Geographic region				
Northeast	3.4	96.6	61	12.6
Midwest	4.6	95.4	109	22.5
South	5.5	94.5	180	37.0
West	6.2	93.8	135	27.9

[a]Due to small sample sizes, American Indian/Alaskan Natives and Asian/Pacific Islanders are included in totals but not included in statistics.

[b]Low income is defined as the bottom 20 percent, middle income is between 20 and 80 percent, and high income is the top 20 percent of all family incomes in 1996.

SOURCE: McMillen, M. (1997). *Dropout Rates in the United States, 1996*. Washington, D.C.: U.S. Department of Education, Office of Educational Research and Improvement, National Center for Education Statistics.

Recent reports of dropout rates in special education support earlier research comparing students with disabilities who left school with their peers without disabilities. For example, studies have consistently shown that students with mild disabilities leave school more often than students without disabilities (Bernoff, 1981; Bruininks, Thurlow, Lewis, & Larson, 1988; Fardig, Algozzine,

TABLE 9.2   Special Education Dropout Rates, Persistence Rates, and Distribution of Dropouts Across Categories

Group/Category	Dropout Rate (Percent)[a]	School Persistence (Percent)	Number of Dropouts	Percent of Dropouts (Within Group)
All disabilities	5.1	94.9	76,608	100.0
Learning disabilities	4.9	95.1	44,244	57.7
Speech or language impairments	3.8	96.2	1,875	2.4
Mental retardation	4.2	95.8	10,270	13.4
Serious emotional disturbance	9.2	89.8	17,370	22.7
Multiple disabilities	1.4	98.6	531	0.7
Hearing impairments	2.5	97.5	570	0.7
Orthopedic impairments	2.4	97.6	412	0.5
Other health impairments	3.8	96.2	1,005	1.3
Visual impairments	2.2	97.8	195	0.2
Autism	1.0	99.0	55	0.1
Deaf-blindness	1.4	98.6	8	0.1
Traumatic brain injury	3.0	97.0	73	0.1

[a]Percentages based on total child count for students ages 14 and older to be comparable with rates used by other agencies.

SOURCE: *Eighteenth Annual Report to Congress on the Implementation of the Individuals with Disabilities Education Act.* Washington, D.C.: Office of Special Education Programs.

Schwartz, Hensel, & Westling, 1985; Hasazi, Gordon, & Roe, 1985; Hess & Lauber, 1985; Kortering & Braziel, 1998; Levin, Zigmond, & Birch, 1985; Lichtenstein, 1987; Owings & Stocking, 1986; Stephenson, 1985; U.S.D.E., 1987, 1988b; Wagner, 1991; White, Schumaker, Warner, Alley, & Deshler, 1980; Zigmond & Thornton, 1985). These findings are exacerbated by studies of the effects of leaving school on students with disabilities.

Special education dropout effects   Examination of the effects of dropping out of school for students with disabilities has been done primarily by looking at their employment status and adjustment. The results clearly indicate that dropping out of school has detrimental effects on the employment attainment of students with mild disabilities. Dropout special education students demonstrate lower employment rates (Edgar, 1987; Hasazi et al., 1985; Hewitt, 1981; Porter, 1982; Zigmond & Thornton, 1985). Furthermore, a lower percentage of time after leaving high school is spent in employment by students who drop out compared to students who graduate.

Functional Dropouts

There is a second type of dropout in schools, but this dropout has received little recognition and even less research. This is the student who attends school but is a functional dropout. Solomon described this type of student as one who remains in school but disengages from the pursuit of academic credentials. He saw this group of dropouts with the same outcomes as traditional dropouts: "They fail to acquire the competencies and credentials necessary for social and economic advancement in adult life" (1989, p. 79). Payne described this phenomenon as well:

> By the time they are of junior high age, if not sooner, many inner-city youngsters behave in ways that seem to unambiguously proclaim their lack of interest in schooling. Teachers are literally bombarded with these signals. Those teachers who hope to work successfully with such youngsters have to convince themselves that what we see of their day-to-day behavior may only be a reflection of more fundamental problems. (1989, p. 113)

The functional dropout is as great a problem as, if not more of a problem than, the student who no longer attends school. The functional dropout continues to sit in the classroom and use taxpayer dollars for instructors and materials, yet he or she may leave school in the same predicament as the actual dropout; both have a lower likelihood of obtaining and keeping a job after high school. Whether the functional dropout somehow benefits from obtaining a graduation diploma (if that happens) and the extent to which students in special education can be considered functional dropouts are unknown. Clearly, additional research is needed in this area.

Dropout Prevention

Many different attempts have been made to prevent high-risk students from dropping out and to reengage students who have already dropped out. These have focused almost exclusively on students in general education, and most have not been investigated adequately or systematically. Programs designed explicitly for dropout-prone students in special education are few in number. Zigmond (1987) suggested that many of the strategies in general education dropout intervention programs already are part of special education programs, such as early identification, individualized approaches, smaller size classes, lower pupil-teacher ratio, vocational education, employment preparation and job training, and counseling. Therefore, existing dropout interventions in general education may be necessary but not sufficient to prevent students with disabilities from dropping out of school.

New perspectives and approaches must be generated to overcome the dropout problem in special education. Edgar (1991) described a comprehensive approach to programming that may keep students with special needs engaged in schools. His approach includes such programs as academic support (tutors, Saturday school, resource teachers) and personal support (case manager, health services, counseling and treatment, prosocial recreation, mentors/benefactors) for students pursuing the academic track in high school. There would also be an alternative track designed specifically to develop work skills and to place students in jobs paying above-poverty-level wages.

Zigmond (1990) proposed four essential components to more effective secondary school programming for students with learning disabilities. First, the program should provide intensive instruction in the basic skills, particularly reading and math. Second, the program should provide instruction in such survival skills as behavior control, behaviors that please teachers, and study and test-taking skills. Third, the program should enable the student to successfully complete those courses required for high school graduation by, for instance, changing graduation requirements or using a consulting teacher to help mainstream teachers adjust mainstream demands to special education students. Fourth, the program should include explicit planning for life after high school; the implementation of this component can vary considerably. According to Zigmond, "The challenge for schools is to construct an efficient and affordable service delivery model with the appropriate combination of special and mainstream education experiences to address these components, and at the same time to develop an appealing and motivating educational program that holds students in school" (pp. 15–66). Zigmond proposed two models that can do this, one that emphasizes preparation for work and one that emphasizes preparation for some type of postsecondary training.

The models proposed by both Zigmond (1990) and Edgar (1991) suggest the use of tracks that accord with the eventual goal of the student's education. This leaves unaddressed, however, the question of when, how, and by whom the goal is to be determined. Clearly, many issues must be addressed as educators attempt to keep high-risk special education students in school and prepare them for life after school.

TRANSITION BEYOND HIGH SCHOOL

According to the latest amendments to the Individuals with Disabilities Education Act (PL 105-17), the term *transition services* means a coordinated set of activities for a student with a disability, designed within an outcome-oriented process, to promote movement from school to postschool activities. Within this context, special education services provided beyond high school include support with postsecondary education, vocational training, integrated employment (including supported employment), continuing and adult education, adult services, independent living, or community participation. These transition services are based on individual student needs, taking into account preferences and interests, and they include instruction, related services, community experiences, the development of employment and other postschool adult living objectives, and when appropriate, acquisition of daily living skills and functional vocational evaluation.

The impetus for focusing attention on the transition from school to postschool activities (usually employment) was the 1983 amendments to the Education of the Handicapped Act Amendments of 1973. In Section 626 of PL 98-199, financial support was provided to an array of demonstration efforts to both stimulate improved programs for secondary special education and to provide coordinated education, training, and related services to help in transitions to employment, vocational training, continuing education, and adult services. Madeleine Will, then assistant secretary for the Office of Special Education and Rehabilitative Services, spoke repeatedly about the need for building a bridge between school and adult experiences. In 1985, an institute devoted to the evaluation and extension of the federal initiative was established at the University of Illinois, Urbana-Champaign. In 1987, a major national longitudinal transition study was funded to collect comprehensive transition data on students with disabilities (Wagner, 1991).

With the enactment of the amendments of PL 94-142 came even more emphasis on transition. The latest law requires that the IEP include a statement of needed transition services beginning no later than age fourteen.

Why was all this attention devoted to postschool transition? For the most part, the efforts on behalf of students with disabilities grew out of a body of follow-up literature that indicated that students with disabilities were leaving school unprepared to work (cf. Rusch & Chadsey, 1998). Halloran succinctly summarized some of the issues when he wrote:

> Some students reach the end of their public school experience poorly prepared for competitive employment or independent living. As students approach the end of their formal schooling we frequently ask what they will be doing after school ends. Unfortunately, when we look back to determine what preparations have been made for students to live and work in our communities we often see a series of disjointed efforts lacking a focus on the skills necessary to confront the new expectations and demands of adult life. (1989, p. xiii)

A number of follow-up studies also indicated that former students who had received special education services did not necessarily fare very well after they left school. Most information obtained after the enactment of PL 94-142 focused primarily on employment, and most studies involved students with mild mental retardation or other mild disabilities (e.g., Chadsey-Rusch & Heal, 1995; Chadsey-Rusch, Rusch, & O'Reilly, 1991; Fardig et al., 1985; Hasazi et al.,

1985; Mithaug, Horiuchi, & Fanning, 1985; Semmel, Cosden, & Konopak, 1985; Wehman, Kregel, & Seyfarth, 1985). Follow-up studies of former students with moderate to severe mental disabilities (e.g., Edgar, 1987; Hasazi et al., 1985; Hawkins, 1984; Thurlow, Bruininks, & Lange, 1989; Wagner, 1995; Wagner, D'Amico, Marder, Newman, & Blackorby, 1992; Wagner, Newman, D'Amico, Jay, Butler, Nalin, Marder, & Cox, 1991; Wehman et al., 1985) indicated similar variability in employment rates and other adjustment indicators. The variability was, however, quite consistently on the low end of the scale (e.g., from 21 percent to 45 percent were employed) for students with moderate to severe disabilities.

The time was right for renewed emphasis on the postschool transition of youths with disabilities. Within two years of the enactment of PL 101-476 in 1991, major changes were to be in place as a result of other landmark legislation, specifically the Americans with Disabilities Education Act (ADA) and the School-to-Work Opportunities Act of 1994 (PL 103-239). The passage of the ADA provided basic civil rights protection to people with disabilities which would allow them to participate in the areas of employment, public accommodations, public services, transportation, and telecommunications on an equal footing with people without disabilities. PL 103-239 established a national framework for states to create school-to-work systems and build on existing employment and transition programs such as tech-prep education, career academics, mentorships, apprenticeships, school-sponsored enterprises, and business-education compacts (Stodden, 1998). It focused on integrating school-based and work-based learning, on integrating academic and vocational learning, and on linking secondary and postsecondary education.

Transition Planning

Beliefs about how to make effective transition services happen vary from one person to the next (Kohler, 1998). Some hold narrow views about the process of planning transition services, focusing primarily on moving a student from high school to an immediate postschool experience. These professionals concentrate on the last one or two years of high school when planning transition services. Others take a broader position on transition, arguing that "all educational programs and instructional activities should be (1) based on the postschool goals of students and (2) developed on the basis of individual needs, interests, and preferences" (Kohler, 1998, p. 180). From this perspective, transition planning includes the following steps.

- Student abilities, needs, interests, and preferences are used to identify appropriate postschool goals.
- School and other educational experiences are provided to prepare students to achieve their postschool goals.
- Students, family members, and other individuals work together to identify appropriate transition services.

Transition planning, then, is the process of deciding what specific services will be appropriate in efforts to improve the lives of individuals with disabilities after high school.

Views on the nature of appropriate transition services also vary from one person to another. For example, some professionals believe that services beyond high school should be provided as part of a lifelong commitment to career development, including continuing education and improvement of daily living skills, person-social skills, and occupational skills (see Brolin & Schatzman, 1989). Others view transition as more of a challenge to interagency cooperation (see Johnson, Bruininks, & Thurlow, 1987). Some see vocational training as the only need, whereas others identify significant personal adjustment needs. Some believe that the transition program should be different for students with learning disabilities or physical disabilities and students with mental retardation. Some argue that personal behavior skills are the most important information in a transition training program, whereas others view an introduction to community services, such as the Division of Rehabilitation Services and Supplemental Security Income, as more critical. These many different approaches raise questions. Should transition programs concentrate on transportation issues (drivers' licenses and special transportation services)? Should they include a focus on housing? Should the only focus be on getting a job? Should self-advocacy be included in all transition programs?

Best practices in providing support for students with disabilities after high school have been studied extensively (Rusch & Millar, 1998). Kohler (1993) reviewed 49 transition-related documents to identify "best practices" supported with empirical evidence. Vocational training, parent involvement, interagency collaboration, and service delivery were among activities cited in more than half the documents. Rusch and Millar (1998) add that participating in early planning; supporting team planning and interagency collaboration; incorporating transition and career planning within the IEP process; focusing on integrated employment opportunities; using functional, community-based curricula; placing students in jobs with potential for improvement; providing ongoing inservice; and evaluating program effectiveness were additional practices supported by research. A summary of the best transition practices is provided in Table 9.3. In general, successful transition programs include the following components (Charner, Fraser, Hubbard, Rogers, & Horne, 1995; Kohler, 1993, 1996; Rusch & Millar, 1998).

- Provision of school- and job-based learning experiences integrated within career guidance opportunities
- Active educational leadership supported by commitment from service providers
- Widespread collaboration and partnership among diverse service providers
- High degrees of student participation
- Creative financing

TABLE 9.3   **Best Practices in Providing Services Beyond High School**

Practice	Key Components/Description
Student-Focused Planning	Individual's needs, preferences, skills, and interests are central focus. Individuals with disabilities are active participants in planning their programs.
Family Involvement	Family members are empowered to participate with specially designed training. Students and families may receive same, similar, or different training experiences.
Collaboration	School personnel, peers, employers, and advocates are active contributors. Multiple and diverse perspectives are critically important to successful transition.
Student Development	Skills and competencies are taught for successful attainment of transition goals. Accommodation and support services are available to facilitate instruction.
Program Integration	Activities and standards are applied to all students to support coherent programs. Separate activities, facilities, and groupings are avoided.

SOURCE: Adapted from Kohler (1996).

Employment and postsecondary education as well as appropriate residential, recreational, and leisure experiences are appropriate goals for transition planning. An example illustrating the transition planning process for employment is provided in Table 9.4.

The Teaching All Students Skills for Employment and Life (TASSEL) model illustrates fundamental features of comprehensive systems designed to assist all students with disabilities in making a smooth transition from school to adulthood (Aspel, Bettis, Test, & Wood, 1999).

- Provide students with options within their educational placements to assist them in meeting their postsecondary goals for employment, living arrangements, education, recreation, and leisure activities.

- Provide student-centered transition planning, supported by assessment of individual skills, abilities, and interests, as well as interagency collaboration and appropriate school experiences for meeting goals after high school.

- Provide options for an academic and/or occupational course of study; completion of academic course of study earns an academic diploma, and completion of occupational course of study earns locally sanctioned occupational diploma.

TABLE 9.4   **Sample Transition Planning Process**

Team Goals	Activities	Responsible Person	Time Line
To establish an individual transition team	1. Contact rehabilitation services to identify counselor 2. Contact developmental disabilities to identify a case manager 3. Identify ancillary staff (speech pathologist, occupational therapist, etc.) for team participation 4. Contact student's parents	Student's special education teacher	Sept. 1, 1999
To write an individual transition plan identifying long- and short-term transition objectives	1. Conduct a transition team meeting as part of the IEP process 2. Identify possible short-term and long-term employment and residential objectives 3. Assign responsibilities for implementation	Individual transition team members: • Special education teacher • Vocational education teacher • Developmental disabilities case manager • Rehabilitation counselor • Parents • Students	Oct. 1, 1999
To identify goals and procedures to assure student is provided with community-based vocational training	1. Identify job training sites for student: (a) Food services (b) Janitorial (c) Micrographics 2. Utilize the supported work model for training 3. Train at least four hours per school day, four days a week, at the job site 4. Monitor and evaluate each position	Individual transition team members: • Special education teacher • Vocational education teacher • Rehabilitation counselor • Developmental disabilities case manager • Occupational and physical therapists • Student	Completed by Sept. 30, 2000

(continued)

TABLE 9.4

Sample Transition Planning Process (Continued)

Team Goals	Activities	Responsible Person	Time Line
To identify a job for students to begin her or his last year of school	1. Survey job market based on findings of job training 2. Establish employer interviews 3. Identify additional skills that require training, i.e., transportation, communication 4. Conduct job placement and training following the supported employment model	Individual transition team members: • Special education teacher • Vocational education teacher • Developmental disabilities case manager • Parents • Employer	Completed by Sept. 1, 2001
To provide supported employment services as needed after graduation	1. Determine a plan for a shift of responsibilities from the school system to adult service agencies 2. Assign responsibilities for job placement and follow-along services 3. Determine a plan for communication among team members and cooperating agencies throughout the transition years	Individual transition team members: • Developmental disabilities case manager • Rehabilitation counselor • Parents • Employer • Special education teacher • Vocational education teacher	June 1, 2002

SOURCE: Wehman, P., Moon, M., Everson, J., Wood, W., & Barcus, J. *Transition from School to Work: New Challenges for Youth with Severe Disabilities.* Paul H. Brookes Publishing Co., P.O. Box 10624, Baltimore, MD 21285-0624. Copyright © 1988. Used with permission.

- Provide opportunities for employment-related experiences within supervised educational settings (e.g., TASSEL students participate in school factory performing work for local businesses with supervision and support necessary for teaching and learning generalizable work skills).

- Provide opportunities for employment-related experiences within supervised job settings (e.g., TASSEL students are provided opportunities to job-shadow employees at local businesses).

- Provide opportunities for paid community-based training with appropriate supervision and support from community transition team composed of representatives from schools, adult service agencies, and local businesses.

- Provide opportunities for competitive employment with assistance in all aspects of finding and keeping a job during the school year.

- Provide opportunities for family involvement in all aspects of transition programming.

Anticipated Services

To support efforts to provide appropriate and effective transitions after high school for students with disabilities, the IDEA requires that the secretary of education collect data on those services anticipated to be needed for students ages 12 to 21 exiting the educational system (U.S.D.E., 1996). Initially, these data were collected annually, but recent changes have mandated their collection every 3 years. Early efforts to collect this information directly from states were plagued by at least two problems. In some cases, state personnel based service needs estimates on the student's disability classification, creating potentially biased findings depending on what groups of students were included. In other cases, data were gathered by school and district personnel who were inexperienced in judging the adult service needs of students leaving the educational system.

To address these problems, the Office of Special Education Programs (OSEP) developed the Performance Assessment for Self-Sufficiency (PASS) system in conjunction with transition experts, state and local administrators, and practitioners in special education and adult services (U.S.D.E., 1996). PASS instruments, which collect information about the functional performance of individuals with disabilities, are completed by teachers on the basis of their knowledge of their students. This information is then fed into an expert system that translates the teacher's assessment into useful information that special education and transition services agencies at all levels can use to anticipate needs and plan services for young adults with disabilities.

The percentages of exiting students with disabilities having primary needs in the 16 adult service categories addressed by PASS is presented in Table 9.5. Primary needs are defined as those needs judged to be essential for the student. The most prevalent primary need was *case management* (80 percent of the total sample). Services to support *alternative education,* which includes programs for

TABLE 9.5   Anticipated Services Needs of Students with Disabilities Beyond High School

Anticipated Adult Services	Percent of Students ($n = 2206$)
Case management	80
Alternative education	51
Services to support postsecondary education	49
Recreation and leisure	41
Communication	35
Social skills training	29
Technological aids	28
Independent living	26
Residential living	26
Ongoing employment-related	22
Mental health	20
Medical and medically related	17
Mobility	15
Family services	12
Specialized transportation	6
No goods or services anticipated	6
Vocational training and job placement	4

SOURCE: U.S. Department of Education. Office of Special Education Programs (OSEP), *Eighteenth Annual Report to Congress.*

continuing adult education, adult basic education (ABE), general education development (GED), adult high school diploma, and adult compensatory or special education and *postsecondary education* were the next common primary needs found among the sampled students. Assistance and training related to *communication services,* including speech/language therapy, interpreter services, reader services, braille training, and tactile interpreting services, were considered primary needs for over one-third of students sampled. In the total group, only 6 percent of the students had no anticipated services

Secondary needs are defined as those needs considered warranted, but which experts felt were not critical (U.S.D.E., 1996). Few students with disabilities were projected as having secondary needs for adult services. No exiting students with disabilities were identified as having secondary needs in the areas of mobility, specialized transportation, medical services, and recreation and leisure services. The most common secondary need was for services to support postsecondary education. These findings are consistent with those of earlier efforts to identify anticipated adult services of individuals with disabilities beyond high school (cf. U.S.D.E., 1995, 1996).

School-to-Work Transition Outcomes

Desired educational outcomes can be specified for all students and then tailored to meet the needs of students with disabilities (Phelps & Hanley-Maxwell, 1997). Efforts to define desired outcomes have taken many directions. Using opinions of prominent business leaders, the U.S. Department of Labor (1991) identified foundation skills, competencies, and personal qualities believed to be essential for success in the world of work in the Secretary's Commission on Achieving Necessary Skills (SCANS) Report. Phelps and Hanley-Maxwell (1997) provide a clear representation of the outcomes delimited in this effort (known hereafter as the SCANS Report):

> Foundational skills refer to basic academic and thinking skills. Included within basic academic skills are the areas of reading (finding, comprehending, and applying printed information), writing to communicate, arithmetic and mathematical operations (basic computational skills, using reasoning to select an appropriate operation and applying it to practical problems), listening (receiving, attending to, interpreting, and responding to verbal messages and other cues), and speaking (organizing ideas and communicating orally). Thinking skills include generating new ideas, decision making and acting, problem solving and implementing, visualizing (to organize, understand, and respond), reasoning to find connections and relationships necessary for problem solving, and continued self-learning. Personal qualities were also deemed essential in this schema for new skills. The following personal qualities are specifically identified . . . as critical for success in today's labor markets: responsibility as shown in effort and perseverance, self-esteem as reflected in self-value and self-view, interpersonal skills that allow effective working with others, self-management (self-assessment, self-monitoring, self-control, and goal setting), and integrity and honesty as shown in using ethics to make decisions. (p. 201)

Specific competencies are derived from the foundational skills and personal qualities that provide a structure for articulating outcomes. The competencies include:

(a) Identifying, organizing, planning, and allocating resources (time, money, human, and material/facilities)

(b) Working with other people (i.e., working in a team, sharing information and skills, responding to customer needs, advocating for oneself, using negotiation and conflict resolution, and responding appropriately to individual differences

(c) Acquiring, organizing, interpreting, and communicating information (includes computer technology)

(d) Understanding interrelationships of complex social, organizational, and technological systems

(e) Securing, applying, and maintaining a variety of technologies (Phelps & Hanley-Maxwell, 1997, p. 202).

Despite the difficulty some students with disabilities would have demonstrating competence in some of its areas, the SCANS Report provides a comprehensive framework of, and is widely recognized as a standard for, important skills and competencies students should have upon leaving high school (cf. Rusch & Chadsey, 1998).

Researchers at the National Center on Educational Outcomes (NCEO) have identified important outcomes for students with disabilities (cf. Thurlow & Elliott, 1998; Ysseldyke, Thurlow, & Shriner, 1992). Within the NCEO model, literacy, self-dependence, satisfaction, social/behavioral skills, contribution/citizenship, and physical/mental health are identified as critical educational outcomes for students with disabilities. Clearly, common themes are evident in the SCANS Report competencies and those designated as important for students with disabilities by the NCEO.

How well do students with disabilities achieve these desired outcomes beyond high school? Research has demonstrated that students with disabilities have poor postschool outcomes (Benz & Halpern, 1987; Edgar 1988; Hasazi, Gordon, Roe, Hull, Fink & Salembier, 1985). The National Longitudinal Transition Study (NLTS) (Blackorby & Wagner, 1996; Wagner, Blackorby, Cameto, & Newman, 1993) provides the most comprehensive data set on outcomes for students with disabilities and "the strongest evidence that students with disabilities are not achieving" key educational outcomes (Phelps & Hanley-Maxwell, 1997, p. 205). Consider the following typical NLTS findings (Marder, 1992; Phelps & Hanley-Maxwell, 1997; U.S.D.E., 1995).

- Overall, youths with disabilities are less likely than their peers to participate in postsecondary education.

- Less than 40 percent of students with mild disabilities enroll in postsecondary academic or vocational programs.

- Overall, youths with disabilities are employed at rates well below their peers.

- Students with disabilities who spent more time in general education are more likely to be employed than their peers who took fewer general education classes.

- Students with disabilities who spent more time in general education earn higher salaries than their peers took fewer general education classes.
- Forty to sixty percent of students with mild disabilities are competitively employed.
- Overall, youths who spent more time in general education were more likely to be participating fully in their communities.
- Less than half of students with mild disabilities are living independently.

School-to-work outcomes are measured regularly; results of these analyses suggest that formidable challenges remain for professionals interested in improving life beyond high school for students with disabilities. With growing national concern for heightened educational standards and continuing reform to improve overall achievement of America's youths, the likelihood is high that widespread improvements in outcomes for students with disabilities will remain difficult to realize. Improving employment, earnings, postsecondary, and life-style opportunities for all students are valued goals for education professionals; however, competing issues created by unresponsive systems continue to create obstacles to full participation of individuals with disabilities in these benefits of the American educational dream. Giving students more voice in their educational lives offers promise in making life beyond high school at least a little better.

Promise of Self-Determination

Quality of life for young adults is characterized by engagement in useful work, achievement in higher education as desired, personal independence, social interaction with peers and other community members, and participation in productive family activities. Over the past 30 years, considerable change has occurred in the services provided to individuals with disabilities who are adjusting to adult life. From primarily custodial care, designed to protect, manage, and control the lives of people with disabilities in segregated environments, America's transition services have become proactive in efforts to provide supports necessary for full participation in family and community life. Gerry and Mirsky (1992) provided five principles to guide adult services.

1. Services for people with disabilities should be guided by the wishes and needs of the individuals themselves and, when appropriate, their families.
2. Services must create flexible conditions within society to reflect and support the diverse and changing needs of people with disabilities.
3. Services must create real opportunities for people with disabilities to participate in productive employment.
4. Services must create collaborative conditions to ensure that people with disabilities have the opportunities and choices that are available to all Americans.
5. Services must ensure that social inclusion of people with disabilities in natural neighborhoods and communities becomes a way of life.

Wehman (1993) added student choice as a critical issue for special education heading into the twenty-first century.

Taking more control over one's life (or giving students more choices) is known as self-determination. It involves the following key concepts: student preferences, interests, abilities, wants, and needs are starting points for all activities; students learn to identify problems and solutions; students learn to generate, implement, and monitor goals and objectives; students take responsibilities for achieving goals; and students learn to express leadership skills and communicate using negotiation and compromise (Wehmeyer, 1998). Self-determination has become a hallmark of providing full and complete transition services (Agran, 1997; Sands & Wehmeyer, 1996; Turnbull, Anderson, Turnbull, Seaton, & Dinas, 1996; Ward, 1996; Wehmeyer, 1992, 1996, 1998). Few practices in education seem as easy to justify as providing students with more involvement in their own lives, and ample models exist to guide efforts in doing so (see Table 9.6); yet few practices are as infrequently implemented as involvement through self-determination (Wehmeyer, 1998).

TABLE 9.6	**Illustrative Self-Determination Programs**	
Program	**Key Concepts**	
ChoiceMaker (Martin & Marshall, 1995)	Seven areas of self-determination are central focus of lesson: self-awareness; self-advocacy; self-efficacy; decision making; independent performance; self-evaluation, and adjustment. A criterion-referenced, self-determination, transition-assessment tool linked to curriculum lessons is also included.	
Group Action Planning (Anderson, Seaton, Dinas, & Satterfield, 1995)	Students working with family members and other professionals formulate action plans across eight areas of daily living: domestic, transportation, employment, financial, recreational, social relationships, behavioral, and community participation.	
Whose Future Is It Anyway? (Wehmeyer & Kelchner, 1995)	Thirty-six sessions introduce students to concepts such as self-awareness, transition decision-making, community resources, transition goals and objectives, communication, and self-advocacy.	
TAKE CHARGE for the Future (Powers, 1996)	Self-help materials and coaching: • To identify transition goals • To organize and conduct transition planning meeting	

	• To achieve goals through application of problem-solving, self-regulation, and collaborative strategies Concurrent mentoring and peer support as well as family involvement
Next S.T.E.P. (Halpern, 1997)	Sixteen lessons in four units: getting started, self-exploration and self-evaluation, developing goals and activities, and putting a plan into place

Over the past three decades, professionals in special education have witnessed substantial financial investments in improving transition services provided to individuals with disabilities (Phelps & Hanley-Maxwell, 1997). This work has resulted in substantial progress in identifying key activities of value in moving young children into preschool and elementary school programs, improving placement changes that occur within schools and identifying key components of effective life changes after high school. For the benefits of all this transition effort to continue, fundamental defining concepts must be broadened. First, clear and explicit goals and performance standards must be included in the individualized education programs of all students with disabilities. As early and as often as possible, this aspect of education should include full and complete involvement of people with disabilities (i.e., self-determination) as well as their families and communities (i.e., collaboration). Additionally, integrated curricula (linking academic, occupational, vocational, and employment outcomes) are essential for forward-thinking, progressive transition services. Finally, changes in teacher education and professional development programs, as well as ongoing research on effectiveness, will be essential for a full and complete realization of transition as a meaningful part of the education of all people with disabilities in the twenty-first century.

Discussion Questions

1. Why is there a need for concern about transitions for students with disabilities other than those occurring when high school is complete?

2. What is the best way to ensure a smooth transition from an early intervention or preschool program to a special education program in an elementary school?

3. Why is it important for a student in special education to stay in school and to be helped to do so by whatever means needed?

4. What are some components of effective transition services provided after high school?

5. To what extent have school-to-work transition services been effective?

Chapter 10
School Reform and Special Education

Our dilemma is that we hate change and love it at the same time; what we really want is for things to remain the same but get better.

—Sydney J. Harris

As the 1990s came to a close, educators continued to write, hear, and speak a language that was already in vogue a decade earlier—*reform, restructuring,* and *excellence* were among the terms more frequently used. The push for educational reform reflected in these terms arose from a series of reports and public opinion polls that pointed to the presence of significant problems in current educational practice. Many of these reports also suggested novel approaches to the solution of the identified problems. These reforms reflected a belief that educators had to deliver more than ever before as they strove, along with businesses and families, toward excellence in education.

School reform has been primarily a general education initiative, even though the potential effects on special education are great. Over time, thinking about general education reform and special education has changed. Near the beginning of the 1990s, there was little to no recognition of students with disabilities in documents about education reform. For example, in its summary of the "education reform decade," the ETS Policy Information Center (1990) had not included a single mention of students with disabilities or even special education. In contrast, by the end of the decade, students with special needs increasingly were recognized as both a challenge to educational reform and a necessary target of it.

In this chapter, we examine what is meant by school reform, restructuring, and the notion of excellence in education, and we look at the relevance of all three to special education. The eight national goals signed into law by President Clinton are discussed in relation to issues and educational goals for students with disabilities, particularly the extent to which the goals and indicators of them reflect any cognizance at all of students served in special education and the implications for students in special education of attempts to meet each goal. We examine the issues that arise for students in special education programs from two large-scale reforms of the 1990s statewide "choice" in education and the push for accountability. Finally, we address some general issues of change in education and the complicating factors that serve as barriers to change in special education.

SCHOOL REFORM, RESTRUCTURING, AND EXCELLENCE IN EDUCATION

Many different initiatives designed to change education for the better, to improve education, have been called school reform. These initiatives include lengthening the school day or setting higher expectations for all students. Restructuring, however, is considered a different approach to reform: "It is a systematic approach that acknowledges the complexity of fundamentally changing the way schools are organized in order to significantly increase student learning. It shifts the focus of reform from mandating what educators do to looking at the results their actions produce" (National Governors' Association, 1990, p. 1). Examples of restructuring include site-based management (decision making carried out at a school site, rather than at a central office), the changing of staff roles (special education teachers serve special education students after school, rather than pulling them out of mainstream classes), the implementation of a higher-order thinking curriculum (emphasis on strategies for learning, for example, rather than on basic skills), and the adoption of an accountability system (student assessment to measure outcomes of learning). Excellence, the desired outcome of reform and restructuring, is the condition in which schools are successful in ultimately preparing students for adulthood.

The Reform Movement in General Education

How did the nation get to the point where it believed there was a critical need to reform or restructure education? The evolving attitude that America's

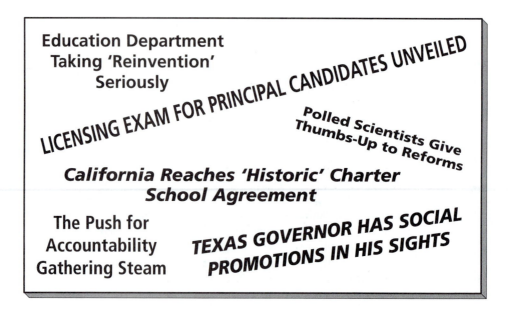

Education Department Taking 'Reinvention' Seriously

LICENSING EXAM FOR PRINCIPAL CANDIDATES UNVEILED

Polled Scientists Give Thumbs-Up to Reforms

California Reaches 'Historic' Charter School Agreement

The Push for Accountability Gathering Steam

TEXAS GOVERNOR HAS SOCIAL PROMOTIONS IN HIS SIGHTS

educational system is in trouble has come from many different reports identifying those qualities in which America's schools are lacking or those areas in which outcomes for American youths are below those for youths from other countries. The reports identifying problems/needs and possible avenues for change have been part of what has been referred to as the "three waves of educational reform."

In 1983, the nation was shocked when the National Commission on Excellence in Education produced its report, *A Nation at Risk: The Imperative for Educational Reform,* which was one of many to appear in this first wave of educational reform. The first wave reports, some of which are summarized in Table 10.1, focused on the dangers of mediocre education to the nation's growth and strength. Most reports emphasized the importance of commitment to excellence by advocating higher standards and "more"—more courses, more homework, more time, and more state and local responsibility. In 1984, President Ronald Reagan presented four national education goals to be reached by the target year 1990:

- To raise high school graduation rates to more than 90 percent
- To raise scores on college admissions tests above the 1985 average
- To make teachers' salaries competitive with entry-level business and engineering graduates' salaries
- To stiffen high school graduation requirements

TABLE 10.1   Selected First-Wave Educational Reform Reports

Report	Focus/Major Points
A Nation at Risk: The Imperative for Educational Reform (National Commission on Excellence in Education, 1983)	This report argues that the nation is at risk because "mediocrity," not excellence, is the norm in education. Recommendations include more time for learning; better textbooks and other materials; more homework; higher expectations; stricter attendance policies; and improved standards, salaries, rewards, and incentives for teachers.
A Placed Called School: Prospects for the Future (Goodlad, 1983)	This report presents recommendations derived from a study of schooling. Included are changes such as establishing smaller schools, ending the tracking system, and requiring a core curriculum of general courses in high school.
Making the Grade (Twentieth Century Fund Task Force on Federal Elementary and Secondary Education Policy, 1983)	This report argues that schools have been forced to play so many roles that they are in danger of forgetting their purpose and that federal government should support local and state efforts because the problems with education are "national and acute in intensity." Recommendations are made for curriculum change, rewards for teachers, and collection of information about education and academic performance of students.
Action for Excellence—A Comprehensive Plan to Improve Our Nation's Schools (Education Commission of the States & Task Force on Education for Economic Growth, 1983)	This report stresses the need for greater intensity and increased productivity throughout the educational system, arguing that technological change and increases in demand for knowledge within the workplace make the current definition of basic skills inadequate. The report argues that a new and higher regard for teachers is essential.
High School: A Report on American Secondary Education (Boyer, 1983)	This Carnegie Report focuses on establishing a core of common learning both to facilitate instruction and to foster connections among schools and workplaces. The need to identify and reward excellence in teaching is also emphasized.

(continued)

TABLE 10.1   Selected First-Wave Educational Reform Reports (Continued)

Academic Preparation for College: What Students Need to Know and Be Able to Do (College Board, Educational Equality Project, 1983)	This report identifies what it takes to do competent and worthwhile college work, with a description of learning outcomes that exceed those in most secondary schools. Better preparation for the collegebound is predicted to spill over and improve the schooling of those who are not collegebound and also to lower the number of high school dropouts.

These goals, while admirable, seemed to ignore the growing population of students considered to be in need of special education services. More of the same hardly seemed the answer to their needs. These goals were feasible only if special education students were considered to be separate from general education students. Only by excluding students with mental retardation, significant emotional and behavioral disorders, or learning disabilities was it possible to think about goals such as a 90 percent graduation rate and higher scores on college entrance exams.

A second wave of educational reform began with the 1986 *Time for Results* report from the National Governors' Association. This and the other reports of the second wave, which are summarized in Table 10.2, emphasized the need to improve school organization and policy as well as the quality of teachers. The governors' report did not argue for more of the same; it argued for changes in the form of improvements. And the need for early educational experiences for children at risk was recognized. This was perhaps the first recognition that children with special needs did exist and that they would require extraordinary procedures and approaches to reach the level required to progress through school successfully and to ultimately attain national goals of excellence. This still was not the same as recognizing the population of children and youths being served in special education, but it did reveal the tip of the iceberg!

The third wave of school reform emphasized more than ever before the needs of children and youths who were at risk or disadvantaged, who had dropped out of school, or whose needs were not being met by the educational system (see Table 10.3). It was argued that to be effective in helping prepare students for the twenty-first century, the educational system would have to be reconstructed. There was a call to reach consensus about national educational goals and strategies to reach them. These calls led eventually to the 1989 education summit of President Bush and the nation's governors and the development of a new set of national education goals.

A fourth wave of educational reform was carried out with the election of one of the governors, who led the effort with President Bush to produce the 1989

TABLE 10.2   Selected Second-Wave Educational Reform Reports

Report	Focus/Major Points
Children in Need: Investment Strategies for the Educationally Disadvantaged (Committee for Economic Development, 1987)	This report focuses on needs specific to children who are disadvantaged, noting that most reform efforts have bypassed this group. Business leaders, educators, and policy makers are urged to look beyond the classroom to establish new partnerships that bolster not only education but also the health and well-being of the whole child.
Educational Achievement: Explanations and Implications of Recent Trends (Congressional Budget Office, 1987)	This report appraises trends in achievement tests scores and their causes. Implications drawn from findings focus on overreliance on test scores for assessing effects of educational initiatives, the importance of improving higher-order skills, and the need to focus on traditionally low-scoring groups such as minorities.
Time for Results: The Governors' 1991 Report (National Governors' Association, 1986)	This report identifies key educational issues for a five-year period: teacher pay, educational recruitment, parental choice of schools, strategies for the poor, school year, technology, college education, and clear, measurable educational goals.
What Works (U.S. Department of Education, 1986)	This report presents research findings and comments on them in the areas of home, classroom, and school. It provides a highly readable translation of technical information, with citations for further reference.

education summit. President Clinton carried forward the concepts from that education summit to produce several education reform laws (e.g., Goals 2000, School to Work Opportunities Act, Improving America's Schools Act). In pushing the reform agenda forward, increased emphasis was given to international comparisons, such as the Third International Mathematics and Science Study (TIMSS) and to the views of businesses about the lack of skills in the graduates of public high schools (see Table 10.4). Despite increasing resistance from conservative groups, the push for reform continues as the century draws to a close.

TABLE 10.3   Selected Third-Wave Educational Reform Reports

Report	Focus/Major Points
Turning Points: Preparing American Youth for the 21st Century (Carnegie Council on Adolescent Development, 1989)	This report identifies the early adolescence period as one in which key decisions are made that affect a person's entire future and provides many recommendations to improve the educational experiences of all middle school students, especially those at risk of being left behind.
America's Shame, America's Hope: Twelve Million Youth at Risk (Smith & Lincoln, 1988)	This report presents itself as an inquiry into the education reform movement of the 1980s, with at-risk youths as the frame of reference. The argument is that despite reform reports, the numbers of at-risk youths have increased. Recommendations are primarily policy related, focusing on legislatures, governors, and commissioners of education.
The Forgotten Half: Non-College Youth in America (William T. Grant Foundation, 1988)	This report calls attention to the needs of youths not planning to go to college to help them move from school to careers, identifies the problem as being in the economy and the paths for youths to enter it, and indicates that education can help but is not the sole solution.
Results in Education: 1988 (National Governors' Association, 1988)	This report describes state efforts to track the results of earlier education reforms, provides information on a state-by-state basis, and summarizes results.
Youth Indicators, 1988: Trends in the Well-Being of American Youth (Office of Educational Research and Improvement, 1988)	This report provides a broad view of the welfare of youths through presentation of statistical information; goes beyond educational indicators to include family structure, economic well-being, drug use, suicide, employment prospects, and so on; and provides a longitudinal perspective.

Parallel Play in School Reform

As young children develop, their social interactions with other children begin as "parallel play." In this type of play, two children may sit side by side without ever having any interchange between them. Yet when asked, they will say that they were playing with each other. This is how school reform began in special education.

TABLE 10.4   Selected Fourth-Wave Education Reform Reports

Report	Focus/Major Points
A Nation Still at Risk: An Education Manifesto (Center for Education Reform, 1998)	This report is representative of several published by conservative educational groups to indicate that the United States is still a nation at risk. It cites poor performance in international comparisons and increased need for remediation of students entering colleges.
Building a System to Connect School and Employment (Council of Chief State School Officers, 1994)	This report documents the issues that must be addressed and resources needed to build a coherent and effective system of youth development and career preparation.
Improving Student Performance: New Strategies for Implementing Higher Standards (Center for Peak Performing Schools, 1993)	This report describes the steps needed to redesign schools, including districtwide reforms (such as new teacher talent, decentralized decision making, etc.) that produce championship schools.
Transforming Education: Overcoming Barriers (National Governors' Association, 1993)	This report examines why progress did meet early expectations for reform. It addresses five categories of barriers (lack of clear direction, weak incentives for change, regulatory and compliance mentality, limited learning opportunities for educators, poor communication) and identifies steps governors can take to promote school reform.

During the time when general education was thinking deeply about educational reform, the Regular Education Initiative was proposed. Despite its name, this was a call from special education for reform in the way services were provided to students with disabilities. It called for a sharing of responsibility by general educators and special educators for these students (Will, 1986). For the most part, debate about the initiative caused great furor among special educators and parents. Some special educators worried about the need for their services if classroom teachers really were to assume responsibility for students with disabilities. Others wondered whether they had the consultation skills required for the shared responsibility espoused by backers of the initiative. Parents expressed concerns about due process rights and about whether their children would be appropriately educated. Personnel in the general education system knew relatively little about the debate until years after it began. The Regular Education Initiative was not viewed as an educational reform in the way that other recommendations were. In Chapter 5, we discussed the Regular Education Initiative and its successor, inclusion, more fully in the context within which it had its greatest impact—debates about appropriate placement of students with disabilities. For educational reform in general, it had limited impact.

EIGHT NATIONAL GOALS FOR EDUCATION

In September 1989, President Bush and the governors from the fifty states met in Charlottesville, Virginia, for a "historic education summit" that for the first time produced goals that all governors supported. The head of the National Governors' Association at the time was Bill Clinton, soon to become president of the United States. He carried forward the six goals into reform legislation called Goals 2000: Educate America Act. While political forces successfully added two goals before the legislation passed in 1993, the original goals (readiness to learn, school completion, student achievement and citizenship, science and mathematics, adult literacy and lifelong learning, and the school environment—safe, disciplined, drug-free) essentially remained intact. The two added goals focused on more process-oriented variables—teacher skills and parent involvement. While each goal included a list of objectives, these soon disappeared from reports on progress toward goals and were replaced by evidence on certain key indicators that formed a U.S. scorecard (see, for example, National Education Goals Panel, 1997).

References to the Goals 2000 legislation all but disappeared from reform language by the end of the 1990s. However, reform rhetoric continued to focus on the *content* of the legislation, especially the standards encompassed in Goal 3 and the discipline and violence encompassed in Goal 7. Still, it is informative to look at each of the goals and the indicators selected to measure progress toward meeting them, and to note the ways in which they recognize (or do not recognize) students with disabilities.

Ready to Learn

The focus on the first educational goal is readiness for learning.

▪ *Goal 1:* By the year 2000, all children in America will start school ready to learn.

This goal originally was the one that most directly recognized the child with a disability and was the only one to use the term *disabled*. This recognition occurred in the first objective of the goal, which stated "All disadvantaged and disabled children will have access to high quality and developmentally appropriate preschool programs that help prepare children for school." With the change in emphasis from objectives to indicators of progress, all references to disability disappeared. Four indicators of readiness to learn were identified and monitored:

- *Children's health index:* Has the United States reduced the percentage of infants born with one or more health risks?
- *Immunizations:* Has the United States increased the percentage of 2-year-olds who have been fully immunized against preventable childhood diseases?
- *Family-child reading and storytelling:* Has the United States increased the percentage of 3- to 5-year-olds whose parents read to them or tell them stories regularly?
- *Preschool participation:* Has the United States reduced the gap in preschool participation between 3- to 5-year-olds from high- and low-income families?

The summary of progress reported by the National Education Goals Panel in 1997 indicated that significant improvement had been made on three of the four indicators. Only the changes found for the last indicator, preschool participation, were considered equivocal. As is evident in the description of that indicator, no attempt was made to measure the access of children with disabilities to preschool programs.

While a definition of "ready for learning" was not provided, many began to question whether, because of the way Goal 1 was stated, elementary schools might shirk their responsibility to get schools ready for children. A Ready Schools Resource Group convened by the National Education Goals Panel identified 10 strategies for schools and community leaders to "strengthen the transition to school and learning" (National Education Goals Panel, 1998):

1. Ready schools smooth the transition between home and school.
2. Ready schools strive for continuity between early care and education programs and elementary schools.
3. Ready schools help children learn and make sense of their complex and exciting world.
4. Ready schools are committed to the success of every child.
5. Ready schools are committed to the success of every teacher and every adult who interacts with children during the school day.
6. Ready schools introduce or expand approaches that have been shown to raise achievement.
7. Ready schools are learning organizations that alter practices and programs if they do not benefit children.
8. Ready schools serve children in communities.
9. Ready schools take responsibility for results.
10. Ready schools have strong leadership.

In discussion of the fourth strategy, children with disabilities are mentioned: "Ready schools have high expectations for children with disabilities, just as they do for all children" (p. 15). The holding of high expectations is tied in this document to "meeting special needs in regular classrooms whenever possible" (p. 15).

School Completion

The completion of high school is the focus of the second national education goal.

> *Goal 2:* By the year 2000, the high school graduation rate will increase to at least 90 percent.

This goal sounds suspiciously similar to the national goal voiced by President Reagan in 1984 and similarly suggests nonrecognition of students with disabilities. Just one indicator was identified for Goal 2:

- *High school completion:* Has the United States increased the percentage of 18- to 24-year-olds who have a high school credential?

While initial discussion of this goal focused on both obtaining high school diplomas and reducing the dropout rate, the selected indicator focuses only on having a high school *credential*. Research has shown that not only do high school graduation requirements vary tremendously from one state to another, but also that a variety of documents are offered at the end of a student's high school years (Thurlow, Ysseldyke, & Reid, 1977). Thus, students with disabilities who do not meet the requirements for a regular high school diploma may earn an IEP diploma, a certificate of completion or attendance, or various other options, depending on where they live. The question of whether this broad definition of successful school completion contradicted calls for stiffer graduation requirements never surfaced.

If the National Education Goals Panel had decided to count only those students earning regular high school diplomas (or various honors diplomas), it is unlikely that success would be demonstrated on this goal. By counting any type of end-of-school document (including IEP diplomas, certificates of completion, etc.), the completion rate of 86 percent remained constant between the baseline year 1990 and the update year 1996 (National Education Goals Panel, 1997).

The notion of dramatically reducing the dropout rate reflected the flip side of the coin. For some time, an implicit assumption held that students in special education were less likely to drop out of school because they were already receiving the extra attention they needed. But evidence suggested that "youth with handicaps, who are entitled to receive appropriate public education until they complete a high school degree or until age 21, also drop out of school at high rates" (Wolman, Bruininks, & Thurlow, 1989, p. 6). In fact, relatively "controlled" studies have generally reported that students with disabilities, whether they attend special education schools or are mainstreamed, are more likely to drop out of school than are students without disabilities (e.g., Bruininks, Thurlow, Lewis, & Larson, 1988; Marder & D'Amico, 1992; Owings & Stocking, 1986; Stephenson, 1985; Wagner, 1991).

If students in special education are already in programs and receiving services much like those now identified as effective for dropout prevention, what must be done to prevent students in special education from dropping out of school? Although this major question was receiving attention as the 1990s began, that attention did not come from the national education goals and the programs identified as reflecting "best practice" for dropout prevention in educational reform. In fact, dropout prevention research focusing on students with disabilities indicated that significantly more intensive interventions were needed to address the needs of youths with disabilities at risk for dropping out of school (Sinclair, Christenson, Evelo, & Hurley, 1998; Thurlow, Christenson, Sinclair, Evelo, & Thornton, 1995).

Student Achievement and Citizenship

Broad notions of achievement and citizenship come together in the third educational goal.

> *Goal 3:* By the year 2000, American students will leave grades 4, 8, and 12 having demonstrated competency over challenging subject matter including English, mathematics, science, foreign languages, civics and government, economics, history, and geography; and every school in America will ensure that all students learn to use their minds well, so they may be prepared for responsible citizenship, further learning, and productive employment in our nation's modern economy.

Six indicators are used to assess progress toward Goal 3:

- *Reading achievement:* Has the United States increased the percentage of students who meet the Goals Panel's performance standards in reading?

- *Writing achievement:* Has the United States increased the percentage of students who can produce basic, extended, developed, or elaborated responses to narrative writing tasks?

- *Mathematics achievement:* Has the United States increased the percentage of students who meet the Goals Panel's performance standard in mathematics?

- *Science achievement:* Has the United States increased the percentage of students who meet the Goals Panel's performance standard in science?

- *History achievement:* Has the United States increased the percentage of students who meet the Goals Panel's performance standard in U.S. history?

- *Geography achievement:* Has the United States increased the percentage of students who meet the Goals Panel's performance standard in geography?

While this goal focuses on demonstrating competency in various content areas and on learning how to use the mind to foster responsible citizenship, further learning, and productive employment, only content knowledge is included in the indicators. To document progress in content area knowledge, data were available for only two of the six content areas—reading and math. For reading, results were either equivocal (grades 4 and 8) or showed decreases in performance (grade 12). For mathematics, results were better, with increases in the percentages meeting performance standards demonstrated at all grades (4, 8, and 12). Yet the numbers also indicate that performance, even when increasing, is not good. For example, the increases in math ranged from 4 percentage points to 9 percentage points, but still was always less than 25 percent of the students meeting standards. The percentages meeting the standard in reading were higher, averaging from 30 percent to 36 percent, yet those were the same as the first time they were measured or lower.

Goal 3 reflects a move toward national and state-by-state assessments of educational indicators such as the National Assessment of Educational Progress. Consideration of the development of a national test for all students similarly reflected this move toward better educational accountability. But the push toward assessment of achievement created many additional questions for educators responsible for students with disabilities. How many students with disabilities, and which ones, should be included in statewide assessments? Is it fair for one state to exclude all students with emotional and learning disabilities from its testing program when another state includes all except those who would be detrimentally affected by the testing experience (in the opinion of a designated team)? (These issues and many others that arise in relation to demonstrating competency were addressed in Chapter 6 and are discussed in greater depth in Chapter 11.)

Teacher Education and Professional Development

The fourth national educational goal, one of the two new goals added by Congress before the passage of the Goals 2000 legislation, addresses preservice and inservice training.

> *Goal 4:* By the year 2000, the nation's teaching force will have access to programs for the continued improvement of their professional skills and the opportunity to acquire the knowledge and skills needed to instruct and prepare all American students for the next century.

Two indicators were identified for this goal:

- *Teacher preparation:* Has the United States increased the percentage of secondary school teachers who hold an undergraduate or graduate degree in their main teaching assignment?

- *Teacher professional development:* Has the United States increased the percentage of teachers reporting that they participated in professional development programs on one or more topics since the end of the previous school year?

Data collected on these indicators were less than adequate. There were no comparison data for the second indicator (only one data point, which suggested that 85 percent of teachers had participated in professional development). The data for the first indicator showed a drop in percentage from the baseline year (1991) to the update year (1994), changing from 66 percent to 63 percent of secondary school teachers holding a degree in the area of their teaching assignment.

Professional development, however, continues to be a hot topic of educational reform. Groups now have put forth or are developing standards for teachers (e.g., National Council for Accreditation of Teacher Education [NCATE], Interstate New Teacher Assessment and Support Consortium [INTASC], and standards are being developed for administrators also (Interstate School Leaders Licensure Consortium [ISLLC]). Professionals in several states must now take tests before they can receive certification or continue teaching, a requirement that has resulted in almost entire teaching forces being unable to pass and state commissioners resigning (Sandham, 1998). Standards have also been developed for special education personnel (Council for Exceptional Children, 1995). Their use for certification has not yet been required.

Mathematics and Science

The fifth goal addresses two specific content areas in the general school curriculum: science and math.

> *Goal 5:* By the year 2000, United States students will be first in the world in science and mathematics achievement.

This fifth goal targets two specific content areas for emphasis because of their significance in international business competition. This concentration is not reasonable for all students unless math is broadly defined as consumer skills or science connotes knowing one's place in the world. This issue and related issues form another pervasive question in special education—what should be the content of instruction? (See Chapter 7 for further discussion.)

Three indicators are used to measure progress toward meeting Goal 5, all of them focusing directly on student achievement and attainment rather than on process indicators related to mathematics and science. The indicators are:

- *International mathematics achievement:* Has the United States improved its standing on international mathematics assessments?
- *International science achievement:* Has the United States improved its standing on international science assessments?
- *Mathematics and science degrees:* Has the United States increased mathematics and science degrees as a percentage of all degrees awarded to:
  - All students?
  - Minorities (blacks, Hispanics, American Indians/Alaskan Natives)?
  - Females?

While comparative data were not available on the first two indicators, attainment of mathematics and science degrees by all groups showed positive changes, from one to three percentage points. Again these indicators include very few students with disabilities.

Adult Literacy and Lifelong Learning

The sixth education goal moves the focus more clearly beyond the school setting to focus on postschool outcomes.

> *Goal 6:* By the year 2000, every adult American will be literate and will possess the knowledge and skills necessary to compete in a global economy and exercise the rights and responsibilities of citizenship.

Three indicators were identified to measure progress on this goal:

- *Adult literacy:* Has the United States increased the percentage of adults who score at or above Level 3 in prose literacy?
- *Participation in adult education:* Has the United States reduced the gap in adult education participation between adults who have a high school diploma or less and those who have additional postsecondary education or technical training?
- *Participation in higher education:* Has the United States reduced the gap between white and black high school graduates who:
  - Enroll in college?
  - Complete a college degree?

  Has the United States reduced the gap between white and Hispanic high school graduates who:

  - Enroll in college?
  - Complete a college degree?

Data were not available to make comparisons from one time to another on the first indicator. Data on the second showed a larger gap between the two groups and thus a negative finding. Data on the third indicator showed no change over time in any of the comparisons.

This goal can be broadly interpreted to cover a goal for successful transition from school to work that has been espoused for students with disabilities (Johnson, Bruininks, & Thurlow, 1987; Phelps & Hanley-Maxwell, 1997; Rusch & Chadsey, 1998; Rusch & Phelps, 1987; Will, 1984). Yet the indicators focus only on literacy levels and educational experiences. These indicators are relatively limited and do not ask, for example, What makes a student qualified for access to a college education? This is a crucial consideration given that youths with disabilities are less likely to enroll in postsecondary education programs than are their peers without disabilities (Fairweather & Shaver, 1991), despite increases in the number of two- and four-year colleges providing services for students with disabilities (Vogel, 1982). Even though students with certain disabilities (such as speech, physical, visual, or hearing impairments) may be more likely to enroll in postsecondary education than students with learning or emotional difficulties, the enrollment of such students is still much lower than for students without disabilities.

Safe, Disciplined, and Alcohol- and Drug-Free Schools

The seventh goal addresses the school environment.

> *Goal 7:* By the year 2000, every school in the United States will be free of drugs, violence, and the unauthorized presence of firearms and alcohol and will offer a disciplined environment conducive to learning.

Four out of seven possible indicators were selected to track progress toward meeting this goal:

- *Overall student drug and alcohol use:* Has the United States reduced the percentage of tenth graders reporting doing the following during the previous year?
  - Using any illicit drug.
  - Using alcohol.
- *Sale of drugs at school:* Has the United States reduced the percentage of tenth graders reporting that someone offered to sell or give them an illegal drug at school during the previous year?
- *Student and teacher victimization:* Has the United States reduced the percentage of students and teachers reporting that they were threatened or injured at school during the previous year?
  - Tenth-grade students
  - Secondary school teachers
- *Disruptions in class by students:* Has the United States reduced the percentage of students and teachers reporting that disruptions often interfere with teaching and learning?
  - Tenth-grade students
  - Secondary school teachers

With information available on the seven data points within the four indicators of this goal (e.g., percentage of drug and alcohol use, percentage of reputed drug dealing, percentage of violence reported by tenth-grade students and secondary school teachers, number of classroom disruptions reported by tenth-grade students and secondary school teachers), two showed no change, four showed negative change, and only one (tenth-grade students reporting having been threatened or injured at school) showed improvement (decreasing from 40 percent to 36 percent).

Goals such as these can be considered appropriate for all students (assuming that students with disabilities are included in health classes where the dangers of alcohol and drugs are likely to be discussed.) This goal, however, probably indirectly contributed to the contentious debate about the rights of students on IEPs when facing disciplinary actions. The 1997 reauthorization of IDEA was delayed many months, in part because of disagreement about whether students with disabilities could be suspended from school without securing special education services for them during their suspension. When the law was passed, discipline was addressed in the section on placement in alternative educational settings. The complexity in the requirements that had to be met before applying disciplinary actions probably contributed to the concern that students with disabilities are not being held to the same standards as other students (see Table 10.5).

This broad goal, which is directed primarily at the content and process of education, is appropriate for all students as long as those with disabilities are included in the health education program. But this goal's actual acknowledgment of the needs of or programs for students with disabilities is questionable. This has been the case in many aspects of the school reform movement. Much of what is proposed would be appropriate if it is adapted to meet the needs of a broad array of students, not just those preparing for college or those at risk for academic failure.

Parental Participation

National education Goal 8, the second of the two new goals introduced before the Goals 2000 bill passed into law, recognizes the contribution that parents and family make to a child's education.

Goal 8: By the year 2000, every school will promote partnerships that will increase parental involvement and participation in promoting the social, emotional, and academic growth of children.

Three indicators were identified for this goal:

- *Schools' reports of parent attendance at parent-teacher conferences:* Has the United States increased the percentage of K to 8 public schools that reported that more than half of their parents attended parent-teacher conferences during the school year?

- *Schools' reports of parent involvement in school policy decisions:* Has the United States increased the percentage of K to 8 public schools that reported that parent input is considered when making policy decisions in three or more areas?

- *Parents' reports of their involvement in school activities:* Has the United States increased the percentage of students in grades 3 to 12 whose parents reported that they participated in two or more activities in their child's school during the current school year?

Data were available for only one of these indicators, the last one, and they showed no difference between the 1993 and 1996 measures of parents' involvement in school activities.

For many of the goals and indicators of them, parent involvement is relevant for students with disabilities. However, because of a history of diffi-

TABLE 10.5 **Examples of Discipline Provisions in the 1997 Amendments to IDEA**

Sec. 615(k). Placement in Alternative Educational Setting.—

(1) Authority of School Personnel.—

   (A) School personnel . . . may order a change in the placement of a child with a disability—

      (i) to an appropriate interim alternative educational setting, another setting, or suspension, for not more than 10 school days (to the extent such alternatives would be applied to children without disabilities); and

      (ii) to an appropriate interim alternative educational setting for the same amount of time that a child without a disability would be subject to discipline, but for not more than 45 days if—

         (I) the child carries a weapon to school or to a school function under the jurisdiction of a State or local educational agency; or

         (II) the child knowingly possesses or uses illegal drugs or sells or solicits the sale of a controlled substance while at school or a school function under the jurisdiction of a State or local educational agency.

   (B) Either before or not later than 10 days after taking a disciplinary action—

      (i) if the local educational agency did not conduct a functional behavioral assessment and implement a behavioral intervention plan for such a child before the behavior that resulted in the suspension . . . , the agency shall convene an IEP meeting to develop an assessment plan to address that behavior; or

      (ii) if the child already has a behavioral intervention plan, the IEP Team shall review the plan and modify it, as necessary, to address the behavior.

cult relations between schools and many parents of students with disabilities, it is less likely that reports from the parents of students with disabilities are included in the data collected to assess progress on this last goal. This lack of data exists despite the belief that parent involvement may be even more important for students with disabilities than it is for other students (see Chapter 11).

Gallup Poll Results on Issues Related to the National Goals for Education

By the late 1990s, opinion polls no longer focused on the "national education goals." They did, however, focus on the content of several of the goals. Some of these were included in the 1997 Gallup poll of 1,517 adults.

- Lack of discipline and inadequate financing are the local school problems most frequently mentioned by respondents. The use of drugs and "fighting, violence, and gangs" are not far behind.

- Do the public schools overemphasize achievement testing? Approximately half (48 percent) believe the current emphasis is appropriate; the remaining half are divided between "too much" (20 percent) and "not enough" (28 percent).

- Children today are getting more parental help with their homework than in earlier years, and Americans in general report an increased willingness to work as unpaid volunteers in their local public schools.

- A small majority of the public (53 percent) is at least somewhat satisfied with the steps being taken to deal with the use of drugs in the local schools. Fifty-two percent of respondents believe an educational approach is the best way to deal with the problem; 42 percent believe severe penalties are best.

- The public gives strong support to "zero tolerance" policies that call for automatic suspension for drug and alcohol possession in school and for carrying weapons of any kind into school.

SOURCE: Results from the 29th annual Gallup Poll of the public's attitudes toward the public schools (Rose, Gallup, & Elam, 1997), pp. 42–43. Rose, L. C., Gallup, A. M., & Elam, S. M. (1997). The 29th annual Phi Delta Kappa/Gallup Poll of the public's attitudes toward the public schools. *Phi Delta Kappan, 79* (1), 41–56.

REFORM, RESTRUCTURING, AND EXCELLENCE IN SPECIAL EDUCATION?

At about the time that the governors and President Bush were discussing the nation's goals for education, the National Council on Disability was preparing a report for the president entitled *The Education of Students with Disabilities: Where Do We Stand?* This report noted that "for the most part school reform efforts have not been directed toward addressing the special challenges that students with disabilities face. There is a perception that students with disabilities have a separate system, called special education [in which they are] better provided for than many other groups of students" (1980, p. 2).

Based on a year-long study, the Council argued that it was time to shift the focus of concern from access to education to the quality of education and student outcomes. The Council found many problems in current educational practice for students with disabilities and reported twenty-eight findings that indicated a need for reform. These findings (see Table 10.6) led the Council to call for the

TABLE 10.6	**Findings on Educational Practice with Students with Disabilities**

1. Parent-professional relationships too often are strained and difficult, and parents and professionals frequently view one another as adversaries rather than as partners. (p. 15)

2. Some parents have difficulty finding appropriate services for their children. (p. 16)

3. Parents and students report that some schools have low expectations for students with disabilities and establish inappropriate learning objectives and goals. (p. 19)

4. Services often are not available to meet the needs of disadvantaged, minority, and rural families who have children with disabilities. (p. 21)

5. Families in the military are not universally entitled to the services or the protections guaranteed under P.L. 94-142. (p. 22)

6. There is a perception that the outcomes of due process hearings are biased in favor of the schools. (p. 24)

7. Many parents are uninformed about their rights under the law. (p. 24)

8. Due process hearings are costly. (p. 25)

9. There is a paucity of attorneys with expertise in special education law available to represent parents. (p. 25)

10. There are no standard qualification or training requirements for hearing officers. (p. 26)

11. There is no national database that includes the routine collection of data regarding due process hearings. (p. 26)

12. There are several commonly agreed upon characteristics to describe what constitutes an effective school. (p. 27)

13. Most school reform initiatives appear to be a response to declining academic achievement, rather than efforts to find ways for schools to meet the diverse needs of all students. (p. 27)

14. An essential aspect of school reform is the professionalization of teaching. (p. 28)

15. School reform efforts have not specifically addressed the diverse needs of students with disabilities. (p. 28)

16. Evaluation procedures, disability classifications, and resulting placement decisions vary greatly among school districts and states, and they often are not related to students' learning characteristics. (p. 29)

17. A highly emotional discussion is taking place about the role of separate schools and the unique instructional needs of students with specific disabilities such as deafness. (p. 31)

18. Special education is a relatively separate system of service delivery. (p. 34)

TABLE 10.6	**Findings on Educational Practice with Students with Disabilities (continued)**

19. In practice, special education has been defined more as an organizational approach to delivering instruction—as part of a placement continuum—than as a specific body of professional expertise. (p. 35)

20. Current pedagogy regarding effective schools and teaching practices can facilitate the integration of special needs students into general classrooms. (p. 36)

21. A strong Federal role in educating students with disabilities is essential. (p. 38)

22. The federal government has not fulfilled its promise of 40% funding of the cost of providing education to students with disabilities. (p. 39)

23. Federal monitoring is an essential aspect of the federal-state partnership. (p. 39)

24. Upon leaving school, students with disabilities and their families often have a difficult time accessing appropriate adult services and/or postsecondary education and training programs. (p. 40)

25. Effective transition planning for high school students with disabilities can facilitate their success in adult life. (p. 41)

26. Graduates with disabilities are more likely to be employed following school if (1) comprehensive vocational training is a primary component of their high school program and (2) they have a job secured at the time of graduation. (p. 42)

27. There are insufficient partnerships between the business community and schools for the purpose of enhancing employment opportunities for students with disabilities. (p. 43)

28. Parent participation during high school facilitates the successful transition of students with disabilities from school to adult life. (p. 44)

NOTE: The report has three additional findings not presented here that reflect an international perspective.

SOURCE: National Council on Disability. (1989). *The Education of Students with Disabilities: Where Do We Stand?* Washington, D.C.: Author. Used with permission.

establishment of a national commission on excellence in the education of students with disabilities to continue an assessment of the status of the education of students with disabilities and to make recommendations about how the quality of education for these students could be enhanced and how improved student outcomes could be realized.

In 1996, the National Council on Disability published another report, this one designed to assess the progress of disability policy in setting an agenda for the future. In its discussion of education issues, the Council summarized the educational system for students with disabilities in the following way:

> Despite progress in the last decade in educating students with disabilities, current federal and state laws have failed to ensure the delivery of a free and appropriate public education for too many students with disabilities. Students with disabilities

often still find themselves in forced and inappropriate isolation, separated from their nondisabled peers. In other situations, students with disabilities are in regular education classrooms with teachers with little or no training in how to educate students with disabilities and without the supports they need. Lack of accountability, poor enforcement, and systemic barriers have robbed too many students of their educational rights and opportunities and have produced a separate system of education for students with disabilities rather than one unified system that ensures full and equal physical, programmatic, and communication access for all students. Parents and students across the country express a high level of frustration with the continued barriers they face to full participation and effective instruction. (p. 50)

Given this assessment of the status of the educational system for students with disabilities, the Council made seven recommendations for the President of the United States to consider:

1. The Congress and state governments should mandate a unified system of education and training that will ensure equal physical, programmatic and communication access to all education programs, facilities and related benefits of education for all students while meeting the individual needs of all students, including those with disabilities. The mandate should include a firm timetable for retraining teachers, changing systems, and training parents and students about the new education policies. . . .

2. The Congress and the Federal Government should ensure that current due process protections for students under IDEA are not weakened and that they are fully enforced.

3. The Congress, the Secretary of Education, state education agencies, and educational organizations should promote the maximal use of modern technology in education. . . .

4. The Secretary of Education and state governors should enforce compliance with federal and state education laws. Local education agencies should be held accountable for student outcomes. . . .

5. The President and heads of relevant Cabinet agencies should more strongly enforce the accessibility provisions of ADA and the Rehabilitation Act and state governments must enforce state accessibility laws to ensure better accessibility in schools for students, parents, teachers, staff and members of the public with disabilities. . . .

6. The President and the Congress should insist on strong enforcement of ADA and the Rehabilitation Act in higher education settings and should develop mechanisms to expand access and support services for students with disabilities who seek to enter or who are participating in postsecondary education. . . .

7. The Secretary of Education and the Secretary of Labor should expand initiatives to promote effective transition from school to work or postsecondary education for all students, both with and without disabilities, with a clear expectation that work is the ultimate goal. (pp. 51–54)

Reform and restructuring in general education necessarily had (and continue to have) an impact on special education. But ideas for reform and reform movements in general education continued to occur without much input from special education. Kaufman, Kameenui, Birman, and Danielson suggested that special education had to change this situation by becoming a master of educational reform:

> In order to be a master of educational reform and not become its victim, special education must not be complacent with the impressive and significant achievements of the past 15 years. Special education must do more than focus on issues of access and inclusion for children with disabilities during these times of reform and change. In order to achieve better results, special educators and parents must assertively seek the knowledge and innovations needed to expand the provision of effective educational experiences and support not only through special education but in regular education, at home, and in the community. It is critical that educational reform and change be viewed as an open-ended journey. The nature of the journey will depend on our inquisitiveness and our resolve to inquire and act. (1990, p. 110)

Well into the 1990s, comprehensive general education reforms were well under way, with as yet unidentified effects, as some of the examples in the next section indicate.

GENERAL EDUCATION REFORMS AND THEIR EFFECTS

There have been many reforms attempted by schools, local education agencies, and state education agencies. The Education Commission of the States (1998b) grouped major education reforms into six broad areas:

- Early childhood education
- Standards/assessment/accountability
- School finance
- Flexibility/governance/choice
- Teacher quality
- Changing the learning environment

For discussion here, we have selected two areas that, by the end of the 1990s, were receiving broad-based attention and were often touted as beneficial to students with disabilities, even if these students had not been considered when the reforms were originally conceptualized: first, the push for educational accountability, sometimes subsumed under the name standards-based reform, and second, choice in education, a reform encompassing the freedom to choose from various alternatives to general public education, including open enrollment options, charter schools, and home schooling.

The Push for Accountability

In some ways, the tremendous push for accountability took off from national education Goal 3, which called for improved student achievement. Closely linked with this goal, from the beginning, was the notion that student achievement had to be measured against defined standards—to specify what students should know and be able to do—and assessments to measure their progress toward meeting those standards. In its discussion of standards, assessments, and accountability, the Education Commission of the States (1998b) stated that *"accountability* systems collect, evaluate, and use data about students and schools to hold educators and others responsible for results" (p. 19). Typically, these systems contain definitions pertaining to how well students must perform. Assessments are the avenues for measuring whether students have met defined standards.

In describing the education accountability systems in the fifty states, the Education Commission of States (1997b) identified two primary types of consequences that are applied: rewards and sanctions. The Commission's analysis revealed that fourteen states had included rewards in their accountability systems, defined in either statute or regulation, while thirty-three states had sanctions. Rewards ranged from cash payments to teachers, to public recognition of accomplishments; sanctions ranged from remediation assistance to takeover and removal of administrators and/or staff (Education Commission of the States, 1997a, 1998a).

Where did special education fit in all this? For the most part, its role in the push for accountability and standards-based reform was minimal to nonexistent. For example, an analysis of state standards documents (Thurlow, Ysseldyke, Gutman, & Geenen, 1998) revealed that while nearly all states boasted that their standards were for all children in the state, few states defined *all* to include children with disabilities. Furthermore, analyses of who actually was involved in developing the standards showed that special education professionals, advocates, or persons with disabilities were rarely involved in the setting of standards to be met by "all" children in the state.

When states were asked directly about whether their standards would apply to students with disabilities, most replied that they would (Rhim & McLaughlin, 1997). Nine states reported that the state standards would *not* apply to students with IEPs, and another four states indicated either that IEP teams would make individual decisions about their applicability to specific students, that the state standards were voluntary, or that IEP students would be required to "accomplish all standards to extent able" (p. 6).

Similarly, a large body of evidence exists on the exclusion of students with disabilities from the assessments used in accountability systems (e.g., Erickson & Thurlow, 1997; McGrew, Thurlow, & Spiegel, 1993; Olson & Goldstein, 1997). This was also evident in states' education accountability reports. As late as 1997, one year before the implementation of the requirement that states report on the performance of students with disabilities in state and district assessments, only eleven states included information on the performance of students with disabilities (Thurlow, Langenfeld, Nelson, Shin, & Coleman, 1998). In contrast, more than half of the states included the number of students receiving special education services and/or the costs of those services.

As might be expected, several issues emerge when consideration is given to the issue of including students with disabilities in standards-based reforms and accountability systems. The Center for Policy Research (1996) suggested that one of the major stumbling blocks was the discord between due process procedures and documenting results:

> Part of the problem is that state accountability is such a complicated undertaking. It involves what is being assessed (for example, "outputs" [versus] "inputs," or state goals [versus] local goals) and a range of consequences for schools that are rated highly or poorly. When federal regulations for special education become interwoven with all of this, the situation becomes even more complicated. Some state officials perceive that if they focus on student results they do so at the peril of maintaining federal due process procedures. Alternatively, they perceive that if they focus on maintaining due process procedures they cannot focus on student achievement. (p. 22)

Based on their tracking of twelve state accountability systems and more in-depth study of four of those systems, the Center for Policy Research identified issues associated with the content of accountability and its implementation. These issues are listed in Table 10.7.

After conducting a broad-based study of students with disabilities and standards-based reform, a National Academy of Sciences committee published a report on its findings (McDonnell, McLaughlin, & Morison, 1997), with recommendations for "states and local communities that have already decided to proceed with standards-based reform and that want to make those reforms consistent with current special education policies and practices" (p. 9). These recommendations (see Table 10.8) represent a fine blending of the requirements of an accountability system and an educational system based on individualization.

The information from these various studies and reports was taken seriously by the federal government in its continuing belief of the need for special education and general education to become more aligned and integrated with each other. In the 1997 amendments to IDEA, requirements related to the students' curriculum, participation in assessments, and public reporting of students' performance push beyond just providing services to a push for accountability for the results of educating students with disabilities.

Choice in Education

In 1985, only those students who had their own (or their parent's) financial resources and those students who resided in a school district with a magnet school program could choose where they received their elementary or secondary education. School placement was determined by where a student lived unless the

TABLE 10.7 **Issues Associated with Accountability Systems**

Content of Accountability	Implementation
General accountability systems that rely heavily on student achievement are inadequate for monitoring the progress of students with disabilities if they are not included in the assessments.	Special education staff are concerned that there is not enough time to monitor special education in all its required dimensions on coordinated review teams.
Accountability systems may mask pockets of poor achievement by schools or populations within schools if data are not collected and reported in sufficient detail.	Districts do not perceive monitoring as coordinated.
State compliance staff feel pulled by federal compliance requirements when a state significantly collapses special education monitoring items into a more general, performance-oriented state format.	Special educators and families worry about the state's motivation for developing integrated monitoring systems.
Parents, teachers, and students are concerned about the potential impact of new graduation and diploma requirements on students with disabilities. Alternatively, some educators and policy makers are concerned that current diploma and graduation requirements may give students with disabilities an unfair advantage in the system.	Special educators and families worry about guaranteeing individual entitlement versus group accountability on common standards.

SOURCE: Issues Identified in State Accountability Systems and Students with Disabilities. Roach, V., Dailey, D., & Goertz, M. (1997) *State Accountability Systems and Students with Disabilities* (Issue Brief). Alexandria, VA: Center for Policy Research.

student or parents could pay for a private school or unless the student lived in a school district that had designed school programs to attract a variety of students, usually in an attempt to meet desegregation goals. By the late 1990s, this had changed dramatically.

Minnesota was the first state to enact a statewide open enrollment law, which was one in a series of choice-in-education policies legislated in this state (programs of excellence; postsecondary enrollment option program, high school graduation incentives program, area learning centers; educational program for pregnant minors and minor parents). The open enrollment law allowed parents of students attending school in Minnesota to enroll their children in any district in the state unless there clearly was not enough space or enrollment would

| TABLE 10.8 | **Recommendations of the National Academy of Sciences Committee on Students with Disabilities and Standards-Based Reform** |

Recommendation 1: States and localities that decide to implement standards-based reforms should design their common content standards, performance standards, and assessments to maximize participation of students with disabilities.

Recommendation 2: The presumption should be that each student with a disability will participate in the state or local standards; however, participation for any given student may require alterations to the common standards and assessments. Decisions to make such alterations must have a compelling educational justification and must be made on an individual basis.

Recommendation 3: The Committee recommends strengthening the IEP process as the formal mechanism for deciding how individual students with disabilities will participate in standards-based reforms.

Recommendation 4: States and localities should revise policies that discourage maximum participation of students with disabilities in the common accountability system and provide incentives to encourage widespread participation.

Recommendation 5: When content and performance standards or assessments are altered for a student with a disability:
- The alternate standards should be challenging yet potentially achievable.
- They should reflect the full range of knowledge and skills that the student needs to live a full, productive life.
- The school system should inform parents and the student of any consequences of these alterations.

Recommendation 6: Even if the individual needs of some students require alterations of the common standards and assessments, the Committee strongly recommends that these students be counted in a universal, public accountability system.

Recommendation 7: Assessment accommodations should be provided, but they should be used only to offset the impact of disabilities unrelated to the knowledge and skills being measured. They should also be justified on a case-by-case basis, but individual decisions should be guided by a uniform set of criteria.

Recommendation 8: States and local districts should provide information to parents of students with disabilities to enable them to make informed choices about their children's participation in standards-based reform and to understand the consequences of those choices.

Recommendation 9: The Committee recommends that before attaching significant stakes to the performance of individual students, those students should be given an opportunity to learn the skills and knowledge expected of them.

(continued)

TABLE 10.8	**Recommendations of the National Academy of Sciences Committee on Students with Disabilities and Standards-Based Reform (Continued)**

Recommendation 10: Given the enormous variability in the educational needs of students, the Committee recommends that policy makers monitor the unintended consequences of participation in standards-based reform, including consequences for students with disabilities.

Recommendation 11: The Committee recommends that states design standards policies that realistically reflect the timelines and resource levels needed to implement standards-based reforms.

Recommendation 12: The Committee recommends a long-term research agenda to address the substantial gaps in knowledge about the schooling of students with disabilities and the impact of standards-based reforms.

SOURCE: Educating One & All: Students with Disabilities and Standards-Based Reform. McDonnell, L. M., McLaughlin, M. J., & Morison, P. (Eds.), *Educating One & All: Students with Disabilities and Standards-Based Reform.* Copyright ©1997 National Academy Press. Reprinted by permission.

interfere with desegregation activities of either the sending or the receiving district. State moneys followed students who used this option.

Since first enacted into law in Minnesota in 1990, evidence of some of the effects has been gathered. Most of this evidence still is limited by the extent to which the choice option is used (Colopy and Tarr, 1994; Funkhouser & Colopy, 1994) or by the public reaction to it (Nathan & Ysseldyke, 1994; Rubenstein, 1992). While there is evidence of benefits to students in terms of self-esteem, attitude, and attendance (Rubenstein, 1992), there do not yet exist "conclusive data on the effects of open enrollment on academic achievement" (Cookson & Shroff, 1997, p. 15).

Open enrollment was one of the most comprehensive and far-reaching educational reform efforts undertaken by a state. At about the same time, President Bush declared that "expanding parents' rights to choose public schools is a national imperative" (*Education Week,* January 18, 1989, p. 1). Within a year of the Minnesota enactment, Nebraska, Iowa, and Arkansas had passed open enrollment legislation. By the end of the 1990s, school choice in one form or another (see Table 10.9) was provided in thirty-nine states and the District of Columbia (Education Commission of the States, 1998b). Most of these states still had relatively limited forms of choice, but thirteen states had open enrollment policies where families could choose from schools outside their home districts.

Among the more recent forms of choice are charter schools, which operate free of most of the rules and regulations governing other schools as long as they adhere to a written contract—a charter—that defines "how the school will be organized and managed, what students will be taught and expected to achieve,

TABLE 10.9	Definitions of Selected "Choice" Plans

Charter schools: Publicly sponsored schools that are free of direct administrative control by the government but are held accountable for student outcomes.

Interdistrict choice: Students are permitted to cross district lines to attend school; state funds follow the student.

Intersectional choice: A choice plan that includes public and private schools.

Intradistrict choice: Students are permitted to choose among schools within a district.

Intrasectional choice: A choice plan that is limited to pubic schools.

Magnet schools: Public schools that offer specialized programs to attract students, often into certain areas to promote racial balance.

Open enrollment: Unlimited interdistrict choice within a state.

Postsecondary options: Students may enroll in college courses at government expense.

Second-chance options: Students who have difficulties in standard public school settings may enter alternative schools or programs.

Voucher plans: Students are assisted in attending the schools of their choice through certificates or cash payments received from the government.

Workplace training: Students are taught a skilled trade through apprenticeships, with costs divided between the employer and the school district.

SOURCE: Definitions provided in *School Choice and Urban School Reform* (Cookson & Shroff, 1997). Cookson, P. W., & Shroff, S. M., (1997). *School Choice and Urban School Reform* (Urban Diversity Series No. 110). New York: Columbia University, ERIC Clearinghouse on Urban and Minority Education.

and how success will be measured" (Education Commission of the States, 1998b, p. 25). Charter schools have spread like wildfire. According to the Education Commission of the States:

> Since 1991, 29 states, the District of Columbia and Puerto Rico have enacted charter school legislation. In these states, nearly 800 charter schools are operating, and their numbers are likely to grow substantially. States follow distinctive approaches to charter school development, and the variations in these approaches profoundly affect the number, type and operation of charter schools in each state. Key variations in the charter laws include how many charter schools are permitted, who grants charters, who may start charter schools and who sets personnel policies. (1998b, p. 25, original footnotes deleted)

Like open enrollment and other choice options, we still have very little data on the effectiveness of charter schools; much of the information we have is in the form of public opinion (Nathan, 1996). What we do know is that it is difficult to describe a typical charter school. One charter school may focus its efforts on technology, another on math and science education, and yet another on working with the community. Some charter schools focus on the needs of students with disabilities, such as Minnesota's Metro Deaf School.

More recent proposed forms of choice include vouchers, where public school funds can be used by students to attend private schools, and home schooling, where parents instruct their children in their own homes. Both forms of choice (vouchers and home schooling) are available to all students. The public believes that vouchers will be most beneficial to higher achieving students (and have little effect on students remaining in the public schools) and that home schooling generally is not good for the nation (Rose et al., 1997).

From the beginning, arguments were made both for and against open enrollment as well as for other "choice" options. The gist of most of the arguments for choice was that no single educational program was best for all children and that parents and schools together had to address the different ways that students learn and how schools could provide the best education for all children (see Boyd & Walberg, 1990; Nathan, 1989). Arguments against choice concentrated on its perceived "real purposes," such as the National Education Association's argument that it would compromise a commitment to free, equitable, universal, and quality public education for every student (Olson, 1989). In all these arguments, little or no mention was made of students with disabilities and the potential impact of an open enrollment policy on this group.

What can students with disabilities expect from the various choice options that now exist in many places in the nation? Some of the most comprehensive research in this area has been conducted by researchers at the University of Minnesota and is summarized by Lange and Ysseldyke (1998). It appears that students with disabilities are participating in the open enrollment form of choice. Very often, the choice of a school is related to what that school can offer to the student.

Students with disabilities are also frequently involved in choice options available to at-risk students. Lange and Ysseldyke (1998) suggest that the second-chance option, in which suspended students may go to a different school or failing students may select an alternative school, is particularly important for students with disabilities, who describe being hassled or teased in the traditional high school. This option seems to provide a "legitimate exit opportunity from high school," one that probably prevents them from dropping out of school.

Lange and Ysseldyke (1998) also report that postsecondary options programs are meeting a need for students with disabilities. Rather than providing the opportunity to gain college credit, this option seems to provide transition experiences for students with disabilities: "More and more high schools in Minnesota are using the [postsecondary] option to provide a transition experience. Often these experiences are actually written into the IEP" (p. 267).

Lange and Ysseldyke express concern about recent discussions among policy makers suggesting that the use of postsecondary options be limited because of concerns about their inappropriate use for remedial rather than college-level work.

Lange and Ysseldyke (1998) suggest that other options will also be used by students with disabilities and that the need for research continues:

> Currently, charter schools are the up-and-coming school choice option: already there are over 400 schools in fifteen states. Twenty-five states have passed legislation. Minnesota was the first state to open a charter school, and in 1995–1996 operators of charter schools reported that 25 percent of charter school students had an individualized education program. If the findings from our research are any indication, there will continue to be substantial participation by students with disabilities in this newer option and others that are developed over the next years. (pp. 268–269)

Lange and Ysseldyke (1998) also note, however, the need for data on the impact of the various choice options on the achievement and other educational outcomes of students with disabilities:

> While the data available from these studies are substantive and informative, they do not address the extent to which the options result in better outcomes for students with disabilities who transfer through a choice option. This is the needed missing link by which to further judge the benefits of changing schools. (p. 269)

So far, these observations have not dispelled some of the early concerns about school choice (based on findings from a study of within-district choice) that it was "a new, improved method of student sorting" in which students with low achievement, students with absence and behavior problems, disabled students, and limited-English-proficient students would still have limited opportunities to participate.

CHANGE IN EDUCATION

A major approach to change in education during the 1990s was large-scale reform, often at the national or state level. A prime example of this was the Kentucky Educational Reform Act (KERA), which essentially was a response to the declaration by the Kentucky Supreme Court that the entire state education system was unconstitutional. Sweeping reforms covered school governance, family supports, staff development, measuring the effect of change, and incentives for improvement. Other states looked to Kentucky's efforts as a model of what they might do.

Attempts to emulate others' reform efforts highlight at least two issues. First, to what extent will programs or reforms that are successful in one place generalize to another; to what extent will programs or reforms that are successful with one population generalize to another? Second, how rapidly can change proceed? And what do we know about the change process that can promote quicker and more effective adoption of changes?

Seymour Sarason on "Obstacles to Change"

How, when, and why new ideas gain currency, get accepted and institutionally implemented, are questions far beyond the purposes of this book. A modest-sized library could be easily filled with the books written on the subject. A fair proportion of these books would be disheartening to read because they chronicle new ideas that have all of the transitory and superficial features of fads and fashions. That is clearly the case in the educational arena, where new ideas have not been in short supply among those within and without the educational establishment. And, in too many cases, where the new ideas deserved consideration, the processes through which they were implemented were self-defeating. Ideas whose time has come are no guarantee that we know how to capitalize on the opportunities, because the process of implementation requires an understanding of the settings in which these ideas have to take root. That understanding is frequently faulty and incomplete. Good intentions married to good ideas are necessary but not sufficient for action consistent with them. In accordance with Murphy's Law, if anything can go wrong it will. The world is not organized in ways that permit it passively to conform to our needs or good ideas, and when the fact interacts with our capacity to oversimplify, and even to delude ourselves, disappointment is not far down the road. That explains Sullivan's Law: Murphy's Law is a gross underestimation.

SOURCE: Sarason, S. B., (1990). *The Predictable Failure of Educational Reform: Can We Change Course Before It's Too Late?* San Francisco: Jossey-Bass, pp. 99–100.

Many individuals have written about the process of change and innovation in education. Some approach the issue from a logical perspective emphasizing technical, rational, and mechanistic characteristics, while others approach it from a sociological perspective emphasizing either a cultural or political point of view (Bennis, Benne, & Chin, 1969; Fullan, 1993). Several writers have addressed change in relationship to specific content areas, such as mathematics (Willoughby, 1990) or specific educational processes, such as staff development (Joyce, 1990). At this time, some professionals question the possible success of planned educational reforms (Pogrow, 1996; Sarason, 1990, 1992, 1993, 1995a). For example:

Schools have been intractable to change and the attainment of goals set by reformers. A major failure has been the inability of reformers to confront this intractability. As a result, each new wave of reform learns nothing from earlier efforts and comes up with recommendations that have failed in the past. What is called reform is based on an acceptance of the system as it has been and is. (Sarason, 1990, pp. xiii–xiv)

Gallup Poll Results on Grading the Schools

Each year since 1986, Gallup interviewers have asked people to rate on a scale of A to F the nation's public schools, their local public schools, and the school that their oldest child attends. Over the eight years, the difference in the percentage of respondents giving ratings of A or B to the nation's schools and to local schools has averaged about 23 percent. The difference between the percentages giving high ratings to the public school the oldest child attends and to the nation's schools has been 47 percentage points. According to the Gallup report, the "obvious conclusion that can be drawn from these figures is that first-hand knowledge of the public schools breeds respect for the public schools."

In response to several articles on reform (see Stringfield, 1995, who edited a special section on studies of education reform for *Phi Delta Kappan*), Sarason (1995b) identified five areas of consensus:

1. Changing one aspect of the education system is extraordinarily difficult, both conceptually and practically. . . .

2. The "system"—by virtue of history, tradition, and overlearned attitudes—is allergic to change. . . .

3. Although we have much still to learn, . . . we have already learned much, *especially about the nature and context of productive learning.* . . .

4. The professional preparation of educators is manifestly inadequate in inculcating the spirit, substance, and complexity of the reform effort. . . .

5. The *initial* object of change is not students, the classroom, or the system; it is the attitudes and conceptions of educators themselves. . . . (p. 84, emphases in original)

The report on reform by the Education Commission of the States (1998b) highlighted four findings about the status of education reform in the United States:

1. An increasingly urgent need exists for better measures of student achievement, as well as more comprehensive and consistent efforts to evaluate the impact of reform on student learning. . . .

2. Significant disconnects exist between what is known to be effective in raising student achievement and the shape and application of some state education reforms. . . .

3. Significant disconnects also exist between the rhetoric of reform and the level of investment in leadership, resources and capacity building. . . .

4. Equity issues, if they continue to be ignored, threaten to undermine even the most promising reforms. . . . (Education Commission of the States, 1998b, pp. 38–40)

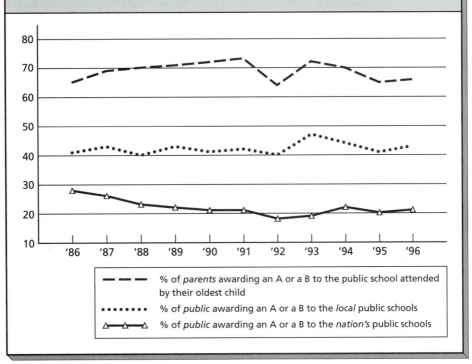

Gallup Poll Results on Grading the Schools

Each year since 1986, Gallup interviewers have asked people to rate on a scale of A to F the nation's public schools, their local public schools, and the school that their oldest child attends. Over the eight years, the difference in the percentage of respondents giving ratings of A or B to the nation's schools and to local schools has averaged about 23%. The difference between the percentages giving high ratings to the public school the oldest child attends and to the nation's schools has been 47 percentage points. According to the Gallup report, the "obvious conclusion that can be drawn from these figures is that firsthand knowledge of the public schools breeds respect for the public schools."

– – – % of *parents* awarding an A or a B to the public school attended by their oldest child

• • • • • • • % of *public* awarding an A or a B to the *local* public schools

△—△—△ % of *public* awarding an A or a B to the *nation's* public schools

Source: 28th Annual Gallup Poll of the Public's Attitude Toward the Public Schools (Elam, Rose, & Gallup, 1996), p. 45.

While the last point made in the ECS report does not refer directly to students with disabilities, it is clear that all the points made about educational reform apply to special education as well as to general education.

While special education clearly has attempted to position itself to participate in general education reform occurring around it, it has its own barriers to change and educational reform. Special educators form their own factions and are unable to reach consensus on such issues as defining categories of disability, accepting inclusion, and defining appropriate instructional interventions for specific types of disabilities. In many ways, these same issues result in special education being divided into various forces that are unable to bring about enough consensus to have an influence on general education.

Discussion Questions

1. What reform activities are currently taking place at the national, state, or local level? To what extent do these activities acknowledge or apply to special education?

2. How might the eight national goals be restated to show that they are goals for all students, including those with disabilities?

3. What are some of the challenges to implementing the recommendations of the National Research Council study on standards-based reform?

4. Prepare an argument for or against open enrollment as a policy for special education?

5. What would be a "road map to reform" for special education today?

Part 3

Issues Reflected in Practice

Chapter 11
Home–School–Community Agency Partnerships

If we could succeed in establishing rather different and closer relations between home and school, such as are aimed at by parent-teacher associations, much might be accomplished.

—Lillian Lincoln, *Everyday Pedagogy* (1915)

Educators have long recognized the importance of working with parents, families, and agencies. The date of the Lincoln quote (above) is 1915. Yet until very recently the focus was on *involving* parents or agencies in school efforts to educate students. And the term used to describe any interrelationship was *collaboration*. In the 1990s there was increased talk about home, school, and community *partnerships* in efforts to reach optimal educational results. As Epstein (1995) indicates, "If educators view students as *children,* they are likely to see both the family and the community as partners with the school in children's education and development." (p. 701)

Professionals' views about parents and their willingness to work collaboratively with them have changed since the mid to late 1980s. There are expanding roles for families in education, and these go beyond the mandates of special education and Title I. Two of the eight national education goals (Goals 1 and 8) implicate parents. Parents have become stronger advocates for the rights of their children, and legal mandates exist for parent involvement in the educational programs of their children. In early education and intervention programs, there has been a movement away from the child as the sole focus of intervention to the family as the unit of intervention. Educators and parents alike now recognize that early intervention, especially intervention with the families of children who have disabilities, is crucial and effective.

Much of the new focus on families and parents is rooted in the work of Bronfenbrenner, who argued that professionals couldn't understand adequately the behavior of the individual student without understanding the influences that the family has on that behavior. The problems students bring to school are becoming increasingly complex. Solution of those problems requires the planning, organization, and management of interventions by multiple sources and varied disciplines. Increasingly, schools are collaborating with community agencies and organizations in delivering interventions. In this chapter we describe the issues school personnel confront as they endeavor to work well with families, parents, and community agencies. *Involvement, collaboration, cooperation, partnership,* and *interface* are terms we often hear these days. We examine some of the issues surrounding these terms and concepts.

HOME-SCHOOL PARTNERSHIPS

Swap (1993) identified four elements of a true partnership. First, there must be two-way communication in which educators and parents listen to one another and work together to create a learning environment in school. Second, school personnel and parents must work together to enhance learning at home and at school. Swap indicates the bidirectional nature of this relationship:

> Parents contribute to children's learning by having high expectations, providing a setting that allows concentrated work, supporting and nurturing learning that occurs in school and elsewhere, and offering love, discipline, guidance and encouragement. Educators develop curriculum and instructional practices and strong relationships with children that create conditions for optimal learning. Parents and educators work together to develop an array of ways parents can be involved in and out of the classroom. (p. 58)

The third element of a true partnership is provision of mutual support. Parent education programs and parental assistance at school are parts of this support. Both groups look for opportunities to recognize formally one another's contributions to child growth and development. The fourth necessary element is joint decision making. Partnerships cannot be forced; they must be built. Swap (1993) outlined strategies schools can use to build two-way communication, make schools welcome places, and communicate expectations for student performance.

The Nature of Parent Involvement

It is very popular these days to talk about parent involvement. The authors of this text regularly attend conferences in which we listen to keynote speakers calling for increased parent involvement and home-school collaboration as essential to solving the problems that schools, children, and families face. Teachers tell us of the need to involve parents in their children's education. Parents sometimes talk about their desire to participate in the education of their children. But what does parent involvement mean, and do professionals and parents really want this meaningful involvement? And even if they do, what improvement does parent involvement contribute to the educational performance of students with disabilities?

To address these issues means investigating the nature of parent involvement. Traditionally, parent involvement has consisted of assistance with fundraising, helping with homework, and volunteering in classrooms. Henderson, Marburger, and Ooms (1986), for instance, differentiated five kinds of parent involvement: parents as partners, as collaborators and problem solvers (helping school personnel solve problems), as audience, as supporters, and as advisers and co–decision makers. Schools involve parents all along the continuum from active involvement to passive reception.

Epstein (1995) differentiated six kinds of parent involvement:

- *Parenting,* in which schools help all families establish home environments to support children as students
- *Communicating,* in which parents and schools work to develop effective two-way communication between home and school focused on school programs and student progress
- *Volunteering,* in which schools recruit and organize parent help and support
- *Learning at home,* in which school personnel provide information and ideas to families about how to help students at home with homework and other activities
- *Decision making,* in which parents are included in school decisions, serve as leaders and representatives on school committees, task force, etc.
- *Collaborating with community,* in which families and school personnel work together to identify and integrate resources and services from the community to strengthen school programs and family practices, and to improve student achievement

Grolnick, Benjet, Kurowski, and Apostoleris (1997) take the position that thinking about parent involvement has been too simplistic. They indicate that typically parent involvement has been measured by looking at attendance at school events, reading at home, and helping with homework. They say, "There is growing consensus that parent involvement cannot be conceived as a unitary phenomenon and that a broad and multidimensional perspective is needed that includes emotional and personal aspects in addition to school-like activities" (p. 538).

While there are many differing definitions of parent involvement, the one proposed by Grolnick and Slowiaczek (1994) picks up on the multidimensional nature of parent involvement. They define parent involvement as "the dedication of resources by the parent to the child within a given domain," and they identify three domains of parent involvement: behavioral, cognitive-intellectual, and personal involvement. They describe the behavioral domain as participation in school activities like parent-teacher conferences and helping with homework at home. Cognitive-intellectual involvement consists of exposing children to intellectually stimulating activities like going to the library and talking about current events. Personal involvement is described as taking personal time with children, and knowing about and keeping abreast of what is going on in school.

Assigning Responsibility

If schools and parents are to work together, identifying who is responsible for what aspects of the education and socialization of children is essential. Where do the responsibilities of parents end and those of the school begin? Since the early 1980s, society has thrust on schools and school personnel an increased set of demands for child rearing, socialization, and the elimination of social problems. Epstein (1990) described parent involvement from the perspective of responsibility for children, child rearing, instruction, and child development. She identified and defined three perspectives on responsibility: separate responsibility, shared responsibility, and sequential responsibility. Separate responsibility stresses the "inherent incompatibility, competition, and conflict between families and schools" (p. 121). "This perspective," according to Epstein "assumes that school bureaucracies and family organizations are directed, respectively, by educators and parents whose different goals, roles and responsibilities are best fulfilled independently" (p. 121). Shared responsibility, which focuses on coordination, cooperation, and complementarity, assumes that families and schools bear joint responsibility for the socialization and education of children together. Sequential responsibility assumes that parents and teachers have primary responsibility for the education and socialization of children at different points in children's lives. It is common from this perspective to presuppose that parents are responsible for child rearing and socialization for the first five or six years of the child's life and that the school takes over once formal schooling starts. The particular perspective a professional or a parent holds on parent involvement influences the extent to which and the method by which parents become involved in their children's educational program.

Just as perspectives vary from one person to another, so do they change from one era to another. In the early nineteenth century, for example, schools were controlled by parents or at least by the community of parents. Lines of demarcation between parent and school responsibility were clear. Schools taught a common curriculum; families taught ethics, values, religion, and ethnicity. Now parents clearly are more involved in making curricular decisions. This involvement derives from several factors. More mothers are highly educated; indeed, many have degrees in teaching but choose not to teach. More parents are knowledgeable about child development and are more engaged in educating infants and toddlers. The federal government has promoted parent involvement by insisting that parents take part in planning IEPs for their children with disabilities (Epstein, 1990).

Parent Involvement and Improved Achievement

There is much rhetoric about parent involvement, so much that it seems logical to suppose that involving parents in students' educational programs will lead to improved educational performance for students. Grolnick et al. (1997) indicate that parent involvement is positively associated with school success, but they also say that we do not know much about the factors that determine how involved parents become. Henderson (1981, 1987) reviewed eighty-five studies of the relationship between parent involvement and student achievement and concluded, "The evidence is now beyond dispute: parent involvement improves student achievement. When parents are involved, children do better in school (1987, p. 1). Others contend that while the correlation between parent involvement in education and student achievement is well documented, there is little evidence of any direct, causal link.

Enhanced pupil performance and achievement are not the only benefits assumed to derive from increased parent involvement. Rich (1987) identified several other reasons for family involvement in student's schooling: promotion of home learning, improved student behavior, family acceptance of children, benefits to parents, teacher's acceptance of students, and benefits to the community. Yet there is no research evidence to indicate that these benefits are actually the results of family involvement. Swap (1993) indicates that parent involvement often promotes nonacademic outcomes, like improved attendance, behavior, and self-esteem.

Partnerships to Reach Higher Standards

Lewis and Henderson (1997) report the results of a meeting of representatives of more than forty organizations concerned with involving parents and communities in school reform. The group met to address ways to get schools, families, and communities involved in advancing school reform and achievement of higher standards. Agreement was reached that family and community members need to be involved in three ways:

- As advocates who insist on excellent public schools that teach to high standards, provide adequate opportunities and extra supports so that students learn, and are open to their families and community.

- As full partners in the process of changing schools, from understanding standards and assessment to taking standards into the classroom, to monitoring the effects on student achievement.

- As participants in the many opportunities for parent engagement that the changes have created. Particularly important are deep, continuous conversations among educators, parents, and students about what we want our children to learn, how it should be taught, and the ways they will apply their knowledge. (p. iv)

There is clear recognition of the urgent need for families, schools, and community agencies to work together, especially in facilitating high achievement and attainment of higher standards for students with disabilities and who are at-risk. Yet there is no consensus on how this might be or ought to be achieved. As Lewis and Henderson (1997) conclude:

> There are no "models" for building parent and community support for school reforms because each school's situation is unique. There is a common, immediate need, however, to mobilize parents and communities, hold everyone accountable for higher student learning, and build the capacity of people to carry out critical reforms. (p. v)

The Home Environment's Influence on Schooling

Much is written on how dysfunctional families produce dysfunctional children, who in turn experience much difficulty in school. Yet this is not always the case. Two of our colleagues at the University of Minnesota, Garmezy and Masten, conducted extensive research on factors related to the development of competence in children and observed that some children, in spite of incredibly adverse circumstances, did end up competent (Masten, Garmezy, Tellegen, Pellegrini, Larkin, & Larsen, 1988); Garmezy and Masten also identified factors that contributed to resilience and development of competence.

Christenson (1990) used a home rating scale to examine differences in educationally relevant home factors among students who were learning disabled, emotionally disturbed, mentally retarded, and nonhandicapped. She looked at routine, organization, lack of stress, security, responsibility, expectations valuing education, support for academics, and support for school. She summed these to produce an index of quality of the home environment and reported that the home environment for students with learning disabilities and students with no disabilities was rated significantly higher than the home environment for students who were emotionally disturbed. (Remember, however, that not every student from a stressed, aversive environment has problems.)

Ysseldyke and Christenson (1993) identified five components of supportive home environments and developed a system to rate the extent to which these are present in the students' homes (the Instructional Environment System). The five components are:

- *Expectations and attributions:* High expectations about schoolwork are communicated to the child, and the value of effort and working hard in school is emphasized.

- *Discipline orientation:* There is an authoritative, not permissive nor authoritarian, approach to discipline, and the child is monitored and supervised by the parents.

- *Home affective environment:* The parent-child relationship is generally positive and supportive.

- *Parent participation:* There is an educative home environment, and others participate in the child's schooling, at home and/or in school.

- *Structure for learning:* Organization and daily routines facilitate the completion of schoolwork, and the child's academic learning is supported.

Ysseldyke and Christenson (1993) argue that student performance in school is enhanced by the presence of these factors.

Parent Control of Children

The August 1, 1990, issue of *Education Week* included a report on enactment of get-tough policies in certain states and localities; these penalized parents for failure to control their children. But where does the responsibility of parents end? In Los Angeles 150 parents have been arrested because their children joined gangs. Wisconsin has adopted policies allowing cuts in welfare payments to parents whose children do not attend school. In Arkansas, Maryland, Mississippi, and Texas, there are threats of fines or jail for parents who refuse to attend parent-teacher conferences. Should schools and society in general police the involvement of parents in children's education? Should parents be punished when the actions they take are deemed to not be in the best educational interest of their children? Who decides?

The Effects of Disabilities on Families

Are families adversely affected by the presence of children with disabilities? Most people believe they are. Yet the research on this issue is mixed. It is risky to say anything about how students with disabilities affect their families. Gartner, Lipskey, and Turnbull argued that the family is the central social institution affecting the life of the child with disabilities, yet they also stated that "to recognize that families are important in the life of a child with disabilities, and vice versa, is to say no more and no less than what is true of all families and all children" (1991, p. 57).

Methodological problems abound in studying the effects of (any kind of) children on their families. Effects differ according to condition and severity (Seligman & Darling, 1989). Effects also differ according to parents' perceptions of whether their children measure up to cultural standards (Epstein, 1990). The interrelationships among factors that affect outcomes are complex. Differing disabilities affect families in varying ways, and the same kind of disability may have radically different effects from one family to the next.

The effects children with disabilities have on their families have also changed significantly with the times. In the not too distant past, medical personnel and laypeople advised parents to avoid raising their children with disabilities and to seek assistance in the form of institutional placement. Parents who chose to keep their children at home were subject to stigma (as children with disabilities were labeled, so too were their parents). Those who put their children in institutions often had to meet the burden of major costs and often looked the other way when their children received shoddy care. Significant changes in social values since the early 1970s have led to the situation in which institutionalization is the exception, not the rule. Families are now expected to assume responsibility for their children with disabilities and to assume responsibilities associated with raising those children. As a result, families with children who have disabilities have become visible.

The families of children with disabilities are perfectly capable of coping with their children. Beavers observed that

> in any family with an identifiably "different" characteristics (e.g., ethnic, extremely rich or poor, military) or member (e.g., schizophrenic, homosexual, celebrity), effective family coping is taken for granted or not noticed, while problematic family interaction is spotlighted. In our study we discovered very early that families with a handicapped child are usually likeable, always interesting, and not stereotypical; they have distinctive family personalities. So, subjectively, we learned to appreciate their resourcefulness and their many strengths. (1989, p. 196)

According to researchers at the Beach Center on Family Disabilities (1995), people learn to cope and some coping mechanisms are constructive; others, unhealthy. Constructive coping mechanisms include seeking support from friends and service providers, embracing spiritual beliefs, and planning/mapping steps to be taken for achieving goals. Unhealthy coping mechanisms include withdrawal and anger. Different families cope in different ways. What works for one family doesn't always work for another. Beach Center personnel identified four cognitive coping strategies:

- *Positive contributions:* The belief that one's child with special needs benefits the family and those outside the family.

- *Meaning:* The belief that a child's special needs exist because of a specific cause or reason.

- *Social comparison:* The belief that one's situation, when compared to that of another, is better or worse than the person with whom the comparison is made.

- *Mastery:* The belief that one has control over some things that happen in the life of a child with special needs.

Parents of children who are disabled go through a predictable set of stages in reacting to the news that their children have disabilities. The stages are the same as those people go through when they learn that they have a serious (terminal) illness: denial, bargaining, anger, depression, acceptance, and stigma.

Students with disabilities do confront their families with challenges over the issue of providing care: care for their everyday needs as well as for their disabilities. Different disabilities confront parents with different care needs. Students with disabilities are often stigmatized, and families can be similarly stigmatized.

FACING CHALLENGES TO HOME-SCHOOL PARTNERSHIPS

Debate About Ways to Increase Parent Involvement

Educators, parents, and researchers generally agree that parent involvement is important. Yet they have differing ideas about how to increase involvement. Henderson et al. (1997) advocated the involvement of parents as partners in the educational enterprise and indicated what they thought schools must do to enable effective family-school partnerships. First, they contend that parents are more likely to be involved in their children's educational programs if the school climate is open, helpful, and friendly, which can be accomplished by putting parent lounges into schools and having set times when parents and teachers have lunch together, among other things.

Second, parents are more likely to become involved in the educational program when there is frequent, clear, two-way communication. They are also more likely to communicate when they are encouraged to comment on school policies and issues and to share in making decisions about programs.

Third, Henderson et al. argue that parents are more likely to become involved when they are treated as collaborators rather than recipients of advice from experts. They say that active efforts must be made to involve parents, especially those who are considered very hard to reach. Schools in which administrators actively express and promote the philosophy of partnership are likely to have high levels of parent involvement, as are schools in which parents are expected to work as volunteers, even after their children finish school. Parent involvement is greater when school personnel make extensive efforts to reach parents who are unavailable.

Grolnick et al. (1997) argue that there is a complex interrelationship among multiple factors that determine the degree of parent involvement in schooling. They contend that demographic factors (e.g., socioeconomic status, single parent) affect the magnitude of parent involvement. But they contend that there is not a direct relationship between these and involvement. Rather, there are many factors that mediate this relationship, including parent attitudes, child characteristics (one of which is disability status), family context (e.g., the amount of stress in the family, social support, and family resources), and classroom factors (e.g., teacher attitudes and behaviors). How parents should be involved in schools, what approach to involvement is best, and how parent involvement can be increased are still topics of debate about which we have limited data, although most educators have strong opinions about them.

Forming Partnerships with Culturally and Linguistically Diverse Families

America's schools are becoming more diverse, and home-school partnerships must be formed with families of students who may differ culturally and linguistically from the teacher. This major issue confronts special educators who often struggle to identify the extent to which the difficulties a student faces in school are due to disabilities and/or cultural differences. Simpson (1996) identified specific strategies and procedures necessary to establishing and maintaining partnerships with ethnic and multicultural families. He stressed the importance of developing an awareness and acceptance of diversity and individual differences. All of us need to understand and accept the fact that members of different cultures may vary in the values they attribute to issues like academic excellence, academic progress, school attendance, homework, competition, and the ways achievement is acknowledged. Simpson provides a few examples. Hispanic families often disapprove of competition in schools; Native American students and families tend to shy away from the use of public praise in social reinforcement programs. Simpson provided a table from the work of Correa and Weismantel (1991) showing the educational implications of specific cultural beliefs. Table 11.1 illustrates the issues that must be considered.

While it is important to acknowledge and accept differences among groups, at the same time it is important that we do not stereotype on the basis of racial, ethnic, or multicultural group membership. We must recognize that there is as much within-group as between-group variation in beliefs, attitudes, and behaviors. Teachers must become familiar with the specific culture, traditions, and backgrounds of the students in their classes and not assume that all members of a particular group are alike.

Simpson (1996) calls attention to the importance of examining one's personal beliefs, prejudices, fears, and concerns regarding groups. In our work we often recommend that students who know they do not like working with specific kinds of students refrain from working with the students (and we work with them on being accepting). This applies to students from specific cultures, nationalities, and races and also to students who display specific kinds of disability conditions (e.g., cerebral palsy, deafness).

Barriers to Collaboration

As might be expected, considerable discussion and disagreement exists in the professional literature about the factors that served as challenges to effective home-school collaboration. And there are differing perspectives on how to overcome some of the barriers. Henderson, Marburger, and Ooms (1986) identified twelve barriers to effective home-school collaboration (see Table 11.2). Some of these same barriers were identified by Imber-Black (1998) and Liontas (1992). (These lists of barriers were combined to form the table.)

TABLE 11.1   **Examples of Cultural Beliefs with Implications for Services**

Ethnic Group	Cultural Beliefs	Implications for Services
Mexican American	Spiritual healing *(curanderos)*	Understand that health-related, special education, or mental health services may be secondary to the family's hope of a cure for the disabled child
Puerto Rican	*Machismo*	Respect the role of the father in family governance
		Understand that the father may be uncomfortable with the child care role
		Provide "male-oriented" activities for parent involvement
		Use male professionals when possible
		Respect the mother's need to postpone decision making until she speaks with her husband
	Compadres	Realize that the extended family system may include godparents, close friends, and neighbors
		Respect the involvement of nonfamily members in the decision-making process for the child's services
		Use extrafamilial subsystems to provide support for parents

SOURCE: Correra & Weismantel (1991).

Note that one of these barriers is the negative stereotypes parents and teachers hold about each other. According to Henderson et al., parents believe that teachers teach too much by rote, parent-teacher conferences are routine and unproductive, teachers send home only bad news, teachers do not follow through on what they say they will do, they do not welcome interactions with parents, and they care more about discipline than about teaching. Teachers believe that parents are not interested in school, they do not show up when asked, they promise but do not follow through, they only pretend to understand what teachers are trying to accomplish, they do children's homework for them, and they worry too much about how other kids are doing.

Leitch and Tangri (1988) identified two categories of barriers to home-school collaboration. First, teachers and parents lack knowledge about how they can use each other more effectively. When Leitch and Tangri asked about

TABLE 11.2   **Barriers to Home-School Collaboration**

Barriers for Parents

- Feelings of inadequacy, failure, and poor self-worth. Many parents see themselves as not very smart and as school failures.
- Negative attitudes or bad experiences with schools.
- Suspicion or anger that schools are not treating them fairly.
- Many low-income parents, as well as those from other cultures, see teachers as authority figures and leave it to the school to educate their children.
- Cultural and language barriers.
- Parents feel anxious about surrendering their children to strangers who may have values different from their own and may inculcate those values in the children.
- The financial pressures of making ends meet becomes primary to worrying about how children are doing in school.
- Economic hardship and unemployment.
- Many parents view schools as unsafe environments.
- Logistical problems. Parents often cannot come to school because they lack access to or are unable to afford transportation to school or childcare for younger siblings. In many instances there are scheduling mismatches between parents and teachers.
- Many homes are socially stressed, and many students who experience difficulties in school are from socially stressed homes. The stress may be such that they contribute to or exacerbate the difficulties students experience in school or take precedence over any difficulties students experience in school.

Barriers for Teachers and Schools

- Commitment: Several school practices have discouraged or completely blocked parent participation.
- School policies sometimes discourage home-school collaboration. For instance, in some schools union contracts specify that volunteers cannot be used for teaching functions.
- Schools do not make parents feel welcome.
- Schools are not held accountable for implementing changes that produce high student achievement, and parents often are unaware of what should be happening for their children.
- A belief that certain parents do not care and will not keep commitments.
- Schools focus on passive parent involvement, failing to recognize the multiple ways that parents can participate effectively in school change.
- Low teacher expectations for at-risk students.
- Teachers worry that parent involvement in decision making decreases teacher independence and autonomy.

(continued)

TABLE 11.2	**Barriers to Home-School Collaboration (Continued)**

- Doubts about their ability to work with some types of parents (e.g., parents who do not speak English, immigrant parents, single parents, parents from specific racial or ethnic groups, at-risk parents).
- Communication from schools focuses on the negative.
- Failing to dwell on the strengths that families have.

Mutual Barriers

- Confusion about the roles of teachers and parents in educating children. Teachers and parents have stereotyped images of one another.
- Parents and teachers are busy. The pressure of having to get many things done in short periods of time interferes with collaboration.
- Concerns about turf and territory.

SOURCES: Table includes barriers (drawn from Liontos (1992), Henderson, Marburger, and Ooms (1986), Lewis & Henderson (1997) and from Imber-Black (1988)).

barriers to collaboration, nearly 50 percent of teachers attributed barriers to parents. Parents saw themselves as primary barriers, whereas teachers said that parents, the system, and themselves were the barriers.

Second, mutual understanding and planning are lacking. "It isn't misperceptions of each other that are the root of home-school problems, it is the lack of specific planning, or, at a more basic level, the lack of knowledge about how each can use the other person more effectively that is the major barrier" (p. 74).

Nevertheless, there is much to support the contention that collaboration between teachers and parents of students with disabilities is greater than that between teachers and students who are not disabled. Recent legislation requires relatively heavy involvement of parents in the assessment of students, in the development of an IEP, in the planning of transition services, and in the setting of career goals and exploration of career options.

OVERCOMING CHALLENGES TO HOME-SCHOOL COLLABORATION

What can school personnel do to help overcome the stated barriers to collaboration? Liontos (1992) indicated that one of the primary factors enabling programs that serve families of at-risk students to overcome barriers is the replacement of old beliefs and assumptions with new ones. Among these new beliefs are the beliefs that all families have strengths, parents can learn new techniques, parents have important perspectives about their children and those perspectives should be drawn upon, most parents really care about their children, cultural differences are both valid and valuable, and many family forms exist and are legitimate. Liontos (1992) also identified five important principles for involving parents:

- A no-fault model in which parents and teachers do not blame each other for student difficulties.

- A nondeficit approach in which teachers respect families for who they are and look for assets and strengths rather than deficiencies and failures.

- Empowerment, or giving parents more control over their lives and their children's education. Parents thus are more able to influence those individuals who affect their lives and the lives of those they care about.

- An ecological approach in which schools and families together see all the connections in a child's world: family, neighborhood or community, church, school.

- Collaboration and partnership among school personnel and families to meet parenting education, counseling, health care, housing, and other needs.

If school personnel work with families on these goals, improved home-school partnerships may result.

Developing Effective Communication Between Parents and School Personnel

Nearly every major report on schooling stresses the role of parents in making education work, and nearly every one of those reports calls attention to "the need for effective communication between parents and school personnel." It is thought that maximum education will occur where families and schools are brought into working relationships and where they communicate.

Epstein (1990) reported that large numbers of parents were excluded from communication with schools. She surveyed parents in 600 Maryland elementary schools and found that more than 30 percent had no conference with a teacher during the year, 60 percent had never talked with a teacher by phone, and most had never engaged in deep or frequent discussion with teachers. At the same time, in the 1987 Metropolitan Life Survey of the American Teacher, most parents (85 percent) and teachers (78 percent) expressed satisfaction with the frequency of contacts between parents and schools. More than 50 percent of the teachers *and* of the parents said they were uneasy or reluctant about approaching the other to talk about the child (Leitch & Tangri, 1988).

A specific issue arises in communication between school personnel and parents of students with disabilities. Students do not receive special education services without first going through a due process hearing. Usually due process hearings are congenial events. Sometimes, however, they are antagonistic, pitting parents against school personnel. When such is the case, it is not an easy matter to resume communication following a hearing.

Empowerment

PL 99-457 specified that school personnel work with families to develop an IFSP. Each state develops rules, regulations, and guidelines for doing so, and each state has a bureaucracy to implement the law. Implementation takes two forms, which Dunst, Trivette, and Deal (1988) called a child-focused model or a family-centered model. In a child-focused model the interventions are expert driven, and the services provided are prescriptive and designed to correct weaknesses. In a family-centered model the interventions are consumer driven and designed to link needs to available services, rather than to create new ones; the services are responsive in nature and are designed to strengthen informal support networks.

School personnel can operate as partners with parents in serving and assisting children, or they can treat parents and children as clients (or patients) who are the recipients of the services to be delivered. In choosing a way in which to operate, they create either empowerment outcomes or dependency outcomes. Professionals can work with parents in an effort to strengthen natural support systems, or they can create new systems. Suppose we want to put in place a system of respite care in which parents of children with disabilities can get relief by having someone serve as a foster parent for a few days or for a weekend. There are two ways to put such a program into effect. We can create a new support system, establishing and training individuals to work as foster parents and provide respite care. Or we can find people with whom the parents already feel comfortable and train those individuals to care for children with disabilities. We can look to create new social services for students or make an effort to use those that are now in place. The more we can rely on natural structures or arrangements, the more we empower parents. When parents have to rely on social service agencies to provide services and make arrangements for them, they may become dependent.

Home Alone: Latchkey Children

The spring 1991 issue of *Teaching Exceptional Children* included a special focus on latchkey children. Why? What is the relationship between children and youths home alone and special education? To what extent is lack of child care and supervision a problem for students with disabilities? Rowland and Robinson (1991) reported on some of these issues: they reported the case of a fourteen-year-old student with mental retardation who was unable to receive day care after school because the center that provided such care did not take children older than twelve. They reported that students with disabilities were dependent on supervision well into adolescence, long after nondisabled peers had become self-sufficient, a problem compounded by the lack of services for students during the summer.

Coleman and Apts (1991) identified the risks to students who are home alone. Such children may not have the cognitive capability and social maturity to fend for themselves. They may lack the physical skills necessary to enter a house and remain at home alone. They may be unable to attend to their basic self-help and self-care needs. They may not know how to protect a house key; get from home to school, and vice versa, on their own; use a telephone; prepare snacks; manage their time; and apply first aid in dealing with emergencies. Decisions to leave children home alone are usually last resort decisions, but parents do often choose to do so. As a result, schools increasingly have to look into after-school programs for students with disabilities and develop instructional programs to enable students to care for themselves.

Homelessness

Homelessness has become a potent issue for special education. Many students with disabilities spend their evenings in homeless shelters and receive their meals from food shelves, some sleep in their cars and do their homework on the steps of a shopping mall, and others live in motels. With no home to return to, they find it difficult to do their homework and attend classes regularly. And for many the doors to a different life, one involving extensive education, are closed.

When is a student homeless? A homeless individual is defined in the Steward B. McKinney Homeless Assistance Act of 1987 as one who lacks a fixed, regular, adequate nighttime residence or has a primary nighttime residence in a supervised publicly or privately operated shelter for temporary accommodation. Until the early 1980s, the American homeless population consisted primarily of men. Each year since then, however, increasing numbers of younger and younger people have become homeless. Of the 2 to 3 million Americans who are homeless each year, 27 percent are children. Families with children constitute approximately 40 percent of people who become homeless (Shinn & Weitzman, 1996).

Consider the changes in the population of homeless individuals from 1987 to 1998. In 1987, the U.S. Conference of Mayors found that families with children were the fastest growing segment of the homeless population. That year, it was estimated that there were 220,000 homeless school-age children and youths, about one-third of whom did not attend school regularly. At that same time, the National Coalition for the Homeless estimated that there were at least two times as many (about 400,000) homeless children. In 1990, the National Law Center on Homelessness and Poverty estimated that 450,000 children and youths were homeless and that another 2 million were precariously housed (Wells, 1989). Now it is estimated that up to 700,000 people are homeless on any given night or that 1.2 to 2 million people experience homelessness during a year (National Law Center on Homelessness and Poverty, 1996). The Children's Defense Fund (1994) estimated that about 100,000 children are homeless each night. Also large numbers of students have been thrown out of their homes by their parents or guardians. When looking at statistics on homelessness, it is important to remember that there is considerable debate about the number of homeless people and there are many ways to account for homelessness. The issue at hand, however, with regard to education, is that homelessness complicates the lives of many students and makes living especially difficult for students with disabilities.

What are the effects of homelessness on pupil achievement and behavior in schools? Most students who are homeless have difficulty attending school regularly, although enrollment figures are improving. Only half of homeless children attended school regularly in 1985; as of 1995, 86 percent attended regularly (Anderson et al., 1995). The McKinney Homeless Assistance Act was amended in 1994 to allow homeless children to attend preschool programs. Less than half do. Enrollment of children who are homeless is hampered by mobility, poor health, inability of schools to obtain past records, transportation, and residency requirements. There are lots of unaccompanied homeless youths and homeless preschoolers. They have difficulty enrolling and attending because of liability and guardianship requirements (Anderson et al., 1995). Success in school is limited by mobility; poor health and nutrition; lack of food, clothing, and/or school supplies; and lack of a stable place to complete homework. Schools report that it is difficult to find students who are homeless when they attempt to conduct evaluations for special education consideration, and that homeless children find it difficult to participate in extracurricular activities and counseling and psychological services, and have trouble accessing before- or after-school care programs. They also report that homeless children are difficult to teach and to provide with developmental assistance because they are so often fleeing domestic violence. Children who are homeless, on the average, score significantly lower on measures of academic achievement than children who have a home (Rafferty & Shinn, 1991).

Most homeless children also live in large urban environments. They see life as temporary; have little structure in their lives; lack continuity; do not have opportunities to establish strong friendships; have no sense of their own space and possessions; and experience repeated shifts in classmates, schools, and curricula. It should not be surprising then to see homeless students who leave projects half-finished, get depressed over leaving familiar places and friends, withdraw, act aggressively, do not complete their homework, fall behind academically, are restless, fight with other students for control of items, have difficulty with transitions, have poor attention span, and demonstrate developmental delays. Students who are homeless can be expected to have major academic deficits and developmental delays. If students who are homeless stay in one place long enough, significant numbers of them will be declared eligible for special education services. How can schools and school personnel combat the effects of homelessness?

INTERAGENCY COLLABORATION

The magnitude of the challenges confronting schools and children is such that they will not be solved by individual organizations or professions operating in isolation. Rather, they will require multidisciplinary and multidimensional approaches.

School personnel must now get involved with other agencies in working on such unfamiliar activities as nutrition programs through the Woman, Infants, and Children (WIC) supplemental feeding program for pregnant women and infants, child care and school nutrition programs, and increased support for food stamps; the Early and Periodic Screening, Diagnosis, and Treatment program with the Medicaid program, child development through Head Start; efforts to increase child support collections; child protective services; and foster care and adoption. The North Central Regional Education Laboratory (1995) put it this way:

> To address both community problems and problems in the service delivery system, many agencies are reworking their organizational thought and practice to emphasize interagency cooperation, coordination, and collaboration. Educational, health, and social service agencies are beginning to recognize that only by working together can they provide services that are integrated rather than fragmented, multidimensional rather than one-dimensional, and continuous rather than sporadic. Still, for agencies accustomed to competition, boundary protection, and categorical funding, recognizing the need to work together is much easier than actually practicing it. (p. 1)

Professionals talk often about interagency interface or collaboration, but few know what it means or what it comprises. In fact, it is extremely difficult to find a definition of interagency collaboration. Essentially, interagency collaboration involves addressing child and family problems and opportunities on a multi-institutional, multiprofessional basis. Key elements of interagency collaboratives include open and honest exchange of ideas across disciplines, programs, and agencies; working together to specify common purposes and identify ways in which separate organizations or professions must change to achieve those purposes; and using formal procedures to help clarify issues, define problems, and make decisions.

McLaughlin and Christensen (1980) identified several reasons for the increased emphasis on interagency efforts to address problems and deliver services. Among these are increased federal initiatives; increased economic pressures; increased pressure from clients, parents, and advocates; the need to reduce duplication of services; and overlap in service definitions. Also affecting interagency collaboration are the pressure for professionals to work together, the fragmented service delivery system, and the multiple funding bases for services. So is interagency collaboration needed? We think so, especially to ensure appropriate placement of students in services, avoid duplication of effort, manage cases across agencies, and promote resource sharing. Collaboration is also needed to facilitate transitions from community or institutional placement to school, prevent disrupted adoptions, and assist individuals in planning their careers.

What does it take to achieve effective collaboration? NCREL (1993) identified guidelines for effective collaboration:

- Involvement of all key players so collaborative decisions and activities receive widespread support and recognition.

- Visionary leadership by individuals who are willing to take risks and facilitate change.
- Shared vision about expected outcomes for the children and families served by the collaborative partners.
- Ownership at all organizational levels and among community members who are involved in the collaborative effort.
- Communication and decision-making processes that work to resolve conflict constructively.
- Identification of collaborative goals and the allocation of funds by individual collaborators to the achievement of those goals.
- Enough time for agency representatives to take a break from their routine responsibilities and be able to work with one another.

The California School to Work Interagency Transition Partnership is an example of an interagency collaborative effort. The partnership involves many agencies working together to provide transition services for youths with disabilities. The collaborative effort involves focus on the individual in transition, the inclusion of the individual and family as partners, working to eliminate barriers to cross-agency work, the reduction of duplication of effort among agencies, the provision of incentives for participating in collaborative work, the use of a common transition planning process, interagency cross-training, and joint efforts to solve barriers that individuals with disabilities face in school-to-work programs.

Interagency collaboration involves hard work. Many professionals are now actively working on models for interagency collaboration. Thus, they continue to identify those elements of shared responsibility and practice that are necessary for the solution of difficult challenges.

Discussion Questions

1. What four elements constitute an effective partnership?
2. Why is parent involvement important for students and educators? Describe the different kinds of parent involvements.
3. What are the five components of supportive home environments? How might student performance in school be enhanced by the presence of these components?
4. What are some difficulties facing homeless students? How might school personnel cope with these difficulties, keeping the students' best interest in mind?
5. What is interagency collaboration and how is it helpful in addressing the needs of students with disabilities?

Chapter 12
Legal Issues

'Tis easier to make certain things legal than to make them legitimate.
—Nicholas Chamfort

Students with disabilities have the legal right to a free appropriate public education. But this leaves the matters of who may be considered disabled, who decides that students have disabilities, and who decides they need to be tested unresolved. Likewise, it does not address the extent to which parents have the right to disagree with decisions the schools make about their children, to refuse to have their children evaluated, and to turn elsewhere, if possible, for help when they disagree with school decisions. Who pays for the very extensive extra services required by some students with disabilities? Should students with disabilities receive the same high school diploma as students without disabilities? Do students who are gifted have the right to special education services (gifted students are not listed in federal legislation)? These and other legal issues permeate special education.

Consider this scenario: Harold is considered emotionally disturbed and suicidal. His parents want to place him in a private residential facility where he can receive round-the-clock supervision and care. The cost for this facility is $50,000 per year. Who pays the cost?

Or consider this scenario: Roberto is a seven-year-old child with AIDS. Is he eligible for special education services, and if so, under what category? And under what circumstances may he be suspended or excluded from school?

The field of special education is loaded with legal questions such as these. Indeed, educators today are as much concerned with matters of litigation and legislation as of education. Since the beginning of the 1970s, the courts and the federal and state legislatures have become deeply involved in the process of schooling, and educators, especially special educators, have been compelled year by year to comply with an ever-larger number of court mandates and laws. Litigation regarding special education has focused on the extent to which the schools, by virtue of administrative arrangements and decisions, deny the equal protection of the law to many students. Earlier litigation concentrated on the right to treatment (education) and due process, but more recently, litigation has addressed the assessment of students and accompanied decision-making practices. Since the late 1970s, many of the methods by which educators assign students to instructional alternatives have been challenged, school assessment practices have been cited as discriminatory, and schools have been charged with failing to provide appropriate education to minority students and/or students with disabilities.

These students have always been with us; it is the attention they receive from the courts and legislatures that makes them more important now. School systems that fail to comply with the mandates of federal legislation are threatened with losing funds appropriated by Congress.

Contemporary litigation and legislation are based on efforts to clarify and in some cases to redefine the fundamental purposes of schooling. Earlier we observed that three ideas directed the development of American education: democracy, nationalism, and individualism. We described the four basic values and ideals of democracy: the worth of the individual, the equality of all individuals, the equality of opportunity, and faith in reason. Two of these ideas—equality of all individuals and equality of opportunity—are rights guaranteed by the equal protection clause (the Fourteenth Amendment) of the U.S. Constitution. The Fourteenth Amendment has been cited as being violated most often when the actions of schools have been tested in the courts. (For a comprehensive treatment of legal issues in special education, see Yell [1998]).

THE ROLES OF LEGISLATURES AND COURTS IN AMERICAN EDUCATION

The idea of public schooling initiated the legislative action that enabled the Commonwealth of Massachusetts to tax its citizens for the purpose of establishing schools and providing children with free education. But until recently, the courts have had a hands-off policy toward the affairs of schools. As Bersoff noted, "There was a time when the behavior of school officials went virtually unexamined by the courts. Pleading lack of expert knowledge, judges were wary of interfering with the discretion of administrators to educate their students" (1979, p. 31). In amplifying his remarks, Bersoff cited a portion of the record in an 1893 case, *Watson* v. *City of Cambridge,* in which the court stated:

Selected, Key Federal Statutes Affecting the Education and Civil Rights of Children and Youths with Disabilities

PL 99-372, The Handicapped Children's Protection Act of 1986.
This law provides for reasonable attorneys' fees and costs to parents and guardians who prevail in administrative hearings or court when there is a dispute with a school system concerning their child's right to a free appropriate special education and related services.

PL 99-457, The Education of the Handicapped Act Amendments of 1986.
This law mandates services for preschoolers with disabilities and established the Part H program to assist states in the development of a comprehensive, multidisciplinary, and statewide system of early intervention services for infants and toddlers (birth to age 3). This law also reauthorized the discretionary programs and expanded transition programs.

PL 100-407, The Technology-Related Assistance for Individuals with Disabilities Act of 1988.
The primary purpose of this law is to assist states in developing comprehensive, consumer-responsive programs of technology-related assistance and to extend the availability of technology to individuals with disabilities and their families. *Assistive technology device* is broadly defined in the law to give the states flexibility in the programs to be developed. Assistive technology services under this law include 8 activities related to developing consumer-responsive services with federal funds.

PL 101-127, The Children with Disabilities Temporary Care Reauthorization Act of 1989.
This law is actually part of a larger federal law, the Children's Justice Act, PL 99-401. Title II of this law includes provisions to fund temporary child care (e.g., respite care) for children who have a disability or chronic illness and crisis nurseries for children at risk of abuse or neglect. In 1989, PL 101-127 extended and expanded this program for two years and included an increase in funding for these programs from $5 million to $20 million in 1990 and 1991. By July 1990, eighty-seven grants were awarded to states to develop and establish respite care programs and crisis nurseries.

PL 101-336, The Americans with Disabilities Act of 1990.
This law, based on the concepts of the Rehabilitation Act of 1973, guarantees equal opportunity for individuals with disabilities in employment, public accommodation, transportation, state and local government services, and telecommunications. The ADA is the most significant federal law ensuring the full civil rights of all individuals with disabilities.

(continued)

Selected, Key Federal Statutes Affecting the Education and Civil Rights of Children and Youths with Disabilities (continued)

PL 101-392, The Carl D. Perkins Vocational and Applied Technology Education Act of 1990.

This law amended PL 98-524 for the purpose of making the United States more competitive in the world economy. This law is closely interwoven with the Education of the Handicapped Act (PL 94-142) toward guaranteeing full vocational education opportunity for youths with disabilities.

PL 101-476, The Education of the Handicapped Act Amendments of 1990.

This law changed the name of EHA to the Individuals with Disabilities Education Act (IDEA). This law reauthorized and expanded the discretionary programs, mandated transition services and assistive technology services to be included in a child's or youth's IEP, and added autism and traumatic brain injury to the list of categories of children and youths eligible for special education and related services.

PL 101-496, The Developmental Disabilities Assistance and Bill of Rights Act of 1990.

This law authorizes grants to support the planning, coordination, and delivery of specialized services to persons with developmental disabilities. In addition, this law provides funding for the operation of state protection and advocacy systems for persons with developmental disabilities. The original law was enacted in 1963 by PL 88-164. In 1987, PL 100-146 significantly expanded the Act to include persons with mental retardation, autism, cerebral palsy, and epilepsy.

PL 105-17, The Individuals with Disabilities Education Act Amendments of 1997.

This law amended PL 101-476, the Individuals with Disabilities Education Act. It contains sweeping amendments that change practices and procedures in assessment and accountability, discipline, personnel preparation, IEP development, discretionary programs, and funding formulas.

SOURCE: Adapted from Home, R. L. (1991). Selected key federal statutes affecting the education and civil rights of children and youths with disabilities. *News Digest,* 1(1), p. 13. Used with permission of the National Information Center for Children and Youth with Disabilities.

The management of schools involves many details, and it is important that a board of public officers . . . having jurisdiction to regulate the internal affairs of the schools should not be interfered with or have their conduct called into question before another tribunal. . . . A jury composed of men of no special fitness to decide educational questions should not be permitted to say that their answer is wrong. (p. 864)

Bersoff also reported that as recently as 1968 the courts maintained a hands-off policy on intervention into the affairs of the school, as evidenced in *Epperson* v. *Arkansas*: "Courts do not and cannot intervene in the resolution of conflicts which arise in the daily operation of school systems and which do not directly and sharply implicate basic constitutional values" (p. 104).

The courts' hands-off policy can be said to have ended with the U.S. Supreme Court's declaration in *Tinker* v. *Des Moines Independent Community School District* (1969) that "students in school as well as out of schools are persons under our Constitution . . . possessed of fundamental rights which the State must respect" (p. 515). Since 1969, according to Bersoff,

> [the Supreme Court] . . . has decided such issues as the reach of compulsory education laws, the requirements of due process prior to infliction of disciplinary and academic sanctions, the immunity of school officials from money damage liability for violations of students' civil rights, the allocation of financial resources to pupils in poor school districts, the education of non–English speaking children, the permissibility of sex-separate high schools, the legality of special admissions programs for minorities, the obligation of colleges and universities to admit handicapped students, and most recently, the validity of system-wide remedies to reduce school segregation. (1979, p. 33)

Over time, special education has undergone radical changes as a result of judicial and legislative actions (see the box on pp. 313–314). But the situation produced by these changes is a dynamic one because the law is always changing. Practices that were followed yesterday may be illegal today, and procedures that are required today may be replaced by others tomorrow. Laws, rules, and regulations change as society's social and economic priorities change. Nevertheless, despite the evolutionary nature of the process, at any time the specific laws, practices, and procedures that govern education are expected to reflect the broad principles of freedom and equality that society through the Constitution has agreed on. As we write this text—even as you read it—Congress, state legislatures, and the courts are shaping public policy in special education by making and interpreting laws that affect how students are treated in the schools.

Where Do Laws and Rules Come From?

Practices in special education today have been shaped mostly by national and state constitutions and laws, administrative regulations and guidelines, court rulings, and the standards and ethics of the profession. The relationship among these elements is shown in Figure 12.1

Federal and state constitutions set forth broad political principles that guide the lawmaking process at both national and state levels, which defines certain elements of education (see the box on p. 317). Administrative rules and regulations are usually written to clarify laws and have the force of law.

The courts interpret these laws, regulations, and guidelines in light of the Constitution and precedent (earlier related judicial decisions, especially those in

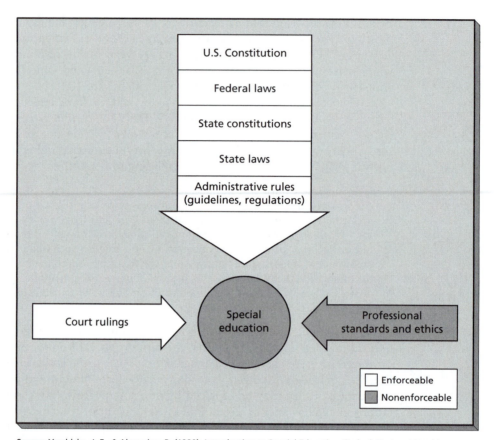

U.S. Constitution

Federal laws

State constitutions

State laws

Administrative rules
(guidelines, regulations)

Court rulings

Special
education

Professional
standards and ethics

☐ Enforceable
■ Nonenforceable

Source: Ysseldyke, J. E., & Algozzine, B. (1990). Introduction to Special Education. 2nd ed. Boston: Houghton Mifflin, p. 41. Used with permission.

the same jurisdiction as that held by the court). Although in theory the courts are not lawmaking bodies, their rulings can change existing law, a situation that by implication gives courts the power to make new laws. As a result, courts regulate who receives special education and what type of special education is provided (Ysseldyke & Algozzine, 1990).

Professional standards and codes of ethics have indirect influence on the practice of special education. The standards that bear most directly on that practice are the Standards for Professional Practice published by the Council for Exceptional Children (CEC). These standards identify instructional responsibilities, behavioral management techniques, the amount of instruction and supervision required to perform support services, responsibilities to parents, and advocacy standards. They also define criteria for professional employment, professional development, and intra- and inter-professional behavior. The CEC Code of Ethics defines broad principles that special educators are responsible for

How Federal Laws and Regulations Are Determined

It is helpful to know how laws are named or referred to. Whenever an Act is passed by the Congress and signed into law by the president, it is given a number, such as PL 94-142. "PL" stands for **Public Law**. The first set of numbers means the session of Congress during which the law was passed. For example, the 94 means the 94th session of the U.S. Congress. The second set of numbers identifies what number the law was in the sequence of passage and enactment during that session. Thus, the 142 means that this was the 142nd law that Congress passed and the president signed during the 94th session of Congress.

It is also important to understand that federal laws are often changed, or amended, regularly. Public Law 94-142, the Education for All Handicapped Children Act, has had several amendments since its passage in 1975. Therefore, it is important to keep up-to-date on these changes because they often affect the delivery of special education, related services, and other programs in your state.

Laws passed by the Congress provide a general framework of policy related to a particular issue. Once a law is passed. Congress delegates to an administrative agency within the executive branch the task of developing detailed regulations to guide the law's implementation. Federal regulations are detailed in the *Code of Federal Regulations (CFR)*. The *CFR* interprets the law, discusses each point of a law, and further explains it. Copies of most federal regulations are available in the public library. The *CFR* is readable and helpful in understanding the laws. State agencies must comply with federal laws and regulations.

At the federal level, special education is an area in which elaborate sets of regulations exist. The regulations for the Education of the Handicapped Act, for example, spell out the procedures and programming that must be provided to children and youths with disabilities so that states will receive federal funds. States may go beyond what is required in the regulations. For example, some states have broader definitions of which children are entitled to special education and, thus, may include gifted children in their special education programming.

SOURCE: Home, R. L. (1991). How Federal Laws and Regulations Are Determined. *News Digest,* 1(1), 2. Used with permission.

upholding and advancing. . . . For the most part, in special education as in general education, professional standards and ethical codes are not enforceable; they do not have the power of law. But this does not mean that they are not important. Although a school district would not take legal action against a teacher for unethical conduct, it probably would take formal action to dismiss the teacher. (pp. 44–45)

Courts, legislatures, and administrative agencies act as checks on one another in the lawmaking and rule-making process. To illustrate this interaction, Rothstein

(1990) cited activities regarding who pays attorneys' fees. In 1975, Congress passed PL 94-142, which did not specify responsibility for paying attorneys' fees incurred as part of due process hearings. In 1984, the Supreme Court decided in *Smith* v. *Robinson* that parents could not recover the money they spent on attorneys' fees. In 1986, Congress responded to that decision by passing the Handicapped Children's Protection Act, which said that in some situations attorneys' fees could be paid by school districts. The issue is now being argued in the lower courts, and there is pressure on personnel in the U.S. Department of Education to develop guidelines to aid school districts and parents in deciding when attorneys' fees can be reimbursed. The issue may again rise to the Supreme Court level.

It is hard to identify the extent to which specific court rulings affect individual school districts and even specific states because there are actually fifty-one separate court systems in the United States. There are three levels of federal courts: the U.S. Supreme Court, the appeals courts, and federal district courts. Each state has a supreme court, a court of appeals, and trials courts (see Fisher and Sorenson [1985] for a picture of the various levels and alternative paths a judicial controversy can take). The rulings of the courts are applicable only in their specific jurisdiction. Supreme Court rulings apply everywhere in the United States and its territories. The rulings of a U.S. appeals court apply only in the region served by that court. The rulings of a state trial court are applicable only in the area in that state served by the court.

There are many ways in which we could share with you the critical legal issues confronting the fields of special and remedial education. The most comprehensive treatment of legal issues in special education to date is a 1998 text by Mitchell Yell entitled *The Law and Special Education*. Yell's text is an issues-oriented text, and legal cases are organized by specific issues. The text is must reading for those concerned about legal issues in special education. We deal with essentially the same issues as does Yell, but we have organized them in the same way in which our textbook is organized. We have relied heavily on Yell's work in clarifying our own thinking on the issues. Those who want more specifics and details regarding these issues are encouraged to read Yell.

Definitional Issues

When provisions for education are specified in law, they are not necessarily accompanied by corresponding definitions. Thus, a law can declare that students be educated in the least restrictive environment but leave the definition of LRE to the courts and to local education agencies to decide. As a result, several complex definitional issues have been debated in the courts, and the outcomes have directly affected the life opportunities of many students.

The Definition of a Disability   One of these issues is what constitutes a disability. The Education for all Handicapped Children Act listed eleven categories of disabling conditions eligible for services. Thirteen specific disability categories are listed in the 1997 Amendments to the Individuals with Disabilities Education Act. Some groups (for example, students who are gifted) are not covered by the legislation, and students who need related services but do not require special education may be excluded. There are major questions regarding the extent to which students who have chronic infectious diseases (hemophilia, AIDS, tuberculosis) are eligible for special education. The courts have taken positions on such issues. For example, in *Espino* v. *Besteiro* (1981), a district court in Texas required that the school air-condition a classroom for a single student who could not regulate his body temperature. In *Antkowiak* v. *Ambach* (1986), a district court in New York ruled that a gifted student who had anorexia was eligible for placement in the Devereaux Treatment Center at no cost to her parents because her anorexia was due to underlying emotional disturbance. In *Roe* v. *Commonwealth of Pennsylvania* (1986), a Pennsylvania district court ruled that a student with an IQ lower than 130 was not entitled to special education for gifted students. In *School District of Nassau County* v. *Arline* (1987), the U.S. Supreme Court ruled that a student with tuberculosis could be considered a person with a disability under Section 504 of the Rehabilitation Act.

The Definition of Right to Education   An important court decision that set the stage for later litigation, including that in *Arline,* was *Tinker* v. *Des Moines Independent Community School District* (1969). The issue it addressed was the right of students to wear black armbands to protest the Vietnam War. The Supreme Court ruled that children and youths were "persons" under the Constitution and had First Amendment rights independent of their parents, and it reaffirmed that children and youths did not lose their civil rights when they attended school. The establishment of the principle that children and youths are persons who have rights was later cited in many judicial rulings relating to special education.

The courts have also tried to define the concept of the right to education. In *Mills* v. *Board of Education* (1972), the district court in Washington, D.C., ruled that all students with mental retardation had the right to a free appropriate education and that denial of due process to such students constituted violation of the Fourteenth Amendment. In *PARC* v. *Commonwealth of Pennsylvania* (1972), the court required the Pennsylvania Department of Education to engage in extensive efforts to locate and evaluate all students who were mentally retarded and who were not enrolled in school. In *City of Cleburne* v. *Cleburne Living Center* (1985), the U.S. Supreme Court ruled that students with disabilities did not have the special protection of the law and that people with disabilities should be treated like everyone else. In *Plyler* v. *Doe* (1982), the court said that even though individuals who were mentally retarded would not be given special treatment under the law, their education would.

The Definition of Provision of Services   Another issue taken up by the courts is where to draw the line in providing education and services to students—are there some students who are so disabled that it does not make sense to involve them in an instructional program? Courts have concluded that all students with disabilities, regardless of the severity of their disabilities, can benefit from education and are therefore covered under the IDEA. For example, in *Timothy W. v. Rochester School District* (1989), the U.S. Court of Appeals for the First Circuit ruled that Timothy W., a paraplegic child with severe cerebral palsy, profound mental retardation, brain damage, and cortical blindness was eligible for services under the IDEA. The issue of where to draw the line has been settled: no student with a disability can be denied services under the IDEA, no matter how severe the disability.

The Definition of Appropriate Education   For much of the 1970s and early 1980s, the substantive issues in court cases were eligibility, access to special education, and bias in assessment. Since the early 1990s, however, courts have been addressing the issue of the appropriateness of services students receive and in the process have been faced with defining "free and appropriate." In 1977, the U.S. Department of Health, Education, and Welfare defined appropriate education as "the provision of regular or special education and related aids and services that . . . are designed to meet individual educational needs of handicapped persons as adequately as the needs of nonhandicapped persons." In the *Rowley* case, the Supreme Court further defined appropriate education as "educational instruction specially designed to meet the unique needs of the handicapped child, supported by such services as are necessary to permit the child to 'benefit' from the instruction" (1982, p. 19). As might be imagined, the courts are still struggling with the question of when students are in a position to benefit from their educational experiences.

Unfortunately, however, these two definitions of appropriate education do not help in identifying the actual or intended meaning of the term *appropriate*. Is an adequate education appropriate, and if so, what is adequate? This dilemma is complicated by the fact that an operational definition of appropriate education would require a statement of the goals of education, which raises a host of other questions. What are the goals of education? How do they differ for students with disabilities and their nondisabled peers? To what extent are these goals even attainable?

Categorization, Classification, and Eligibility Issues

The courts regularly intervene in classification, placement, fee payment, categorization, labeling, and eligibility matters. Because students must be declared eligible for special education services before these can be provided and in most states students must be formally labeled or categorized to receive services, the courts have addressed the extent to which specific students are members of categories and the extent to which students ought to be categorized. In many cases, the substantive issue has been bias in assessment that has resulted in assignment of students to stigmatized categorical groups.

Classification Classification has been repeatedly addressed by the courts. In 1967, Judge Wright rendered an important decision in the case of *Hansen* v. *Hobson,* which brought suit on behalf of black students who were assigned in disproportionate numbers to lower ability groups or lower tracks in the Washington, D.C., schools. The chief argument was against the practice of using pupil performance on standardized aptitude and achievement tests to make grouping or placement decisions. Judge Wright ruled:

> The evidence shows that the method by which track assignments are made depends essentially on standardized aptitude tests which, although given on a system-wide basis, are completely inappropriate for use with a large segment of the student body. Because these tests are standardized primarily on and are relevant to a white middle class group of students, they produce inaccurate and misleading test scores when given to lower class and Negro students. (p. 514)

The courts have been able to demonstrate again and again that educational placements based on pupil performance on ability or achievement tests result in the disproportionate placement in lower tracks of minority students and of those from lower socioeconomic backgrounds. The courts have ruled that these readily observable instances constitute a denial of equal protection of the law.

Placement Educators today advocate a continuum of placements for students with disabilities, with the placements varying in degree of restrictiveness. Within such a model, placement in a residential facility is seen as very restrictive. According to Rothstein (1990), *Kruelle* v. *New Castle Country School District* (1981) was the earliest major decision on residential placements, and it is "still cited as a standard on the issue" (1990, p. 150). Paul Kruelle was a child with profound retardation for whom the district court recommendation full-time residential placement. The U.S. circuit court of appeals upheld the district court recommendation. Both courts ruled that the child required continuous and consistent supervision and that such supervision was not available in the six-hour school program.

The courts can go so far as to mandate placement out of state, as a circuit court did in *Antkowiak* v. *Ambach* when it ruled that the school district had to pay for the child to be enrolled at the Devereaux Treatment Center in Pennsylvania. One category of students for whom placement arguments have been especially prevalent is deaf students. Educators and parents regularly debate whether students who are deaf should attend regular schools or separate facilities. In *Lachman* v. *Illinois State Board of Education* (1988), the circuit court upheld a district court ruling that the child could be educated in a general school where his educational needs could be met in an appropriate manner.

In debating placement issues such as mainstreaming and least restrictive environment, the courts have also considered the extent to which students have the right to placement with their age-appropriate peers. The issue becomes whether the students have the right to attend not only general classes but which general classes. The issue is unsettled. The Supreme Court in *Hendrick-Hudson District Board of Education* v. *Rowley* noted that an appropriate placement must approximate the grade levels used in the state's regular education system.

Payment of Fees   The courts have addressed the payment of fees by school districts for students to attend private schools. In *Burlington School Committee* v. *Department of Education* (1985), the lower courts asked the Supreme Court for a ruling on the meaning of "appropriate education." Michael Panaco, a first-grader with a specific learning disability, was enrolled in a private school because his parents contended that he was not receiving an education that met his unique needs in the local public school. The Court noted that "where a court determines that a private placement desired by the parents was proper under the Act and that an IEP calling for placement in a public school was inappropriate, it seems clear beyond cavil that appropriate relief includes . . . placing the child in a private school" (p. 231). The Court ruled that the most important element of PL 94-142 was an appropriate educational program, wherever it took place.

Categorization   In addition to debating specific placements, the courts get into the categorization argument. They may, for example, rule in individual cases whether a specific student meets the criteria for being classified as mentally retarded, learning disabled, or some other condition. Many court cases have focused on the other health impaired category and have asked whether students who have chronic illnesses are eligible for services under this category. For example, in *School Board of Nassau County* v. *Arline*, the court ruled that a student with tuberculosis could be considered disabled and a member of the other health impaired category.

Assessment Issues

The courts have regularly entered disputes between parents and schools over whether students should be assessed and how. Courts have gotten involved most often when the issue has been the use of test results in making decisions to place students in allegedly inferior educational environments. In a consent decree reached as part of *Diana* v. *State Board of Education* (1970), the state of California agreed to test all children whose primary language was not English in both their primary language and English. They eliminated "unfair verbal items" from tests, reevaluated all Mexican American and Chinese students enrolled in classes for students with mental retardation by using only nonverbal items and testing them in their primary language, and developed IQ tests that would reflect Mexican American culture and would be standardized only on Mexican Americans. The case of *Diana* arose when the parents of Mexican American students entered into a class-action suit against the state, arguing that the assignment of Mexican American students to classes for students with mental retardation on the basis of their performances on standardized intelligence tests was discriminatory. In *Covarubias* v. *San Diego Unified School District* (1971), a consent decree established the right of the plaintiffs and only those plaintiffs to monetary damages as a result of their misclassification as having disabilities.

Schools and state education agencies have been charged with discriminatory intent when their assessment practices resulted in the disproportionate assignment of blacks and minority students to special education classes. Although educators and psychologists have been unable to reach a consensus on the meaning of nondiscriminatory assessment, PL 94-142 mandated schools to select and administer assessment devices in racially and culturally nondiscriminatory ways. As early as 1967, the court had ruled in *Hansen* v. *Hobson* that the standardized tests employed by the Washington, D.C., schools for making tracking decisions were inappropriate for use with black students because the tests were developed and standardized on white middle-class students. In *Lora* v. *New York City Board of Education* (1978), the assessment procedures of the school district were cited as inadequate and discriminatory. But contrast the decisions in the *Larry P.* and *PASE* cases: whereas in *Larry P.* v. *Riles* (1979) the California State Supreme Court declared the IQ tests that were used to place black students in classes for students with mental retardation as discriminatory, in *PASE* v. *Hannon* (1980) the Illinois district court ruled that two standard intelligence tests were not biased against black children. Without a clear definition of terms such as *biased, discriminatory,* and *nondiscriminatory,* decisions on whether tests exhibit these characteristics are at best problematic. As a result, several questions regarding the recent litigation and legislation are still unanswered:

1. How big a difference may (or must) be observed in the test performance of blacks and whites before the test is considered biased?
2. If intelligence tests are banned, how will MR placement be determined?
3. What is race?
4. To what extent are classes for students with disabilities a dead end?

The Magnitude and Validity of Testing

Recent court cases have mandated that testing be limited (*Larry P.* v. *Riles*) and expanded (*Frederick L.* v. *Thomas* [1978]; *Lora* v. *New York City Board of Education*). What, then, should educators do? Should intellectual assessment be discontinued, or should more and better intelligence tests be administered to identify the increasing number of students with disabilities? What are the standards for better tests of intelligence?

According to PL 94-142, tests must be validated for the purposes for which they are used. In *Larry P.* v. *Riles,* Judge Peckham ruled that school personnel could use intelligence tests to make EMR placement decisions about black students only if before doing so they could demonstrate that the tests they planned to use were valid for making EMR placement decisions for black students. Sarason and Doris pointed out, however, that anyone who sets for himself the task of collecting, describing, and criticizing intelligence tests either currently in use or advertised for use has staked out at least half a career. In the face of such a bewildering array of tests, conceptions, and criticisms, it is understandable if one concludes that far from being naked, the emperor not only has a surfeit of clothes but he is wearing them all at the same time. This is said to suggest that as one gets overwhelmed pursuing test after test and tries to organize the various underlying conceptions into some coherent framework, one may well conclude that the concept of intelligence has all the characteristics of an inkblot onto which people have projected meanings on the basis of which they wish to urge other people to see what they see, to "measure" it in the same way they do. (1979, p. 30)

Courts and legislatures have ordered that tests be validated for the purposes for which they are used. Yet examination of some of the purposes for which tests are employed in special and remedial education reveals that educators cannot achieve compliance with the mandate. Tests are used to differentiate individuals; to identify those who are mentally retarded, learning disabled, and emotionally disturbed; and to spot those who have incipient learning disabilities. They are used to identify children who have limited intelligence, body image problems, auditory sequential memory deficits, or figure-ground pathology or who suffer from hysteria, hypochondriasis, and depression. But educators are not certain what these terms mean and what these conditions are and have no idea of what to do (with any degree of validity) when they find them. Sarason and Doris observed that definitions of conditions such as mental retardation, learning disabilities, and emotional disturbance are constantly shifting because they reflect changing societal values and attitudes:

Why define intelligence and mental retardation? Why measure them? We can now formulate an answer: in the realm of human behavior and actions, the need to define and measure always reflects dominant social needs as the society at the time perceives them, and these perceptions are inevitably colored by moral or value judgments. Neither the substance of definitions nor the types of measuring devices to which they give rise are neutral, dispassionate affairs, although the effectiveness with which the culture transmits these dominant perceptions to us ordinarily obscures how rooted in the culture we and the definitions are. What we take to be "natural" and objective is not free from the influences of social time and place. (1979, p. 36)

How can educators demonstrate the validity of tests for measuring things that are neither defined nor conceptualized? Current measures of traits, aptitudes, and abilities do not provide empirical evidence for their validity as measures of those traits, aptitudes, and abilities.

The courts have also entered into the debate about appropriate assessment by ruling on the meaning of informed consent for evaluations, payment for evaluations, and specific evaluation procedures and limitations. For example, in *Seals* v. *Loftus* (1985), the court ruled that the school had to pay for extensive out-of-school neurological and psychological evaluations. In *Matty T.* v. *Mississippi*

Department of Education (1981) and in *Luke S.* v. *Louisiana Department of Education* (1983), the issue was the timeliness and appropriateness of assessment procedures used with black students. The district courts ordered the state departments of education to develop procedures whereby school personnel could and would engage in prereferral interventions before referring students for evaluations. The court also ruled that such evaluations had to be completed quickly following formal referral. Recently, states have begun to require that student promotion and graduation be based on satisfactory performance on minimum competency tests. In *Debra P.* v. *Turlington* (1984), the court ruled that students with disabilities could be required to take such minimum competency tests as long as it could be shown that the tests covered the content of the curriculum to which the students were exposed. In *Brookhart* v. *Illinois State Board of Education* (1984), the court ruled that minimum competency tests were valid when used with students with disabilities.

Instruction Issues

Given that under IDEA students with disabilities are granted the right to a free appropriate education, it should come as no surprise that the courts have been heavily involved in litigation regarding instruction, specifically, appropriate instruction. As we noted earlier, the courts have tried to define appropriate education. They have also addressed extended services, right to psychological services and counseling as part of instruction, delivery of health services, provision of "extra" services, and parental participation in the development of IEPs. In *Hendrick-Hudson Board of Education* v. *Rowley* (1982), the Court overturned a lower court ruling that had required a school to provide an interpreter for a deaf student. The case began when Amy Rowley's parents asked the school to provide a sign language interpreter in their deaf daughter's class on a full-time basis. The school was providing speech therapy, use of a hearing aid, and a tutor for one hour a day and had offered sign language instruction to those of Amy's teachers who wanted it. But the school refused to put an interpreter in Amy's classroom. The Supreme Court ruled that the school was acting within its rights. In writing the decision for the court, Justice Rehnquist stated that schools did not have to develop the maximum potential of students with disabilities; they just had to give students access to educational opportunities.

In *Irving Independent School District* v. *Tatro* (1984), the issue was the responsibility of a school to provide a medical procedure, in this case, catheterization, to a student with a disability. Chief Justice Burger writing for the majority reasoned that

> a service that enables a handicapped child to remain at school during the day is an important means of providing the child with the meaningful access to education that Congress envisioned. Services like CIC [clean, intermittent catheterization, which involves washing a small metal tube called a catheter, inserting the catheter in the bladder to allow urine to drain, pulling the catherter out, and wiping the

> bladder region] that permit a child to remain at school during the day are not less related to the effort to educate than are services that enable the child to reach, enter, or exist in the school. (p. 104)

Burger went on to say that catheterization, because it could be carried out by a school nurse, was a related, not a medical, service. Schools are not required to provide medical services that have to be administered by a physician (with the exception of some assessment and diagnostic services); but they must provide services that can be carried out by a school nurse.

In *Frederick L.* the issue was provision of "appropriate" educational services to students who had learning disabilities, whereas in *Lora* the issue was delivery of "appropriate educational services" to students who were emotionally disturbed. A number of services are specifically listed in PL 94-142 as related services that are to be made available to the child; included are psychological services and counseling. In *Max M.* v. *Illinois State Board of Education* (1986), the Illinois court ruled that parents could be reimbursed for psychological and psychiatric services the child received out of school, but the Court also put some limitations on the amount of reimbursement.

Another issue addressed by the courts is precisely with whom the school should communicate. Given the relatively high divorce rate, schools are faced with making decisions about which parent they should contact. In *Fay* v. *South Colonie Central School District* (1986), the Second Circuit Court of Appeals indicated that schools did not have to communicate routine announcements to both parents with legal custody but that parents with legal custody had access to students' records.

School Outcomes Issues

The recent move to specification of outcomes for students has not been tested by the courts. Yet in a real sense the courts have been concerned with outcomes for some times. We see court intervention in outcomes in several "malpractice suits." In *Meiner* v. *Missouri* (1982), the U.S. circuit court held that damages were never available as a remedy for alleged educational malpractice. In *Manecke* v. *School Board* (1985), the circuit court ruled that damages might be available as a remedy for malpractice, but it did not specify the conditions in which such damages might be awarded. And there is considerable variation in court decisions on whether states are immune from damages.

Early Intervention

In 1986 Congress amended PL 94-142 and extended all rights and protections of the law to preschoolers with disabilities. Effective in the 1990–1991 academic year, all states that applied for funds under PL 94-142 had to provide free appropriate education to all children with disabilities aged 3 through 5.

At the same time, as part of PL 99-457. Congress established a new state grant program for infants and toddlers with disabilities. Eligible for early intervention are children from birth through age 2 who are delayed in development or at risk of substantial delay in development. The states have the authority to specify the criteria for deciding whom to serve.

To receive the federal funds available as part of PL 99-457, states must have an agency that administers the services and an interagency coordinating council to help develop programs and services. By the 1990–1991 academic year, statewide early intervention systems had to be in place, providing all eligible infants and toddlers with multidisciplinary assessments, individualized programs, and case management services.

PL 99-457 specified that each school district use a multidisciplinary assessment to develop an individualized family service plan (IFSP) for each student. The IFSP must include:

- A statement of the student's present level of cognitive, social, speech and language, and self-help development
- A statement of the family's strengths and needs related to enhancing the student's development
- A statement of the major outcomes expected for the student and family
- Criteria, procedures, and timelines for measuring progress
- A statement of the specific early intervention services necessary to meet the unique needs of the student and family, including methods, frequency, and intensity of service
- Projected dates for initiation and expected duration of services
- The name of the person who will manage the case
- Procedures for transition from early interventions into a preschool program

Transition Issues

PL 105-17, passed in 1997, requires that transition planning begin when a student reaches the age of 14.

The courts have addressed a number of what we call "transitional issues": suspension, graduation requirements, and dropout.

Suspension In *Honig* v. *Doe* (1988), the Supreme Court reaffirmed the decision of a lower court that schools could not exclude students with disabilities, particularly emotional disabilities, because of their behavior. The case involved the suspension of two students who were receiving special education services in the San Francisco school district. The students (called John Doe and Jack Smith in the decision) had been expelled for different reasons.

Student Doe had been placed in a developmental center for students with disabilities. While attending school, he assaulted another student and broke a window. When he admitted these offenses to the principal, he was suspended for five days. The principal referred the matter to the school's student placement committee with the recommendation that Doe be expelled. The suspension was continued indefinitely as permitted by California state law, which allowed suspensions to extend beyond five days while expulsion proceedings were being held.

Student Smith's IEP stated that he was to be placed in a special education program in a general school setting on a trial basis. Following several incidences of misbehavior, the school unilaterally reduced his program to half-day. Although his grandparents agreed to the reduction, the school district did not notify them of their right to appeal. A month later Smith was suspended for five days when he made inappropriate sexual comments to female students. In accordance with California law Smith's suspension also was continued indefinitely while expulsion proceedings were initiated by the school placement committee (Yell, 1989).

The case went through several levels of courts, eventually ending up in the Supreme Court. Justice Brennan, writing for the majority, stated that schools could not unilaterally exclude students with disabilities. When placement was being debated, the child had to remain in the current educational setting unless school officials and parents agreed otherwise. The decision left a number of questions unanswered (Yell, 1998): In what ways can these students be disciplined? How should the schools deal with students who are a danger to themselves or others but whose parents do not consent to removal?

Graduation Requirements   According to Rothstein, "The issue of graduation requirements involves two different questions of obligation by educational agencies. The first is whether diploma requirements may be imposed on students with disabilities. The second is whether there is any obligation to a disabled student once the diploma has been awarded" (1990, p. 174).

In *Brookhart* v. *Illinois State Board of Education,* a suit was brought on behalf of fourteen elementary and secondary students who were disabled and were required to pass a minimum competency test to receive a high school diploma. The district court ruled that the plaintiffs did not have to pass the minimum competency test because the test did not assess the content of their curriculum. Rather than receiving the standard high school curriculum, the object of the test, the students had received unique instruction as specified in their IEPs. The court ruled that if the students has been given notice early enough of the requirement to pass the minimum competency test, their IEPs could have been adjusted to include the content of the tests. Because the test did not include the content of the curriculum for the students (as ruled earlier in *Debra P.* v. *Turlington*), the students did not have to pass the tests to graduate. They did, however, have to meet two other graduation requirements: completion of seventeen course credits and fulfillment of the state's graduation requirements. We are not aware of a court case in which the court has taken action on whether the school may issue different diplomas to students who are disabled.

Dropout   In what conditions can a student with disabilities drop out of school? Rothstein raised a number of issues about dropouts but stated clearly that these issues have not really been addressed by the courts. She described the dilemmas as follows:

> In many states, students are not required to attend school beyond a certain age, usually around 14 to 16. This raises an interesting question as to whether a student who is receiving special education may elect to stop attending school. For example, a student who has reached 16 in a state where 16 is the cutoff for mandatory attendance may wish to stop attending school. If that student is receiving some programming for a learning disability, for example, what is the obligation of the school to try to keep that student in school? Is there any greater obligation for that student than there is for a student who is not receiving special education? What happens if the parents do not care? Is there any greater obligation to try to persuade the parents to "force" the child to attend because the student is receiving special education? Once the student becomes 18, the parents no longer have the legal power to force the student to attend anyway. (1990, pp. 178–179)

Disciplining Students with Disabilities

The Individuals with Disabilities Act Amendments of 1997 included a section affecting the discipline of students with disabilities. School officials can suspend students with disabilities or unilaterally change their placement to an appropriate setting for up to ten school days. Following the ten days, however, a school official must provide educational services to a student. Whether the ten-day limit is consecutive or not remains unsettled, although the Office of Special Education considers the limit to apply to ten consecutive days in a school year.

If a student with disabilities brings a weapon to school or a school function or knowingly possesses, uses, or sells illegal drugs at a school or school function, school officials may unilaterally place the student in an interim alternative educational setting for up to forty-five days. Similarly, an impartial officer can order a forty-five-day interim placement if school officials have convincing evidence that the student is substantially likely to injure him- or herself or others and that they have made reasonable, although unsuccessful, efforts to minimize the risk of harm.

When school officials seek a change of placement, suspension, or expulsion, a review of the relationships between a student's disability and misconduct, called a manifestation determination, must be conducted by the student's IEP team. If the term concludes that there is no relationship between the disability and misconduct, the same disciplinary procedures that would be imposed on all students, including expulsion, may be used. Educational services cannot be discontinued.

Economic Issues

Provision of special education services costs school districts extra money. Specialized equipment, additional resources, and specially designed transportation equipment are all part of the picture. School districts are reimbursed by state departments of education for portions of the salaries of special education teachers. The courts have intervened in disputes over who pays for special education, the extent to which cost is the responsibility of local education agencies (LEA) versus state education agencies (SEA), and the extent to which parents may be reimbursed for the fees they pay to attorneys who assist them in achieving an appropriate educational program for their children.

When local school districts fail to provide services for students, courts sometimes have to decide whether the state is then responsible for providing services. Although several circuit courts have ruled that the state is responsible, the U.S. Supreme Court has not ruled on the issue. States and local education agencies also get into disputes about who is responsible for paying for the educational programs of specific children. Such cases usually arise when the student is a resident of one district but the services are provided in a neighboring district or state or when the student requires very expensive educational interventions. The courts' rulings have typically been different for each case.

In *Burlington School Committee* v. *Department of Education,* the U.S. Supreme Court ruled that reimbursement for private school tuition was an appropriate form of relief for a court to grant. In *Smith* v. *Robinson* (1984), the school district had agreed to place Thomas Smith, a youngster with cerebral palsy and physical and emotional disabilities, in a day treatment program at a hospital in Rhode Island. After a period of time, the school district informed the parents that the Rhode Island Department of Mental Health, Retardation, and Hospitals would have to take over the expense of the program. The state supreme court ruled that the duty of funding the educational program rested with the local school, not the state. The parents appealed the case to a federal district court and in addition asked for payment of attorneys' fees. The district court agreed with the parents, but the court of appeals did not. The U.S. Supreme Court ruled that parents were responsible for paying the attorneys' fees.

Schools encounter excess costs in providing services to students with disabilities. The courts regularly get involved in disputes about who pays the excess costs. In *Bevin* v. *Wright* (1987), a district court in Pennsylvania ruled on the extent to which the Pittsburgh school district was responsible for paying the costs of home nursing services that enabled a 7-year-old girl with severe physical and mental disabilities to attend school. The court ruled that the costs were clearly beyond those intended by the law and would have to be borne by the parents. The court cited the Supreme Court ruling in *Rowley,* arguing that although "all children with disabilities are entitled to some form of education tailored to their individual needs and abilities, it does not require school districts to provide the best possible education without regard to expense."

Home-School Collaboration Issues

The courts have dealt with the definition of "parents" for purposes of legislation relevant to students with disabilities. The law specifies that the term *parents* is intended to include grandparents, stepparents, surrogate parents, or guardians who have legal responsibility for children. As noted above in our discussion of *Fay* v. *South Colonie School District,* schools should communicate important information (anticipated changes in enrollment, solicitation of informed consent for testing) to both parents if the parents are separated or divorced and both have legal custody.

Unresolved Issues

The courts have not resolved all the major legal issues about delivery of special education services to students with disabilities. In the following list, we provide a sample of unresolved issues to spur your thinking and discussion (also see Rothstein, 1990; Yell, 1998).

- Where should the line be drawn in the provision of services? How many students should be served in special education?

- How can the general class be thought of as the least restrictive environment if in it teachers are supposed to deliver individualized instruction for students with disabilities?

- If a 17-year-old student who is receiving special education services wants to drop out of school, may she or he?

- To what extent are specific tests (or items on tests) biased?

- If a 19-year-old student accepts a high school diploma, is he or she still eligible to receive special education services? The law says such services are available until age 21.

- Should scarce resources be used to upgrade the teaching of "average" students or to provide special education services to students with disabilities?

- When students who require extensive services change districts, who pays for the costs of educating the students?

- What remedy do parents have when schools do not comply with procedural requirements?

- If a student with disabilities can survive in a general classroom with supports, is the student automatically entitled to the supports? Who pays for the supports?

- What is an alternate assessment, and specifically, who should take alternate assessments?
- Who is responsible for paying for the educational services received in a juvenile detention center by students with disabilities?
- What happens if a student needs a particular service and the district does not have the money to pay for it?
- What relief (in terms of respite care) is available to parents of students with disabilities? Who pays for it?
- What happens if placement in a separate facility is clearly the least restrictive placement for a student, but there is no certified special education teacher in the facility?
- Should schools be required to keep both parents informed of a child's progress if the parents are divorced? Under what conditions can one parent prohibit the other from access to a student's records or notification regarding school events?
- Is a student who needs only related services but not special education considered disabled?
- Does least restrictive placement require placement with age-appropriate peers?
- Is it permissible to have separate scout troops for students with disabilities?

Discussion Questions

1. Why do you suppose it has taken so much legal activity to get school districts to allow students with disabilities to attend school and to provide appropriate services for these students?
2. How does IDEA 1997 address the issue of disciplining students with disabilities?
3. Discuss any of the unresolved issues cited at the end of this chapter.

Chapter 13
Economic Issues in Special Education

THE ROLE OF GOVERNMENT IN EDUCATION

FINANCIAL ISSUES
The Cost of Special Education
Payment for Special Education Services
Funding Formulas
Funding Incentives and Disincentives
Are We Spending Too Much on Special Education?
The Influence of Funding Patterns on Research
Cost of Transportation
Cost of Teacher Salaries

EFFICIENCY ISSUES
What Should Be Considered as "Benefits"?
Equity Versus Efficiency
No Matter the Cost?
The Cost Versus the Benefit of Prevention

DISCUSSION QUESTIONS

As a nation, we now invest more in education than in defense. But the results have not improved, and we're not coming close to our potential or what is needed.

—George Bush, in *American 2000*

Special education is supported by federal, state, and local school district tax dollars. Historically, federal funds have been allocated to states based on the numbers of students with disabilities who are receiving special education and related services. States with large numbers or percentages of students declared entitled to services received proportionately more money. The 1997 Amendments to IDEA (PL 105-17) made major changes in the ways in which federal dollars are given to states.

Each of the states has different policies and procedures for allocating special education aid (federal and state monies) to local school districts. Local school districts differ considerably in the amount of local tax dollars they spend on special education. Because special education has evolved in response to how money is allocated to education, it can be argued that funding navigates the direction of special education.

When educators and other school personnel are asked to describe the economic issues in special education, they point to measures of productivity, how districts fund special education, who pays for what, and when costs become more important considerations than benefits. They want to know if and how the costs of education will rise in the first decade of the twenty-first century, whether the cost of educating a student in a self-contained classroom is greater, and if students with disabilities who graduate from high school can expect to enjoy greater earnings than those who drop out of school before graduation.

Yet not all these are economic, or strictly economic, issues. Indeed, discussion of economic or cost issues can never be considered independently from matters of social value, appropriateness, and effectiveness. And there are trade-offs among these considerations. Suppose administrators in the Jefferson county schools decide that they must reduce their expenditures for provision of special education services and that the way to accomplish this is to reduce the number of salaried special education teachers by combining small classes of students in various parts of the district. Costs for salaried personnel will decrease, while transportation costs will increase.

In other circumstances, however, "cost issues are often secondary in relationship to policy directives or important social values" (Lewis, Bruininks, & Thurlow, 1989, p. 483). Society may decide, through court action or legislation, that certain students are entitled to a free appropriate education and that the cost of providing this service may be secondary. Or a court may rule that a school district is negligent in the inappropriate assessment of and placement of minority students in special education classes and that the school district must reeducate its psychological services personnel regardless of the cost of doing so.

In this chapter we discuss two kinds of economic issues—issues of finance, such as the costs of delivering services and allocating resources to students with special needs, and issues of efficiency, such as the relationship between costs and outputs, cost-effectiveness, and productivity. This classification of the issues is not as distinct as it first seems because the economic issues presented here have social and political dimensions or ramifications. We begin by examining the role of government in the provision of education so we can differentiate the regulatory, financial, and administrative role of government in education.

THE ROLE OF GOVERNMENT IN EDUCATION

In Chapter 2 we observed that governments establish schools to prepare the young to assume society's responsibilities. (Yet parents operating independently of government intervention can and do establish schools.) Governments intervene in education, and specifically in special education, for several reasons:

1. Governments intervene to protect minors because, as common thinking goes, they are unable to stand up for their own rights, and parents and society will not necessarily do so.

2. Government agencies intervene because the benefits of education to society (rather than to the individual) are large and therefore must be protected. Such benefits include the establishment of a strong national defense, the provision of an educated citizenry, the inculcation of common values, the belief in and practice of democracy, social cost reductions (in the form of decreased crime, increased health, and decreased unemployment), and equality of opportunity.

3. Government agencies intervene to ensure freedom and prevent the creation of monopolies: because provision of education is a state, rather than a federal, responsibility, this prevents monopolistic control of education.

4. Governments intervene to facilitate the efficiency of operation that is thought to result from central control of resources.

5. Governments intervene to ensure equity of access for all children and youths, regardless of disability, race, or gender.

Government intervention is of three types: regulation, finance, and administration. Government regulation takes the form of requirements, such as those specifying that all students must attend school and that schools must provide services to all students. Government finance of education varies according to how high in the system the student is. Because at higher levels the student derives more individual benefits from education, he or she is expected to pay more of the costs. At lower levels, education is subsidized by state and local agencies. Government administration occurs through state and federal agencies, which regularly send teams of personnel to monitor compliance with corresponding rules and regulations.

FINANCIAL ISSUES

As a social service, education in general and special education in particular must complete for dollars with highways, sanitation, and other services. To the extent that members of society value special education more than other services, special education is financed more heavily. Government spending patterns influence public policy on the education of students with disabilities (though the converse is also true). Policy makers also decide which education programs to emphasize: preschool programs, basic primary education for young children, programs to keep adolescents from dropping out of school, or vocational programs for illiterate adults.

The Cost of Special Education

Estimating the cost of providing special education services is difficult. The best we can do is cite national averages. In nearly all instances, the largest cost component for educating students with disabilities is personnel costs. About 80 percent of the funds for special education are used to pay teachers and other direct-services personnel. Remaining costs comprise transportation, food, health, and rehabilitation services.

The cost of providing services varies as a function of the nature and severity of the disability condition. Students with limited vision may need to work with computers that have special software to translate text to large print and to display the letters in white with a black background. They may also need special ergonomic furniture that reduces fatigue from sitting for long hours at a computer screen. Shell reported that

> it is not uncommon for one child to require a traveling chair, a stand-in table, a tilt table, and a wheelchair desk built or modified to the chair's specifications. The cost of this equipment can easily exceed $7,000 per child. Many kinds of equipment must be replaced as the child's functional ability changes or as the child's size increases. Special equipment to use in teaching self-feeding skills or for communication with children having limited oral language can also push the equipment cost per child into the thousands. (1981, p. 8)

A tenuous balance exists between society's willingness to provide special education and related services to students with disabilities and society's ability to pay for these services. In times of financial prosperity, attempts to limit services or the number of students declared eligible for services are few. When school districts have plenty of money to spend on educating students with disabilities, diagnostic personnel are encouraged to locate and identify as many students with disabilities as possible. When funds are limited, however, concerns grow about the large number of students being declared entitled to special education services.

Payment for Special Education Services

Who pays for special education services, and how much do they pay? In a few instances, parents, private industry, or private organizations pay for the provision of special education services. This is especially true when services are provided in private schools or in private residential facilities. More generally, however, the public—through federal, state, or local tax dollars—pays the cost of educating exceptional students. Yet according to personnel at the Center for Special Education Finance in Palo Alto, California, nobody really knows how much is spent on special education each year. According to Chambers, Parrish, Lieberman, and Wolman (1998), "There are no comprehensive and accurate data sources that indicate what public schools in the U.S. are spending on special education services" (p. 2), and "There are no current, uniform data sources that track expenditures for special education services at the federal or state level" (p. 4).

The U.S. Department of Education's Office of Special Education Programs stopped requiring states to collect cost data after the 1987–1988 school year because of concerns about accuracy. When the Center for Special Education Finance surveyed states in the 1994–1995 school year, only twenty-four were able to report their statewide special education costs. And only thirteen of those states said they were "highly confident" of their data. The average per-pupil expenditure for special education varied widely among the twenty-four states, with figures ranging from $2758 in Indiana to $8501 in Connecticut. Half of the states reported that the state government paid for at least 50 percent of the special education costs for each student with a disability. Prior to enactment of the Education for All Handicapped Children's Act in 1975, it is estimated that about 8 percent of funding for the education of students with disabilities came from federal sources. In Table 13.1 we show variability among states in expenditures for special education; per-pupil expenditures; percentages of support from federal, state, and local sources; and the extent to which state personnel were confident in the data they reported.

When special education costs were last formally estimated (1987–1988), it was estimated that $19.3 million was spent. The Center for Special Education Finance estimated that costs now range from about $30 billion to $34.8 billion. U.S. Department of Education Statistics indicate that about $4.5 billion was appropriated by the federal government for special education grants to states in 1998 and that President Clinton has proposed about $4.5 billion for 1999. So about 7 to 8 percent of the cost of special education is paid by the federal government.

The question of who is responsible for funding programs and services for students with disabilities is actively debated among and within the different levels of government. Debate is especially intense when federal laws mandate services that state or local education agencies are expected to pay for. Ultimately, the schools are responsible for providing all services that students need, including related services. They must work with local agencies to determine who pays for which service. What happens if schools are unable to raise needed funds? They have to pay for related services themselves. This process has serious implications. When funds are limited, administrative personnel may discourage teachers and other from recommending needed related services.

Even when funds are not limited, special education competes with general education for financial resources. From all the funds provided for education, moneys must be allocated among general education, special education, and other entitlement programs (e.g., school improvement programs, Goals 2000 funding, Title I, bilingual education). When a state increases the percentage of moneys allocated to special education, moneys allocated to other kinds of education and services typically go down.

Funding Formulas

States typically allocate special education moneys to local districts using a specific formula. Parrish (1996, p. 5) described four kinds of funding and defined each as follows:

1. *Pupil weights:* "Two or more categories of student-based funding for special programs, expressed as a multiple of regular education aid." For example, Georgia provides 2.27 times the general education funding for students with learning disabilities or speech disorders; and 5.54 times the general education funding for students who are deaf-blind, profoundly mentally retarded, visually impaired and blind, hearing impaired and deaf, and orthopedically handicapped.

TABLE 13.1 Special Education Expenditures as Reported by States: 1993–1994*

State (n = 24)	Total Expenditure*	Associated Student Special Education Count**	Average Special Education Expenditure per Student	Percentage of Support by Source			Confidence in Data
				Federal	State	Local	
California	$3,070,700,000 [A]	550,293 [A]	$5,580	5%	71%	24%	SC
Colorado	$260,337,092 [A]	76,374 [B]	$3,409	9%	31%	60%	HC
Connecticut	$627,331,211	73,792	$8,501	4%	37%	59%	HC
Florida	$1,470,186,087 [B]	290,630 [A]	$5,059	6%	56%	38%	C
Indiana	$350,430,294 [B]	127,079	$2,758	17%	63%	20%	NC
Iowa	$277,700,000 [B]	65,039 [B]	$4,270	11%	70%	19%	HC
Kansas	$326,106,608 [B]	47,489	$6,867	7%	54%	39%	HC
Louisiana	$427,924, 416	108,317 [B]	$3,951	6%	94%	0%	C
Maine	$145,000,000 [B]	30,565	$4,744	8%	59%	33%	HC
Maryland	$757,328,777	95,752	$7,909	5%	26%	69%	HC
Massachusetts	$1,065,523,416	149,431	$7,131	6%	30%	64%	HC
Michigan	$1,334,000,000 [B]	188,703 [C]	$7,069	6%	34%	60%	HC
Minnesota	$689,656,932 [A]	96,542 [A]	$7,114	6%	70%	24%	NC
Missouri	$436,778,659	121,419 [D]	$3,597	10%	30%	60%	C
Montana	$54,865,132	17,881	$3,068	14%	60%	26%	HC
Nevada	$202,369,114	24,624	$8,218	4%	40%	56%	C
New Mexico	$250,000,000 [B]	45,364	$5,511	9%	90%	1%	SC
North Carolina	$344,809,332 [C]	142,394	$2,422	15%	76%	9%	HC
North Dakota	$54,560,122	12,180	$4,479	10%	31%	59%	SC
Rhode Island	$147,300,000	25,143	$5,858	5%	36%	59%	HC
South Dakota	$61,618,034	15,208	$4,052	13%	49%	38%	HC
Vermont	$79,155,945	10,131 [E]	$7,813	5%	39%	56%	HC
Virginia	$608,692,266	129,498 [A]	$4,700	9%	23%	68%	C
Wisconsin	$630,000,000 [A]	95,552	$6,593	6%	62%	32%	C
All reporting states	$13,929,607,674	2,581,905	$5,395	7%	53%	40%	
Highly confident or confident states	$9,514,260,326	1,750,477	$5,435	7%	44%	49%	

*States reported for the 1993–94 school year except as designated below:
[A] 1992–93
[B] 1994–95
[C] 1990–91

**Count of students reported by the state associated with the reported total expenditure. Includes age range 3–21 except as designated below:
[A] Includes age range 0–22
[B] Includes age range 0–21
[C] Includes age range 0–26
[D] Includes age range 3–22
[E] Includes age range 5–22

Confidence in Data:
HC: Highly confident
C: Confident
SC: Somewhat confident
NC: Not confident

SOURCE: Chambers, J. G., Parrish, T., Lieberman, J. C., and Wolman, J. M. (1998). What Are We Spending on Special Education in the U.S.? CSEF Brief No. 8. Palo Alto, CA: Center for Special Education Finance.

2. *Resource-based:* Funding based on "allocation of specific special education resources (e.g., teachers or classroom units); classroom units are derived from prescribed staff/student ratios, by disabling condition, or by type of placement."

3. *Percent reimbursement:* "Funding is based on a percentage of allowable or actual expenditures." In some states, districts are given reimbursement of a percentage of what the state permits them to spend per student or a percent of what they can show it actually costs.

4. *Flat grant:* A fixed funding amount per student or per unit.

Parrish provided a table showing the kind of funding formula used in each state. The table is reproduced as Table 13.2.

With the new Individuals with Disabilities Act, there is a push toward census-based funding. Until moneys that go to states exceed $4.9 billion, state grants will be calculated on the basis of child count. When this $4.9 billion is exceeded, a new permanent formula will be used as follows:

> 85% of the funds above the base amount will be distributed based on states' relative share of the entire school-age population, and 15% of the funds above the base year amount will be distributed based on states' relative share of the entire school-age population in poverty. (Verstegen, Parrish, & Wolman, 1998, p. 1)

A growing number of states now use census-based funding (Massachusetts, Montana, North Dakota, South Dakota, Pennsylvania, and Vermont). At the time we prepared this chapter California and Illinois were considering census-based funding. Because funding for special education will not reach $4.9 billion for several years, states will not be compelled to move in that direction for some time. The provisions are now law, so we expect that any changes states make in their funding formulas will be toward census-based funding. The federal dollars that support the implementation of public laws on the education of students with disabilities are distributed to the states as formula grants based on the number of students being served. In the Individuals with Disabilities Education Act Amendments of 1997, the funding formula was revised. The funding formula remains based on the number of students served until federal appropriations reach $4.9 billion. Federal appropriations above that level will be allocated according to a population-based formula, with an adjustment for poverty rates.

Funding Incentives and Disincentives

Several issues arise when states use categorical funding formulas. There is a natural tension between separate, highly categorical funding and overall educational reform objectives that favor more unified schooling systems (McLaughlin & Warren, 1992). And when moneys are differentially allocated to categories of students, there are incentives to classify students into the categories that are reimbursed at higher rates. Biklen put it this way:

TABLE 13.2 State Special Education Funding Systems and Reform, 1994–1995

State	Current Funding Formula	Basis of Allocation	State Special Ed $ for Target Population Only	Implemented Reform Within Last 5 Years	Considering Major Reform
Alabama	Flat grant	Special ed. enrollment	✓	✓	✓
Alaska	Pupil weights	Type of placement			✓
Arizona[1]	Pupil weights	Disabling condition			✓
Arkansas	Pupil weights	Type of placement	✓		✓
California	Resource-based	Classroom unit	✓		✓
Colorado	Flat grant	Special ed. enrollment	✓	✓	
Connecticut	% reimbursement	Actual expenditures			✓
Delaware	Resource-based	Classroom unit	✓		✓
Florida	Pupil weights	Disabling condition			✓
Georgia	Pupil weights	Disabling condition	For 90% of funds		✓
Hawaii	Pupil weights	Placement & condition			
Idaho	% reimbursement	Actual expenditures	✓	✓	
Illinois	Resource-based	Allowable costs		✓	✓
Indiana	Pupil weights	Disabling condition			✓
Iowa	Pupil weights	Type of placement			✓
Kansas	Resource-based	No. of special ed. staff	✓		
Kentucky	Pupil weights	Disabling condition		✓	
Louisiana	% reimbursement	Actual expenditures	✓	✓	✓
Maine	% reimbursement	Allowable costs	✓		✓
Maryland	Flat grant	Special ed. enrollment			✓
Massachusetts	Flat grant	Total district enrollment		✓	
Michigan	% reimbursement	Allowable costs	✓		✓
Minnesota	% reimbursement	Actual expenditures	✓		✓
Mississippi	Resource-based	No. of special ed. staff	✓		
Missouri	Resource-based	No. of special ed. staff	✓	✓	✓
Montana	Flat grant	Total district enrollment		✓	
Nebraska	% reimbursement	Allowable costs	✓		✓
Nevada	Resource-based	Classroom unit	✓		
New Hampshire	Pupil weights	Type of placement			✓
New Jersey	Pupil weights	Placement and condition			
New Mexico	Pupil weights	Services received			✓

It is not hard to imagine the programmatic imperatives that can derive from such funding mechanisms. If state reimbursement rates provide more funding for learning disabilities than for "slow learners" or underachievers, for example, the ranks of students labeled "learning disabled" can be expected to expand. Similarly, if a state provides near total funding for certain types of services (e.g., for private or state residential schools), and a far less substantial allotment for serving students in their home districts, local school boards might be tempted to "place" more students outside the district. These effects of fiscal incentives have been well documented. (1989, p. 9)

In those states in which teacher unit funding* is used, there is a disincentive for identification of students as disabled because schools that identify large numbers of students end up with larger classes, not necessarily with more money for their programs. The only time schools receive more money is when they employ more personnel. This becomes a critical issue when teachers' unions battle with local school districts over class sizes and cost issues. School districts then look to state departments of education to change allocation rules and funding formulas.

Parrish (1996) found that those states with resource-based funding systems tended to provide more money to more restrictive settings. The more students in restrictive settings, the more money the district received.

A third issue that arises is whether special education funding should be adjusted on the basis of student poverty. One side argues that states should get money based on numbers of students, while the other side argues that high-poverty states should receive a larger proportion of funding. McLaughlin and Owings (1993) found no significant relationship between poverty and overall rates of identification of students with disabilities. But for students with learning disabilities—the category of students that might be expected to be most affected by at-risk conditions related to sustained and intensified poverty—they found a significant negative relationship. Parrish (1996) reported finding a significant positive relationship between the percentage of students in poverty and the percentage of students in special education.

Are We Spending Too Much on Special Education?

In 1996 the Phi Delta Kappa/Gallup Poll of the Public's Attitudes Toward the Public Schools reported that 47 percent of adults thought that America is spending too little on provision of services to students with special needs, 41 percent thought that about the right amount is being spent, while only 5 percent said too much is being spent (Elam, Rose, & Gallup, 1966). Parrish (1996) estimated that about $32 billion a year is spent on provision of special education services, and that we spend about 2.3 times as much educating students with disabilities as we spend on educating general education students. It is clear that people believe that there are not enough resources to provide educational services to all students, and some people believe that provision of special education services drains resources from the general education budget. And clearly there is significant growth in the numbers of students identified as disabled and in need of special education services. Wolman and Parrish (1996) respond to the question of escalating special education costs this way:

> Enrollments clearly continue to grow and, as expected, contribute to rising costs. However, special education cost information is neither sufficiently current nor adequate to clarify the magnitude, causes, and implications of this growth.
>
> Are expenditures rising faster than should be expected or accepted, and is special education encroaching on general education resources? If yes, to what

*Teacher unit funding is a type of resource-based funding (see p. 339–340). Monies are allocated based on the number of teachers of students with disabilities.

extent is this due to the shifting of costs previously borne by other public agencies and also to the overall constraints placed on education budgets, especially in relation to other labor-intensive public sector activities such as health care and public safety? (p. 7)

The Influence of Funding Patterns on Research

The research priorities established by the U.S. Department of Education usually determine the direction of research activities in special education. During the 1950s and 1960s, the federal government made mental retardation a research priority, and centers for research on mental retardation were established across the country. As funding priorities changed, new centers were established and old ones changed their names and expanded their missions. During the mid- and late 1970s, institutes were funded to conduct research on learning disabilities and on early intervention. In the 1980s, there was less federal support for research on learning disabilities; instead, support shifted to research on students with severe disabilities and transition services for older students with disabilities. In the early 1990s, emphasis was on early childhood education, while in the late 1990s there was a balanced program of research, with comparable funding of research on assessment and accountability, development of effective interventions, policy research, and research across the age span (early childhood, elementary, secondary, and transition). Decisions to shift research efforts are often motivated by economics: researchers go "where the money is."

Cost of Transportation

School districts incur extra costs in the provision of transportation to students who are disabled. Such students often must be transported long distances to receive appropriate educational services, and they must often be transported using special equipment (buses designed for wheelchairs, equipped with oxygen, etc.). Lewis et al. noted that

> transportation costs within special education have always been recognized as a necessary component for the delivery of such educational services; however, the magnitude of such costs has not always been appreciated. For example, it is important to note that in almost every case of special education service by an external agency in this study there were significant concurrent transportation costs to the district beyond just tuition charges. Although daily transportation costs for special education students being served by external agencies averaged only $6, as compared to average daily tuition rates of $12, in almost half of the individual student cases daily transportation costs exceeded or almost equaled the average daily tuition rate being charged by the external agency to which the student was being transported. In this study, transportation costs represented almost one-half of all costs to the district in sending students out to external agencies. (1989, p. 481)

Cost of Teacher Salaries

Teacher salaries become an issue because it is thought by general education teachers (and sometimes the general public) that the provision of special education means hiring additional personnel who have specialized training and who are paid at rates higher than those of general education teachers. This is not always the case, however. Lewis et al. reported that

> contrary to conventional wisdom, the average salaries of teachers in special education within the district under study were less than those of regular teachers by over 11 percent—i.e., $25,335 versus $28,500. It is typically assumed that because teachers in special education necessarily must have additional training and licensure in their respective service areas (generally after initial certification as regular teachers), and with salary schedules closely aligned with such training and experience, the average salaries in special education will necessarily exceed those of regular teachers. Consequently, it often is assumed that the average cost of instructional staff in special education will inherently always be more expensive than regular instruction. This case study indicates that these assumptions and results are not necessarily always true. The teaching staff of regular classes in this school district apparently also had considerable advanced training and experience and/or the special education personnel in this district were, on average, younger than the staff of regular instruction. (1989, p. 481)

When there are disparities in salary between general and special education teachers, several issues arise. For example, a disparity in salaries will have an effect on self-esteem: teachers who are paid less may view themselves as worth less. Disparities may also affect expectations: an administrator may expect more of teachers who are paid more, less of those who are paid less. Differences in self-esteem and expectation may in turn translate into differences in teacher performance, with those who are paid less performing in accord with their perceptions of the "low regard" with which they are held. Finally, salary disparities may have an impact on peer relations: teachers' relations with one another may be negatively affected when there are salary disparities.

EFFICIENCY ISSUES

For the most part, the efficiency and productivity of special education have received only minimal attention in both the research and policy literature because special educators have been concerned with matters of finance, specifically with the cost of providing special education services. The examination of the relationships between costs and outcomes is quite new to special education.

What Should Be Considered as "Benefits"?

If educators are to look at the extent to which students with disabilities profit from special education, what factors should be considered as benefits? There are no "typically used" indicators of benefits: sometimes educators talk about academic outcomes as benefits (improved academic skills, usually as evidenced through an achievement test), yet such an indicator is hardly useful when it comes to students with disabilities. In this case, educators consider the extent to which provision of services to such students results in increased output (earnings, contributions to the tax base), reduced use of alternative programs (institutional environments), reduced program costs, and improved quality of life. Indicators of benefits from schooling are measured in terms of employment status (competitive paid employment, sheltered paid employment, no employment), earned income, participation in the work force (hours worked per week), financial independence (receipt of Social Security benefits, receipt of Medicaid, possession of an independent checking account), community adjustment, and degree of independence in living arrangements (group home, foster care, independent living). Those who study the benefits of education for students with disabilities, especially those who want to know whether education is efficient, must make tough choices in selecting outcomes indicators. At issue is whether to select academic indicators, personal/social/affective indicators, or quality of life indicators. Also at issue is whether indicators should differ as a function of the severity of an individual's disability.

Equity Versus Efficiency

The most efficient provision of services to students is not always the most equitable. Take, for instance, the provision of vouchers to parents so that they can send their children to any school they choose. This practice is widely advocated as well as widely abhorred, and there are financial and efficiency arguments for and against such open enrollment.

Advocates of open enrollment argue that provision of vouchers and choice will result in a market-driven school system in which schools become competitive (to attract or retain students) and improve their quality. They argue that structural change in schools will come only through the withholding of resources. They point out that schools that lose students will either cut back, close, or get better and that this will result in improved efficiency.

Those who argue against choice say that the practice of providing parents with vouchers will result in the use of those vouchers primarily by parents of upper- and upper-middle-class students, parents who can afford to pick up some of the costs of transporting students and who are aware enough of their options to take advantage of them. Opponents argue that provision of vouchers will result in increased social stratification.

No Matter the Cost?

When individuals or groups believe they have been abused or shortchanged by the educational system, they sometimes take it on themselves to redress wrongs through litigation. Parents of children who were mentally retarded sued the Pennsylvania Department of Education for alleged exclusion of their children from the educational system. Parents of students with learning disabilities in Philadelphia sued the school district for failure to provide their children with an "appropriate" education. The courts sometimes mandate that educators take action, no matter the costs, to redress wrongs.

When instances of alleged abuse become very frequent, or when there are repeated court cases on the same or similar issues, legislatures take remedial action. In the late 1960s and early 1970s, there were many instances in which professional associations advocacy groups, or individuals sued school districts for failure to provide access to educational services for students with disabilities, for exclusion of services (or changes in placement without due process), for alleged bias in assessment, and for inappropriate placement. In 1975, President Gerald Ford signed the Education for All Handicapped Children Act into law. That law included provisions that mandated access, fair assessment, due process, and placement in least restrictive environments. Cost was not an issue. The social value of the ideals outweighed funding considerations.

The Cost Versus the Benefit of Prevention

Many educational programs have been developed for the purpose of preventing later school difficulties and then providing costly educational interventions (see box p. 346). One example of such a program is Project Head Start. Instituted as part of President Lyndon Johnson's War on Poverty, Head Start has been funded for more than twenty years. The program was started in an effort to close the experiential gap between children who were disadvantaged by virtue of their family's social and economic status and those who were not. The children were given preschool experiences that would enable them to be on an even footing with nondisadvantaged children when they entered school. The program is a compensatory education program, not a special education program. There are, of course, some students with disabilities who participate in the program.

Has the program worked? Has participation in preschool intervention put the children on an even footing; has it reduced or eliminated later academic difficulty; has it saved society money in the long run? Lee, Brooks-Gunn, and Schnur recently addressed these questions by comparing disadvantaged children who attended Head Start, other preschool programs, and no preschool. They reported that

> Large initial group differences were observed between Head Start children and both comparison groups, with those in Head Start at a disadvantage on nearly every demographic and cognitive measure. Adjusting for initial background and cognitive differences, Head Start children showed significantly larger gains on the Preschool Inventory and Motor Inhibition tests than either comparison group, with Black children in Head Start (especially those of below-average initial ability) gaining the most. However, despite substantial gains, Head Start children were still behind their peers in terms of absolute cognitive levels after a year in the program.

It Is Cheaper, Easier, and More Effective To:

1. Keep people from falling into poverty in the first place rather than to get them out later.

2. Keep all kinds of families intact rather than arrange adoption and foster care facilities later.

3. Keep students performing at grade level by "front loading" resources toward those most at risk, rather than telling them at the *end* of third grade that they failed when no effort was made to provide the resources that could have meant success.

4. Keep people out of prisons rather than trying to rehabilitate them later.

5. Keep low-income people in an expanding supply of affordable housing rather than increasing the number of homeless families, often with children and one or more full-time workers.

6. Keep mass transit so that low-income workers can continue to have jobs, housing, and some freedom.

7. Keep kids from getting sick (or hungry) rather than providing massive programs for curing (or feeding) them after the damage has been done.

Although these points are obvious, it is estimated by the author that we spend in general 15 percent of our money on prevention programs and *85 percent* on rather ineffective "cures" in all social service areas.

SOURCE: Hodgkinson, H. L. (1989). *The Same Client: The Demographics of Education and Service Delivery Systems* (p. 27). Washington, D.C.: Institute for Educational Leadership, Center for Demographic Policy. Used with permission.

> Head Start proved an impressive instrument of short-term change, even compared with other preschool experience. Gains in behaviors other than intelligence suggest that the effects may not be limited to the cognitive domain. (1988, p. 210)

The Committee for Economic Development has called for full funding of Head Start three times in the past three years, and it has maintained that

> education is an investment, not an expense. If we can ensure that all children are born healthy and develop the skills and knowledge they need to be productive, self-supporting adults, whatever is spent on their development and education will be returned many times over in higher productivity, incomes, and taxes and in lower costs for welfare, health care, crime, and myriad other economic and social problems. (1991, p. 15)

Full funding of Head Start and other preventive programs designed to ensure adequate development and early education of poor children would cost about $9

The High Cost of Failure

Businesspeople know that it is less expensive to prevent failure than to try to correct it later. Early intervention for poor children from conception to age 5 has been shown to be a highly cost-effective strategy for reducing later expenditures on a wide variety of health, developmental, and educational problems that often interfere with learning. Long-term studies of the benefits of preschool education have demonstrated returns on investment ranging from $3 to $6 for every $1 spent. Prenatal care has been shown to yield over $3.38 in savings on the costs of care for low-birth-weight babies. Early immunization for a variety of childhood diseases saves $10 in later medical costs. Supplementing nutrition for poor women, infants, and children yields a $3 payback in savings on later health care costs.

At the same time, the costs of not intervening early can be astronomical.

- Every "class" of dropouts earns about $237 billion less than an equivalent class of high school graduates during their lifetimes. As a result, the government receives about $70 billion less in tax revenues.

- Each year, taxpayers spend $16.6 billion to support the children of teenage parents.

- About 82 percent of all Americans in prison are high school dropouts, and it costs an average of $20,000 to maintain each prisoner annually. In comparison, a year of high-quality preschool costs about $4,800 and has been shown to decrease the rate of arrest in the teenage years by 40 percent.

SOURCE: Research and Policy Committee of the Committee for Economic Development. (1991). *The Unfinished Agenda: A New Vision for Child Development and Education.* New York: Committee on Economic Development. Used with permission.

billion more than is currently spent. At issue is whether funds should be spent on such preventive and developmental programs or on other national priorities, such as defense, transportation, and housing.

Discussion Questions

1. Identify some of the ways in which the federal government and the state in which you live regulate, finance, and administer special education services.

2. Identify at least three financial incentives for identifying students in your state as disabled and in need of special education services.

3. How do you believe we should calculate the costs and the benefits of special education? How might the two be compared?

Chapter 14
Results of Schooling

Learning is like rowing upstream; not to advance is to drop back.

—Chinese proverb

Along with the increased emphasis in the early 1990s on school reform (see Chapter 9) came questions about the results of education. As the nation set goals for education, it also began to think more specifically than before about the expected results of education. Chester Finn, former secretary of education, described the shift as one away from the *process* of education (who teaches, how many students per teacher, etc.) and toward the *results* of education (Finn, 1990a). As might be expected, the stress on educational results first emerged in general education with little or no regard for special education. In fact, the emphasis on academic excellence was frequently translated into results that placed students in special education even more at risk in the educational system.

Interest in school results came first from general education's struggle with repeated evidence that education was not effective for large numbers of students. The American business community likewise began to emphasize the results of schooling and their importance for the nation's future in a complex and competitive world: "In an earlier industrial era, the economy did not need to ensure that every child was well educated, partly because the available labor pool was large enough and partly because unskilled manual labor and low-skilled manufacturing jobs were sufficiently plentiful and well-paid to absorb those without higher level skills. This is no longer the case" (Committee for Economic Development, 1991, p. 2). Interest in results was given even more impetus when the emphasis on national education goals was at its peak, particularly when the focus was on Goal 3 (see Chapter 10) and its implication that there needed to be higher, more challenging standards of what students should know and be able to do. Even when the attention given to the national education goals waned, the belief in the need for challenging academic standards remained, embraced by liberals and conservatives alike.

In this chapter, we examine what kinds of results have been deemed desirable, giving due emphasis to standards. We then identify the many issues that arise from the emphasis on identifying and collecting data on results. These issues range from the identification of critical domains and the development of appropriate indicators to how information is used. We also examine several of the effects of educational policies based on results (e.g., graduation requirements, minimal competency tests, retention/social promotion, grades, and grading), and the additional issues they raise. Finally, we provide data on the results of schooling for students with disabilities, using data available in state accountability reports.

IDENTIFYING DESIRED EDUCATIONAL RESULTS

In 1993, an article in *Education Week* reported that national efforts to identify standards in various academic and nonacademic content areas had a combined budget of nearly $10 million (Viadero, 1993). No accounting was even attempted for the many state efforts under way to define standards. Standards are statements of criteria against which comparisons can be made (Ysseldyke, Thurlow, & Shriner, 1992). According to Shriner, Ysseldyke, and Thurlow (1994), they are "statements about what is important, and they are sometimes established for the purpose of changing an existing situation" (p. 1). Those advocating for standards-based change argue that standards can drive change because they remove ambiguity about expectations, compare students to goals rather than to each other, and allow assessments to be equitable ("When Standards Drive Change," 1998).

Content standards define what students are to know and what they are to be able to do. Performance standards define how well students must perform on the content standards. Content and performance standards were the standards of interest during the 1990s. Opportunity to learn standards (also called service delivery standards), which were initially introduced along with content and performance standards to indicate the "quality of a school's (or district's) capacity and performance in educating its students" (National Council for Education Standards and Testing, 1992, p. E-5), soon disappeared from the conversation. States enthusiastically jumped into standards-setting activities. By 1997, all but one state had in place or were developing content standards (American Federation of Teachers, 1997a).

National and State Standards

By the mid-1990s, at least eleven national-level groups were working on developing standards in various content areas. The first group, the National Council of Teachers of Mathematics (1989) produced a set of highly respected, innovative standards that served as a model for other standards-setting groups. Mathematics standards were followed by science standards (National Research Council), which also were fairly well received. Other content areas in which standards were being set included arts (Consortium of National Arts Education Associations, 1994), civics (Center for Civic Education, 1994), economics (National Council on Economic Education, 1997), English (International Reading Association & National Council of Teachers of English, 1996), foreign languages (National Standards in Foreign Language Education Project, 1996), geography (Geography Education Standards Project, 1993), history (National Center for History in the Schools, 1996), physical education (National Association for Sports and Physical Education, 1995), social studies (National Council for the Social Studies, 1994), and others.

The national standards-setting efforts almost ended because of issues that arose related to the standards developed by two of the groups. First, the English standards were delayed in production, and the federal funding was pulled (Diegmueller, 1994). Finally, when the English standards were presented in draft form after alternative funding was secured, they were attacked as too general and of little use for guiding practice (Burke, 1996). Second, the history standards were strongly attacked as portraying a biased view of history—too much emphasis on victimization of women, minorities, and third-world countries (Diegmueller, 1995).

By the time that revisions were being considered (Diegmueller & Viadero, 1995), the idea of a national set of standards had fallen into disfavor. States rights reigned again, and the need for states to develop their own standards was emphasized. When the importance of state standards was recognized, most states were already well on their way toward developing their own standards. The content areas in which states have developed standards are shown in Table 14.1. States differ in the specific content areas addressed by standards, and they differ in the nature of the standards that are developed. In fact, in some states different groups developed the standards in different content areas, resulting in inconsistencies in the nature of standards within a single state.

Grading the Standards

Standards developed by states received much attention by people interested in educational reform. Among the groups monitoring states' standards was the

TABLE 14.1 Content Areas in Which States Have Developed Content Standards

State	Eng	Math	Sci	SS	Art	PE	Hlth	Mus	ForL	Oth
Alabama	✓	✓	✓	✓	✓	✓	✓	✓	✓	✓
Alaska										✓
Arizona	✓	✓	✓		✓	✓	✓		✓	✓
Arkansas	✓	✓	✓	✓					✓	
California										
Colorado	✓	✓	✓	✓						✓
Connecticut										✓
Delaware	✓	✓	✓	✓						
Florida	✓	✓	✓	✓	✓	✓	✓			✓
Georgia										✓
Hawaii										✓
Idaho	✓	✓	✓	✓	✓	✓	✓			✓
Illinois	✓	✓	✓	✓	✓	✓	✓		✓	
Indiana	✓	✓	✓	✓						
Iowa										
Kansas	✓	✓	✓	✓	✓					✓
Kentucky										✓
Louisiana	✓	✓	✓	✓	✓				✓	✓
Maine										✓
Maryland										✓
Massachusetts	✓	✓	✓				✓			✓
Michigan										✓
Minnesota										✓
Mississippi	✓	✓	✓	✓	✓					✓
Missouri										
Montana										✓
Nebraska										✓
Nevada										✓
New Hampshire										✓
New Jersey										✓
New Mexico										✓
New York	✓	✓		✓	✓	✓	✓		✓	✓
North Carolina										✓
North Dakota	✓									✓
Ohio	✓	✓		✓	✓				✓	
Oklahoma										✓
Oregon										✓
Pennsylvania										✓
Rhode Island	✓	✓	✓				✓			
South Carolina	✓	✓	✓		✓		✓		✓	
South Dakota	✓	✓	✓	✓			✓		✓	
Tennessee	✓	✓	✓	✓		✓	✓		✓	✓
Texas										✓
Utah	✓	✓	✓	✓	✓		✓	✓	✓	✓
Vermont										✓
Virginia	✓	✓	✓	✓						
Washington	✓	✓	✓	✓	✓	✓	✓			
West Virginia										✓
Wisconsin										✓
Wyoming										

Note: Eng = English; Sci = Science; SS = Social Studies; PE = Physical Education; Hlth = Health; Mus = Music; ForL = Foreign Language; Oth = Other.

Example of State Standards in Science

In science, students in Missouri public schools will acquire a solid foundation which includes knowledge of

1. Properties and principles of matter and energy.
2. Properties and principles of force and motion.
3. Characteristics and interactions of living organisms.
4. Changes in ecosystems and interaction of organisms with their environments.
5. Processes (such as plate movement, water cycle, air flow) and interactions of earth's biosphere, atmosphere, lithosphere, and hydrosphere.
6. Composition and structure of the universe and the motions of the objects within in it.
7. Processes of scientific inquiry (such as formulating and testing hypotheses).
8. Impact of science, technology, and human activity on resources and the environment.

SOURCE: From Missouri's "Show Me" standards.

American Federation of Teachers (1997a). Each year this group would produce a document entitled *Making Standards Matter* in which it would evaluate states' standards in the core academic areas of English/language arts, mathematics, science, and social studies. Of course, their ratings reflected certain beliefs about what standards should be like, including that they should (1) include the four core academic subjects (English, math, science, and social studies), (2) be clear and specific enough to provide the basis for a common core curriculum, (3) have assessments aligned with them, and (4) be benchmarked against the academic expectations of other high-achieving countries.

Other groups with slightly different views of what standards should be like soon also began to evaluate states' standards (Finn, Petrilli, & Vanourek, 1998; Joftus & Berman, 1998). Among the criteria used to grade state standards were rigor, clarity, and likelihood of their boosting student achievement. The importance of perspective in judging standards is obvious when the three sets of ratings are compared (see Table 14.2 on page 353).

While all this about standards was going on, important questions were emerging about how students with disabilities fit within the standards-based education movement. According to Raber and Roach (1998), among the issues that needed to be addressed were:

- To what extent are special educators involved in the *development* (as opposed to merely reacting to or reviewing) of state policies to promote standards-based reform? . . .

TABLE 14.2 Grades Given to States' Content Standards in English and Math

State	English			Math			State	English			Math		
	AFT	Frd	CBE	AFT	Frd	CBE		AFT	Frd	CBE	AFT	Frd	CBE
Alabama	B	D	C–	B	B	C	Montana	D	—	C–	D	F	F
Alaska	D	—	D–	C	C	D–	Nebraska	—	—	—	D	F	C–
Arizona	C	B	B+	B	B	B+	Nevada	C	—	—	C	—	—
Arkansas	D	—	C+	D	F	B–	New Hampshire	B	D	B+	B	C	A–
California	A	—	B+	B	A	—	New Jersey	D	F	B–	D	C	A
Colorado	B	F	C–	B	D	B+	New Mexico	D	—	D	C	F	B–
Connecticut	F	—	—	B	D	B+	New York	C	C	B	C	B	B+
Delaware	B	D	C+	B	C	B+	North Carolina	B	—	C	B	A	B
Florida	B	D	C	A	D	C+	North Dakota	D	—	C–	C	D	C
Georgia	B	B	—	B	B	C+	Ohio	B	F	C	A	A	B+
Hawaii	C	F	C	B	F	C	Oklahoma	B	C	C–	B	F	B
Idaho	B	F	—	B	F	—	Oregon	B	F	C	B	D	B
Illinois	C	B	A	B	D	B–	Pennsylvania	C	—	B–	B	D	B+
Indiana	D	F	D	B	C	B–	Rhode Island	D	—	C+	D	F	B
Iowa	—	—	—	—	—	—	South Carolina	D	—	C	B	D	B
Kansas	D	F	C+	D	D	B+	South Dakota	D	—	—	D	F	—
Kentucky	D	—	C–	C	D	B	Tennessee	D	F	C–	D	C	—
Louisiana	D	—	D+	D	F	C+	Texas	C	B	B–	B	B	B
Maine	D	—	B–	D	F	B–	Utah	B	C	C–	B	B	A–
Maryland	D	—	C	B	F	B+	Vermont	D	—	B+	D	C	B+
Massachusetts	B	A	B	C	F	B	Virginia	A	B	B–	A	B	B
Michigan	C	F	B+	C	F	B+	Washington	B	D	B–	C	F	B
Minnesota	D	F	C–	D	—	B–	West Virginia	B	—	B	A	B	A–
Mississippi	D	D	C–	B	B	B	Wisconsin	B	C	B+	B	C	B+
Missouri	C	F	B–	C	F	B–	Wyoming	—	—	—	—	—	—

Sources: AFT ratings are from American Federation of Teachers (1997a), *Making Standards Matter.* These ratings were translated from the pie representations used by AFT, so that no filled part = F, 1/4 filled = D, 1/2 filled = C, 3/4 filled = B, and all filled = A. Frd (Fordham) ratings are from Finn, Petrilli & Vinourek (1998), *The State of State Standards.* The A–F grades were used in the original Frd document. CBE (Council of Basic Education) ratings are from Joftus & Berman (1998), *Great Expectations? Defining and Assessing Rigor in State Standards for Mathematics and English Language Arts.*

- How appropriate are new state standards and curriculum frameworks for the diversity of students in the schools, including students with disabilities? (p. 44)

These questions were raised by Thurlow, Ysseldyke, Gutman, and Geenen (1998) in their analysis of the inclusion of students with disabilities in state standards documents. They looked at both the extent to which individuals who know students with disabilities were involved in the development process and the extent to which students with disabilities were identified as being a target group of students for the standards. They summarized their findings as follows:

> While most states indicate that their standards are for "all" students, only 13 states specifically state that "all" includes students with disabilities. Furthermore, those involved in the development of standards rarely were individuals who know students with disabilities. Only eight states indicated specifically that these individuals were included in standards development. (p. i)

Thus, a major reform effort, one that provided the context for looking at the results of education, proceeded with little consideration of students with disabilities. Yet one might ask, How would the content standards change if students with disabilities were considered? Shouldn't the desired content remain the same? Perhaps it is the performance standards that would be changed for students with disabilities. But this approach leads to questions about whether lower performance standards would simply reflect low expectations for students who, if instructed properly, might achieve higher standards.

Desired Results for Students with Disabilities

Prior to the 1990s and the emphasis on standards, there were calls to identify important outcomes of education for students with disabilities and to produce information on the progress of students with disabilities in relation to those outcomes. At that time, the lists of important outcomes for students with disabilities often were different from those for students in general education. Even though there were many areas of overlap (e.g., achievement, school participation, postsecondary experiences/status), some of those identified for students with disabilities were not identified as important for students in general education (e.g., quality of life, work readiness). Similarly, some of the outcomes identified for general education were not included in lists for students with disabilities (e.g., creative thinking/problem solving, interpersonal/organizational skills).

As the focus turned from outcomes to standards, the question remained of whether students with disabilities needed to meet different standards from those to be met by students without disabilities. If states' standards were broad enough, they could encompass all students, including students with disabilities (Thurlow, Elliott, & Ysseldyke, 1998). An example of a broad standard would be "the ability to use quantitative information in ways needed to be successful in one's next environment." Conversely, an example of a narrow standard would be "the ability to use algebraic procedures to solve complex mathematical problems."

The problem with broadening states' standards to be more appropriate for all students was that states' standards were being graded in terms of how specific they were, a higher grade reflecting greater specificity. Specific standards tend to be viewed as more rigorous than standards presented in more general terms. Whether to use more general or specific standards continues to be a source of much debate in education.

A National Research Council Panel (McDonnell, McLaughlin, & Morison, 1997) studied standards-based education and students with disabilities. The panel made two recommendations that addressed the conflict:

Recommendation 1: States and localities that decide to implement standards-based reforms should design their common content standards, performance standards, and assessments to maximize participation of students with disabilities. (p. 197)

Recommendation 2: The presumption should be that each student with a disability will participate in the state or local standards; however, participation for any given student may require alterations to the common standards and assessments. Decisions to make such alterations must have a compelling educational justification and must be made on an individual basis. (p. 198)

What are alterations to common standards? How does one determine that there is a compelling educational justification to make alterations in standards? If a standard is altered, doesn't that mean that the assessment methodology must be different?

States dealt with these issues in different ways. Even before in 1997 amendments, states were divided on whether they were identifying outcomes for all students or separate outcomes for students with disabilities. For example, the Connecticut Department of Education (1988) made the assumption that outcome measures for special education should be essentially the same as for general education. Connecticut developed a common core of learning (CCL) that identified outcomes for all children. The CCL has three overall groups of outcomes (attitudes and attributes, skills and competencies, and understanding and application of competencies) organized into four categories for special education (student participation, academic competencies, attitudes and attributes, and graduate follow-up data—independent living skills). Another approach, to identify specific outcomes for individuals with specific categories of disability, was taken by the Michigan Department of Education through the Center for Quality Special Education, which identified lists of outcomes for students with autism, educable mental impairment, emotional impairment, hearing impairment, learning disabilities, physical and other health impairments, preprimary impairment, severe multiple impairments, speech and language impairments, trainable mental impairment, and visual impairment.

Because the individualized educational program (IEP) typically has been the focus of accountability in special education, questions are often raised about why the IEP does not satisfy the need for evidence of the results of education for students with disabilities. The rationale for not using the IEP generally focuses on the individualized and nonsystematic nature of IEPs and on the difficulty of aggregating across IEPs to develop an overall picture of the results of education of students with disabilities. While the IEP continues to serve as a tool for documenting students' goals and programs, it probably cannot serve as a basis for documenting the results of education for students with disabilities.

COLLECTING DATA ON EDUCATIONAL RESULTS

Many issues arise in identifying results that are appropriate for students in special education (results that, it is hoped, mesh with general education results) and in collecting data on these results. Four of these issues merit consideration here:

What are the critical results domains? Is different information needed at different levels? How do educators accommodate the heterogeneity of the student population? How do educators measure results?

Critical Domains

Whether the domains of outcomes for students with disabilities should be different from those for students without disabilities is a fundamental question in the consideration of critical outcome domains. Although most efforts in outcomes assessment have focused on developing measures of achievement, other areas have been identified as being important (e.g., see Burstein, 1989; Creech, 1990). Among these other domains are student participation and access; student status after completion of secondary school; and student attitudes, expectations, and aspirations. Even within general education, there is concern about the lack of tools for measuring cognitive and conative aspects of learning. Snow (1989) claimed that learners should be able to develop conceptual structures, procedural skills, learning strategies, self-regulatory functions, and motivational orientations. The recognition of these aspects of learning means a new consensus must be reached concerning the domains that should be emphasized in schools and the educational indicators that will be used to monitor an evaluate the outcomes.

Information Needed at Different Levels

Information on educational results is important to the teacher in the classroom, to the school district trying to document the success of its educational programs, to the state being compared, and to the nation involved in international comparisons. The multiple levels at which outcome information can be used has created much confusion about identifying outcomes and collecting data on them. The teacher in the classroom needs information on outcomes for individual students so that programs and learning time can be adjusted for each student; at this level outcomes have to be fairly specific. At the district level, desired results can be broader, even though they must still be specific enough to identify schools where problems may exist. At the state level, outcomes can be even broader and often system-level. The same is true at the national level. The international level requires that outcomes be broad enough to span the "gulfs of nationality, language, and culture" (Barrett, 1990).

The differences among possible outcomes identified at three different levels (international, national, and state) are shown in Table 14.3. As the table illustrates, information from each level could feed into the next higher level, and not all information at one level would have to be used at the next level. Likewise, tests could vary as a function of individual needs, not just grade. For example, a typical third-grade student might be required to complete a standardized reading test, a student with severe visual impairments might be required to read from a large-print book, and a student with severe mental retardation might be required to point out the sign that would be by the men's, rather than the women's, restroom.

TABLE 14.3   Possible Outcomes at Different Administrative Levels

Level	Outcome Domain	Outcome Indicator	Comments
International (information from nations)	Achievement	Percent meeting competency standard in math in grade 8 Percent meeting competency standard in reading in grade 8	Competency requirements might vary for individual students. A specific grade would be selected at which education was comparable across nations (before some students might be excluded from schools).
	Satisfaction	Percent parents happy with education of student in grade 8	
National (information from states or a national sampling plan)	Achievement	Percent meeting competency standard in math in grades 4, 8, and 12 Percent meeting competency standard in communication (reading, writing) in grades 4, 8, and 12 Percent meeting competency standard in leisure area (physical, artistic, etc.) in grades 4, 8, 12	Competency requirements might vary for individual students. Three grades would be selected to have better indication of education across grades.
	Satisfaction	Percent parents happy with education of students in grades 4, 8, and 12	
	Participation	Percent receiving certificate, GED, or diploma for successful school completion Percent dropping out of school at ages 16 and 17	Outcomes beyond achievement and satisfaction would be added but still at a system level (percent with certain characteristics).
	Transition readiness	Percent rated as having skills needed for next role (postsecondary education or work)	
State (information from districts or a state sampling plan)	Achievement	Percent meeting competency standard in math in grades 1 to 12 Average score of students on appropriate math exam in grades 1 to 12 Percent meeting competency standard in reading in grades 1 to 12	

(continued)

TABLE 14.3   Possible Outcomes at Different Administrative Levels (*Continued*)

Level	Outcome Domain	Outcome Indicator	Comments
State (information from districts or a state sampling plan)	Achievement	Average score of students on appropriate reading exam in grades 1 to 12	
		Percent meeting competency standard in writing in grades 1 to 12	
		Average score of students on appropriate writing exam in grades 1 to 12	
		Percent meeting competency standard in leisure area in grades 1 to 12	
		Average score of students on appropriate leisure exam in grades 1 to 12	
		Percent meeting competency standard in social studies/social skills in grades 1 to 12	
	Satisfaction	Percent parents happy with education of student in grades 1 to 12	
	Participation	Percent receiving certificate for successful school completion	
		Percent receiving GED for successful school completion	
		Percent receiving diploma for successful school completion	
		Percent dropping out of school at ages 14, 15, 16, and 17	
		Percent attending postsecondary education institution one year after high school	
		Percent in employment one year after high school	
	Transition readiness	Percent rated as having skills needed for next role (postsecondary education or work)	
		Percent retained in grade	

Student Population Heterogeneity

Questions must be raised about how the heterogeneity of the student population will be taken into account in a system of outcome indicators. The issue of making fair comparisons among states, schools, or students when the makeup of the student population differs also must be addressed. At the broadest level, these issues involve determining how to integrate general education indicators with special education indicators. As educators move from outcome domains to sub-domains of outcomes and to indicators of outcomes, the issue of differences in students will have to be addressed. Students with severe mental disabilities may have to complete different kinds of tasks than students with sensory disabilities. Perhaps different weights will have to be applied to different kinds of tasks, or perhaps scores will have to be adjusted as a function of the numbers of students with disabilities who have been included in an indicator. These are difficult issues that educators are certain to face again and again as the nation continues to push for educational accountability.

Measurement of Results

Many argue that there is a need for better assessment measures and particularly that tests should not be the only means of assessing educational results (e.g., Cronbach et al., 1980; Glaser, 1988; Shepard, 1989b). Among the questions that should be raised are:

What are the most appropriate assessment tools?

How should new dimensions of learning be measured?

Who should make decisions about appropriate tools and their role in monitoring the system?

What are the desired technical characteristics of outcomes indicators?

What level of construct validity must be attained for an indicator to be useful?

Should measurement approaches used in general education outcomes assessment influence measurement approaches in special education outcomes assessment?

EFFECTS OF POLICIES RELATED TO EDUCATIONAL RESULTS

Results-related policies have been enacted at many different levels. At the local and state levels, policies in the late 1980s and through the 1990s focused primarily on graduation requirements, graduation exams, retention in grade/social promotion, and grading practices. For example, graduation requirements were made stiffer so that America could be sure that those graduating really had gained some meaningful skills. Graduation exams had the goal of making sure that students could either meet high standards or show some minimal levels of mastery before moving ahead in school. Retention in grade and the determination of course grades were woven into the fabric of policies in the schools. Each of

Remarks to the Republican Governor's Conference, Miami, November 21, 1997

Data from the Third International Mathematics and Science Study (TIMSS) show U.S. eighth graders' performance in mathematics and science to be mediocre and disappointing. We are slightly above the international mean in science and below it in mathematics—but in both cases we are in the middle. . . .

However, results from the fourth grade TIMSS assessment suggest that we do not *begin* behind the children of the rest of the world, but we *fall* behind them during the middle school years. . . .

Differences in achievement across nations appear to be related to the specific topics different countries choose to emphasize in their curriculum. Emphasizing different topics amounts to different visions of what is important in mathematics and science. The key to understanding U.S. performance is related to our nation's lack of an intellectually coherent vision of what we want our children to know in mathematics and science. No such vision dominates practice in the United States. In this respect, we differ from all of the top achieving countries and from most of the nations that participated in TIMSS.

Not having such a coherent vision at its core, the U.S. educational system exhibits several distinctive features which are related to educational achievement. These features include:

- Curricula that are a mile wide and an inch deep—lacking any real focus
- State frameworks that are like long laundry lists lacking coherence across the topics
- A static view of what is basic that keeps repeating the same topics from grade to grade
- A middle school curriculum that is not intellectually challenging or world class in standard
- A system of tracking students in mathematics that gives a different curriculum to different groups of students
- Classroom instruction that mirrors the lack of focus and coherence in the curriculum

SOURCE: Press Release, Michigan State University, East Lansing, MI (http://ustimss. msu.edu/whatsnew.htm).

these policies had particular effects or the potential for effects on students in special education. At the national level, policy makers began to talk about a national test that would go beyond the NAEP. In mid-1991, President Bush endorsed an educational policy that called for voluntary tests for *every* student in grades 4, 8, and 12 in math, English, and science. This idea was carried forward by President Clinton, who proposed voluntary national tests, standards-based tests that would provide comparable data across states, in reading and mathematics. The tests were to be voluntary: states would decide whether they would use them. Despite funding for the development of these tests, they soon became part of political controversy about state control of education and the extent to which national tests would drive a national curriculum. The challenges of including all students in these tests were among the issues addressed by those developing the national tests.

Graduation Requirements

Graduation from high school has been tied for more than eighty years to the Carnegie unit, defined as five hours of related work per week or five periods of forty to sixty minutes for at least thirty-six weeks (Shaw & Walker, 1981). The Carnegie unit was established to define the requirements that had to be met by students entering an institution of higher education for the institution to qualify for Carnegie Pension funds for retired professors. Despite its initial purpose, the unit was quickly adopted as a way to define high school graduation requirements; typically this is done in terms of both a minimum number of units and a distribution scheme of the content areas in which units had to be obtained. The reform movement has led many states to increase the number of Carnegie units required for graduation as a way of stiffening graduation requirements. Graduation requirements have changed in several ways over the years. The number of states with graduation policies increased to where all but three states in the mid-1980s had policies regulating the minimum number of Carnegie units, courses, or course hours required for graduation (Bodner, Clark, & Mellard, 1987). That number had fallen to one state by the late 1990s (Guy, Shin, Lee, & Thurlow, 1998). Hall and Gerber (1985) also had noted the trend toward increasing the number of Carnegie units required for graduation, a trend that later translated into increased requirements for the completion of academic units (Bodner et al., 1987). Thurlow, Ysseldyke, and Reid (1997) documented the continuing trend of increasing these kinds of requirements for graduation.

Policy makers recognized the possibility that stiffening course requirements for graduation might have negative consequences for many students (such as increased rates of dropping out of school). Yet studies did not bear this out (see Kaufman, McMillen, & Bradby, 1992), enabling organizations like the Education Commission of the States (1997) to say:

> Contrary to many predictions, requiring a larger academic core for high school graduation is not associated with a higher high school dropout rate; indeed, research over the past decade indicates that students work harder to meet higher expectations and actually drop out of school at a lower rate. (p. 8)

This research, however, did not address students with disabilities.

Carnegie units, course hours, and types of classes, of course, are not the only requirements that may be imposed on students earning a high school diploma. Instead of Carnegie units, some states present their requirements in terms of class hours. Many states supplement their Carnegie unit or class requirements with graduation exams that students must pass to earn a diploma. Still other states have implemented requirements for community service before a diploma can be obtained (see Guy, Shin, Lee, & Thurlow, 1999). To complicate matters even more, some states determine graduation requirements at the local level, sometimes within the framework of state guidelines and sometimes not.

Students with disabilities, particularly those with mild disabilities, are required to fit into graduation requirements in different ways. Oftentimes these adaptations are established informally by schools or districts. In some cases, students with disabilities have to meet the same requirements as all other students. In other cases, they are allowed to take special courses to fulfill credit requirements for Carnegie units; alternatively, for credit to be awarded, students have to be taught by a teacher certified in the subject matter (a special education course could count if the teacher was certified in the content area as well as in special education). In still other cases, credits for participation in a special program are counted but are applied only toward an alternate document, such as a certificate of completion; this method seriously limits those students considering postsecondary education and even some of those hoping to obtain a job following completion of school. In some cases, each local education agency determines its own policy.

The most recent analysis of states' graduation requirements for students with disabilities (Guy, Shin, Lee, & Thurlow, 1999) confirms this picture of variability and confusion when it comes to students with disabilities and graduation requirements. Surveys of general and special education state-level personnel in all fifty states revealed that states have complex systems involving different exit options, requirements for graduation, and decision makers. While the standard diploma is available to all students in all states, states differ from that point on. Among the varied exit documents available to students are certificates; graduation and high school certificates; certificates of attendance, achievement, attainment, completion, and IEP; and IEP, adjusted, occupational, and honors diplomas.

To obtain a standard diploma, 41 states required the completion of Carnegie course units, but the actual number of units required varied from 14.5 to 24. States that did not require completion of Carnegie units either had different credit unit systems or left the determination of credits to local districts. However, for students with disabilities, these requirements were altered in several ways. In some states, modified courses were counted; in others, some credit requirements could be waived. In other states, the number of credits required could be reduced, or performance criteria could be lowered. In some states, students simply had to meet their IEP goals and objectives to obtain a standard diploma. In fact, for the twenty-four states that had only credit requirements for graduation (i.e., no graduation exam), only two states did not allow any changes in the requirements for students with disabilities.

Raber and Roach (1998) provide a fairly accurate picture of the variability in high school graduation standards for students with disabilities, describing the situation as one in which there is a great deal of interpretation by parents, teachers, and administrators. They give several examples of the "wiggle room" (flexibility) created when IEPs can supersede state graduation policies by describing the systems in three states:

In California, Pennsylvania, and Missouri, graduation requirements for students with IEPs are the same as those for other students—except for any adjustments that the IEP team makes. An IEP team may alter the graduation requirements for a particular student by, for example, requiring six credits in mathematics instead of nine. As long as the student completes the requirements on the IEP, the student can graduate with a regular diploma. . . .

The California, Pennsylvania, and Missouri policies are not only subject to influence, but they are skewed toward parents who know how to negotiate the system. . . . One California district that we studied has recently set new graduation requirements, and students must now have a 2.0 grade point average along with the proper credits to graduate. Parents of students with disabilities in this district who know how the system of exemption works have requested an IEP meeting to have courses that their child has failed or done poorly in removed from those required for graduation. As a result, the student's grade point average increases, thus increasing the likelihood that the student will graduate with a standard diploma. (p. 41)

This picture becomes more complicated because many states add graduation exams to their list of graduation requirements, and students must pass them to obtain a standard diploma. (The use of graduation exams and other high-stakes exams for students is discussed in the next section.)

The practice of allowing students to leave the regular school setting to earn a high school equivalency diploma by taking General Educational Development (GED) tests generates several questions for special educators. The largest number of people earning GED are those age 19 and younger (see Figure 14.1).

In 1997, approximately 2300 individuals used a special edition of the GED, that is, an audiocassette, Braille, or large print version of the test. In addition, 3000 individuals requested learning disabilities accommodations, such as time extensions, reading devices, answer marking, and other types of accommodations. Is the GED a viable alternative to the standard high school diploma? Is it achievable when the standard diploma is not because intensive tutoring can be obtained? Does the GED give students with disabilities the skills they need for entry into either work or some type of postsecondary education?

Although there has been much discussion of the issues surrounding stiffer graduation requirements and the potential effects of alternative school completion documents, researchers have not directly assessed these effects. Kortering, Julnes, and Edgar (1990) attempted to address the graduation issue by looking at pertinent components of the U.S. Constitution, the Rehabilitation Act, PL 94-142, and their legal interpretations in case law. They noted that "courts have limited their reviews of cases pertaining to special education students and graduation to procedural concerns" (p. 12). The authors concluded their discussion by stating, "We have the opportunity, if not absolute duty, to define, in practice and outcome, what constitutes the graduation of special education students. A necessary first step is to establish, at the local level, how and when to graduate special education students" (p. 13). Until we are able to do as Kortering et al. suggested, it is not possible even to obtain a good assessment of the suggested differential effects of varying exit documents (e.g., Higgins, 1979).

FIGURE 14.1   **GED Credentials Earned by Age Groups**

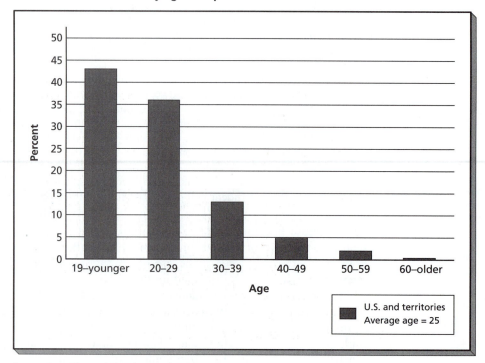

Source: From *Who took the GED? GED 1997 Statistical Report.* Washington, DC: American Council on Education, 1998. Used with permission of GED Testing Service, American Council on Education.

Graduation Exams

The notion that students must meet certain standards before graduating or moving from one grade to the next is not new. Minimal competency testing (MCT), the forerunner of today's graduation exams, was popular in the 1970s. By the end of the 1980s, nearly half the states had some kind of minimal competency testing program in place (see Bodner et al., 1987; "State Education Statistics," 1988). With the surge in educational reform and calls for high standards, the MCT language was replaced by terms like *graduation exams* and *exit exams.* In 1997, however, the American Federation of Teachers (AFT) noted that, of the twenty states with exit exams (most to award diplomas, but some to award diploma endorsements), only half were based on tenth-grade standards or higher. The exit exams for seven states were based on standards for seventh, eighth, or ninth grade, and three were not even based on standards.

According to the Council of Chief State School Officers (Bond, Roeber, & Connealy, 1998), twenty-five states had exams in 1997 used for student accountability purposes (graduation, promotion, endorsements) (see Figure 14.2); eighteen states had exams used to determine whether a student received a high school

FIGURE 14.2   Assessment Purposes

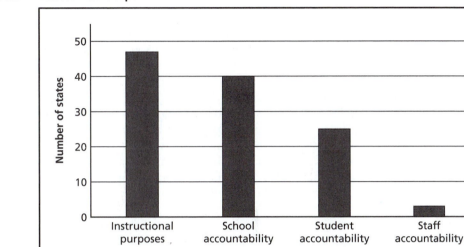

Source: From L. Bond, E. Roeber, and S. Connealy, *Trends in State Student Assessment Programs: Fall 1997.*
Council of Chief State School Officers. Washington, DC: 1998. Reprinted by permission.

diploma. These exams were lauded by some as significantly increasing student achievement (see Bishop, 1997), while decried by others as contributing to high dropout rates, especially among minorities (see Jacobson, 1998). An evaluation conducted by FairTest (Neill, 1997), a national center for "fair and open testing," identified two states (Minnesota and New York) with not only a graduation test, but also an "acceptable alternative." In both of these states, however, political winds have changed. Initial plans to allow the state to certify alternative assessments have been changed; the legislatures in both states have determined that no alternatives will be allowed for the graduation exam.

Just as the course requirements for students with disabilities to graduate are unclear, so are the participation and/or performance requirements on graduation exams. Guy, Shin, Lee, and Thurlow (1998) found that, of the twenty states that in 1998 required students to pass a graduation exam as well as earn a specific number of credits, most allowed students with disabilities to meet course requirements by taking different courses or earning fewer credits, but they did not change the requirement to pass the exam at the same level as other students. This approach is legally defensible and has been supported by several court cases (Freedman, 1997). In some states, however, students with disabilities can be exempted from the graduation exam but still earn a regular diploma (Thurlow, Ysseldyke, & Reid, 1997). With these kinds of alterations, it becomes very difficult to know much about the skills of those students with disabilities who earn high school diplomas. Nevertheless, the pros and cons of these types of tests for students with disabilities continue to be argued (Langenfeld, Thurlow, & Scott, 1997), just as they do for students in general (e.g., Marion & Sheinker, 1998).

Retention in Grade/Social Promotion

One strategy for dealing with school failure is to have students repeat a grade. Many students in special education programs are older than their classmates because they have repeated a grade. About 25 percent of students with disabilities have repeated a grade, compared to about 8 percent of students without disabilities (National Center for Education Statistics, 1997). The notion of retaining students at one grade level for a second time (more commonly known by students as "flunking") is consistent with the notions of school reform and the striving for educational excellence. Students should not be promoted for social reasons or for maintenance of self-esteem but rather only when the basic skills required for starting the next grade have been mastered. Of course, these viewpoints create considerable difficulty for students in special education programs, who often must have demonstrated below-grade performance to qualify for special education services.

According to the Council of Chief State School Officers (Roeber, Bond, & Connealy, 1998), in 1997 six states had exams that determined whether a student moved from one grade to the next. This number seemed likely to increase because of growing political pressures to stop "social promotion," which is the "practice of moving students from grade to grade regardless of their academic ability to do the work required at the next level" (American Federation of Teachers, 1997b). In its report, with the catchy title *Passing on Failure,* AFT stated:

> Social promotion is an insidious practice that hides school failure and creates problems for everybody—for kids, who are deluded into thinking they have learned the skills to be successful or get the message that achievement doesn't count; for teachers, who must face students who know that teachers wield no credible authority to demand hard work; for the business community and colleges that must spend millions of dollars on remediation; and for society that must deal with a growing proportion of uneducated citizens, unprepared to contribute productively to the economic and civic life of the nation.
>
> The public believes that students should earn the right to move from grade to grade; they should demonstrate that they have mastered the knowledge and skills required of them. Students should know that performance counts. If students can't do the work they should not go forward. (p. 5)

These words, echoed by most candidates for governor during the 1998 campaigns, have significant implications for many students, not just students with disabilities.

In a comprehensive book on grade retention edited by Shepard and Smith (1989), the effects of grade retention are highlighted, along with popular beliefs about the effects of retention. Shepard and Smith (1989) concluded on the basis of multiple methods, operations, and perspectives about retention that retention in grade has no benefits for either school achievement or personal attainment; retention is strongly related to later dropping out of school; two years of kindergarten, even when one year is labeled a "transition program," fail to enhance achievement or solve the problem of inadequate school readiness; and from the students' perspective, retention is conflict laden and hurtful. Despite all this, an "abiding faith in the merits of retention" exists among teachers, parents, and educational reformers.

If not done grade by grade, then it is argued (e.g., Education Commission of the States, 1997) that retention should be implemented at least when considering whether a students moves from one level of education to the next (e.g., elementary school to middle school). Since the Shepard and Smith study, there has been some evidence that the effects of grade retention do not have to be negative. This is particularly true if something different is done for the student during the retention year. In a reassessment of the effects of retention in the primary grades, Alexander, Entwisle, and Dauber (1994) provided evidence of the benefits of retention. Others, however, have argued that students with learning disabilities are the least likely to benefit from grade retention (McLeskey, Lancaster, & Grizzle, 1995).

One alternative to grade retention is to assume an outcomes-based education approach in which students are to reach certain goals regardless of how long it takes. Grades would no longer be a needed organizational structure for the school. Nevertheless, not all students in a school would progress unless outcomes and goals were carefully defined, criteria varied according to individual characteristics, and appropriate instruction were provided.

Grading Practices

Grading practices are often the subject of debate, with concerns frequently expressed about their usefulness or meaningfulness. Grade inflation was a common concern during the 1990s, in part because students seemed to be receiving adequate grades and graduating from high school, yet not possessing the skills needed for the world of work or successful entry into postsecondary education settings (see Bracey, 1998, for a rebuttal of the belief that grade inflation exists).

Grading systems typically vary as a function of the student's grade level (Robinson & Craver, 1989). Letter grades are most common in junior and senior high schools. In primary schools, checklists or rating scales are used more often. Report card grades seem to cause considerable difficulty for teachers in general education who have students with disabilities in their classes. Carpenter and his associates (Carpenter, 1985; Carpenter, Grantham, & Hardister, 1983) described many of the pertinent issues that arose in grading students with disabilities. In reviewing the recommendations for grading practice made by numerous professionals, they found that these recommendations could be divided into those promoting different standards (e.g., lowered grading standards, contract with students), those identifying different grading vehicles (e.g., pass-fail system, multiple marking system), and those suggesting different logistics (e.g., daily grading, individualized grading plan in the IEP).

The limited research on grades has found that students with learning disabilities tend to receive lower grades than low-achieving students (Donahoe & Zigmond, 1990) and that across the nation, high school students with all types of disabilities tend to have grade point averages of C+ or lower (Rossi, Herting, & Wolman, 1997; Valdes, Williamson, & Wagner, 1990). Mainstream teachers tend to give D grades to students with learning disabilities simply for showing up for class or for appearing interested (Zigmond, Levin, & Laurie, 1985). Educators tend to prefer grading students with disabilities on the basis of effort, attitude, level of ability, and participation, rather than on the basis of performance, preparedness, attendance, and completion of assignments (Carpenter & Grantham, 1985). These practices raise the issue of grading policies and what students are learning in mainstream classes. Is it fair to place students where they do not learn and then allow them to pass to the next grade? How can educators ensure that students learn in the mainstream classroom and receive an earned passing grade?

A second issue is the use of the same or of a different grading system for students with disabilities. Early research suggested that grading policies for mainstreamed youth with disabilities were usually unwritten, even if they existed, and more often were individual teacher, rather than school, policies (Carpenter & Grantham, 1985). Later research suggested that this had changed. Findings from a national survey (Polloway, Epstein, Bursuck, Roderique, McConeghy, & Jayanthi, 1994) indicated that 65 percent of the districts had grading policies, and that more than half of these included modifications for grading students with disabilities.

A third issue is the purpose of grades (to determine successful completion of a course, to indicate standing relative to all others in the class) and the basis for grade assignments (competence, effort, relative standing to others). Chandler identified grades as one of the main sources of friction between the special education teacher and the general class teacher. He argued that grades are sacrosanct in the general education system, with the argument being something like "If the child should be taught differently, why isn't he in a special classroom?; if he is in a regular classroom, then why can't he take a test like everyone else?; if he is graded differently, isn't that debasing the grades?" (1983, p. 242).

DATA ON THE RESULTS OF SCHOOLING FOR STUDENTS WITH DISABILITIES

As the number of students receiving special education services has increased and the cost of providing special education services has grown, there have been more and more calls for data on the outcomes of providing all these services. Pulling these data from existing data collection programs (both national and state) was one of the first assignments of the National Center on Educational Outcomes (NCEO), devoted solely to identifying the important outcomes of education for students with disabilities and to assisting federal agencies and states in assessment practices to obtain data on the important outcomes. Very early in its attempts to pull these data, NCEO discovered that students with disabilities, for the most part, had been left out of these large-scale data collection programs (McGrew, Thurlow, Shriner, & Spiegel, 1992; National Academy of Education, 1993). NCEO worked with both federal agencies and states to change this situation.

Not Much, but Some

By the last 1990s, notable changes had occurred in the participation of students with disabilities in large-scale assessments. Yet there was still considerable room for improvement. Among the earliest programs to include students with disabilities were special studies conducted by the National Center for Education Statistics (NCES). One of the studies was the National Education Longitudinal Study (Ingels & Quinn, 1996; Rossi, Herting, & Wolman, 1997), which followed students from grade 8 through grade 12, and then two years past high school. Another study was the Adult Literacy Survey (Kirsch, Jungeblut, Jenkins, & Kolstad, 1993), designed to assess the literacy levels of adults. In 1996, for the first time, NCES made it a point to increase the participation of students with disabilities in our nation's report card, the National Assessment of Educational Progress (NAEP) and provided accommodations to help increase that participation (O'Sullivan, Reese, & Mazzeo, 1997; Reese, Miller, Mazzeo, & Dossey, 1997). All of these efforts focused almost exclusively on the academic achievement or literacy of youths or adults.

Similarly, changes occurred in the participation of students with disabilities in state-level assessments. In the early 1990s, the majority of states included 10 percent or less of their students with disabilities in the state assessment (U.S. Department of Education, 1995). By 1997, this number had increased dramatically, and of course, starting in 1998, reports on the participation and performance of students with disabilities on state and district assessments were required by the 1997 amendments to IDEA. Still, in an analysis of 1997/1998 state reports, only thirteen states actually reported performance data for students with disabilities (Ysseldyke, Thurlow, Langenfeld, Nelson, & Teelucksingh, 1998).

Poor Performance Documented

The findings about the academic achievement or literacy of individuals with disabilities from these data collection activities were bleak. Almost universally, individuals with disabilities performed poorly on the measures administered. The first reports of how individuals with disabilities performed on large-scale assessments came from the National Adult Literacy Survey (NALS), which assessed prose literacy (e.g., editorials, news stories, poems, fiction), document literacy (job applications, payroll forms, transportation schedules, maps, tables, graphs), and quantitative literacy (applying arithmetic operations—balancing a checkbook, figuring a tip, completing an order form, determining interest on a loan).

Of the more than 26,000 adults who were surveyed, a significant percentage reported having some type of condition (illness, disability, or impairment). The discrepancies were great between the performance of adults without any type of illness, disability, or impairment and the performance of those individuals reporting emotional conditions, learning disabilities, mental retardation, and physical disabilities (see Table 14.4). Most adults with disabilities were at the lowest level of performance, while the most frequently achieved level for the total population was Level 3 (see Figure 14.3 for descriptions of the levels).

FIGURE 14.3 Descriptions of Literacy Levels in the National Adult Literacy Survey

	Prose	Document	Quantitative
Level 1 *0–225*	Most of the tasks in this level require the reader to read relatively short text to locate a single piece of information which is identical to or synonymous with the information given in the question or directive. If plausible but incorrect information is present in the text, it tends not to be located near the correct information.	Tasks in this level tend to require the reader either to locate a piece of information based on a literal match or to enter information from personal knowledge onto a document. Little, if any, distracting information is present.	Tasks in this level require readers to perform single, relatively simple arithmetic operations, such as addition. The numbers to be used are provided and the arithmetic operation to be performed is specific.
Level 2 *226–275*	Some tasks in this level require readers to locate a single piece of information in the text; however, several distractors or plausible but incorrect pieces of information may be present, or low-level inferences may be required. Other tasks require the reader to integrate two or more pieces of information or to compare and contrast easily indentifiable information based on a criterion provided in the question or directive.	Tasks in this level are more varied than those in Level I. Some require the readers to match a single piece of information; however, several distractors may be present, or the match may require low-level inferences. Tasks in this level may also ask the reader to cycle through information in a document or to integrate information from various parts of a document.	Tasks in this level typically require readers to perform a single operation using numbers that are either stated in the task or easily located in the material. The operation to be performed may be stated in the question or easily determined from the format of the material (for example, an order form).
Level 3 *276–325*	Tasks in this level tend to require readers to make literal or synony-mous matches between the text and information given in the task, or to make matches that require low-level inferences. Other tasks ask readers to integrate informa-tion from dense or lengthy text that contains no organizational aids such as headings. Readers may also be asked to generate a response based on information that can be easily identified in the text. Distracting information is present, but is not located near the correct information.	Some tasks in this level require the reader to integrate multiple pieces of information from one or more documents. Others ask readers to cycle through rather complex tables or graphs which contain information that is irrelevant or inappropriate to the task.	In tasks in this level, two or more numbers are typically needed to solve the problem, and these must be found in the material. The operation(s) needed can be determined from the arithmetic relation terms used in the ques-tion or directive.

	Prose	Document	Quantitative
Level 4 *326–375*	These tasks require readers to perform multiple-feature matches and to integrate or synthesize information from complex or lengthy passages. More complex inferences are needed to perform successfully. Conditional information is frequently present in tasks at this level and must be taken into consideration by the reader.	Tasks in this level, like those at the previous levels, ask readers to perform multiple-feature matches, cycle through documents, and integrate information; however, they require a greater degree of inferencing. Many of these tasks require readers to provide numerous responses but do not designate how many responses are needed. Conditional information is also present in the document tasks at this level and must be taken into account by the reader.	These tasks tend to require readers to perform two or more sequential operations or a single operation in which the quantities are found in different types of displays, or the operations must be inferred from semantic information given or drawn from prior knowledge.
Level 5 *376–500*	Some tasks in this level require the reader to search for information in dense text which contains a number of plausible distractors. Others ask readers to make high-level inferences or use specialized background knowledge. Some tasks ask readers to contrast complex information.	Tasks in this level require the reader to search through complex displays that contain multiple distractors, to make high-level text-based inferences, and to use specialized knowledge.	These tasks require readers to perform multiple operations sequentially. They must disembed the features of the problem from text or rely on background knowledge to determine the quantities or operations needed.

Source: U.S. Department of Education. National Center for Education Statistics, National Adult Literacy Survey, 1992.

Data from the National Education Longitudinal Study (NELS) are limited because of evidence of some systematic exclusion that occurred during the baseline year. Although the data collection program discovered this problem and attempted to correct it, this limitation must be kept in mind. Nevertheless, the data from NELS showed that students with disabilities (whether teacher identified or parent identified) scored lower on math and reading proficiency tests than did their peers. While the majority of students without disabilities scored at Level 3 or Level 4 (where levels were defined similar to the NALS levels), most students with disabilities scored at Level 1 or Level 2. Students with multiple problems and with learning disabilities tended to perform below all other disability categories.

It is expected that data from the 1996 National Assessment of Educational Progress in science and mathematics will produce similar results. These data were still being prepared for publication in 1999.

State data generally reflect findings about the academic achievement of students with disabilities that are similar to national data. For the thirteen states that publicly reported on the performance of their students with disabilities before they were required to do so by the 1997 amendments to IDEA, all showed that students with disabilities were performing below the total population of students. This occurred regardless of content area or student grade. When placed on a common metric of the percentage of students meeting specified criteria, from 30 percent to 50 percent fewer students with disabilities met the criteria than students overall.

TABLE 14.4 Performance of Individuals with Disabilities Compared to Total Population

Group	Average Score	Percentage at Each Performance Level				
		Level 1	Level 2	Level 3	Level 4	Level 5
Prose Literacy						
Total population	272	21	27	32	17	3
Emotional condition	225	48	24	18	8	2
Learning disability	207	58	22	14	4	1
Mental retardation	143	87	3	5	3	1
Physical disability	231	44	30	19	6	1
Document Literacy						
Total population	267	23	28	31	15	3
Emotional condition	224	45	28	17	8	3
Learning disability	203	60	22	13	4	1
Mental retardation	147	86	5	6	3	0
Physical disability	226	47	29	18	6	0
Quantitative Literacy						
Total population	271	22	25	31	17	4
Emotional condition	215	51	23	17	8	2
Learning disability	200	60	21	14	4	1
Mental retardation	117	89	4	6	1	0
Physical disability	228	45	26	21	7	1

Source: *Adult Literacy in America,* Washington, DC: National Center for Education Statistics, 1993.

One state has examined the performance of students with disabilities and general students over four years during which intensive educational reform activities occurred (Trimble, 1998). Although more evident at grade 4 than at grade 8 or 11, there was evidence that the performance of students with disabilities was improving at a faster rate than that of general students, even though the performance of students with disabilities was below that of general students.

As mentioned previously, the data from large-scale national and state data collection programs focus almost entirely on academics when reporting on the performance of students. Occasionally there are data on dropout rates or attendance, but rarely are there data on how individuals with disabilities perform after they leave school. One source of data that goes beyond academics is the Survey of Americans with Disabilities conducted jointly by the National Organization on Disability and Louis Harris & Associates (1998). This survey of 1000 individuals with disabilities found wide gaps in employment rates between those with disabilities and those without (29 percent versus 79 percent work). Similar gaps exist in income level (34 percent versus 12 percent in poverty), and high school completion (40 percent versus 90 percent completing high school). In addition to these areas, the survey found that individuals with disabilities less often socialized with close friends, relatives, or neighbors (69 percent versus 84 percent) or went to a restaurant (33 percent versus 60 percent) at least once a week. Consistent with these gaps, only 33 percent of individuals with disabilities were very satisfied with life, while 61 percent of individuals without disabilities indicated this level of satisfaction.

The National Longitudinal Transition Study (Wagner, D'Amico, Marder, Newman, & Blackorby, 1992; Wagner, Newman, D'Amico, Jay, Butler-Nalin, Marder, & Cox, 1991) was a study designed specifically to follow students with disabilities after leaving school. Two years out of school, only 15 percent of students with disabilities had attended a postsecondary school, 30 percent had not held a paid job, 40 percent of those employed worked only part time, and 20 percent had been arrested. Findings for some specific groups, such as students with emotional disabilities, were worse (Wagner, 1995). Three to five years out of school findings revealed improvements in participation in postsecondary school (25 percent) and employment (19 percent had not held a job; 22 percent worked part time), as well as in the frequency of independent living arrangements.

Discussion Questions

1. How would you describe a set of outcome domains that would apply to all students?

2. The inclusion of students with disabilities in standardized testing is a much debated issue. What are some of the perspectives on this issue?

3. One approach to a common system for measuring attainment of outcomes is to develop a national test or a set of national tests. How would you do this so that all students could participate?

4. What alternative strategies to grades can be used to keep track of students' progress in school? Is there a way to merge the IEP with general education indicators of progress toward outcomes?

Chapter 15
Continuing Challenges

THE FUTURE OF SPECIAL EDUCATION
Preparing People Versus Preparing Professionals
Reform Versus Resignation
Assessing Students Versus Assessing Outcomes
Continuing Choices Versus Historical Challenges
Performance Versus Postulates
Self-Determination Versus Societal Responsibility
Reform Versus Renewal

SPECIAL EDUCATION AND THE FUTURE
Educating All Children
Understanding Fundamentals of General and Special Education
Shifting Assessment and Instructional Paradigms
Putting Practical Perspectives on Learned Concepts
An Ounce of Prevention Is Worth a Pound of Cure
An Ounce of Pretention Is Worth a Pound of Manure
An Ounce of Intervention Is Worth a Pound of Assure

DISCUSSION QUESTIONS

We find that whole communities suddenly fix their minds upon one object, and go mad in its pursuit; that millions of people become simultaneously impressed with one delusion, and run after it, till their attention is caught by some new folly more captivating than the first.

—Charles Mackay

Special education is a subsystem of general education, but whether this will always be the case we do not know. Nor can we say whether special education will continue to be organized categorically, how assessment practices will evolve, what conditions special education teachers will encounter, and how school reform will affect special education. In short, we do not believe that we can predict the future of special education because the direction of special education has been shaped by a mixture of social, legal, political, philosophical, and financial realities and will continue to be so influenced. Who would have anticipated the degree of progress that has been made in the past two decades?

Nevertheless, we do have some thoughts on where special education is going. As you read through this chapter, however, we hope you will recognize the precarious nature of making statements about the future, especially where special education is concerned.

THE FUTURE OF SPECIAL EDUCATION

Views of the future are typically presented differently by the optimist and by the pessimist. To the optimist, the glass is always half full; to the pessimist, it is half empty. Nobody really knows if the glass is empty or full. Perceptions control most of human behavior, and the perceptions people have about training, educational reform, assessment, human responsibility, educational choice, and performance measurement will control the destiny of these matters for the future of special education. The competing perspectives that characterize contemporary opinions about these and other areas of professional practice will drive efforts to improve special education in the next century.

Preparing People Versus Preparing Professionals

The issues that will shape the direction of personnel training efforts in special education for this century will be grounded in past and current practices and in the views people hold about the nature of teaching and its professional development. Some of these issues center on the differences between special and general education teachers, between prepared and unprepared teachers, and among special education teachers. Other issues address the public's expectations of special education teachers, whether these teachers are the only ones who can deliver services to exceptional children, and if not, what expectations attach to other professionals providing services. Still other issues look at who is preparing teachers of exceptional students and what expertise the teachers need or possess.

In regard to the last set of issues, Pugach and Lilly argued that "teacher education programs tend to follow rather than lead the field of practice" (1984, p. 48). This is largely due to the simple fact that universities prepare students to work in schools that are controlled by regulations and requirements originating in state departments of education:

> Universities prepare students to compete for real jobs in real schools and must therefore be sensitive to professional conditions, as well as hiring practices and criteria, in K–12 schools.
>
> Universities offer teacher education programs through a maze of state regulations for program approval and teacher certification that are nearly always reflective of current and past practice in education, not future trends or directions. (Lilly, 1989, p. 144)

In the years following the passage of PL 94-142, the demand for special education personnel grew at unprecedented rates as school districts delivered more and varied services to broader numbers and wider age ranges of students with disabilities (U.S. Dept. of Education, 1990a). The need for qualified personnel to work with students with special learning needs will probably continue in this century. Because special education populations have been steadily growing, there is no reason to believe that this growth will subside; in fact, new groups of children and youths with special learning needs (e.g., children with AIDS, crack babies, language minority students with learning problems) are increasingly appearing as "hot topics" in professional journals (Barnes, 1986; Cantwell & Baker, 1991; Centers for Disease Control, 1987a, 1987b; Fradd & Correa, 1989; Jason et al., 1990; Shaywitz & Shaywitz, 1991). At the same time, teacher attrition rates in special education are increasing, and enrollments in and graduations from personnel preparation programs are declining (U.S. Dept. of Education, 1990b).

The decline in recruitment, the growth in reported personnel shortages, the projections of teacher retirements, the expansion of services, and the increase in the number of students receiving special education make personnel preparation concerns central and critical. Although the status of these current conditions "signal an impending crisis" in the provision of services to students with disabilities, they also represent only a portion of the problems related to meeting personnel needs in special education (U.S. Dept. of Education, 1990b, p. 39247). Local school districts also report high levels of need for staff other than teachers (see Table 15.1).

The largest category of special education personnel employed in recent years was teachers of students with specific learning disabilities, who accounted for 85,853 (27.6 percent) of all employed, fully certified teachers and 6,897 (32.7 percent) of employed, not fully certified teachers (U.S.D.E., 1996). The next largest group of special education teachers taught in classes in which students with several disabilities were served (i.e., cross-categorical classes). The largest number of vacant positions was in the area of speech or language impairments (30.1 percent of all vacant positions), followed by specific learning disabilities (21.1 percent) and cross-categorical (15.3 percent). Eighty-seven percent of the employed, fully certified teachers and 62.5 percent of the teachers not fully certified were retained from the previous year (U.S.D.E., 1996).

In recent years, more than 300,000 personnel other than special education teachers were employed to work with students with disabilities. Teacher aides accounted for more than 60 percent of employed, fully certified other personnel; 64.2 percent of employed, not fully certified other personnel; and 35.2 percent of vacant, other personnel positions (U.S.D.E., 1996). Psychologists, nonprofessional staff, and other professional staff were the next largest groups of other personnel providing services to students with disabilities. Nearly one-third of all reported other personnel vacancies were in occupational therapist, physical therapist, and psychologist positions.

The continuing need for qualified teachers creates concern in many school districts. Over the past ten to fifteen years, various studies, commissions, and national reports have identified a widespread failure to ensure that America's public schools are staffed with quality teachers (see Ingersoll, 1998). This national tragedy, in turn, had reformers pushing for tougher standards and more rigorous coursework in efforts to upgrade the teaching force. An important source of misunderstanding in measuring problems associated with finding and keeping qualified teachers) is the "out-of-field" teacher (i.e., teachers assigned to

TABLE 15.1   Personnel Needs in Special Education

Type of Personnel	Fully Certified	Not Fully Certified	Vacant Positions	Total Positions
Teachers				
Specific learning disabilities	85,853	6,897	771	93,522
Speech/language impairments	36,807	1,655	1,097	39,559
Mental retardation	39,342	2,530	353	42,225
Serious emotional disturbance	26,171	3,608	373	30,151
Multiple disabilities	7,118	520	67	7,705
Hearing impairments	5,738	285	84	6,107
Orthopedic impairments	2,684	239	126	3,049
Visual impairments	2,433	1,439	68	2,640
Other health impairments	2,065	239	43	2,347
Autism	1,418	285	24	1,727
Traumatic brain injury	110	23	2	136
Deaf-blindness	102	13	3	118
Cross-categorical	84,534	4,501	559	89,534
Other Personnel				
Teacher aides	189,011	12,968	1,286	203,265
Psychologists	20,104	424	336	20,864
Nonprofessional staff	18,844	1,452	165	20,461
Other professional staff	18,053	3,002	139	21,194
Supervisors/administrators	14,502	344	161	15,007
School social workers	11,026	462	106	11,595
Diagnostic staff	8,464	76	167	8,707
Counselors	7,269	127	108	7,504
Occupational therapists	5,331	207	459	5,997
Physical education teachers	4,971	251	60	5,282
Vocational education teachers	4,123	115	97	4,335
Physical therapists	3,536	131	390	4,057
Work study coordinators	1,407	85	42	1,534
State level supervisors	1,021	10	39	1,070
Audiologists	836	22	22	880
Recreation therapists	256	61	8	325
Rehabilitation counselors	179	—	8	193
Interpreters	2,209	470	60	2,739

SOURCE: U.S. Department of Education. (1996). Eighteenth Annual Report to Congress on the Implementation of the Individuals with Disabilities Education Act. Washington, D.C.: Office of Special Education Programs.

teach subjects that do not match training or education). A teacher certified to teach students with serious emotional disturbance teaching students with learning disabilities is teaching out-of-field. A teacher with learning disabilities preparation teaching students with serious emotional disturbance is an out-of-field teacher. While little research has been completed on this phenomenon in special education, data in general education illustrate that out-of-field teaching has profound effects on satisfaction and supply and demand conditions (Ingersoll, 1998). Considerable study of this important influence on special education personnel preparation and staffing practices remains to be done.

Current practices allow some local school district administrators and state education agency personnel to waive preparation requirements so that people with emergency or restricted certification can fill positions on a temporary or permanent basis (Goodlad, 1990; Ingersoll, 1998). Alternative certification is a "generic term applied to any non-traditional route to certification which permits an individual who does not hold an appropriate certificate to begin teaching while pursuing the appropriate certificate through a supervised program of academic study and 'on the job' training" (Olson, 1990, p. 1). The extent of these practices has been estimated to be high (e.g., almost all states make some provision for alternative certification), and their impact on special education remains a topic of future research. There is concern that the impact will not be positive because, by definition, these "professionals" are not fully qualified to teach students in special education. A serious issue will surface if efforts to compare "qualified and unqualified" teachers produce inconsequential differences in terms of outcomes that matter to students. Indeed, there is some evidence that categorical certification has little to do with teacher effectiveness.

Observing that teachers certification and training programs typically adhere to the same categorical delineations as student-based identification systems, Marston (1988) examined academic achievement of students taught by teachers prepared in the same or different categorical certification programs. His results were less than complimentary for categorical training perspectives:

> LD students taught by LD teachers do not improve more than LD students taught by EMR teachers. Likewise, EMR pupils instructed by EMR licensed teachers do not improve more than EMR students taught by teachers with LD certification. Rather, both LD and EMR pupils make similar gains when taught by teachers with varying certification. (Marston, 1987, p. 427)

Concerns about the quality and quantity of special education teachers have also led to the development of alternative preparation programs. Traditional university-based training programs are being replaced or supplemented with school district–based offices designed to provide continuing and entry-level teachers with courses and information necessary to practice in public schools. The perspectives of these programs vary greatly in terms of the academic preparation and field experiences needed for completion (U.S. Dept. of Education, 1990b), and concern for their effects on alternative certification practices is evident in most states (Olson, 1990).

For years, private schools have been staffed with a pool of people with strong content knowledge but little professional preparation. Many public school teachers, "desperate for better education experiences for their own children, are strapping themselves financially to send their children to private schools, which they believe are doing a better job of quality education" (Glasser, 1990, p. 6). As the search for better schools continues, comparisons of the teaching styles provided by people trained and entering education along different paths will likely become common.

How will the preparation of teachers change as a result of concern for current practices and the future? Nobody knows, but professionals have prepared predictive platforms and proposed plenty of postulates as planks in the bridge that must be built to move from the present state of affairs to a more desirable one. For example, Lilly predicted that

> separate systems of teacher preparation in special education [would] go the way of separate systems of education for children [and that for] programs for preparing teachers of students labeled "mildly handicapped" (or "learning disabled," "behaviorally disordered," or "educable or mildly mentally retarded") special education as a separate entity in teacher education [would] disappear. (1989, p. 146)

He based his prediction on observations of interest in a system of national teacher certification (Carnegie Forum, 1986) and on increasing incentives for continuing education and advancement for practicing teachers.

Concerned by persistent patterns of neglect in professional preparation efforts, Goodlad presented nineteen "essential presuppositions—as postulates—to guide our journey through the teacher education landscape and, ultimately, to shape our evaluation of it" (1990, p. 191). The postulates that he believed would shape the future of teacher education follow (pp. 191–192):

Postulate 1. Programs for the education of the nation's educators must be viewed by institutions offering them as a major responsibility to society and be adequately supported and promoted and vigorously advanced by the institution's top leadership.

Postulate 2. Programs for the education of educators must enjoy parity with other campus programs as a legitimate college or university commitment and field of study and service, worthy of rewards for faculty geared to the nature of the field.

Postulate 3. Programs for the education of educators must be autonomous and secure in their borders, with clear organizational identity, constancy of budget and personnel, and decision-making authority similar to that enjoyed by the major professional schools.

Postulate 4. There must exist a clearly identifiable group of academic and clinical faculty members for whom teacher education is the top priority; the group must be responsible and accountable for selecting students and monitoring their progress, planning, and maintaining the full scope and sequence of the curriculum, continuously evaluating and improving programs, and facilitating the entry of graduates into teaching careers.

Postulate 5. The responsible group of academic and clinical faculty members described above must have a comprehensive understanding of the aims of education and the role of schools in society and be fully committed to selecting and preparing teachers to assume the full range of educational responsibilities required.

Postulate 6. The responsible group of academic and clinical faculty members must seek out and select for a predetermined number of student places in the program those candidates who reveal an initial commitment to the moral, ethical, and enculturating responsibilities to be assumed.

Postulate 7. Programs for the education of educators, whether elementary or secondary, must carry the responsibility to ensure that all candidates progressing through them possess or acquire the literacy and critical-thinking abilities associated with the concept of an educated person.

Postulate 8. Programs for the education of educators must provide extensive opportunities for future teachers to move beyond being students of organized knowledge to become teachers who inquire into both knowledge and its teaching.

Postulate 9. Programs for the education of educators must be characterized by a socialization process through which candidates transcend their self-oriented student preoccupations to become more other-oriented in identifying with a culture of teaching.

Postulate 10. Programs for the education of educators must be characterized in all respects by the conditions for learning that future teachers are to establish in their own schools and classrooms.

Postulate 11. Programs for the education of educators must be conducted in such a way that future teachers inquire into the nature of teaching and schooling and assume that they will do so as a natural aspect of their careers.

Postulate 12. Programs for the education of educators must involve future teachers in the issues and dilemmas that emerge out of the never-ending tension between the rights and interests of individual parents and special-interest groups, on one hand, and the roles of schools in transcending parochialism, on the other.

Postulate 13. Programs for the education of educators must be infused with understanding of and commitment to the moral obligation of teachers to ensure equitable access to and engagement in the best possible K–12 education for all children and youths.

Postulate 14. Programs for the education of educators must involve future teachers not only in understanding schools as they are but in alternatives, and how to effect needed changes in school organization, pupil grouping, curriculum, and more.

Postulate 15. Programs for the education of educators must assure for each candidate the availability of a wide array of laboratory settings for observation, hands-on experiences, and exemplary schools for internships and residencies; they must admit no more students to their programs than can be assured these quality experiences.

Postulate 16. Programs for the education of educators must engage future teachers in the problems and dilemmas arising out of the inevitable conflicts and incongruities between what works or is accepted in practice and the research and theory supporting other options.

Postulate 17. Programs for educating educators must establish linkages with graduates for purposes of both evaluating and revising these programs and easing the critical early years of transition into teaching.

Postulate 18. Programs for the education of educators, in order to be vital and renewing, must be free from curricular specifications by licensing agencies and restrained only by enlightened, professionally driven requirements for accreditation.

Postulate 19. Programs for the education of educators must be protected from the vagaries of supply and demand by state policies that allow neither back door "emergency" programs nor temporary teaching licenses.

Clearly strong emotion has emerged from efforts to postulate "what ought to be" if teacher education is to make substantive gains in improving what has passed as professional practice for quite some time (Johnson, 1990; Lilly, 1989; Wise, 1990). The education of special educators will surely profit from similar soul-searching, and the benefits that will accrue if these postulates are put into practice will serve special educators well.

Reform Versus Resignation

The 1980s and 1990s will probably be seen as the decades of school reform. Many different initiatives designed to improve education can be grouped under the rubric of school reform. Approaches ranging from simple administrative practices such as lengthening the school day or setting higher expectations for students to full-scale restructuring of educational systems (e.g., providing open enrollment options) have been proposed in efforts to change education (Goens & Clover, 1990). Interest in school reform has generated considerable local, state, and national activity. Beginning with identification of the sad state of affairs characterized as an educational system and ending with articulated goals and questions related to how to achieve them, efforts to improve education moved rapidly during the last quarter century.

But not everybody believes education can be reformed, at least not in its present state. Sarason painted a particularly bleak picture:

When I say that schools have been intractable to reform, I mean that for the large majority of students, including most from nonpoverty backgrounds, the declared aims of schooling are empty rhetoric that bears little relationship to their social experience. Further, I mean that failure of educational reform derives from a most superficial conception of how complicated settings are organized: their structure, their dynamics, their power relationships, and their underlying values and axioms. Schools today are not what they were twenty or thirty years ago. They have changed but in the spirit of the popular song containing the line "I am true to you in *my* fashion," which means that the changes are cosmetic and not fundamental. Schools will remain intractable to desired reform as long as we avoid confronting (among other things) their existing power relationships. (1990, p. 5)

He argued that a fundamental error in conceptualizing how to change the system is the traditional misplacement of blame for school failure onto a litany of inappropriate villains (e.g., inadequate teachers; irresponsible parents; irrelevant or inadequate curricula; unmotivated students from whom too little is expected, demanded, or obtained; improvement-defeating bureaucracies; inadequate or inappropriate promotion and graduation standards; and lack of the competitiveness that goads organizations to progress in other arenas). He saw the alteration of power relationships in classrooms and schools as a first step in improving educational systems.

Alternative perspectives on power are also at the base of other proposals to radically alter educational systems. Building on the principles postulated by Deming that transformed Japan into the "world's richest country," Glasser (1990, p. 3) called for movement from boss management to lead management as the only way really to achieve quality schools. Under boss management, the power rests with the boss, and the needs of the boss are more important than those of the workers:

1. The boss sets the jobs and, without consulting the workers, establishes the standards for what workers are to do. Bosses do not compromise or consult; workers adjust to the job as the boss defines it.

2. The boss usually tells, rather than shows, the workers how the work is to be done and rarely asks for input about how a job might be done better.

3. The boss (or a designated representative) inspects the work. Because workers are not involved in this process, they often settle for just enough quality to get by the evaluation of the boss.

4. When workers resist, the boss uses punishment, power, and coercion to obtain compliance and in doing so creates a workplace in which workers and managers are constant adversaries.

By substituting teacher for boss and student for worker, the parallels to educational workplaces become transparent and serve as sufficient basis for considering lead management as an alternative for improving educational systems. As Deming put it, "The goal is clear. The productivity of our systems must be increased. The key to change is the understanding of our managers, and the people to whom they report, about what it means to be a good manager" (quoted in Glasser, 1990, p. 31). The principles of lead management illustrate what this means:

1. The leader engages the workers in a discussion of the quality of the work to be done and the time needed to do it so that they have a chance to add their input. The leader makes a constant effort to fit the job to the skills and the needs of the workers.

2. The leader (or a worker designated by the leader) shows or models the job so that the worker who is to perform the job sees exactly what the manager expects. At the same time, the workers are continually asked for their input as to what they believe may be a better way.

3. The leader asks the workers to inspect or evaluate their own work for quality, with the understanding that the leader accepts that they know a great deal about how to produce high-quality work and will therefore listen to what they say.

4. The leader is a facilitator in that he shows the workers that he has done everything possible to provide them with the best tools and workplaces as well as a noncoercive, nonadversarial atmosphere in which to do the job. (Glasser, 1990, pp. 31–32)

Clearly much of what passes as instruction in contemporary classrooms bears strong resemblance to boss management and little resemblance to lead management (see Table 15.2). And even though we see the principles of lead management as truly promising alternatives for reforming education, we believe the likelihood of significant changes happening is very small—not because people do not want to change but because they are resigned to ineffective reform strategies that address the wrong problems and ask the wrong questions. This is evident in efforts to explain the failure of school reform to correct education's errant course adequately (Glasser, 1990; Sarason, 1990) and in efforts to improve assessment and other important practices.

Assessing Students Versus Assessing Outcomes

States are mandating changes in their assessment practices. Some states are merging special education with general education, breaking down barriers that required specific kinds of low-level performances on tests to permeate. School districts are enabling assessors to engage in new roles and new activities. School psychologists are now working as behavior management specialists and collaborative consultants, rather than as psychometric robots. University preparation programs, like the one at the University of Minnesota, are changing the way they train assessors. They are moving away from training professionals to administer the major intelligence tests and instead educating them in ecological appraisal, assessment of instructional environments, curriculum-based measurement, portfolio assessment, and collaborative problem solving. Indeed, the National Association of School Psychologists published an entire compendium of alternative educational delivery systems (Graden, Zins, & Curtis, 1988). Practitioners who spoke in the past of norm-referenced appraisal, technical adequacy, aptitude × treatment interactions, and bias in assessment now talk about performance-based assessment, neuropsychological appraisal, curriculum-based measurement, assessment of instructional environments, and assessment anchored to outcomes. It would be easy to conclude that a major revolution is taking place in assessment practices.

But the more we have read and the more we observe assessment practices in schools, the more we doubt that fundamental change is taking place. We get discouraged. We repeatedly ask ourselves questions such as "Will those who assess children really discontinue their heavy reliance on tests?" "What are the incentives for people to change their practices?" "Will training programs really adapt the way they train professionals?" "Will we ever see an end to the practice of describing child pathology as the focus of assessment?"

In fact, society has changed significantly over the past three decades, and students now enter school with significantly more problems (and individually with many more severe problems) than they did in the early 1970s. Schools are undergoing restructuring and reform. Yet assessment practices today look, for the most part, as they did in 1970, and there is little reason to believe they will

TABLE 15.2 **Comparison of Completing Instructional Management Styles**

Boss Management	Lead Management
Boss teacher sets the learning agenda, and students are expected to comply because it is right to do so. Students have little or no say in the process.	Lead teacher discusses content, defining critical aspects and explaining why specific topics are taught and how students can use them in their daily lives.
Boss teacher tells students to work independently and sets specific dates for assignments and tests. Students are seldom asked for input on instructional goals or methods. Preset curriculum targets control instructional time.	Lead teacher answers immediate questions and uses small cooperative groups as primary work structures. Teacher uses student input about when test should be given. Competency and quality are the rule. Amount of time needed to master a task does not control instruction.
Boss teacher grades students using preset standards. Students pass if they meet minimum standards (e.g., D or better), and plenty of students are failing.	Lead teacher involves students, as individuals and as members of groups, in evaluating the quality of their classwork, homework, and test performances.
Boss teacher gives students little authority. Control and compliance with rules for behavior are hallmarks of the management style, and plenty of time is spent "disciplining" students.	Lead teacher continually facilitates by talking to students and listening to their input on how to keep the classroom a good place to learn.

change. Sure, the social, political economic, and cultural happenings since 1970 have influenced assessment practices, but they have not led to fundamental change. Assessment practices in the future will probably look much like they look today. Some assessors will engage in curriculum-based measurement and prereferral intervention, monitor data on pupil progress, focus at the preschool level, and engage in multidisciplinary problem solving. Most, we believe, will continue to function as psychometric robots. Jack Bardon, in a keynote address to the North Carolina Association of School Psychologists (October 1990), pointed out that "Assessment practices are whatever professionals make of them. They are a function of the styles, knowledge base, characteristics, demeanor, professional biases, creativity, temperament, savvy, wisdom, energy, assertiveness, etc. of the individual assessor more so than they are a function of what the field is or somebody says it should be."

We hope we are wrong. Perhaps when all is said and done, change will come about by chaos. McGarry contended that enduring changes require the reformation of entire networks of interlocking elements, that chaos provides the most fertile source for new structures, and that attempts to change assessment practices by adjusting one factor at a time will fail. McGarry argued further that

> change can occur gradually, but only if major sections of the cultural network change incrementally, until an entirely new network has been created. An easier way to make incremental change, however, is to initiate it at a cusp in the organizational life—at a time when the former structure is collapsing in the face of a changed environment or from exhaustion of its own internal energies. (1990, p. 15)

Continuing Choices Versus Historical Challenges

What will the future look like if choice is fully implemented in more states? When we talk about choice we mean the perspective that grew in the 1980s regarding the potential for marketplace influences to work in education. According to this concept, if educational institutions were subjected to the laws of the marketplace, consumers would show their desire for quality products and, as a result, schools would begin to "clean up their act" so that they would not go out of business. The result would be increases in the number of good schools and decreases in the number of bad and not-so-good schools.

But even as the notion of educational choice picked up speed, questions were raised about what it meant for students with disabilities. Would students with disabilities or their parents participate in the opportunity for choice? Would it make a difference in a program that was so heavily influenced by federal funding? And did parents really know what programs were the best for their children with unique educational needs? These and many other questions will continue to face us if the nation moves toward increased educational choice.

Performance Versus Postulates

Will educators ever really be concerned about what difference special education makes, or will they continue to give lip service to propositions and postulates about what "ought to be" evaluated? Few states assess the educational outcomes of students with mild disabilities beyond what is required by federal mandates (e.g., dropout rate, anticipated need for services). And for the most part few states have the resources to do more in the area of outcomes assessment than what is required by law. If this is the case, how can educators expect to give more than lip service to the notion of evaluating the effectiveness of special education? Even if states did have the resources to evaluate special education, would they know what to collect for outcome data and how?

There are many basic questions related to outcomes assessment that have not yet been solved. For example:

- To what extent should effectiveness indicators for students with disabilities differ from effectiveness indicators for students without disabilities?

- Should desired outcomes for students with disabilities be noncategorical?

- Should desired outcomes differ as a function of severity of disability?
- Should desired outcomes differ as a function of developmental level?
- Should professionals be gathering data on outcomes at the level of the individual, the building, the district, or the state?

Even if states did know the answers to these and other questions, so what? If educators are not yet able to link outcomes back to programs, what difference does worrying about outcomes make?

Self-Determination Versus Societal Responsibility

Not that long ago people in America, and other countries as well, thought that it was the responsibility of society to take care of those individuals who supposedly were not able to take care of themselves. At the beginning of the twentieth century, Americans were very concerned with promoting reproduction of only the most capable individuals. Individuals with disabilities, particularly those with mental impairments, were held in very low regard. Not until the middle of the twentieth century did Americans begin to recognize that they had been mistreating people with disabilities. Progress was slow, but the move was toward realizing that every individual could be valued. In 1985, Dybwad was quoted as saying, "Thirty-five years ago parents revolted and protested the neglect and exclusion of their children with mental retardation. The most significant progress since that time has been the emergence of individuals with mental retardation as persons in their own right. As fellow human beings claiming their place in our society" (Lovett, 1985, p. 89).

Since that time, individuals with disabilities and their advocates have begun to recognize that citizens have a right not just to be valued but also to make decisions for themselves. They have a right to self-determination. The notion was eloquently stated by Williams:

> In this final analysis, we are *all people first*. Isn't this what the Declaration of Independence tells us: that we are *all people first and foremost*? And that as such we are endowed with certain inalienable rights and that among these are the right to life, liberty and the pursuit of happiness.
>
> But, without being afforded the right and opportunity to make choices in our lives, we will never obtain full, first class American citizenship. This is why we are here today: to reassert these fundamental rights and lay claim to them as ours. (1989, p. 16)

But despite the apparent acceptance of this concept, the issue still remains: do Americans with disabilities now enjoy the right to self-determination, and if so, what limits, if any, to self-determination obtain? Does society believe that even if an individual cannot make the best decisions for him- or herself, that individual still has the right to make those decisions, no matter what the individual's mental abilities or physical capabilities might be? For example, is society willing to allow the individual who graduates from high school under alternative graduation criteria for students who received special education services to make the decision to attend college, even though the individual has no possible chance of success there? Or is society willing to allow a young couple with mental retardation to make the decision to have children?

Or does our society believe that some individuals must be protected from their own decisions and that society must be protected as well? Is societal responsibility a cover-up for society's unwillingness to allow all individuals with disabilities the right to self-determination? Do we believe that, to protect itself, society must assume greater responsibility for making decisions for others, particularly those with disabilities?

The ambivalence of society toward self-determination for all people can be seen in common special education practices. According to Taylor (1988), the concepts of least restrictive environment, cascade of services, and continuum of placements, although progressive when first proposed, do not provide necessary direction for the achievement of self-determination or independence and represent stumbling blocks to full inclusion of people with disabilities in all aspects of life. Taylor identified the following flaws in the least restrictive environment principle:

- The LRE principle favors less restriction in placements but implies that more restrictive environments are appropriate for some people. Principles and practices are not well developed for deciding when a more (or less) restrictive placement is appropriate for a particular person.

- The LRE principle confuses intensity of service with service environments. There is little evidence to support the assumption that certain types of services can be provided only in more segregated, more restrictive environments.

- The LRE principle is based on a model in which students have to demonstrate that they are "ready" for less restrictive placements before they can be placed in them. There is little evidence supporting the belief that more restrictive environments prepare people for life in less restrictive settings.

- The LRE principle supports professional decision making and limits how individuals participate in their own placement decisions. Appropriateness of a placement is more often based on professional judgments than on individual choices or desires.

- The LRE principle sanctions infringements on people's rights by focusing on acceptable amounts of restriction. Deciding that no measure of restriction would be appropriate supports rights currently enjoyed by people without disabilities.

- The LRE principle defines when movement should occur and ignores interpersonal relations of individuals. Friendships and a sense of community may be ignored if people must go to least restrictive environments simply because they are ready and the new settings are judged appropriate.

- The LRE principle directs attention to setting, rather than to services provided in programs. There is little evidence to support the equation of the restrictive nature of a program with the place in which it is provided.

These types of issues will continue to plague special education, education in general, and society as a whole. Americans must examine the extent to which they still limit the self-determination of others through legislation that excludes certain small businesses from the requirements for assuring accessibility to all, through policies that propose a national test for schools that systematically excludes most students served in special education, and through neighborhood restrictions on the presence of housing for individuals with various forms of disabilities. Americans will continue to struggle with issues surrounding the notions of social responsibility and the rights of all individuals to make choices for themselves.

Reform Versus Renewal

Will special education be different ten, twenty, or a hundred years from now? Nobody knows. Will national education goals and a continuing resurgence of interest in reform make a difference in how America's schools look in the future? Again, nobody knows. Based on historical analyses and the well-articulated views of some (see Glasser, 1990; Sarason, 1990), the answer is probably "not unless drastic reform changes how schools are structured and organized." Nevertheless, the future is not so bleak for professionals who believe that renewal should replace reform as the driving force in improving education.

McPherson (1991, p. 17) provided the following illustrations of how reform and renewal differ:

- Reform is for institutions; renewal is for individuals.
- Reform adds something new; renewal recaptures what already exists.
- Reform assumes blame; renewal begins with faith.
- Reform is imposed, often by groups outside education; renewal is contractual, an agreement between willing partners.
- Reform is for the many; renewal is for the one.
- Reform can be codified rather easily; renewal is difficult to describe.

For special education to prosper in the future, it is time for both reform and renewal to happen. Efforts at reform and renewal must be taken seriously, not swept aside as unnecessary or unprofessional. Whether reform or renewal captivates the ideals and actions of future special educators, there is plenty of hard work ahead, and the demand for quick, simple solutions that has captured the interest of many contemporary practitioners will probably be replaced by a sincere, realistic recognition that the forces of change move very slowly in education, one person at a time.

When we think about the future, we see the need for reform and renewal in several areas of practice. Clearly, conditions in general education require restructuring for special education to avoid destruction by the sheer numbers of students believed to need special services. We also think that systems for classifying and funding special education programs require radical reform. Finally, instructional practices require renewed attention if children and youths with special learning needs are to continue profiting from special education services.

SPECIAL EDUCATION AND THE FUTURE

During the last century, special education moved from a segregated, isolationist position to a position of prominence within America's educational system, responsible in large part for many interventions and practices that have changed the lives of individuals with disabilities and their families and friends. Four areas should continue to be addressed if special education is to enjoy similar success and have similar effects in the twenty-first century.

First, educators will have to expand their views on who will succeed in America's schools; the perspective of one educational system for all students will become more prominent. Similarly, the roles and expectations of personnel providing services to students with disabilities will have to expand, and boundaries between specific professionals responsible for special education will blur. To foster acceptance of all students and increased collaboration, special education practices of questionable efficacy will need to be altered; it will become increasingly unacceptable to exercise professional practice without concern for accountability, evidence, or outcomes. Concern for outcomes will expand professional interest in intervention. It will become unacceptable to place a student in special education for long periods without providing evidence that what happens in the name of special education is beneficial.

Educating All Children

Increased diversity has become a primary characteristic of American's schools, and education must be responsive to the growing needs of an increasingly diverse society. America's racial profile is rapidly changing. Between 1980 and 1990, the rate of increase in the population for white Americans was 6 percent, while the rate of increase for racial and ethnic minorities was much higher: 53 percent for Hispanics, 13.2 percent for African Americans, and 107.8 percent for Asians. At the century mark, almost 300 million people, nearly one of every three, is either African American, Hispanic, Asian American, or American Indian. As a group, minority children comprise an ever larger percentage of the public school student population, and schools require increasing modifications in their practices to meet their needs. At the same time, it has become increasingly apparent that many students from diverse cultural, linguistic, and racial backgrounds have been misidentified, misclassified, and misplaced in special education.

A popular solution to these problems is multicultural education:

An overall goal of multicultural education is to help all students develop their potential for academic, social, and vocational success. Educational and vocational options should not be limited by sex, age, ethnicity, native language, religion, class, or exceptionality. Educators are given the responsibility to help students contribute to, and benefit from, our democratic society. Within our pluralistic society, multicultural education values the existing diversity, positively portrays that diversity, and uses that diversity in the development of effective instructional categories for students in the classroom. In addition, multicultural education should help students think critically about institutionalized racism, classism, and sexism. (Gollnick & Chinn, 1990, p. iii)

Broadly conceived and practiced, multiculturalism is a pervasive force in modern society that supports the complexities of culture and illustrates the benefits of listening to multiple voices in moving society forward. As Obiakor and Utley (1997) pointed out, "The recognition of these multiple voices highlights multiple capabilities, competencies, and intelligences that individuals bring to classrooms, colleges, and communities" (p. 102).

Obiakor (1998) addressed issues and solutions related to multicultural education of exceptional learners. The perspective he presented has strong implications for improving educational opportunities for all students. It does not mean creating separate classrooms for each cultural group, nor does it mean creating different educational experiences for students from different cultural backgrounds. It *does* mean focusing education for all students on a few universal principles. According to Obiakor (1998), to educate multicultural learners, especially those with exceptionalities, educators must (1) understand the fundamentals of general and special education, (2) shift assessment and instructional paradigms, and (3) put practical perspectives on learned concepts.

Understanding Fundamentals of General and Special Education

The aims of multicultural education are very similar to those of general and special education. Whether students are in general or special education programs, teachers must (1) stimulate them intellectually by presenting novel ideas, (2) assist them in maximizing their full potential by understanding their strengths and weaknesses, (3) prepare them for the future by focusing on their positive energies, (4) create nurturing environments by empowering them, (5) collaborate and consult with their parents by regarding them as equal partners, and (6) provide support mechanisms for growth and development by becoming problem solvers. The idea must not be to create or give labels and hope that students match their labels, or that educational experiences are tailored to characteristics implied in the labels. The idea must be to educate all children for life (Debruyn, 1984).

For multicultural learners with exceptionalities, general and special educators must understand their multidimensional classroom, school, and community problems. These learners confront expectations that are counterproductive to their sacred existence as human beings (Banks, 1999; Obiakor, 1994; Siccone, 1995). They are frequently at risk of (1) misidentification, (2) discriminatory referral and assessment, (3) undue processes, (4) disempowerment, (5) misinstruction, and (6) improper inclusion/exclusion in educational programming

(Ford, Obiakor, & Patton, 1995; Grossman, 1998; Obiakor & Schwenn, 1995, 1996; Obiakor & Utley, 1997; Utley & Obiakor, 1997; Winzer & Mazurek, 1998). As Winzer and Mazurek indicated:

> Special education can no longer be concerned solely with the nature of a disabling condition and appropriate intervention strategies tailored for a particular disability. With the composition of the school-aged population shifting to encompass more students from culturally diverse backgrounds, bilingual homes, and economically disadvantaged families, the need for special services in the schools increases, and special educators must consider a broader range of characteristics that specifically include (but are certainly not restricted to) cultural and linguistic difference. Today and in the future, schools must develop programs, teaching methods, and resources to teach a diverse body and improve special education service delivery for exceptional learners from a wide variety of cultural and linguistic backgrounds. (p. 1)

Shifting Assessment and Instructional Paradigms

Multidimensional problems call for multidimensional solutions. There must be shifts in power and paradigms on how students are identified, assessed, placed, and instructed. It is dangerous to prejudge students' capabilities, strengths, and weaknesses. Gardner (1993) stated that general and special educators must "recognize and nurture all of the varied human intelligences, and all of the combinations of intelligences" (p. 12). They must begin early to create multicultural environments that build multidimensional self-concepts of students (Obiakor, 1994; Siccone, 1995). For example, Siccone suggested that a teacher ask him- or herself the following instructional questions:

- Am I tailoring my curriculum so that it is relevant to my students—their interests and ambitions as well as their cultural identity?

- Am I aware of my students' various learning styles, and do my teaching strategies reflect this awareness?

- Are the books and other materials I use reflective of diversity—ethnicity, culture, race, class, gender, age, [disability], and so forth?

- Are the images on the walls, bulletin boards, and so forth also reflective of diversity? (p. 187)

To shift paradigms, general and special educators must avoid illusory conclusions about multicultural students who look, learn, talk, and behave differently. They must authenticate their assessments by documenting students' behaviors in various learning and teaching situations. Such documentations must (1) be culturally sensitive (Hilliard, 1995; Midgette, 1995); (2) include nontraditional assessment methods such as work samples, student interviews, and student journals (Armstrong, 1994; Erickson, 1992; Karr & Wright, 1995; Mehring, 1996); and (3) be related to nonprejudicial instructions (Banks, 1999; Grossman, 1998; Obiakor, 1994, 1998). The perspective of one education for all students must become a reality.

Putting Practical Perspectives on Learned Concepts

General and special educators must practice what they preach. They must use divergent techniques to teach multicultural learners with exceptionalities. To look for the "magic pill" that can cure educational "problems" for multicultural learners is not realistic. Educators must be trained to value individual and cultural differences (Ford et al., 1995; Obiakor, 1994, 1997; Obiakor & Algozzine, 1995; Obiakor & Utley, 1997); they must be aware of the emotional first-aid needed to address crises confronting their students (Obiakor, Campbell-Whatley, Schwenn, & Dooley, 1998; Obiakor, Mehring, & Schwenn, 1997). In these areas, preservice and in-service programs can be very beneficial. It is unproductive to spend time bemoaning the existence of multicultural education as a new paradigm—this new paradigm can be taught, learned, and put into proper practical perspectives. In the words of Price (1991),

> I wonder, frankly, how we can bemoan the phenomena of tribalization and multi-culturalism in our society if we are doing so little to eliminate the economic and educational disparities which fuel them. The appropriate antidote for increased separatism is a culture of inclusiveness which would infuse every facet of our society. To my mind, the blame for balkanization rests more with those who have the power to include but won't, and less with those on the outside who are barred entry. (p. 8)

Efforts must be made to recruit, retain, graduate, and place individuals from diverse backgrounds to be successful in America's classrooms (Obiakor & Utley, 1997; Ward, 1996). Traditional models have failed to produce practitioners who understand the possible interactions between exceptionalities and cultural diversities. According to Obiakor and Utley, "[I]t is the professional responsibility of teacher educators to help prospective teachers expand their knowledge, beliefs, and attitudes toward people who differ from them" (p. 105).

It is common knowledge that poorly prepared teachers teach poorly. Even when people have acquired mastery over what they have been taught, they sometimes find it difficult to apply their skills productively. When multicultural students are taught by teachers who do not understand their cultures, symbols, or values, the whole concept of individualized educational programming fails. Additionally, when instructions lack practical pedagogical power and appear divorced from students' realities, the students suffer. As a consequence, general and special educators must (1) know who they are and who their students are, (2) learn the facts when they are in doubt, (3) change their way of thinking, (4) use resource persons (e.g., parents, guardians, and community members), (5) build self-concepts, (6) teach with multidimensional techniques, (7) make the right choices, and (8) continue to learn (see Obiakor, 1994). To make classroom teaching multicultural in special and general education programs, teachers must put the perspectives they have been taught into practice (Banks, 1999; Gay, 1992; Grossman, 1998).

An Ounce of Prevention Is Worth a Pound of Cure

About 3 to 5 percent of the school population is referred for special education each year, and most of the students who are referred end up in special education programs (Algozzine, Christenson, & Ysseldyke, 1982). If special education is to improve, changes in referral practices are essential. We wish to see the following changes:

- Special and general education teachers develop collaborative teaching models so students remain in general classes.

- Special and general education teachers develop prereferral intervention practices that work and use them so students remain in general classes.

- Special and general education teachers share responsibility for students with special learning needs.

In the best of all possible worlds, general and special education teachers work with all students. There is no reason for the skills of special education teachers to be applied only to students with disabilities. Similarly, the benefits of education with people without disabilities for students with special learning needs are widely accepted. There is no reason special areas of instruction such as sign language or study skills should be taught only to some students. Any student needs to learn what any other student needs to learn to be able to get along better in the world of the future. Just as it was judged unfair to segregate students of color in separate but equal facilities because of the stigma attached to separation and because of the deprivation of interaction with students of other backgrounds, it should be judged unfair to separate and restrict learning experiences on the basis of perceived need (unless the need is judged universal) or learning characteristics. There is no reason why special education and general education have to be organized and have to function as they do today. The models for collaborative teaching have simply not been clearly articulated, proposed, and practiced.

Referring students for placement in special education programs takes time and costs money. The extensiveness of referral practices controls an important instructional variable; that is, time spent gathering assessment data, waiting for assessment information, and making decisions is too often time spent not teaching students with special learning needs. But time spent developing, implementing, and modifying classroom instructional practices prior to referral is time well spent teaching students with special learning needs. If teachers believe that more education should be provided in general classrooms, the search for successful prereferral interventions will be more successful. Convincing them that this is how it should be will not be easy because for years they have been told that the right place for students with disabilities is outside the classroom in "special" environments.

Only by encouraging teachers to share responsibility for students with special learning needs will special education change from a separate but equal system to one that speaks for unitary interests and provides effective teaching in classrooms for all children. There is no reason why special education teachers cannot have homerooms just like those of other teachers. There is no reason why special education teachers have to teach only students with special learning needs. There is no reason why special education should be provided only after a student has been referred by a general classroom teacher.

An Ounce of Pretention Is Worth a Pound of Manure

There are more students classified with learning disabilities than any other category of special education. The practice continues despite convincing evidence that there is no defensible system for doing it. Similar controversies are evident for most categories of special education. Typically, the practice of classifying and labeling students is justified as a method of providing funding for students in need of special education. We think it is time to start viewing classification differently. We wish to see special and general educators call a moratorium on identification and classification practices and embrace alternative ways to fund special education and provide resources for students with special learning needs.

Considerable evidence exists to suggest that current identification and classification practices are biased. Students who meet criteria share many characteristics with students who do not meet criteria, just as students who are considered normal also share many of the same characteristics. The benefits of classifying students are generally valued more by the people who do the classifying than by the people who are classified. If professionals stop classifying students for at least a year, they may just find out that they can exist without doing it forever.

When the federal government develops a defense budget, it does so without regard for how many people have special learning needs. When universities develop budgets, they generally do so using past levels of funding and projected cost-of-living increases. It is not necessary to continue classifying students to justify special education funding. Using past levels of resource allocations and reasonable levels of yearly increases, administrators can develop reasonable federal, state, and local budgets that will include appropriate support for special education. In fact, when general education budget are developed, they are created without regard to the number of students who fit other categories (e.g., sex, race, geographic region). There is no reason why special education should be funded or provided *only after* a student has been classified.

An Ounce of Intervention Is Worth a Pound of Assure

A free appropriate education is guaranteed by federal law. Placing students in special education programs, however, does *not* guarantee or assure that they will receive free appropriate education. Receiving an individualized educational program does not either. Being placed in a special class does not guarantee that principles embodied in the least restrictive environment concept will be adhered to in the program that is provided there. We think it is time to start viewing intervention differently. We wish to see special and general education teachers demonstrate effective techniques when working with all children and youths.

Teaching is systematic presentation of content assumed necessary for mastery within an area of instruction. Effective teachers plan their instructional presentations based on their knowledge of what their students currently know. They manage their instructional presentations and modify their teaching based on feedback from their students. Whether they teach students with gifts and talents, mild disabilities, severe disabilities, or no disabilities, in preschool, elementary, secondary, or college programs, effective teachers plan, manage, deliver, and evaluate their instructional presentations. There is no magic here: good teaching is good teaching, and the best way to improve education is one person at a time.

Working together, educators can identify problems and point to areas needing solutions. Working individually, educators can make a difference. If every teacher changes the way students with special learning needs are treated, education will be improved. If 100 teachers change the way students with special learning needs are treated, education will be improved. If one teacher changes the way students with special learning needs are treated, education will be improved. It is time to think globally but act locally in efforts to improve education in general and special education in particular.

We end this book as another book was ended:

> We are reminded of the story of two frogs who fell into a cream can. They swam around for a while discussing the fact that it would be nearly impossible to get out of the can. One frog, bemoaning this fact, finally gave up, sank to the bottom of the can, and drowned. The other frog worked vigorously, swimming around the can so fast and so hard that the cream turned to butter, thereby giving the frog a "platform" from which to escape. (Ysseldyke & Algozzine, 1984, pp. 430–431)

We encourage you to do whatever you can to improve the practice of special education.

Discussion Questions

1. Some people believe that teachers are born, not made. They see few problems in allowing people with nontraditional education backgrounds to enter the teaching profession. What do you think?

2. What models have characterized societal attitudes toward people with disabilities? Do you think all people are capable of making their own decisions? What does the term *self-determination* mean to you?

3. What barriers control how teachers interact when providing special education services? What differences in elementary, middle, and high school exacerbate these problems?

4. What can be done to ensure that cultural differences are addressed appropriately in school assessment practices?

REFERENCES

Abeson, A., & Zettel, J. (1977). The end of the quiet revolution: The Education for All Handicapped Children Act of 1975. *Exceptional Children, 44,* 115–128.

Abikoff, H. (1991). Cognitive training in ADHD children: Less to it than meets the eye. *Journal of Learning Disabilities, 24,* 205–209.

Adler, J. (1998, November 2). "Tomorrow's child." *Newsweek,* pp. 54–64.

Administration on Developmental Disabilities. (1988). *Mapping the future for children with special needs: P.L. 99-457.* Des Moines: University of Iowa.

Agran, M. (Ed.) (1997). *Student-directed learning: Teaching self-determination skills.* Pacific Grove, CA: Brooks/Cole.

Alberto, P. A., & Troutman, A. C. (1986). *Applied behavior analysis for teachers* (2nd ed.). Columbus, OH: Merrill.

Alexander, K. L., Entwisle, D. R., & Dauber, S. L. (1994). *On the success of failure: A reassessment of the effects of retention in the primary grades.* Cambridge, England: Cambridge University Press.

Algozzine, B. (1991). Observations to accompany analyses of the tenth annual report to Congress. *Exceptional Children, 57,* 217–275.

Algozzine, B. (1992). *Behavior problem management: Educator's resource service-revised.* Gaithersburg, MD: Aspen Publishers.

Algozzine, B., & Algozzine, K. (1990). *Help identifying gifted and high-achieving students (HIGHS): Examiner's manual.* Charlotte, NC: Decision Products.

Algozzine, B., Christenson, S., & Ysseldyke, J. E. (1982). Probabilities associated with the referral to placement process. *Teacher Education and Special Education, 5*(3), 19–23.

Algozzine, B., Morsink, C. V., & Algozzine, K. M. (1988). What's happening in self-contained special education classrooms? *Exceptional Children, 55,* 259–265.

Algozzine, B., Salvia, J., & Ysseldyke, J. (1984). Who should teach the difficult-to-teach students? *Educators Forum, 6,* 4–5.

Algozzine, B., Schmid, R., & Mercer, C. D. (1981). *Childhood behavior disorders: Applied research and educational practice.* Rockville, MD: Aspen Systems.

Algozzine, B., & Ysseldyke, J. E. (1983). Learning disabilities as a subset of school failure: The oversophistication of a concept. *Exceptional Children, 50,* 242–246.

Algozzine, B., & Ysseldyke, J. E. (1986). The future of the LD field: Screening and diagnosis. *Journal of Learning Disabilities, 19,* 394–398.

Algozzine, B., & Ysseldyke, J. E. (1987). In defense of different numbers. *Remedial and Special Education, 8*(2), 53–56.

Algozzine, B., Ysseldyke, J. E., & Elliott, J. L. (1997). *Strategies and tactics for effective instruction.* (2nd ed.). Longmont, CO: Sopris West.

Algozzine, B., Ysseldyke, J. E., & McGue, M. (1995). Differentiating low-achieving students: Thoughts on setting the record straight. *Learning Disabilities Research & Practice, 10*(3), 140–144.

Allington, R. L., & McGill-Franzen, A. (1989). Different programs, indifferent instruction. In D. K. Lipsky & A. Gartner (Eds.), *Beyond separate education: Quality education for all* (pp. 75–97). Baltimore, MD: Brookes.

Almond, P., Tindal, G., & Stieber, S. (1997). *Linking inclusion to conclusions: An empirical study of participation of students with disabilities in statewide testing programs* (State Assessment Series, Oregon Report 1). Minneapolis, MN: University of Minnesota, National Center on Educational Outcomes.

American Association of Colleges for Teacher Education. (1991). Teacher education programs eliminated in Oregon budget cuts. *AACTE Briefs, 12*(4), 1–2.

American Association on Mental Retardation. (1992). *Mental retardation: Definition, classification, and systems of supports* (9th ed.). Washington, DC: Author.

American Council on Education. (1998). *Who took the GED? GED 1997 statistical report.* Washington, DC: Author.

American Educational Research Association (AERA), American Psychological Association (APA), and National Council on Measurement in Education (NCME). (1985). *Standards for Educational and Psychological Testing.* Washington, DC: American Psychological Association.

American Federation of Teachers. (1997a). *Making standards matter 1997.* Arlington, VA: Author.

American Federation of Teachers. (1997b). *Passing on failure: District promotion policies and practices.* Arlington, VA: Author.

American Psychiatric Association. (1979). *Diagnostic and statistical manual of mental disorders (DSM III).* Washington, DC: Author.

American Psychiatric Association. (1982). *Diagnostic and statistical manual of mental disorders* (3rd ed.). Washington, DC: Author.

American Psychiatric Association. (1994). *Diagnostic and statistical manual of mental disorders* (4th ed., DSM-IV). Washington, DC: Author.

Anderson, E. L., Seaton, K., Dinas, P., & Satterfield, A. (1995). *Group action planning: An innovative manual for building a self-determined future.* Lawrence, KS: Full Citizenship.

Anderson, L. (1995). *An evaluation of state and local efforts to serve the educational needs of homeless children and youth*. Washington, DC: United States Department of Education.

Angoff, W. H., & Ford, S. F. (1971). *Item-race interaction on a test of scholastic aptitude*. Princeton, NJ: Educational Testing Service.

Annie E. Casey Foundation. (1998a). *1998 kids count: A pocket guide on America's youth*. Baltimore, MD: Author.

Annie E. Casey Foundation. (1998b). *1998 kids count data book: Overview*. Baltimore, MD: Author.

Annie E. Casey Foundation. (1998c). *1998 kids count data book: State profiles of child well-being*. Baltimore, MD: Author.

Armstrong, T. (1994). *Multiple intelligences in the classroom*. Alexandria, VA: Association for Supervision and Curriculum Development.

Arter, J. A., & Jenkins, J. R. (1979). Differential diagnosis—prescriptive teaching: A critical appraisal. *Review of Educational Research, 49,* 517–556.

Asch, A. (1984). Personal reflections. *American Psychologist, 39,* 551–552.

Asch, A. (1989). Has the law made a difference? What some disabled students have to say. In D. K. Lipsky & A. Gartner (Eds.), *Beyond separate education: Quality education for all* (pp. 181–205). Baltimore, MD: Brookes.

Aspel, N., Bettis, G., Test, D. W., & Wood, W. M. (in press). An evaluation of a comprehensive system of transition services. *Career Development for Exceptional Individuals*.

Association for Persons with Severe Handicaps. (1981). Resolution on intrusive interventions. *TASH Newsletter, 7,* 1–2.

Badon, J. (1982). The psychology of school psychology. In C. R. Reynolds & T. B. Gutkin (Eds.), *The Handbook of school psychology* (pp. 3–14). New York: Wiley.

Baer, D., & Bushell, D. (1981) The future of behavior analysis in the school? Consider its recent past, and then ask a different question [Special issue]. *School Psychology Review, 10*(2).

Bailey, D. B. (1989). Issues and directions in preparing professionals to work with young handicapped children and their families. In J. J. Gallagher, P. L. Trohanis, & R. M. Clifford (Eds.), *Policy implementation & PL 99-457: Planning for young children with special needs* (pp. 97–132). Baltimore, MD: Brookes.

Bailey, D. B. (1994). Working with families of children with special needs. In M. Wolery & J. S. Wilbers (Eds.), *Including children with special needs in early childhood programs* (pp. 23–44). Washington, DC: National Association for the Education of Young Children.

Ball, D. L. (1993). With an eye on the mathematical horizon. Dilemmas of teaching elementary school mathematics. *Elementary School Journal, 93,* 373–397.

Banks, J. A. (1999). *An introduction to multicultural education* (2nd ed.). Boston, MA: Allyn and Bacon.

Barabasz, M., & Barabasz, A. (1996). Attention deficit disorder: Diagnosis, etiology and treatment. *Child Study Journal, 26*(1), 1–36.

Bardon, J. (1982). The psychology of school psychology. In C. R. Reynolds & T. B. Gutkin (Eds.), *The handbook of school psychology* (pp. 3–14). New York: Wiley.

Bardon, J. (1991). Keynote Address at North Carolina Association of School Psychologists. Atlantic Beach, NC, October, 1991.

Barnes, D. M. (1986). Brain function decline in children with AIDS. *Science, 232,* 1196.

Barnes, K. E. (1982). *Preschool screening: The measurement and prediction of children at risk.* Springfield: IL: Thomas.

Baron, J. B. (1990, October). Use of alternative assessments in state assessment: The Connecticut experience. Paper presented at the OERI conference on *The promise and peril of alternative assessment.* Washington, DC: Office of Educational Research and Improvement.

Barrett, M. J. (1990, November). The case for more school days. *The Atlantic,* pp. 78–106.

Bayley, N. (1965). Consistency and variability in the growth of intelligence from birth to 18 years. *Journal of Genetic Psychology, 75,* 96.

Beach Center on Family Disabilities (1995).

Beavers, J. (1989). Physical and cognitive handicaps. In L. Combrinck-Graham (Ed.), *Children in family contexts: Perspectives on treatment.* New York: Guilford.

Bechtold, E. (1989). Doing what works. In T. Vandercook, S. Wolff, & J. York (Eds.), *Learning together . . . Stories and strategies* (p. 36). Minneapolis, MN: Institute on Community Integration, University of Minnesota.

Becker, G., & Jauregui, J. (1985). The invisible isolation of deaf women: Its effect on social awareness. In M. Degan & N. Brooks (Eds.), *Women and disability: The double handicap* (pp. 23–26). New Brunswick, NJ: Transaction.

Behrmann, J. (1990). Caring for and educating the children of drug-using mothers: A challenge for society and schools in the 1990s. *Counterpoint, 11*(2), 15.

Beirne-Smith, M., & Deck, M. D. (1989). A survey of postsecondary programs for students with learning disabilities. *Journal of Learning Disabilities, 22,* 456–457.

Beirne-Smith, M. Ittenbach, R. F., & Patton, J. R. (1998). *Mental retardation* (5th ed.). Upper Saddle River, NJ: Prentice-Hall.

Bennis, W. G., Benne, K. D., & Chin, R. (Eds.). (1969). *The planning of change* (2nd ed.). New York: Holt, Rinehart and Winston.

Benz, M. R., & Halpern, A. S. (1987). Transition services for secondary students with mild disabilities: A statewide perspective. *Exceptional Children, 53,* 507–514.

Bereiter, C. (1969). The future of individual differences. *Harvard Educational Review, 39,* 162–170.

Berkel, D., & Gaylord-Ross, R. (1989). The concept of transition: Historical and current developments. In D. E. Berkell & J. M. Brown (Eds.), *Transition from school to work for persons with disabilities* (pp. 1-21). New York: Longman.

Berlin, G., & Duhl, J. (1984). *Educational equity and economic excellence: The critical role of second chance and basic skills and job training programs.* New York: Ford Foundation.

Berman, C., & Lourie, I. S. (1988). Mental health issues in early intervention programs. *OSERS News in Print, 1*(4), 9.

Bernoff, L. (1981). *Early school leavers: High school students who left school before graduating, 1979–1980* (Publication No. 404). Los Angeles: Unified School District, Research and Evaluation Branch.

Berry, G. L., & Lopez, C. A. (1977). Testing programs and the Spanish-speaking child: Assessment guidelines for school counselors. *School Counselor, 24,* 261–269.

Bersoff, D. N. (1979). Regarding psychologists testily: Legal regulation of psychological assessment in the public schools. *Maryland Law Review, 39,* 27–120.

Bijou, S. W. (1971). Environment and intelligence: A behavioral analysis. In R. Cancro (Ed.), *Intelligence: Genetic and environmental contributions.* New York: Grune and Stratton.

Biklen, D. (1989). Redefining education. In D. Biklen, D. L. Ferguson, & A. Ford (Eds.), *Schooling and disability* (pp. 1–24). Chicago: National Society for the Study of Education.

Biklen, D., Ferguson, D. L., & Ford, A. (1989). *Schooling and disability: Eighty-eighth yearbook of the National Society for the Study of Education* (pp. 1–24). Chicago: University of Chicago Press.

Biklen, D., Ford, A., & Ferguson, D. L. (1989). Elements of integration. In D. Biklen, D. L. Ferguson, & A. Ford (Eds.), *Schooling and disability: Eighty-eighth yearbook of the National Society for the Study of Education* (pp. 256–272). Chicago: University of Chicago Press.

Binet, A., & Simon, T. (1916). *The development of intelligence in children.* Baltimore, MD: Williams and Wilkins.

Bishop, J. H. (1997). *Do curriculum-based external exit exam systems enhance student achievement?* (Paper #97-28). Ithaca, NY: Cornell University, Center for Advanced Resource Studies.

Bishop, K. K. (1988). Maternal and child health activities for 0–5 year olds: An overview. *OSERS News in Print, 1*(4), 8.

Blackman, H. P. (1989). Special education placement: Is it what you know or where you live? *Exceptional Children, 55,* 459–462.

Blackorby, J., & Wagner, M. (1996). Longitudinal postschool outcomes of youth with disabilities: Findings from the National Longitudinal Transition Study. *Exceptional Children, 62,* 399–413.

Blair, C., & Ramey, C. T. (1997). Early intervention for low-birth-weight infants and the path to second-generation research. In M. J. Guralnick (Ed.), *The effectiveness of early intervention* (pp. 77–97). Baltimore: Paul H. Brookes.

Bloom, B. (1964). *Stability and change in human characteristics.* New York: Wiley.

Bodner, J. R., Clark G. M., & Mellard, D. F. (1987). *State graduation policies and program practices related to high school special education programs: A national study.* Lawrence: University of Kansas, Department of Special Education. (ERIC Document Reproduction Service No. ED 294 347)

Bogdan, R., & Kugelmass, J. (1984). Case studies of mainstreaming: A symbolic interactionist approach to special schooling. In L. Barton & S. Tomlinson (Eds.), *Special education and social interests* (pp. 83–97). London: Croom Helm.

Bogdan, R., & Taylor, S. (1976). The judged, not the judges: An insider's view of mental retardation. *American Psychologist, 31,* 47–52.

Bond, L., Roeber, E., & Connealy, S. (1998). *Trends in state student assessment programs: Fall 1997.* Washington, DC: Council of Chief State School Officers.

Bower, E. M. (1969). *Early identification of emotionally handicapped children in school* (2nd ed.). Springfield, IL: Charles C. Thomas.

Bower, E. M. (1982). *Early identification of emotionally handicapped children in school* (3rd ed.). Springfield, IL: Thomas.

Boyd, W. L., & Walberg, H. J. (Eds). (1990). *Choice in education: Potential and problems.* Berkeley, CA: McCutchan.

Boyer, E. L. (1983). *High school: A report on American secondary education.* Princeton, NJ: Carnegie Foundation for the Advancement of Teaching.

Braaten, S., Kauffman, J. M., Braaten, B., Polsgrove, L., & Nelson, C. M. (1988). The regular education initiative: Patent medicine for behavioral disorders. *Exceptional Children, 55,* 21–28.

Bracy, G. W. (1998, November). Better than ever: Grade inflation and the extinction of the .400 hitter. *American School Board Journal, 185*(11), 50–51.

Braddock, J. H., & McPartland, J. M. (1993). Education of early adolescents. *Review of Research in Education 19,* 135–170.

Bradley, A. (1990, October 3). Goals for urban schools offered by boards group. *Education Week,* p. 10.

Brandt, R. (1989). On parents and schools: A conversation with Joyce Epstein. *Educational Leadership, 47*(2), 24–27.

Brantlinger, E. (1997). Using ideology: Cases of nonrecognition of the politics of research and practice in special education. *Review of Educational Research, 67,* 425–459.

Bredekamp, S., & Copple, C. (Eds.). (1997). *Developmentally appropriate practice in early childhood programs* (rev. ed.). Washington, DC: National Association for the Education of Young Children.

Bricker, D. (1989). Essential features for early intervention programs in the 1990's. *Intitute on Community Integration IMPACT, 2*(2), 4–5.

Bricker, D. D., Bruder, M. B., & Bailey, E. (1982). Developmental integration of preschool children. *Analysis and Intervention in Developmental Disabilites, 2,* 207–222.

Bricker, D., & Cripe, J. J. W. (1992). *An activity-based approach to early intervention.* Baltimore: Brookes.

Bricker, D., & Slentz, K. (1989). Personnel preparation: Handicapped infants. In M. C. Wang, H. J. Walberg, & M. C. Reynolds (Eds.), *The handbook of special education research and practice* (Vol. 3, pp. 319–346). Oxford: Pergamon.

Brightman, A. J. (1984). *Ordinary moments: The disabled experience.* Baltimore, MD: University Park Press.

Brolin, D. E., & Schatzman, B. (1989). Lifelong career development. In D. E. Berkell & J. M. Brown (Eds.), *Transition from school to work for persons with disabilities* (pp. 22–41). New York: Longman.

Brooks-Gunn, J., Denner, J., & Klebanov, P. (1994). Families and neighborhoods as contexts for education. In E. Flaxman & A. Harry Passow (Eds.), *Changing populations changing schools* (pp. 233–252). Chicago: National Society for the Study of Education.

Broudy, H. S. (1978). Conflicts in school programs. *Today's Education, 67,* 24–27.

Brown, D. T. (1979). Issues in accreditation, certification, and licensure. In G. Phye & D. Reschly (Eds.), *School psychology: Perspectives and issues* (pp. 88–116). New York: Academic.

Brown, L., & York, R. (1974). Developing programs for severly handicapped students: Teacher training and classroom instruction. In L. Brown, W. Williams, & T. Crowder (Eds.), *A collection of papers and programs related to public school services for severely handicapped students* (pp. 1–18). Madison, WI: Madison Public Schools.

Bruininks, R. H., Thurlow, M. L., Lewis, D. R., & Larson, N. W. (1988). Post school outcomes for students in special education and other students one to eight years after high school. In R. H. Bruininks, D. R. Lewis, & M. L. Thurlow (Eds.), *Assessing outcomes, costs and benefits of special education programs* (pp. 9–111). Minneapolis: University of Minnesota, University Affiliated Programs.

Bryant, D. M., Burchinal, M., Lau, L. B., & Sparling, J. J. (1994). Family and classroom correlates of Head Start children's developmental outcomes. *Early Childhood Research Quarterly, 9,* 289–309.

Bryant, D., & Maxwell, K. (1997). The effectiveness of early intervention for disadvantaged children. In M. J. Guralnick (ed.), *The effectiveness of early intervention* (pp. 23–46). Baltimore, MD: Paul H. Brookes.

Burcham, B. G., & Carlson, L. B. (1994). Attention deficit disorder: School-based practices. In Chesapeake Institute, *Executive summaries of research syntheses and promising practices on the practices on the education of children with attention deficit disorder* (pp. 43–51). Washington, DC: Chesapeake Institute.

Burke, J. (1996, April 3). "National standards for English: The importance of being vague." *Educational Week, 15*(28), 35.

Burstein, L. (1989). *NESAC outcomes subcommittee: Idea paper.* Washington, DC: National Forum on Educational Statistics Committee.

Butler-Nalin, P., Marder, C., & Shaver, D. M. (1989). *Making the transition: An explanatory model of special education students' participation in post-secondary education.* Menlo Park, CA: SRI.

Byers, J. (1989). AIDS in children: Effects on neurological development and implications for the future. *Journal of Special Education, 23,* 5–16.

Cahir, W. J. (1997, July 17). "Individuals with disabilities education act analysis" (Special Supplement). *Education Weeek, 30*(137), pp. 1–28.

Cahir, W. J. (1998, April 13). "IDEA rules mandates IEP rewrites, clarify suspensions" (Special Supplement). *Education Daily, 31*(70).

California State Department of Education. (1986). *California Dropouts. A status report.* Sacramento: CA.

Callahan, R. E. (1961). *An introduction to education in American society.* New York: Knopf.

Can Ivan read better than Johnny? (1961, May 27). *Saturday Evening Post,* pp. 30–33.

Cantwell, D. P. (1996). Attention deficit disorder: A review of the past 10 years. *Journal of the American Academy of Child and Adolescent Psychiatry, 35*(8), 978–987.

Cantwell, D. P., & Baker, L. (1991). Association between attention deficit-hyperactivity disorder and learning disorders. *Journal of Learning Disabilities, 24,* 88–95.

Carlberg, J., & Kavale, K. (1980). The efficacy of special versus regular class placement for exceptional children: A metaanalysis. *The Journal of Special Education, 14,* 294–309.

Carmichael Olson, H., & Burgess, D. M, (1997). Early intervention for children prenatally exposed to alcohol and other drugs. In M. J. Guralnick (Ed.), *The effectiveness of early intervention* (pp. 109–145). Baltimore: Paul H. Brookes.

Carnegie Council on Adolescent Development. (1989). *Turning points: Preparing American youth for the 21st century.* New York: Carnegie.

Carnegie Forum on Education and the Economy. (1986). *A nation prepared: Teachers for the twenty-first century.* New York: Carnegie Corporation.

Carnevale, A. P., Gainer, L. J., & Meltzer, A. S. (1988). *Workplace basics: The skills employers want.* Alexandria, VA: American Society for Training and Development, U.S. Department of Labor, Employment, and Training Administration.

Carpenter, D. (1985). Grading handicapped pupils: Review and position statement. *Remedial and Special Education, 6*(4), 54–59.

Carpenter, D., & Grantham, L. B. (1985). A statewide investigation of grading practices and opinions concerning mainstreamed handicapped pupils. *Diagnostique, 11*(10), 31–39.

Carpenter, D., Grantham, L. B., & Hardister, M. P. (1983). Grading mainstreamed handicapped pupils: What are the issues? *Journal of Special Education, 17*(2), 183–188.

Carta, J. L., Atwater, J. B., Schwartz, I. S., & McConnell, S. R. (1993). Developmentally appropriate practices and early childhood special education: A reaction to Johnson and McChesney Johnson. *Topics in Early Childhood Special Education, 13,* 243–254.

Carter, J., & Sugai, G. (1989). Survey on prereferral practices: Responses from state departments of education. *Exceptional Children, 55,* 298–302.

Casto, G., & Mastropieri, M. A. (1986). The efficacy of early intervention programs for handicapped children: A meta-analysis. *Exceptional Children, 52,* 417-424.

Catterall, J. S. (1988). *Dropping out of school in the north central region of the United States: Costs and consequences.* Los Angeles: North Central Regional Educational Laboratory.

Center, D. B. (1990). Social maladjustment: An interpretation. *Behavioral Disorders, 15*(3). 141–148.

Center for Civic Education. (1994) *National standards for civics and government.* Calabasas, CA: Author.

Center for Educational Reform. (1998). *A nation still at risk: An education manifesto.* Washington, DC: Author.

Center for Peak Performing Schools (1993). *Improving student performance: New strategies for implementing higher standards.* Greeley, CO: Author.

Center for Policy Research. (1996). *What will it take? Standards-based education reform for all students.* Alexandria, VA: Author.

Centers for Disease Control. (1987a). Classification system for human immunodeficiency virus (HIV) infection in children under 13 years of age. *Morbidity and Mortality Weekly Report, 36,* 225–230.

Centers for Disease Control. (1987b). Human immunodeficiency virus infection in the United States: A review of current knowledge. *Morbidity and Mortality Weekly Report, 36* (Suppl. S-6), 1–19.

Chadsey-Rusch, J., & Heal, L. (1995). Building consensus from transition experts on social integration and outcomes. *Exception Children, 62,* 165–186.

Chadsey-Rusch, J., Rusch, F. R., & O'Reilly, M. F. (1991). Transition from school to integrated communities. *Remedial and Special Education, 12,* 22–33.

Chambers, J. G., Parrish, T. B., Lieberman, J. C., & Wolman, J. M. (1998). What are we spending on special education in the U.S.? CSEF Brief No. 8. Palo Alto, CA: Center for Special Education Finance, American Institutes for Research.

Chandler, J. N. (1983). Making the grade. *Journal of Learning Disabilities, 16,* 241–242.

Charner, I., Fraser, B. S., Hubbard, S., Rogers, A., & Horne, R. (1995). Reforms of the school-to-work transition: Findings, implications, and challenges. *Phi Delta Kappan, 40,* 58–59.

Children's Defense Fund (1994). *The state of America's children 1994.* Washington, DC: Author.

Children with Attention Deficit Disorders. (1988). *Attention deficit disorders: A guide for teachers.* Plantation, FL: Author.

Christenson, S. L. (1990). Differences in students' home environments: The need to work with families. *School Psychology Review, 19,* 505–517.

Christenson, S. L., Thurlow, M. L., & Ysseldyke, J. E. (1987). *Instructional effectiveness research: Implications for effective instruction of handicapped students* (Monograph No. 4). Minneapolis: University of Minnesota, Institute for Research on Learning Disabilities.

Christenson, S. L., & Ysseldyke, J. E. (1989). Assessing student performance: An important change is needed. *Journal of School Psychology, 27,* 409–426.

Christenson, S. L., Ysseldyke, J. E., & Thurlow, M. L., (1987). *Instructional psychology and models of school learning: Implications for effective instruction of handicapped students* (Monograph No. 2). Minneapolis: University of Minnesota, Institute for Research on Learning Disabilities.

Christenson, S. L., Ysseldyke, J. E., & Thurlow, M. L. (1989). Critical instructional factors for students with mild handicaps: An integrative review. *Remedial and Special Education, 10,* 21–31.

Cipollone, A. (1986). *The unity of school dropout literature for comprehensive high schools,* Unpublished manuscript.

Cline, D. H. (1990). A legal analysis of policy initiatives to exclude handicapped/disruptive students from special education. *Behavioral Disorders, 15*(3), 159–173.

Cobb, R. B., & Neubert, D. A. (1998). Vocational education: Emerging vocationalism. In F. R. Rusch & J. G. Chadsey (Eds.), *Beyond high school: Transition from school to work* (pp. 101–126). Belmont, CA: Wadsworth.

Cohen, D. L. (1991, April 17). Expressing 'alarm' N.A.E.S.P. votes to oppose retaining pupils in grade. *Education Week,* p. 4.

Cohen, H. J., Grosz, J., Ayoob, K., & Schoen, S. (1997). Early intervention for children with HIV infection. In M. J. Guralnick (Ed.), *The effectiveness of early intervention* (pp. 193–206). Baltimore: Paul H. Brookes.

Cohen, S. A. (1976). The fuzziness and the flab: Some solutions to research problems in learning disabilities. *Journal of Special Education, 10,* 129–136.

Cohen, S., Semmes, M., & Guralnick, M. J. (1979). Public Law 94-142 and the education of preschool children. *Exceptional Children, 45,* 279–285.

Cohn, S. J., Cohn, C. M., & Kanevsky, L. S. (1988). Giftedness and talent. In E. W. Lynch & R. B. Lewis (Eds.), *Exceptional children and adults: An introduction to special education* (pp. 456–501). Glenview, IL: Scott Foresman.

Coleman, M. (1986). *Behavior disorders: Theory and practice.* Englewood Cliffs, NJ: Prentice-Hall.

Coleman, M., & Apts, S. (1991). Home-alone risk factors. *Teaching Exceptional Children, 23,* 36–38.

College Board. (1983). *Academic preparation for college: What students need to know and be able to do.* New York: Educational Equality Project.

Colopy, K. W., & Tarr, H. C. (1994). *Minnesota's public school choice options.* Washington, DC: Policy Study Associates. (ERIC Reproduction Service No. ED 376 585).

Committee for Economic Development. (1985). *Investing in our children: Business and the public schools.* New York: Author.

Committee for Economic Development. (1987). *Children in need: Investment strategies for the educationally disadvantaged.* New York: Author.

Committee for Economic Development. (1991). *The unfinished agenda: A new vision for child development and education.* Washington, DC: Author.

Comptroller General. (1981). *Disparities still exist in who gets special education.* Washington, DC: General Accounting Office.

Congressional Budget Office. (1987). *Educational achievement: Explanations and implications of recent trends.* Washington, DC: Author.

Connecticut Department of Education. (1988). *Plan for statewide evaluation of special education programs.* Hartford, CT: Author.

Consortium of National Arts Education Associations. (1994). *National standards for arts education: What every young American should know and be able to do in the arts.* Reston, VA: Music Educators National Conference.

Cookson, P. W., & Shroff, S. M. (1997). *School choice and urban school reform* (Urban Diversity Series No. 110). New York: Columbia University, Institute for Urban and Minority Education.

Copperman, P. (1978). *The literacy hoax: The decline of reading, writing and learning in the public schools and what we can do about it.* New York: Morrow.

Correa, V., & Weismantel, J. (1991). Multicultural issues related to families with an exceptional child. In M. J. Fine (Ed.), *Collaboration with parents of exceptional children* (pp. 83–102). Brandon, VT: Clinical Psychology Publishing Company.

Council for Children with Behavior Disorders. (1990a). Position paper on the provision of service to children with conduct disorder. *Behavioral Disorders, 15*(3), 180–189.

Council for Children with Behavior Disorders. (1990b). Position paper on the use of behavior reduction strategies with children with behavioral disorders. *Behavioral Disorders, 15,* 225–260.

Council for Exceptional Children. (1995). Record number of special education students served in 1993–94. *CEC Today, 2*(6), 1, 5.

Council for Exceptional Children. (1995). *What every special educator must know: The international standards for the preparation and certification of special education teachers.* Reston, VA: Author.

Council for Exceptional Children. (1990). *Policy manual,* Sections 8.315 and 8.316. Reston, VA: Council for Exceptional Children.

Council of Chief State School Officers. (1990). State education indicators: 1989. Washington, DC: Author.

Council of Chief State School Officers. (1994). *Building a system to connect school and employment.* Washington, DC: Author.

Crack babies in preschool suggest problems ahead for schools. (1990). *Counterpoint, 11*(1), 7.

Creech, J. D. (1990). *Educational benchmarks.* Atlanta: Southern Regional Education Board.

Criswell, E. (1981). Behavioral perspective of emotional disturbance. In B. Algozzine, R. Schmid, & C. D. Mercer (Eds.), *Childhood behavior disorders: Applied research and educational practice* (pp. 113–143). Rockville, MD: Aspen Systems.

Cromwell, R. L., Blashfield, R. K., & Strauss, J. S. (1975). Criteria for classification systems. In N. Hobbs (Ed.), *Issues in the classification of children* (Vol. 1, pp. 4–25). San Francisco: Jossey-Bass.

Cronbach, L. J. (1969). Heredity, environment, and educational policy. *Harvard Educational Review, 39,* 190–199.

Cronbach, L. J., Ambron, S. R., Dornbusch, S. M., Hess, R. D., Hornik, R. C., Phillips, D. C., Walker, D. F., & Weiner, S. S. (1980). *Toward reform of program evaluation: Aims, methods, and institutional arrangements.* San Francisco, CA: Jossey-Bass.

Cronbach, L. J., Furby, L. (1970). How should we measure "change"—or should we? *Psychological Bulletin, 74,* 68–80.

Cross, C. (1990, October). Paper presented at the OERI conference on the promise and peril of alternative assessment. Washington, DC: Office of Educational Research and Improvement.

Cruickshank, W. M. (1977). Least restrictive placement: Administrative wishful thinking. *Journal of Learning Disabilities, 10*(4), 193–194.

Cuban, L. (1990). Four stories about national goals for American education. *Phi Delta Kappan, 72,* 265–271.

Cubberley, E. P. (1922). *A brief history of education.* Boston: Houghton Mifflin.

Cubberley, E. P. (1934). *Readings in public education in the United States.* Boston: Houghton Mifflin.

Curtis, M. J., & Batsche, G. M. (1991). Meeting the needs of children and families: Opportunities and challenges for school psychology training programs. *School Psychology Review, 20,* 565–577.

D'Alonzo, D. (1996). Identification and education of students with attention deficit and attention deficit hyperactivity disorders. *Preventing School Failure, 40*(2), 88–94.

Daniel, P. T. R. (1997). Educating students with disabilities in the Least Restrictive Environment, *Journal of Educational Administration, 35*(5), 397–410.

Danielson, L. C., & Bellamy, G. T. (1989). State variation in placement of children with handicaps in segregated environments. *Exceptional Children, 55,* 448–455.

Darling-Hammond, L. (1990). Achieving our goals: Superficial or structural reforms. *Phi Delta Kappan, 72,* 286–295.

Davies, S. P. (1976). The institution in relation to the school system. In M. Rosen, G. R. Clarke, & M. S. Kivitz (Eds.), *The history of mental retardation* (pp. 225–239). Baltimore, MD: University Park Press.

Davis, J. (1989). The regular education initiative: What professionals think. Unpublished doctoral dissertation, Michigan State University.

Davis, J. C., & Maheady, L. (1990). *The regular education initiative: What do three groups of educational professionals think?* Manuscript submitted for publication.

DeBruyn, R. L. (1984, April 16). Upholding the tenets of education. *The Master Teacher, 15,* 1.

Degan, M., & Brooks, N. (1985). Introduction—women and disability: The double handicap. In M. Degan & N. Brooks (Eds.), *Women and disability: The double handicap* (pp. 1–5). New Brunswick, NJ: Transaction.

Deming, W. E. (1982). *Out of the crisis.* Cambridge, MA: MIT, Center for Advanced Engineering.

Deno, E. (1970). Special education as developmental capital. *Exceptional Children, 37,* 229–240.

Deno, S. L. (1986). Formative evaluation of individual student programs: A new role for school psychologists. *School Psychology Review, 153,* 358–374.

Deno, S., & Mirkin, P. (1977). *Data-based program modification: A manual.* Reston, VA: Council for Exceptional Children.

Deshler, D. D., & Schumaker, J. B. (1988). An instructional model for teaching students how to learn. In J. L. Graden, J. E. Zins, & M. J. Curtis (Eds.), *Alternative educational delivery systems: Enhancing educational options for all students* (pp. 391–412). Silver Spring, MD: National Association of School Psychologists.

DeWeerd, J., & Cole, A. (1976). Handicapped children's early childhood program. *Exceptional Children, 43,* 155–157.

DeYoung, A. J., Huffman, K., & Turner, M. E. (1989). Dropout issues and problems in rural America, with a case study of one central Appalachian school district. In L. Weiss, E. Farrar, & H. G. Petrie (Eds.), *Dropouts from school: Issues, dilemmas, and solutions* (pp. 55–77). Albany: State University of New York Press.

Diegmueller, K. (1994, March 30). "English group loses funding for standards," *Education Week, 13*(27), pp. 1, 9.

Diegmueller, K. (1995, October 18). "Revise history standards, two panels advise." *Education Week, 15*(7), pp. 1, 11.

Diegmueller, K., & Viadero, D. (1995, November 15). "A short history of the standards." *Education Week, 15*(11), pp. 31, 33.

Dix, D. (1976). Memorial to the legislature of Massachusetts. In M. Rosen, G. R. Clark, & M. S. Kivitz (Eds.), *The history of mental retardation* (Vol. 1, pp. 47–58). Baltimore, MD: University Park Press.

Doll, E. (1924). Current problems in mental diagnosis. *Journal of Psycho-Asthenics, 29,* 298–308.

Donahoe, K., & Zigmond, N. (1990). Academic grades of ninth-grade urban learning-disabled students and low-achieving peers. *Exceptionality, 1*(1), 17–27.

Donnellan, A. M., Negri-Shoultz, N., Fassbendes, L., & LaVigna. G. (1988). *Progress without punishment: Effective approaches for learners with behavior problems.* New York: Teachers College Press.

Don't expect me to be perfect. (1990, Special issue summer/fall). *Newsweek,* p. 62.

Dunkin, M. J. (1987). Teaching: Art or science? In M. J. Dunkin (Ed.), *The International Encyclopedia of Teaching and Teacher Education* (p. 19). New York: Pergamon.

Dunst, C. J., Trivette, C. M., & Deal, A. G. (1988). *Enabling and empowering families: Principles and guidelines for practice.* Cambridge, MA: Brookline Books.

Dwyer, C. A. (1976). Test content in mathematics and science: The consideration of sex. Paper presented at the annual meeting of the American Educational Research Association.

Dwyer, K. P. (1990). Making the Least Restrictive Environment work for children with serious emotional disturbance. *Preventing School Failure, 34*(3), 14–21.

Dykman, R. A., Ackerman, P. T., & Raney, T. J. (1994). Research synthesis on assessment and characteristics of children with attention deficit disorder. In Chesapeake Institute, *Executive summaries of research syntheses and promising practices on the education of children with attention deficit disorder* (pp. 4–21). Washington, DC: Chesapeake Institute.

Early years. (1991, April 17). *Education Week,* p. 7.

Edgar, E. (1987). Secondary programs in special education: Are many of them justifiable? *Exceptional Children, 53,* 555–561.

Edgar, E. (1991). Providing ongoing support and making appropriate placements: An alternative to transition planning for mildly handicapped students. *Preventing School Failure, 35*(2), 36–39.

Edgar, E. (1998). Employment as an outcome for mildly handicapped students: Current status and future directions. *Focus on Exceptional Children, 21,* 1–8.

Edgar, E., & Hayden, A. H. (1984–1985). Who are the children in special education and how many children are there? *Journal of Special Education, 18,* 523–539.

Edgerton, R. B. (1967). *The cloak of competence.* Berkeley: University of California Press.

Edmonds, R. R. (1982). Programs of school improvement: An overview. *Educational Leadership, 40,* 4–11.

Educational Policies Commission (1938). *The purposes of education in American democracy.* Washington, DC: National Education Association, American Association of School Administrators.

Education Commission of the States, Task Force on Education for Economic Growth. (1983). *Action for excellence: A comprehensive plan to improve our nation's schools.* Denver: Author.

Educational Commission of the States. (1997a). *A policymaker's guide to incentives for students, teachers, and schools.* Denver, CO: Author.

Education Commission of the States. (1997b). *Education accountability systems in 50 states.* Denver, CO: Author.

Education Commission of the States. (1998a). *Designing and implementing standards-based accountability systems.* Denver, CO: Author.

Education Commission of the States. (1998b). *The progress of education reform: 1997.* Denver, CO: Author.

80,000 women of child-bearing age may have AIDS virus, study says. (1991, April 10). *Education Week,* p. 2.

Ekstrom, R. B., Goertz, M. E., Pollack, J. M., & Rock, D. A. (1986). Who drops out of high school and why? Findings from a national study. *Teachers College Record, 8*(3), 356–373.

Elam, S. M., Rose, L. C., & Gallup, A. M. (1996). The 29th annual Phi Delta Kappa/Gallup Poll of the public's attitudes toward the public schools. *Phi Delta Kappan, 78*(1), 41–59.

Elkind, D. (1969). Piagetian and psychometric conceptions of intelligence. *Harvard Educational Review, 39,* 171–189.

Elliott, S. (1994) U.S. Congress, Office of Technology Assessment (1992).

Elliott, S. N., Witt, J. C., & Kratochwill, T. R. (1991). *Selecting, implementing and evaluating classroom interventions.* Silver Spring, MD: National Association of School Psychologists.

Engelmann, S., Granzin, A., & Severson, H. (1979). Diagnosing instruction. *Journal of Special Education, 13,* 355–365.

English, K., Goldstein, H., Shafer, K., & Kaczmarek, L. (1997). Promoting inter- actions among preschoolers with and without disabilities: Effects of a buddy skills training program. *Exceptional Children, 63*(2), 229–243.

Epps, S., Ysseldyke, J. E., & McGue, M. (1984). Differentiating LD and non-LD students: I know one when I see one. *Learning Disability Quarterly, 7,* 89–101.

Epstein, J. (1990, April 4). Large numbers of parents are excluded from commu- nication. *Education Week,* p. 8.

Erickson, M. T. (1992). *Behavior disorders of children and adolescents: Assessment, etiology, and intervention* (2nd ed.). Englewood Cliffs, NJ: Prentice Hall.

Erickson, R. N., & Thurlow, M. L. (1997). *State special education outcomes 1997.* Minneapolis, MN: University of Minnesota, National Center on Educational Outcomes.

ETS Policy Information Center. (1990). *The education reform decade.* Princeton, NJ: Educational Testing Service.

Fairweather, J. S., & Shaver, D. M. (1991). Making the transition to postsec- ondary education and training. *Exceptional Children, 57,* 264–270.

Famous educator's plan for a school that will advance students according to abil- ity. (1958, April 14). *Life,* pp. 120–121.

Fardig, D. B., Algozzine, R. F., Schwartz, S. E., Hensel, J. W., & Westling, D. L. (1985). Post-secondary vocational adjustment of rural, mildly handicapped stu- dents. *Exceptional Children, 52,* 115–121.

Farina, A., Thaw, J., Felner, R. D., & Hust, B. E. (1976). Some interpersonal con- sequences of being mentally ill or mentally retarded. *American Journal of Mental Deficiency, 80,* 414–422.

Farrell, E. E. (1908). Special classes in the New York City schools. *Journal of Psycho-Asthenics, 13,* 91–96.

Favell, J. E., Azrin, N. H., Baumeister, A. A., Carr, E. G., Dorsey, M. F., Forehand, R., Foxx, R. M., Lovaas, O. I., Risley, T, R., Romanczyk, R. G., Schroeder, S. R., & Solnick, J. V. (1982). The treatment of self-injurious behav- ior. *Behavior Therapy, 13,* 529–554.

Ferguson, D. L. (1989). Severity of need and educational excellence. In D. Bilken, D. L. Ferguson, & A. Ford (Eds.), *Schooling and disability: Eighty-eighth yearbook of the National Society for the Study of Education* (pp. 25–58). Chicago: University of Chicago Press.

Ferguson, D., & Asch, A. (1989). Lessons from life: Personal and parental perspectives on school, childhood, and disability. In D. Bilken, D. Ferguson, & A. Ford (Eds.), *Schooling and disability: Eighty-eighth yearbook of the National Society for the Study of Education* (pp. 108–140). Chicago: University of Chicago Press.

Fessler, M. A., Rosenberg, M. S., & Rosenberg, L. A. (1991). Concomitant learning disabilities and learning problems among students with behavioral/emotional disorders. *Behavioral Disorders, 16,* 97–106.

Figueroa, R. A., Fradd, S. H., & Correa, V. I. (1989). Bilingual special education and this special issue. *Exceptional Children, 56,* 174–178.

Fine, M. (1986). Why urban adolescents drop into and out of public high school. *Teachers College Record, 87*(3), 393–409.

Fine, M., & Asch, A. (1988). Disability beyond stigma: Social interaction, discrimination, and activism. *Journal of Social Issues, 44*(1), 3–22.

Finn, C. E. (1990a). The biggest reform of all. *Phi Delta Kappan, 71,* 584–592.

Finn, C. E. (1990b). Why we need choice. In W. L. Boyd & H. J. Walberg (Eds.), *Choice in education: Potential and problems* (pp. 3–20). Berkeley, CA: McCutchan.

Finn, C. E., Petrilli, M. J., & Vanourek, G. (1998). *The state of state standards* (Fordham Report, vol. 2, no. 5). Washington, DC: Thomas B. Fordham Foundation.

Fiore, T. (1994). Research synthesis on education intervention for students with attention deficit disorder. In Chesapeake Institute, *Executive summaries of research syntheses and promising practices on the education of children with attention deficit disorder* (pp. 36–42). Washington, DC: Chesapeake Institute.

Fiore, T. A., Becker, E. A., & Nero, R. C. (1993). Educational interventions for students with attention deficit disorder. *Exceptional Children, 60*(2), 163–173.

Fischer, L., & Sorenson, G. P. (1985). *School law for counselors, psychologists, and social workers.* New York: Longman.

Ford, B. A., Obiakor, F. E., & Patton, J. M. (1995). *Effective education of African American exceptional learners: New perspectives.* Austin, TX: Pro-Ed.

Forest, M. (1987). Keys to integration: Common sense ideas and hard work. *Entourage, 2,* 16–20.

Forgione, P. D. (1998). *Achievement in the United States: Progress Since A Nation at Risk?* Washington, DC: U.S. Department of Education, Office of Educational Research and Improvement, National Center on Education Statistics. [Available online—http://nces.ed.gov/Pressrelease/reform/].

Forness, S. T., Youpa, D., Hanna, G. L., Cantwell, D. P., & Swanson, J. M. (1992). Classroom instructional characteristics in attention deficit hyperactivity disorder. Comparison of pure and mixed subgroups. *Behavioral Disorders, 17*(2), 115–125.

Fort, S. J. (1900). Special school for special children. *Journal of Psycho-Asthenics, 5,* 28–38.

Fowler, S. A., Chandler, L. K., Johnston, T. E., & Stella, M. E. (1988). Individualizing family involvement in school transitions: Gathering information and choosing the next program. *Journal of the Division for Early Childhood, 12,* 208–216.

Fradd, S. H., & Correa, V. I. (1989). Hispanic students at-risk: Do we abdicate or advocate? *Exceptional Children, 56,* 105–110.

Freedman, M. K. (1997). *Testing, grading, and granting diplomas to special education students.* Horsham, PA: LRP Publications.

Friedman. (1972). *Introduction to statistics.* New York: Random House.

Frost, J. L. (1968). *Early childhood education rediscovered.* New York: Holt, Rinehart, and Winston.

Fuchs, D. (1991). Mainstream assistance teams: A prereferral intervention system for difficult-to-teach students. In G. Stoner, M. Shinn, & H. Walker (Eds.), *Interventions for achievement and behavior problems* (pp. 241–268). Silver Spring, MD: National Association of School Psychologists.

Fuchs, D., Featherstone, N., Garwick, D. R., & Fuchs, L. S. (1984). Effects of examiner familiarity and task characteristics on speech and language-impaired children's test performance. *Measurement and Evaluation in Guidance, 16*(4), 198–204.

Fuchs, D., & Fuchs, L. (1988). Evaluation of the adaptive learning environment model. *Exceptional Children, 55,* 115–127.

Fuchs, D., & Fuchs, L. (1990). Making educational research more important. *Exceptional Children, 57,* 102–107.

Fuchs, D., & Fuchs, L. S. (1986). Test procedure bias: A metaanalysis of examiner familiarity effects. *Review of Educational Research, 56*(2), 243–262.

Fuchs, D., & Fuchs, L. S. (1994). Inclusive schools movement and the radicalization of special education reform. *Exceptional Children, 60,* 294–309.

Fuchs, D., & Fuchs, L. S. (1994/1995). Sometimes separate is better. *Educational Leadership, 52*(4) 22–26.

Fuchs, D., & Fuchs, L. S. (1995, March). What's 'special' about special education? *Phi Delta Kappan, 76*(7), 522–540.

Fuchs, D., Fuchs, L. S., Benowitz, S., & Barringer, K. (1987). Norm-referenced tests: Are they valid for use with handicapped students? *Exceptional children, 54,* 263–272.

Fuchs, D., Fuchs, L. S., Dailey, A. M., & Power, M. H. (1985). The effect of examiners' personal familiarity and professional experience on handicapped children's test performance. *Journal of Educational Research, 78*(3), 141–146.

Fuchs, D., Fuchs, L. S., & Fernstrom, P. (1993). A conservative approach to special education reform: Mainstreaming through transenvironmental programming and curriculum-based measurement. *American Educational Research Journal, 30,* 149–177.

Fuchs, D., Fuchs, L. S., Garwick, D. R., & Featherstone, N. (1983). Test performance of language-handicapped children with familiar and unfamiliar examiners. *Journal of Psychology, 114,* 37–46.

Fuchs, D., Fuchs, L. S., Mathes, P. H., & Simmons, D. (1997). Peer-assisted strategies: Making classrooms more responsive to diversity. *Americn Educational Research Journal, 34*(1), 174–206.

Fuchs, D., Fuchs, L. S., Power, M. H., & Dailey, A. M. (1985). Bias in the assessment of handicapped children. *American Educational Research Journal, 22,* 185–198.

Fuchs, D., Zern, D. S., & Fuchs, L. S. (1983). Participants' verbal and nonverbal behavior in familiar and unfamiliar test conditions: An exploratory analysis. *Diagnostique, 8,* 159–169.

Fuchs, L., & Deno, S. L. (1991). Paradigmatic distinctions between instructionally relevant measurement models. *Exceptional Children, 57,* 488–500.

Fuchs, L., & Fuchs, D. (1986). Linking assessment to instructional interventions: An overview. *School Psychology Review, 15*(3), 318–324.

Fullan, M. (1993). Innovation, reform, and restructuring strategies. In G. Cawelti (Ed.), *Challenges and achievements of American education (1993 Yearbook of the Association for Supervision and Curriculum Development)* (pp. 116–133). Alexandria, VA: ASCD.

Funkhouser, J. E., & Colopy, K. W. (1994). *Minnesota's open enrollment option: Impacts on school districts.* Washington, DC: Policy Studies Associates. (ERIC Reproduction Service No. ED 376 587).

Gadsden, V., Wagner, D., & Hirschhorn, L. (1990). Workplace literacy: Studying the workplace. *Literacy Research Newsletter, 6*(1), 1, 3.

Gage, N. L. (1978). The yield of research on teaching. *Phi Delta Kappan, 60,* 229–235.

Gage, N. L. (1990). Dealing with dropout problems. *Phi Delta Kappan, 72,* 280–285.

Gallagher, J. J. (1970). Three studies of the classroom. In J. J. Gallagher, G. A. Nuthall, & B. Rosenshine (Eds.), *Classroom observation* (pp. 74–108). Chicago: Rand McNally.

Gallagher, J. J. (1976). The sacred and profane uses of labeling. *Mental Retardation, 14,* 3–7.

Gallagher, J. J. (1988). National agenda for educating gifted students: Statement of priorities. *Exceptional Children, 55,* 107–114.

Gardill, M. C., DuPaul, G. J., & Kyle, K. E. (1996) Classroom strategies for managing students with attention-deficit/hyperactivity disorder. *Intervention in School and Clinic, 32*(2) 89–94.

Gardner, H. (1983). *Frames of mind: The Theory of multiple intelligences.* New York: Basic Books.

Gardner, H. (1993). *Multiple intelligences: The theory in practice.* New York: Basic Books.

Garnett, K. (1996). *Thinking about inclusion and learning disabilities: A teacher's guide.* Reston, VA: Council for Exceptional Children.

Garrett, J. E., & Brazil, N. M. (1989). *Categories of exceptionality: A ten-year follow-up.* Unpublished manuscript.

Gartner, A., & Lipsky, D. K. (1987). Beyond special education: Toward a quality system for all students. *Harvard Educational Review, 57,* 367–395.

Gartner, A., Lipsky, D., & Turnbull, D. (1991). *Supporting families with a child with a disability.* Baltimore, MD: Brookes.

Gay, G. (1994). *At the essence of learning: Multicultural education.* West Lafayette, IN: Kappa Delta Pi.

Geography Education Standards Project. (1993). *The national geography standards: Geography for life.* Washington, DC: National Council for Geographic Education.

Gerber, M. M. (1984). The Department of Education's sixth-annual report to Congress on PL 94-142: Is Congress getting the full story? *Exceptional Children, 51,* 209–224.

Gerber, M. M., & Levine-Donnerstein, D. (1989). Educating all children: Ten years later. *Exceptional Children, 56,* 17–27.

Gerry, M. H., & Mirsky, A. J. (1992). Guiding principles for public policy on natural supports. In J. Nisbet (Ed.), *Natural supports in school, at work, and in the community for people with severe disabilities* (pp. 341–346). Baltimore, MD: Paul H. Brookes.

Gersten, R., & Woodward, J. (1990). Rethinking the regular education initiative: Focus on the classroom teacher. *Remedial and Special Education, 11*(3), 7–16.

Gersten, R., Baker, S., & Pugach, M. (in press). Contemporary research on special education teaching.

Gersten, R., Vaughn, S., Deschler, D., & Schiller, E. (1997). What we know about using research findings: Implications for improving special education practice. *Journal of Learning Disabilities, 30*(5), 466–476.

Giangreco, M. F., Dennis, R., Cloninger, C., Edelman, S., & Schattman, R. (1993). "I've counted Jon": Transformational experiences of teachers educating students with disabilities. *Exceptional Children, 59*(4), 359–372.

Gickling, E., & Havertape, J. (1981). Curriculum-based assessment. In J. Tucker (Ed.), *Non-test-based assessment: A training module* (pp. 189, 409). Minneapolis: National School Psychology Inservice Training Network.

Gilhool, T. K. (1989). The right to an effective education: From Brown to PL 94-142 and beyond. In D. K. Lipsky & A. Gartner (Eds.), *Beyond separate education: Quality education for all* (pp. 243–253). Baltimore, MD: Brookes.

Glaser, R. (1988). Cognitive and environmental perspectives on assessing achievement. In *Assessment in the service of learning: Proceedings of the 1987 ETS invitational conference* (pp. 71–83). Princeton, NJ: Educational Testing Service.

Glasser, W. (1990). *The quality school: Managing students without education.* New York: Harper and Row.

Goens, G. A., & Clover, S. I. R. (1990). *Mastering school reform.* Boston: Allyn and Bacon.

Goetz, L., & Sailor, W. (1990). Much ado about babies, murky bathwater, and trickle down politics: A reply to Kauffman. *Journal of Special Education, 24,* 334–339.

Goldman, R. D., & Hewitt, B. N. (1976). Predicting the success of black, Chicano, Oriental and white college students. *Journal of Educational Measurement, 13,* 107–117.

Goldstein, H., Arkell, C., Ashcroft, S., Hurley, O., & Lilly, S. (1975). Schools. In N. Hobbs (Ed.). *Issues in the classification of children* (Vol. 2, pp. 4–61). San Francisco: Jossey-Bass.

Gollnick, D. M., & Chinn, P. C. (1990). *Multicultural education in a pluralistic society* (3rd ed.). New York: Merrill.

Good, T., & Brophy, J. (1986). The social and institutional context of teaching: School effects. In *Third handbook of research on teaching* (pp. 161–193). New York: American Educational Research Association.

Goodlad, J. I. (1979a). Can our schools get better? *Phi Delta Kappan, 60,* 342–347.

Goodlad, J. I. (1979b). *What schools are for.* Bloomington, IN: Phi Delta Kappa Education Foundation.

Goodlad, J. I. (1983). *A place called school: Prospects for the future*. New York: McGraw-Hill.

Goodlad, J. I. (1990). Better teachers for our nation's schools. *Phi Delta Kappan, 72,* 184–194.

Gordon, E. W. (1971). Methodological problems and pseudo issues in the nature-nurture controversy. In R. Canero (Ed.), *Intelligence: Genetic and Environmental Contributions* (pp. 240–251). New York: Grune and Stratton.

Gorham, K. A., Des Jardins, C., Page, R., Pettis, E., & Scherber, B. (1976). Effect on parents. In N. Hobbs (Ed.), *Issues in the classification of children* (Vol. 2, pp. 154–188). San Francisco: Jossey-Bass.

Gough, P. B. (1990). Moving beyond rhetoric. *Phi Delta Kappan, 72,* 259.

Graden, J. L., Casey, A., & Bonstrom, O. (1985). Implementing a prereferral intervention system: Part II: The data. *Exceptional Children, 51,* 487–496.

Graden, J. L., Casey, A., & Christenson, S. L. (1985). Implementing a prereferral intervention system: Part I: The model. *Exceptional Children, 51,* 377–384.

Graden, J. L., Zins, J., & Curtis, M. (1988). *Alternative educational delivery systems*. Washington, DC: National Association of School Psychologists.

Greenburg, D. (1984). The 1984 annual report to Congress: Are we better off? *Exceptional Children, 51,* 203–208.

Greenburg, D. E. (1989). The tenth annual report to Congress: One more ride on the merry-go-round. *Exceptional Children, 56,* 10–13.

Greenwood, C. R., Carta, J. J., Hart, B., Kamps, D., Terry, B., Arreaga-Mayer, C., Atwater, J., Walker, D., Risley, T., & Delquadri, J. (1992). Out of the laboratory and into the community: 26 years of applied behavior analysis at the Juniper Gardens Children's Project. *American Psychologist, 47,* 1464–1474.

Greer, J. V. (1990). The drug babies. *Exceptional Children, 56,* 382–384.

Grissmer, D. W., Kirby, S. N., Berends, M., & Williamson, S. (1994). *Student achievement and the changing American family*. Santa Monica: RAND Corporation.

Grolnick, W. S., & Slowiaczek, M. L. (1994). Parents' involvement in children's schooling: A multidimensional conceptualization and motivational model. *Child Development, 65* (1), 237–252.

Grolnick, W., Benjet, C., Kurowski, C. O., & Apostoleris, N. H. (1997). Predictors of parent involvement in children's schooling. *Journal of Educational Psychology, 89*(3), 538–548.

Grosenick, J. K., & Huntze, S. (1980). *National needs analysis in behavior disorders: A model for a comprehensive needs analysis in behavior disorders*. Columbia: University of Missouri, Columbia.

Grossman, H. (1973). *Manual on terminology and classification in mental retardation.* Baltimore, MD: Garamond/Pridemark.

Grossman, H. (Ed.). (1983). *Manual on terminology and classification in mental retardation* (rev. ed.). Washington, DC: American Association on Mental Deficiency.

Grossman, H. (1998). *Ending discrimination in special education.* Springfield, IL: Charles C. Thomas.

Grossnickle, D. R. (1986). *High school dropouts: Causes, consequences, and cure* (Fastback 242). Bloomington, IN: Phi Delta Kappa Educational Foundation.

Guess, D. (1988). Problems and issues pertaining to the transmission of behavior management technologies from researchers to practitioners. In R. H. Horner (Ed.), *Behavior management and community integration for individuals with developmental disabilities and severe behavior problems.* Washington, D.C.: U.S. Office of Special Education and Rehabilitative Services.

Guralnick, M. (1997a). Introduction: Directions for second-generation research. In M. J. Guralnick (Ed.), *The effectiveness of early intervention.* Baltimore: Brookes.

Guralnick, M. (1997b). Second-generation research in the field of early intervention. In M. J. Guralnick (Ed.), *The effectiveness of early intervention* (pp. 3–20). Baltimore: Brookes.

Guralnick, M. J. (Ed.) (1997c). *The effectiveness of early intervention.* Baltimore, MD: Brookes.

Guy, B., Shin, H., Lee, S., & Thurlow, M. L. (1999). *State graduation requirements for students with and without disabilities* (Technical Report 24). Minneapolis, MN: University of Minnesota, National Center on Educational Outcomes.

Hagen, E. (1980). *Identification of the gifted.* New York: Teachers College Press.

Hahn, A., Danzberger, J., & Lefkowitz, B. (1987). *Dropouts in America. Enough is known for action.* Washington, DC: Institute for Educational Leadership.

Hall, J., & Gerber, P. (1985). The awarding of Carnegie units to learning disabled high school students: A policy study. *Educational Evaluation and Policy Analysis, 7*(3), 229–235.

Hall, V., Greenwood, C., & Delquadri, J. (1976). *The importance of opportunity to respond to children's academic success.* Kansas City, KS: Juniper Gardens Children's Center.

Hallahan, D. P., & Kauffman, J. M. (1977). Labels, categories, behaviors: ED, LD, and EMR reconsidered. *Journal of Special Education, 11,* 139–149.

Hallahan, D. P., & Kauffman, J. M. (1989). *Exceptional children* (4th. ed.). Englewood Cliffs, NJ: Prentice-Hall.

Hallahan, D. P., & Kauffman, J. M. (1997). *Exceptional learners*. Boston: Allyn and Bacon.

Hallahan, D. P., Keller, C. E., & Ball, D. W. (1986). A comparison of prevalence rate variability from state to state for each of the categories of special education. *Remedial and Special Education, (7)* 2, 8–14.

Halloran, W. (1989). Foreword. In D. E. Berkell & J. M. Brown (Eds.), *Transition from school to work for persons with disabilities* (pp. xiii–xvi). New York: Longman.

Hamblin-Wilson, C., & Thurman, S. K. (1990). The transition from early intervention to kindergarten: Parental satisfaction and involvement. *Journal of Early Intervention, 14,* 55–61.

Hanft, B. (1988). Occupational therapy and early intervention. *OSERS News in Print, 1*(4), 11.

Harp, L. (1991, March 13). Senate subcommittee samples views on need for national achievement test. *Education Week,* p. 35.

Harrington, M. (1962). *The other America.* Baltimore, MD: Penguin.

Hartman, W. T., & Fay, T. (1996). *Cost effectiveness of instructional support teams in Pennsylvania. CSEF Policy Paper No. 9.* Palo Alto, CA: Center for Special Education Finance, American Institutes for Research.

Hasazi, S. B., Gordon, L. R., & Roe, C. A. (1985). Factors associated with the employment status of handicapped youth exiting high school from 1979 to 1983. *Exceptional Children, 51,* 455–469.

Hasazi, S., Gordon, L., Roe, C., Hull, M., Fink, R., & Salembier, G. (1985). A statewide follow-up on the post high school employment and residential status of students labeled "mentally retarded." *Education and Training of the Mentally Retarded, 20,* 222–234.

Haskins, R. (1989). Beyond metaphor: The efficiency of early childhood education. *American Psychologist, 44,* 274–282.

Hatlin, P. H., Hall, A. P., & Tuttle, D. (1980). Education of the visually handicapped. In L. Mann & D. A. Sabatino (Eds.), *Fourth review of special education.* New York: Grune and Stratton.

Hawkins, J. A. (1984). *Follow-up study of special education graduates: Class of 1983.* Rockville, MD: Department of Educational Accountability. (ERIC Document Reproduction Services No. Ed 256–786)

Hawley, R. A. (1990). The bumpy road to drug-free schools. *Phi Delta Kappan, 72,* 310–314.

Haywood, H. C. (1979). What happened to mild and moderate mental retardation? *American Journal of Mental Deficiency, 83,* 429–431.

Heller, K. A., Holtzman, W., & Messick, S. (1982). *Placing children in special education: A strategy for equity.* Washington, DC: National Academy Press.

Henderson, A. T., Marburger, C. L., & Ooms, T. (1986). *Beyond the bake sale: An educator's guide to working with parents.* Washington, DC: National Committee for Citizens in Education.

Hendrick, I. G., & MacMillan, D. L. (1989). Selecting children for special education in New York City: William Maxwell, Elizabeth Farrell, and the development of ungraded classes, 1900–1920. *Journal of Special Education, 22,* 395–418.

Henley, M., Ramsay, R., & Algozzine, B. (1998). *Characteristics of and teaching strategies for students with mild disabilities.* Boston: Allyn and Bacon.

Hennessy, J. J., & Merrifield, P. R. (1976). A comparison of the factor structures of mental abilities in four ethnic groups. *Journal of Educational Psychology, 68(6),* 754–759.

Hess, A. G., & Lauber, D. (1985). *Dropouts from the Chicago public schools: An analysis of the classes of 1982, 1983, 1984.* Chicago IL: Chicago Panel on Public School Finances.

Hess, F. (1987). *A comprehensive analysis of the dropout phenomenon in an urban school system.* Paper presented at the annual meeting of the American Educational Research Association.

Heward, W. L., & Orlansky, M. D. (1989). *Exceptional Children* (3rd ed.). Columbus, OH: Merrill.

Hewitt, S. K. N. (1981). *Learning disabilities among secondary in-school students, graduates, and dropouts.* Unpublished doctoral dissertation, University of Minnesota, Minneapolis.

Higgins, S. (1979). *Policy options regarding graduation and their impact on handicapped students.* Reston, VA: Council for Exceptional Children. (ERIC Document Reproduction Service No. ED 191 200)

Hilliard, A. S. (1995). Culture, assessment, and valid teaching for the African American student. In B. A. Ford, F. E. Obiakor, & J. M. Patton (Eds.), *Effective education of African American exceptional learners: New perspectives* (pp. ix–xvi). Austin, TX: Pro-Ed.

Hirsch, J. (1971). Behavior-genetic analysis and its biosocial consequences. In R. Caucro (Ed.), *Intelligence: Genetic and environmental contributions* (pp. 88–106). New York: Grune and Stratton.

Hirshoren, A., & Umansky, W. (1977). Certification for teachers of preschool handicapped children. *Exceptional Children, 44,* 191–193.

Hobbs, N. (1975). *Issues in the classification of children.* San Francisco: Jossey-Bass.

Hodgkinson, H. L. (1985). *All one system: Demographics of education—kindergarten through graduate school.* Washington, DC: Institute for Educational Leadership.

Hodgkinson, H. L. (1989). *The same client: The demographics of education and service delivery systems.* Washington, DC: Institute for Educational Leadership, Center for Demographic Leadership.

Hodgkinson, H. L. (1992). *A demographic look at tomorrow.* Washington, DC: Institute for Educational Leadership.

Hollowood, T. M., Salisbury, C. L., Rainforth, B., & Palombaro, M. M. (1994/1995). Use of instructional time in classrooms serving students with and without severe disabilities. *Exceptional Children, 61*(3), 242–253.

Home alone. (1991, March 6). *Education Week,* p. 3.

Horn, J. L. (1924). *The education of exceptional children: A consideration of public school problems and policies in the field of differentiated education.* New York: Century.

How federal laws and regulations are determined. (1991). *News Digest, 1*(1), 2.

Howe, S. G. (1848). *Report of commission to inquire into the conditions of idiots of the Commonwealth of Massachusetts* (Senate Document No. 51). Boston: State Department of Education.

Howell, K. W. (1986). Direct assessment of academic performance. *School Psychology Review, 15*(3), 324–335.

Hudson, F., Graham, S., & Warner, M. (1979). Mainstreaming: An examination of the attitudes and needs of regular classroom teachers. *Learning Disability Quarterly, 3,* 558–562.

Hunt, P., Farron-Davis, F., Beckstead, S., Curtis, D., & Goetz, L. (1994). Evaluating the effects of placement of students with severe disabilities in general education versus special classes. *The Journal of the Association of Persons with Severe Handicaps, 19*(3), 200–214.

Hurley, O. L. (1989). Implications of PL 99-457 for preparation of preschool personnel. In J. J. Gallagher, P. L. Trohanis, & R. M. Clifford (Eds.), *Policy implementation & PL 99-457: Planning for young children with special needs* (pp. 133–145). Baltimore, MD: Brookes.

Hurley, R. (1969). *Poverty and mental retardation: A causal relationship.* New York: Random House.

Hyman, I. A. (1979). Will the real school psychologist please stand up? III. A struggle of jurisdictional imperialism. *School Psychology Digest, 8,* 174–180.

Imber-Black, E. (1988). *Families and larger systems.* New York: Guilford.

Indicators Panel. (1990). *Three draft outlines of the final report of the Special Study Panel on Education Indicators, appendix* (Staff report). Washington, DC: National Center for Education Statistics.

Ingels, S. J., & Quinn, P. (1996). *Sample exclusion in NELS:88. Characteristics of base year ineligible students, changes in eligibility status after four years* (NCES 96-723). Washington, DC: U.S. Department of Education, Office of Educational Research and Improvement, National Center for Education Statistics.

Ingersoll, R. M. (1998). The problem of out-of-field teaching. *Phi Delta Kappan, 79,* 773–776.

Inman, D., Prebish, S. L., & Salganik, L. H. (1990). *Summary profiles: State education indicator systems.* Washington, DC: Pelavin.

Interagency Committee on Learning Disabilities. (1987). *Learning disabilities: A report to the U.S. Congress.* Washington, DC: U.S. Department of Health and Human Services.

International Reading Association & National Council of Teachers of English. (1996). *Standards for the English language arts.* Urbana, IL: NCTE.

Jacobs, J. (1986). *Educating students with severe handicaps in the regular education program, all day, every day.* Paper presented at the annual conference of the Association for Persons with Severe Handicaps, San Francisco, CA.

Jacobson, J. W., & Mulick, J. A. (1996). *Manual on diagnosis and professional practice in mental retardation.* Washington, DC: American Psychological Association.

Jacobson, L. (1998, June 24). State capitals: State graduation tests raise questions, stakes. *Education Week, 17*(41), p. 22.

Jason, L. A., Betts, D., Johnson, J. H., Weine, A. W., Warren-Sohlberg, M. L., Shinaver, C. S. I., Neuson, L., Filippelli, L., & Lardon, C. (1990). Prompting competencies in high-risk transfer children. *Special Services in the Schools, 1–2,* 21–36.

Jensen, A. (1967). *Estimation of the limits of heritability of traits by comparison of monozygotic and dizygotic twins.* Washington, DC: National Academy of Sciences.

Jensen, A. R. (1968a). Patterns of mental ability and socio-economic status. *Proceedings of the National Academy of Sciences, 60.* 1330–1337.

Jensen, A. R. (1968b) Social class, race, and genetics: Implications for education. *American Educational Research Journal, 5,*1–42.

Jensen, A. R. (1969) How much can we boost IQ and scholastic achievement? *Harvard Educational Review, 39,* 1–123.

Jensen, A. R. (1976). Test bias and construct validity. *Phi Delta Kappan, 58,* 340–346.

Jensen, A. R. (1979). *Bias in mental testing*. New York: Free Press.

Joftus, S., & Berman, I. (1998). *Great expectations: Defining and assessing rigor in state standards for mathematics and English language arts* (Special Report). Washington, DC: Council for Basic Education.

Johns, B. (1991). Highlights of the new IDEA. *DLD Times, 8*(2), 5.

Johnson, D. R., Bruininks, R. H., & Thurlow, M. L. (1987). Meeting the challenge of transition service planning through improved interagency cooperation. *Exceptional Children, 53,* 522–530.

Johnson, J. M., & Pennypacker, H. S. (1980). *Strategies and tactics of human behavioral research*. Hillsdale, NJ: Earlbaum.

Johnson, T. W. (1990). Taking a first step toward reform. *Phi Delta Kappan, 72,* 202–203.

Jones, R. L., Gottlieb, J., Guskin, S., & Yoshida, R. K. (1978). Evaluating mainstream programs: Models, caveats, considerations, and guidelines. *Exceptional Children, 44,* 588–601.

Joyce, B. (1990). *Changing school culture through staff development*. Alexandria, VA: Association for Supervision and Curriculum Development.

Joyce, B., & Weil, M. (1972). *Models of teaching*. Englewood Cliffs, NJ: Prentice-Hall.

Kagan, S. L. (1990). Readiness 2000: Rethinking rhetoric and responsibility. *Phi Delta Kappan, 72,* 272–279.

Kagan, S. L., Moore, E., & Bredekamp, S. (1995). *Considering children's early development and learning: Toward shared belief and vocabulary*. Washington, DC: National Education Goals Panel.

Kamin, L. J. (1975). Social and legal consequences of IQ tests as classification instruments: Some warnings from our past. *Journal of School Psychology, 13,* 317–323.

Kantrowitz, B. (1990, Summer/Fall special issue). Homeroom [Special issue]. *Newsweek*, pp. 50–54.

Karaim, R. (1990, December 11). High incidence of alcohol abuse causing defects, retardation in babies, experts say. *St. Paul Pioneer Press*, p. 3.

Karnes, M. B., & Zehrbach, R. R. (1977). Early education of the handicapped: Issues and alternatives. In B. Spodek & H. J. Walberg (Eds.), *Early childhood education*. Berkeley, CA: McCutchan.

Karr, S., & Wright, J. V. (1995). Assessment: Proper use for persons with problem behaviors. In F. E. Obiakor & B. Algozzine (Eds.), *Managing problem behaviors: Perspectives for general and special educators* (pp. 63–95). Dubuque, IA: Kendall/Hunt.

Katz, I. (1981). *Stigma: A social psychological analysis.* Hillsdale, NJ: Erlbaum.

Kauffman, J. M. (1977). *Characteristics of children's behavior disorders.* (2nd ed.). Columbus, OH: Merrill.

Kauffman, J. M. (1980). Where special education for disturbed children is going: A personal view. *Exceptional Children, 46,* 522–527.

Kauffman, J. M. (1985). *Characteristics of children's behavior disorders.* (3rd ed.). Columbus, OH: Merrill.

Kauffman, J. M. (1989a). *Characteristics of children's behavior disorders.* (4th ed.). Columbus, OH: Merrill.

Kauffman, J. M. (1989b). The regular education initiative as Reagan-Bush education policy: A trickle-down theory of education of the hard-to-teach. *Journal of Special Education, 23,* 256–278; *24,* 319–325.

Kauffman, J. M. (1997). *Characteristics of emotional and behavioral disorders of children and youth.* Upper Saddle River, NJ: Prentice Hall.

Kauffman, J. M., Gerber, M. M., & Semmel, M. I. (1998). Arguable assumptions underlying the regular education initiative. *Journal of Learning Disabilities, 21,* 6–12.

Kauffman, J. M., & Hallahan, D. P. (1990). What we want for children: A rejoinder to REI proponents. *Journal of Special Education, 24,* 340–345.

Kauffman, J. M., & Hallahan, D. P. (Eds.). (1995). *The illusion of full inclusion: A comprehensive critique of a current special education bandwagon.* Austin, TX: Pro-Ed.

Kauffman, J. M., Lloyd, J. W., & McKinney, J. D. (1988). [Special issue]. *Journal of Learning Disabilities, 21*(1).

Kaufman, M. J., Kameenui, E. J., Birman, B., & Danielson, L. (1990). Special education and the process of change: Victim or master of educational reform? *Exceptional Children, 57,* 109–115.

Kaufman, P., McMillen, M., & Bradby, D. (1992). *Dropout rates in the United States: 1991.* Washington, DC: National Center for Education Statistics.

Kavale, K. A., Fuchs, D., & Scruggs, T. E. (1994). Setting the record straight on learning disability and low achievement: Implications for policymaking. *Learning Disabilities Research & Practice, 9*(2), 70–77.

Keogh, B. K. (1988). Improving services for problem learners: Rethinking and restructuring. *Journal of Learning Disabilities, 21,* 19–22.

Killoran, J., & Tingey, C. (1989). Staff development in early intervention. In C. Tingey (Ed.), *Implementing early intervention* (pp. 79–94). Baltimore, MD: Brookes.

Kirk, S. A. (1977). General and historical rationale for early education of the handicapped. In N. E. Ellis & L. Cross (Eds.), *Planning programs for early education of the handicapped* (pp. 28–46). New York: Walker.

Kirk, S. A., & Gallagher, J. J. (1986). *Educating exceptional children* (5th ed.). Boston: Houghton Mifflin.

Kirk, S. A., & Gallagher, J. J. (1989). *Educating exceptional children* (6th ed.). Boston: Houghton Mifflin.

Kirsch, I. S., Jungeblut, A., Jenkins, L., & Kolstad, A. (1993). *Adult literacy in America: A first look at the results of the national adult literacy survey.* Washington, DC: U.S. Department of Education, Office of Educational Research and Improvement, National Center for Education Statistics.

Kirst, M. W. (1990). *Accountability: Implications for state and local policy makers. Policy Perspectives.* Washington, DC: U.S. Department of Education, Information Services Office of Educational Research and Improvement.

Knoff, H. M. (1985). Attitudes toward mainstreaming: A status report and comparison of regular and special educators in New York and Massachusetts. *Psychology in the Schools, 22,* 411–418.

Koegel, L. K., Koegel, R. L., & Dunlap, G. (1996). *Positive behavioral support: Including people with difficult behavior in the community.* Baltimore: Brookes.

Kohler, P. D. (1993). Best practices in transition: Substantiated or implied? *Career Development for Exceptional Individuals, 16,* 107–121.

Kohler, P. D. (1996). Preparing youths with disabilities for future challenges: A taxonomy for transition programming. In P. D. Kohler (Ed.), *Taxonomy for transition programming: Linking research to practice* (pp. 1–62). Champaign-Urbana, IL: University of Illinois, Transition Research Insitute.

Kohler, P. D. (1998). Implementing a transition perspective in education. In F. R. Rusch & J. G. Chadsey (Eds.), *Beyond high school: Transition from school to work* (pp. 179–205). Belmont, CA: Wadsworth.

Kontos, S., & File, N. (1993). Staff development in support of integration. In C. A. Peck, S. L. Odom, & D. Bricker (Eds.), *Integrating young children with disabilities into community programs: Ecological perspectives on research and implementation* (pp. 169–186). Baltimore: Brookes.

Kortering, L. J., & Braziel, P. M. (1998). School dropout among youth with and without learning disabilites. *Career Development for Exceptional Individuals, 21,* 61–74.

Kortering, L. J., Julnes, R., & Edgar, E. B. (1990). An instructive review of the law pertaining to the graduation of special education students. *Remedial and Special Education, 11*(4), 7–13.

Kreitzer, A. E., Madaus, G. F., & Haney, W. (1989). Competency testing and dropouts. In L. Weiss, E. Farrar, & H. G. Petrie (Eds.), *Dropouts from school: Issues, dilemmas, and solutions* (pp. 129–152). Albany: State University of New York Press.

Lambert, N. (1981). *Diagnostic and technical manual, AAMD adaptive behavior scale-school edition.* Monterey, CA: CTB/McGraw-Hill.

Lambert, N. (1981). School psychology training for the decades ahead. *School Psychology Review, 10, 2.*

Lange, C. M., & Ysseldyke, J. E. (1998). School choice policies and practices for students with disabilities. *Exceptional children 64,(2), 255–270.*

Langenfeld, K., Thurlow, M., & Scott, D. (1997). *High stakes testing for students: Unanswered questions and implications for students with disabilities* (Synthesis Report 26). Minneapolis, MN: University of Minnesota, National Center on Educational Outcomes.

LaVor, M. (1972). Economic opportunity amendments of 1972, Public Law 92-424. *Exceptional Children, 39,* 249–253.

Lavor, M. (1979). Federal legislation for exceptional persons: A history. In F. Weintraub, A. Abeson, J. Ballard, & M. LaVor (Eds.), *Public policy and the education of exceptional children.* Reston, VA: Council for Exceptional Children.

LaVor, M., & Harvey, J. (1976). Headstart, Economic Opportunity, Community Partnership Act of 1974. *Exceptional Children, 42,* 227–230.

Lee, V. E., Schnur, E., & Brooks-Gunn, J. (1988). Does Head Start work? A 1-year follow-up comparison of disadvantaged children attending Head Start, no preschool, and other preschool programs. *Developmental Psychology, 24(2),* 210–222.

Lehr, C. A., Ysseldyke, J. E., & Thurlow, M. L. (1987). Assessment practices in model early childhood education programs. *Psychology in the Schools, 24,* 390–399.

Leitch, M. L., & Tangri, S. S. (1988). Barriers to home-school collaboration. *Educational Horizons, 66,* 70–74.

Lentz, F. E., & Shapiro, E. S. (1986). Functional assessment of the academic environment. *School Psychology Review, 15(3),* 346–357.

Lerner, J. (1985). *Learning disabilities* (4th ed.). Boston: Houghton Mifflin.

Lerner, J. (1997). *Learning disabilities.* Boston: Houghton Mifflin.

Lerner, J., Lowenthal, B., & Egan, R. (1998). *Preschool children with special needs: Children at-risk, children with disabilities.* Boston, MA: Allyn & Bacon.

Lessen, E. I., & Rose, T. L. (1980). State definitions of preschool handicapped populations. *Exceptional Children, 46,* 467–469.

Levin, E., Zigmond, N., & Birch, J. (1985). A follow-up study of 52 learning disabled students. *Journal of Learning Disabilities, 18,* 2–7.

Levy, L., & Rowitz, L. (1973). *The ecology of mental disorders.* New York: Behavioral Publications.

Lewis, A. C. (1990) The murky waters of monitoring achievement of the national goals. *Phi Delta Kappan, 72,* 260–261.

Lewis, A. C., & Henderson, A. T. (1997). *Urgent message: Families crucial to school reform.* Washington, DC: Center for Law and Education.

Lewis, D. R., Bruininks, R. H., & Thurlow, M. L. (1989). Cost analysis for district-level special education planning, budgeting, and administrating. *Journal of Education Finance, 14*(4), 466–484.

Lezotte, L. W. (1989). School improvement based on the effective schools research. In D. K. Lipsky & A. Gartner (Eds.), *Beyond separate education: Quality education for all* (pp. 25–37). Baltimore, MD: Brookes.

Lichtenstein, R., & Ireton, H. (1984). *Preschool screening: Identifying young children with developmental and educational problems.* Orlando, FL: Grune and Stratton.

Lichtenstein, S. J. (1987). *A study of selected post-school employment patterns of handicapped and nonhandicapped graduates and dropouts.* Unpublished doctoral dissertation, University of Illinois, Urbana-Champaign.

Lilly, M. S. (1989). Teacher preparation. In D. K. Lipsky & A. Gartner (Eds.), *Beyond separate education: Quality education for all.* Baltimore, MD: Paul H. Brookes.

Lincoln, D. F. (1903). Special classes for feeble-minded children in the Boston public schools. *Journal of Psycho-Asthenics, 7,* 83–93.

Linn, R. L. (1990, October). Discussant to paper by Resnick presented at the OERI Conference on the Promise and Peril of Alternative Assessment. Washington, DC.

Linn, R. L., & Herman, J. L. (1997, February). *Standards-led assessments: Technical and policy issues in measuring school and student progress.* CSE Technical Report 426. Los Angeles, CA: UCLA, National Center for Research on Evaluation, Standards, and Student Testing (CRESST).

Liontos, L. B. (1992). *At-risk families & schools: Becoming Partners.* Eugene, OR: ERIC Clearinghouse on Educational Management.

Lipsky, D. K., & Gartner, A. (1987). Capable of achievement and worthy of respect: Education for the handicapped as if they were full-fledged human beings. *Exceptional Children, 54*, 69–74.

Lipsky, D. K., & Gartner, A. (1989a). *Beyond separate education: Quality education for all.* Baltimore, MD: Brookes.

Lipsky, D. K., & Gartner, A. (1989b). Building the future. In D. K. Lipsky & A. Gartner (Eds.), *Beyond separate education: Quality education for all* (pp. 255–290). Baltimore, MD: Brookes.

Lloyd, J. W., Crowley, E. P., Kohler, F. W., & Strain, P. S. (1988). Redefining the applied research agenda: Cooperative learning, prereferral, teacher consultation, and peer-mediated interventions. *Journal of Learning Disabilities, 21*, 43–52.

Lockwood, A. V. (1978). Accommodating learning disabilities: Creating the Least Restrictive Environment. *Illinois Schools Journal, 58*(4), 33–36.

Louis Harris and Associates, Inc. (1998). *The Metropolitan Life Survey of the American Teacher 1998: Building family-school partnerships: Views of teachers and students.* New York, NY: Louis Harris and Associates, Inc.

Lovett, H. (1985). *Cognitive counseling and the person with special needs: Adapting behavioral approaches to the social context.* New York: Praeger.

Lovitt, T. (1978). Reactions to planned research. Paper presented at the Roundtable Conference on Learning Disabilities. Minneapolis, MN: Institute for research on Learning Disabilities.

Ludlow, B. (1989). Shortage of qualified special education personnel declared national emergency. *American Association on Mental Retardation News and Notes, 2*(3) 1–5.

Lynn, L. (1983). The emerging system for educating handicapped children. *Policy Studies Review, 2*, 21–35.

Lynn, R. (1979). *Learning disabilities.* New York: Free Press.

Lyon, R. (1983). Subgroups of learning disabled readers: Clinical and empirical identification. In H. Myklebust (Ed.), *Progress in learning disabilities* (Vol. 5, pp. 67–94). New York: Grune and Stratton.

Lyon, R. (1985). Identification and remediation of learning disabilities subtypes: Preliminary findings. *Learning Disabilities Focus, 1*(1), 21–35.

Maag, J. E., & Reid, R. (1994). Attention-deficit hyperactivity disorder: A functional approach to assessment and treatment. *Behavioral Disorders, 20*(1), 5–23.

Macchiarola, F. J. (1989). Foreword. In D. K. Lipsky & A. Gartner (Eds.), *Beyond separate education: Quality education for all* (pp. xi–xix). Baltimore, MD: Brookes.

Mack, J. (1985). An analysis of state definitions of severely emotionally disturbed children. In Council for Exceptional Children's, *Policy options report*. Reston, VA: Author.

MacMillan, D. L., Balow, I. H., Widaman, K. F., Borthwick-Dubby, S., & Hendrick, I. G. (1990). Methodological problems in estimating dropout rates and the implications for studying dropouts from special education. *Exceptionality, 1*(1), 29–39.

Madden, N. A., & Slavin, R. E. (1983). Mainstreaming students with mild handicaps: Academic and social outcomes. *Review of Educational Research, 53,* 519–569.

Maheady, L., & Algozzine, B. (1991). The regular education initiative: Can we proceed in an orderly and scientific manner? *Teacher Education and Special Education, 14,* 66–73.

Mann, D. (1986). Can we help dropouts: Thinking about the undoable. *Teachers College Record, 87*(3), 307–323.

Mann, L. (1979). *On the trail of process*. New York: Grune & Stratton.

Marder, C. (1992). *How well are youth with disabilities really doing?* Menlo Park, CA: SRI International.

Marder, C., & D'Amico, R. (1992). *How well are youth with disabilities really doing? A comparison of youth with disabilities and youth in general*. Washington, DC: U.S. Department, SRI International Contract 300-87-0054.

Marion, S. F., & Sheinker, A. (1998). *Issues and consequences for state-level minimum competency testing programs* (State Assessment Series, Wyoming Report 1). Minneapolis, MN: University of Minnesota, National Center on Educational Outcomes.

Marston, D. (1987). Does categorical teacher certification benefit the mildly handicapped child? *Exceptional Children, 53,* 423–431.

Marston, D. (1987–88). The effectiveness of special education: A time series analysis of reading performance in regular and special education settings. *Journal of Special Education, 21,* 13–26.

Marston, D. (1989). Measuring progress on IEPs: A comparison of graphing approaches. *Exceptional Children, 55,* 38–44.

Martin, E. W. (1995). Case studies on inclusion: Worst fears realized. *The Journal of Special Education, 29*(2), 192–199.

Martin, J. E., & Marshall, L. H. (1995). Choicemaker: A comprehensive self-determination transition program. *Intervention in School and Clinic, 30* (3), 147–157.

Martin, R. (1975). *Legal challenges to behavior modification: Trends in schools, corrections, and mental health*. Champaign, IL: Research Press.

Massachusetts Advocacy Center. (1986). *The way out: Student exclusion practices in Boston middle schools.* Boston: Author.

Masten, A. S. (1989). Resilience in development: Implications of the study of successful adaptation for developmental psychopathology. In D. Cicchetti (Ed.), *The emergence of a discipline: Rochester Symposium on Developmental Psychopathology* (Vol. 1, pp. 261–294). New York: Cambridge University Press.

Masten, A. S., Garmezy, N., Tellegen, A., Pellegrini, D. S., Larkin, K., & Larsen A. (1988). Competence and stress in school children: The moderating effects of individual and family qualities. *Journal of Child Psychology and Psychiatry, 29,* 745–764.

Matluck, J. H. & Mace, B. J. (1973). Language characteristics of Mexican American children: Implications for assessment. *Journal of School Psychology, 11,* 365–386.

Matuszek, P., & Oakland, T. (1972). *A factor analysis of several reading readiness measures for different socioeconomic and ethnic groups.* Paper presented at the annual meeting of the American Educational Research Association.

McBride, J. W., & Forgnone, C. (1985). Emphasis of instruction provided LD, EH, and EMR students in categorical and cross-categorical resource programs. *Journal of Research and Development in Education, 18*(4), 50–54.

McCollum, H., & Turnbull, B. J. (1989). *Educational indicators.* Washington, DC: Policy Study Associates.

McCollum, J. A. (1987). Early interventionists in infant and early childhood education programs. *Topics in Early Childhood Special Education, 7*(3), 24–25.

McDonnell, J., Sheehan, M., & Wilcox, B. (1983). *Effective transition from school to work and adult services: A procedural handbook for parents and teachers.* Lane County, OR: Lane County Education Service District.

McDonnell, L. M., McLaughlin, M. J., & Morison, P. (Eds.). (1997). *Educating one & all: Students with disabilities in standards-based reform.* Washington, DC: National Academy Press.

McGill-Franzen, A. (1987). Failure to learn to read: Formulating a policy problem. *Reading Research Quarterly, 22,* 475–490.

McGregor, G., & Vogelsberg, R. T. (1998). *Inclusive schooling practices: Pedagogical and research foundations.* Pittsburgh: Allegheny University of the Health Sciences.

McGrew, K., Thurlow, M. L., Shriner, J. G., & Spiegel, A. N. (1992). *Inclusion of students with disabilities in national and state data collection programs* (Technical Report 2). Minneapolis, MN: University of Minnesota, National Center on Educational Outcomes.

McGrew, K. S., Thurlow, M. L., & Spiegel, A. N. (1993). An investigation of the exclusion of students with disabilities in national data collection programs. *Educational Evaluation and Policy Analysis, 15*(3), 339–352.

McKinney, J. D. (1984). The search for subtypes of specific learning disabilities. *Journal of Learning Disabilities, 17,* 43–50.

McKinney, J. D. (1988). Research on conceptually and empirically derived subtypes of specific learning disabilities. In M. C. Wang, H. J. Walberg, & M. C. Reynolds (Eds.), *The handbook of special education: Research and practice* (pp. 253–282). Oxford: Pergamon.

McKinney, J. D. (1989). Longitudinal research on the behavioral characteristics of children with learning disabilities. *Journal of Learning Disabilities, 22,* 141–150, 165.

McKinney, J. D., & Hocutt, A. M. (1988). Policy issues in the evaluation of the regular education initiative. *Learning Disabilities Focus, 4,* 15–23.

McKinney, J. D., Montague, M., & Hocutt, A. M. (1993). Educational assessment of students with attention deficit disorder. *Exceptional Children, 60*(2), 125–131.

McKinney, J. D., Montague, M., & Hocutt, A. M. (1994). Research synthesis on the assessment and identification of attention deficit disorder. In Chesapeake Institute, *Executive summaries of research syntheses and promising practices on the education of children with attention deficit disorder* (pp. 22–35). Washington, DC: Chesapeake Institute.

McKinney, J., & Speece, D. (1986). Academic consequences and longitudinal stability of behavioral subtypes of learning disabled children. *Journal of Educational Psychology, 78,* 365–372.

McLaughlin, J. A., & Christensen, M. (1980). *A study of interagency collaborative agreements to discover training needs for special education administrators.* Washington, DC: Bureau of Education for the Handicapped.

McLaughlin, M. (1990). The Rand change agent study revisited: Macro perspectives and micro realities. *Educational Research, 19*(9), 11–16.

McLaughlin, M. J., & Owings, M. (1993). Relationships among state's fiscal and demograhic data and the implementation of PL 94-142. *Exceptional Children, 34,* 247–261.

McLaughlin, M. J., & Warren, S. H. (1992). *Issues and options in restructuring schools and special education programs.* College Park, MD: University of Maryland.

McLaughlin, M. J., & Warren, S. H. (1994, November). The costs of inclusion: Reallocating financial and human resources to include students with disabilities. *The School Administrator, 51*(10), 8–12, 16–19.

McLaughlin, M. J., & Warren, S. H. (1994). *Resource implications of inclusion: Impressions of special education administrators at selected sites.* Palo Alto, CA: American Institutes of Research.

McLean, M. E., & Odom, S. L. (1993). Practices for young children with and without disabilities: A comparison of DEC and NAEYC identified practices. *Topics in Early Childhood Special Education, 13,* 274–292.

McLeskey, J., Lancaster, M., & Grizzle, K. L. (1995). Learning disabilities and grade retention: A review of issues with recommendations for practice. *Learning Disabilities Research & Practice, 10*(2), 120–128.

McLeskey, J., Skiba, R., & Wilcox, B. (1990). Reform and special education: A mainstream perspective. *Journal of Special Education, 24,* 319–325.

McMillen, M. (1997). *Dropout rates in the United States, 1996.* Washington, DC: U.S. Department of Education, Office of Educational Research and Improvement, National Center for Education Statistics.

McNulty, B. A. (1989). Leadership and policy strategies for interagency planning: Meeting the early childhood mandate. In J. J. Gallagher, P. L. Trohanis, & R. M. Clifford (Eds.), *Policy implementation & PL 99-457: Planning for young children with special needs* (pp. 147–167). Baltimore, MD: Brookes.

McPherson, R. B. (1991, April 10). Reform versus renewal. *Education Week,* p. 17.

McWilliam, R. A. (1992). *Family-centered intervention planning: A routine-based approach.* Tucson, AZ: Communication Skill Builders.

McWilliam, R. A. (Ed.). (1996). *Rethinking pull-out services in early intervention: A professional resource.* Baltimore: Brookes.

Mehring, T. A. (1996). Authentic assessment—the link to special education. In A. F. Rotatori, J. O. Schwenn, & S. Burkhardt (Eds.), *Advances in special education: Assessment and psychopathology issues in special education* (Vol. 10, pp. 177–200). Greenwich, CT: JAI Press.

Meisels, S. J. (1985). *Developmental screening in early childhood: A guide* (rev. ed.). Washington, DC: National Association for the Education of Young Children.

Meisels, S. J. (1987). Uses and abuses of developmental screening and school readiness testing. *Young Children, 42*(2), 4–6, 66–73.

Mercer, C. D., Forgnone, C., & Wolking, W. (1976). Definitions of learning disabilities used in the United States. *Journal of Learning Disabilities, 9,* 376–386.

Mercer, J. (1973). *Labeling the mentally retarded.* Berkeley: University of California Press.

Mercer, J., & Ysseldyke, J. E. (1977). Designing diagnostic-intervention programs. In T. Oakland (Ed.), *Psychological and educational assessment of minority children* (pp. 70–90). New York, NY: Brunner/Mazel.

Mehrens, W. A., Popham, W. J., & Ryan, J. M. (1998). How to prepare students for performance assessments. *Educational Measurement: Issues and Practice, 17* (1), 18–22.

Michigan State University. (1997). "Remarks to the Republican Governor's Conference, Miami, November 21, 1997" (Press Release: http://ustimss.msu.edu/whatsnew.htm)

Midgette, T. E. (1995). Assessment of African American exceptional learners: New strategies and perspectives. In B. A. Ford, F. E. Obiakor, & J. M. Patton (Eds.), *Effective education of African American exceptional learners: New perspectives* (pp. 3–26). Austin, TX: Pro-Ed.

Mid-South Regional Resource Center. (1986). *Effectiveness indicators for special education: A reference tool.* Lexington, KY: Author.

Mikulecky, L. (1990). National adult literacy and lifelong learning goals. *Phi Delta Kappan, 72,* 304–309.

Miles, B. S., & Simpson, R. L. (1989). Regular educators' modification preferences for mainstreaming mildly handicapped children. *Journal of Special Education, 22,* 479–491.

Miller, D. L., & Miller, M. A. (1979). The Education for All Handicapped Act: How well does it accomplish the goal of promoting the Least Restrictive Environment for education? *DePaul Law Review, 28*(2), 321–350.

Mills, P. E., Cole, K. N., Jenkins, J. R., & Dale, P. S. (1998). Effects of differing levels of inclusion on preschoolers with disabilities. *Exceptional Children, 65*(1), 79–90.

Minnesota Department of Education. (1989). *A progress report on the evolution of a Minnesota vision for outcome-based education.* St. Paul: Author, Instructional Effectiveness Division.

Mirkin, P. K. (1980). In J. E. Ysseldyke & M. L. Thurlow (Eds.), *The special education assessment and decision-making process: Seven case studies* (Research report no. 44), pp. 100–113. Minneapolis: University of Minnesota, Institute for Research on Learning Disabilities.

Mithaug, D. E., Horiuchi, C. N., & Fanning, P. N. (1985). A report on the Colorado statewide follow-up survey of special education students. *Exceptional Children, 55,* 230–239.

Montie, J. All kids learn. In T. Vandercook, S. Wolff, & J. York (Eds.), *Learning together . . . Stories and strategies* (p. 6). Minneapolis, MN: Institute on Community Integration, University of Minnesota.

Moore, D. R., & Davenport, S. (1990). School choice: The new improved sorting machine. In W. L. Boyd & H. J. Walberg (Eds.), *Choice in education: Potential and problems* (pp. 187–224). Berkeley, CA: McCutchan.

Moores, D. F. (1978). *Educating the deaf: Psychology, principles, and practices.* Boston: Houghton Mifflin.

Moores, D. F. (1982). *Educating the deaf: Psychology, principles, and practices* (2nd ed.). Boston: Houghton Mifflin.

Morsink, C. V., Thomas, C. C., & Correa, V. I. (1990). *Interactive teaming.* Columbus, OH: Merrill.

Mullis, I. (1990). *The NAEP Guide: A description of the content and methods of the 1990-1992 assessments.* Washington, DC: NAEP.

Myers, B. J., Carmichael Olson, H., & Kaltenbach, K. (1992). Cocaine-exposed infants: Myths and misunderstandings. *Zero to Three, 13*(1), 1–5.

Myers, P., & Hammil, D. C. (1990). *Learning disabilities.* Austin, TX: PRO-ED.

NASBE. (1992). *Winners all: A call for inclusive schools.* Alexandria, VA: National Association of State Boards of Education.

NASBE. (1995). *Winning ways: Creating inclusive schools, classrooms and communities.* Alexandria, VA: National Association of State Boards of Education.

Nash, E. D. (1901). Special schools for defective children. *Journal of Psycho-Asthenics, 6,* 42–48.

Nathan, J. (1990). *Public schools by choice: Expanding opportunities for parents, students, and teachers.* Minneapolis: Free Spirit Publishing Co.

Nathan, J. (1996). Possibilities, problems, and progress: Early lessons from the charter movement. *Phi Delta Kappan, 78*(1), 18–23.

Nathan, J., & Ysseldyke, J. (1994). What Minnesota has learned about school choice. *Phi Delta Kappan, 75*(9), 682–688.

National Academy of Education. (1993). *The Trial State Assessment: Prospects and realities.* Stanford, CA: Stanford University, National Academy of Education.

National Association for Sport and Physical Education. (1995). *Moving into the future: National standards for physical education.* Reston, VA: Author.

National Association of State Directors of Special Education. (1990). *Education of the Handicapped Act Amendments of 1990 (PL 101-476): Summary of major changes in Parts A through H of the act.* Washington, DC: Author.

National Association of State School Nurse Consultants. (1990). *Delegation of nursing care in a school setting.* Washington, DC: Author.

National Center for Education Statistics. (1997). *The condition of education 1997* (NCES 97-388). Washington, DC: U.S. Department of Education, Office of Educational Research and Improvement, NCES.

National Center for Education Statistics. (1998). *Digest of education statistics 1997* (NCES 98-015). Washington, DC: U.S. Department of Education.

National Center for Education Statistics. (1998). *The condition of education.* Washington, DC: U.S. Department of Education, Office of Educational Research and Improvement.

National Center for History in the Schools. (1996). *National standards for history: Basic edition.* Los Angeles, CA: Author.

National Center on Educational Outcome (1997). *1997 State Special Education Outcomes.* Minneapolis, MN: University of Minnesota, National Center on Educational Outcomes.

National Commission on Excellence in Education. (1983). *A nation at risk: The imperative for educational reform.* Washington, DC: U.S. Government Printing Office.

National Council for the Social Studies. (1994). *Expectations of excellence: Curriculum standards for social studies.* Washington, DC: Author.

National Council of Teachers of Mathematics. (1989). *Curriculum and education standards for school mathematics.* Reston, VA: Author.

National Council on Disability. (1989). *The education of students with disabilities: Where do we stand?* Washington, DC: Author.

National Council on Disability. (1996). *Achieving independence: The challenge for the 21st century.* Washington, DC: Author.

National Council on Economic Education. (1997). *Voluntary national content standards in economics.* New York: Author.

National Council on Education Standards and Testing. (1992). *Raising standards for American education.* Washington, DC: U.S. Government Printing Office.

National Education Association, Department of Superintendence. (1922). *Ideals of public education.* Chicago: Author.

National Education Association, Instruction, N. C. o. t. P. o. (1963). *Deciding what to teach.* Washington, DC: Author.

National Education Association. (1979). Teacher opinion poll. *Today's Education, 68,* 10.

National Education Goals Panel. (1997). *Special early childhood report 1997.* Washington, DC: Author.

National Education Goals Panel. (1997). *The national education goals report summary.* Washington, DC: Author.

National Education Goals Panel. (1998). *Ready schools.* Washington, DC: Author.

National Governors' Association. (1986). *Time for results: The governors' 1991 report on education.* Washington, DC: Author.

National Governors' Association. (1988). *Results in education: 1988.* Washington, DC: Author.

National Governors' Association. (1990a, July). *National goals for education* (Draft document). Washington, DC: Author.

National Governors' Association. (1990b). *State actions to restructure schools: First steps.* Washington, DC: Author.

National Governors' Association. (1993). *Transforming education: Overcoming barriers.* Washington, DC: Author.

National Joint Committee on Learning Disabilities. (1987). Learning disabilities and the preschool child. *DLD Times, 4*(3), 5–10.

National Law Center on Homelessness and Poverty. (1990). *Shut out: Denial of education to homeless children.* Washington, DC: Author.

National Organization on Disability and Louis Harris and Associates. (1994). *Survey of Americans with disabilities.* Washington, DC: Author.

National Research Council. (1996). *National science education standards: Introducing the national science education standards.* Washington, DC: National Academy Press.

National Society for the Prevention of Blindness. (1966). *Estimated statistics on blindness and vision problems.* New York: Author.

National Standards in Foreign Language Education Project. (1996). *Standards for foreign language: Preparing for the 21st century.* Yonkers, NY: Author.

NCREL and North Central Regional Education Laboratory are the same 1993 & 1995, from p. 309 of text.

Neill, M. (1997). *Testing our children: A report card on state assessment systems.* Cambridge, MA: National Center for Fair & Open Testing (FairTest).

Neisser, U. (1967). *Cognitive psychology.* New York: Appleton-Century-Crofts.

Neisworth, J. T., & Greer, J. G. (1975). Functional similarities of learning disability and mild retardation. *Exceptional Children, 42,* 17–21.

Nelson, C. M., & Rutherford, R. (1990). Troubled youth in public schools. In P. Leone (Ed.), *Troubled and troubling youth: Multidisciplinary perspectives* (pp. 38–60). Newbury Park, CA: Sage.

NESAC. (1990). *A guide to improving the national education data system.* Washington, DC: U.S. Department of Education, National Center for Education Statistics.

Neuspiel, D. R. (1993). Cocaine and the fetus: Mythology of severe risk. *Neurotoxicology and Terattology, 15,* 305–306.

Newland, T. E. (1969). *Blind learning aptitude test.* Champaign, IL: Author.

Newland, T. E. (1973). Assumptions underlying psychological testing. *Journal of School Psychology, 11,* 316–322.

Newland, T. E. (1980). Assessing the cognitive capability of exceptional children. In W. Cruickshank (Ed.), *Psychology of exceptional children and youth* (pp. 38–61). Englewood Cliffs, NJ: Prentice-Hall.

Nietupski, J. A. (1995). The evolution of the LRE concept for students with severe disabilities. *Preventing School Failure, 39*(3), 40–46.

Nix, F. W. (1977). The Least Restrictive Environment. *Volta Review, 79*(5), 287–296.

Norby, J., Thurlow, M. L., Christenson, S. L., & Ysseldyke, J. E. (1990). *The challenge of complex school problems.* Austin, TX: Pro-Ed.

Nuttall, E. V., Landurand, P. M., & Goldman, P. (1984). A critical look at testing and evaluation from a cross-cultural perspective. In P. C. Chinn (Ed.), *Education of culturally and linguistically different exceptional children* (pp. 42–62). Reston, VA: Council for Exceptional Children.

Obiakor, F. E. (1994). *The eight-step multicultural approach: Learning and teaching with a smile.* Dubuque, IA: Kendall/Hunt.

Obiakor, F. E. (1997, Spring). Shifting paradigms: Responding to cultural diversity in teacher preparation programs. *DDFL News, 7,* 6–7.

Obiakor, F. E. (1998). Multicultural education of exceptional learners: Issues and solutions. Manuscript submitted for publication.

Obiakor, F. E. (1998). *Racism in the classroom: Lessons from real life "personal" cases.* Emporia, KS: Emporia State University.

Obiakor, F. E., & Algozzine, B. (1995). *Managing problem behaviors: Perspectives for general and special educators.* Dubuque, IA: Kendall/Hunt.

Obiakor, F. E., Campbell-Whatley, G., Schwenn, J. O., & Dooley, E. (1998). Emotional first-aids for exceptional learners. In A. F. Rotatori, J. O. Schwenn, & S. Burkhardt (Eds.), *Advances in special education: Issues, practices and concerns in special education* (Vol. 11, pp. 171–185). Greenwich, CT: JAI Press.

Obiakor, F. E., Mehring, T. A., & Schwenn, J. O. (1997). *Disruption, disaster, and death: Helping students deal with crises.* Reston, VA: The Council for Exceptional Children.

Obiakor, F. E., & Schwenn, J. O. (1995). Enhancing self-concepts of culturally diverse students: The role of the counselor. In A. F. Rotatori, J. O. Schwenn, & F. W. Litton (Eds.), *Advances in special education: Counseling special populations* (Vol. 9, pp. 191–206). Greenwich, CT: JAI Press.

Obiakor, F. E., & Schwenn, J. O. (1996). Assessment of culturally diverse students with behavior disorders. In A. F. Rotatori, J. O. Schwenn, & S. Burkhardt (Eds.), *Advances in special education: Assessment and psychopathology issues in special education* (Vol. 10, pp. 37–57). Greenwich, CT: JAI Press.

Obiakor, F. E., & Utley, C. A. (1997). Rethinking preservice preparation for teachers in the learning disabilities field: Workable multicultural strategies. *Learning Disabilities Research & Practice, 12,* 100–106.

Odom, S. L., Deklyen, M., & Jenkins, J. R. (1984). Integrating handicapped and nonhandicapped preschoolers: Developmental impact on nonhandicapped children. *Exceptional Children, 51*(1), 41–48.

Office of Educational Research and Improvement. (1988). *Youth indicators, 1988: Trends in the well-being of American youth.* Washington, DC: U.S. Department of Education.

Office of Juvenile Justice and Delinquency Prevention. (1995). *Juvenile offenders and victims: A national report.* Pittsburgh, PA: National Center for Juvenile Justice.

Olson, C. O. (1990). *Alternative certification guidelines.* Raleigh: NC Department of Public Instruction.

Olson, J. F., & Goldstein, A. (1997). *The inclusion of students with disabilities and limited English proficient students in large-scale assessments: A summary of recent progress* (NCES 97-482). Washington, DC: U.S. Department of Education, Office of Educational Research and Improvement.

Olson, L. (1989, January 9). Minnesota's education leadership: Leitmotif for policy issues looming. *Education Week,* pp. 1, 20.

O'Meara, P. (1998, October 20). "Fetal surgery may give spina bifida baby a better chance." *Roseville Little Canada Review,* pp. 6, 11.

"On cases of contagion." (1987, March 4). *New York Times,* p. A21.

O'Neil, J. (1994/1995). Can inclusion work? A conversation with Jim Kauffman and Mara Sapon-Shevin. *Educational Leadership, 52*(4), 7–11.

O'Sullivan, C. Y., Reese, C. M., & Mazzeo, J. (1997). *NAEP 1996 science report card for the nation and the states.* Washington, DC: U.S. Department of Education, Office of Educational Research and Improvement, National Center for Educational Statistics.

Owings, J., & Stocking, C. (1986). *High school and beyond, a national longitudinal study for the 1980's: Characteristics of high school students who identify themselves as handicapped.* Washington, DC: National Center for Education Statistics. (ERIC Document Reproduction Service No. ED 260 546)

Palincsar, A. S., & Klenk, L. (1992). Fostering literacy learning in supportive contexts. *Journal of Learning Disabilities, 25*(4), 211–225, 229.

Pallas, A. (1987). *Center for Education Statistics: School dropouts in the United States.* Washington, DC: U.S. Department of Education, Office of Educational Research and Improvement.

Parrish, T., Chambers, J., & Matsumoto, C. (1994). *Estimating the cost of enabling special needs populations to achieve high standards of learning.* Palo Alto, CA: American Institutes of Research.

Parrish, T. B. (1996). *Special education finance: Past, present, and future.* Policy Paper No. 8 Palo Alto, CA: Center for Special Education Finance, American Institutes for Research.

Parrish, T. B., O'Reilly, F., Duenas I., & Wolman, J. (1997). *State special education finance systems. 1994–95.* State Analysis Series. Palo Alto, CA: Center for Special Education Finance, American Institutes for Research.

Patton, J. P., Prillaman, D., & Van Tassal-Baska, J. (1990). The nature and extent of programs for the disadvantaged gifted in the United States and territories. *Gifted Child Quarterly, 34*(3), 94–96.

Payne, C. (1989). Urban teachers and dropout-prone students: The uneasy partners. In L. Weiss, E. Farrar, & H. G. Petrie (Eds.), *Dropouts from school: Issues, dilemmas, and solutions* (pp. 113–128.). Albany: State University of New York Press.

Pelham, W. E. (1993). Pharmacotherapy for children with attention-deficit hyperactivity disorder. *School Psychology Review, 22*(2), 199–227.

Peterson, N. L. (1987). *Early intervention for handicapped and at-risk children: An introduction to early childhood special education.* Denver: Love.

Phelps, L. A., & Hanley-Maxwell, C. (1997). School-to-work transitions for youth with disabilities: A review of outcomes and practices. *Review of Educational Research, 67*(2), 197–226.

Phillips, V., & McCullough, L. (1990). Consultation-based programming: Instituting the collaborative ethic in schools. *Exceptional Children, 56,* 291–304.

Pitsch, M. (1991a, April 3). Congress provides funds to fight infant mortality. Education Week, p. 26.

Pitsch, M. (1991b, January 23). Hispanic graduation rates lags others', A.C.E. finds. *Education Week,* p. 4.

Pogrow, S. (1996). Reforming the wannabe reformers: Why education reforms almost always end up making things worse. *Phi Delta Kappan, 77*(10), 656–663.

Polloway, E. A., Epstein, M. H., Bursuck, W. D., Roderique, T. W., McConeighy, J. L., & Jayanthi, M. (1994). Classroom grading: A national survey of policies. *Remedial and Special Education, 15*(3), 162–170.

Ponessa, J. (1996, January 24). Wash. schools chief reveals she has AIDS virus. *Education Week*, p. 11.

Ponsford, J., Sloan, S., & Snow, P. (1995). *Traumatic brain injury: Rehabilitation for everyday adaptive living*. Hillsdale, NJ: Erlbaum.

Pool, H., & Page, J. A. (1995). *Beyond tracking: Findings success in inclusive schools*. Bloomington, IN: Phi Delta Kappa Educational Foundation.

Porter, A. C. (1990). *Assessing national goals: Some measurement dilemmas*. Paper presented at the 1990 ETS Invitational Conference Proceedings: The assessment of National Educational Goals.

Porter, S. H. (1982). Employment characteristics of handicapped graduates and dropouts. *Adult Literacy and Basic Education, 6*(4), 238–244.

Preprimary enrollment. (1991). *Education Week, 10*(28), 7.

Price, H. B. (1991, Fall). Multicultural education: The debate. *Humanities in the South*, pp. 1–8.

Pugach, M. (1987). The national reports and special education: Implications for teacher education. *Exceptional Children, 53*, 308–314.

Pugach, M. (1990). The moral cost of retrenchment in special education. *Journal of Special Education, 24*, 326–333.

Pugach, M., & Lillp, M. S. (1984). Reconceptualizing support services for classroom teachers: Implications for teacher education. *Journal of Teacher Education, 35*(5), 48–55.

Purkey, S., & Smith, M. (1985). School reform: The district policy implications of the effective schools literature. *Elementary School Journal, 85*(3).

Pyecha, J. (1980). *A national survey of individualized education programs (IEPs) for handicapped children*. Research Triangle Park, NC: Research Triangle Institute.

Quay, H.C. (1973). Special education: Assumptions, techniques, and evaluative criteria. *Exceptional Children, 40*, 165–170.

Raber, S., & Roach, V. (1998). *The push and pull of standards-based reform*. Alexandria, VA: Center for Policy Research on the Impact of General and Special Education Reform.

Rafferty, Y., & Shinn, M. (1991). The impact of homelessness on children. *American Psychologist, 46* (11), 1170–1179.

Raines, J. C. (1995). Appropriate versus least restrictive: educational policies and students with disabilities. *Social Work in Education, 18*(2), 113–127.

Ralph, J. (1989). Improving education for the disadvantaged: Do we know whom to help? *Kappan, 70*(5), 378–385.

Ramsey, R., & Algozzine, B. (1990). Teacher competency testing: What are special education teachers expected to know? *Exceptional Children, 53,* 574–578.

Ramsey, R. S., & Algozzine, B. (1991). Teacher competency testing: What are special education teachers expected to know? *Exceptional Children, 57,* 339–344.

Reddaway, J. L. (1990). Discussant to paper entitled *NAEP: A national report card for education and the public.* Paper presented at the 1990 ETS Invitational Conference Proceedings: The Assessment of National Educational Goals.

Reese, C. M., Miller, K. E., Mazzeo, J., & Dossey, J. A. (1997). *NAEP 1996 mathematics report card for the nation and the states.* Washington, DC: U.S. Department of Education, Office of Educational Research and Improvement, National Center for Education Statistics.

Reform plan for schools. (1957, September 2). *Life,* pp. 123–136.

Reinert, H. (1967). *Children in conflict.* St. Louis, MO: Mosby.

Renzulli, J. (1979). *What makes giftedness?* Los Angeles: National and State Leadership Training Institute of the Gifted and Talented.

Reschly, D. J. (1997). *Disproportionate minority representation in general and special education: Patterns, issues, and alternatives.* Des Moines, IA: Iowa Department of Education, Bureau of Special Education, and Mountain Plains Regional Resource Center at Drake University.

Reschly, D., & Ysseldyke, J. (1995). School psychology paradigm shift. In A. Thomas & J. Grimes (Eds.), *Best practices in school psychology—III.* Bethesda, MD: National Association of School Psychologists.

Resnick, L. (1990, October). *Assessment and educational standards.* Paper presented at the OERI conference on the Promise and Peril of Alternative Assessment. Washington, DC. October 29.

Reynolds, C. J. (1991, Winter). Viewpoint, *The Forum,* p. 1.

Reynolds, M. C. (1978). Final notes. In J. Grosenick & M. Reynolds (Eds.), *Teacher education.* Minneapolis: University of Minnesota, Leadership Training Institute/Special Education.

Reynolds, M. C., & Birch, J. W. (1982). *Teaching exceptional children in all America's schools.* Reston, VA: Council for Exceptional Children.

Reynolds, M. C., Wang, M. C., & Walberg, H. J. (1987). The necessary restructuring of special and regular education. *Exceptional Children, 53,* 391–398.

Rhim, L. M., & McLaughlin, M. J. (1997). *State level policies and practices: Where are students with disabilities?* College Park: University of Maryland, Institute for the Study of Exceptional Children and Youth.

Rhodes, W. C. (1967). The disturbing child: A problem of ecological management. *Exceptional Children, 33,* 449–455.

Rhodes, W. C. (1970). A community participation analysis of emotional disturbance. *Exceptional Children, 37,* 309–314.

Rhodes, W. C., & Tracy, M. L. (1972). *A study of child variance: Conceptual models* (Vol. 1). Ann Arbor: University of Michigan.

Rich, D. (1987). *Schools and families.* Washington, DC: National Education Association.

Richert, S. E. (1987). Rampant problems and promising practices in the identification of disadvanaged gifted students. *Gifted Child Quarterly, 31*(4), 149–154.

Riese, W. (1959). *A history of neurology.* New York: M. D. Publications.

Rivera-Batiz, F. (1990). *Quantitative literacy and the likelihood of employment among young adults in the U.S.* Paper presented at the annual meeting of the American Educational Research Association, San Francisco.

Roach, V., Dailey, D., & Goertz, M. (1997). *State accountability systems and students with disabilities* (Issue Brief). Alexandria, VA; Center for Policy Research.

Roach, V., Halvorsen, A., Zeph, L., Giugno, M., & Caruso, M. (1997). Providing accurate placement data on students with disabilities in general education settings. *Consortium on Inclusive Schooling Practices Issue Brief, 2*(3), 1–10.

Robinson, G. (1983). *Effective schools: A summary of research.* Arlington, VA: Educational Research Service.

Robinson, G. E., & Craver, J. M. (1989). *Assessing and grading student achievement.* Arlington, VA: Educational Research Service.

Robinson, N., & Robinson, H. (1976). *The mentally retarded child.* New York: McGraw-Hill.

Roeber, E., Bond, L., & Connealy, S. (1998). *Annual survey of state student assessment programs: Fall 1997* (Vol. II). Washington, DC: Council of Chief State School Officers.

Rogan, J., Lajeunesse, C., McCann, P., McFarland, G., & Miller, C. (1995). Facilitating inclusion: The role of learning strategies to support secondary students with special needs. *Preventing School Failure, 39*(3), 35–39.

Rose, L. C., Gallup, A. M., & Elam, S. M. (1997). The 29th annual Phi Delta Kappa/Gallup Poll of the public's attitudes toward the public schools. *Phi Delta Kappan, 79*(1), 41–44.

Rossi, R., Herting, J., & Wolman, J. (1997). *Profiles of students with disabilities as identified in NELS:88* (NCES 97-254). Washington, DC: U.S. Department of Education, Office of Educational Research and Improvement, National Center for Education Statistics.

Rotberg, I. C. (1990). I never promised you first place. *Phi Delta Kappan, 72,* 296–303.

Rothstein, L. F. (1990). *Special education law.* New York: Longman.

Rothstein, R., & Miles, K. H. (1995). *Where's the money gone? Changes in the level and composition of education spending.* Washington, DC: Economic Policy Institute.

Rourke, B. P. (1985). *Neuropsychology of learning disabilities: Essentials of subtype analysis.* New York: Guilford.

Rowland, B. H., & Robinson, B. E. (1991). Latchkey kids with special needs. *Teaching Exceptional Children, 23,* 34–35.

Rubenstein, M. C. (1992). *Minnesota's open enrollment option.* Washington, DC: Policy Studies Associates. (ERIC Document Reproduction Service No. ED 353 686)

Rueda, R. (1989). Defining mild disabilities with language-minority students. *Exceptional Children, 56,* 121–128.

Rumberger, R. W. (1987). High school dropouts: A review of issues and evidence. *Review of Educational Research, 57,* 101–121.

Rusch, F., & DeStefano, L. (1989). Transition from school to work: Strategies for young adults with disabilities. *Interchange, 9*(3), 1–8.

Rusch, F. R., & Chadsey, J. G. (Eds.) (1998). *Beyond high school: Transition from school to work.* Belmont, CA: Wadsworth.

Rusch, F. R., & Millar, D. M. (1998). Emerging transition best practices. In F. R. Rusch & J. G. Chadsey (Eds.), *Beyond high school: Transition from school to work* (pp. 36–59). Belmont, CA: Wadsworth.

Rusch, F. R., & Phelps, I. A. (1987). Secondary special education and transition from school to work: A national priority. *Exceptional Children, 53,* 487–492.

Rutter, M. (1978). Diagnosis and definition. In M. Rutter & E. Schopler (Eds.), *Autism: A reappraisal of concepts and treatment* (pp. 31–45). New York: Plenum Press.

Ruttiman, A., & Forest, M. (1986). With a little help from my friends: The integration facilitator at work. *Entourage, 1,* 24–33.

Sacks, O. (1985). *The man who mistook his wife for a hat and other clinical tales.* New York: Harper Collins.

Sailor, W. (1989). The educational, social, and vocational integration of students with the most severe disabilities. In D. K. Lipsky & A. Gartner (Eds.), *Beyond separate education: Quality education for all* (pp. 53–74). Baltimore, MD: Brookes.

Salisbury, C., & Chambers, A. (1994). Instructional costs of inclusive schooling. *Journal of the Association for Persons with Severe Handicaps, 19*(3), 215–222.

Salvia, J., & Ysseldyke, J. E. (1998). *Assessment.* Boston: Houghton Mifflin.

Salvia, J., & Ysseldyke, J. E. (1981). *Assessment in special and remedial education* (2nd ed.). Boston: Houghton Mifflin.

Salvia, J., & Ysseldyke, J. E. (1991). *Assessment* (5th ed.). Boston: Houghton Mifflin.

Sameroff, A. J., & Zax, M. (1973). Schizotaxia revisited: Model issues in the etiology of schizophrenia. *American Journal of Orthopsychiatry, 43,* 744–754.

Samuels, S. J. (1981). Characteristics of examplary reading programs. In J. Guthrie (Ed.), *Comprehension and teaching: Reviews of research.* Newark, DE: International Reading Association.

Sandham, J. L. (1998, July 8). Mass. chief resigns in protest amid test flap. *Education Week, 17* (42), p. 20.

Sands, D. J., & Wehmeyer, M. L. (Eds.). (1996). *Self-determination across the life span: Independence and choice for people with disabilities.* Baltimore: Paul H. Brookes.

Sapon-Shevin, M. (1988). Working towards merger together: Seeing beyond distrust and fear. *Teacher Education and Special Education, 11,* 103–110.

Sarason, S. B. (1990). *The predictable failure of educational reform.* San Francisco: Jossey-Bass.

Sarason, S. B. (1992). *The case for change: Rethinking the preparation of educators.* San Francisco: Jossey-Bass.

Sarason, S. B. (1993). *Letters to a serious education president.* Newbury Park, CA: Corwin Press.

Sarason, S. B. (1995a). *School change: A personal development.* New York: Teachers College Press.

Sarason, S. B. (1995b). Some reactions to what we have learned. *Phi Delta Kappan, 77*(1), 84–85.

Sarason, S. B., & Doris, J. (1979). *Educational handicap, public policy, and social history.* New York: Free Press.

Sashkin, M., & Egermeier, J. (1993). *School change models and processes: A review and synthesis of research and practice.* Washington, DC: U.S. Department of Education, Office of Educational Research and Improvement Programs for the Improvement of Practice.

Sautter, R. C. (1994). Who are today's city kids? Beyond the "deficit model." *City Schools, 1,* 6–10.

Schenck, S. J. (1980). The diagnostic/instructional link in individualized education programs. *Journal of Special Education, 14,* 337–345.

Scheyneman. (1976). *Validating a procedure for assessing bias in test items in the absence of an outside criterion.* Paper presented at the annual conference of the American Educational Research Association.

Schnepf, A. (1994). Introducing inclusion: A View from Clark County. *The Principal Letters: Practices for Inclusive Schools, 16*(4), 1–6.

School Dropouts. (1986). *Everybody's problem.* Washington, DC: Institute for Educational Leadership.

Schumaker, J. B., & Deshler, D. D. (1994/1995). Secondary classes can be inclusive, too. *Educational Leadership, 52*(4), 50–51.

Schumaker, J. B., Deshler, D. D., & McKnight, P. (1989). *Teaching routines to enhance the mainstream performance of adolescents with learning disabilities.* (Final Report). Lawrence: University of Kansas.

Schumaker, J. B., Deshler, D. D., & McKnight, P. C. (1991). Teaching routines for content areas at the secondary level. In G. Stoner, M. Shinn, & H. Walker (Eds.), *Interventions for achievement and behavior problems* (pp. 473–494). Silver Spring, MD: National Association of School Psychologists.

Seiger-Ehrenberg, S. (1985). Educational outcomes for a K–12 curriculum. In A. L. Costa (Ed.), *Developing minds: A resource for teaching thinking* (pp. 7–10). Washington, DC: Association for Supervision and Curriculum Development.

Selden, R. W. (1990). *State indicator systems in education.* Washington, DC: Council of Chief State School Officers.

Selected, key federal statutes affecting the education and civil rights of children and youth with disabilities. *News Digest 1*(1), 13.

Seligman, M., & Darling, R. B. (1989). *Ordinary families, special children: A systems approach to childhood disability.* New York: Guilford.

Seligmann, J. (1990, Special issue, summer/fall). Chance of a lifetime. *Newsweek,* pp. 68–72.

Semmel, D. S., Cosden, M. A., & Konopak, B. (1985). *A comparative study of employment outcomes for special education students in a cooperative work placement program.* Paper presented at the annual convention of the Council for Exceptional Children.

Semmel, M. I., Gerber, M. M., & MacMillan, D. L. (1995). A legacy of policy analysis research in special education. In J. M. Kauffman & D. P. Hallahan (Eds.), *The illusion of full inclusion: A comprehensive critique of a current special education bandwagon* (pp. 39–57). Austin, TX: Pro-Ed.

Shane, H. (1969). Editorial: The renaissance of early childhood education. *Phi Delta Kappan, 50*(369), 412–413.

Shanker, A. (1994/1995). Full inclusion is neither free nor appropriate. *Educational Leadership, 52*(4), 18–21.

Shapiro, E. (1996) Academic skill problems: Direct assessment and intervention. New York: Guilford.

Sharpe, M. N., York, J. L., & Knight, J. (1994). Effects of inclusion on the academic performance of classmates without disabilities. *Remedial and Special Education, 15*(5), 281–287.

Shavelson, R. J. (1990). *What alternative assessment looks like in science.* Paper presented at the OERI conference on the Promise and Peril of Alternative Assessment.

Shavelson, R., McDonnell, L., & Oakes, J. (1989). *Indicators for monitoring mathematics and science education.* Santa Monica, CA: RAND.

Shaw, R. C., & Walker, W. (1981). High school graduation requirements—from whence did they come? *NASSP Bulletin, 65,* 96–102.

Shaywitz, S. E., & Shaywitz, B. A. (1991). Introduction to the special series on attention deficit disorder. *Journal of Learning Disabilities, 24,* 68–71.

Shea, T. M. (1978). *Teaching children and youth with behavior problems.* St. Louis, MO: Mosby.

Shell, P. (1981). Straining the system: Serving low-incidence handicapped students in an urban school system. *Exceptional Education Quarterly, 2,* 1–10.

Shepard, L. A. (1989a). A review of research on kindergarten retention. In L. A. Shepard & M. L. Smith (Eds.), *Flunking grades: Research and policies on retention* (pp. 64–78). London: Falmer.

Shepard, L. A. (1989b). Why we need better assessments. *Educational Leadership, 46*(7), 4–9.

Shepard, L. A., & Smith, M. L. (1989). *Flunking grades: Research and policies on retention.* London: Falmer.

Shinn, M., & Weitzman, B. C. (1996). Homeless families are different. In J. Baumohl (Ed.), *Homeless in America: A reference book.* New York, NY: National Coalition for the Homeless.

Shonkoff, J. P., Hauser-Cram, P., Krauss, M. W., & Upshur, C. C. (1992). Development of infants with disabilities and their families. *Monographs of the Society for Research in Child Development, 57* (6, Serial No. 230).

Short, E. J., Feagans, L., McKinney, J. D., & Appelbaum, M. I. (1986). Longitudinal stability of LD subtypes based on age- and IQ-achievement discrepancies. *Learning Disability Quarterly, 9,* 214–225.

Shriner, J., Ysseldyke, J. E., Gorney, D., & Franklin, M. J. (1991). Alternative explanations for variability in prevalence of students who are gifted and talented. Minneapolis, MN: Unpublished.

Shriner, J. G., Ysseldyke, J. E., Gorney, D., & Franklin, M. J. (1993). Examining prevalence at the ends of the spectrum: Giftedness and disability. *Remedial and Special Education, 14*(5), 33–39.

Shriner, J. G., Ysseldyke, J. E., & Thurlow, M. L. (1994). Standards for all American students. *Focus on Exceptional Children, 28*(5), 1–19.

Siccone, F. (1995). *Celebrating diversity: Building self-esteem in today's multicultural classrooms.* Boston, MA: Allyn and Bacon.

Silberman, C. E. (1970). *Crisis in the classroom: The remaking of American education.* New York: Random House.

Silver, L. B. (1990). Attention deficit-hyperactivity disorder: Is it a learning disability or related disorder? *Journal of Learning Disabilities, 23,* 394–397.

Simpson, R. (1996). *Working with parents and families of exceptional children and youth.* Austin, TX: Pro-Ed.

Sinclair, M. F., Christenson, S. L., Evelo, D. L., & Hurley, C. M. (1998). Dropout prevention for youth with disabilities: Efficacy of a sustained school engagement procedure. *Exceptional Children, 65*(1), 7–21.

Singer, J., & Butler, J. (1987). The Education for All Handicapped Children Act: Schools as agents of social reform. *Harvard Educational Review, 57,* 125–152.

Skiba, R., & Deno, S. (1991). Terminology and behavior reduction: The case against "punishment." *Exceptional Children, 57,* 298–313.

Sleeter, C. E. (1986). Learning disabilities: The social construction of a special education category. *Exceptional Children, 53* 46–54.

Smith, M. L., & Shepard, L. A. (1989). Flunking grades: A recapitulation. In L. A. Shepard & M. L. Smith (Eds.), *Flunking grades: Research and policies on retention* (pp. 214–236). London: Falmer.

Smith, R. C., & Lincoln, C. A. (1988). *America's shame, America's hope: Twelve million youth at risk.* Chapel Hill, NC: MDC. (ERIC Document Reproduction Service No. ED 301 620).

Smith, S. W. (1990). Comparison of individualized education programs (IEPs) of students with behavioral disorders and learning disabilities. *Journal of Special Education, 24,* 85–100.

Smith, S. W., & Simpson, R. L. (1989). An analysis of individualized education programs (IEPs) for students with behavioral disorders. *Behavioral Disorders, 14,* 107–116.

Smith, T. E. C., Price, B. J., & Marsh, II, G. E. (1986). *Mildly handicapped children and adolescents.* St. Paul, MN: West.

Snow, R. E. (1989). Toward assessment of cognitive and conative structures in learning. *Educational Research, 18*(9), 8–14.

Solomon, R. P. (1989). Dropping out of academics: Black youth and the sports subculture in a cross-national perspective. In L. Weiss, E. Farrar, & H. G. Petrie (Eds.), *Dropouts from school: Issues, dilemmas, and solutions.* (pp. 79–93). Albany: State University of New York Press.

Spady, W. G. (1988). Organizing for results: The basis of authentic restructuring and reform, *Educational Leadership, 46*(2), 4–8.

Speece, D. L., McKinney, J. D., & Appelbaum, M. I. (1985). Classification and validation of behavioral subtypes of learning disabled children. *Journal of Educational Psychology, 77,* 67–77.

Stacey, N., Alsalam, N., Gilmore, J., & To, D. (1988). *Education and training of 16- to 19-year-olds after compulsory schooling in the United States.* Washington, DC: U.S. Government Printing Office.

Stainback, S., & Stainback, W. (1985). *Integration of students with severe handicaps in the regular classroom.* Reston, VA: Council for Exceptional Children.

Stainback, S., & Stainback, W. (1989). Classroom organization for diversity among students. In D. Bilken, D. Ferguson, & A. Ford (Eds.), *Disability and society: Eighty-eighth yearbook of the National Society for the Study of Education* (pp. 195–207). Chicago: University of Chicago Press.

Stainback, S., Stainback, W., & Forest, M. (1989). *Educating all students in the mainstream of regular education.* Baltimore, MD: Brookes.

Stainback, W., and Stainback, S. (1984). A rationale for the merger of special and regular education. *Exceptional Children, 51,* 102–111.

Stainback, W., & Stainback, S. (1987). Integration versus cooperation: A commentary on "Educating children with learning problems: A shared responsibility." *Exceptional Children, 54,* 66–68.

State education statistics. (1988, March). *Education Week,* pp. 18–19.

Stebbins, L., St. Pierre, R., Proper, E., Anderson, R., & Cerva, T. (1977). *Education on experimentation: A planned variation model.* Cambridge, MA: ABT Associates.

Stein, J. U. (1994). Total inclusion or least restrictive environment? *Journal of Physical Education, Recreation and Dance, 65*(9), 21–25.

Stephenson, R. S. (1985). *A study of the longitudinal dropout rate: 1980 eighth-grade cohort followed from June, 1980 through February, 1985.* Miami FL: Dade County Public Schools.

Sternberg, R. J. (1985). *Beyond IQ: A triarchic theory of human intelligence.* Cambridge: Cambridge University Press.

Stevens, L. J., & Price, M. (1991). *Special education for the 1990's: New and/or increasing populations.* Wayne, PA: Radnor Township School District.

Stixrud, W. R. (1982). *Plaintalk about early education and development.* Minneapolis: University of Minnesota, College of Education, Center for Early Education and Development.

Stock, J. R., Newbord, J., Wnek, L. L., Schenck, E. A., Gabel, J. R., Spurgeon, M. S., & Ray, H. W. (1976). *Evaluation of Handicapped Children's Early Education Program (HCEEP): Final Report* (Contract No. EC-0-74-0402). North Carolina, OH: Battelle Center for Improved Education.

Stodden, R. A. (1998). School-to-work transition: Overview of disability legislation. In F. R. Rusch & J. G. Chadsey (Eds.), *Beyond high school: Transition from school to work* (pp. 60–76). Belmont, CA: Wadsworth.

Strauss, A. A., & Lehtinen, L. E. (1947). *Psychopathology and education of the brain-injured child.* New York: Grune and Stratton.

Stringfield, S. C. (Ed.). Special section on studies of education reform. *Phi Delta Kappan, 77*(1), 15–40, 60–85.

Strully, J. (1986). *Our children and the regular classroom: Or why settle for anything less than the best?* Paper presented at the meeting of the Association for Persons with Severe Handicaps.

Swan, W. W. (1980). The Handicapped Children's Early Education Program. *Exceptional Children, 47,* 12–16.

Swanson, J. M. (1994). Research synthesis on the effects of stimulant medication on children with attention deficit disorder: A review of reviews. In Chesapeake Institute, *Executive summaries of research syntheses and promising practices on the education of children with attention deficit disorder* (pp. 52–56). Washington, DC: Chesapeake Institute.

Swart, E. (1990). So, you want to be a 'professional.' *Phi Delta Kappan, 72,* 315–319.

Swap, S. A. (1990). *Parent involvement and success for all children: What we know now.* Boston, MA: Institute for Responsive Education.

Talbot, M. E. (1964). *Edward Seguin: A study of an educational approach to the treatment of mentally defective children.* New York: Teachers College Press.

Taylor, S. (1988). Caught in the continuum: A critical analysis of the principle of the least restrictive environment. *Journal of the Association for Persons with Severe Handicaps, 13*(1), 41–53.

Thorndike, R. M., & Lohman, D. F. (1990). *A century of ability testing.* Chicago, IL: Riverside Publishing Company.

Thornton, H., & Zigmond, N. (1986). Follow-up of post-secondary age LD graduates and dropouts. *LD Research, 1*(1), 50–55.

Thurlow, M. L., Bruininks, R. H., & Lange, C. (1989). *Assessing post-school outcomes for students with moderate to severe mental retardation* (Project Report No. 89–1). Minneapolis: University of Minnesota, Department of Educational Psychology.

Thurlow, M., Christenson, S., Sinclair, M., Evelo, D., & Thornton, H. (1995). *Staying in school: Strategies for middle school students with learning and emotional disabilities.* Minneapolis: University of Minnesota, College of Education and Human Development, Insititute on Community Integration. (ERIC Document Reproduction Service No. 398 671).

Thurlow, M. L., Christenson, S. L., & Ysseldyke, J. E. (1987). *School effectiveness research: Implications for effective instruction of handicapped students* (Monograph No. 3), Minneapolis: University of Minnesota, Institute for Research on Learning Disabilities.

Thurlow, M., & Elliott, J. (1998). Student assessment and evaluation. In F. R. Rusch & J. G. Chadsey (Eds.), *Beyond high school: Transition from school to work* (pp. 265–296). Belmont, CA: Wadsworth.

Thurlow, M. L., Elliott, J. L., & Ysseldyke, J. E. (1998). *Testing students with disabilities: Practical strategies for complying with district and state requirements.* Thousand Oaks, CA: Corwin Press.

Thurlow, M. L., & Gilman, C. J. (1999). Issues and practices in the screening of preschool children. In E. V. Nuttall, I. Romero, & J. Kalesnik (Eds.), *Assessing and screening preschoolers: Psychological and educational dimensions* (pp. 72–93). Boston: Allyn and Bacon.

Thurlow, M. L., Langenfeld, K. L. H., Nelson, J. R., Shin, H., & Coleman, J. E. (1998). *State accountability reports: What are states saying about students with disabilities?* (Technical Report 20). Minneapolis: University of Minnesota, National Center on Educational Outcomes.

Thurlow, M. L., O'Sullivan, P. J., & Ysseldyke, J. E. (1986). Early screening for special education: How accurate? *Educational Leadership, 44*(3) 93–95.

Thurlow, M. L., & Ysseldyke, J. E. (1979). Current assessment and decision-making practices in model LD programs. *Learning Disability Quarterly, 2,* 15–24.

Thurlow, M. L., Ysseldyke, J. E., & Christenson, S. L. (1987). *Student cognitions: Implications for effective instruction of handicapped students.* Minneapolis: University of Minnesota, Institute for Research on Learning Disabilities.

Thurlow, M. L., Ysseldyke, J. E., Gutman, S., & Geenen, K. (1998). *An analysis of students with disabilities in state standards documents* (Technical Report 19). Minneapolis: University of Minnesota, National Center on Educational Outcomes.

Thurlow, M. L., Ysseldyke, J. E., & O'Sullivan, P. (1985). *Preschool screening in Minnesota: 1982–83* (Research Report No. 1). Minneapolis: University of Minnesota, Early Childhood Assessment Project. (ERIC Document Reproduction Service No. ED 269 950)

Thurlow, M. L., Ysseldyke, J. E., & Reid, C. L. (1997). High school graduation requirements for students with disabilities. *Journal of Learning Disabilities, 30*(6).

Thurlow, M. L., Ysseldyke, J. E., Weiss, J. A., Lehr, C. A., O'Sullivan, P. J., & Nania, P. A. (1986). *Policy analysis of exit decisions and follow-up procedures in early childhood special education programs* (Research Report No. 14). Minneapolis: University of Minnesota, Early Childhood Assessment Project.

Tilly III, W. D., & Flugum, K. R. (1995). Ensuring quality interventions. In A. Thomas & J. Grimes (Eds.), *Best practices in school psychology III* (3rd Ed.) (pp. 485–500). Washington, DC: National Association of School Psychologists.

Tilly III, W. D., Grimes, J. P., & Reschly, D. J. (1993). Special education system reform: The Iowa story, *Communique, 22,* (insert).

Tilly, W. D., Knoster, T. P., Kovaleski, J., Bambara, L. Dunlap, G., & Kincaid, D. (1998). *Functional Behavioral Assessment: Policy Development in Light of Emerging Research and Practice.* Alexandria, VA: National Association of State Directors of Special Education.

Timothy W. v. Rochester, New Hampshire School District, 875 F2d. 954 (1st Cir. 1989).

Tingey, C., & Stimell, F. (1989). Increasing services through interagency agreements, volunteers, and donations. In C. Tingey (Ed.), *Implementing early intervention* (pp. 63–78). Baltimore, MD: Brookes.

Tittle, C. K. (1973). Women and educational testing. *Phi Delta Kappan, 55,* 118–119.

Tolor, A., & Brannigan, G. C. (1975). Sex differences reappraised: A rebuttal. *Journal of Genetic Psychology, 127,* 319–321.

Trachtman, G. (1981). On such a full sea. *School Psychology Review, 10,* 138–181.

Trimble, S. (1998). *Performance trends and use of accommodations on a statewide assessment* (State Assessment Series, Maryland/Kentucky Report 3). Minneapolis: University of Minnesota, National Center on Educational Outcomes.

Tucker, J. A. (1980). Ethnic proportions in classes for the learning disabled: Issues in nonbiased assessment. *Journal of Special Education, 14,* 93–105.

Tucker, J. A. (1989). Less required energy: A response to Danielson and Bellamy. *Exceptional Children, 55,* 456–458.

Turnbull, A., Anderson, E., Turnbull, H. R., Seaton, K., & Dinas, P. (1996). Enhancing self-determination through group action planning: A holistic emphasis. In D. J. Sands & M. L. Wehmeyer (Eds.). *Self-determination across the life span: Independence and choice for people with disabilities* (pp. 233–252). Baltimore: Paul H. Brookes.

Twentieth Century Fund, Task Force on Federal Elementary and Secondary Education Policy. (1983). *Making the grade.* New York: Author.

Ullman, L. P., & Krasner, L. (1969). *A psychological approach to abnormal behavior.* Englewood Cliffs, NJ: Prentice-Hall.

Ullman, L., & Krasner, L. (1969). *A socio-psychological approach to abnormal behavior.* Englewood Cliffs, NJ: Prentice-Hall.

U.S. Department of Education. (1980). U.S. Department of Education Second Annual Report to Congress. Washington, DC: USDE.

U.S. Department of Education. (1986). *Statistics of state school systems: Revenues and expenditures for public elementary and secondary education.* Washington, DC: Author.

U.S. Department of Education. (1986b). *What works: Research about teaching and learning.* Washington, DC: Author.

U.S. Department of Education. (1987). *To assure the free appropriate public education of all handicapped children: Ninth annual report to Congress on the implementation of the Education of the Handicapped Act.* Washington, DC: Author.

U.S. Department of Education. (1989a). *Digest of education statistics.* Washington, DC: National Center for Education Statistics.

U.S. Department of Education. (1989b). *To assure the free appropriate public education of all handicapped children: Eleventh annual report to Congress on the implementation of the Education of the Handicapped Act.* Washington, DC: Author.

U.S. Department of Education. (1990 September 25). Improving the retention of special education teachers. *Federal Register, 55*(186), 39247–39249.

U.S. Department of Education. (1991). *Thirteenth annual report to Congress on the implementation of the Individuals with Disabilities Education Act.* Washington, DC: Author.

U.S. Department of Education. (1994). *Sixteenth annual report to Congress on the implementation of the Individuals with Disabilities Education Act.* Washington, DC: Author.

U.S. Department of Education. (1995). *Seventeenth annual report to Congress on the implementation of the Individuals with Disabilities Education Act.* Washington, DC: Office of Special Education Programs.

U.S. Department of Education. (1996). *Eighteenth annual report to Congress on the implementation of the Individuals with Disabilities Education Act.* Washington, DC: Office of Special Education Programs.

U.S. Department of Education. (1997). *Nineteenth annual report to Congress on the implementation of the Individuals with Disabilities Education Act.* Washington, DC: Office of Special Education Programs.

U.S. Department of Health and Human Services. (1993). *Eighth special report to the U.S. Congress on alcohol and health* (NIH Publication No. 94-3699). Washington, DC: U.S. Government Printing Office.

U.S. Department of Justice, Civil Rights Division, Coordination and Review Section. (1990). *Americans with Disabilities Act requirement: Fact sheet.* Washington, DC: Author.

U.S. Department of Labor. (1991). *What work requires of schools: A SCANS report for America 2000.* Washington, DC: Author.

U.S. General Accounting Office. (1981). *Disparities still exist in who gets special education.* Washington, DC: U.S. Government Printing Office.

U.S. News and World Report, (1957, March 15), pp. 38–44.

U.S. News and World Report, (1961, September 4), p. 45.

U.S. Office of Education. (1977). Assistance to states for education of handicapped children: Procedures for evaluating specific learning disabilities. *Federal Register, 42,* 65082–65085.

U.S. Senate. (1975, June 2). *Education for All Handicapped Children Act* (No. 94-168).

Valdes, K. A., Williamson, C. L., & Wagner, M. M. (1990). *The national longitudinal transition study of special education students* (Vol. 1). Menlo Park, CA: SRI International.

Vandercook, T., Walz, L., Doyle, M. B., York, J. L., & Wolff, S. (1995). *Inclusive education for learners with disabilities.* Minneapolis: University of Minnesota, College of Education and Human Development.

Vanderwood, M., McGrew, K., & Ysseldyke, J. (1998). Why we can't say much about students with disabilities during educational reform. *Exceptional Children, 64,* 359–370.

Van Sickle, J. H. (1908–1909). Provision for exceptional children in the public schools. *Psychological Clinic, 2,* 102–111.

Van Tassel-Baska, J., Patton, J., & Prillaman, D. (1989). Disadvantaged gifted learners at-risk for educational attention. *Focus on Exceptional Children, 22*(3), 1–16.

Vasquez, J. (1972). Measurement of intelligence and language differences. *Aztlan, 3,* 155–163.

Vaughn, S., & Schumm, J. S. (1995). Responsible inclusion for students with learning disabilities. *Journal of Learning Disabilities, 28*(5), 264–270.

Ventura, S., Martin, J., Curtin, S., & Matthews, T. J. (1998). *Report of final natality statistics, 1996.* Washington, DC: National Center for Health Statistics.

Verstegen, D. A. (1998). *Landmark court decisions challenge state special education funding.* Palo Alto, CA: American Institutes of Research.

Verstegen, D. A., Parrish, T. B., & Wolman, J. (1998). A look at changes in the finance provisions for grants to states under the IDEA amendments of 1997. *CSEF Resource,* Winter, 1997–98. Palo Alto, CA: American Institutes for Research.

Viadero, D. (1988, March 30). Researchers' critique escalates the debate over "regular education" for all students. *Education Week,* p. 20.

Viadero, D. (1989, October 25). Drug-exposed children pose special problems. *Education Week,* pp. 1, 10–11.

Viadero, D. (1990, September 5). Study of drug-exposed infants finds problems in learning as late as age 3. *Education Week,* p. 15.

Viadero, D. (1991, March 27). Law to aid handicapped infants faces critical test. *Education Week,* pp. 1, 28–29.

Viadero, D. (1993, June 16). Guide to national efforts to set subject matter standards. *Education Week,* pp. 16–17.

Vitello, S. J. (1988). Handicapped students and competency testing. *Remedial and Special Education, 9*(5), 22–27.

Vogel, S. A. (1982). On developing LD college programs. *Journal of Learning Disabilities, 15,* 518–528.

Wagner, M. (1989). *National transition longitudinal study.* Palo Alto, CA: SRI.

Wagner, M. (1991). *Dropouts with disabilities: What do we know? What can we do? A report from the National Longitudinal Transition Study of Special Education Students.* Washington, DC.: U.S. Department of Education, Office of Special Education Programs.

Wagner, M. (1991). *School completion of students with disabilities: What do we know? What can we do?* Paper presented at the Annual Leadership Conference for State Directors of Special Education.

Wagner, M. M., D'Amico, R., Marder, C., Newman, L., & Blackoby, J. (1992). *What happens next? Trends in postschool outcomes of youth with disabilities.* Menlo Park, CA: SRI International.

Wagner, M. M., Newman, L., D'Amico, R., Jay, E. D., Butler-Nalin, P., Marder, C., & Cox, R. (1991). *Youth with disabilities: How are they doing?* Menlo Park, CA: SRI International.

Wagner, M., Blackorby, J., Cameto, R., & Newman, L. (1993). *What makes a difference? Influences on postschool outcomes of youth with disabilities.* Menlo Park, CA: SRI International.

Walker, B. J. (1991). Convention highlights reading assessment changes. *Reading Today, 8*(4).

Wallace, A. (1973). Schools in revolutionary and conservative societies. In F. Lanni & E. Story (Eds.), *Cultural relevance and education issues* (pp. 38–49). Boston: Little, Brown.

Wang, M. C. (1980). Adaptive instruction: Building on diversity. *Theory into Practice, 19*(2), 122–127.

Wang, M. C. (1981). Mainstreaming exceptional children: Some instructional design and implementation considerations. *Elementary School Journal, 81,* 194–221.

Wang, M. C. (1985). *Toward achieving excellence for all students.* Washington, DC: National Center for Educational Statistics. (ERIC Document Reproduction Service No. ED 272 572).

Wang, M. C. (1989). Adaptive instruction: An alternative for accommodating student diversity through the curriculum. In D. Lipsky & A. Gartner (Eds.), *Beyond separate education: Quality education for all* (pp. 99–119). Baltimore, MD: Brookes.

Wang, M. C., & Birch, J. (1984). Comparison of a full-time mainstreaming program and a resource room approach. *Exceptional Children, 51,* 33–40.

Wang, M. C., & Lindvall, C. M. (1984). Individual differences and school learning environments. In E. W. Gordon (Ed.), *Review of research in education* (pp. 161–225). Washington, DC: American Educational Research Association.

Wang, M. C., Reynolds, M. C., & Walberg, H. J. (1986). Rethinking special education. *Educational Leadership, 44*(1), 26–31.

Wang, M. C., Reynolds, M. C., & Walberg, H. J. (1987). *Repairing the second system for students with special needs.* Paper presented at the Wingspread Conference on the Education of Children with Special Needs.

Wang, M. C., & Walberg, H. J. (1988). Four fallacies of segregationism. *Exceptional Children, 55,* 128–137.

Ward, J. L. (1996, Fall). Diversity in the special education training force. *NCPSE News, 1,* (1) 6.

Ward, M. J. (1996). Coming of age in the age of self-determination: A historical and personal perspective. In D. J. Sands & M. L. Wehmeyer (Eds.). *Self-determination across the life span: Independence and choice for people with disabilities* (pp. 1–14). Baltimore: Paul H. Brookes.

Wehman, P. (1993). Transition from school to adulthood for young people with disabilities: Critical issues and policies. In R. C. Eaves & P. J. McLaughlin (Eds.), *Recent advances in special education and rehabilitation.* (pp. 178–192). Boston, MA: Andover Medical.

Wehman, P., Kregel, J., & Seyfarth, J. (1985). Transition from school to work for individuals with severe handicaps: A follow-up study. *Journal of the Association of the Severely Handicapped, 10*(3), 132–136.

Wehman, P., Moon, M., Everson, J., Wood, W., & Barcus, J. (1988). *Transition from school to work: New challenges for youth with severe disabilities.* Baltimore, MD: Paul H. Brookes.

Wehmeyer, M. L. (1992). Self-determination and the education of students with mental retardation. *Education and Training in Mental Retardation, 27,* 302–314.

Wehmeyer, M. L. (1996). Self-determination as an educational outcome: Why is it important to children, youth, and adults with disabilities?. In D. J. Sands & M. L. Wehmeyer (Eds.). (1996). *Self-determination across the life span: Independence and choice for people with disabilities* (pp. 15–34). Baltimore: Paul H. Brookes.

Wehmeyer, M. L. (1997). Self-directed learning and self-determination. In M. Agran (Ed.), *Student-directed learning: Teaching self-determination skills* (pp. 28–59). Pacific Grove, CA: Brooks/Cole.

Wehmeyer, M. L. (1998). Student involvement in transition-planning and transition-program implementation. In F. R. Rusch & J. G. Chadsey (Eds.), *Beyond high school: Transition from school to work* (pp. 206–233). Belmont, CA: Wadsworth.

Wehmeyer, M. L., & Kelchner, K. (1995). *Whose future is it anyway? A student-directed transition planning process.* Arlington, TX: The Arc National Headquarters.

Weinberg, L. A., & Weinberg, C. (1990). Seriously emotionally disturbed or socially maladjusted? A critique of interpretations. *Behavioral Disorders, 15*(3), 149–158.

Wells, A. S. (1989). Educating homeless children. *Digest* (ERIC Clearinghouse on Urban Education, Institute for Urban and Minority Education). New York: Teachers College.

Wells, S., Bechard, S., & Hamby, J. V. (1989). *How to identify at-risk students. Solutions and strategies.* Clemson, SC: Clemson University, National Dropout Prevention Center.

Werner, H., & Strauss, A. A. (1941). Pathology of figure-background relation in the child. *Journal of Abnormal and Social Psychology, 36,* 236–248.

When Standards Drive Change. (1998, March). *Strategies, 5*(2), 1–3.

White, K. R., & Boyce, G. C. (Eds). (1993). Comparative evaluations of early intervention alternatives [special issue]. *Early Education and Development, 4.*

White, K. R., & Casto, G. (1989). What is known about early intervention. In C. Tingey (Ed.), *Implementing early intervention.* (pp. 3–20). Baltimore, MD: Paul H. Brookes.

White, K. R., & Greenspan, S. P. (1986). An overview of effectiveness of preventive intervention programs. In I. R. Berlin & J. Noshpitz (Eds.), *Basic handbook of child psychiatry* (pp. 87–123). New York: Basic Books.

White, W. J., Schumaker, J. B., Warner, M. M., Alley, G. R., & Deshler, D. D. (1980). *The current status of young adults identified as learning disabled during their school career.* (Research Report No. 21). Lawrence: University of Kansas, Institute for Research in Learning Disabilities.

Whiteman, M., & Deutsch, M. (1968). Social disadvantage as related to intellective and language development. In M. Deutsch, I. Katz, & A. Jensen (Eds.), *Social class, race, and psychological development.* New York: Holt, Rinehart and Winston.

Wilder Foundation. (1996). *Social outcomes for our community: Entering the 21st century.* St. Paul, MN: Wilder Research Center.

Will, M. (1984). *OSERS program for the transition of youth with disabilities: Bridges from school to working life.* Washington, DC: U.S. Department of Education, Office of Special Education and Rehabilitative Services.

Will, M. (1986). *Educating children with learning problems: A shared responsibility.* Washington, DC: U.S. Department of Education, Office of Special Education.

William T. Grant Foundation, Commission on Work, Family, and Citizenship. (1988). *The forgotten half: Non-college youth in America*. Washington, DC: Author.

Williams, D. L., & Chavkin, N. F. (1989). Essential elements of strong parent involvement programs. *Educational Leadership, 47*, 18–20.

Williams, R. (1989, January 9–10). *Creating a new world of opportunity: Expanding choice and self-determination in lives of Americans with severe disability by 1992 and beyond*. Paper presented at the National Conference on Self-Determination, Arlington, VA.

Williams, R. J., & Algozzine, B. (1979). Teachers' attitudes toward mainstreaming. *Elementary School Journal, 80*(2), 63–67.

Willoughby, S. S. (1990). *Mathematics education for a changing world*. Alexandria, VA: Association for Supervision and Curriculum Development.

Winzer, M. A., & Mazurek, K. (1998). *Special education in multicultural contexts*. Upper Saddle River, NJ: Prentice-Hall.

Wise, A. E. (1990). Policies for reforming teacher education. *Phi Delta Kappan, 72*, 200–202.

With goals in place, focus shifts to setting strategy. (1990, March 7). *Education Week*, pp. 1, 20.

Wolery, M., & Bredekamp, S. (1994). Developmentally appropriate practice and young children with special needs: Contextual issues in the discussion. *Journal of Early Intervention, 18*, 331–341.

Wolery, M., & Fleming, L. A. (1993). Implementing individualized curriculum in integrated settings. In C. A. Peck, S. L. Odom, & D. Bricker (Eds.), *Integrating young children with disabilities into community programs: Ecological perspectives on research and implementation* (pp. 109–132). Baltimore: Brookes.

Wolery, M., & McWilliam, R. A. (1998). Classroom-based practices for preschoolers with disabilities. *Intervention, 34*(2), 95–102, 117.

Wolman, C., Bruininks, R. H., & Thurlow, M. L. (1989). Dropouts and dropout programs: Implications for special education. *Remedial and Special Education, 10*(5), 6–20, 50.

Wolman, J. M., & Parrish, T. B. (1996). Escalating special education costs: Reality or myth? *The CSEF Resource*. Palo Alto, CA: Center for Special Education Finance, American Institutes for Research.

Wood, F. H. (1990). [Special issue]. *Behavioral Disorders, 15*(3), 139.

Woods, P. A., Sedlacek, W. E., & Boyer, S. P. (1990). Learning disability programs in large universities. *NASPA Journal, 27*(3), 248–256.

Wyche, L. G. (1989). The tenth annual report to Congress: Taking a significant step in the right direction. *Exceptional Children, 56*, 14–16.

Yates, A. J. (1954). The validity of some psychological tests of brain damage. *Psychological Bulletin, 51,* 359–379.

Yeager, R. C. (1990, September). The Reader's Digest home eye test. *Reader's Digest,* pp. 93–100.

Yell, M. L. (1989). *Honig* v. *Doe:* The suspension and expulsion of handicapped students. *Exceptional Children, 56,* 60–69.

Yell, M. L. (1998). *The law and special education.* Upper Saddle River, NJ: Merrill.

Yell, M. L., & Shriner, J. G. (1997). The IDEA Amendments of 1997: Implications for special and general education teachers, administrators, and teacher trainers. *Focus on Exceptional Children, 30*(1), 1–19.

York, J., & Tundidor, M. (1995). Issues raised in the name of inclusion: Perspectives of educators, parents, and students. *Journal of the Association for Persons with severe handicaps, 20*(1) 31–44.

York, J., Vandercook, T., Macdonald, C., Heise-Neff, C., & Caughey, E. (1992). Feedback about integrating middle-school students with severe disabilities in general education classes. *Exceptional Children, 58*(3), 244–258.

Young, B. A., & Smith, T. M. (1996). The social context of education. In National Center for Education Statistics, *The condition of education.* Washington, DC: U.S. Department of Education, Office of Educational Research and Improvement.

Ysseldyke, J. E. (1973). Diagnostic-prescriptive teaching: The search for aptitude-treatment interactions. In L. Mann & D. A. Sabatino (Eds.), *The first review of special education* (pp. 1–37). New York: Grune and Stratton.

Ysseldyke, J. E. (1982). Remediation of ability deficits in adolescents: Some major questions. In L. Mann, L. Goodman, & L. Wiederholt (Eds.), *The Learning disabled adolescent* (pp. 37–61). Boston: Houghton Mifflin.

Ysseldyke, J. E. (1989). Editor's note. *Exceptional Children, 56,* 7.

Ysseldyke, J. (1997). What we know about participation of students with disabilities in assessment and accountability systems. Presentation to the Wyoming Department of Education.

Ysseldyke, J. E., & Algozzine, B. (1982). *Critical issues in special and remedial education.* Boston: Houghton Mifflin.

Ysseldyke, J. E., & Algozzine, B. (1983). LD or not LD: That's not the question! *Journal of Learning Disabilities, 16,* 29–31.

Ysseldyke, J. E., & Algozzine, B. (1984). *Introduction to special education.* Boston: Houghton Mifflin.

Ysseldyke, J. E., & Algozzine, B. (1995). *Introduction to special education* (2nd ed.). Boston: Houghton Mifflin.

Ysseldyke, J. E., & Algozzine, B. (1995). *Special education: A practical approach for teachers.* (3rd ed.). Boston: Houghton-Mifflin.

Ysseldyke, J. E., Algozzine, B. A., & Mitchell, J. (1982). Special education team decision making: An analysis of current practice. *Personnel and Guidance Journal, 60,* 308–313.

Ysseldyke, J. E., Algozzine, B., Richey, L., & Graden, J. (1982). Declaring students eligible for learning disability services: Why bother with the data? *Learning Disability Quarterly, 5,* 37–44.

Ysseldyke, J. E., Algozzine, B., Shinn, M., & McGue, M. (1982). Similarities and differences between underachievers and students classified as learning disabled. *Journal of Special Education, 16,* 73–85.

Ysseldyke, J. E., Algozzine, B., & Thurlow, M. (1992). *Critical issues in special and remedial education.* Boston: Houghton Mifflin.

Ysseldyke, J. E., & Christenson, S. L. (1987). Evaluating students' instructional environments. *Remedial and Special Education, 8,* 17–24.

Ysseldyke, J. E., Dawson, M., Lehr, C., Reschly, D., Reynolds, M., Telzrow, K. (1997). *A blueprint for the future of training and practice in school psychology—II.* Bethesda, MD: National Association of School Psychologists.

Ysseldyke, J., Krentz, J., Elliott, J., Thurlow, M., Erickson, R., & Moore, M. (1998). *NCEO framework for educational accountability.* Minneapolis, MN: University of Minnesota, National Center on Educational Outcomes.

Ysseldyke, J. E., & Marston, D. (1990). The use of assessment information to plan instructional interventions. In T. Gutkin & C. Reynolds (Eds.), *The Handbook of School Psychology* (2nd ed., pp. 663–684). New York: Wiley.

Ysseldyke, J. E., & Thurlow, M. L. (1980). *The psychoeducational assessment and decision-making process: Seven case studies* (Research Report No. 44). Minneapolis: University of Minnesota, Institute for Research on Learning Disabilities.

Ysseldyke, J. E., Reynolds, M. C., & Weinberg, R. A. (1984). *School psychology: A blueprint for the future of training and practice.* Minneapolis: National School Psychology Inservice Training Network.

Ysseldyke, J. E., Thurlow, M. L., & Christenson, S. L. (1987). *Teacher effectiveness and teacher decision making: Implications for effective instruction of handicapped students.* Minneapolis: University of Minnesota, Institute for Research on Learning Disabilities.

Ysseldyke, J. E., Thurlow, M. L., Kozleski, E., & Reschly, D. (1998). *Accountability for the results of educating students with disabilities: Assessment conference report on the new assessement provisions of the 1997 Individuals with Disabilities Education Act.* Minneapolis: University of Minnesota, National Center on Educational Outcomes.

Ysseldyke, J., Thurlow, M., Langenfeld, K., Nelson, J. R., & Teelucksingh, E. (1998). *Educational results for students with disabilities: What do the data tell us?* Minneapolis: University of Minnesota, National Center on Educational Outcomes.

Ysseldyke, J. E., Thurlow, M. L., O'Sullivan, P., & Bursaw, R. A. (1986). Current screening and diagnostic practices in a state offering free preschool screening since 1977: Implications for the field. *Journal of Psychoeducational Assessment, 4,* 191–203.

Ysseldyke, J. E., Thurlow, M. L., Shriner, J.G. (1992). Outcomes are for special educators too. *Teaching Exceptional Children, 25,* 36–50.

Ysseldyke, J. E., Thurlow, M. L., Weiss, J. A., Lehr, C. A., & Bursaw, R. A. (1985). *An ecological study of school districts with high and low preschool screening referral rates* (Research Report No. 6). Minneapolis: University of Minnesota, Early Childhood Assessment Project. (ERIC Document Reproduction Service No. ED 269 955).

Ysseldyke, J. E., Vanderwood, M.L., & Shriner, J.G. (1997). Changes over the past decade in special education referral to placement probability. *Diagnostique, 23* (1), 193–201.

Zigmond, N. (1987). *Convergent studies of LD students at risk for dropping out of high school: An overview.* Paper presented at the annual convention of the American Educational Research Association, Washington, DC.

Zigmond, N. (1990). Rethinking secondary school programs for students with disabilities. *Focus on Exceptional Children, 23*(1), 1–22.

Zigmond, N., & Baker, J. M. (1995). Concluding comments: Current and future practices in inclusive schooling. *Journal of Special Education, 29*(2), 245–250.

Zigmond, N., Jenkins, J., Fuchs, D., Deno, S., & Fuchs, L. (1995). When students fail to achieve satisfactorily: A reply to McLeskey and Waldron. *Kappan, 77*(4), 303–306.

Zigmond, N., Levin, E., & Laurie, T. (1985). Managing the mainstream: An analysis of teacher attitudes and student performance in mainstreaming high school programs. *Journal of Learning Disabilities, 18,* 535–541.

Zigmond, N., & Thornton, H. (1985). Follow-up of postsecondary age learning disabled graduates and dropouts. *Learning Disabilities Research, 1*(1), 50–55.

AUTHOR/SOURCE INDEX

SUBJECT INDEX

DATE DUE